Emerging Practices in Cost Management

1993 EDITION

BARRY J. BRINKER
EDITOR

WARREN GORHAM LAMONT

ii

ISSN 0-7913-1597-5
Library of Congress Card No. 90-71250

Contributing Authors

Thomas L. Albright
Assistant Professor, University of Alabama, Tuscaloosa, Alabama
CHAPTER K3

Felix F. Amenkhienan
Associate Professor, Radford University, Radford, Virginia
CHAPTER G5

John Antos
President, Antos Enterprises, Dallas, Texas
CHAPTER B7

Mohsen Attaran
Professor, California State University, Bakersfield, California
CHAPTER C6

Jon W. Bartley
Professor of Accounting, North Carolina State University, Raleigh, North Carolina
CHAPTER A8

Sidney J. Baxendale
Professor, University of Louisville, Louisville, Kentucky
CHAPTER J4

William K. Beckett
Plant Manager, Pratt & Whitney Canada, Longueuil, Quebec
CHAPTER C5

Scott Belser
Partner, Waterman & Miller, San Francisco, California
CHAPTER L1

Roger Beynon
President, Gulliver Ritchie Associates, Inc., Dallas, Texas
CHAPTER D6

Keki R. Bhote
Senior Corporate Consultant, Motorola, Inc., Schaumburg, Illinois
CHAPTER J3

Wayne G. Bremser
Professor, Villanova University, Villanova, Pennsylvania
CHAPTER I3

John P. Campi
President, Genesis Consulting Group, Racine, Wisconsin
CHAPTER B4

David A. Carlson
Assistant Professor, University of Colorado, Boulder, Colorado
CHAPTER B2

Lawrence P. Carr
Assistant Professor, Babson College, Wellesley, Massachusetts
CHAPTERS E1, K5

Judith Cassidy
Assistant Professor, University of Mississippi, University, Mississippi
CHAPTER C3

Bruce E. Committe
Lawyer and CPA, Own Account, Arlington, Virginia
CHAPTER I2

Khiem Dang
Project Manager, The Spectrum Management Group, Wallingford, Connecticut
CHAPTER C5

A. Lynn Daniel
Principal, The Daniel Group, Charlotte, North Carolina
CHAPTER E2

Mark C. DeLuzio
Vice-President of Finance, Jacobs Vehicle Equipment Company, Bloomfield, Connecticut
CHAPTER C1

Glenn DeSouza
President, Strategic Quality Systems, Inc., Belmont, Massachusetts
CHAPTER E4

Denis Detzel
Managing Director of Research and Organizational Development, The Hay Group, Philadelphia, Pennsylvania
CHAPTER E3

Dileep G. Dhavale
Professor, Clark University, Worcester, Massachusetts
CHAPTER C4

Mark L. Fagan
Principal, Temple, Barker & Sloane, Lexington, Massachusetts
CHAPTER E6

Joseph Fisher
Assistant Professor, Dartmouth College, Hanover, New Hampshire
CHAPTER H3

Steven A. Fisher
Associate Professor of Accounting, California State University—Long Beach, Long Beach, California
CHAPTER A3

Gary B. Frank
Associate Professor, The University of Akron, Akron, Ohio
CHAPTER A3

Robert A. Garda
Director, McKinsey & Company, Inc., Cleveland, Ohio
CHAPTER I1

Andrew Geller
*Managing Director of Worldwide Strategy and Organizational Effectiveness,
The Hay Group, Philadelphia, Pennsylvania*
CHAPTER E3

Peter G. Gerstberger
CEO, The Berwick Group, Inc., Boston, Massachusetts
CHAPTER H2

Joel D. Goldhar
Professor, Illinois Institute of Technology, Chicago, Illinois
CHAPTER D1

Vijay Govindarajan
*Professor of Strategy and Controls, Dartmouth College, Hanover,
New Hampshire*
CHAPTERS L3, L4

Forrest B. Green
Associate Professor, Radford University, Radford, Virginia
CHAPTER G5

Thomas G. Greenwood
Materials Manager, Carrier Corporation, Knoxville, Tennessee
CHAPTER B5

D. Jacque Grinnell
Professor, University of Vermont, Burlington, Vermont
CHAPTER I2

John Gurrad
Director of Business Planning, American President Lines, Oakland, California
CHAPTER L1

H. James Harrington
International Quality Advisor, Ernst & Young, San Jose, California
CHAPTER J6

Cynthia D. Heagy
Assistant Professor, University of Houston—Clear Lake, Houston, Texas
CHAPTER K4

Jan P. Herring
Vice-President, The Futures Group, Inc., Glastonbury, Connecticut
CHAPTER F4

Anita S. Hollander
Assistant Professor, Florida State University, Tallahassee, Florida
CHAPTER K2

Charles T. Horngren
*Edmund W. Littlefield Professor of Accounting, Stanford University, Stanford,
California*
CHAPTER G3

Steven M. Hronec
Partner, Arthur Andersen & Co., Chicago, Illinois
CHAPTER D5

Christopher D. Ittner
Assistant Professor, University of Pennsylvania, Philadelphia, Pennsylvania
CHAPTER E1

Richard L. Jenson
Assistant Professor of Accounting, Utah State University, Logan, Utah
CHAPTER A8

H. Thomas Johnson
Retzlaff Professor of Cost Management, Portland State University, Portland, Oregon
CHAPTER A7

Arnold S. Judson
Chairman, Gray-Judson-Howard, Inc., Cambridge, Massachusetts
CHAPTER L2

Ilene K. Kleinsorge
Assistant Professor, Oregon State University, Corvallis, Oregon
CHAPTER A4

Robert O. Knorr
Partner/Practice Executive, Meritus Consulting Services, New York, New York
CHAPTER J2

Philip Kotler
Professor, Northwestern University, Evanston, Illinois
CHAPTER D4

Stewart Lamond
Partner, Coopers & Lybrand Consultants, Sydney, Australia
CHAPTER B8

David Lei
Assistant Professor, Southern Methodist University, Dallas, Texas
CHAPTER D1

Alan S. Levitan
Associate Professor, University of Louisville, Louisville, Kentucky
CHAPTER J4

Michael P. Licata
Assistant Professor, Villanova University, Villanova, Pennsylvania
CHAPTER I3

John B. MacArthur
Assistant Professor, University of Northern Iowa, Cedar Falls, Iowa
CHAPTERS A5, A6, C2

Arun Maira
Head, Manufacturing Management Consulting Group, Arthur D. Little, Cambridge, Massachusetts
CHAPTER D2

Lawrence S. Maisel
Managing Director, Maisel Consulting Group, Stamford, Connecticut
CHAPTER H1

James R. Martin
Professor, The University of South Florida, Tampa, Florida
CHAPTER F2

Brian H. Maskell
Vice-President, Unitronix Corporation, Mount Laurel, New Jersey
CHAPTER H4

Francis V. McCrory
Senior Associate, The Berwick Group, Inc., Boston, Massachusetts
CHAPTER H2

J. Stanton McGroarty
Consultant, The Stanton Group, Rockford, Illinois
CHAPTER G3

C.J. McNair
Associate Professor, Babson College, Wellesley, Massachusetts
CHAPTER D3

John A. Miller
Partner, Miller-Newlin & Co., Houston, Texas
CHAPTERS B1, E1

Thomas O. Miller
Vice-President of Marketing and Customer Support, Norand Corporation, Cedar Rapids, Iowa
CHAPTER K1

Michael R. Ostrenga
Principal, Ernst & Young, Milwaukee, Wisconsin
CHAPTER J1

Bruce Pfau
National Practice Director of Quality Management, The Hay Group, Philadelphia, Pennsylvania
CHAPTER E3

R. Steven Player
Senior Manager, Arthur Andersen & Co., Dallas, Texas
CHAPTER A7

Lawrence A. Ponemon
Associate Professor, Babson College, Wellesley, Massachusetts
CHAPTER K5

Peter L. Primrose
Director of Diploma, University of Manchester Institute of Science and Technology, Manchester, England
CHAPTER G4

Frank R. Probst
Professor, Marquette University, Milwaukee, Wisconsin
CHAPTER J1

Robert Putrus
Senior Manufacturing Consultant, Digital Equipment Corporation, Farmington Hills, Michigan
CHAPTER C7

Donald W. Ramey
Adjunct Professor, Washington State University, Seattle, Washington
CHAPTER G2

Manash R. Ray
Assistant Professor, Lehigh University, Bethlehem, Pennsylvania
CHAPTER B3

James M. Reeve
Professor, University of Tennessee, Knoxville, Tennessee
CHAPTER B5

Harold P. Roth
Professor, University of Tennessee, Knoxville, Tennessee
CHAPTERS K2, K3

Wendi K. Schelb
Graduate Student, The University of South Florida, Tampa, Florida
CHAPTER F2

Theodore W. Schlie
Associate Professor, Lehigh University, Bethlehem, Pennsylvania
CHAPTER B3

John K. Shank
Noble Professor of Managerial Accounting, Dartmouth College, Hanover, New Hampshire
CHAPTERS L3, L4

William A. Sherden
Vice-President, Temple, Barker & Sloane/Strategic Planning Associates, Lexington, Massachusetts
CHAPTER J5

Michael D. Shields
Professor, San Diego State University, San Diego, California
CHAPTER L5

Harvey N. Shycon
Director, Arthur D. Little, Cambridge, Massachusetts
CHAPTER E5

Richard C. Snyder
Graduate Student, The University of South Florida, Tampa, Florida
CHAPTER F2

Lewis J. Soloway
Principal, Cost Management Strategies, Pasadena, California
CHAPTER B6

Jeffrey S. Sparling
Graduate Student, The University of South Florida, Tampa, Florida
CHAPTER F2

Paul J. Stonich
Vice-President, United Research, Morristown, New Jersey
CHAPTER D4

Dan W. Swenson
Assistant Professor, University of Idaho, Moscow, Idaho
CHAPTER C3

Takao Tanaka
Professor, Tokyo Keizai University, Tokyo, Japan
CHAPTER F1

Ray D. Tanner
International Logistics Manager, Hewlett-Packard, Corvallis, Oregon
CHAPTER A4

Ronald Teichman
Associate Professor, Babson College, Wellesley, Massachusetts
CHAPTER D3

Hal Thilmony
Manager of Financial Systems Implementation, Kingsford Products Company, Oakland, California
CHAPTER A2

Peter B.B. Turney
Chief Executive Officer, Cost Technology, Portland, Oregon
CHAPTER A1

Dominique V. Turpin
Professor, International Institute for Management Development, Lausanne, Switzerland
CHAPTER F3

Thomas P. Vance
Partner, Arthur Andersen & Co., Dallas, Texas
CHAPTER A7

Jewell G. Westerman
Vice-President, Temple, Barker & Sloane/Strategic Planning Associates, Lexington, Massachusetts
CHAPTER J5

Allen R. Wilkie
Director of Planning & Financial Systems, GenCorp Polymer Products, Akron, Ohio
CHAPTER A3

S. Mark Young
Associate Professor, University of Southern California, Los Angeles, California
CHAPTERS B2, L5

Contents

PART C

Advanced Manufacturing Techniques

PART D

Competitive Environment and Change Management

Preface

This—the third edition of *Emerging Practices in Cost Management*—is a book of current readings about modern cost management. As in previous editions, most of the articles reprinted here come from the *Journal of Cost Management*, though we have also included articles from the *Journal of Business Strategy, Corporate Controller, Financial and Accounting Systems,* and *Information Systems Management.* Taken as a whole, the 65 articles published together here provide what is undoubtedly the most comprehensive and most current collection of articles about cost management available.

Note that *Emerging Practices in Cost Management* is part of a family of publications about cost management published by Warren Gorham Lamont. First comes the *Journal of Cost Management,* a quarterly journal that provides current coverage of all important topics in cost management. Since 1987, the *Journal of Cost Management* has published ground-breaking articles about activity-based costing, activity-based management, target costing, and performance measurement. The *Journal of Cost Management* also publishes regular columns, software reviews, and opinion pieces. The third and newest member of this family of publications about cost management is the *Handbook of Cost Management,* which was published in 1992 and is updated yearly. This reference book covers the waterfront: It provides in-depth, up-to-date guidance about every important cost management topic.

Defining Cost Management

Accounting terminology is notoriously imprecise, and the term "cost management" is no exception. This is perhaps inevitable, given that "cost management" combines two terms ("cost accounting" and "management account-ing") that are themselves subject to frequent misinterpretation. These terms are often considered synonymous, but are at other times used to mean quite different things.

Cost management builds on both cost accounting and management accounting and assumes a knowledge of both. Nonetheless, cost management is not cost accounting if cost accounting is taken to mean the costing of inventory for financial reporting purposes. Similarly, cost management is not the same as management (or managerial) accounting, if by management accounting we mean the calculation (for purposes of management control) of variances between actual and standard costs. Although these characterizations of cost accounting and management accounting grossly oversimplify the scope, depth, and complexity of both cost accounting and management accounting, they at least help to place cost management in context.

If we try to define cost management directly (rather than by the back-door approach of saying what cost management is *not*), we might say that cost management is a set of techniques and methods for controlling and improving a company's activities and processes, its products and services. The ultimate purpose of cost management is to provide information that companies must have to provide the value, quality, and timeliness that customers demand in a global economy.

Elements of Cost Management

Most people would agree about the basic tools, techniques, and methods that together constitute cost management. They include (in no particular order):

- Performance measurement;
- Activity-based costing;
- Activity-based management;
- Quality costs and total quality management;

- Continuous improvement;
- Strategic cost management and value chain analysis;
- Target costing;
- Life cycle costing;
- Business reengineering and process improvement; and
- Investment justification and asset deployment.

Despite general agreement about the elements of cost management, passionate disagreements have arisen over the aims, applications, and relative importance of certain aspects of cost management, especially activity-based costing (ABC).

The origins of ABC lie in the recognition that traditional cost systems often report distorted product costs. Although product costing was the initial focus of ABC, some practitioners, consultants, and academics now prefer other terms (e.g., activity analysis, activity-based cost management, activity-based management, or activity accounting) to make it clear that product costing is just part of the picture. After all, simply reallocating the same costs does nothing to increase customer value. The emphasis must therefore be on improving processes to eliminate waste and, thus, delivering higher-quality, lower-cost products or services to customers. This can be accomplished through the proper use of activity-based management and appropriate performance measures.

Acknowledgments

In addition to thanking the many authors and editors who made this book possible, I particularly want to thank Mike Roberts (former program manager of the cost management systems program at Computer-Aided Manufacturing—International and now president of the Cost Management Institute) and the other editors of the *Journal of Cost Management*: John Kammlade of Lexmark International, Bob Eiler of Price Waterhouse, and Larry Maisel of Maisel Consulting Group.

At Warren Gorham Lamont, Paul Wendell has provided encouragement, sound advice, and practical guidance over the years. Jill Uhlfelder and Debbie Kovatch have also been instrumental in preparing this issue.

Finally, I thank my family—Darlene, Mark, and Amy—for their help and support.

BARRY J. BRINKER

PART *A*

Activity-Based Costing

What an Activity-Based Cost Model Looks Like[1]

Peter B.B. Turney

The modern activity-based costing model has two dimensions: a costing dimension and a process dimension. The *cost* dimension contains cost information about resources, activities, and cost objects. It supports economic evaluations of the strategy and operations of an organization. The *process* dimension contains performance information about the work done in the organization. This information supports judgments about why work is done and how well it is performed. The process dimension brings the world of operations directly into the heart of the cost system. This article explains this new, more comprehensive view of activity-based costing and activity-based management.

A new definition of activity-based costing (ABC) was published in the last issue of the *Journal of Cost Management*. The definition reads as follows:

Activity-based costing—A methodology that measures the cost and performance of activities, resources, and cost objects. Resources are assigned to activities, then activities are assigned to cost objects based on their use. Activity-based costing recognizes the causal relationship of cost drivers to activities.[2]

In contrast to earlier definitions of ABC, which focused only on product costing,[3] this definition includes a wide range of cost and performance information. This expanded definition was selected for the glossary because it was believed to be descriptive of the practice of ABC in the early 1990s, and because an ABC model based on this definition is a powerful tool for improvement.[4]

Two-dimensional ABC

An ABC model based on this definition has two main views. The first is the *cost assignment view,* which is the vertical part of the model shown in Exhibit 1.[5] It reflects the need that organizations have to assign costs to activities and cost objects (including customers as well as products) to analyze critical decisions. These decisions have to do with issues such as the following:

- Pricing;
- Product mix;
- Sourcing;
- Product design; and
- Setting priorities for improvement efforts.

The second part of the ABC model is the *process view,* which is the horizontal part of the model shown in Exhibit 1. The process view reflects the need that organizations have for a new category of information—information about what causes work, and how well that work is done. Organizations use this type of information to help improve performance and to increase the value received by customers.

The ABC cost assignment view

The cost assignment view identifies the significant activities of an organization and attaches costs to them. It also assigns costs to cost objects that use the activities.

Knowing the cost of activities makes it easier to understand why resources are used. Moreover, the information provided makes it much easier to address such questions as:

- Which activities require the most resources?

Exhibit 1. *Activity-Based Management*
(Cost Assignment and Process Views)

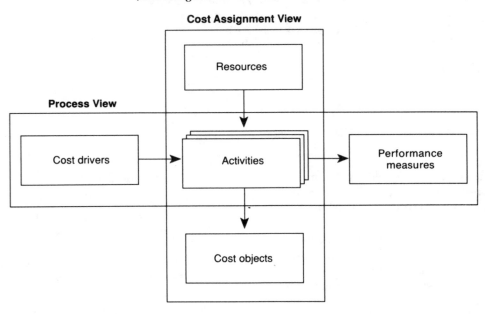

- What types of resources are required by these activities? and
- Where are the opportunities for cost reduction?

Cost objects. Cost objects take ABC far beyond product costing. For example, some ABC systems include the customer as a cost object. This makes sense, because customers often vary in their needs for support. Also, customer-support activities are costly in many companies. The use of customers as a cost object takes costing into new areas of an organization. Customer-support activities, for example, invariably take place outside the manufacturing plant—in marketing, order entry, and customer service.

Building blocks of the cost assignment view

The cost assignment view is constructed from several building blocks. The three main blocks are:

1. Resources;
2. Activities; and
3. Cost objects.

Resources are connected to activities via *resource drivers,* and activities to cost object via

activity drivers. Activity centers, cost elements, and cost pools also help describe the model (see Exhibit 2).

Resources are economic elements directed toward the performance of activities. They are the sources of cost. Resources in a manufacturing company include direct labor and direct material, production support (such as the salary cost of material procurement staff), indirect costs of production (such as the cost of power for heating the plant), and costs outside production (such as advertising). Examples of resources found in both manufacturing and service companies include the salaries of professionals and office support staff, office space, and costs of information systems.

Resources flow to *activities,* which are processes or procedures that cause work. In a customer service department, for example, activities can include processing orders, solving customer difficulties with products, processing returned products, and testing returned products (see Exhibit 3).

Typically, related activities are enclosed in an *activity center.* An activity center is a cluster of activities, which are usually clustered by

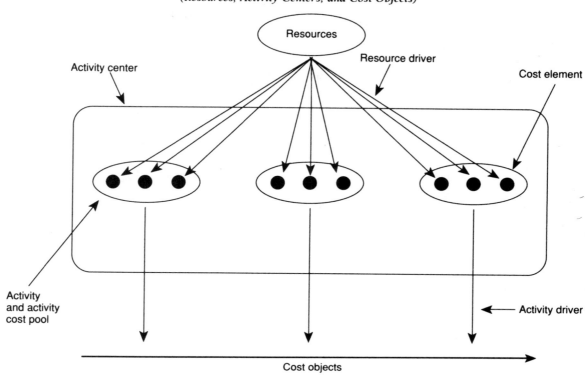

Exhibit 2. *Activity-Based Management*
(Resources, Activity Centers, and Cost Objects)

function or process. In Exhibit 3, for example, the activity center contains all customer service activities.

Various factors, referred to as *resource drivers,* are used to assign costs to activities. These factors are chosen to approximate the use of resources by the activities. In Exhibit 3, customer service cost is traced to three activities. (It is assumed that the cost of resources used in the customer service department has already been determined.) The percentages shown (60 percent, 20 percent, and 20 percent) are based on estimates of the effort expended on each activity. This would be the case, for example, in a ten-person department, if six employees work full-time at solving customer problems, while the other four split their time between processing and testing returns.

Each type of resource traced to an activity (e.g., the salary cost of processing returns) becomes a *cost element* in an *activity cost pool.* The activity cost pool is the total cost associated with an activity.

Each activity cost pool is traced to cost objects via an *activity driver.* The activity driver is a measure of the use of the activity by the cost objects. It is used to assign resources from the activities to the cost objects.

To relate this back to Exhibit 3, each activity has a unique activity driver to trace its cost to the products. "Solving product problems," for example, is traced to products based on the number of telephone calls. This is reasonable because the product that creates the most problems for customers is likely to generate the most phone calls.

The *cost object* is the final point to which cost is traced. A cost object is the reason why work is performed in the company. It may be a product or a customer. Engineering, producing, marketing, selling, and distributing a product require a number of activities. Supporting a customer is also comprised of a number of activities. The cost traced to each product or customer reflects the cost of the activities used by that cost object.

Exhibit 3. *Activities in a Customer Service Department*

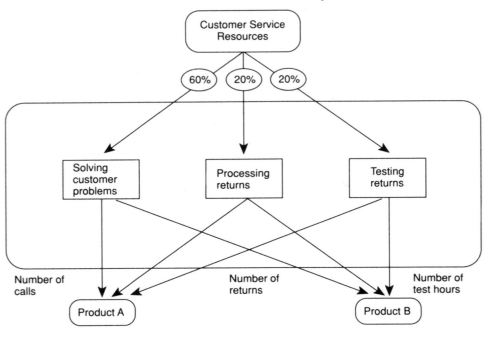

This vertical flow of information in ABC defines the economics of the company and the organization of work within it. It also provides the basic building blocks for creating accurate and useful cost information about the strategy and operations of the company.

Process view of ABC

The horizontal part of the ABC model contains the process view (see Exhibit 1). It provides information about the work done in an activity and the relationship of this work to other activities.

To expand on this, a *process* is a series of activities that are linked to perform a specific goal. Each activity is a customer of another activity and, in turn, has its own customers. In short, activities are all part of a "customer chain," with all activities working together to provide value to the outside customer.[6]

At a value manufacturer, for example, metal is melted in the foundry and then forwarded to molding. Molding pours the molten metal into molds, allows them to cool, and passes them on to an activity that breaks and removes the mold to reveal the parts inside. All

these activities—and many more—work together to provide finished valves to the company's customers.

On a more detailed level, the process view of ABC includes information about cost drivers and performance measures for each activity or process in the customer chain. These cost drivers and performance measures are primarily nonfinancial. They are useful in helping to interpret the performance of activities and processes.

Cost drivers. *Cost drivers* are factors that determine the work load and effort required to perform an activity. They include factors relating to the performance of prior activities in the chain, as well as factors internal to the activity.

Cost drivers tell you *why* an activity (or chain of activities) is performed. Specifically, activities are performed in response to prior events. Scheduling a batch of parts, for example, is a response to a customer order or the scrapping of inventory—the why. In turn, scheduling the parts requires setting up equipment—the effort.

Cost drivers also tell *how much effort* must be expended to carry out the work. A defect in the part or data received from a prior activity, for example, can increase the effort required. A requisition containing the wrong part number requires correction prior to completing a purchase order. An engineering drawing that fails to reflect the current process causes additional effort during machine setup.

Cost drivers are useful because they reveal opportunities for improvement. A reduction in the defect rate for incoming requisitions, for example, allows wasted effort and resources to be eliminated in the purchasing activity.

Performance measures. *Performance measures* describe the work done and the results achieved in an activity. They tell *how well* an activity is performed. They communicate how an activity is meeting the needs of internal or external customers. They include measurements of:

- The efficiency of an activity;
- The time required to complete an activity; and
- The quality of work done.

The *efficiency* aspect is judged by first determining the activity's output volume. This is then compared to the resources needed to sustain that activity and its output level. For example, the number of molds processed in a month is computed for a molding activity. This measure of output is then divided into the resources required by that activity during the month. The result is a cost per mold, say $20, which may be compared with internal or external standards of efficiency.

Still another dimension of performance is the *time* required to complete an activity. Measures of elapsed time are indirect measures of cost, quality, and customer service. The longer it takes to perform an activity, the greater the resources required. These additional resources include the salaries of staff required to do the work and the cost of equipment used to carry out the work. Also, the longer it takes, the more likely it is that work will have to be redone to correct mistakes or defects. Conversely, the shorter the elapsed time, the quicker the activity's response will be to changes in customer demand.

A third aspect of performance is *quality.* For example, what percent of the molded parts need to be reworked, and what percent are scrapped? The higher this percent is, the lower the quality of the activity, the higher its overall cost, and the greater the detrimental influence will be on the next activity in the process. The value received by the customer may eventually be diminished as well.

Performance measures focus attention on the important aspects of activity performance and stimulate efforts to improve.

The process view reflects the need that organizations have for a new category of information—information about what causes work, and how well that work is done.

Operational intelligence. To recap, the ABC process view provides *operational intelligence* about the work going on in a company. This includes information about the external factors determining how often the activity is performed, and the effort required to carry it out. Operational intelligence also includes information about the performance of an activity, such as its efficiency, the time it takes to perform the activity, and the quality with which it is carried out.

An illustration of two-dimensional ABC

Exhibit 4 illustrates how two-dimensional ABC works. The total resource pool of $6 million is the total budget for the procurement department. $450,000 of this cost is traced directly to the purchasing activity. (The resource drivers include estimates of effort expended on the activity and a specific measurement of the use of supplies.) The cost of the purchasing activity is traced to part numbers via the number of purchase orders per part number (the activity driver).

The number of purchase orders measures the output of the activity (the number of times the activity was performed). Other performance measures include the number of errors made, the number expedited, and the elapsed

Exhibit 4. *Illustration of Two-Dimensional ABC*

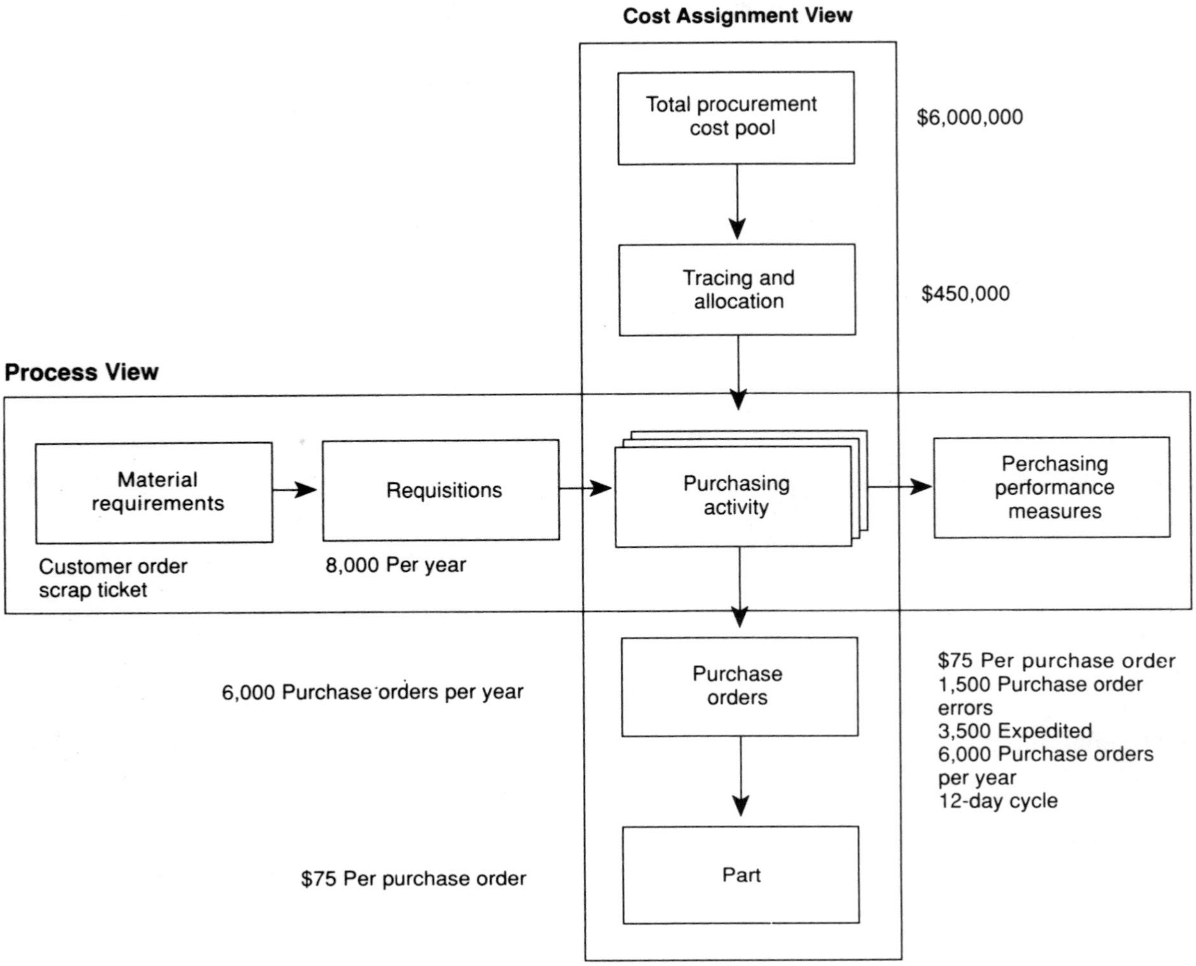

Cost Assignment View

Total procurement cost pool — $6,000,000

Tracing and allocation — $450,000

Process View

Material requirements
Customer order scrap ticket

Requisitions
8,000 Per year

Purchasing activity

Perchasing performance measures

6,000 Purchase orders per year

Purchase orders

$75 Per purchase order
1,500 Purchase order errors
3,500 Expedited
6,000 Purchase orders per year
12-day cycle

$75 Per purchase order

Part

---

time required to complete a purchase order. A volume of 6,000 purchase orders and an activity cost of $450,000 yields a cost per purchase order of $75.

In this example, the activity driver and the performance measure of output are one and the same. This matching of activity driver and performance measure is common in activity-based costing, though there are exceptions.

For example, if the number of purchase orders per part number is not captured by the company's information system, an alternative activity driver (such as the number of different parts) is required. Alternatively, if the effort required to complete a purchase order varies systematically from one type of part to another, a different activity driver (such as a direct measurement of the effort involved) may be necessary.

On the input side, the activity must cope with a volume of incoming requisitions of 8,000. A requisition is not a cost driver of the purchasing activity. Rather, it is the paperwork, or "trigger," that initiates the work.

The volume of requisitions is determined by two cost drivers—the number of customer orders and the number of scrap tickets. Customer orders and scrap tickets are factors that trigger preparation of a purchase requisition (and the need to complete a purchase order).

Exhibit 4 shows the demand for the purchasing activity coming from purchases of parts.

The level of work, however, is determined by the cost drivers—demand for end products (number of customer orders) and the quality of the parts and their processing (the number of scrap tickets). An improvement in the quality of a machining activity, for example, reduces the number of scrap tickets and, in turn, reduces both the number of requisitions and the demand for purchasing replacement parts.

Performance is monitored by several measures. The cost per purchase order averages $75. The frequency of errors is one in four (1,500 out of 6,000 per year). Over half the purchase orders were expedited rather than completed in the normal processing cycle. It took an average of twelve days to complete the processing of a purchase order.

Conclusion

A modern ABC model has two dimensions. The cost dimension contains cost information about resources, activities, and cost objects. It supports economic evaluations of the strategy and operations of an organization.

The process dimension contains performance information about the work done in the organization. It supports judgments about why work is done and how well it is performed.

The process dimension brings the world of operations directly into the heart of the cost system. Cost and nonfinancial information join forces to provide a total view of the work done, thus facilitating management of activities and the improvement of performance. ▲

Notes
1. Adapted from Peter B.B. Turney, *Common Cents: The ABC Performance Breakthrough* (Portland, Ore.: Cost Technology, 1992).
2. Norm Raffish and Peter B.B. Turney, "Glossary of Activity-Based Management," *Journal of Cost Management* (Fall 1991): 53–63. This glossary was first published as *The CAM-I Glossary of Activity-Based Management*, ed. Norm Raffish and Peter B.B. Turney (Arlington, Texas: Computer Aided Manufacturing-International, Inc., 1991).
3. See, e.g., Robin Cooper, "The Rise of Activity-Based Costing—Part One: What Is An Activity-Based Cost System?" *Journal of Cost Management* (Summer 1988): 45–54. This article contains a product costing definition of ABC, and describes a model that is consistent with this definition.
4. See Turney, *Common Cents: The ABC Performance Breakthrough*, Chaps. 7, 8, 9, for examples of successful applications of activity-based costing.
5. Exhibits 1 and 4 were adapted from figures included in *The CAM-I Glossary of Activity-Based Management*, eds. Raffish and Turney, which is the basis for the article, "Glossary of Activity-Based Management," Norm Raffish and Peter B.B. Turney eds., *Journal of Cost Management* (Fall 1991): 54–63.
6. Richard J. Schonberger, *Building a Chain of Customers: Linking Business Functions to Create the World Class Company* (New York: Free Press, 1990).

Product Costing: One Set of Books or Two?

Hal Thilmony

Most companies that have implemented activity-based costing (ABC) continue to use their traditional cost system to value inventories and record variances in the general ledger. This is true even though ABC systems generate more accurate product costs than traditional systems. This article challenges the notion that two product costing systems are needed. In addition to comparing and contrasting information that an ABC and a traditional cost system might generate for a hypothetical manufacturing plant, the article shows how a single ABC system can be used to satisfy the strategic, operational, and fiscal reporting needs of a company.

As activity-based costing (ABC) gains credibility, more and more companies are entering the software race. Currently, the most popular software packages continue to run on personal computers (PCs).[1] This stand-alone approach is a relatively inexpensive way to start an ABC pilot and deliver quick results. The use of PC-based software, however, leaves the impression that ABC is an off-line cost modeling tool that is separate and distinct from a company's integrated financial reporting system.

This impression is further reinforced by articles that advocate multiple cost systems.[2] As a result, companies that implement ABC end up supporting two systems for developing product costs: a traditional cost system to value inventories and record variances in the general ledger, and an ABC system to provide activity and product cost information for strategic and operational analyses.

Why not one cost system?

ABC has proven to be a better methodology for developing product costs than traditional cost systems.[3] Why, then, is there a reluctance to use ABC product costs for standard costing? Do companies really need two cost systems? And if two systems are used, does each cost system create value, or does the existence of multiple cost systems simply create confusion?

The following arguments are frequently advanced in support of two cost systems:

1. Incorporating ABC costing into the general ledger closing process requires too much number crunching and data maintenance; and
2. Since ABC costs are designed for strategic and operational improvement analyses, they cannot meet the fiscal reporting needs of internal or external audiences.

These arguments have merit, but they overlook a possible middle ground where cost information is developed in a single system and then modified (i.e., adjusted, aggregated, or decomposed) to meet the needs of various users. This is not a new concept. Many companies, for example, adjust the inventory values reported in their general ledgers to meet tax reporting requirements.

One cost accumulation and reporting system

As companies experiment with ABC and begin to understand its power for managing activity and product-level costs, questions about the need for two product cost systems arise—first in the cost accounting department and eventually at higher levels of corporate management. Until these questions are answered, someone will inevitably be required ". . . to manage the repercussions that are bound to occur when two systems report different product costs and thus suggest two different courses of action."[4]

A properly designed cost system—one that captures the business processes and activities of the company in a single cost accumulation and reporting system—can provide:

- Cost knowledge to support strategic analyses (e.g., product pricing);
- Reliable standard costs for valuing inventories;
- A sound basis for calculating and understanding variances;
- A path to continuous improvement opportunities (by using attributes to identify value added and cost of quality);
- An internal benchmark for initiatives on cost savings; and
- A method to generate and manage operational budgets.

This list may sound like a cost accountant's fantasy, but it can be a reality.

Case study

The case study given in the following sections illustrates:

- How a traditional cost system might convert budget data into product cost standards;
- How this same budget data is used in an activity-based product costing system; and
- How the two systems would approach the development of actual product costs and variance reporting based on actual spending.

As a starting point, Exhibit 1 shows the budgeted costs and production volumes, and also the actual costs and production volumes for a plant that makes two products: Product 1 and Product 2. (Note that, although this example uses only two products for the sake of simplicity, the value of ABC as a product costing tool increases dramatically as the number and diversity of products increase and the source of costs shifts from direct to indirect categories.)

Traditional approach to product costing

Traditional approaches to product costing tend to use relatively simple allocation methodologies. While these methodologies satisfy the inventory valuation requirement imposed by generally accepted accounting principles, they normally overlook the unique relationships that exist between activity spending and product complexity.

Exhibit 1. *Plant Operating Costs and Volumes*

	Budget	Actual
Production center 1		
Direct labor	$15,000	$20,000
Direct labor benefits	3,000	4,000
Operating supplies	2,000	2,000
Subtotal	20,000	26,000
Production center 2		
Direct labor	60,000	45,000
Direct labor benefits	12,000	9,000
Operating supplies	8,000	6,000
Subtotal	80,000	60,000
Overhead costs		
Indirect labor	80,000	90,000
Indirect labor benefits	16,000	17,000
General supplies	5,000	8,000
Contracts	25,000	28,000
Plant depreciation	24,000	24,000
Subtotal	150,000	167,000
Total Operating Cost	**$250,000**	**$253,000**
Production volumes (cases)		
Product 1	100,000	110,000
Product 2	200,000	180,000
Total Production Volume	**300,000**	**290,000**

Traditional standard product costs. Exhibit 2 shows a traditional approach to assigning costs to products. Budgeted production center costs ($100,000) are allocated to products based on machine hours, and budgeted overhead costs ($150,000) are allocated to products based on production volumes.

The machine-hour allocation recognizes the relative efficiency of the processing and packaging equipment of the two production centers. In this example, the equipment runs at 80 cases per hour to make Product 1, versus 40 cases per hour to make Product 2. In both centers, the equipment requires the attention of two operators. Given the budgeted production volumes, Product 1 will require 1,250 hours of machine time over the course of the year, versus 5,000 hours for Product 2.

Since the costs incurred in the overhead cost pools do not vary based on machine-hours, these costs are allocated to products based on production volumes. The traditional system yields a fully-absorbed standard cost of $0.70 for Product 1 and $0.90 for Product 2.

Traditional actual product costs

Exhibit 3 shows how the actual spending ($253,000) is assigned to product. First, pro-

Exhibit 2. *Standard Product Costs (Traditional Approach)*

Category	Budget	Allocation Basis	Allocation Quantity Product 1	Allocation Quantity Product 2	Total Cost Product 1	Total Cost Product 2	Unit Cost Product 1	Unit Cost Product 2
Production center 1	$ 20,000	Machine hours	1,250		$20,000		$0.20	
Production center 2	80,000	Machine hours		5,000		$80,000		$0.40
Overhead pool	150,000	Cases	100,000	200,000	50,000	100,000	0.50	0.50
Total	$250,000				$70,000	$180,000	$0.70	$0.90

Exhibit 3. *General Ledger Cost & Variance Reporting (Traditional Approach)*

	Total	Product 1	Product 2
Inventory value (@ standard)	$239,000	$77,000	$162,000
Variances:			
Production spending	(8,000)	4,000	(12,000)
Overhead spending	17,000	13,345	3,655
Overhead volume	5,000	(5,000)	10,000
Subtotal	14,000	12,345	1,655
Total Actual Production Costs	**$253,000**	**$89,345**	**$163,655**
Total Unit Costs (Actual)		$0.81	$0.91

duction volume is recorded in the general ledger's inventory accounts based on the standard cost for each product. The difference between the actual spending and the inventoried cost is then captured in the following three variances:

1. *Production spending variance*, which is derived by comparing actual direct labor spending to the costs that should have been incurred under a flexible budget (i.e., the standard production center rate times the actual production for the period).

   Calculation for Product 1:
   $26,000 − ($0.20 × 110,000 cases) = $4,000

2. *Overhead spending variance*, which is computed by comparing the total actual overhead costs times each product's percent of actual production volume, less the total budgeted overhead costs times each product's percent of budgeted volume.

   Calculation for Product 1:
   ($167,000 × 110,000/290,000) − ($150,000 × 100,000/300,000) = $13,345

3. *Overhead volume variance*, which is the difference between budgeted and actual

production volumes, times the standard overhead rate.

Example for Product 1:
(100,000 − 110,000) × $0.50 = ($5,000)

Under the traditional approach, actual product costs are calculated by adding the allocated portions of each variance to the original product cost standard. As Exhibit 3 shows, the actual unit cost of Product 1 and Product 2 is thus $0.81 and $0.91 respectively.

ABC approach to product costing

One of the first steps under an ABC system is to assign costs to the activities that consume

Exhibit 4. *Assignment of Costs to Activity Centers*

Activity Centers	Budget	Actual
Production center 1	$20,000	$26,000
Production center 2	80,000	60,000
Purchasing	25,000	32,000
Quality control	30,000	33,000
Maintenance	5,000	6,000
Warehousing	75,000	81,000
Plant sustaining	15,000	15,000
	$250,000	$253,000

Exhibit 5. *Product Characteristic Profiles*

Activity Center	Characteristic	Profiles Product 1	Product 2
Production	Number of machine hours per 1,000 cases of product	12.5	25.0
Purchasing	Number of POs per 1,000 cases of product	10.0	7.5
Quality control	Number of QC tests per 1,000 cases of product	4.0	1.0
Maintenance	Number of maintenance hours per 1,000 cases of product	0.8	0.6
Warehousing	Number of pallets moved per 1,000 cases of product	25.0	25.0

Exhibit 6. *Standard Product Costs (ABC Approach)*

Activity Center	Budget $	Assignment Basis	Quantity Consumed Product 1	Product 2	Total Cost Product 1	Product 2	Unit Cost Product 1	Product 2
Production center 1	$20,000	Machine hours	1,250		$20,000		$0.20	
Production center 2	80,000	Machine hours		5,000		$80,000		$0.40
Purchasing	25,000	Purchase orders	1,000	1,500	10,000	15,000	0.10	0.08
Quality control	30,000	QC tests	400	200	20,000	10,000	0.20	0.05
Maintenance	5,000	Maintenance hours	80	120	2,000	3,000	0.02	0.02
Warehousing	75,000	Pallets moved	2,500	5,000	25,000	50,000	0.25	0.25
Plant sustaining	15,000	Production volume	100,000	200,000	5,000	10,000	0.05	0.05
Total	$250,000				$82,000	$168,000	$0.82	$0.84

the costs. Generally, the number of activities in an ABC system depends on the purpose of the system. An ABC system that supports continuous improvement (also called activity-based management, or ABM) requires more activities than a system that is designed merely to improve product costing.

ABC software packages that are currently available can handle a vast amount of detail. For that reason, these off-line systems should continue to be used for the number-crunching that goes into activity cost management. These systems can also roll lower-level activity costs into higher-level activity centers. For example, the cost of activities such as ordering materials, contacting vendors, recording receipts, and paying invoices can all be combined into a single activity center: Purchasing. Using *activity-center* costs, rather than *activity-level* costs, to record inventory values and variances in the general ledger substantially reduces the burden placed on the general ledger during the closing process.

Exhibit 4 shows the result of restating budget and actual costs by activity center. Five of these activity centers (purchasing, quality control, maintenance, warehousing, and plant sustaining) describe what was previously in-

cluded in the traditional system's single overhead cost pool.

ABC standard product costs. The next step under the ABC approach is to identify the unique demands that each product places on the activity centers. These unique demands are captured in product characteristic profiles such as those shown in Exhibit 5.

The profiles for Product 1 and Product 2 reflect activity cost consumption rates based on 1,000 cases of product. For example, the production of 1,000 cases of Product 1 requires 10 purchase orders, while the production of 1,000 cases of Product 2 requires only 7.5 purchase orders.

Using the product profile rates to trace costs from the activities (where the spending occurs) to the products that require the spending is the essence of ABC. Exhibit 6 shows the development of product costs using the ABC approach. The standard cost for Product 1 is $0.82 per case and the standard cost for Product 2 is $0.84.

Note that since plant-sustaining costs (e.g., general plant depreciation) do not vary with any other product characteristic, volume is used as a default cost-assignment method to

Exhibit 7. *Actual Product Costs (ABC Approach)*

Activity Center	Actual $	Assignment Basis	Quantity Consumed Product 1	Product 2	Total Cost Product 1	Product 2	Unit Cost Product 1	Product 2
Production center 1	$26,000	Machine hours	1,375		$26,000		$0.24	
Production center 2	60,000	Machine hours		4,500		$60,000		$0.33
Purchasing	32,000	Purchase orders	1,100	1,350	14,367	17,633	0.13	0.10
Quality control	33,000	QC tests	440	180	23,419	9,581	0.21	0.05
Maintenance	6,000	Maintenance hours	88	108	2,694	3,306	0.03	0.02
Warehousing	81,000	Pallets moved	2,750	4,500	30,722	50,278	0.28	0.28
Plant sustaining	15,000	Production volume	110,000	180,000	5,690	9,310	0.05	0.05
Total	$253,000				$102,892	$150,108	$0.94	$0.83

Exhibit 8. *General Ledger Cost & Variance Reporting (ABC Approach)*

	Total	Product 1	Product 2
Inventory value (@ standard)	$241,400	$90,200	$151,200
Variances:			
Production	(8,000)	4,000	(12,000)
Purchasing	7,500	3,367	4,133
Quality control	2,000	1,419	581
Maintenance	1,100	492	608
Warehousing	8,500	3,224	5,276
Plant sustaining	500	190	310
Subtotal	11,600	12,692	(1,092)
Total Actual Production Costs	**$253,000**	**$102,892**	**$150,108**
Total Actual Unit Costs		$0.94	$0.83

allow all costs to be fully absorbed. By absorbing all the costs that go into the traditional system, ABC product costs can be readily compared to traditional product costs. However, when performing strategic product cost analyses, such arbitrarily assigned costs as plant-sustaining costs can be easily backed out of a product's unit cost computation.

ABC actual product costs. The same methodology that was used to develop ABC product cost standards can be used to calculate actual product costs. Exhibit 7 shows how actual product costs are calculated using ABC software.

Activity-based product costs can also be developed in a manner that more closely corresponds to the traditional approach. This alternative ABC approach is shown in Exhibit 8. Actual production is valued in the general ledger inventory accounts using the ABC product cost standards. Variances are then calculated against each activity center.

Using the purchasing activity center as an example, each purchase order (PO) costs $10. This rate is calculated by dividing the cost of the activity center ($25,000) by the number of POs (2,500) that are needed, based on the forecasted production volumes. Given the actual production volume, however, only 2,450 POs should have been needed. At $10 per PO, the cost of the purchasing activity center should have been $24,500. Since the actual cost of the activity center is $32,000, the difference ($7,500) represents an unfavorable variance.

Like the traditional approach, each ABC-generated variance can be assigned to product. Again, using purchasing as the example, Product 1 would receive $3,367 of the total variance because it consumed 1,100 of the 2,450 POs needed to support the actual production volume (1,100/2,450 × $7,500).

One advantage that ABC has over traditional costing is the calculation of variances by ac-

Exhibit 9. *Activity Center Cost Trend Report*

		Full Year Budget	1st Qtr	2nd Qtr	3rd Qtr	4th Qtr	Full Year Actual
Production Center 1	Cost:	$20,000	$6,000	$6,000	$10,000	$4,000	$26,000
	Machine hours:	1,250	250	375	500	250	1,375
	Cost/machine hour:	$16.00	$24.00	$16.00	$20.00	$16.00	$18.91
Production Center 2	Cost:	$80,000	$20,000	$8,000	$12,000	$20,000	$60,000
	Machine hours:	5,000	1,500	500	1,000	1,500	4,500
	Cost/machine hour:	$16.00	$13.33	$16.00	$12.00	$13.33	$13.33
Purchasing	Cost:	$25,000	$7,500	$6,200	$9,500	$8,800	$32,000
	Purchase orders:	2,500	650	450	700	650	2,450
	Cost/purchase order:	$10.00	$11.54	$13.78	$13.57	$13.54	$13.06
Quality Control	Cost:	$30,000	$6,500	$7,000	$11,250	$8,250	$33,00
	Quality control tests:	600.0	140.0	140.0	200.0	140.0	620.0
	Cost/quality control test:	$50.00	$46.43	$50.00	$56.25	$58.93	$53.23
Maintenance	Cost:	$5,000	$1,700	$1,600	$1,400	$1,300	$6,000
	Maintenance hours:	200	52	36	56	52	196
	Cost/maintenance hour:	$25.00	$32.69	$44.44	$25.00	$25.00	$30.61
Warehousing	Cost:	$75,000	$19,000	$20,000	$21,000	$21,000	$81,000
	Pallets moved:	7,500	2,000	1,250	2,000	2,000	7,250
	Cost/pallet moved:	$10.00	$9.50	$16.00	$10.50	$10.50	$11.17

tivity center. Under the traditional approach, all favorable and unfavorable variances associated with various indirect areas (e.g., purchasing and maintenance) are aggregated and obscured in a single overhead cost pool. As a result, the traditional approach provides virtually no information to help analyze or control overhead spending.

Exhibit 10. *Two Systems vs. One*

Two Product Costing Systems:

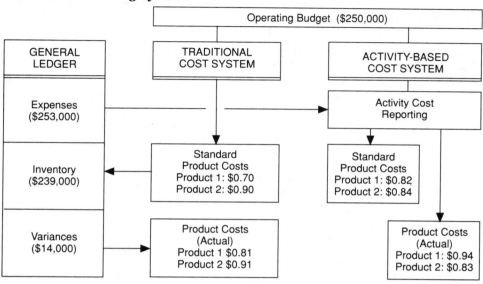

One Product Costing System:

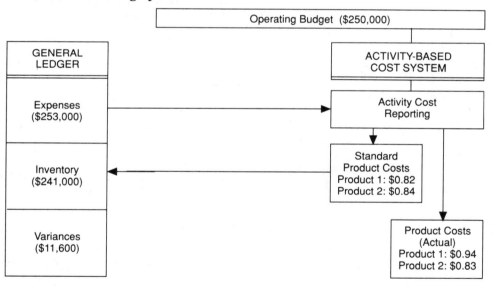

If desired, activity variances can be further subdivided into spending and volume components based on the product profile rates. The availability of actual rates, such as the actual number of purchase orders processed rather than the theoretical number, would also allow the calculation of efficiency variances for each activity center.

Activity cost reporting

An ABC system permits another level of cost reporting that is not available in a traditional cost system. In addition to product cost reports, ABC systems can generate a variety of activity cost reports.

The sample report in Exhibit 9 graphs the cost trends for each activity center over four quarters. In addition to the budgeted and actual costs of each activity center, the report shows the number of activity drivers (e.g., machine-hours, purchase orders, quality control (QC) tests, maintenance hours, and pallets moved) that correspond to each activity center. These drivers are essentially performance measurements that, when combined with cost data, give plant personnel a better understanding of how the work that they perform affects costs.

Activity cost reports serve multiple purposes. First and foremost, they satisfy a major reporting gap—the measurement of continuous improvement—for both the direct production and the overhead areas of responsibility. This measurement of continuous improvement can be extremely motivational.

Activity cost reports also give visibility to possible problem areas. For example, the cost per PO increased substantially during the last three quarters in the Purchasing activity center. This increase in per unit cost may indicate poor vendor performance (e.g., an increase in the quantity of raw materials that had to be returned to vendors because of quality problems), low productivity in the purchasing area (e.g., a change in personnel that requires additional training), or a change in the way materials are ordered and paid (e.g., the installation and testing of a new voucher payment system). Significant shifts in cost driver rates generally highlight the need for some type of action. In many cases, the mere tracking of activity driver information motivates the early detection and resolution of problem areas.

Two cost systems or one?

As companies gain confidence in the ability of ABC systems to support operational and strategic cost analyses, they will begin to question the need for a separate system to value inventories and record budget-to-actual variances. Exhibit 10 illustrates, in a graphical format, several issues that should be considered when deciding whether to continue with two product costing systems or to migrate to a single system.

The following observations can be drawn from Exhibit 10:

1. Two product cost systems generate sub-
stantially different calculations of standard and actual product costs. According to the traditional system, Product 2 costs more to produce than Product 1. The ABC system yields the exact opposite conclusion.

2. Variances can be calculated under either system. While the total amount of the variance is about the same, the ABC variances focus on activity centers, while the traditional system lumps all indirect spending into a single overhead cost pool. (See also Exhibits 3 and 8.)

3. The ABC system provides activity cost reports to support operational cost analyses. Such reports are not available in the traditional system.

4. Supporting two product cost systems requires some level of redundant effort.

A single activity-based cost accumulation and reporting system can satisfy the strategic, operational, and fiscal reporting needs of a company more effectively and more efficiently than maintaining two cost systems. The major ingredients for success within a single system are as follows:

*   Designing enough activity-level detail into the system to satisfy operational cost management needs;
*   Modifying cost reports to meet the requirements of different users; and
*   Minimizing the level of detail that is used to value inventories and report variances in the general ledger. ▲

Reprinted from *Journal of Cost Management*, Winter 1993, pp. 37–44. Copyright © 1993 by Warren Gorham Lamont, a division of Research Institute of America Inc. All rights reserved. Used by permission.

Notes
1. James P. Borden, "Software for Activity-Based Management," *Journal of Cost Management* (Fall 1991): 6–36.
2. See Robert A. Bonsack, "Does Activity-Based Costing Replace Standard Costing?" *Journal of Cost Management* (Winter 1991): 46–47; Robert Kaplan, "One Cost System Isn't Enough," *Harv. Bus. Rev.* (January/February 1988): 61–66; Kelvin Cross and Richard Lynch, "Accounting for Competitive Performance," *Journal of Cost Management* (Spring 1989): 20–28.
3. Robin Cooper and Robert S. Kaplan, "Measure Costs Right: Make the Right Decisions," *Harv. Bus. Rev.* (September/October 1988): 96–103.
4. Robin Cooper, "Implementing an Activity-Based Cost System," *Journal of Cost Management* (Spring 1990): 34.

Implementing Activity-Based Costing: Lessons From the GenCorp Experience

Steven A. Fisher, Gary B. Frank, and Allen R. Wilkie

GenCorp Polymer Products overcame an information crisis by developing and implementing a new activity-based costing (ABC) system. GenCorp learned among other lessons, that it is possible to implement ABC in a traditional manufacturing setting without outside help. Other results of the implementation include a better understanding of cost relationships, a costing system that links product costing and pricing, and a global performance measurement system applied across functional areas to enhance understanding of plant performance and profitability.

To be relevant and reliable, accounting must be responsive to management's information needs and decision models. If the information system loses its responsiveness and becomes the captive of accountants, its usefulness to management is undermined. Consequently, effective system design requires a partnership between accountants and information users.

The case reported here demonstrates how one company, GenCorp Polymer Products (GPP), overcame an information crisis by developing a new activity-based costing system through the joint efforts of its accounting department and management. The task force approach to system development involved accounting information users from all functional areas of the business. The outcomes of this effort included enhanced understanding of cost relations, a revised costing system that linked product costing and pricing, and a global performance measure applied across functional areas to enhance understanding of plant performance and profitability. GenCorp's experience illustrates how human potential can be tapped when management encourages open cooperation across functional areas to achieve total cost control. It also demonstrates that activity-based costing is widely applicable if accountants and managers can break out of established patterns of cost analysis to reconsider the underlying assumptions driving their analysis.

The lessons of the GenCorp experience are widely applicable for corporate and plant controllers. Activity-based costing in high-technology settings has been publicized widely, perhaps leading some corporate controllers to assume that it is inapplicable in more traditional manufacturing operations. However, GenCorp's experience illustrates that the thrust of activity-based costing is to identify the causal factors driving production costs and to modify costing systems to structure decision and pricing models around those crucial variables. This emphasis makes firms' costing systems responsive to today's rapidly changing manufacturing technologies.

Background on plant, process, and product

GenCorp's case involves a plant with a long history and several "lives," over which both the technology used and products produced had changed, but the costing system had failed to respond. GPP's Mogadore, Ohio, plant was built in 1915 by the India Rubber Company and was at one time used to produce bicycle tires. It was converted to latex production during World War II and subsequently has been expanded several times. It currently is the world's largest producer of styrene/butadiene latex.

The production process. GPP's manufacturing process produces synthetic rubber compounds through polymerization using styrene and butadiene as the primary reactive monomers. The system technology is a modified batch basis controlled by a process computer. The plant originally was designed for decentralized monitoring and control that allowed only a dozen product formulations. The shift to a centralized process control technology enabled the plant to expand product variety, and the plant currently produces more than 50 different latex products.

Products include both custom formulations to specific customer requirements as well as standardized products that fit general purpose categories. Both classes of product are produced within the same reactor vessels that are consequently the rate-determining plant equipment. The Mogadore plant's 18 reactors range in size from 3,500 to 7,500 gallons, with an average of 6,000 gallons. Production cycles through the reactors vary according to product from 10 to 40 hours, with an average of 15 to 16 hours. The manufacturing process, from the time the raw materials reach the storage site until finished products are shipped, is controlled by a Foxboro 1A process computer.

Cost allocation based upon direct labor had been appropriate under the original plant technology, but changes in the manufacturing process resulted in cost allocation patterns that were biasing management decisions.

Product characteristics. Latex is used in the manufacture of numerous goods: glossy paper found in magazines or annual report covers; binders to hold tufted carpet together; binders for disposable diapers and paper towels; web saturants, such as is used in masking tape; and tire cord adhesives that help bonding. These different markets have the common feature of multiple competing producers. Consequently, product prices are market set based on price points established by competing formulations.

It is GenCorp's competitive strategy to emphasize product quality while maintaining competitive pricing. This strategy provided the impetus for moving from batch production, characterized by decentralized produc-

tion control and monitoring, toward a process technology controlled by computer. As a consequence, GPP has experienced a shift of production labor from that of a high direct labor component to virtually 100% indirect labor.

Identifying information needs

GPP was satisfied with its costing system from the time of its plant acquisition in 1952 until 1985 when the plant reached operating capacity. The system provided the information necessary for cost accumulation, cost allocation, and the valuation of inventory for financial reporting. It was not structured specifically for accurate product pricing or for production capacity allocation decisions. In 1985, when plant capacity was reached, the inadequacies of the existing cost system became apparent. Top management realized that the existing system did not provide the information needed to allocate production capacity; instead, management was forced to make those decisions intuitively.

Recommendations made by the cost accounting group and by the financial controller about which products to limit evoked strong reactions from the president of the company. He was convinced that accounting's numbers were wrong. The president questioned whether a link existed between GPP's product costing and the real world of production, product pricing, and marketing.

GPP's standard costing system used direct labor hours as the basis for allocating overhead to production. But when GPP's accountants studied the production process, their analysis failed to disclose any direct labor component other than one production worker involved in limited mixing operations. Cost allocation based on direct labor had been appropriate under the original plant technology, but changes in the manufacturing process resulted in cost allocation patterns that were biasing management decisions. The problem was further compounded because plant overhead was allocated equally to reactors, despite their varying capacities. Additionally, products ran through the reactors at different speeds and yields. Consequently, production scheduling influenced costs attached to individual products. The overall result was that the cost allocation system led to suspect results and distorted profit assessments.

Forming the intervention team

As a result of reaching capacity limits, GPP was forced to evaluate the existing system critically. GPP management recognized that the outputs generated by the costing system failed to provide relevant information for individual functional area managers to assess each output's impact on overall profitability. Technical personnel had a directive to reformulate products to improve reactor runs, but they had no means to identify the products on which to focus. Production and maintenance realized that some products ran through the plant more easily than others did and caused less reactor downtime for cleaning, but the analysis from the existing costing system did not indicate that these were profitable products. Marketing knew what products could be sold readily, but they were uncertain that product prices covered the "true" costs.

Top management supported a total review and overhaul of the costing system. Decisions had to be made to improve divisional profitability, and the existing system did not provide the needed direction. GPP's management then made a crucial choice in supporting an intervention team approach for system development and implementation. Management recognized that the plant was a complex socio-technical system that would function well only if all functional areas could reach accord on the information system requirements and goals. They decided to create an internal intervention team to assess the plant's information needs and make recommendations for system change.

The intervention team proposed by the group controller and ratified by management included members drawn from all business functions: the heads of the technical group, manufacturing group, and marketing group, and the controller. The team initially questioned what factors determined product cost. All functional area managers identified information important to their function. This procedure generated an "ideal" information model to be compared with the existing management information system.

As the team identified information uses, it became apparent that different functions had pursued different priorities and that no single performance goal was followed. The manufacturing manager favored high-volume, short cycle-time products that also minimized reactor cleaning. Manufacturing's goals often conflicted with the technical manager's objective of product and process innovation: such innovation resulted in short-term production losses until learning curve effects could develop. The marketing manager wanted production of anything that he could sell in large quantities cheaply. Conversely, the controller evaluated products in terms of their margins. As a result of their initial analyses, the intervention team recognized that their success would depend upon defining a common goal: they needed to identify a common denominator that had relevance across all functional areas.

System analysis to determine cost drivers

The team established two interrelated goals. Their first goal was to identify the activities driving production costs. Second, they needed to structure a new cost allocation system for product costing. The team identified two primary data sources: (1) historic production and cost data and (2) personal interviews. Production and cost data were subjected to extensive trend analysis, but the interpretation of results relied on input from wide-ranging interviews. The team interviewed maintenance people, computer control personnel, technicians and technical managers, sales representatives, and customers to define their information needs. The parameters of the decision problem had expanded far beyond the initial concern for capacity allocation. From this system analysis, the team identified six variables driving plant costs:

- Raw material recipe.
- Material cost.
- Reactor loading.
- Reactor cycle time.
- Reactor cleaning time.
- Frequency of cleaning.

Based on their enhanced understanding of cost behaviors, the team redefined cost pools to include all labor and overhead as conversion cost. Analysis had revealed that 93% to 94% of labor and overhead costs were fixed over the relevant production range.

Revision of the cost allocation system proved to be a more formidable task. The existing allocation system had been driven by a production mind set. However, the intervention team had determined that the revised system must encompass the concerns of production and of sales and also have relevance for the technical area. Numerous alternatives were investigated and rejected, because they did not relate to controllable variables affecting product profitability.

Developing a new cost system

A major breakthrough occurred when the team focused on the factor limiting production output: reactor capacity ultimately drove plant profitability. The team concentrated on the pounds produced in a reactor-hour; a common denominator had to be specified, because reactors varied in size but any product could be processed through any reactor. The solution was for the technical group to recast product standards based on an assumed reactor size, a 6000-gallon reactor.

Having defined a standard production denominator, the team addressed the specification of a global performance measure that would encompass the marketing, production, purchasing and technical areas. The intervention team agreed that the performance measure should encourage goal congruence across

---

A major breakthrough occurred when the team focused on the factor limiting production output: reactor capacity ultimately drove plant profitability.

---

functional areas and assess individual efforts toward plant profitability. Finally, it should support strategic decision-making by GenCorp's management.

The performance measure proposed by the team is a product-profit velocity (PPV) ratio that measures profit generated by each product, emphasizing controllable factors that are influenced by all the functional areas. Table 1 presents the basic PPV formula. The formula relates product revenue and cost to allow management to evaluate the individual profit potential of products. Product revenue per

Table 1. *The Product Profit Velocity Formula*

Product Revenue Per Standardized Reactor Run	−	Materials and Freight Out	=	Standardized Product Contribution Margin
Standardized Product Contribution Margin	+	Product's Standard Processing Time	=	Product Profit Velocity (PPV)
Product Revenue Per Standardized Reactor Run	=	Product Price Per Pound	×	Standard Pounds Per Standard Reactor Run

standardized reactor run, adjusted for direct materials and freight-out, is defined as the standardized product contribution margin. That contribution margin divided by the product's standard processing time yields the product's PPV loading. This formula allows products to be ranked by profitability and enables GPP to direct attention and efforts toward improving profitability of products falling at the lower end of the scale.

Implementing the new system

The new costing system is designed to link product costing to pricing and to highlight points at which functional areas could contribute to improve product profitability. Top management wholeheartedly endorsed the proposed revisions. Data requirements of the new costing methodology were met by the existing information system that already collected data on batch sizes, reactor cleaning times, cycle times, material costs, and selling prices. Management determined that the PPV ranking was an ideal means to direct all functions toward improving total profit of the Mogadore facility. However, instead of mandating changes, the intervention team conducted a series of meetings with department heads to explain the concept of the PPV ratio and to indicate what actions they could take to improve profitability.

Next, products were ranked by their PPV ratio. The PPV ranking has become the locus of efforts to improve bottom-line profitability of the latex operation. Not only does this ranking identify the most profitable products, but, more importantly, it identifies products needing improvement. The company instituted regular meetings of functional managers to evaluate products in the bottom 10% of the PPV rankings. Each functional area contributes; marketing reviews competitors' product pricing and evaluates customer reaction to potential price increases; the technical group considers modifications to product formulation to improve processing; purchasing assesses raw material prices and alternative suppliers; manufacturing reviews scheduling to reduce cycle times and cleaning cycle frequency. The resulting incremental improvements to product PPV have improved plant profitability and have increased cooperation dramatically between functional areas.

Table 2 presents a truncated PPV ranking to illustrate how the PPV ranking differs from the ranking by contribution margin-per-pound that was calculated previously in the standard cost system. Under the old methodology, Products F and B with the highest contribution margins would have been assessed as the most profitable products, and sales efforts would have been focused on those products. In fact, it would not have hurt the company to sell as much of Product F as it could, but Product B was a "loss leader" due to low pounds-per-reactor run. The PPV ranking reveals that Product A is the company's most profitable product, because it runs efficiently in terms of pounds-per-reactor hour, but Product A's contribution margin is low and led to misleading results under the old system.

Use and benefits of the new system

The lapsed time from problem identification until the new system was implemented was six months. Developmental costs were insignificant since the analysis was conducted by participants on personal computer spreadsheets. The system did not supplant the origi-nal costing system but is run parallel with it; for consistency, management has chosen to continue costing products under the old system for external financial reporting.

Evaluation of products by PPV rating has resolved the question of capacity allocation that caused the crisis giving rise to the task force. However, the continuing significance of unanticipated consequences of system change is dramatic. Management had projected product mix modifications; the product mix now emphasizes products with high PPV ratings. However, to implement the change, a new budget process has been established in which functional managers regularly meet to plan the volume of product production and product sales. Viewing pricing as a controllable variable has caused pricing structures to be reassessed and a new target pricing system to be established that ties sales price to the PPV rating and to desired returns on investment. Sales personnel now are evaluated on their ability to meet the target price derived from the PPV rating.

The system has been incorporated into the company's strategic planning and capital budgeting models. It has been used to identify favorable product market opportunities and to assess the company's competitive market position on a product-by-product basis. Its input into the capital budgeting model has been used to justify plant expansion at the Mogadore facility as well as construction of a new latex plant at a different location.

Most striking of all the changes derived from the system development and implementation is the morale effect evident across the plant. The intervention team approach to the capacity allocation problem evolved into a near-total organizational development effort. The crisis was a precipitating event that motivated management to support an overall system review. The intervention team functioned as an internal change agent. Its review of information needs identified goal inconsistency across functional areas. Development of the PPV ratio tied product costing and pricing together and emphasized factors controllable by all functional areas. Existence of the new global performance measure encouraged goal congruity and cooperation that has had a discernable impact in improving plant morale at all levels.

Table 2. *PPV Ranking of Products*

Ranking	Product	Contribution Margin	Pounds Per Reactor Hour	PPV
1	A	.15	2,000	300
2	F	.30	900	270
3	D	.20	1,250	250
4	E	.19	1,200	228
5	C	.12	1,800	216
6	B	.28	500	140

ACTIVITY-BASED COSTING

Lessons from the GenCorp experience

Due to the complexity and cost, management information system review and modification are tasks that firms only reluctantly undertake. As a negative consequence, systems that fail to evolve may generate data that misleads management decisions. Manufacturing companies are complex socio-technical systems that function most effectively when their organizational structure and accounting and information systems correspond to the technology employed. However, system correspondence may be transitory since technology evolves in response to competitive market changes. GPP's costing system originally corresponded to plant technology and provided necessary decisional information. Technology changed at GPP, but there was no automatic feedback mechanism to adjust the information system to reflect these changes.

Once alerted to the dysfunctional aspects of their information system, GenCorp management moved decisively to remedy the situation. Their experience provides several lessons for other manufacturing companies. First, activity-based costing is applicable not only in high-technology environments but also in traditional manufacturing. Cost drivers may be more numerous in technologies involving multiple production stages, but the activity-based costing philosophy remains constant: identify cost behaviors by focusing on activities that drive costs.

GenCorp recognized that functional managers are often in the best position to identify cost drivers even though they may not have been trained in activity-based costing. Consequently, the second lesson learned from the GenCorp experience is that in-house expertise is often available. It is not imperative for companies to resort to external consultants to move toward activity-based costing.

Finally, the active involvement of all functional areas in the systems revision caused functional managers to accept the new system readily. Commitment toward goals is an absolute precondition for success in information system revision. GPP's intervention team approach was suited ideally to building the group identity and adherence to macroplant goals that made it possible to implement the PPV evaluation system rapidly.

To maintain relevance, management accounting must move beyond cost aggregation to cost engineering. If management accountants maintain a narrow and deterministic view of their function, opportunities are lost to manage costs and prices to enhance corporate profit. Each company's situation is unique, and no clear action blueprint can be provided. However, when companies support the philosophy that accounting is an integral part of the management team, there is greater assurance that the information capabilities of the costing system will remain a source of competitive advantage. ▲

Reprinted from *Corporate Controller*, September/October 1990, pp. 15–20. Copyright © 1990 by Faulkner & Gray. All rights reserved. Used by permission.

Activity-Based Costing: Eight Questions to Answer Before You Implement

Ilene K. Kleinsorge and Ray D. Tanner

By now, managers from companies of all sizes have read about activity-based costing (ABC) or even attended conferences about ABC. Many are now trying to reap the benefits that ABC offers. But the rush to understand and implement ABC has caused some issues to be poorly understood. To summarize these issues, this article identifies eight questions people often ask about ABC. Companies that answer these eight questions before implementing ABC are more likely to have successful ABC systems.

Many accountants, engineers, and marketers have embraced activity-based costing (ABC) because it seems to correct many of the failings of traditional cost accounting. ABC is based on the idea that activities consume resources and products consume activities, and it addresses the problems of managing people who work in these activities. An important result of managing activities and reducing non-value-added activities should be lower costs.

Traditional costing focuses on *outputs* or *products* and on *full-absorption costing*. ABC, by contrast, focuses on *inputs* or *activities* and on *relevant costs*. ABC is consistent with the operating philosophies of total quality management (TQM) and just in time (JIT). All three focus on processes and activities; all three also encourage the elimination of waste. In layman's terms, ABC, TQM, and JIT focus on the work of the organization rather than on outputs.

Here are eight questions that people often ask about ABC. These questions summarize issues that have been poorly understood until now. By answering these eight questions, compa-

nies that implement ABC are more likely to succeed.

Question 1. Is top management outwardly committed to ABC?

ABC is not the concern of accountants alone. Since ABC involves fundamental changes in how a business is managed, the effects of ABC will be noticed throughout the organization. ABC certainly involves people who work in accounting, but it also requires the input and cooperation of people who work in marketing, research and development, manufacturing, service, quality assurance, personnel, facilities, order administration, logistics, and the legal department.

Studies about organizational change emphasize how important it is to obtain the commitment of top managers for any new system. If people perceive that top managers are merely paying lip service to ABC, the message will be that ABC is just another program that will pass—in other words, that ABC is not important.[1]

A lack of commitment on the part of top management may be indicated by the conduct of business as usual and the delegation of an ABC implementation to others. When top management has a history of not being involved in change or of grasping at every new fad that comes on the scene without following through, employees will conclude that "this, too, will pass." Management at the highest levels of a company must show commitment to ABC in ways that are visible to subordinates.

Management can show support for ABC by:

- Actively participating in ABC implementation;
- Attending training sessions;

- Actively using the ABC system or methodology; and
- Establishing performance measures that are realistic, measurable, and published internally.

Once an ABC system is initiated, management must be prepared to support the implementation by providing additional short-term resources. When management shows this level of commitment, the organization will begin to believe that it "must be important, or they wouldn't be spending money on it."

Question 2. Is the firm ready for change?

In a stable organization, dissatisfaction with current affairs can become quite vocal at the operational level and can actually prepare the organization for change. However, management should determine that employees are ready for change before important changes are undertaken.

In many companies, the "champion" of ABC should probably come from some functional area other than accounting. In today's business environment, many people may have no faith in the current accounting system, yet they may not believe that adopting ABC is the best course of action. Bringing operational parts of the organization other than accounting into the decision will help pull the organization together behind a successful implementation of ABC.

Pilot projects. Employees must believe that changes to ABC will improve matters. Rhetorical support of ABC should be avoided in favor of positive action. Instead of trying to implement ABC plantwide, the company should select an early demonstration or pilot project that will quickly demonstrate payoffs to managers and staff.[2]

Education. Educating the work force about ABC before the change is also important. In any implementation of ABC, operational data must be collected. If those who are implementing ABC go into the organization without educating employees about ABC, the data they collect may be biased.

For example, if a material handler is asked to participate in time-and-motion studies or interviews about the activities of a packaging operation, the employee may slant his answers to match what he sees as a threat to his job ("Yes boss, it takes me *five* minutes to package that material for shipment."). The employee might also tell the interviewer what he thinks the interviewer wants to hear ("Yes boss, it takes me *one* minute to package that material for shipment.").

Interviewers should take the time to explain why the information is needed—at least in general terms. For example, the interviewer might say that the company is looking for ways to improve profitability by managing activities, thus making employees more effective in their jobs. In this way, the material handler is more likely to give an unbiased answer ("Yes boss, it takes me about *two* minutes to package that material for shipment . . . but I could do it in less time if production would deliver the material to the shipping area instead of leaving it in the aisle."). Of course, the company must be up-front about the fact that some employees may have to be reassigned to new positions if their jobs are eliminated as a result of a reorganization. Change is not always easy for employees or employers. (See question seven below for ideas on how to reduce tension and increase cooperation in the dynamic environment created by ABC.)

Question 3. Do performance measurement and reward systems take ABC into account?

Managers pay attention to those performance measures that result in valued outcomes (e.g., pay raises, promotions, recognition, and bonuses). Therefore, if a business is serious about using ABC, ABC must become integral to performance evaluation. Failure to include ABC measures and to link them visibly to valued outcomes sends the message that ABC is unimportant and can be assigned a low priority without consequences.[3]

Managers must ensure that benefits are associated with the use of an ABC system. If the outcomes of reliance on ABC are perceived as negative, the accuracy of the system will degrade and the implementation may well fail. Negative outcomes include perceived loss of control or of power, reduced prestige, increased interference, and increased paperwork. For example, a company will typically run an ABC system parallel to the traditional cost system. Employees will therefore expect more paperwork. They may also be uncertain about how ABC reports will be used and how the reports will affect their work.

As far as employees know, the company is changing the rules of the game when it introduces ABC. Until the reward system demonstrates that rewards are tied to the new performance evaluation rules, employees will experience confusion and dissonance. The ultimate goal is for employees to gain confidence that using ABC will cause the company to make better decisions based on more equitable and meaningful allocations costs.

Question 4. Do performance measures help you manage the "forest" or the individual "trees"?

The ultimate measure of success must always be customer satisfaction, not successful management of activities. Competitive position in the global economy depends primarily on two things:[4]

- Listening to the voice of the customer; and
- Continuously eliminating work that adds no value to the customer.

As customers' wants and needs change, activities that can be identified as value-added may change. With the implementation of a new information system like ABC, it is very easy to assume that proper management of activities will automatically bring success—even though the company may utterly fail to consider the impact of those activities on the ultimate customer.

One of the weaknesses of traditional management practice is the demand for efficiency in each department, which too often leads to increased work-in-process and ending inventories—and, thus, to higher inventory costs.[5] Optimizing each activity does not necessarily lead to a more productive company as a whole; often the contrary is true. Companies must therefore establish overall performance measures that monitor and encourage both managers and employees to take the "forest" view rather than the "tree" view.

Question 5. Does the cost system emphasize managing activities rather than managing costs?

Probably the most exciting difference between traditional product costing and ABC is the direct influence ABC can have on nonfinancial operations management. The notion that managing activities efficiently will reduce total costs is fundamental to ABC.[6]

Most managers are far too attuned to managing isolated product costs. Unfortunately, product costs often contain significant elements of uncontrollable fixed costs. Decisions to decrease individual unit costs may not succeed in decreasing total plant costs. On the contrary, independent product-cost decisions could actually increase total plant costs. One result could be several isolated operations with individually optimized unit costs that are suboptimal when taken as a whole.

For example, consider two functions—receiving and material picking—from a typical distribution operation in which a product is matched to an order. Taken separately, the manager of each function attempts to achieve the lowest cost that still meets the service goals of the function. Thus, the receiving manager might decide that the most effective cost structure would be a linear flow of inbound product throughout the day rather than all at once, i.e., all inbound freight arriving the first thing each morning. This would allow the receiving function to eliminate a person, and thus reduce costs. The material picking manager, however, might decide that the lowest costs for his department would result from "wave" picking, which means that all orders for a particular product are pulled at once.

If both managers act to achieve the lowest possible costs for their two departments, the resulting costs for the distribution center as a whole might actually increase. For example, receiving will not be able to support the picking department's needs if the receiving staff is reduced when the material pickers require product in big batches to meet their wave-picking needs. The easy fix would be to increase inventory so that material is always ready. However, higher inventory means higher costs. Moreover, to achieve a steady flow of inbound freight to the receiving department, freight carriers would probably incur additional costs that they would then pass along to the receiving department.

In this example, the managers of the two functions lose sight of the distribution center as a whole. Unknowingly, they drive up total costs by practicing micromanagement. Worst of all, each area loses sight of its customers (including "customers" *within* the firm), who consequently suffer longer turnaround time for orders, more distribution errors due to the erratic picking process, and increased product cost.

Question 6. Have you "kept it simple"?

Although a company probably wants a system that perfectly mirrors the business, the detail and EDP resources needed to achieve perfection come at a great cost. As an ABC system becomes more complex and detailed, the cost of added detail ultimately outweighs the benefit gained from increased accuracy.

An ABC system should be as accurate as it reasonably can be, but the costs of implementing the system must justify the desired improvements in managing the business. For this reason, companies should do a cost-benefit analysis that considers the costs of:

• Data collection;
• Data maintenance;
• Time required to keep the ABC system up-to-date;
• Staffing; and
• Computer and software requirements.

These costs should be weighed in light of the accuracy needed from the ABC system to appropriately model the business. There is a direct trade-off between cost and the resulting accuracy of the ABC system. The more complex the ABC system, the higher the direct cost and the greater the probability that users will become overwhelmed by the details provided by the system.[7]

The axiom that "it is more important to be approximately right than precisely wrong" is appropriate to an ABC implementation (remember to apply the 80/20 rule). For example, in the distribution center example given previously, assume that eight cost drivers add 1 percent to the cost structure and provide enough data and control to reduce total costs by 5 percent, for a net tangible reduction of 4

percent. Adding another eight drivers to the system (thus bringing the total to sixteen cost drivers) might conceivably bring about another 5 percent reduction in cost. However, the incremental cost of data needed for the additional eight drivers is likely to cost much more than the incremental 5 percent saved. The point is to expend effort on those activities where significant rewards are possible.

As an ABC system is redefined, additional non-value-added functions are likely to be discovered. This improves the tangible cost benefit. However, in looking for non-value-added activities, don't let the system become too complex. The system will have the largest positive effect if it is widely understood and simple.

An ABC implementation requires a long-term focus, because neither tangible nor intangible benefits are likely to be experienced immediately. Companies should probably plan to spend one to three years learning about and implementing ABC, and cost-benefit studies should take this into consideration.

Question 7. Are you prepared to reassign or terminate personnel as excess resources are identified?

Once opportunities for savings begin to appear after an ABC system is in place, a company is likely to find that potential savings are often tied to staffing. Managers must be ready to make staffing adjustments, which means reassigning, retraining, transferring, or terminating employees.

To reduce tension and to increase cooperation among the remaining employees, the company may want to have a process in place to retrain, relocate, and appropriately reassign employees who can fit the new needs of the organization. Ultimately, the people retained will appreciate that they still have their jobs. As long as the company treats those employees who are laid off fairly, most employees will remain cooperative and retain their motivation to work toward the goals of the company.

Staffing is one of the more difficult aspects of an ABC implementation, yet it is essential to the success of the business. A company's manager must assume that competitors (domestic and international) are also making these difficult choices and—by cutting non-value-added activities—becoming more cost-effective. If a company has more non-value-added costs than its competitors, sooner or later its products or services will become more expensive.

Employees need to have the correct skills; they must not spend their time performing non-value-added activities. Managers and employees must use ABC to identify value-added functions and eliminate functions that do not directly relate to the company's success. The good news is that ABC implementations take time—as do retraining, redeployment, and thoughtful terminations. Management must understand these challenges and be prepared to make these changes.

Question 8. Do you understand that ABC is a management system—not a costing system?

ABC is not in accordance with generally accepted accounting principles, and for a good reason: All costs need not be absorbed or included in product costs under ABC, because ABC costs are not intended for use in inventory valuation. Instead, the purpose of ABC costs is to provide information for managing the business.

Conclusion

A review of the above questions should make it clear that the primary issues involved in ABC implementation are *management* issues, not *costing* issues. An ABC system does not replace the company's cost accounting department, because ABC is a management system, not a costing system.

The questions that this article raises point to the fact that ABC has much more to do with managing people than it has to do with the direct management of costs. The best summary of these eight questions is simply to remember the human element. The real challenge and problems lie in the human side of the cost management system, not the technical side.[8]

Education cannot be stressed enough. People must be treated as thinking individuals who can understand what is needed and can provide valuable input into what may be needed. On the negative side, the greatest implementation difficulties of any system also have to do with employees. If management provides tangible assurances that employees' best interests are being considered, the employees will work to achieve success for the company.

ABC supports a shift in how businesses operate to a much more humanistic approach. ABC should bring rewards to those organizations that commit the time and resources required to view the workplace from the standpoint of activities. ▲

Notes
1. Wendell L., French and Cecil H. Bell, Jr., *Organization Development Behavioral Science Interventions for Organization Improvement* (Englewood Cliffs, N.J.: Prentice Hall, 1984).
2. R. Lewicki, "Team Building in the Small Business Community: The Success and Failure of OD," in P. Mirvis and D. Berg, eds., *Failures in Organization Development and Change* (New York: Wiley-Interscience, 1977).
3. Edward E. Lawler, III, *Pay and Organization Development* (Reading, Penn.: Addison-Wesley, 1983).
4. H. Thomas Johnson, "Managing Costs Versus Managing Activities—Which Strategy Works?" *Financial Executive* (Jan.–Feb. 1990): 32–36.
5. Eliyahu M. Goldratt and Jeff Cox, *The Goal* (Croton-on-Hudson, N.Y.: North River Press, 1986).
6. H. T. Johnson, "Activity-Based Information: A Blueprint For World-Class Management Accounting," *Managing Accounting* (June 1988): 23–30.
7. R. Cooper, "Implementing an Activity-Based Cost System," *Journal of Cost Management* (Spring 1990): 33–42.
8. Thomas B. Lammert and Robert Ehrsam, "The Human Element: The Real Challenge in Modernizing Costs Systems," *Management Accounting* (July 1987): 32–37.

Activity-Based Costing: How Many Cost Drivers Do You Want?

John B. MacArthur[1]

This article describes a decentralized approach to choosing and implementing activity-based costing (ABC) systems, as illustrated by the experiences of Deere & Company and Fisher Controls. The article points out that the key questions that local plant managers must answer in decentralized, multinational companies are: "What sort of ABC system—and how many cost drivers—do we *want*?"

Activity-based costing (ABC) has been widely heralded as a better approach (or family of approaches) than traditional costing methods for identifying the cost of various activities within business organizations. ABC is particularly useful in companies with multiple products or services, because product or service complexity usually requires expensive overhead support activities, which need careful cost management. Simplistic volume-based allocation methods used by conventional costing systems often produce distorted unit costs for products or services.

Identification of the activities that cause costs to be incurred facilitates more precise costing of products and services, the reduction or elimination of non-value-added activities, and improved identification of the profitability of individual products and services. However, the benefits from ABC should be weighed against the costs involved in establishing and maintaining a more complex costing system (even at the local plant level), especially for decentralized companies. The "bottom-up," evolutionary development of ABC systems to meet all parties' needs was adopted by Hughes Aircraft.[2] The importance of "ownership" of a new cost system by all management

levels has been pointed out by the experience of such companies as Caterpillar.[3]

The decentralized approach to selecting and implementing ABC systems is further illustrated by the experiences of Deere & Company (Deere) and Fisher Controls (Fisher). These two major manufacturing companies, both with headquarters in the Midwest, have for cost/benefit reasons opted for different degrees of complexity in their respective corporate ABC models. However, the ABC models in both companies are similar in that they permit local plant managers to select the particular kind of ABC system that they want.

The experience at Deere & Company

Deere is a leading manufacturer of equipment for agriculture, construction, forestry, public works, and lawn and grounds care; it also operates major financial services businesses. Deere is a multinational corporation with seventeen North American and nine foreign factory locations. The company provides its goods and services on six continents. Deere has operated for more than 150 years and is well known for the quality, reliability, and durability of its products.

Deere was an early pioneer of ABC and, in fact, coined the name "activity-based costing" for the new costing approach that its cost accountants developed in 1984. The development of ABC occurred in a pilot study at the John Deere Harvester Works (Harvester Works) and in a separate study of the screw machining area of John Deere Component Works (Component Works). The improved knowledge of product costs from the Component Works pilot study resulted in more competitive bidding and transfer pricing, improved process scheduling for parts manufacture, and more efficient machine configurations.[4] The model developed at the Harvester Works was programmed into a fully functional, on-line corporate costing system.

Systems vary according to local needs. Since the Component Works and Harvester Works studies, ABC cost systems have been installed at many other Deere plant locations. The systems vary according to the costing needs perceived by local plant management. These ABC systems have helped to improve product quality and reduce manufacturing costs in both discrete parts manufacturing and continuous production environments.[5] For example, the ABC system at the John Deere Foundry, Waterloo, more accurately calculates the costs of individual castings by assigning overhead on the basis of the manufacturing activities required for the production of castings. The use of ABC has brought about greater accuracy in costing new castings for both internal and external customers. Previously, most overhead costs were allocated on the basis of direct labor dollars.

Typical ABC installations at Deere plants employ ten to fifteen cost drivers to assign the costs for twenty to sixty activities. A few examples of Deere activities and cost drivers are shown in Exhibit 1. Some cost drivers are considered basic to a functioning ABC system; others are considered optional cost drivers that may be useful for the needs of particular plants. Experience has shown that some cost drivers (e.g., machine hours) are generally applicable to Deere operations because of common activities that are present in all the Deere plants in which an ABC system has been implemented.

ABC systems improve the accuracy of cost allocation to manufactured parts through the use of appropriate cost drivers. They also show the content of overhead assigned to a part through the definition of activities (such as setup), thus facilitating better decision making. ABC information on the activities, cost drivers, and costs associated with particular parts and products is available to management to aid in the decision process.[6] For example, Deere has used ABC information for various what-if cost studies and also to identify the cost of alternative routings for new parts. More precise costing has also helped

Exhibit 1. *Examples of Deere & Company Activities and Cost Drivers*

Overhead Activity	Cost Drivers
Machine operations	Machine hours[a]
Setup	Setup hours[a]
Production scheduling	Manufacturing orders[a]
Inspection	Pieces inspected[b]
Shipping	Shipping hours[b]

[a] Basic cost drivers.
[b] Optional cost drivers.

plant management make product-mix and sourcing decisions.

In one recent plantwide reorganization at Deere, ABC cost information was used to evaluate non-value-added activities such as material handling and setups. The ABC data assisted management in reorganizing machine tools into manufacturing cells. The benefits from improved costing accuracy and more helpful cost disclosure were deemed to outweigh the costs of designing, implementing, and operating a more complex ABC system in this local plant.

"On-line calculator system." ABC data can be manipulated on-line by manufacturing personnel using what is called an "on-line calculator system." This system provides detailed ABC information such as the incremental cost of a specified part and the actual machine run time and related overhead to produce a particular part on a specified operation. Users can identify the relevant costs for a particular decision and make on-line simulations. By using the on-line calculator system, users can thus simulate the expected costs of new products and new parts. In essence, computerized ABC systems have made it possible for Deere manufacturing personnel to understand and manage their product costs more effectively.

In most Deere installations, local plant management has chosen to use the corporate ABC model that was developed at the Harvester Works, though optional cost drivers have been added to meet local needs. For example, one Deere factory modified the material handling portion of the corporate ABC system so that it would work in tandem with the plant's implementation of a just-in-time approach to production and purchasing.

Choosing cost drivers. Most Deere plants want detailed cost drivers for activities defined to the department level. Some plants want even more detailed cost information (e.g., down to the machine center level) so that they can monitor and accurately allocate costs of resources such as capital investment, power, and maintenance. The experience gained from implementing the corporate ABC model at different plants over the years has made it possible to adapt the corporate model quickly enough to meet the needs of most Deere plants. Two plants, however (both of them foundries for casting metals), chose not to select some variant of the corporate model.

Two plants that went their own way. The two Deere foundries developed their own ABC systems for two related major reasons:

1. Foundry management wanted to add some unique cost drivers not then present in the corporate system; and
2. At the time, the corporate model would have taken longer to program to meet local needs than local management desired.

By taking the initiative in the development of ABC, the two foundries obtained the timely cost information that they wanted for sourcing decisions, pricing, and process evaluation. However, foundry management did solicit the help of corporate management to gain a proper understanding of ABC principles and data development.

In summary, a decentralized approach to choosing a cost system makes it easier to gain the commitment of local plant management to a new ABC system.[7]

The experience at Fisher Controls

Fisher Controls is the leading supplier of process control products and services in such diverse industries as chemicals, oil and gas, pulp and paper, and power. Fisher operates twenty major manufacturing and nonmanufacturing sites in ten countries and has sales and service capabilities in virtually every country in the world. Fisher's manufacturing is conducted in nine major facilities in seven countries.

In late 1988, Fisher's Marshalltown site established a multidisciplinary team to explore alternate costing techniques to address the inadequacies of conventional costing systems that used volume-based allocation methods (i.e., direct labor hours and direct materials costs). Factors prompting this review included increases in:

*   Global competition;
*   Quality standards;
*   Factory automation (which has reduced direct labor costs); and
*   Factory overhead (which requires careful cost management and more refined allocations to cost objects).

The Marshalltown team's primary objective was to improve the accuracy of standard product cost. The team developed an ABC model that is comprehensive enough to properly cost the significant activities of Fisher's manufacturing operations, but still is manageable under the existing cost system. For example, the number of cost drivers was restricted to minimize the amount of time and other resources needed to reprogram the cost system. More recently, Fisher has purchased ABC software to help structure further cost system developments. Examples of Fisher's activities and cost drivers are shown in Exhibit 2.

Non-value-added activities and nonmanufacturing costs. As Fisher and other companies have discovered, an important by-product of identifying key cost drivers for allocation purposes is the discovery and costing of non-value-added activities. While efforts are made to lower the costs of value-added activities, simultaneous efforts are underway at Fisher to eliminate such non-value-added activities as:

*   Expediting;
*   Inspecting;
*   Material handling;
*   Setup; and
*   Storage.

The intent is to expand ABC analysis to consider such nonmanufacturing costs as distribution, marketing, administration, and technical activities.

Fisher is educating its managers on the benefits of activity-based management. Top man-

Exhibit 2. *Examples of Fisher Controls Activities and Cost Drivers*

Overhead Activity	Cost Drivers
Purchasing and receiving	Number of purchase orders
Shop order handling	Number of shop orders
Valve assembly support	Number of customer requisitions
Setup and teardown	Number of operations
Inspection	Number of operations

agers have strongly encouraged plant managers to adopt ABC in their plants as an important factor in remaining globally competitive. As a result, the implementation of ABC is also well under way in the Fisher plant at Sherman, Texas. As at Deere, local managers can adopt whatever ABC model they want.

Interdisciplinary ABC development teams

At Deere, ABC development teams primarily involve members from:

- Accounting;
- Manufacturing engineering; and
- Computer systems.

In addition, manufacturing, product engineering, and quality engineering personnel actively participate in developing data for ABC.

At Fisher, ABC teams include representatives from:

- Applications engineering;
- Assembly;
- Cost accounting;
- Industrial engineering;
- Inventory control;
- Machine shop;
- Product engineering; and
- Human resources.

Such interdisciplinary involvement in ABC projects leads to the development of cost systems that generally satisfy the overall requirements of plants; it also provides common ground for dialogue between managers of the various factory functions. The ABC approach can even develop into a management style or strategy for continuous improvement of an organization by focusing the attention of managers toward resource allocation at the activity level.

What ABC system do you want?

The big question that managers of plants at Deere and Fisher must answer is: "What ABC system do you want?" This is a different question from: "What ABC system do you *need*?" or "Which cost drivers *should be* implemented?"[8]

The question: "What ABC system do you want?" implies a "bottom-up," participatory approach to the design of cost systems—one that allows the decision makers (i.e., the users of the cost system) to request the information that will help them run their operations more efficiently. The corporate controller's costing specialists can use their functional expertise to help design and implement an ABC system that satisfies the local requirements. This approach is consistent with the decentralized approach taken at both Deere and Fisher.

The questions: "What ABC system do you *need*?" and "Which cost drivers *should be* implemented?" on the other hand, are normative and suggest more of a "top-down," autocratic approach to the development of a cost system—one imposed, in other words, by the "experts" at corporate headquarters. (This may, nevertheless, be a valid approach in more centralized corporate organizations.)

Corporate vs. local development of ABC

A corporate ABC system has the advantage of being an "off the shelf" variant with a proven track record in other settings. However, plant managers may still perceive the net benefits of a locally designed ABC system to outweigh the net benefits of adopting a modified version of an established corporate model. In companies that have a participatory management style, a similar result may be achieved by permitting sufficient flexibility to be built into a corporate ABC system so that it can accommodate the wishes of local plant management teams.

Especially in decentralized organizations such as Deere and Fisher, local plant managers may not use cost data generated by a corporate ABC system that is imposed on them. This problem may be exacerbated if the corporate ABC model is highly complex and expensive. A complex ABC system will not be cost beneficial if the ABC information is largely unused by plant managers. Therefore, corporate proponents of the merits of ABC must do a good job of marketing a more sophisticated cost system to local managers. As is usually the case, the behavioral benefits and costs associated with new cost systems are important considerations, although they may be hard to measure.

Local development of an ABC system has the advantage of adding a further ABC model to the corporate costing repertoire for future consideration by other plants. To keep information production costs to a sensible level, a locally developed ABC system will likely be a compromise version based on the requests of managers within the plant. Otherwise, it would be necessary to have several different ABC systems running simultaneously within each plant to provide the various types of unique cost information requested by the individual subunit managers. Such micro-ABC systems are not likely to be viable on cost-benefit grounds. In any case, the necessary expertise and time to develop an on-site, tailor-made ABC system may not exist in smaller plants.

Whether an ABC system is a corporate or locally developed model, users will likely want to start with only a limited number of cost drivers so that they will not be overwhelmed with complexity. Cost drivers can be added later as the need becomes apparent to local managers. In this way, decentralized plants select the ABC system and specific cost drivers that they want.

Final thoughts

Choosing an appropriate ABC system for a particular plant is never easy. There are tangible and intangible benefits and costs associated with, for example, the selection of many

rather than few cost drivers. Each plant must weigh the cost of extra time, effort, and other resources against the perceived benefits from more detailed and precise costing.

The experiences of both Deere and Fisher illustrate that a single ABC system is unlikely to be appropriate for all operating units within a large, global company. ABC systems are thus likely to be introduced into individual plants gradually over a number of years as local managers realize their need for more precise cost information. Therefore, key questions that local managers must answer (especially in a decentralized organization) before making changes in their cost systems are: "What sort of ABC system—and how many cost drivers—do we *want*?" ▲

Reprinted from *Journal of Cost Management*, Fall 1992, pp. 37–41. Copyright © 1992 by Warren Gorham Lamont, a division of Research Institute of America Inc. All right reserved. Used by permission.

Notes
1. The author wishes to thank Deere & Company and Fisher Controls for permitting details of their ABC systems to be discussed in this article. In particular, the author wants to thank Duane R. Lemke and Eric Sandberg of Deere & Company and Jim Sullivan and Deborah Vogeler of Fisher Controls for their contributions to this article.
2. Jack Haedicke & David Feil, "In a DOD Environment Hughes Aircraft Sets the Standard for ABC," *Management Accounting* (Feb. 1991): 30.
3. Lou F. Jones, "Product Costing at Caterpillar," *Management Accounting* (Feb. 1991): 41.
4. Robert S. Kaplan, "John Deere Component Works (A)," *Harvard Business School Case Series 187-107* (Rev. Nov. 1987); and Robert S. Kaplan, "John Deere Component Works (B)," *Harvard Business School Case Series 187-108* (Rev. Nov. 1987).
5. See the comparison of ABC for discrete part versus continuous process environments in Thomas L. Albright & James M. Reeve, "A Case Study on the Impact of Material Yield Related Cost Drivers on Economic Improvement," *Journal of Management Accounting Research* 20–43. (Fall 1992). Also see James M. Reeve, "Cost Management in Continuous-Process Environments," *Journal of Cost Management* (Spring 1991): 22–34.
6. A report that communicates this information is called a "bill of activities" in "Glossary of Activity-Based Management," Norm Raffish & Peter B.B. Turney, eds., *Journal of Cost Management* (Fall 1991): 58; and Peter B.B. Turney, *Common Cents: The ABC Performance Breakthrough* (Hillsboro, Ore.: Cost Technology 1991): 163–165, 208.
7. The importance of carefully selecting the way in which an ABC system is introduced into a company is discussed in Steven M. Hronec, "How a Controller Communicates the Change to ABC," *Corporate Controller* (Sept./Oct. 1990): 5–7.
8. See examples of such questions in Robin Cooper, "The Rise of Activity-Based Costing—Part Three: How Many Cost Drivers Do You Need, and How Do You Select Them?" *Journal of Cost Management* (Winter 1989): 34.

Zero-Base Activity-Based Costing

John B. MacArthur[1]

This article reports the recent experience of a major Midwestern manufacturing company that developed an activity-based costing (ABC) system as its *first* costing system—in effect, a "zero-base ABC system." This company's experience illustrates that a functioning ABC system can be implemented at a reasonable cost. Although ABC systems are more complex than typical conventional costing systems, this case study shows that ABC can be cost-justified by smaller companies as well as by large, long-established companies.

The emergence of activity-based costing (ABC) systems as potential replacements for traditional costing systems is well documented.[2] The identification of cost drivers that are not related to volume, as well as volume-related cost drivers, can lead to more accurate product cost measurement, especially if a company manufactures a wide variety of products that differ in their utilization of activities, and if the number of units in production batches vary widely by product.[3] Costing non-value-added activities can also help companies manage costs.

Cases have been reported of companies that replace their existing costing system with full-blown ABC systems, while others adopt a more evolutionary approach by making more moderate changes to their existing cost systems.[4] This article complements such studies by reporting the recent experience of a major Midwestern manufacturing company that developed an ABC system as its *first* costing system—in effect, a "zero-base ABC system." This company's experience illustrates that a functioning ABC system can be implemented at a reasonable cost. Although ABC systems

tend to be more complex than typical conventional costing systems, ABC can be cost-justified by smaller companies as well as by larger, long-established companies.

Case study: Bertch Cabinet Mfg., Inc.

Bertch Cabinet Mfg., Inc. (Bertch) started production in 1977 in a converted barn with only one product: bathroom vanities. Through a combination of high-quality work and competitive pricing, however, Bertch soon expanded its operations and product lines. By 1991, the company had achieved an annual sales volume of more than $25 million, which put Bertch in the top 10 percent of cabinet manufacturers.

Bertch conducts business in five modern facilities, including a building that was recently completed. Together, these facilities provide over 187,000 square feet for production. Bertch employs state-of-the-art equipment in its factories. As Exhibit 1 shows, Bertch is divided into six operating divisions and a support division, the Transportation Division.

"Seat of the pants" costing

Bertch's world-class manufacturing was not matched by its costing information. Product cost information was provided on an *ad hoc* basis, and a periodic inventory system was used. Manufacturing overhead was applied to inventory using direct labor dollars.

Despite having limited cost information, Bertch was successful for at least two reasons:

- It had a young, highly motivated management team and a workforce that was committed to efficient manufacturing, the production of quality products, and providing quality service to customers;

Exhibit 1. *Bertch Divisions and Product Lines*

Kitchen Cabinet Division	Bath Cabinet Division	Cultured Marble Top Division	Mirror Division	Semi-Custom Division	Production Support Division	Transportation Division
800 models custom	80 models stock	480 models	Unlimited variations	New division	Parts & panel sizing	Own trucks, trailers & tractors

• It operated in a highly competitive market in which prices were largely set by external market forces, which meant that cost information was not needed in establishing prices.

Nonetheless, pressure started growing at Bertch to have a world-class costing system to properly support manufacturing operations.

Competitive pressures

Competitive pressures increased as the cabinet market moved into the mature stage of the product life cycle. This market pressure was exacerbated by the worldwide recession of 1990–1991. Several of Bertch's competitors were even forced out of business. In such a heightened competitive environment, Bertch management recognized the need to have more accurate cost information to identify the profitability of the company's various products.[5] Management also wanted to determine how significant non-value-added activities (setups, for example) were in the company. Having this information would make it possible for managers to begin reducing, or possibly even eliminating, nonproductive activities.

The increasing complexity of Bertch's operations intensified line management's dissatisfaction with existing cost information and further stimulated demand for a more accurate and informative costing system.[6] Symptoms of the increasing complexity were as follows:

• A rapid growth in Bertch's product line from one product to a widely diverse range of products, as shown in Exhibit 1;
• A wide variety of operating activities that are used to varying degrees in manufacturing the different products; and
• The addition of advance technology machines, which increased the proportion of overhead in total production costs.

In a complex manufacturing environment with relatively high levels of overhead, the use of a single unit-level application base (typically direct labor cost) is not likely to produce accurate product costs. Moreover, significant overhead costs need careful cost management.

The implementation of ABC at Bertch

In summer 1991, Bertch employed a senior accounting major to help identify the resources consumed by the various production activities and also to cost the activities consumed by the products during a recent period. The ABC pilot study was conducted using a Lotus 1-2-3 spreadsheet and the book *Common Cents* as a primary reference guide for the implementation of ABC.[7] The company decided to initiate a pilot ABC study in the Mirror Division (Mirror) and the Cultured Marble Top Division (Marble Top) because it was thought that activity analysis would be easiest in those two divisions.

Designing a pilot study for quick returns on an investment in ABC is advantageous for at least the following three reasons:

• Swift returns shorten the payback period for the ABC project investment;
• Early returns help managers determine the worth of ABC with a minimum investment of time and other resources;
• Speedy returns generate early momentum in support of ABC and encourage further adoption of ABC by other divisions.

Mirror Division

Each of the machines, receiving, and shipping were identified as suitable activity centers for the Mirror study. Resource drivers (first-stage cost drivers)[8] were identified to track the resources consumed by each activity center. For example, managers were interviewed to identify the time devoted to various activities as a basis for assigning their salaries and salary-related costs to the activity centers.

The activity drivers (second-stage cost drivers)[9] for Mirror were unit-level drivers, such as the lineal footage of glass processed through a machine for each product, because non-volume-related activities were minimal. For example, through observation and interviews with Mirror personnel, it was determined that setup time was relatively insignificant. Moreover, since the basic raw material input was sheets of glass, the purchasing department manager did not perceive any differences in the order costs for different products. Exhibit 2 shows examples of Mirror activities and activity drivers.

The Mirror operation is a divergent rather than a convergent process, and therefore is without the front-end component complexity that is typical of a convergent process (such as high-production scheduling costs).[10] The common glass raw material is processed into a variety of mirror products. It is also without the end-product variety complexity expected of a divergent process (such as high marketing costs), because most of its output is transferred to other divisions of Bertch.[11]

Initially, the major benefits for Mirror from ABC stemmed from the selection of appropriate resource and activity drivers (see Exhibit 2). For example, some mirrors require holes for lights. Since the number of holes varies according to the type of mirror, the number of holes is used as the activity driver to assign the costs of the drilling activity to the mirrors. This driver correctly measures the resources in the drilling activity center consumed by the various types of mirrors.

The various mirrors do not all follow the same routing through the production processes. Mirrors should not receive a share of the indirect costs of activity centers through which they are not processed. This distinction between products is not possible under a traditional costing system that uses a single allocation base (such as direct labor cost) to assign the indirect costs of a department (consisting of many different activities) to all products that flow through the department. This approach ignores whether or not particular products receive any benefit from all the

Exhibit 2. *Examples of Mirror Division Activities and Activity Drivers*

Activity	**Activity Driver**
Mirror cutting	Square inches of mirror surface
Mirror safety backing	Lineal inches of mirror length
Mirror beveling	# Oval mirrors
Drilling mirror holes	# holes

production activities in the department. For this reason, conventional costing is sometimes referred to as the "peanut butter" approach to cost assignment, because indirect costs are spread uniformly across all products by means of a single allocation base.[12]

Under the Bertch ABC system, indirect costs are assigned to mirrors only by activity centers that process the mirrors. This is particularly important in Bertch because one expensive Mirror activity center (one that has a high-cost machine) is used only by a small number of mirror types. Managers were eager to learn the ABC cost of these mirrors to help establish internal and external prices.

Cultured Marble Top Division

Unlike the Mirror Division, the Cultured Marble Top Division's various products all go through the same operations. Raw materials costs differ, as do the size and design of the various cultured marble tops. Batch-level costs are also more significant in the Marble Top than in the Mirror Division.

For example, mold preparation is labor intensive, because each mold requires taping before processing. Setup times are also significant when changing from one type of mold to another. The costs of setup are maintained for purposes of cost management, but, initially at least, it was decided not to separately assign setup costs to products using batch-level activity drivers (e.g., setup time or number of setups). Instead, setup costs are included as part of the indirect cost of the particular activity centers to which they relate and are assigned to Marble Top products using the various unit-level activity drivers of particular activity centers. This helps to keep the costs of collecting information to a minimum for the initial ABC system. Exhibit 3 shows examples of Marble Top's activities and activity drivers.

Activity	Activity Driver
Mold preparation	# molds prepared
Grinding	# tops ground
Buffing	# tops buffed
Shipping & packaging	# tops shipped

An interesting problem was encountered with regard to costing the molds used for making the cultured marble vanity tops. The molding process involves seven distinct activities. The bottom mold is first taped in preparation for the filling activity. The second activity is to apply a gel-coat finish to the bottom mold. The third activity is machine-filling of the matrix into the bottom mold. A top mold hat is next placed on the bottom mold base and extra matrix is added to completely fill the mold. Subsequently, the molds pass through the remaining three activities of removing the top mold hat, mold hat waxing, and demolding. On average, the molds last for seven years with proper routine maintenance (such as regular Duracoating) and repair work when necessary.

The problem facing Bertch was whether to allocate the mold costs to all the activity centers through which each mold travels, to allocate the cost to one representative activity center (e.g., mold filling) only, or to keep the molds as a separate cost center. After much consideration and consultation,[13] Bertch decided to create a separate activity center for mold preparation. Sensible resource drivers could not be determined for assigning mold costs to all the activity centers through which the molds travel. In addition, the activity drivers are different for each of these activity centers, and none is particularly appropriate for the mold costs.

Each mold benefits several time periods and many units of product. The mold preparation activity center costs (that is, mold depreciation, the cost of the wooden pallets on which the molds travel, and repair and maintenance costs) should be assigned to the cultured marble tops on the basis of the estimated number of units to benefit from each type of mold (they differ in size). As Exhibit 3

shows, the selected activity driver for the mold preparation activity center is the number of molds prepared.

ABC limitations

The mold allocation problem outlined previously highlights an important limitation of ABC analysis. It is sometimes claimed that ABC is useful in making decisions such as whether to make or buy a component.[14] However, not all ABC costs at the product level are incremental costs.[15] For example, outsourcing the manufacture of a particular cultured marble top would most probably reduce such mold costs as repair and maintenance, but not the significant sunk cost of mold depreciation. Only the future costs of replacing the redundant molds would be saved. Essentially, ABC product costs represent more accurate estimates of the *long-run*, strategic costs of providing goods and services.[16] Care should thus be exercised in determining both the long-run and the short-run costs that are incremental to a particular make-or-buy decision.

Further developments since the ABC pilot study

Since the completion of the ABC pilot study at the end of summer 1991, the Mirror Division has used ABC information to help price glass products sold to outside customers. For the first time, managers have cost of sales information by style and size of mirror and by cultured marble top. This information helps managers evaluate the long-term profitability of these products. The supervisors of the Mirror and Marble Top Divisions compile weekly reports on the time spent by labor at the activity centers identified in the ABC pilot study. The labor information is used by upper-management for evaluating labor efficiency.

As a result of the ABC pilot study, Mirror and Cultured Marble Top managers have also been made aware of the nature and cost of non-value-added activities; this information is used to help manage the costs of such activities. Examples of non-value-added activities are shown in Exhibit 4.

Bertch management concluded that the initial ABC pilot study was a success, so in summer 1992 it purchased personal computer (PC)

Exhibit 4. *Examples of Mirror Division and Marble Top Division Non-Value-Added Activities*

Mirror Division	Marble Top Division
Changing wheels on beveling machines	Receiving materials
Washing glass particles from mirrors	Mold protective coating
Counting and checking mirrors	Quality control sampling
Cleaning up	Cleaning up

software to continuously maintain the cost records on an ABC basis. In the future, activity analyses will be conducted in the remaining five Bertch divisions. Eventually, Bertch plans to integrate the ABC costing records with the general ledger system on a mainframe computer.

Final thoughts

The early experiences at Bertch indicate that a successful "zero-base" ABC system can be implemented for a modest investment. Usable results were obtained using a relatively straightforward ABC PC system that uses only unit-level activity drivers for the initial model. The gradual introduction of batch-level, product-level, and facility-level activity drivers can proceed as the ABC model is developed to meet the growing needs of the company. ▲

Notes

1. The author wishes to thank Bertch Cabinet Mfg., Inc. for allowing details of their ABC system to be discussed in this article and also anonymous referees for their helpful comments about this article. In particular, the author wishes to thank Pamela D. Bishop, Dawn L. Cutsforth, and Mark D. Fober for their contributions to this article.
2. For example, see James P. Borden, "Review of Literature on Activity-Based Costing," *Journal of Cost Management* (Spring 1990): 5–12; and Alfred King, "The Current Status of Activity-Based Costing: An Interview with Robin Cooper and Robert S. Kaplan," *Management Accounting* (September 1991): 22–26.
3. See Robin Cooper, "The Rise of Activity-Based Costing—Part Two: When Do I Need an Activity-Based Cost System?" *Journal of Cost Management* (Fall 1988): 41–48; and Robin Cooper, "The Rise of Activity-Based Costing—Part Three: How Many Cost Drivers Do You Need, and How

Do You Select Them?" *Journal of Cost Management* (Winter 1989): 34–46.
4. For example, see the contrasting experiences of companies described in Robin Cooper, "Cost Classification in Unit-Based and Activity-Based Manufacturing Cost Systems," *Journal of Cost Management* (Fall 1990): 4–14, and of Deere & Company and Fisher Controls in John B. MacArthur, "Activity-Based Costing: How Many Cost Drivers Do You Want?" *Journal of Cost Management* (Fall 1992): 37–41.
5. See support for this viewpoint under "Myth 7: The market sets prices so we do not need product costs" in Peter B.B. Turney, "Ten Myths About Implementing an Activity-Based Cost System," *Journal of Cost Management* (Spring 1990): 29.
6. The characteristics identified in this section are among those suggested to indicate potential for an ABC system in Charles T. Horngren & George Foster, *Cost Accounting: A Managerial Emphasis,* 7th ed. (Englewood Cliffs, N.J.: Prentice-Hall Inc. 1991): 157.
7. Peter B.B. Turney, *Common Cents The ABC Performance Breakthrough* (Hillsboro, Or.: Cost Technology 1991).
8. For a definition of "resource driver," see "Glossary of Activity-Based Management," Norm Raffish & Peter B.B. Turney, eds., *Journal of Cost Management* (Fall 1991): 61.
9. For a definition of "activity driver," see *id.* at 57.
10. For a comparison of ABC in convergent versus divergent processes, see Thomas L. Albright and James M. Reeve, "A Case Study on the Impact of Material Yield Related Cost Drivers on Economic Improvement," *Journal of Management Accounting Research* (Fall 1992): 20–43; and James M. Reeve, "Cost Management in Continuous-Process Environments," *Journal of Cost Management* (Spring 1991): 22–34. The latter article states that "[m]ost discrete-part environments can be characterized as a convergent process" in which "components are fabricated, finished, inspected, and assembled into subassemblies, which are then assembled into a complete unit" (page 22). The same article goes on to describe "[c]ontinuous-manufacturing processes . . . as a divergent process" in which: "[c]ommon raw material streams are routed through a common process. This stream of material is eventually split into many different end products . . ." that "vary from the original raw material stream by slight differences in how they are processed, or because of the introduction of minors (additives), such as color." (page 22).
11. *Id.*
12. Charles T. Horngren and George Foster, *Cost Accounting: A Managerial Emphasis,* 7th ed. (Englewood Cliffs, N.J.: Prentice-Hall Inc. 1991): 407.
13. Informal contacts were made by the author with Robin Cooper (Claremont Graduate School) and Peter B.B. Turney (CEO, Cost Technology Inc.) to obtain their thoughts on this question.
14. See James A. Brimson, *Activity Accounting: An Activity-Based Costing Approach* (New York: John Wiley & Sons, Inc. 1991): 77, 170–171; and Peter B.B. Turney, *Common Cents The ABC Performance Breakthrough,* (Hillsboro, Or.: Cost Technology 1991): 281–282.
15. For additional discussion on the limitations of ABC, see Douglas Sharp and Linda F. Christensen, "A New View Of Activity-Based Costing," *Management Accounting* (September 1991): 32–34; H. Thomas Johnson, "It's Time to Stop Overselling Activity-Based Concepts," *Management Accounting* (September 1992): 26–35; and Robert W. Koehler, "Triple Threat Strategy," *Management Accounting* (October 1991): 30–34.
16. See H. Thomas Johnson, "Activity Management: Reviewing the Past and Future of Cost Management," *Journal of Cost Management* (Winter 1990): 4–7.

Pitfalls in Using ABC Cost-Driver Information to Manage Operating Costs

H. Thomas Johnson, Thomas P. Vance, and R. Steven Player

Activity-based costing (ABC) has proved so useful in understanding product costs that managers may be tempted to rely on ABC information to help manage their operating costs. Managers can and should use ABC information to understand and eliminate activities—that is, the work that people do. But ABC information reflects a company's *existing* processes rather than the way the processes *should* be. Companies that make operating decisions to economize on activity drivers may be ignoring what they should be doing to compete and to achieve long-term profitability.

The story has a familiar ring: an auto component manufacturer found itself in a bind. Beset by foreign competition in a mature product line, it had refused to cut prices below what it believed were already unprofitable limits. Instead, it had expanded its sales of newer, more sophisticated products that appeared to have very high margins. Despite this quick action to shift toward a "richer" product mix, the company was soon hemorrhaging red ink and facing potential bankruptcy.

Management called in outside experts to advise them on product costing. Using activity-based costing (ABC), they found that the company was perversely abandoning its most profitable product lines and replacing them with lines that barely broke even, if at all.

Scarcely a controller alive today hasn't heard about the power of ABC to save companies from making disastrous product-mix decisions based on traditional cost information. But the tool has proven so useful in understanding product costs that managers increasingly are relying on the same information to help manage their operating costs. In many cases this use of ABC is impeding efforts to compete and profit in the customer-driven global economy.

It doesn't have to be that way. Managers can use activity-based cost information to manage operating costs—in both manufacturing and service companies—with one caveat. ABC can be an extremely powerful tool for the purpose if it is used to understand and eliminate activities—in other words, the work people do. It is not if it's used only to understand and manipulate "drivers," such as the number of setups or the number of purchase orders. Only when people look behind those drivers to the activities that surround them can they use activity-based costs to manage operating costs successfully.

The pitfall: focusing only on drivers

As it's currently used by most companies, activity-based costing is a misnomer: the tool seldom costs activities; it usually costs drivers. While focusing on drivers is a good way to understand the costs of specific products, it's a dangerous way to make operating decisions.

Useful for product decisions

ABC is useful for making product decisions because it provides a way to estimate indirect costs: it assigns costs to products according to the demands each product makes on the company's overhead resources.

A two-stage approach is used to conduct most ABC analyses. The thrust of the design, which was originally codified by Robin Cooper of Harvard Business School, is to identify a relatively small set of overhead cost drivers (say 6 to 12) in stage one and to trace indirect costs to each driver. In stage two, the company determines the percentage of the

Figure 1. *"Activity"-Based Product Costing (ABC)*

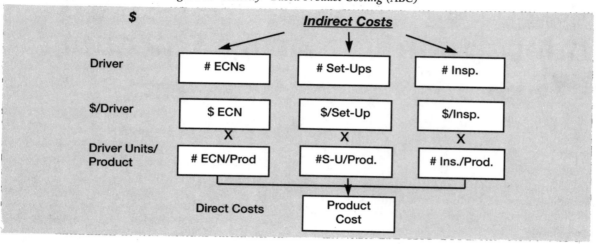

drivers consumed by each product or service. The result is an estimate of the indirect costs of each product based on such drivers as engineering change notices (ECNs), setups, and inspections (see Figure 1).

For example, consider purchase orders, a common indirect cost driver. Suppose it costs $100 to process purchase orders for the total output of a plant for one day—say ten cars. If each car requires the same direct labor, the old accounting methods would distribute the cost equally to all units at $10 a car. However, one car might be a custom model in which half the parts are nonstandard and must be ordered individually. Using the new methodology of ABC, that car might be assigned $50 in purchasing overhead while the remaining $50 is allocated to the other nine cars.

This kind of cost-driver information is excellent for marketing decisions. In pricing, for instance, it helps marketing managers confirm their suspicions that a company has been overestimating the cost of standard products. It also helps in evaluating the profitability of your product mix. With this kind of information, managers in tough, competitive situations can "know when to hold and know when to fold." Products with lower margins will be an easier discard. Those with higher margins will clearly be worth fighting for.

To reliably cost a wide array of products that consume resources in diverse ways, it is very important to accurately trace resource consumption to the products that demand the resources. Two-stage, multiple-driver ABC analysis does that very well.

Dangerous for operating decisions

But danger lurks when companies use the same driver-cost information to manage operating costs. The drivers specify "what" but not "why." When managers try to use them to reduce operating costs, they are accepting the company's current processes as a given and are simply trying to reduce the number of units for each cost driver—for example, by getting rid of products that require a large number of purchase orders. They are not considering how the customer will respond to the change.

This is a natural extension of a philosophy that has prevailed for the last 40 years in American business: the belief that profitability comes from scale economies and high-volume business. In the fifties and sixties it may have been the right answer. Low unit cost was the chief source of competitive advantage, so manufacturers produced long runs of stan-

Companies that make operating decisions to economize on activity drivers are ignoring what they should be doing to compete and to achieve long-term profitability.

dardized products in large-scale facilities. Large inventories hedged against uncertain quality and inflexibility, usually causing total costs to rise. But more output could always offset more costs. The catch phrase was "making it up on volume"—assuming customers could always be persuaded to purchase the excess output at a price above variable cost.

But in a global economy, when the customer is in the driver's seat demanding high quality and customized products, flexibility is much more important. In this environment, "making it up on volume" is the wrong answer. Companies that make operating decisions to economize on activity drivers are ignoring what they should be doing to compete and to achieve long-term profitability. Long runs and large batches cannot raise profitability when customers want differentiated products. That kind of market requires fast changeover and small lots.

To articulate these dangers, let's examine a couple of composite cases that bring into focus the difficulties of several actual companies. The first case involves the auto component manufacturer mentioned at the beginning of the article. The results of ABC were eye-opening for this company: they found that product costs varied by as much as 300% from what they had thought.

They soon began to take a hard look at the cost drivers. One insight the new ABC data revealed was how much it really cost to set up machines every time an order for a batch of components was released to the shop floor. The old cost accounting system pooled setup costs with all other indirect factory costs and spread them over components in proportion to direct labor hours. Components ordered in large lots that kept machines running steadily for long periods of time absorbed the same overhead cost per unit (including setup costs) as components ordered in small lots that required more frequent and costlier setup. Obviously, the old costing system did not reveal the true cost of handling small lots produced in short runs. The ABC system, however, by pooling setup costs separately from other indirect costs and applying them to components in relation to their demands for setup time, eliminated that distortion and put the costs where they belonged—on the small lots.

The new information prompted management to alter its pricing and operations practices. They cut prices of components produced in large lots and charged a premium to buyers ordering small lots. They also discouraged the sales staff from taking orders from buyers who insisted on frequent delivery of small quantities.

A manufacturer of personal computers and electronic measurement equipment followed a similar path in applying ABC information to operations. Management had always costed products by pooling all factory overhead and allocating it over direct labor hours. Thus, the cost accounting system did not reliably differentiate among costs of several printed circuit boards that were fabricated through very different processes, such as three different types of component insertion (dip, axial, and manual) and two types of soldering (wave and manual). Consequently, costs of boards with substantial numbers of manually inserted components were not significantly different from costs of boards with components inserted automatically. This was counter-intuitive to what every design engineer believed to be the true costs of printed circuit boards.

The company installed an ABC system to give product design engineers more reliable information about the cost of design decisions. In the new system, indirect costs (essentially all costs except materials and purchased components) were pooled separately for automatic and manual insertion. It confirmed that manual insertion procedures cost several times as much as auto-insertion. However, auto-insertion machines could not operate reliably in spaces as small as human hands could. Therefore, designs for products made on auto-insertion machines had to space components further apart and further from the edge of a board. That meant trading off lower auto-insertion costs for somewhat larger boards. Nevertheless, design engineers proceeded to design manually-inserted boards out of existence.

In both of these cases, the information helped management see ways to reduce costs and improve short-term profits by altering product mix or process mix. But, long-term, both companies were destined to watch the market pass them by. In both cases management failed to ask two crucial questions:

1. Do consumers really want the product?
2. If so, how can activity analysis help us identify changes in the way we work so we can produce it efficiently and effectively?

To drive competitive and profitable operations in a customer-driven global economy, companies must give customers what they want, not persuade them to purchase what the company presently produces at lowest cost. If customers favor small lots and smaller electronic products, then companies must respond, even when it costs more.

Looking behind the drivers to reduce activities

To compete well today, companies need information about the work people do and the time they take to do it—activity information. Achieving global competitiveness, identified with total customer satisfaction, means reducing "wasted" activities that actually constrain the company's ability to be responsive to customer needs. For example, many companies are trying to eliminate some of the activities involved in handling a customer complaint or setting up a new product on the manufacturing line. To accomplish those changes, companies must really understand what activities are taking place in their organizations and why.

Using activity analysis to cost activities

Activity analysis, pioneered in the 1960s and 1970s by General Electric and expanded upon by Arthur Andersen & Co. in the late 1970s, has helped hundreds of companies see nonintuitive ways to reduce costs by changing the way work is done, not by realizing economies with greater volumes of products customers don't really want.

For example, in 1978 Arthur Andersen used activity analysis to help the Dairy Equipment Company in Milwaukee, Wisconsin, reduce costs. Management of the Dairy Equipment Company, maker of stainless steel milk cooling tanks, observed that at one plant the second shift required more workers (53 as opposed to 47) and more overtime to produce the same amount of product as the first shift. Their charge to the project team was to

make the second shift just as productive as the first.

Challenging current activities to ask why they're taking place is what really allows companies to achieve competitive and profitable operations.

If the team had begun by searching for cost drivers they probably would have identified things such as inspections and setup times. The natural instinct would have been to manage the frequency of inspections and setups on the second shift.

Instead, the team began by defining, tracing, and estimating the time spent on activities during both shifts, such as receiving and stocking, setting up and changing over, inspecting and testing, reworking, waiting, housekeeping, expediting, and maintaining equipment (see Figure 2). To their surprise, they found that the second shift had about the same number of setups, inspections, and reworking. But they spent three times as much of their time performing these and other indirect activities such as stocking, handling materials, maintaining equipment and looking for parts. Why? First, supervisors and support personnel went home at 5 PM every day and left the second shift to fend for themselves. Second, personnel always started inexperienced workers on the second shift.

Instead of taking the traditional approach of laying off workers, the team recommended that the company hire two materials expediters and one supervisor for the second shift. Even after the additional $80,000 in salaries, increased productivity led to an annual reduction in total labor costs and overtime premiums of $145,000—all in 1978 dollars, of course. When the company rolled out these concepts to its other plants, the annual savings amounted to $660,000.

The same approach is being applied today, in service companies as well as manufacturing operations. Last year Weyerhaeuser Mortgage Company, under competitive pressure to re-

Figure 2. *Activity Analysis at Dairy Equipment Company*

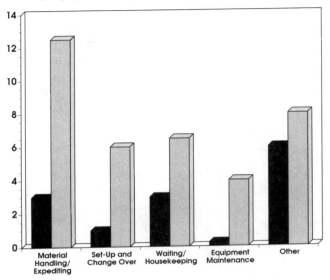

duce costs, wanted to improve its profitability. Using activity analysis, the project team was able to identify non-value added activities and streamlining opportunities. This allowed Weyerhaeuser to understand the impact of changes such as flattening their organization, consolidating locations, and eliminating activities that did not justify their costs. These and other changes led to total savings of over $17 million.

Challenging the activities to reduce cost

Challenging current activities to ask why they're taking place is what really allows companies to achieve competitive and profitable operations. And it works at companies of any size. Small companies have tackled activity analysis projects using a PC spreadsheet, and larger companies have gone so far as to create their own software. The point in either case is to begin with the "work" people do: the activities that go on in the company.

A project team usually begins this kind of activity analysis by building an extensive "dictionary" of key activities under each of the company's functions. The supervisor of each area then creates a table showing all the people involved in each of the key activities and estimates the percentage of time they spend on each activity. When the table is finished, the "Aha's!" surface. A glance across

columns begins to tell the company about irrationalities and abnormalities in carrying out a particular activity.

For example, one shop in a large telecommunications company found that its people spent almost 30% of their time in various types of rework activity. No one had ever questioned the necessity of any of this work, but then no one had ever really examined the nature of the work. The activity analysis team found the causes of the rework. When they were eliminated, the company was able to redeploy and eliminate almost one-quarter of the shop's work force.

Once a table of activities has been built, the project team enters the cost of each activity, based on fully loaded payroll and controllable non-payroll costs (see Figure 3). At this point cost drivers can be agreed upon and costed, opening the way for defining costs by product, customer, distribution channel, etc. Modern software tools improve and speed the process enormously.

The result is a map for managing operations—something managers have been crying out for. With this activity map you know where the costs lie and you can begin to wrestle meaningfully with the question of how to reduce them. The basis for deciding ultimately what to do about costly activities is

Figure 3. Sample of "Menu" Activity Analysis

Acct No	ACTIVITY (in thousands of Dollars)	SALES — Industrial Supply and Maint.	SALES — Contractors	PURCHASING — Plumbing	PURCHASING — Electrical	PURCHASING — HVAC	MANUFACTURING — Design Engr.	MANUFACTURING — Plant	MANUFACTURING — Mfg. Admin.	MANUFACTURING — Inspt	WAREHOUSING — Chicago	WAREHOUSING — Rockford	DELIVERY — Chicago	DELIVERY — Rockford	Accounting	EDP
1.0	ACQUIRE AND ENTER ORDERS															
1.1	Sales Planning and Forecasting	3	21													
1.2	Market Research	4	22													
1.3	Acquire and Develop Accounts	4	96													
1.4	Advertising and Sales Promotion		22												4	
1.5	Sales Call Preparations	4	32													
1.6	Travel Time	9	142													
1.7	Customer Sales Call	5	105													
1.8	Technical Support - Manufacturers	8	33	2	2	1	3									
1.9	Technical Support - Customers		118							2						
1.10	Customer Product Surveys		21						1							
1.11	Taking Telephone Orders	28				6										
1.12	Order Processing	27	10			10										
1.13	Over-the-Counter Orders	5									7					
1.14	Special Orders	18	43													
1.15	Order Expediting	21	44													
1.16	Update Order Book and Check Stock Status	6	54													
1.17	Order Editing		31													
1.18	Customer Inquiries	6	13													
1.19	Customer Complaints	8	52													
1.20	Credit Memos	2	21													
1.21	Rockford Warehouse Invoice Delivery															
1.22	Handle Salesmen's Inquiries	26														
1.23	Problem Solving	6	100			3										
1.24	Special Order Handling		20													
1.25	Sales Training	6	55													
1.26	Salesmen's Performance Review	21	21													
1.27	Idle Salesmen Time		34													
1.28	Officers Involvement	2					3									
	TOTAL	217	1110	2	2	20	3									
2.0	ACQUIRE AND CONTROL MERCHANDISE															
2.1	Vendor Selection	2	1	2												
2.2	Product Line Planning	1	3	2	3											
2.3	Purchase Order Preparation and Processing	3	3													
2.4	Expedite Purchase Orders															
2.5	Schedule Vendor Deliveries															
2.6	Receiving - Physical Handling															
2.7	Receiving - Check-in and Paperwork															
2.8	Straight Stock of Merchandise															
2.9	Breakdown and Repack - Pipe															
2.10	Breakdown and Repack - Fittings															
2.11	Breakdown and Repack - Pther															
2.12	Vendor Return															
2.13	Vendor Problems															
2.14																

to consider the satisfaction they deliver to customers. If an activity helps satisfy a customer want, you certainly need to continue it, but you may have an opportunity to reduce its cost. If an activity is not satisfying customer wants you should work toward eliminating it.

Some companies try to categorize activities into "value-added" and "non-value-added." We are increasingly convinced that a better way to describe activities is to say that all are necessary until a change in the way work is done makes some activity unnecessary. No one consciously performs "non-value" activities. But by analyzing activities and expeditiously reorganizing your operations you can always reduce activities, and often you can eliminate the need for entire groups of activities.

Take the case of the American manufacturer that had defined inspections as a major cost driver. Many ABC experts would consider reducing the cost of inspections in products by consolidating inspection in one location, purchasing inspection hardware so that inspectors could check larger volumes, investing in training and software to facilitate sampling, and removing products that con-

---

All the activity analysis in the world isn't going to help in the long run if you mindlessly seek scale economies with high utilization rates and high output.

---

sume most of the inspecting activities. Instead, by examining its activities the company discovered how to eliminate inspections entirely. They improved linkages between processes, reduced batch sizes, reduced changeover times, and empowered workers to correct problems as they occurred.

Once a company's activities have been mapped, management has a much better data base for estimating activity costs and for making product mix decisions. For example, if the auto components manufacturer had used activity analysis to question its processes it

might well have decided to keep producing small-batch products. And the computer manufacturer would have assessed the tradeoff between automatic and manual insertion of circuit boards in terms of customer satisfaction.

As the experience of these companies show, it's easy to get the cart before the horse in using activity analysis. Whether you use the term ABC or "activity analysis," if your goal is to improve operations, the tool should be used to assess activities first—in terms of satisfying customer wants—and then to cost products and other units. Companies need to do both, but in the right order.

Testing activity analysis in your company

Management teams who are interested in using activity analysis to create a roadmap for making operational decisions should:

1. Select a pilot that's a likely candidate for cost reduction—a department, plant, or business unit. Companies often are aware of opportunities to improve competitiveness and profitability; they just need a roadmap for pinpointing the source and the degree of waste. Start activity analysis in a spot where you know there will be a strong payoff. That will create momentum for a wider program and help overcome any skepticism that may exist.

2. Conduct an activity analysis that really focuses on changing activities, not just managing drivers. All the activity analysis in the world isn't going to help in the long run if you mindlessly seek scale economies with high utilization rates and high output. Indeed, with that mindset at work, managers looking at the costs of "drivers" will tend to economize on drivers by using them sparingly in hopes of cutting costs as such. The results often diverge greatly from what customers find satisfactory. If your mindset tells you to satisfy customers by improving flexibility, then you will do what is needed to achieve small lots, short leadtimes, and defect-free output. It follows that the steps you take probably will lead to faster changeover, less work, and—incidentally—lower costs.

If American companies had been using activity costing throughout the last 20 years would they have competed better and profited more? The answer is, maybe. It depends on what kind of information they had been using. Information that really defines, questions, and costs activities—not just drivers—is what is needed for managing operations better. ▲

Reprinted from *Corporate Controller*, January/February 1991, pp. 26–32. Copyright © 1991 by Faulkner & Gray. All rights reserved. Used by permission.

Applying ABC to Product Design

Jon W. Bartley and Richard L. Jenson

To take full advantage of activity-based costing (ABC) for strategic decision making, companies need to develop multiple cost models tailored to the different decisions managers face. In particular, the greatest opportunity to influence product costs significantly occurs during the product design phase. The accuracy of cost estimates during the design phase has a direct impact on the success of a project. Accurate cost estimates through the use of ABC concepts can lead to an optimal product design and thus significantly reduce product development costs.

Activity-based costing (ABC) is rapidly gaining acceptance as a management accounting technique. Its primary advantages are derived from the process of allocating indirect costs on the basis of output, or output characteristics, rather than direct-labor hours or dollars. In addition to providing more accurate cost data, ABC gives management a better understanding of cost drivers, the factors that determine the ultimate cost of the product. This better understanding allows managers to improve their strategic decisions with respect to product design, the production process, and marketing strategy.

To take full advantage of the ABC concept as a strategic decision-making tool, controllers will need to develop multiple cost models tailored to the different decisions managers face. The normal ABC system is designed to maximize the accuracy of product costs using all information available at the completion of the production process. However, managers make many strategic decisions during the initial phases of product design when information about the product's final form and production process is incomplete. As a result, financial managers cannot develop a normal ABC model. For example, if a company using target costing needs to modify the design and production process of a new product to match a required cost profile before production begins, it must develop specialized cost estimation models to make the necessary trade-offs.

Often, the greatest opportunity to influence product costs significantly occurs during the project's design phase, and as a result, the accuracy of cost estimates during the design phase has a direct impact on the success of a project. Errors in estimation are especially devastating when a company must bid on projects—underestimates lead to unprofitable contracts while overestimates lead to contracts lost to competitors. Accurate cost estimates contribute to the selection of an optimal product design and reduce product development costs, often by a significant amount.

Figure 1 illustrates the normal relationship of estimated costs to the final costs of developing a new product. Underestimates of costs can lead to dramatic cost overruns and typically are more serious than overestimates. Consider a situation where the estimates of engineering effort on a project with a rigid timetable are too low and lead to understaffing. By the time the actual scope of the project becomes apparent, the project will be significantly behind schedule. Adding large numbers to new personnel in the late stages of a project inevitably results in complex staffing and coordination problems that reduce efficiency and cause cost overruns. If changes in the product design are necessary to compensate for higher than expected costs, even greater cost overruns occur.

Although it may seem counterintuitive, overestimates of costs also lead to higher product

Figure 1. *Relationships Between Estimated and Final Costs*

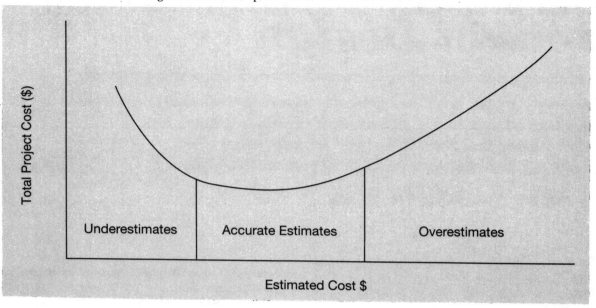

development costs. Human nature is such that overly generous budgets often become self-fulfilling prophecies. Goldplating in the form of unnecessarily elaborate product design is a common outcome of cost estimates that contain a great deal of padding. Even when management determines that a project is overstaffed in the early stages, it may be difficult to reduce the staffing commitment rapidly enough to avoid a major cost overrun.

These problems can be avoided by using activity-based models that rely on a reduced set of cost drivers for which cost estimating relationships (CERs) can be reliably estimated, even before production has begun. The model uses an output-based approach to identifying cost drivers that is inherent in activity-based costing rather than the traditional bottom-up approach to cost estimation.

ABC vs. conventional cost estimation

Cost analysts use a variety of procedures to estimate new product cost. One common approach used during product design is to make ad hoc comparisons of the proposed product to existing, similar products. If managers have not identified the cost drivers, it is very difficult for them to assess the relevant differences among products, much less differences in cost. When it can be used, the tradi-

tional engineering, bottom-up approach to cost estimation offers greater accuracy, but at a high cost because estimation of individual component costs can be time consuming and expensive. Further, bottom-up estimation may not be feasible because the proposed project can only be described at a high level of abstraction during its design phase.

The key concept of ABC that improves cost estimation models is the direct linking of costs to either product output or output characteristics. For example, the cost of manufacturing an airplane might be estimated as a function of maximum weight, range, and airspeed rather than the sum of the costs of the airframe, engine, electronics, and other components. Thus, the cost estimation process is not dependent on detailed and costly specifications of product design and does not prejudge product design.

When controllers use output-based cost estimation models during product design, they normally discover the relationship of costs to output characteristics by analyzing data for existing products. They use statistical analysis to measure the empirical relationships among the physical and performance characteristics of products (cost drivers) and their ultimate cost. These empirical relationships, the CERs, form the cost estimation model that is often described as a parametric model because of the statistical estimation of the model parameters (the CERs). The key distinction between output-based cost estimation models and traditional bottom-up models is that output-based models are based on the costs of output or performance characteristics of the complete product rather than the costs of the components that make up the product.

The advantages of output-based cost estimation include the following:

- Output-based estimates can be made during all phases of a project, including the design phase during which traditional empirical estimation models may not be feasible.
- Output-based estimates can be made for projects involving new technology or a scale of activity not previously undertaken.
- Output-based models are less costly to develop than bottom-up cost models that require detailed information about project components.
- Output-based models can be used for services as well as tangible products.
- Output-based cost models are easily manipulated to answer what-if questions that facilitate performance/cost trade-offs during the project's design phase. In contrast, bottom-up cost models are often very expensive to manipulate.

An illustration of output-based cost estimation

To illustrate the process, we examine the development of an output-based cost estimation model for a computer software programming effort. The example illustrates the potential simplicity of the estimation models, as well as their application outside the more common manufacturing setting.

Lake Computer, Inc., an integrated computer and software company specializing in interactive computer graphics, high performance computerized simulation systems, and computer-aided industrial design (CAID) software, needed to develop an output-based model for estimating the cost of programming enhancements to the company's manufacturing resource planning (MRP) database management system. The MRP database management system includes software for bill-of-materials, inventory, material require-

ments planning, customer order entry, and production scheduling.

The supervisor responsible for maintaining Lake Computer's MRP database management system needs cost estimates to evaluate requests for system enhancements and manage individual programming projects. Users continually request enhancements to the MRP system in order to expand the capabilities of the system and to respond to changing business conditions. Typical software modifications include new reports, new display formats, and the addition of new controls for the MRP system. Although these projects are normally small in size, the major resource required, programming hours, is constrained. As a result, the supervisor needs estimates of programming effort to manage the programming staff and the MRP system.

The supervisor has a fixed number of programmers, all of whom have similar skill levels. Because programming projects are typically small in size, the only variable costs that are relevant to the supervisor's decision to undertake a project are the costs of employing the programming staff. Lake Computer's cost estimation model is actually a model that estimates programming effort. The estimated programming effort (programming hours) is directly related to the opportunity cost of undertaking a new software project, and programming hours can be easily converted into dollars of cost based on current compensation levels. Even for large software development projects, companies often prefer models that estimate programming duration because they are more generalizable than models based on a specific compensation structure.

Lake Computer implemented an output-based cost estimation model involving four steps:
1. Identification of physical, performance, and other output characteristics that may influence product costs. The level of abstraction will depend on the phase of the project in which the cost estimate is to be made.
2. Building a database of costs and the potentially relevant project characteristics known as cost drivers.
3. Statistical analysis of the database to determine the cost estimating relationships (CERs). This is typically done with re-

gression analysis if the database has an adequate number of observations.

4. Validation of the model by testing it on independent projects.

Step 1: Identification of cost drivers. The cost drivers are unique to the particular product or service for which the cost model is being developed. Initially, it may be necessary to examine a large set of variables in order to discover the cost drivers. In the case of Lake Computer, the model must be based on the very abstract descriptions of the software product available when a customer asks for an MRP system enhancement.

Traditional cost allocation models assign software cost based primarily on the number of lines of code. Although the number of lines of computer code is known with certainty at the completion of a given project, it is obviously unknown at the beginning of a project. As a result, Lake Computer's cost estimation model is based on a novel set of output-oriented variables. The model is based on an abstract model of software output characteristics consisting of objects, operations performed on the objects, and interfaces among the objects. This model was used to identify characteristics of software that were likely to be cost drivers.

Objects are the major components of a computer application system, and they represent the real-world entities being modeled by the software. Within the system, data files represent these real-world entities. Operations are manipulations performed on or by the objects using program algorithms. An interface is a dependency among objects that requires some form of message passing between objects within the software.

The simplest model of software programming effort containing the three cost drivers is an additive model of the form:

$$\text{Hours} = b_0 + b_1\text{OBJ} + b_2\text{OP} + b_3\text{INT}$$

where: Hours = total programming effort in hours (or days) required for completion of the programming task

OBJ = number of objects
OP = number of operations
INT = number of interfaces among objects.

Step 2: Building the database. Based on his records, the MRP system supervisor analyzed 18 system software enhancement projects. He used a simple worksheet to provide an abstract description of each program enhancement from the user's perspective, rather than the programmer's. The descriptions focused on output characteristics (i.e., what the program was to accomplish rather than how it was to be implemented). Consider the following program description:

"Display the status of the inventory by inventory bin location, display the extended cost by bin location, and display the total inventory."

The Lake Computer worksheet analyzing this program description is shown in Table 1.

The resulting variable count is four objects, three operations, and two interfaces. Using his programming records, the supervisor also obtained the hours of programming effort and identified individual programmers for each project.

Step 3: Statistical analysis to identify the CERs. The supervisor then used regression analysis to estimate the coefficients of the model. It may be necessary to examine several combinations of variables and various data transformations before the best estimation model is identified. The results of the initial regression for model 1 are presented in

Table 1. *Cost Estimation Worksheet*

Operation	Object	Interface	Object
Display	Status of inventory	By	Inventory bin location
Display	Extended cost	By	Inventory bin location
Display	Total inventory		

Table 2. *Cost Estimation Models of Software Programming Effort*

	Linear Model 1	Nonlinear Model 2
Intercept	−0.63 (.55)*	6.90 (.01)
OBJ	4.40 (.03)	.14 (.01)
OP	1.36	(.32)
INT	−1.51	(.70)
Adjusted R^2	.24	.40
F-statistic	2.83 (.08)	12.54 (.01)

* The significance levels for the model coefficients are based on one-tailed t-tests.

Table 2. The coefficient of the OBJ cost driver was statistically significant, but the coefficients of OP and INT were not significantly different from zero. Thus, a reduced model should perform as well as the three-variable model.

Model 1 was based on the assumption that a linear relationship existed between the cost drivers and programming effort. In output-based cost analysis, nonlinear relationships are common, and as a result, the supervisor examined several nonlinear models using routine variable transformations that are available in most commercial regression programs. In every case the objects cost driver provided substantially all of the predictive power.

The model with the best fit to the data (the highest adjusted R^2) was the nonlinear single-variable model, model 2, in which the objects cost driver was transformed to be the constant e (2.718) raised to the power equal to the number of objects (see Table 2). Model 2 has the form:

$$\text{Hours} = b_0 + b_1 * e^{\text{OBJ}}$$

The adjusted R^2 of model 2 is .40 which is less than the .80–.95 range that can be obtained for activity-based cost models developed from actual cost data obtained after production is underway. The lower model fit occurs because the cost estimation model relies on a smaller number of cost drivers. The data for many cost drivers are unknown during the planning phase of a product; for example, the number of lines of code in a software program is an important cost driver that remains unknown until the program is virtually complete. Output-based cost estimation models can be continuously improved by the addition of cost drivers as the design phase progresses and the final product becomes more clearly defined.

There is a high correlation between the number of objects and the number of interfaces so it is not surprising that a reduced model performs well. In addition, model 2 is consistent with the well-known existence of diseconomies of scale for software programming. That is, as the size and complexity of the project increases, the necessary programming effort increases at an increasing rate. Figure 2 illustrates this nonlinear relationship between the number of objects and programming effort.

Step 4: Validation of the cost estimation model. The final step in the development of an output-based model is the validation of the model's predictive ability before its application for strategic decision making. Lake Computer used the jackknife prediction procedure in which each project was held out in turn, and the model was estimated using the remaining 17 projects. The company measured model's accuracy in predicting programming hours for the holdout project and then repeated this process, holding out each project in turn. The combined predictive performance of the 18 models provides a measure of the cost estimation model's performance when it is applied to independent software projects.

Often, the greatest opportunity to influence product costs significantly occurs during the project's design phase.

Predictive accuracy can be measured in several ways. The magnitude of relative error (MRE) measures the percentage error of the forecast, and it is one of the most easily understood measures of accuracy. The formula for MRE is the absolute value of:

$$\frac{\text{actual amount} - \text{predicted amount}}{\text{actual amount}}$$

The mean and the median of the MRE were calculated for each model. In order to give more weight to larger projects, a weighted

Figure 2. *Relationship Between Number of Objects and Programming Effort*

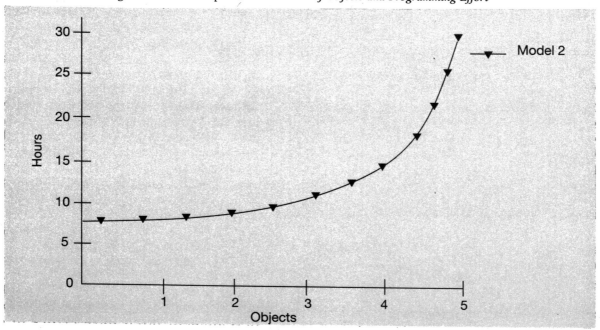

magnitude of relative error (WMRE) for each prediction was calculated as follows:

$$\frac{MRE \times \text{actual amount for the project}}{\text{mean of all project amounts}}$$

By weighting the MREs in this way, the risk associated with larger project size is recognized in the measure of accuracy.

Table 3 contains the error measures for the full linear model and the single-variable nonlinear model. It is apparent that the single-variable nonlinear model 2 is more accurate than model 1. Thus, the validation results are consistent with the differences in statistical fit of the models reported in Table 2.

The MREs are substantially greater than the WMREs for both models, indicating that the

models are less accurate for small programs than for large programs. By examining the individual forecast errors. Lake Computer discovered that the programming hours for the two smallest projects were significantly overestimated by both of the models. Apparently, these projects did not fall within the relevant range of the cost estimating relationships calculated. As a result, these models were reestimated, omitting the two smallest projects. The mean MRE was reduce to .72 and .52 for models 1 and 2, respectively.

Although errors averaging 52% may appear to be large, this degree of accuracy is very good for estimates made at the beginning of the design phase of a software project. Nonempirical estimates made during the early stages of software development often have errors in excess of 100%. The nature of software programming is such that significant variability of cost is the norm, and one would expect more accurate estimates in most manufacturing environments.

As a final test of the validity of the cost estimation models that were developed, the company examined the relationship between programmer experience and programming hours and found that it was not possible to

Table 3. *Error Measures for the Cost Estimation Models*

	Linear Model 1	Nonlinear Model 2
Original 18 Projects		
Mean MRE	1.22	.98
Median MRE	.53	.40
Mean Weighted MRE	.64	.45
Reduced Set of 16 Projects		
Mean MRE	.72	.52

improve the predictive model by adding a variable for programmer experience. This is not too surprising since only one programmer had less than three years' experience and it has typically been found that programming productivity is relatively constant for programmers with more than two years' experience.

Conclusion

The flexibility, low cost, and objectivity of output-based cost estimation make this procedure an important tool for cost accountants and cost analysts. Potential applications include estimating costs and cost estimating relationships (CERs) for use in target costing, design-to-cost contracts, and contract bidding. The application of ABC concepts to the estimation of costs for use in strategic decisions allows managers to improve corporate performance by replacing seat-of-the-pants guesses with empirically derived estimates of costs. ▲

PART *B*

Activity-Based Management

The Best Way to Implement an Activity-Based Cost Management System

John A. Miller

Managers need more than accurate product costs; they need information to help them improve productivity, effectiveness, and decision making so that they can eliminate inefficiency, redundancy, bureaucracy, and waste. Activity-based management is designed to accomplish these goals by focusing on activities rather than costs. Its emphasis is on providing relevant information about business processes and activities throughout an organization, not just on the manufacturing floor. This article explains a methodology for implementing activity-based management.

During the past several years, management leaders in many industries have reported that traditional accounting and cost accounting systems are not providing the relevant information that they need to plan, control, and make decisions about their businesses. Many of these reports charge that accounting systems, specifically cost accounting systems, have not kept pace with the advances in manufacturing technology (e.g., materials requirements planning (MRP), computer-aided design (CAD), just-in-time (JIT), flexible manufacturing systems (FMS), robotics). The conclusions most often reached are that existing cost accounting systems and cost management practices do not support the objectives of automated manufacturing and that traditional methods of allocating overhead on the basis of direct labor are misleading and distort product cost.

An alternative to traditional methods that has been gaining acceptance is activity-based costing. Simply defined, activity-based costing traces costs to operational information about the activities of the business—what people and machines actually do in the organization. Activity-based costing determines which activities products consume and calculates product cost on that basis. Because most of the literature and discussion about activity accounting and activity-based costing is centered on large organizations that have invested heavily in automated manufacturing, there is a tendency to link the need for these new cost accounting systems directly to factory automation and product costing. This is a narrow view of activity accounting. Particularly narrow is the importance placed on product costing.

Accounting information goes beyond price-setting guidelines

Certainly, understanding product cost is important. But would the knowledge that a product's cost was understated by 25% lead to higher sales prices, cost reduction programs, improved production processes, or management action? Hopefully, it would not. Hopefully, product sales prices are determined based upon market conditions and that nothing is left on the table, given a market-share objective. Hopefully, cost reduction and improvement efforts are an ongoing responsibility of managers, and management is not inspired to take action only when it discovers that a particular product cost is higher than expected. There is, of course, strategic value to knowing product cost from the standpoint of product profitability and the potential to discontinue a product line that is losing money.

But managers require more than just accurate product cost information to compete effectively in today's world markets. They need information that enables them to improve productivity, effectiveness, and decision-making so that they can eliminate inefficiency, redundancy, bureaucracy, and waste.

Activity-based cost management (ABCM) is a tool to fill this management need. ABCM focuses on activities, not just costs. The emphasis is placed on providing relevant information on business processes and activities over the entire organization, not just the manufacturing plant. ABCM specifies a chart of activities (see Table 1) that, when completed, provides management with information as to (1) the cost-effectiveness of their activities (value added and nonvalue added); (2) the efficiency under which activities are carried out; (3) the cause of cost (cost drivers); and (4) the products or product lines that consume the activities (resources) of the business.

Activity-based costing determines which activities products consume and calculates product cost on that basis.

Accounting departments today typically do not report this kind of cost information about their businesses. Rather, they report cost by department on the basis of expense type (e.g., salaries, travel and entertainment, utilities, rent, and supplies). They report what amount is *spent for* and by whom, but they fail to report what the money is *spent on*. Companies spend money *on* the activities of the business—to do budgets, to make sales calls, to develop new products, or to purchase goods and services. In most companies, however, the cost of these business activities is unknown.

For example, take budgets. In most companies, if asked how much it costs to do the annual budget, the department budget for planning would be reviewed to determine the cost of doing the budget. But what really happens in a company? The annual budget involves much more time and resources than just the planning department. Virtually everyone in a company is involved in one way or another with the annual budget. Sales people make sales forecasts, manufacturing people estimate raw material requirements, purchasing people estimate purchase prices, and every department head prepares a department budget. But where are these total costs of doing the budget accumulated?

In case you think this is insignificant, consider *Fortune* magazine's April 9, 1990, cover story. "Cost Cutting: How to do it Right," which reported that Gary Ames of US West Communications spent three months asking 7,000 middle managers what they did every hour of every day. He was shocked to learn that 350 people were involved in drawing up the annual budget. With this knowledge, Ames set a goal of reducing this number to 100. If US West Communications achieves its goal, 250 people who formerly worked on the budget will be available to work on business activities that can contribute to the success of the company. That's the value of activity analysis—knowing what cost is spent *on*, so that cost can be compared to benefits received.

Managers often are surprised when they define the business processes and activities of their business and learn how few resources are spent on those key activities that build competitive advantage. It is more surprising to learn the amount of inefficiency, redundancy, and waste included in operations and resources consumed by activities that have nothing to do with whether the business is successful. Often, the perception of what goes on in the business is completely different from what actually happens.

Unfortunately, the cost associated with business processes and activities is not readily available in most companies and must be dug out of the organization. But the effort generally is well rewarded.

Developing activity-based cost information

Following eight general steps guides a controller's collection of activity-based cost information (see Table 2) and produces a chart of activities. Each step involves data gathering, ongoing interviews of key personnel, and analysis:

1. Gain top management input on the scope and use of ABCM. Like any effort that involves

Table 1. *Activity-Based Cost Management*

Chart of Accounts	Processes and Activities	Cost Effectiveness			Efficiency			Cost Drivers		Product Line Profitability		
					Output		Cost per Unit of Output			Product Line 1	Product Line 2	Product Line N
		Value Added	Non-Value Added	Total	Measure	Volume		Measure	Volume			
Salaries	Process 1											
	Activity 1											
	Activity 2											
	Activity 3											
Materials	Process 2											
	Activity 1											
Supplies	Activity 2											
	Activity 3											
	*											
Facility Costs	*											
	*											
Transportation Costs	Process N											
	Activity 1											
	Activity 2											
	Activity N											

the use of resources, management commitment is required. Management must believe that the commitment of resources will produce a result. More importantly, management must be willing to take action with the information that will be developed.

To improve time management for an entire organization, managers should do for the organization what is done for the individual—monitor how time is spent and what it's spent on.

---

2. Specify activities. This is one of the most important steps, because it involves defining what's important to the business and a significant amount of time will be spent gathering data, including cost and specifics about these activities. Activities should be defined in a way that captures the most important aspects of the business (core activities) but not at such a detail level to represent tasks. Once defined activities can be grouped under major

categories of business processes. As a general guideline, 10 to 12 major business processes should represent 80% of the cost structure of the business.

3. Select time frame and organize data. Determine which period will be converted from traditional to activity-based. For example, the conversion could involve the previous month, previous year, current month, or the annual budget. Once the period is determined, obtain traditional general ledger department expense types and financial data.

4. Trace cost to each activity. This the most time-consuming and detailed step, involving interviews, analyses, and inspections of detail cost information. The substeps are:

- Determine time allocation for total personnel for each activity.
- Trace total labor costs (salary and fringe) to activities, based upon time allocation.
- Trace nonsalary costs to activities.

Caution must be exercised when using interviews of personnel to determine how they spend their time on various activities. This is because the way people actually spend their time is different than the way they think they spend it. That's why in sophisticated activity-

Table 2. *Steps to Create Chart of Activities*

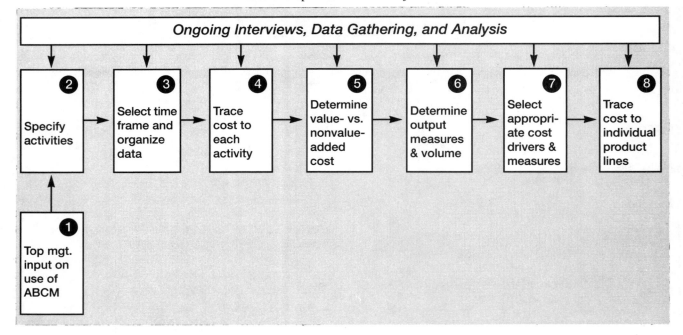

based systems, people complete time cards that indicate activities on which they spent their time. There is generally a high level of resistance when white-collar workers are asked to fill out time cards. However, this resistance often can be overcome when two points are considered:

- In many companies, the total cost of employees (salary, fringe benefits, and items like electricity, supplies, travel, and meals, which are consumed by individual employees) can represent 50% or more of the cost structure of the business. There are very few companies where the total cost of employees is insignificant. It is reasonable for management to monitor this significant cost and know exactly what employees are doing on a week-to-week basis.
- Any good time management course advises that, to improve the use of an individual's time, a time log should be kept to learn exactly how time is spent. To improve time management for an entire organization, managers should do for the organization what is done for the individual—monitor how time is spent and what it's spent on.

5. *Determine value vs. nonvalue added cost.*
Once the total cost of each activity is known, the next step is to determine that portion

which is value vs. nonvalue added from a customer's point of view. Customers are defined in the broad sense to include customers outside the organization (those who buy the products or services offered by the company) and customers inside the company who use the product or services of others. Making nonvalue added cost visible is one of the ABCM's biggest benefits, but also one of the most difficult.

The difficulty arises from no one wanting to be labeled as nonvalue added or acknowledging that they may be responsible for waste. However, the empirical data shows that for many companies the cost of nonvalue added activities can represent 25% or more of the cost structure of a business. Making the determination of value vs. nonvalue added requires a considerable amount of judgment and skill, plus an ability to look at things from a customer's viewpoint. Perhaps the simplest approach is not to consider the nonvalue added portion of cost at all. Rather, from the perspective of a customer, look at the activities and tasks being performed and decide which add value. All remaining costs then would be reported as nonvalue added.

6. *Determine output measures and volume.*
Once the cost of activities is known, it is nec-

essary to measure the efficiency (productivity) under which these activities are carried out. This is done by measuring the cost per unit of output (total for the activity cost divided by the volume measurement) produced by the activity.

As an example, consider the business process of purchasing goods and services. Activities and costs that may be part of this process include the preparation of purchase orders and requisitions, vendor qualification, receiving and inspection of incoming goods, payments of vendor invoices, and engineering time to prepare drawing or specifications to accompany the purchase order. An output measure for this business process might be the number of purchase orders processed. An output measure for the activity of paying vendor invoices might be the number of checks prepared. Dividing cost by the volume of the output measurement yields a cost per unit of output, which in this example would be the cost per purchase order and cost per check.

Productivity improvements are achieved by eliminating nonvalue added costs and activities that don't need to be done at all through improvement efforts like total quality management and JIT. The efficiency measurement must be selected carefully and represent a good measure of productivity. In some cases, the volume information for the most meaningful measurement may be difficult or costly to obtain. In these cases, some other measurement may be more appropriate from a cost standpoint, because the volume information is more readily attainable.

7. Select appropriate cost drivers and measures. A cost driver is a factor that has a direct influence on the cost and performance of activities. Cost drivers should explain why an activity's costs go up or down. Cost drivers are valuable because they enable management to focus on the cause of cost in their organizations.

Many companies assume that manufacturing overhead is driven by direct labor—the more direct labor, the more overhead—so reducing direct labor results in less overhead. However, studies[1] have shown that manufacturing overhead in many companies is driven not by direct labor but by the number of transactions and level of complexity on the plant floor. In these studies, significant correlations were found between the number of part numbers, number of engineering change notices, and number of transactions on the shop floor with the amount of overhead. The correlation existed because significant amounts of overhead were required to balance, account, execute, confirm, and keep track of all the various part numbers, engineering change notices, and transactions. In companies such as these, cost reduction is best achieved by attacking the root cause of cost by reducing the number of part numbers, engineering change notices, and transactions. The result will be less overhead.

8. Trace costs to individual product lines. Products consume activities. Because we know the cost of each activity and what drives its cost, cost drivers can be used to determine which products are consuming activities. This is done in proportion to the cost drivers used by each product or product line. For example, if the number of move transactions was the cost driver for activity No. 1 and product line A accounted for 10% of the total move transactions, then 10% of the total cost for activity No. 1 would be assigned to product line A.

A three- to six-person team should implement an ABC system during a period of four to six months. This recommendation stands regardless of the size of the business.

Once completed, the chart of activities can be used on both a horizontal and vertical basis to manage the business. Individual activities and business processes can be monitored on a horizontal basis to determine the efficiency and effectiveness under which they are carried out. On a vertical basis, managers can review the overall efficiency of the organization and determine areas of emphasis. Product managers will learn how the entire cost structure of the business relates to individual products or product lines.

Table 3. *ABCM Implementation Schedule*

Steps	Time (Months)	Results
1. Top management input on use of ABCM	bar ≈ month 0.5–1	Management commitment
2. Specify activities	bar ≈ month 1–2	Visability of key activities and processes
3. Select time frame and organize data	bar ≈ month 1.5	Time boundaries for analysis
4. Trace cost to each activity	bar ≈ month 1–3	Cost of key processes and activities
5. Determine value- vs. nonvalue-added cost	bar ≈ month 1.5–4	Visability of nonvalue-added cost and assessment of waste
6. Determine output measures and volume	bar ≈ month 2.5–4	Preliminary performance data
7. Select appropriate cost drivers and measures	bar ≈ month 3–4.5	Cost driver analysis
8. Trace cost to individual product lines	bar ≈ month 4–5	Estimating and pricing data Product line profitability Target costing

Months: 1 2 3 4 5 6

Implementation: small team, big results

Implementing an activity-based cost management system requires a commitment of resources on an initial and ongoing basis as well as a willingness to take action to improve the activities of the business. Without improvement efforts to reduce and eliminate nonvalue added costs, the preparation of the chart of activities specified under ABCM would be a waste of company resources.

For those who choose to make the initial implementation commitment, a three- to six-person team should be assigned to the project on a full-time basis for a period of four to six months. This recommendation stands regardless of the size of the business. The variable is the scope of the project. For very large businesses, the resources and time line may enable the project team to look only at two or three major business processes and perhaps 25 to 35 significant activities. Smaller businesses may be able to complete the entire conversion within a six-month period. A typi-cal implementation schedule is set forth in Table 3.

Key factors for a successful implementation include:

1. A cross-functional team. Comprised of various disciplines within the organization, the team should have an accounting department representative.

2. The company's best and brightest. Team members must be well respected by company personnel and must have demonstrated previously an ability to be flexible, innovative, and forward-thinking.

3. An environment promoting waste-reduction without a threat of job losses. If ABCM is perceived as a witch-hunt designed to eliminate people or find out which managers are wasteful, the effort is doomed to failure. All companies have waste. The best companies develop an environment in which employees constantly look for ways to eliminate waste and do so without the threat of losing their jobs.

4. An easy-to-succeed first project. Rather than select the most difficult activities and business processes of the organization, select an area where information is easy to come by and might involve only two or three departments. Experience and success will breed confidence to take on the more difficult aspects of the business. As the initial activities are defined, concentrate on improvement and a reduction of waste as a means to finance the ongoing effort.

5. Considerations of a pilot project. Especially in large organizations, pick a small operation or plant for implementation. This reduces the amount of resources initially committed to the effort and allows managers to test the benefits received.

6. Consideration of outside professional expertise. Select a person or firm with experience who can recommend improvement efforts that will be beneficial to the company.

Summary

Traditional cost and financial accounting systems report information that often is designed for outside investors, regulatory agencies, and banks but is of little use to management. Managers need information about the business that will enable them to improve productivity, effectiveness, efficiency, and decision-making.

What's missing is financial and operational information about the business activities that are performed by the people and machines that make up the organization. Only by looking at what people and machines actually do can management begin to look at ways to improve. That's what activity-based cost management is all about—to identify the core activities of the business, to determine the value added and nonvalue added costs associated with these activities, and to measure the improvement in productivity so that management can judge the success of their improvement efforts. As markets continue to get more competitive, continual improvements and greater productivity are conditions for long-term survival.

There are hundreds of examples where U.S. manufacturers can ship raw materials to other countries for processing and return finished goods to us at a cost less than if the product was made here and the shipping costs were avoided altogether. It's not all because of low-cost workers. In many cases, it is attributable to the inefficiency, bureaucracy, and waste that U.S. manufacturers have allowed to creep into their U.S. operations. As accountants, we must take a proactive position to eliminate waste, inefficiency, redundancy, and bureaucracy by providing our management leaders with information about the costs of what the business actually does so that actions to improve can be taken. ▲

Activity-Based Total Quality Management at American Express

David A. Carlson and S. Mark Young

Product costing and a quality strategy are related in the sense that both seek answers to the difficult questions of how and where information workers spend their time. This article illustrates how activity-based costing contributes not only to the achievement of accurate product costs, but also to improved quality at American Express Integrated Payment Systems (IPS). Activity costs at IPS were determined by asking each manager to estimate the time that his department spends on each activity, then splitting those activity estimates across each product line. To achieve the objectives of total quality management (TQM), these activity costs were augmented with perceptual data that various stakeholders expressed about the activities. The article suggests how similar approaches to TQM can benefit other service organizations or the service functions of manufacturing companies.

A
t American Express, a commitment to total quality management (TQM) comes from the top. The Chairman, CEO, and Chief Quality Officer at American Express is James D. Robinson III, who stresses that quality must be integrated with business strategy. As a result, business unit heads must present their strategy for quality improvements as part of their annual budget and business plans.

As of 1992, each American Express business unit must undergo a self-assessment based on the criteria specified in the guidelines for the Malcolm Baldrige National Quality Award. American Express wants to ensure that its investments in training and technology are paying off.

Will the changes at the American Express business units improve the bottom line? The activity-based costing (ABC) method used at American Express Integrated Payment Systems (IPS) in Denver can help answer this question.[1]

TQM and ABC at American Express

IPS manages one of the oldest financial services American Express has: American Express Money Orders. Introduced in 1882, customers use money orders to pay bills and make mail-order purchases. Money orders provide a stable source of income that has helped support IPS's entry into markets for similar financial services, including:

- American Express MoneyGram, which is a relatively new and rapidly growing service that lets consumers transfer funds around the world, usually within minutes;
- American Express Official Checks, which are negotiable instruments that financial institutions use as substitutes for their own disbursement items (e.g., teller checks and loan checks); and
- Cash Management Services, a service that works as an electronic clearinghouse to collect, concentrate, and disburse funds and data for corporations and financial institutions.

Early in 1990, IPS instituted a TQM philosophy that would involve all 1,000 employees in the Denver metro area. Charlie Fote, the president of IPS, hired Brian Higgins as director of quality assurance to lead this initiative.

Fote and other IPS executives were unaware of any particularly troublesome quality problems; in fact, IPS was (and remains) a service leader in the markets it serves. Instead, the reason for pursuing TQM was to expand IPS's competitive advantages by improving service and to increase income without increasing costs.

Defining continuous improvement. Defining continuous improvement in a service organization is a difficult task. In defining and measuring quality, the quality assurance staff at IPS tried to answer the following questions:

- In the spirit of TQM, how do our customers and suppliers feel about the reliability of the activities we perform or about the contribution that those activities make toward their requirements?
- What do our employees do that contributes value to our services or that advances our company's mission?
- Conversely, what do our employees do that does not contribute value?

The restructuring imperative

In an article in the *Harvard Business Review*, Stephen S. Roach states:

> Services need an accounting framework that can identify which activities add the most value. . . . Activity-based managerial accounting is a step in the right direction, but much more work in this area remains to be done. . . . It should go without saying that a metric for quality is equally important. Admittedly, quality in the service sector is hard to define.[2]

As this quotation suggests, the improvement of white-collar productivity has not been embraced by business leaders, probably because of the nature of knowledge work. Poor productivity is difficult (if not impossible) to remedy. Many people consider knowledge work unstructured, self-directed, and intangible. It is often difficult to relate activity costs to the value provided. Nonetheless, improving white-collar productivity is not a hopeless task. Many managers simply do not understand the difficulties associated with assessing and improving the productivity of knowledge workers; they also lack the tools needed to adequately address the problem. IPS appears to have made important progress, however.

Activity-based TQM

The TQM initiative at IPS began by getting all employees involved in continuous im-

provement efforts. Customer satisfaction, vendor satisfaction, and employee satisfaction were processes that were assessed regularly, and efforts were made to gain a better understanding of the activities and performance measures at IPS.

Activity analysis began in the customer service department and telephone operations and quickly became interwoven with concerns about product costing. In particular, senior management wanted to manage growth better by gaining a better understanding of the fixed versus variable costs for each product line. Product costing was connected with the quality strategy because both efforts tried to answer the difficult questions of how and where information workers spent their time.

ABC is central to recent efforts to redesign cost accounting systems to account for a wide variety of changes that have occurred in high-technology manufacturing and service firms. These changes require accountants and all other employees to alter their mindsets away from cost accounting toward "cost management." Cost management emphasizes an active approach to planning and managing an organization's costs, whereas cost accounting usually focuses on the historical reporting of costs.[3]

Cost management integrates consideration of corporate strategy, which leads to the notion of strategic cost management (SCM),[4] which is closely related to the *functional administrative control technique* (FACT) approach used at IPS (see Exhibit 1). Managers at IPS have explicitly tied the results of FACT studies to achievement of the company's TQM strategy and its product strategies.

Value engineering

The FACT approach has its roots not in accounting but in value engineering, which is a technique for increasing the *value* of a product or organization rather than simply decreasing its cost. A product-oriented value engineering study, for example, would first create a functional description of a physical product, then map the product's parts onto the functions that those parts perform. Thus, a costed functional description is produced. Customers' requirements are balanced with the costs of the functions in assessing value.

Exhibit 1. *Activity-Based Total Quality Management*

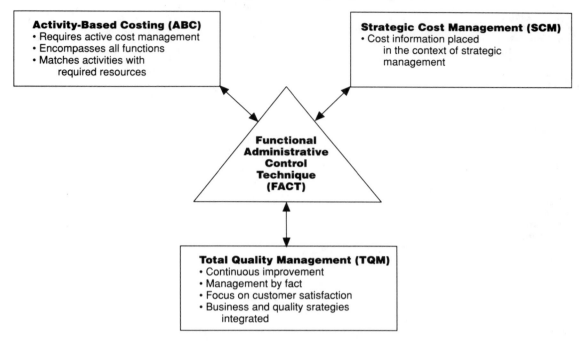

Cross-functional analysis. During the 1960s, General Electric refined some of the value engineering disciplines developed during the 1940s, which had proved useful in reducing material costs. GE's refinement, which is called *cross-functional analysis*, was designed to examine cross-functional effort applied to organizational activities.

Using cross-functional analysis, a business model is constructed that contains the activities performed throughout an entity. Typically, 150–200 such activities are defined and grouped into major business processes. Effort and cost are then recast into this business model. The contribution of each functional organization is examined to identify specific activities that are unique or that contain duplication, redundancy, or overlap. An organization's resources are then redeployed—added to some activities or reduced in others—to increase the value of the business to employees and to customers. Brian Higgins worked as a value engineer when he began

designing FACT in 1972; his efforts began with no knowledge of GE's cross-functional analysis.[5]

Phases of a FACT project plan

As Exhibit 2 shows, FACT uses a five-phase project plan for analyzing and improving organizational performance. Although the duration of a complete FACT project varies according to the scope and complexity of the organization, a project can usually be completed within sixteen weeks.

Project planning phase. The first phase—the project planning phase—is guided by the FACT project leader, who carefully selects a small team to conduct the study. Depending on the scope of the project, from two to ten people may be required, either part or full time. The project leader typically introduces the objectives and plan for the FACT study in a meeting of all managers involved.

Exhibit 2. *FACT Project Plan*

☐ **Project Planning**
  • Understand the scope and structure of the organization to be studied
  • Establish the hierarchy of activities
  • Plan the duration of the project and identify critical milestones
☐ **Data Collection**
  • Interview all managers, and selected customers and vendors
  • Document interviews
  • Enter data into FACT database
☐ **Synthesis**
  • Run reports from FACT database
  • Identify major issues
☐ **Data Analysis**
  • Select opportunities for change
  • Perform analyses using FACT data
  • Identify preliminary recommendations
☐ **Recommendations**
  • Prepare final report
  • Present recommendations to executive management

Data collections phase. In the data collection phase, FACT project team members gather information by using standardized data collection forms. They conduct interviews with three questions in mind:

1. What does the organization do?
2. What does it cost to do what it does?
3. What is the acceptance or worth of what it does?

Interviewers use questions that provoke managers, customers, and vendors to identify problem areas and possible opportunities for change. Interviewees are asked to imagine how the organization would look if everything worked perfectly, then to respond to the questions accordingly.

For each primary activity that affects the interviewee, three questions are asked:

1. If the organization worked in the most efficient and effective manner, how would things be organized, and how would the activity be performed?
2. What inhibits the organization from working in the most efficient and effective manner?
3. How else can the activity be provided?

Final three phases. The last three phases of a FACT project plan are crucial for building consensus among the team members and management. Specialized corrective action teams are established at the start of the data analysis phase. These teams champion changes through the collaborative participation of all affected individuals, departments, customers, and suppliers. A corrective action team retains control of the project until final recommendations are presented to management, and often until final implementation is completed.

As Higgins point out, crucial assumptions are made when (as in many traditional accounting systems) a large proportion of product costs are allocated from pools of overhead expense. One half of IPS's expenses, for example, were allocated overhead, but the accountants at IPS admitted that they were comfortable with only 15 percent of the allocations.

The improvement of white-collar productivity has not been embraced by business leaders, probably because of the nature of knowledge work.

For example, data processing expenses were allocated to products based on the volume of transactions. Since IPS processes hundreds of thousands of money order transactions per day, money orders received the lion's share of data processing allocations, even though everyone admitted that MoneyGram's on-line systems were more CPU-intensive per transaction. Higgins concludes, "You have to question the assumptions people made when their decisions are based on allocating huge overhead pools to products. Such assumptions are often wrong!" By directly allocating expenses to activities and to products, a more accurate picture can be obtained.

Defining activities

The foundation of the FACT model lies in the concept of an activity—i.e., a response to the question "What does the organization do?"

An activity can best be stated as a brief verb-noun description of a process: for example,

Exhibit 3. *Activity Hierarchy*

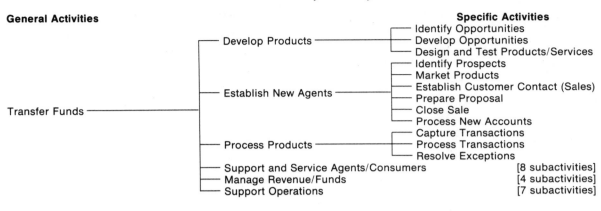

General Activities

Specific Activities

- Develop Products
  - Identify Opportunities
  - Develop Opportunities
  - Design and Test Products/Services
- Establish New Agents
  - Identify Prospects
  - Market Products
  - Establish Customer Contact (Sales)
  - Prepare Proposal
  - Close Sale
  - Process New Accounts
- Process Products
  - Capture Transactions
  - Process Transactions
  - Resolve Exceptions

Transfer Funds

- Support and Service Agents/Consumers — [8 subactivities]
- Manage Revenue/Funds — [4 subactivities]
- Support Operations — [7 subactivities]

"resolve customer problems" or "coordinate corrective action." Unlike GE's cross-functional analysis and many applications of ABC, FACT derives significant benefits from using a hierarchical structure of activities (see Exhibit 3). Thus, a response to the question "How is an activity performed?" leads from left to right in Exhibit 3 from the general to the more specific activities in the hierarchy.

Conversely, a response to the question "Why is an activity performed?" leads from specific to more general activities (i.e., from right to left in Exhibit 3). This structure permits both macro- and micro-level analyses of an organization. The level of detail expressed by these activities depends on the purpose for which the FACT model will be used.

FACT has been applied to individual work groups as small as five people as well as to organizations having 1,000 employees and overhead expenses exceeding $60 million. In small departments, for example, the activities may address such processes as "document customer problem" or "reconcile invoices," whereas in large organizations the activities are conceptualized at a higher level (e.g., "research market," "establish pricing," or "identify inventory variation"). Exhibit 3 shows the top levels of an activity hierarchy for IPS.

Linking activities to business and quality strategies

FACT begins by defining the costed hierarchy of activities, but it does not end there. An activity structure provides the basis for assembling information that can later be used in creating and evaluating solutions to problems and in linking activities to business and quality strategies (see Exhibit 4).

Managers follow an incremental process for constructing an organizational model that begins with the definition of a costed activity set. Each activity's cost is determined by assigning a fraction of each person's time (and therefore salary) or a fraction of a departmental expense item to a particular activity. Thus, all the organization's costs are allocated to the activity hierarchy. The fractions are determined by a variety of methods (e.g., time sampling or interviews with managers), depending on the scope of the organization. Once costs are allocated, additional information is collected and related to the model.

Nonfinancial information

The principal nonfinancial information used consists of attitudes of customers and suppliers—those who receive the outputs of the organization and those who supply its inputs. This attitudinal information includes both quantified variables and statements of perceptions (see the box "Customer and Supplier Comments" in Exhibit 4).

Quantified data consists of rating each activity for its contribution and reliability on ten-point scales. Perceptual data includes verbal comments that provide either favorable or unfavorable opinions about one or more ac-

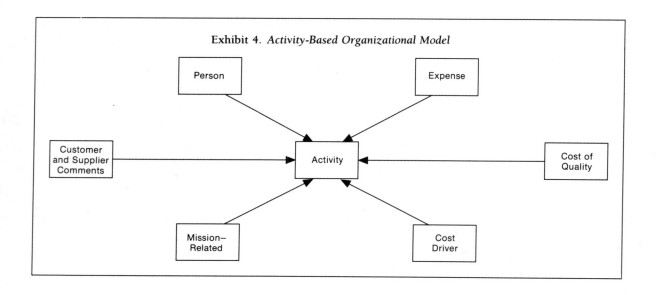

Exhibit 4. *Activity-Based Organizational Model*

tivities. This data is crucial for satisfying the objectives of TQM. The Malcolm Baldridge criteria place 30 percent of their emphasis on customer satisfaction; the activity hierarchy provides a framework for comprehensive assessment of satisfaction across the total business.

Classifying activities as mission-related or not

Each activity is also classified as being either mission-related or not (see Exhibit 4). Information about cost drivers—i.e., those events or environmental situations that cause costs to be incurred—may also be associated with each activity. These two information sources work in tandem to tell managers which activities contribute to accomplishing business strategies and how costs are generated.

Cost of quality

Activities may be associated with one of the four "cost of quality" categories (i.e., prevention, appraisal, internal failure, and external failure) or with the "cost of business" (e.g., advertising or production).

Many companies have spent years developing an accounting system that can estimate the cost of quality (though few service organizations attempt such analyses). Using FACT, however, an accurate estimate can be pro-

duced in a matter of hours. Although many people express disbelief that the cost of quality can be computed so quickly, with an activity and cost database as extensive as the one developed for a FACT study, the assignment becomes straightforward. The activities are so detailed that each one is simply assigned to a cost of quality category or split between two categories. (The activity "train agents," for example, is a cost of prevention, while "resolve customer problems" is a cost of external failure.) Computing cost of quality thus becomes trivial; all that has to be done is to sum the activity costs in each category.

A FACT study is a relatively short—but intensive—process. After data is collected, the information is entered into a proprietary software program, which produces summary reports for analysis. The study of all 1,000 employees at IPS took about two months to gather all the data, then another two months to analyze the data and to develop initial recommendations. Since the FACT team consisted of twelve part-time members, it was possible to conduct the study without disrupting ongoing organizational processes.

Restructuring through FACT analysis

In discussions of advanced manufacturing technologies, it is often stated that implementation of just-in-time processes uncovers a "hidden factory" of overhead expenses for logistical, balancing, quality, and change transactions, all of which account for a large portion of the effort expended in production.[6] Similarly, service organizations may discover overhead expenses that were previously obscure by identifying "hidden service providers." This point is clearly illustrated by a situation uncovered through the FACT study at IPS. The following example provides a fictionalized example of this situation.

Example of MIS manager. John, the vice-president of management information systems at IPS, spends several thousands of dollars

---

Many managers simply do not understand the difficulties associated with productivity of knowledge workers or else they lack the tools needed to adequately address the problem.

---

each year traveling to customer sites. Under the conventional accounting system, these expenses were charged to the travel accounting in his department. Meanwhile, directors of customer service departments for each product line reviewed their respective budgets and believed they were managing all costs of customer service. As FACT revealed, however, customer service costs were higher than the costs indicated by the conventional cost system. Since 100 percent of John's travel was related to supporting customers and resolving their problems, all his travel costs were allocated to the subactivities "support and service agents and consumers." As this example shows, IPS discovered that John was a hidden service provider; the true cost of customer service was higher than had been thought.

Example of controller. The controller at IPS also discovered hidden service providers. Costs related to the activity "administer financials" range far beyond the Accounting Department's budget as it exists in typical cost accounting systems. At first glance, the controller believed that the FACT data were

wrong, because the reported costs were twice what he expected. After reviewing the details, however, he agreed that the numbers were right. Managers throughout the company "help" the controller with such activities as "budget/forecast operations" or "document employee travel and entertainment expenses (T&E)." Similarly, in the Human Resources Department, all managers contribute to the activities "hire exempt employees" or "review employee performance." In each of the three examples, the actual cost incurred to provide these activities far exceeds the apparent cost shown in the respective department's budget.

The realization that actual activity costs often significantly exceed or fall short of presumed costs is of central importance in promoting and guiding restructuring. Restructuring is promoted by creating disenchantment with the status quo; it is guided by providing a sound basis for restructuring decisions.

Promoting efforts to restructure

Managers resist change[7]—or, at least, they resist unfounded or unjustified change. Once a foundation has been laid and changes justified, however, resistance quickly breaks down and may even turn into enthusiasm.

The examples of hidden service providers given previously illustrate one way that resistance to change was overcome at IPS. Other means were used that were also based on the data collected during the initial phases of FACT. Pareto analysis, which is commonly taught as an analytical technique in quality circles, involves sorting a set of items into descending order and focusing quality improvements on the top of the list—i.e., on the largest items.

A Pareto analysis of activity costs is illuminating; managers are often surprised to discover how large a large fraction of total cost occurs because of only few activities. It is also surprising to note *which* activities show up at the top of the list. Managers often have an intuition that the cost of some activity cost is too high, but intuition alone cannot justify significant investments. The relative positions of activity costs, however, can provide information that was previously unavailable for justifying corrective investments. A similar list of activity costs can be produced for each

Exhibit 5. *Cross-Product Analysis*

Activity	Product A	Product B	Product C
1 Develop Products etc.			
4 Support and Service Agents	3%	7%	5%
41 Receive and Document Inq.	1.5%	2%	2%
42 Handle Agent Problems	0.5%	3.5%	0.7%
43 Supply Agents etc.	1.0%	2.5%	2.3%
Totals	**100%**	**100%**	**100%**

category of the cost of quality. Having this list allows managers to focus on the top offenders in each area.

Focusing attention on the top of a sorted list, however, tells only one half of the story. When Higgins gave one IPS executive an eight-page list of activity costs for the Money-Gram product, the executive was prepared to throw away the last seven pages and focus on reducing the largest activity costs on page one. Higgins, however, pointed out that the activities at the bottom of the list are also candidates for attention, because important activities may not be receiving enough resources. For example, a costly activity at the top of the list may represent an internal or external failure cost, while an ignored activity at the bottom of the list may represent a preventive item that, with a small investment, could dramatically reduce the failure-related activity. This example illustrates the difference between value analysis and cost reduction.

Cross-functional and cross-product summaries of activity costs. Perhaps the most powerful analyses enabled by the FACT process are cross-functional and cross-product summaries of activity costs. A matrix is constructed with an indented list of the activity hierarchy on the left side and either the major functional areas or the product families across the top.

As the fictionalized example in Exhibit 5 shows, the percentage of cost allocated to the activity "support and service agents" has a wide variance across products. Exhibit 3 shows that the total cost of this activity is divided among eight subactivities. By itself, this observation is interesting, but of limited value. The obvious next question is "Why?". Fortunately, the FACT model provides a response.

A FACT study includes a record of how each person's time (and therefore salary) is allocated to activities. A department's expense items (other than personnel) are also allocated to the activity. (Note that a department does not allocate its personnel costs as one cost pool.) Thus, if an activity's total cost is out of line or if the cost is oddly split between product lines, the supporting data is easily available for explaining these anomalies. In general, this audit trail of detailed data is crucial for investigating activity costs.

Comparing ratios of activities. If the old cliche "numbers speak louder than words" applies anywhere, it applies here. The numbers are arrived at through a logical estimation process that is validated through a structured interview with each manager.

Although the numbers may be only estimates, the ratios of activity costs provide powerful information. Suppose, for example, that the ratio between the activities "resolve agent problems" and "train agents" is 20 : 1. Even if the respective costs are off by 10 percent or even by 25 percent, the size of the ratio still suggests a potential problem and a way to solve it—namely, to reduce agent problems by increasing training. A similar conclusion may be drawn from an analysis of the cost of quality. Agent problems (a cost of external failure) may be reduced by investing in agent training (a cost of prevention). The data provided by FACT support either of these analyses.

Cost of quality has been faulted by the quality expert W. Edwards Deming, who asserts that if you focus on process improvement, the cost of quality will take care of itself. The ease of computing cost of quality within the FACT framework, however, can motivate efforts to change the status quo and to restructure.

Guiding firms in restructuring

To avoid the slash-and-burn mentality of most cost-cutting efforts, a better basis must be provided for decision making. Stephen Roach warns that "cost cutting must be judicious" if service organizations are to avoid the problem that occurred when the manufacturing sector sold its future short by trading long-term capacity requirements for the sake of near-term financial gain.

One of the most useful mechanisms for guiding restructuring is cost driver analysis. Cost drivers cause activities to be performed. They may be positive (customer orders) or negative (customer complaints). By eliminating negative cost drivers, the associated activity costs are also reduced.

During the data collection phase of FACT, each activity is identified as being either mission-related or not (see Exhibit 4). Employees may spend disproportionate time on activities that are not directly related to the mission of their work group. Efforts to restructure the organization should focus on shifting effort toward mission-related activities. For example, are members of the sales department performing the activity "close sales," or are they instead "resolving agent problems" or "preparing department reports"? Only the first activity contributes to the department's mission.

Major work activities are often diffused across the organization. Many different individuals may be involved in an activity that represents only a few full-time-equivalent employees. When activities are highly fragmented, they should automatically be subjected to further analysis. Though some activities should remain distributed among managers, consolidating activities may improve performance. (Budgeting, personnel reviews, and similar tasks are examples of normally fragmented activities that contribute to effective management.)

Empowerment vs. enforcement

The way that FACT information is used can have an important impact. This warning is especially true in promoting a successful TQM strategy, which must have the support and involvement of every employee. If a company uses data about misallocations of resources as a stick that is used to beat people, employees are unlikely to give their heartfelt commitment to creating and implementing improvements or to producing accurate estimates of activity costs.

Downsizings. There are exceptional situations when an activity-based analysis is the best means for quickly downsizing an organization that is having severe profitability problems. Unless FACT is carefully managed, however, it is likely to be viewed as an axe for paring organizational fat. While this approach is superior to the slash-and-burn mentality that cuts necessary activities along with the fat, the benefits are unlikely to become long-term, strategic changes.

Product costing was related to the quality strategy because both tried to answer the difficult questions of how and where information workers spent their time.

The approach IPS uses seeks to empower corrective action teams to develop and implement changes. These teams are armed with copious data for guiding their efforts in the most fruitful directions. FACT process facilitators serve as consultants to the corrective action teams by helping them interpret *their* data and teaching them additional data analysis techniques to restructure their respective organizations, to refocus their efforts, and to refine their processes. This approach is consistent with TQM objectives (e.g., instilling attitudes to promote continuous improvement and establishing quantitative performance measures to assess quality level and monitor improvement).

Implications for service organizations

At IPS, FACT has provided valuable insight into operations and yielded substantial savings in several operational areas. Not surprisingly, FACT uncovered information that could result from a similar study conducted in a manufacturing organization, including:

- High cost areas;
- Costs for systems changes; and
- A more accurate estimation of overhead costs.

At IPS, however, the study went further to identify less tangible—but no less valuable—opportunities for quality improvement.

"The study was helpful in creating a fact base for potential organizational improvements," said Eula Adams, an executive vice-president at IPS who has twenty years of audit experience at a large accounting firm. "In the past, these kinds of changes at service firms were driven largely by opinion—by what people thought would work. Our study provides a solid fact base and, consequently, justification for changing the organization."

Support for organizational improvements. According to Adams, the study garnered support for organizational improvements by identifying areas of overlap and duplication and by focusing attention on non-value-added activities. "Overlap and noncontributing areas are usually fairly evident in manufacturing environments, but that wasn't necessarily the case in the service sector, until now. This study was helpful in identifying those opportunities and indicating how we might address them."

Bob Kuhnemund, the chief financial officer at IPS, agrees with Adams's assessment. He believes that the study is helping to link customer satisfaction to specific organizational activities. "In addition to hard numbers, it helped us develop an understanding for mission-related activities—what's hot and what's not. That's extremely helpful from an organizational perspective and can have a dramatic impact on overhead costs—reducing in some areas and increasing in others."

Documented savings. Just two months after the FACT study was completed and results tabulated, IPS documented savings in several areas totaling more than $1 million. While creating considerable savings, the changes also created some equally dramatic customer service improvements.

Dan Carrington, vice-president of Money-Gram Operations at IPS, stated that information from FACT led to new ways of streamlining the operating processes of some very important customer functions for MoneyGram. "Normally," he said, "improvements like these are associated with large one-time expenses. But we realized savings of $350,000 and improved the speed of providing these services. These are the kinds of changes we have to make because we're competing in what many people perceive to be a commodity service area. Also, we have a competitor with more experience; we have to set ourselves apart from their way of doing business."

ABC results. In spite of the rather unlikely emergence of ABC within the Quality Assurance Department at IPS, these testimonials point to the fact that ownership and backing of the FACT approach to cost management transcends the quality function. As Higgins concludes, "The FACT results have now become Accounting's numbers. They own it. But we're also finding out that other areas can own it too—areas like customer service and operations." IPS is currently considering ways of supplementing its existing cost accounting systems with an activity-based approach based on the initial FACT study.

Tying TQM to the bottom line

The FACT project plan provides a structure and methodology for assessing the current situation: where effort is being expended and what value those efforts have from a customer's viewpoint. An activity-based model is used for this assessment, and a number of approaches have been described for guiding a firm's restructuring decisions. But an answer has not been supplied to the CEO's concern about whether the investment that American Express has made in TQM can be tied to improvements in the bottom line.

Using ABC to quantify expected benefits. The results of TQM efforts in a service organization—changes to processes that affect an activity's performance—can be measured by using activity costs to quantify the expected benefits of the change and by computing a return on investment. For finer resolution, activity costs may be separated by department, product, employee classification (e.g., manager, individual contributor, or clerical), or all of the above to better estimate the benefits of a proposed change.

In relatively small-scale FACT studies, activity costs can be traced according to the percentage of time devoted by individual employees. These cost savings can then be accumulated by activity for an accurate estimate of the benefits derived from TQM. These analyses are often performed within corrective action teams at IPS as they progress through the phases of the FACT project plan.

Summary

In the same article mentioned near the beginning of this article, Stephen Roach concludes by saying: "Only with the proper measurement tools in hand can services assess restructuring options." FACT provides such a tool. Roach suggests that an activity-based value analysis can assist banks in reallocating information technology away from low-value-added activities (e.g., transaction processing and administration) toward more analytical applications (e.g., interest-rate swaps).

To more directly address Roach's concern about redeploying information technology in a firm, FACT might be extended to allocating capital investments to the activity hierarchy. A cross-functional analysis could then yield summaries of information technology investment by functional area for each activity. In a similar manner, both expenses and capital investments could be summarized for those activities related to two or more competitive strategies (or for nonmission-related activi-

ties) to analyze the relative cost consumed by each one. If costs of strategies are dramatically out of line with strategic priorities, some form of restructuring would be indicated. ▲

Notes

1. Subsequent to implementing activity-based costing, IPS and a related group of companies within American Express were spun off into First Data Corporation, an independent corporation which is 54 percent owned by American Express. This article continues to refer to the relationship that IPS had with American Express at the time that this study was conducted.
2. See S.S. Roach, "Service Under Siege—The Restructuring Imperative," *Harv. Bus. Rev.* (Sept.–Oct. 1991): 82–91.
3. See. H.T. Johnson and R.S. Kaplan, *Relevance Lost: The Rise and Fall of Management Accounting* (Boston: Harvard Business School Press, 1987).
4. Strategic cost management, as described by John Shank ("Strategic Cost Management: New Wine, or Just New Bottles?" *Journal of Management Accounting Research* (Fall 1989): 47, calls for integrating strategic considerations into activity-based costing.
5. See T.C. Fowler and B. Higgins, "Organization Analysis Made Easy," *Society of American Value Engineers Conference Proceedings* (Southfield, Mich.: Society of American Value Engineers, 1974): 3.1–3.7; and B. Higgins and C.M. Dice, "Quantifying White-Collar Functions," *National Productivity Review* (Summer 1984): 288–302.
6. See J.G. Miller and T.E. Vollmann, "The Hidden Factory," *Harv. Bus. Rev.* (Sept.–Oct. 1985): 142–150.
7. See M.D. Shields and S.M. Young, "A Behavioral Model for Implementing Cost Management Systems," *Journal of Cost Management* (Winter 1989): 17–27, for a summary of the factors that contribute to the resistance of an organization and its employees to change.

Activity-Based Management of Innovation and R&D Operations

Manash R. Ray and Theodore W. Schlie

This article discusses the use of activity-based management (ABM) for innovation and for research and development operations. The fast-growing literature on activity-based costing (ABC) and ABM has so far focused primarily on the use of ABC and ABM in manufacturing and product costing, but they can also be used for other purposes, such as design for manufacturability, process design, overhead value analysis, and performance measurement. This new focus results from an increasing awareness that traditional cost accounting systems are irrelevant because of the poor fit between traditional cost systems and advanced manufacturing systems.

Computer Aided Manufacturing-International, Inc. (CAM-I) has defined activity-based management (ABM) as:

> "A discipline that focuses on the management of activities as the route to improving the value received by the customer and the profit achieved by providing this value. The discipline includes cost driver analysis, activity analysis, and performance measurement. Activity-based management draws on activity-based costing as its major source of information."[1]

CAM-I has defined activity-based costing (ABC) as:

> "A system that maintains and processes financial and operating data on a firm's resources, activities, cost objects, cost drivers, and activity performance measures. It also assigns cost activities and cost objects."[2]

ABM as it has been applied so far generally involves the following steps:

- Identification of activities;
- Distinguishing between value-adding and non-value-adding activities for specific products or services;
- Tracing the sequence of product or service flows through activities;
- Assigning cost and time values to each activity;
- Establishing linkages between activities within functions and across functions;
- Making product or service flows more efficient;
- Reducing non-value-adding activities;
- Analyzing two or more related activities to see if trade-offs among such activities lead to cost reduction; and
- Continuous improvement.

The question arises, however, whether ABM can be successfully applied to the management of functions other than manufacturing—specifically, to the innovation and the research and development (R&D) function.

Cost management and R&D

In the literature about R&D, several articles discuss the problems of applying conventional accounting systems to R&D—e.g., in monitoring and controlling R&D spending and in financial evaluation of R&D projects.[3] Some authors have called for improved management accounting systems for R&D by suggesting subsystems that segregate operating and strategic development expenses.[4]

Little attention has been paid to the possibility of controlling innovation or R&D operations through the reporting and analysis of activities associated with the innovation process. This article discusses such an application and raises several critical issues that must be addressed to make this possible. Note that throughout the article, the term *ABM* is used rather than the term *activity-based costing* to highlight the fact that such applications pertain to all operational areas of business. This choice of terms moves away from the somewhat restrictive notion that activities should be analyzed only to arrive at "true" product costs.

Why innovation/R&D?

High-technology companies, which traditionally have extensive R&D or product development functions, now face an environment characterized by accelerated technological change, shortened product life cycles, and global competition. In this dynamic environment, product development should be a continuous process in which criteria for terminating a product's life cycle can be established even before the product is introduced. This process requires the continuous management and evaluation of product development activities and rapid redeployment of scarce resources toward uses that offer better opportunities.[5]

Traditional approaches to product development have involved such sequential phases as:

- Concept development;
- Feasibility testing;
- Development process;
- Product design;
- Pilot production;
- Final production; and
- Commercialization.

Recently, companies such as Canon, Honda, NEC, Epson, 3M, Xerox, and Hewlett-Packard have adopted multidisciplinary team approaches that involve overlapping development phases.[6] Evidence suggests that such integrated approaches can lead to shorter launch periods and improved manufacturing performance.[7]

Life-cycle accounting. The attention now being paid to product development has resulted from shortened product life cycles and from the emergence of time to market and flexibility as competitive weapons for high-tech firms. This has led to the concept of *product life-cycle accounting.* In high-tech companies that use advanced manufacturing technologies, most of the production costs of a new product (85 percent) are widely believed to be committed *before* the product is ever produced.[8] Therefore, it is important to control

production costs in the early development stages of a product's life cycle (i.e., even though these costs are *incurred* much later).[9] The shorter product life cycles in high-tech industries also impose the requirement that product development costs be recovered within a shorter time.

In the product innovation literature, several studies have examined the factors that contribute to innovation or product development success.[10] One survey of 300 firms or divisions, for example, reports that managers of successful new product had taken an integrated approach to new product development and commercialization.[11] Another study[12] describes the problems that lead to high rates of new product failure, the presence of too many new products that are not truly innovative, and perceptions about products having poor quality and value. Two problems identified were as follows:

1. That commercialization was often viewed as separate from the development process; and
2. That most new product development processes were designed for products with long product life cycles.

This information clearly points toward the need for intelligent cost management in innovation/R&D operations, because a major portion of total product costs are *designed in* early in the product's life cycle. Given that products with short life cycles must get to the market in as short a time as possible, ABM may prove relevant if it is moved upstream from manufacturing.

ABM in the R&D function. ABM could be incorporated into innovation/R&D operations either within the R&D function itself or across all functions involved in the innovation process.

ABM of the R&D function would resemble the use of ABM in manufacturing. This would involve:

- Defining R&D activities;
- Tracing idea flows through activities;
- Distinguishing between value-added and non-value-added activities;
- Assigning time and cost values to activities;
- Making idea flows more efficient; and
- Striving for continuous improvement.

ABM in the innovation process. The innovation process, on the other hand, ranges from R&D through engineering design, manufacturing, marketing, and successful launch. Incorporation of ABM in the innovation process would involve careful evaluation of cross-functional trade-offs between linked activities. For example, an ABM system might identify situations in which increased investment (costs) in a product development activity might be more than offset by time or cost benefits in downstream activities in manufacturing. The result would be a net benefit for the innovation process as a whole.

ABM and innovation/R&D

ABM should be considered for use in innovation/R&D management with the following attainable objectives in mind:

- Better management of R&D activities and budgets;
- Better management of linkages and communication between functions involved in new product development (i.e., research, development, engineering, manufacturing, and marketing); and
- Innovation/R&D information that is more coherent and useful to top management.

The use of ABM should lead to a better understanding of the relationship between activities and early life cycle times and costs. ABM should enable managers to identify and focus on product development practices that contribute to inefficiencies; it should also identify individual activities that make up the major portion of non-value-added time and costs.

Bill of activities. The generation and analysis of a "bill of activities" (i.e., for product development) should enable management to relate activities to the following four project outcome factors:

1. Realization of specified performance features;
2. Attainment of specified factory cost objectives;
3. Meeting of the development schedule; and
4. Staying within the project budget.[13]

Value chains. The use of ABM should also lead to better management of linkages and to enhanced communications between different functional areas. Michael Porter illustrates the importance of this aspect by describing the firm as a "collection of activities that are performed to design, produce, market, deliver, and support its product."[14] According to Porter, all these activities can be represented using a *value chain,* which divides a firm into its strategically relevant activities.

Activities in a firm's value chain are linked to each other since the value chain itself is a system of interdependent activities. Managing *linkages* can lead to optimization and better coordination, often resulting from trade-offs between activities to achieve a desired result.[15] Top management has a key role to play in managing cross-functional linkages, since any specific functional manager may resist increasing his own costs for the benefit of a downstream functional manager unless the trade-offs are recognized, approved, and taken into account in budget allocations and in evaluations of managers' performance. ABM puts all functional activities on a common baseline and thus enhances communication between functional managers and to top management concerning cross-functional trade-offs.

R&D and marketing

The product innovation literature includes several studies that examine the interaction of R&D and marketing in new product development projects.[16]

A major problem in this area is managing communications and linkages. Surveys have shown that there are complaints in each camp about the following issues:

- Timeliness and validity of information;
- Presentation of data in an understandable manner; and
- Consistency and usefulness of information.

These frictions are also present in the interfaces between product development, engineering, and manufacturing—specifically in the issue of design-for-manufacturability.

The use of ABM provides a common denominator for effective communications among these groups as well as with top management. For example, ABM should enable product engineering professionals to better understand the impact of different designs on manufacturing cost. New CAD technology gives them the flexibility to make desirable modifications easily and quickly.[17] Therefore, a design change or specification change request that is generated by a market survey can be analyzed in terms of alternative activities needed to accomplish it in product development, engineering, manufacturing, and marketing functions. The cost and time impacts of those activities can be evaluated in terms of the four project outcome factors referred to earlier (i.e., realization of performance specifications, attainment of factory cost targets, staying within the development budget, and meeting the development schedule).

This process requires the continuous management and evaluation of product development activities and rapid redeployment of scarce resources toward uses that offer better opportunities.

It should be noted that some project management systems used in engineering design may already be a form of ABM. Thus it might be feasible to isolate a product "champion" and to undertake an exploratory activity analysis.[18]

Value to top management

Some of the most important benefits of ABM should accrue to top management. Traditionally, top managers have received too much information, but not enough of the right kind. ABM should allow top managers to prioritize the project outcome factors of performance specifications, factory costs, development budget, and development schedule, *then* examine activities that relate to these factors.

Relevant questions. Before ABM is implemented for innovation/R&D management, it should be preceded by a careful feasibility study. Issues that should be considered are presented below in the form of relevant questions:

- Has the use of ABM changed or improved management decision making in functions

where it has been tried? What implications do such experiences have for innovation/R&D management?

- Can ABM be used in R&D for performance measurement in terms of development cycle times, budget, "better" innovations, target specifications, and target factory cost? Will it bring about new or better R&D performance measures? Which?
- Can ABM better communicate or justify development budgets? How?
- Can ABM better answer questions of "What have you done for me lately?"
- Can ABM link R&D activities to support product lines throughout their life cycles?
- Can ABM aid investment analysis of new product projects or manufacturing systems in terms of recovery of development costs?
- Can ABM better handle risk or uncertainty aspects of R&D management?

Classification issues

Several classification issues need to be addressed to develop a framework for the application of ABM to the innovation process.

Innovation functions and activities might be categorized in terms of:

- Research;
- Development;
- Design engineering;
- Applications engineering; and
- Technical services.

High-tech industries might be broadly classified in terms of:

- Materials processing;
- Discrete parts fabrication and assembly; and
- Project engineering.

Important classification issues relate to whether ABM (and perhaps cost management in general) applies equally well in all R&D settings. Several authors have stressed that some innovation processes, by their very nature, are not conducive to formal procedures and control.[19] This may only be true of the earlier stages of the research process. Other studies have reported that experienced innovators allow informal, nonstandardized procedures in the initial stages. Once the product proposition is approved, formal controls are exercised to ensure a timely and successful launch. A successful new product development program needs to be managed and controlled so that "new products are launched into the marketplace at the right time to counter competitive threats and to ensure the firm's survival and growth."[20]

Definition of activities. The definition of activities in different R&D settings poses a problem for activities that make up the early stages of the product development process. At earlier stages of the research process, activities may seem more like chaos than discrete and separable functions. A solution would be to start identifying and defining activities at the postproduct-approval stage. The challenge

---

Managers of successful new products take an integrated approach to new product development and commercialization.

---

is not insurmountable, because the product innovation literature contains exhaustive listings of specific sequential activities that make up the product development process. Moreover, a wealth of historical data may already be available in R&D departments of corporations willing to start a pilot project.

Activity issues

The following additional issues relating to activities must be addressed before a framework for implementation can be developed:

- Is it possible to distinguish between value-adding and non-value-adding activities in the innovation/R&D processes?
- Are there conditions under which innovation activities have or do not have value?
- Do customers (both internal and external customers) of innovation/R&D activities recognize trade-offs between linked activities? Are they willing to pay for the up-front investment costs?
- How can one assign a value to an innovation activity whose costs are incurred now but whose value is not realized until much later in the life cycle?
- When do innovation activities in effect constitute downstream cost commitments?

Linkage issues

Several linkage issues must be considered to develop a framework for the incorporation of ABM into the innovation process. These include the following issues:

- Can ABM link innovation/R&D to the goals and competitive strategies of the firm?
- Can ABM enhance the formation and management of cross-functional product development or design teams?
- How can ABM enhance design-for-manufacturability (i.e., cost implications of new designs, design changes, and design complexity)?
- How can ABM enhance design for customer demand?
- How can ABM enhance product customization and the development of product families?

The potential of ABM to link innovation/ R&D to the goals and strategies of the firm may constitute its most important linkage benefit. Modern corporations exhibit multiple and complex goals, objectives, strategies, and policies. For example, one survey that was conducted to identify technical, marketing, and firm innovation strategies[21] revealed:

- Four technology strategies (defensive imitator, process developer, aggressive specialist, and aggressive innovator);
- Four marketing strategies (defense imitator, market defender, market penetrator, and innovative marketer); and
- Three strategic groupings (risk avoiders, risk balancers, and innovators).

Apparently, therefore, firms can maintain different combinations of technology and marketing strategies for different products or product families. These combinations translate into differential emphasis on project outcome factors and key activities that need to be monitored and controlled. The use of ABM can yield a system that can track the *relevant* product development activity for each product or product family. ABM would therefore be of value to a system in which technological and marketing strategies are translated into project outcome factors and key activity standards.

Multifunctional product development teams. The formation of multifunctional product development teams and their management is another important linkage issue. Several studies have evaluated the effectiveness of alternative project structures such as functional, functional matrix, balanced matrix, project matrix, and project teams.[22] An ABM system that identifies key activities and recognizes linkages among activities may provide valuable input toward evaluation of alternative project structures.

The setting up of an ABM system should not treat the project structure as given. In fact, the activity analysis that precedes installation of ABM systems may have value in designing R&D project structures that facilitate the recognition of linkages with other functional areas. The linkages between ABM and product design have been discussed earlier in the article. ABM systems for innovation should have room for flexibility to account for customization and design for manufacturability.

Implementation issues

Most of the issues discussed so far affect the implementation of ABM systems for innovation/R&D management. However, the following issues deserve separate mention:

- How has ABM been effectively implemented in other functions? What are the implications for R&D?
- Who should be the ABM initiator? If it is top management, what is the composition of an "ideal" implementation team? What level of involvement should outside consultants have?
- What are the different routes to ABM implementations (e.g., through pilot projects)?
- How should resistance be dealt with? What determines transferability to other parts of the firm?
- How will the culture of the R&D organization affect receptivity to ABM?

Summary and conclusions

This article considers the application of ABM to the management of innovation/R&D operations. A study during the early 1980s indicated that the industrial sector was expecting significant increases in profits from new prod-

ucts.[23] Given the changing nature of global competition at present, this reliance on new products will only become stronger during the 1990s.

With high-tech firms using "time-to-market" as a competitive weapon in markets characterized by short product life cycles, the use of ABM for innovation/R&D operations is a plausible management action. This article explores the feasibility of such an application of ABM and identifies several key issues that should be addressed before a framework for applying ABM in innovation/R&D can be

---

Given that products with short life cycles must get to the market in as short a time as possible, ABM may prove relevant if it is moved upstream from manufacturing.

---

developed. As indicated by the issues related to classification, activity (definition), linkage, and implementation, incorporating ABM into the R&D function can be both challenging and rewarding. The potential benefits of applying ABM to innovation R&D operations are so great and so crucial to the future international competitiveness of U.S. companies that research and action must begin now. ▲

Notes
1. Norm Raffish & Peter B.B. Turney, eds., "Glossary of Activity-Based Mangement," *Journal of Cost Management* (Fall 1991): 53–63.
2. *Id.*
3. See, e.g., Paul E. Nix & Richard M. Peters, "Accounting for R&D Expenditures," *Research Technology Management* (Jan.-Feb. 1988): 39–41; Maurice S. Newman, "Accounting for Research and Development," *Research Technology Management* (July-Aug. 1988): 6–7; Lynn W. Ellis, "What We've Learned Managing Financial Resources," *Research Technology Management* (July-Aug. 1988): 21–38; and Lynn W. Ellis, "Viewing R&D Budgets Financially," *Research Management* (May-June 1984): 35–40.
4. Lynn W. Ellis & Robert G. McDonald, "Reforming Management Accounting to Support Today's Technology," *Research Technology Management* (Mar.-Apr. 1990): 30–34.

5. G.D. Hughes, "Managing High-Tech Product Cycles," *Academy of Management Executives* (May 1990): 44–55.

6. H. Takeuchi & I. Nonaka, "The New Product Development Game," *Harv. Bus. Rev.* (Jan.-Feb. 1986): 137–146.

7. Arnold O. Putnam, "A Redesign for Engineering." *Harv. Bus. Rev.* (May-June 1985): 139–144.

8. C.J. McNair, William Mosconi, & Thomas Norris, *Meeting the Technology Challenge: Cost Accounting in a JIT Environment* (Montvale, N.J.: National Association of Accountants 1988).

9. Hank Johannson, "The Revolution in Cost Accounting," *P&IM Review and APICS News* (Jan. 1985): 42–46.

10. See, e.g., Roger J. Calantone & Robert G. Cooper, "New Product Scenarios: Prospects for Success," *Journal of Marketing* (Spring 1981): 48–60; Robert G. Cooper, "New Product Strategies: What Distinguishes the Top Performers?" *Journal of Product Innovation Management* (Sept. 1984): 151–164; and Roy Rothwell, "Factors for Success in Industrial Innovation," *Project SAPPHO—A Comparative Study of Success and Failure in Industrial Innovation* (Brighton, UK: Science Policy Research Unit, University of Sussex 1972).

11. Roger J. Calantone & C. Anthony di Benedetto, "An Integrative Model of the New Product Development Process: An Empirical Validation," *Journal of Product Innovation Management* (Sept. 1988): 201–215.

12. Yoram Wind & Vijay Mahajan, "New Product Development Process: A Perspective for Reexamination," *Journal of Product Innovation Management* (Dec. 1988): 304–310.

13. The four project outcome factors have been identified by Milton D. Rosenau, Jr., "Schedule Emphasis of New Product Development Personnel." *Journal of Product Innovation Management* (Dec. 1989): 282–288.

14. Michael E. Porter, *Competitive Advantage: Creating and Sustaining Superior Performance* (New York: The Free Press 1985).

15. *Id.* at ch. 2.

16. See, e.g., A.K. Gupta, S.P. Raj, & D. Wilemon, "The R&D-Marketing Interface in High-Technology Firms," *Journal of Product Innovation Management* (Mar. 1985): 12–24; W.L. Shanklin & J.K. Ryans, *Marketing High Technology* (Lexington, Mass.: Lexington Books: 1984); Ashok K. Gupta & David Wilemon, "The Credibility-Cooperation Connection at the R&D-Marketing Interface," *Journal of Product Innovation Management* (Mar. 1988): 20–31; and William E. Souder, "Managing Relations Between R&D and Marketing in New Product Development Projects," *Journal of Product Innovation Management* (Mar. 1988): 6–19.

17. Peter B.B. Turney, "Using Activity-Based Costing to Achieve Manufacturing Excellence," *Journal of Cost Management* (Summer 1989): 23–31.

18. Such an analysis would involve tracing the product development process in terms of key activities and comparing these to product development exercises that were not as successful.

19. See, e.g., C. Gresov, "Designing Organizations to Innovate and Implement: Using Two Dilemmas to Create a Solution," *Columbia Journal of World Business* (Winter 1984): 63–67; and J.B. Quinn, "Managing Innovation: Controlled Chaos," *Harv. Bus. Rev.* (May-June 1985): 73–84.

20. F. Axel Johne & Patricia A. Snelson, "Success Factors in Product Innovation: A Selective Review of the Literature," *Journal of Product Innovation Management* (June 1988): 114–128.

21. Klaus Brockhoff & Alok K. Chakrabarti, "R&D/Marketing Linkage and Innovation Strategy: Some West German Experiences," *IEEE Transactions on Engineering Management* (Aug. 1988): 167–174.

22. See, e.g., Erik W. Larson & David H. Gobeli, "Organizing for Product Development Projects," *Journal of Product Innovation Management* (Sept. 1988): 180–190.

23. "New Products Management for the 1980s" (corporate document, Booz Allen & Hamilton, Inc. 1981).

It's Not as Easy as ABC

John P. Campi

Activity-based costing (ABC) should not be considered a stand-alone initiative. Instead, it is one of a number of initiatives required by organizations that seek world-class status. Taken together, those initiatives (including just-in-time manufacturing, total quality maintenance, cellular manufacturing, focused factories, and others) are understood to constitute a fundamentally different *business process* than the one U.S. companies have used in the past. This new business process has been called *activity-based management,* or ABM. Unlike ABC, ABM is not viewed as an accounting exercise concerned with developing better product cost data. A failure to understand the new business process approach called ABM has led to a number of disappointing or even unsuccessful ABC implementations.

One of the first public conferences about activity-based costing (ABC) took place in March 1989. By then, ABC had received national attention because of an article in *Business Week*[1] the preceding summer called "The Productivity Paradox." Because of this article, Computer Aided Manufacturing-International (CAM-I)—which had previously been a little-known research consortium for the study of applications of computer technology to advanced manufacturing—first received national recognition for the work of its cost management systems (CMS) project.

At that time, the primary thrust of CAM-I's CMS program was research into advanced cost management initiatives, which included the following topics:

- ABC;
- Performance measurement;
- Life cycle cost management; and
- Investment justification.

Documentation of a methodology and implementation guide for ABC was already under way.

A growing market for cost management specialists

Heightened awareness about CAM-I's work and a growing recognition of the failure of traditional cost management systems quickly caused the demand for qualified cost management specialists to outstrip the supply.

The conference in early 1989 clearly demonstrated a level of confusion that persists even today about the intent and application of ABC. This confusion is understandable when we consider how difficult it is to move away from research to actual applications of the findings of research.

On the whole, the publicity about ABC was a mixed blessing. Although the publicity gained support for CAM-I's research, it generated such a high level of interest (and high expectations), that a market for "ABC expertise" exploded. That market demand has been filled, in many cases, by unskilled practitioners.

Note that the CAM-I research never viewed ABC as a stand-alone initiative, but rather as one of a number of initiatives required by organizations that sought world-class status. Today, those initiatives are understood to be a fundamentally different *business process* than the one U.S. companies have understood and used in the past. This new business process has been called *activity-based management,* or ABM. The lack of understanding of this business process approach has ultimately led to failed or disappointing ABC implementations.

A "quick fix"

What were the results that companies expected from ABC? Like many other initiatives that U.S. companies have rushed to adopt, ABC has been seen as a "quick fix" for declining profitability or productivity. Thus, too many companies have viewed just-in-time (JIT) manufacturing, total quality management (TQM), cellular manufacturing, focused factories, ABC, or this year's newest addition to the alphabet soup of management's tool box as "hot buttons" that will supposedly solve all their problems.

U.S. companies have generally failed to examine the underpinning of management training and also to challenge the basic business process employed. Evidence exists throughout the world of different—and better—business processes, though we tend to dismiss them and attribute other countries' success to "cultural differences."

U.S. businesses too often take it for granted that our way of doing business is the best way. Nowhere is this prejudice more pronounced than in the financial community. FASB promulgations, for example, are written with no apparent concern about the effect that accounting changes will have on the competitiveness of U.S. business in global markets.

The need for benchmarking. U.S. companies must start benchmarking their business principles and processes against "best in class" practices globally, rather than automatically assuming that our methods (which were developed when the United States did indeed dominate world markets) are superior. It is this mind-set of infallibility that has allowed international competitors to dominate the international markets for steel, machine tools, and automotive markets in recent years.

ABC is a classic example of this desire for a quick fix. When the article in *Business Week* was published, ABC was only one facet of CAM-I's ongoing research about advanced cost management. In fact, ABC was not even the cornerstone of the effort, but merely one component. Instead, ABM is the cornerstone, because it involves gaining a view of an organization's *entire* business practice (the latest CAM-I research in this area, for example, is called the project on "quality customer/quality supplier relationships").

Unlike ABC, ABM is not viewed as an accounting exercise concerned with developing better product cost data. One analogy that comes to mind when comparing ABC to ABM might be that ABC is to advanced cost management what a windshield is to an automobile: It allows us to see our surroundings and our direction, but it's not the vehicle itself.

ABM involves a comprehensive paradigm shift in management—one that involves moving away from the traditional functional view of organizational structure toward one that facilitates a cross-functional view of the effectiveness of activities and business processes. It must affect the culture of the entire organization. ABC is simply the language used to communicate in this new environment. Many less-than-successful implementations of ABC have occurred because the companies failed to change their business processes—that is, they failed to make the paradigm shift that is required for ABC to succeed. Many of those who have taught and written about ABC have also failed to recognize this critical element of the change process.

Cultural change

For ABC to work, it must be one of a set of cultural change initiatives. ABM is the umbrella structure for the cultural change mandated by today's global competition. As Exhibit 1 shows, this set of initiatives includes:

- TQM;
- JIT;
- Total customer satisfaction;
- Time-based competition;
- Employee empowerment;
- Focused factories;
- Continuous flow process; and
- Cellular manufacturing.

If companies that decide to adopt advanced cost management initiatives fail to understand the need for these other initiatives, implementations of ABC are unlikely to succeed.

Some companies, incidentally, believe that an ABC system must be "fully embedded" (as opposed, for example, to a stand-alone ABC

Exhibit 1. *The New Business Process Paradigm*

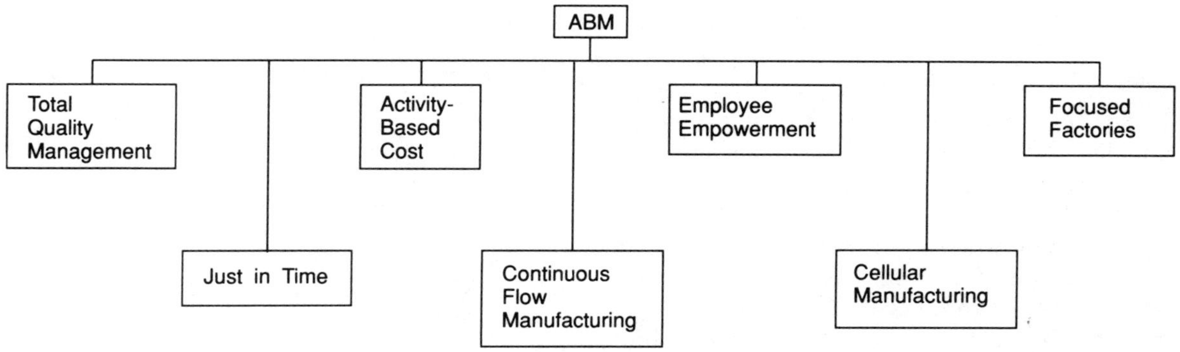

```
                        ┌─────┐
                        │ ABM │
                        └──┬──┘
   ┌───────────┬──────────┼──────────┬───────────┐
┌──┴──────┐  ┌─┴─────┐  ┌─┴──────┐  ┌─┴───────┐  ┌┴────────┐
│ Total   │  │Activity│ │Employee│  │ Focused │
│ Quality │  │-Based  │ │Empower-│  │Factories│
│Management│ │ Cost   │ │ ment   │  │         │
└─────────┘  └───┬───┘  └────────┘  └─────────┘
      ┌──────┐ ┌─┴────────┐ ┌──────────┐
      │Just in│ │Continuous│ │ Cellular │
      │ Time  │ │  Flow    │ │Manufactur│
      │       │ │Manufactur│ │  ing     │
      └───────┘ └──────────┘ └──────────┘
```

Total Quality Management · Activity-Based Cost · Employee Empowerment · Focused Factories · Just in Time · Continuous Flow Manufacturing · Cellular Manufacturing

---

system on a microcomputer). This is not the case. Having one comprehensive system that provides all financial and managerial data needed by management is not essential, although it may well be the ultimate goal.

What is ABM?

What, then, is ABM, and how can both manufacturing and service organizations use ABM to manage their future (as opposed to being managed by the future)? First, ABM is *not* a new cost system. Second, it is not simply a new software package to install on a mainframe (as many people with financial training felt they could do with ABC). Third—and most important—ABM is not business as usual.

Re-education. ABM requires a re-education of the organization, from the executive suite to the shop floor. To effectively compete in a global marketplace, organizations must completely understand the business processes required to support their goods and services in order to meet customer needs. *Activities* are the common denominator in the business process analysis. World-class competitors will find it increasingly essential to understand how their business processes, and therefore their activities, perform against the "best in class" globally.

Traditional management training in the United States has focused almost obsessively on the financial statements of publicly traded corporations as the primary measure of performance. This financial focus was acceptable when the vast majority of competitors used consistent financial performance measures in common capital markets.

For nearly forty years (until about 1970) this was true for U.S. companies, which dominated global marketplaces. Today, however, capital markets have changed. Today, large institutional investors that participate in U.S. capital markets face legal constraints on ownership of publicly traded companies, which is not the case abroad (e.g., in Germany, Japan, and many other foreign countries). Institutional investors abroad can therefore take longer-term views of their major investments in public companies. Financial reporting and the gyrations of capital markets therefore have quite different impacts abroad.

The only universal measures for global competition today involve the time and resource consumption of activities that support business processes (and thus add value in delivering a superior product or service to the market). This is a "total cost management" approach that looks at both financial and nonfinancial data to measure "best in class" performance, whether in terms of quality, throughput time to market, or life cycle cost to the consumer of the goods or services.

What, then, should organizations do? How do firms that want to survive and then attain world-class status assure themselves of a successful implementation of advanced management initiatives? What are the critical success factors? How can an organization be energized in a manner that will foster rather than inhibit the change process? The sections below attempt to answer these questions.

Leadership and risk management

Today's corporate leaders realize the international global threat, but often they are not aware of one of the primary causes for their organizations' continual decline—the continued focus on short-term financial measures to the exclusion of all else. (As mentioned previously, many of the world's formidable competitors abroad do not face this never-ending pressure to meet short-term financial goals.) While international competitors have focused on performance measures that address the critical success factors of quality, speed to market, customer satisfaction and total cost, the narrow-minded focus of too many U.S. companies is on earnings per share for the next quarterly report.

As George C. Lodge's new book "*Perestroika For America*" states:

> "Today, managers of the Fortune 500 are forced to discern shareholders' desires from the transactions of gifted traders on Wall Street whose objectives are purely financial: a return—and a quick one at that—on what they have invested for their clients, the owners. These traders could scarcely have less interest in the long-run health of the firms their actions sustain or destroy.[2]"

Similarly, in a recent article[3] Lester Thurow, Dean of the Sloan School of Management at MIT, suggested the need for fundamental changes in this country's capital markets. It is quite obvious that this type of change will occur only over an extended period of time, but it is imperative that business leaders realize the problems caused by the disparity between the performance measures that really matter and the financial measures on which U.S. companies are actually evaluated.

Although awareness of the problem has grown, too often it manifests itself in the form of disjointed management initiatives, such as narrow focuses on ABC, JIT, TQM, or employee involvement. All these initiatives are essential to world-class performance, but many organizations have embarked on major initiatives without understanding the broader context in which these initiatives must be viewed. In other words, the activities, or business processes, that must exist to support or

change these initiatives have not been understood.

Uncoordinated, piecemeal initiatives. Many companies, for example, have taken up the banner of quality without being able to define those activities that add value to the quality initiative. Similarly, JIT has been attempted without involving suppliers (who must, of necessity, be involved in planning and implementing JIT). Lip service has also been paid to employee empowerment, yet many companies have trouble defining just what empowerment means. And, of course, ABC systems have been implemented that involve only financial parts of the organization because (supposedly) "ABC is a new accounting system for better product costs."

The paradigm shift that must occur in U.S. business involves more than just product costs, quality, or empowerment. Instead, U.S. companies need to adopt a completely different approach. Regardless of the traditional financial reporting being done for publicly traded corporations, management must focus on the performance criteria that *all* global competitors can use as common denominators—the productivity and efficiency of activities that support value-adding business processes, which must deliver the highest value at the lowest total cost (i.e., the lowest total life cycle cost, which includes the ultimate disposal cost to the end-use consumer).

This can be accomplished only by fundamental modifications to organizational structures so that activities and business processes that cross functional boundaries can be managed. ABM provides a framework for just such an approach. ABM is a business process approach that focuses on the activities required to support the business processes for getting goods and services to the market.

Management's commitment

ABM requires extensive re-education of the entire organization. For this to occur, the initiative must come from the top of the organization. If senior management is not committed to a sweeping change in philosophical approaches to management, ABM will never become embedded in the mind-set or culture of the company.

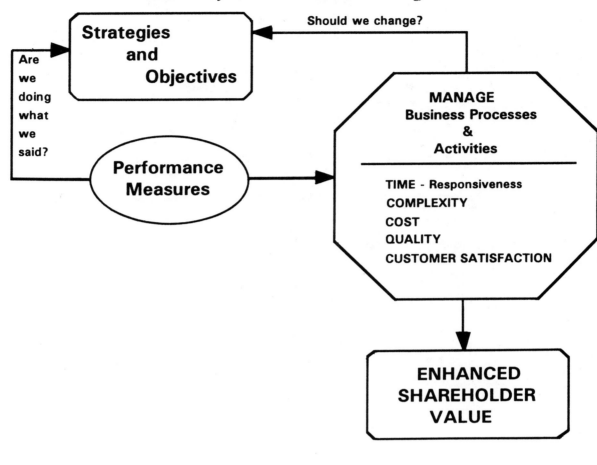

Exhibit 2. *Performance Measurement Must Be Strategy Driven*

Every major effort undertaken by management—be it JIT, continuous flow manufacturing, TQM, or ABC—requires an understanding of the activities that support those efforts. Therefore, ABM is not a new and different effort, but a facilitator of *all* these management initiatives. It gives an organization a common basis for understanding how to evaluate cause and effect to facilitate productivity.

Revolutionary change. We have seen unprecedented change over the past twenty years. Dramatic changes have occurred almost daily: Germany has been reunited, and the Union of Soviet Socialist Republics has ceased to exist. Even though we have witnessed these major paradigm shifts, we seem to be baffled and surprised by the rapidly changing business

environment we face. It seems as if those who were closest to the international marketplace in the past—U.S. businessmen and women—are the most surprised and disoriented.

The change process: making it happen

The first order of business for companies that seek to compete in today's global markets is to recognize the revolutionary changes that have occurred in the environment. They should then focus on establishing a senior-level, cross-functional team to evaluate and continually monitor the competitive factors affecting the global marketplace.

Performance measurement must be the focus of this key group of executives. The performance measurement system must provide consistent measures of global competitiveness

Exhibit 3. *Performance Measurement Balanced Set*

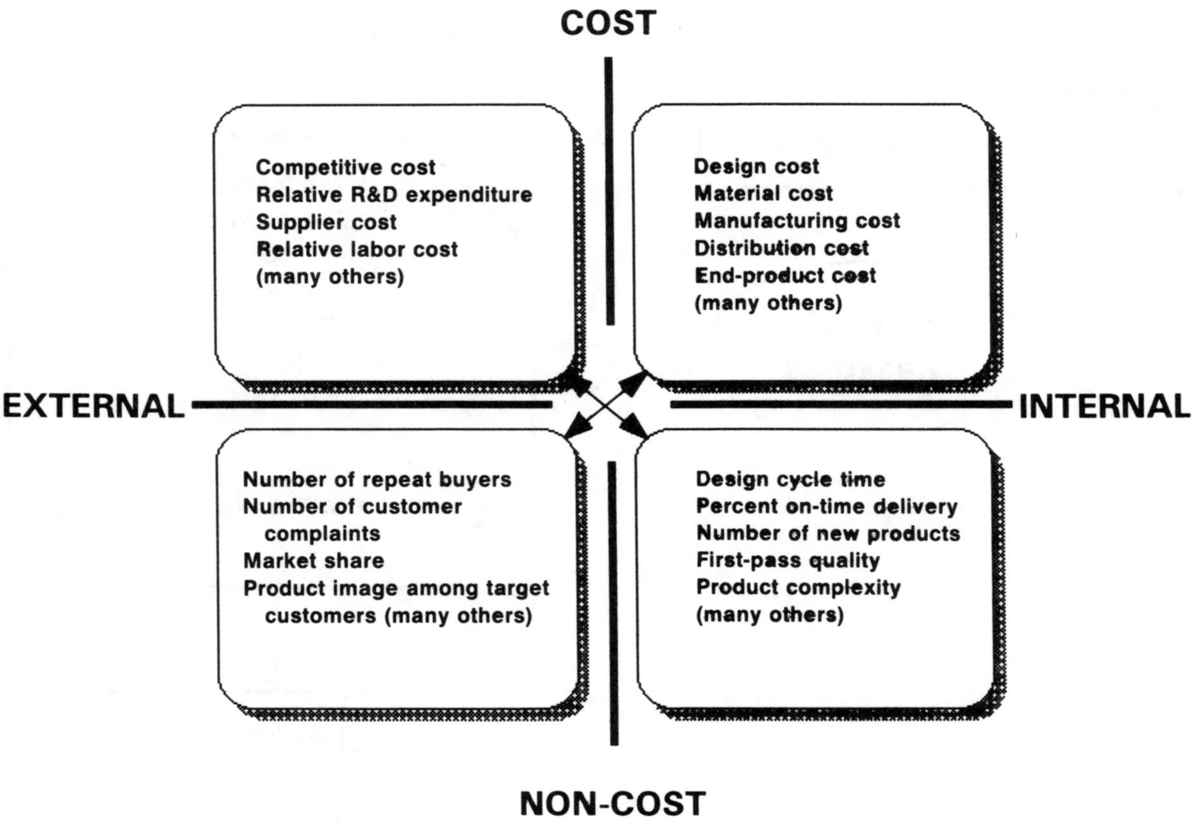

COST

EXTERNAL

Competitive cost Relative R&D expenditure Supplier cost Relative labor cost (many others)	Design cost Material cost Manufacturing cost Distribution cost End-product cost (many others)

Number of repeat buyers
Number of customer
  complaints
Market share
Product image among target
  customers (many others)
	Design cycle time
	Percent on-time delivery
	Number of new products
	First-pass quality
	Product complexity
	(many others)

INTERNAL

NON-COST

while also acknowledging the national financial measures that continue to influence performance in stock markets. This senior management team must champion the change process by re-educating the work force. Only through such high-level encouragement will organizations be willing to assume the risk associated with the revolutionary changes that are required.

Performance measurement

Performance must be clearly defined before it can effectively be measured. This effort to define must be driven by the strategy of the firm, as Exhibit 2 illustrates. This requires great effort to ensure that the strategy is communicated throughout the organization. Although this sort of communication has always been a management imperative, it takes on increased meaning as ABM is applied to business processes, for these business processes must be linked with an organization's strategy to increase shareholder value. Global compet-

itiveness requires the use of a balanced set of performance measures, as Exhibit 3 illustrates. Companies must be able to evaluate financial and nonfinancial effectiveness both internally and externally.

Effective use of these performance measures ultimately should lead to reduced dependence on financial reporting as the only ongoing performance criteria that matters. By benchmarking "best in class" in the business processes employed, companies can focus on the continuous improvement of processes and of the activities that support these processes, as Exhibit 4 illustrates. Continuous improvement is enhanced by tying the reward system not simply to financial performance, but also to the continuous improvement of activities that advance the strategy of the organization and thus improve the business processes of the firm. This will ultimately lead to improved financial performance, even if the accounting rules are not consistent between competing companies in different parts of the

Exhibit 4. Benchmarking "Best in Class"

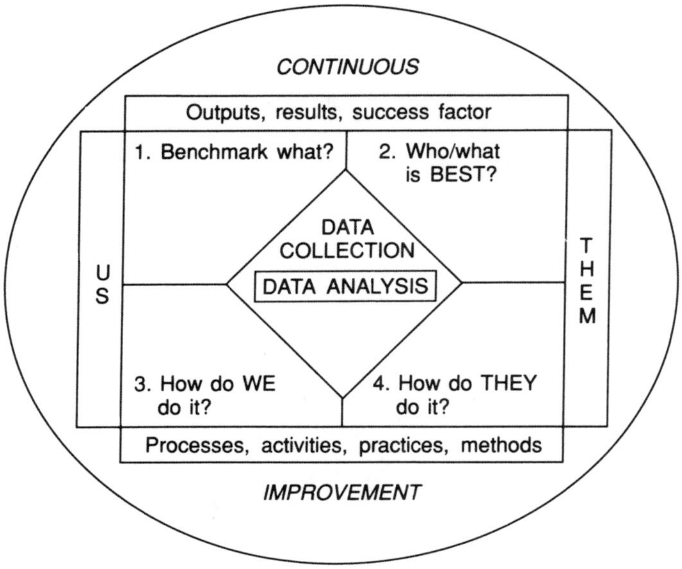

world. (Note that the FASB has an ongoing project about the standardization of accounting rules throughout the world. However, if financial performance—regardless of international measurement inconsistencies—is driven by critical success factors such as quality, customer satisfaction, and time to market, companies that focus on continual improvement of activities that support their business practices will ultimately reap dividends in their financial performance.) Ultimately, the enhancement of shareholder value is the common objective of all global competitors.

By implementing ABM, an organization empowers its work force to participate in substantive ways by improving the activities they perform. By focusing on the activities that must be performed to supply goods or services, employees derive a sense of accomplishment that, when linked to a responsive reward system, establishes a true culture of empowerment.

Conclusion

No, it is not as easy as ABC. The most remarkable attribute of Americans and of U.S. industry has been our ability to meet challenges with insight and ingenuity. There is no question that this country's industrial base can meet the global challenge. The only ques-

tion is how many of our industries have to be decimated before we rise to the challenge. The steel, machine tools, automobile, and (possibly) computer chip industries have already sustained unprecedented damage.

We must not allow our dominance of world markets in the past to cloud our vision of the "new order" in today's world. It will take unprecedented cooperation between the leaders of government, industry, and our unions to forge a new and responsive industrial base for the global challenges that lie ahead. The reunification of Germany, the rise of the European Economic Community, and the emergence of new democracies in Eastern Asia all pose economic challenges and opportunities that will play an ever-increasing role in emerging global markets. ▲

Notes
1. Otis Port, "The Productivity Paradox," *Business Week* (June 6, 1988): 100–111.
2. George C. Lodge, *Perestroika for America—Restructuring Business-Government Relations for World Competitiveness* (Boston: Harvard Business School Press 1990), 6.
3. Lester Thurow, "Let's Learn From the Japanese," *Fortune* (November 18, 1991): 30.

Activity-Based Cost Management for Continuous Improvement: A Process Design Framework

Thomas G. Greenwood and James M. Reeve

Activity-based costing frameworks were originally designed to support strategic decision making about products and customers. This article outlines a comprehensive activity-based architecture for supporting operational decision making. The architecture described here supports costing of a process hierarchy, product costing, high-order cost driver relationships, and process modeling and planning decisions.

I n the area of organizational intervention, many consulting firms have espoused the advantages afforded by broad activity analyses and modeling of complex organizations. Although all the firms employ proprietary methodologies for which information is limited, there appears to be a consistent theme in terms of the sequence of events recommended for achieving improved performance through activity analysis. These events include:

1. The identification of activities performed throughout an organization;
2. An analysis of the value of the respective activities; and
3. An analysis of the horizontal integration of activities with respect to business processes.

The only criticism of the current applications of activity analysis for organizational intervention is that they are usually employed as senior-level management projects that result, primarily, in broad inferences regarding the effective utilization of employees. Although these efforts benefit the organization by providing senior management with new insights into how work is actually performed, there appears to be no hooks to bind these programs to ongoing continuous improvement

initiatives at lower levels in the management control structure. What we find is that these programs are excellent, strategic "front ends" for more in-depth activity analysis. However, the current methodologies do not offer the type of cost and performance tracking needed for continuous improvement programs. Specifically, these methodologies are not designed to be downwardly compatible with existing process layers within the organization. (In this context, downward compatibility implies that the activity structure can overlay a more detailed activity cost allocation and performance tracking scheme.) If this capability existed, strategic inferences from these front-end projects could be projected downward to the individual activity level in the form of specific cost and performance targets.

Activity-based costing

The motivation for activity-based costing (ABC) derives from a need to adjust inequities in traditional volume-based allocation techniques for indirect manufacturing costs.[1] The basic premise of these new cost system designs is that various production actions that are similar should be classified together as activities. For example, all the actions associated with setup operations throughout the plant may be associated with the activity "setup." The resources consumed by the occurrence of an activity are then pooled to form an activity cost pool in the first stage of the allocation scheme. In the second stage, these cost pools are allocated to various cost objects (mostly products) using a single activity driver for each cost pool. In these systems, the primary objective is clearly aimed at attributing costs to products in a manner commensurate with the respective demands they place on production and nonproduction systems. Since the emphasis is on product costing, these allocation schemes allow certain expediencies, such as the pooling of multiple resource categories and activities; these expediencies tend to diffuse management's ability to discern the actual cost of activities or process segments.[2] Two other factors limit the scope of inferences that can be made from the cost data collected by these systems. The first factor is that only product-related activity drivers are assumed to affect the cost of activities. The second factor is that a strictly proportional relationship is assumed between the level of demand for a given cost object driver and commensurate marginal changes in the cost of activities. While this assumption is satisfactory for product costing, there is serious question about its validity in cost estimating and pro forma analysis.

Current limitations of ABC

There are several significant problems associated with the use of current activity analysis methodologies to promote continuous improvement. *First*, recent periodicals are replete with articles that allude to the potential benefits of using activity-based information to foster process-oriented improvements. However, there is an apparent void in the literature of any comprehensive methodology actually designed to relate cost and performance information to processes at the activity level. The categorization of activities as "value-added" or "non-value-added" is simply insufficient for providing performance feedback and insights into operational improvement.

The current initiatives outlined in the literature are either top-down activity analysis systems designed for organizational intervention or detailed cost systems motivated by product costing or other strategic needs. The ABC paradigm advanced by Cooper is very effective for the application of product costing. However, since activity costs are pooled by cost driver instead of being associated with the appropriate business process, the actual process cost information is not preserved for management control and continuous improvement of processes. What is missing is a design to support *activity-based, process-oriented cost management.*

Another problem associated with the use of current activity analysis methodologies is that, although there have been many references to the need for a cost simulation capability to support business decision making, the present systems are reactive in design. Hence, they provide only inferential associations between current conditions and actual production costs. What is needed is a methodology that:

- Directly associates costs with specific activities; and
- Clearly delineates the relationships between product (and process) characteristics and production costs. Moreover, the methodology that is needed must associate the impact of activity changes with actual changes in resource spending by utilizing the actual cost behavior pattern between activities and resources. The methodology explained in this article allows managers to predict activity and process costs under alternative product design and production scenarios.

Yet another potential problem is an emerging "simplification" philosophy toward cost control in repetitive manufacturing environments. The current trend is to streamline and downplay the importance of variance reporting, work-in-process tracking, and other traditional financial reporting tools. Hewlett-Packard, Daihatsu, and other practitioners of just-in-time (JIT) manufacturing have discontinued standard variance reporting; they have implemented other steps to simplify their accounting systems. This trend has been misconstrued by some to mean a reduced emphasis on the importance of cost management. Clearly, this is not the case. For example, Japanese practitioners of JIT expend significant resources toward providing process cost data to support "cost down" efforts.[3]

The position taken in this article is that the principal objective of an activity-based management system must be to reveal the details about the cost of process activities. A clear distinction should be made between this objective and fiduciary requirements for financial reporting. Current efforts to simplify financial reporting requirements by eliminating inventory levels in the bill of material structure and employing post-deduct techniques to reduce inventory transactions are reasonable objectives. However, these initiatives should not be construed as indicating a reduction in the importance of cost-based decision support. Following the lead of some of our Japanese counterparts, we must develop new methodologies to support process-oriented cost information for decision making.

A process-based activity architecture

The following description captures the essence (but by no means the detail) of the architecture of such a cost system. The field site for testing this architecture is an organization that manufactures fan coil units for residential air conditioning systems. The operations consist of cellular fabrication and assembly of fan coils within a JIT production environment. This cost system is designed to provide operational relevance, so its structure differs significantly from some of the cost systems espoused in the JIT literature.

Exhibit 1 illustrates the activity architecture of this approach. The architecture is designed to maintain information at the organizational unit level. This is critical when estimating the impact of product and process changes, as discussed later. First, resource categories are constructed by aggregating the budgetary line-item costs in the organization (starting at the left of Exhibit 1). Frequently, it is useful to aggregate these items into major categories of cost, such as supplies, tooling, and direct labor. This example considers thirteen resource categories, four of which are illustrated in Exhibit 1. These major categories can be broken into resource subcategories . (which are not illustrated) according to differences in costs within a particular category. For example, the direct labor resource category can be constructed to capture different labor-grade classifications across the facility. The construction of resource categories allows the designer to aggregate general ledger line items to reduce the complexity of the system. This is important, because the design retains the resource category or subcategory definitions down into the activity structure. This is essential for conducting cost simulations, as is demonstrated later.

Organizational units. Resource categories are aggregated into functional departments (organizational units), as illustrated by mainte-

nance, evaporative coil production, and manufacturing engineering departments. At this point, the design has simply traced general ledger items by broadly defined resource categories to the organizational unit level. The next step is to bring these costs down into the activities of the enterprise (moving left to right in Exhibit 1).

The methodology views the organization as a hierarchy of embedded processes. The hierarchy for a sample process (from the highest to lowest levels), as illustrated in Exhibit 1, is:

Hierarchy	*Process*
Process level (05)	Production
Subprocess level (05A)	Evaporative coil cell
Production process segment (05A1)	Fin production
Activity (05A1-05)	Press breakdown

The activity is the lowest level at which data is captured. From this level, cost and performance data can be rolled up into the higher levels of the process hierarchy. This process hierarchy gives the product manager a wealth of information from a cross-functional perspective about how costs are incurred in doing work. The activity information provides the basis for mapping cost consequences across organizational boundaries. It can also provide the basis for supporting process budgeting and performance evaluation.

In Exhibit 1, the press breakdown (05A1-05) activity is detailed. Within this activity, the resource category information is maintained. It is at this intersection that the vertical detail of the organization chart merges with the horizontal detail of the process information. The activities are coded by process, but the resource categories within the activities are coded by resource category and department. This structure is similar to cost systems within the project engineering environment.

Consumption basis. The consumption basis for a resource category can be thought of as a resource cost driver.

It is the basis on which cost within the resource category is consumed by the activity. For example, consider the direct labor resource category (06-52) within the press breakdown activity (05A1-05). The consumption basis is full-time equivalents (FTEs). For

Exhibit 1. *Activity Architecture*

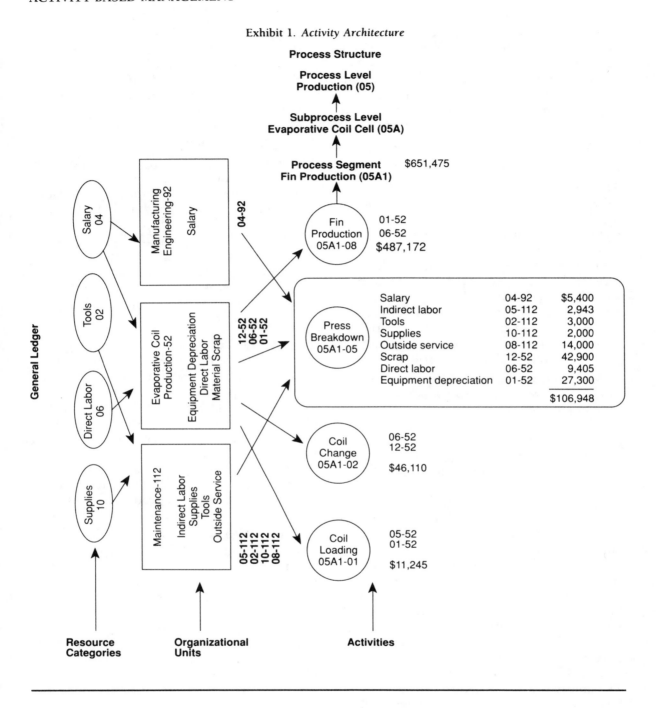

example, assume that the commitment in department 52 (evaporative coil production) for the direct labor resource category is eight operators (FTEs) and that the total dollar commitment to this resource category from the general ledger is $250,800. The activity of press breakdown consumes .3 FTEs. Therefore, the total operator resource commitment to the press breakdown activity is determined by multiplying the factor .0375 × $250,800, or $9,405. (The activity consumption factor (.0375) is determined simply as .3 ÷ 8, which is the ratio of FTEs committed to the breakdown activity to the total direct labor commitment in department 52.)

Resource category costs. As Exhibit 1 shows, eight resource categories contribute to the

Exhibit 2. *Activity Hierarchical Structure*

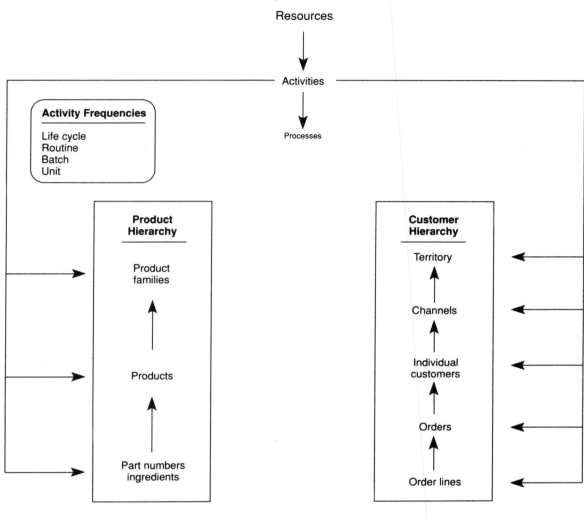

activity of press breakdown repairs. The sum of the resource category costs within the breakdown activity totals $106,948. The immediate observation is that this represents more than 16 percent ($106,948 ÷ $651,475) of the total cost of activities within the fin production (05A1) process segment. Not only this, but a significant source of the cost of the press breakdown activity is the depreciation from lost time and material scrap. This information provides direction toward cost reduction efforts.

Hierarchies

In addition to cost information, each activity also provides performance, hierarchy level, and activity frequency information. The classifications of activity type and frequency require some elaboration. The trend of current ABC discussions, as established by Cooper and Kaplan, has been to categorize activities into a four-level hierarchy (unit, batch, product sustaining, and facility sustaining) for purposes of tracing costs of activities to product.[4] Our thinking runs along a similar path, but we believe that the hierarchy should not include unit and batch levels, for these represent *frequencies* with which activities occur. In this system, therefore, activities are categorized by both hierarchy and frequency. This hierarchy is illustrated in Exhibit 2. Basically, an activity can be related to a product, process, or customer hierarchy. A product hierarchy has part numbers or ingredients at the lowest level and builds up to completed products, which (in turn) build up to product families. For example, activities on the vendor side of the value chain frequently are associated at the part-number level, while those at the customer side attach to the end-product code or family level. Likewise, many activities, such as marketing or sales-related activities, can be attached to the customer, channel, or territory level. The frequencies are defined in Exhibit 3. Exhibit 4 provides an example of different combinations of activity frequencies for the product hierarchy.[5]

Performance objectives

In the case of the press breakdown activity, the performance objectives are the time to replace the die, time to replace the punch, and depreciation from lost machine time. The press breakdown activity falls into the "process" activity hierarchy, and its frequency is routine. The occurrence of the machine breakdown event occurs randomly and is governed by a probability distribution for which parameters may be tracked (e.g., mean time between failure).

From a management perspective, understanding the nature of routine activities that are triggering events for subsequent sequences (networks) of activities affords a tremendous advantage. The accepted term for such a routine triggering event is a *cost driver*. Defective materials, customer inquiries and returns, material shortages, and engineering change orders are examples of cost drivers that have significant cost impacts because they perturb the steady-state nature of the system and touch off a whole series of activities. In the press breakdown activity example, the nature of the event is captured within the single activity called "press breakdown." What becomes even more interesting is when the event causes a series of activities to occur across a number of processes. The nature of these events can only be captured by mapping the activity network of the event. (Activity networks and how they can be used to manage systems are discussed later in this article.)

Once this basic activity database is constructed, the report-writing capabilities are

Exhibit 3. *Activity Frequency Definitions*

Frequency Definitions

Unit: Activities performed once per unit.

Batch: Activities performed once per batch.

Periodic:

Routine: Activities performed routinely to sustain a product or process. These activities can be part of either normal operations or exception events. Exception events are termed *cost drivers*. Routine activities are generally expensed to the final cost object.

Product Life Cycle: Activities performed at given points during the life cycle of a given product. These activities add long-term value to the cost object (e.g., product or customer) and are generally capitalized to the final cost object.

Exhibit 4. *Examples of Activities for Various Hierarchy and Frequency Combinations*

Activity Frequency	Product Hierarchy Level	
	Part Number	Product
Unit	Machining or fabricating individual parts through a work center	Processing or packing activities of final product
Batch	Quality sampling of incoming purchase part lots	Warehouse picks of individual orders of product
Routine	Activities related to part number engineering changes	Customer return activity on defective shipments
Life Cycle	Numerical control programming activities for part number tool paths	Research, development, and testing for a new product

multidimensional. Examples include activity costs by resource category, process segment costs by activity, process segment costs by resource category, and process segment costs by organizational unit.

Product costing

The product costing approach uses a multiple-driver perspective based on product attributes (PAs). PAs distinguish various products with respect to characteristics that affect resource consumption during both production and nonproduction processes. The product costing methodology is illustrated in

Exhibit 5. *The Product Costing Calculation Methodology*

Product Attributes	→	Input Factors	→	Product Allocation Factors (PAFs)

Examples	**Examples**	
PA1: Number of rows	IF1: Unit volumes	Functions for each activity using input factors.
PA2: Fins per inch	IF2: Weight volume	
PA3: Aluminum weight	IF3: Presswork complexity	
PA4: Percent volume mix	IF4: Machine consumption demands	
PA5: Machine time		

Exhibit 5. PAs are used to construct input factors, which (in turn) are used to construct product allocation factors (PAF).

The table below illustrates attributes of fan coils that are critical to resource consumption:

- Mix volumes;
- Machine times; and
- Physical design characteristics, such as the number of rows of holes or weight of raw material stock.

The intent of the system is to provide a table of PAs that can be used as the basis for determining the functional relationship between the activity and product. To construct the complete functional relationship, the PAs must be converted into input factors (IFs). The IFs are, in turn, used to construct the final functional relationship between activity and product. These are the PAFs. The rationale for the layered-table approach is to maintain and easily display the building blocks of the cost allocation scheme to all users. The calculation hierarchy through linked tables provides an easy approach toward simulating changes in the functional relationships, design attributes, and input variables.

Intermediate input variable calculations. The first step is to relate the PAs above with inter-mediate input variable calculations. There can be any number of intermediate input variable calculations, though only a few are illustrated in Exhibit 6.

Once the IFs are determined, the final PAFs can be determined. Exhibit 7 illustrates the use of the PAFs in determining the product cost of Product 1. The PAFs for each activity are determined from the engineering relationships between the product and that activity. Consider the press breakdown activity. Products will consume this activity according to the following formula:

$$\text{Unit volume} \times \text{machine time} \times \text{press complexity}$$

This is fairly straightforward: High volume, high machine time per unit, and complex products should cause relatively more breakdown activities than products with opposite characteristics. Product 1 has a low unit volume and low machine time per unit. These characteristics offset the relatively high complexity rating, thus resulting in a PAF of only .117. Hence, only 11.7 percent of the activity cost is allocated to Product 1. In a similar way, the coil loading and changing activities are consumed by aluminum weight. Low-volume, light-gauge products consume less coil-change resources than high-volume,

Product Attributes	Product 1	Product 2	Product 3	Product 4
Product Attributes	*Product 1*	*Product 2*	*Product 3*	*Product 4*
PA1: No. of rows	2	2	2	3
PA2: Fins per inch	11	14	11	14
PA3: Aluminum weight	7.0	12.0	18.5	23.5
PA4: Percent volume mix	15	35	40	10
PA5: Machine time	0.33	0.35	0.50	0.95

Product Attributes (PAs) for Four Fan Coil Products

Exhibit 6. *Intermediate Cost Drivers From Product Attributes*

Input Factor 1: The unit volumes in the product mix

Equation: IF1 = PA4 × product line volume

Example: IF1(PROD 1) = .15 × 300,000 = 45,000

Product 1	Product 2	Product 3	Product 4
45,000	105,000	120,000	30,000

Input Factor 2: Weight volume in pounds

Equation: IF1 = (PA3 × PA4)/SUM TOTAL

Example: IF2(PROD 1) = (7 × .15) ÷ (7 × .15 + 12 × .35 + 18.5 × .4 + 23.5 × .1) = .07

Product 1	Product 2	Product 3	Product 4
.07	.28	.493	.157

Input Factor 3: Presswork complexity (draw complexity)

Equation: Ratio of difficulty scale based on PA2, 14 FPI = 1; 11 FPI = 1.25

Product 1	Product 2	Product 3	Product 4
1.25	1.0	1.25	1.0

Input Factor 4: Machine time (ratio of comparison to average)

Equation: IF4 = PA5/(SUM(PA5) ÷ (no. of products))

Example: IF4(PROD 1) = .33 ÷ ((.33 + .35 + .5 + .95) ÷ 4) = .62

Product 1	Product 2	Product 3	Product 4
.62	.66	.94	1.78

Exhibit 7. *Product Cost Calculation for Product 1*

Activity	Activity Amount	PAF Function	PAF	Product 1 Cost
Fin production	$487,172	(IF1 × IF4)/SUM (IF1 × IF4)	.106	$51,640
Coil load	$11,245	IF2	.07	787
Press breakdown	$106,948	(IF1 × IF3 × IF4)/ SUM(IF1 × IF3 × IF4)	.117	12,513
Coil change	$46,110	IF2	.07	3,228
Total cost				$68,168/
Unit volume				45,000
Unit cost				$1.52

heavy-gauge products. The PAFs reflect this logic.

The PAFs represent the insight of engineers on the relationship between production activities and the attributes of products. From this information, it is possible to provide a modeling tool for evaluating the impact of changes in both product and process design. The result of product and process design changes are reflected by appropriate changes in the PA file. The cost effects of attribute changes are captured, in turn, by the functional relationships. For example, the complexity factor for fins per inch (PA2) can be changed in the product attribute file if:

- The process is improved so that the complexity penalty is removed; or
- Products are redesigned to have fourteen fins per inch (the low-complexity input factor).

The next section discusses advancing the system design to accommodate process cost modeling and planning decisions. The design characteristics necessary to accomplish these objectives are new.

Exhibit 8. *Resource Cost Information for the Current Condition*

Activity Index	Activity Description	Resource Category Index	Resource Category Description	Consumption Basis	Activity Allocation
05A1-01	Aluminum coil loading	05-52	Material handler	FTE	$4,000
		01-52	Forklift depreciation	Unit	$145
		12-52	Scrap	Lbs.	$3,900
05A1-02	Aluminum coil changing and feeding	06-52	Operator	FTE	$18,810
		12-52	Scrap	Lbs.	$27,300
05A11-01	Kanban recycle	04-33	Material planner	FTE	$1,650
05A11-02	Material receiving	05-41	Material handler	FTE	$60,000
		01-41	Forklift depreciation	Unit	$8,700
05A11-03	Production cell resupply	05-52	Material handler	FTE	$68,000
		01-52	Forklift depreciation	Unit	$8,555

Process cost modeling and planning

To this point, this article has described a basic activity model for purposes of evaluating the activity, process, and product cost of a baseline (i.e., existing, or as is) condition. A principal concern to operating managers is assessing the impact of change on spending patterns in the business and on resource deployment throughout the organization. To accomplish these objectives, a model must be able to simulate resource levels as a result of process improvement initiatives, product design variations, and production mix changes. In this way, the model becomes a simulation tool, much like the cost tables used in Japan and Germany. However, three basic advantages of this approach over cost tables are:

1. The cost-function relationships are explicitly stated;
2. The design framework incorporates actual cost behavior patterns in determining short-term spending changes; and
3. The cost of overhead resources are integrated within a clearly defined activity framework.

The following example demonstrates this approach. Note that the activity relationships can be quite complex; this explanation is purposely simplified to show how it works.

Example. Suppose operating managers within the fin production process segment are considering a change in the unit weight of the aluminum coil stock from 4,000 pounds to 8,000 pounds. Since all products use the same gauge and width of coil, coil changes are not affected by product changes. Management wishes to assess the cost impact of implementing the coil weight change. This is not a product costing question, but a cost management question. The following sections explain how to resolve the issue.

Determine activities influenced by decision

The first step is to identify the activities that will be influenced by the process or product change. Exhibit 8 shows the activities affected by the coil weight decision. As can be seen, the activities of aluminum coil loading (05A1-01) and aluminum changing and coil feed (05A1-02) from the product costing example provided previously are included as activities that may be influenced by a coil weight change. In Exhibit 8, note that the total cost of the aluminum coil loading activity is less than the value reflected in previous exhibits. This occurs because some of the resource category costs are not affected by this decision, and thus they were not included in Exhibit 8. Additional activities within the process structure are also included as part of this analysis. As in the product costing model, the resource categories within each activity are maintained within the database. This is important, because actual spending is planned at the resource category level. Organizations do not fund activities directly; instead, they provide the employees and equipment needed to perform activities. Since the cost profiles of equipment and employees will be different, a separation must be maintained.

Determine spending profiles of resource categories

The next step in the analysis process is to construct spending profiles for each of the resource categories affected by the coil weight change decision. These profiles should capture the short-term expenditure profile for the resource category as a function of the consumption basis (i.e., the resource, or first-stage, driver). Exhibit 9 may help to explain the issues involved. The top of Exhibit 9 illustrates the cost behavior assumption for purposes of product costing. The relationship between the consumption of a resource category and an activity is strictly proportional, as is the relationship between cost objects and activities. This assumption is appropriate for product costing, because the decision scenarios that incorporate product costs are of a long-term nature.

The proportionality assumption has led some to criticize ABC as inaccurate in terms of reflecting the actual consumption of resources. It is argued, for example, that dropping a product will not necessarily mean that the consumption of activities and resources will necessarily go down by the amount implied by the ABC model. This argument fails to distinguish between two different *uses* of an activity model. For product costing purposes, the flow of costs is from resource category to activity to cost object. Strict proportionality can be assumed for this purpose, because all costs are variable in the long term.

For purposes of operational decision support and simulation modeling, however, the flow of analysis is in the opposite direction. Specifically, when the economic question revolves around what will happen to resource spending due to operational changes, then the cost flow is from activities back to resource categories. This distinction is critical to understanding this framework. The coil change decision involves understanding how spending at the resource categories will be influenced by changes in activities that will result from this process change. The question revolves around how activity changes affect actual spending back at the resource categories. This is clearly different than product costing, which is concerned only with attaching resource costs to products through activi-

Exhibit 9. *Cost Behavior Patterns for Product Costing and Resource Management*

Cost Behavior Pattern for Product Costing

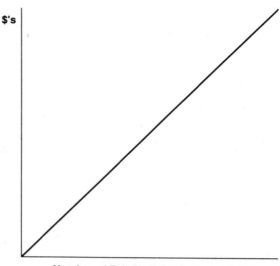

Number of Full-Time Equivalents (FTEs)

Cost Behavior Pattern for Resource Management

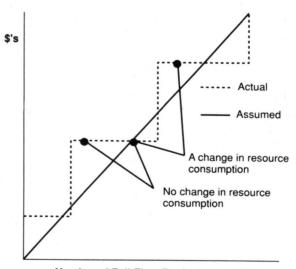

Number of Full-Time Equivalents (FTEs)

ties. What is unique about this model is that it is robust enough to support both product costing and operational decision making.

Operational decisions regarding process improvements are clearly of a shorter time horizon. As a result, the assumption of proportionality is no longer sufficient. The actual cost behavior pattern within a resource category must be used to understand the impact on short-term deployment of resources. This is illustrated in the graph at the bottom of Exhibit 9. In the case of the operator resource category (06-52), the actual spending follows a step function with every increment in headcount. Spending changes occur only when full-time employees are added or removed.

What is provided by this architecture is an activity framework that allows operating managers to model the impact of process changes, then to roll them up into resource categories to assess whether a step (i.e., an FTE in this case) is breached. Only if a step is removed or added will actual spending be affected. As a result, the model can be used to detect short-term spending changes from product and process changes. Again, this is a different use than the product costing application of ABC.

All resource categories have their own cost function profiles. For example, manpower resource categories will be step functions based on FTEs, equipment-based categories will have larger step functions based on changes in equipment units (such as number of forklifts), and scrap will have a linear function based on pounds of material generated.

ciled at the organizational level. To illustrate further, suppose that a manager is interested in determining if a change in coil weight will change the number of operators in the department. This determination can be made only by accumulating all activities that are consumed by operators and determining if the coil weight change will affect enough of these activities to cause a change in operator FTEs to do the work. Since operators are involved in many activities, only a complete reconciliation at the resource category level can provide the needed insights to fully evaluate the spending impact.

Develop the engineering relationships from activities back to resource categories

This step is one of the most challenging. The engineering impact of a coil weight change within an activity must be captured to discover the influence on spending. This is different than allocating from the resource category down to activity for purposes of product costing. This step requires specific modeling of the impact of the decision. In this example, management wishes to assess the cost impact of an increase in coil weight. Intuitively, one would expect an increase in coil weight to have the following impact on selected activities:

Activities	Cost Impact	Rationale
Coil loading	Decrease	Less loading frequency.
Coil changing	Decrease	Scrap occurs on each coil change, therefore, less coil changes will result in less scrap.
Kanban recycle	Decrease	Larger coils lead to fewer moves and, thus, fewer Kanban pulls.
Material receiving	Unknown	Trade-off between less receipts, but greater handling difficulty of larger coils.
Production cell resupply	Unknown	Trade-off between less moves, but greater handling difficulty of larger coils.

Reconcile activities at the resource category

Once the spending profiles for each resource category are identified, all activities that use a particular resource must be modeled under the baseline and proposed operating environment. The reason for this logic is straightforward: Although activities consume resources, it is organizational units that are the resource providers. Hence, resources must be recon-

The issue, of course, is how to translate these intuitions into functional form. A complete description of the functional relationships for all resource cost categories and activities requires a complex set of table relationships. One set of these relationships is illustrated here for the material handler (05-52) resource category. The material handlers in department 52 are responsible for three activities: alumi-

Exhibit 10. *Functional Relationship Between Activities and Material Handler Resource Category*

Activity Index	Description	Functional Form
05A1-01	Aluminum coil load	FTE = (time to load coil) × (number of coil changes per hour)/60
05A2-01	Copper coil load	FTE = (coil changes per hour) × (time to change coil)/60
05A11-03	Cell resupply	FTE = (travel time to cell + time to handle pallet) × (average pallets per delivery × average delivery per hour)/60

num coil loading, cell resupply, and copper coil loading. Copper coil loading is not influenced by the aluminum coil weight change, but needs to be part of the analysis in order to know the complete FTE impact of a weight change. (Ignoring any activity at the resource category level will misstate the location on the cost function profile where the current and proposed options will lie, so all activities must be included.)

Exhibit 10 provides a summarized version of the functional relationships between the activities and material handling resource category. In the actual database, a series of linked tables are used to convey all the information. Each row represents the unique functional form for the indicated activity. For example, the aluminum coil load activity is defined as:

$$FTE = (CD1 \times CD2) \div 60,$$
= (time to load a coil × number of coil changes required per hour),

where

$$CD1 = 5[1 + ((PRCA1 - 4,000) \times .5) \div 4,000],$$
the time to load a coil,

where

PRCA1 = Aluminum coil size; and
$$CD2 = PDCA1 \times PDCA2/PRCA1,$$ the aluminum coil change per hour,

where

PDCA1 = Average units per hour

PDCA2 = Average aluminum per unit

PRCA1 = Aluminum coil size

These sets of equations indicate the impact on the aluminum coil loading activity of coil weight. The equation for cost driver 1 (CD1) relates the time to load a coil to a standard time of five minutes for a 4,000-pound coil with an inflation factor that increases the time required, as a function of coil size, to compensate for the increased difficulty of

handling larger coils. The equation for the second cost driver expresses the average number of coil changes per hour in terms of:

- The product cost attributes (PDCAs) of average units per hour and average weight of aluminum used in the product; and
- The process cost attribute (PRCA) of aluminum coil weight. Naturally, as coil size increases, the number of aluminum coil changes per hour goes down. Therefore, the aluminum coil loading activity is influenced by changes in coil weight in both the number of changes and the time to perform each change. The net benefit is a function of whether the reduction in number of changes compensates for the increased difficulty of each change.

Economic impact of the decision

The functional relationships detailed above are for a single activity reconciled to a single resource category. The complete functional description includes all relevant activities reconciled to all resource categories influenced by this decision. The resulting analysis is both a current level of resource expenditure (based on the existing coil weight) and a proposed level of expenditure based on the new coil weight. The difference between the two conditions provides the economic impact of the decision. Exhibit 11 provides a summary comparison of the current condition with the pro forma scenario.

As can be seen from Exhibit 11, the major contributor to cost savings was the reduction in scrap from using the larger coil sizes. Every coil change causes the system to move out of production equilibrium for an average amount of time. Naturally, reducing the num-

Exhibit 11. *Comparison Summary of Current Operating Scenario Against Proposed Coil Weight Change Scenario*

Resource Consumption Index	Description	Allocation Basis	Current Consumption Level	Pro Forma Consumption Level	Current Consumption Quantity	Pro Forma Consumption Quantity	Current Spending Level	Pro Forma Spending Level	Change in Cost
06-52	Operator	FTE	8.19	8.14	9 FTEs	9 FTEs	$282,150	$282,150	0
12-52	Scrap	Pounds	42,090	27,621	42,090 lbs.	27,621 lbs.	63,135	41,432	+$21,703
05-52	Material handler	FTE	1.35	1.34	2 FTEs	2 FTEs	80,000	80,000	0
01-52	Forklift	Unit	.702	.695	1 Unit	1 Unit	2,900	3,700	−800
01-41	Forklift	Unit	3.53	3.53	4 Units	4 Units	11,800	12,400	−800

Projected cost savings from coil weight change $20,103

ber of coil changes reduces the amount of scrap from this cause. The spending profile of scrap is proportional to the pounds saved, so the reduction in the resource consumption level (pounds) translates directly into cost savings.

It is interesting to note that this analysis indicates that the coil size change did very little to affect the number of forklifts needed to do the work or the number of operator and material handler FTEs. The FTE changes were so small as to prevent a step change in the spending profile. Therefore, both operator and material handler resources do not change because of the coil size change. The cost increase in the forklifts comes from an increased investment in larger forklifts to accommodate the larger coil sizes; the number of forklifts does not change, just the type. The bottom-line analysis is that the coil size change could be supported.

The pro forma cost simulation is tailored to the nature of the decision. The activity framework provides a cost architecture appropriate for modeling various scenarios. The resource categories and activities are built into the framework. The engineer or analyst must provide the functional relationship between the activity and resource category *as a function of the decision variable.* The coil change variable above was a key input to the functional relationships, since this was the focus of the decision. The result is a costing framework that provides, simultaneously, a product costing structure and the needed flexibility for economic analysis and planning.

Process management through activity networks

So far, this article has described an architecture for supporting process management, product costing, and cost simulation. In this section, the article extends the discussion and design principles into the use of activity networks in process management. This is an experimental phase of the architecture, but one that offers great promise. Again, an example from the fan coil manufacturer is used to illustrate the concepts, design attributes, and decision benefits that emanate from activity networks.

The activity architecture discussed previously breaks down cross-functional processes into subprocesses, process segments, and then, finally, to activities. This decomposition was illustrated with an example from the evaporative coil cell. One characteristic of this operation (from an engineering perspective) is that it is a well-defined process. As a result, defining the process hierarchy was a relatively easy exercise. Indeed, such a description is frequently part of the industrial engineer's process analysis work. Such detail is more challenging to determine for indirect and other support systems.

The four process levels (process, subprocess, process segment, and activity) are not well described in the nonproductive processes of the organization. This is where the concept of activity networks becomes important. Interviews are used to determine the resources committed to activities. The activity networks serve as a method of linking sequential activities into coherent process segments and sub-

Exhibit 12. *Activity Network of the Material Acquisition Process (03) and Materials Procurement Subprocess (03A)*

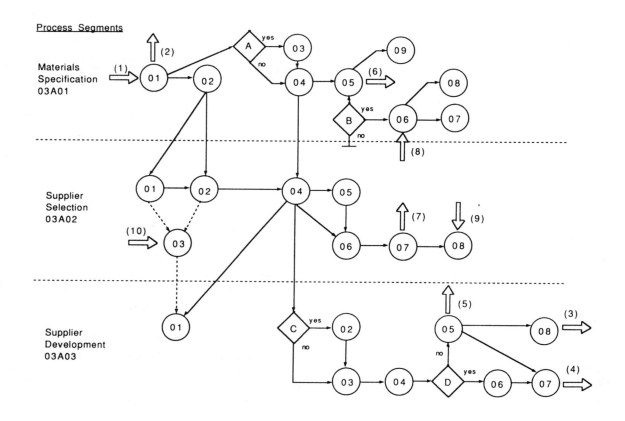

Descriptive Material

Key

08   Activity

→   Activity interdependency

◇   Process flow decision

⇨   Process input/output

------   Activity association

Process Input/Output Descriptions
(1) Input: new/modified part design
(2) Output: material handling/tooling specification requirements
(3) Output: quality planning objectives
(4) Output: quality status metrics
(5) Output: receiving inspection requirements
(6) Output: data for MRP execution
(7) Output: standard cost information
(8) Input: Kanban schedule adjustment and execution problems
(9) Input: production schedule forecast
(10) Input: resolve schedule problems with suppliers

Process Decisions
C–Is a new supplier selected?
D–Is supplier certified for part family?
A–Are existing parts to be discontinued?
B–Will the part be replenished by Kanban?

processes. These process segments and subprocesses are not predefined by the organization. The cost system designer must use the interview process to gain insight into the nature of the activity linkages. The network hierarchy is then validated through additional interviews and adjustments until a consensus is determined. As a result, an activity network is a necessary tool for developing the process-based activity architecture espoused in this article.

An example of an activity network is provided in Exhibit 12. The exhibit illustrates the flow of activities within three process segments that make up the materials procurement subprocess. Each circle represents a separate activity within the segment (the activities are listed in Exhibit 13). In this example, the process segments are linked to form the subprocess, which is a major flow distinction (or channel) that exists within the total material acquisition business process. The result of this analysis is an activity network up to the subprocess level. The network maps interdependencies between activities both within and between process segments.

The schema uses circles to portray activities, which are connected by linkages reflecting both one- and two-way dependencies or associations. Exhibit 12 shows all the activities within a subprocess. Segment boundaries are established to segregate the activities by segment designations, and logic junctions are employed to accommodate branching in the process flow. The large arrows represent routine inputs or outputs that cross subprocess boundaries.

The advantage of activity networks over typical aggregated activity analyses is that they focus management's attention toward a process orientation. This perspective requires managers to address the following process flow considerations:

- First, managers must ensure the horizontal integration of activities across functional domains. The network provides a basis for resourcing processes through the budgetary process.
- Second, the networks allow the manager to improve the orderly processing of routine inputs within process segments. Specifically, the network provides a basis for eval-

Exhibit 13. *Process Hierarchy for the Materials Acquisition Process (03)*

Process: Materials Acquisition (03)

Subprocesses:
- 03A   Materials procurement
- 03B   Materials requirement planning
- 03C   Material ordering
- 03D   Material transportation
- 03E   Material receiving, inspection, storage, and handling

Materials Procurement (03A)

Process: Segments and Activities

03A01—Material Specification
- 01   Evaluate part specification
- 02   Purchase part-price estimating
- 03   Develop part obsolescence report
- 04   Establish ECO effective date
- 05   Establish/maintain bill of materials
- 06   Establish/update *kanban* plan
- 07   Establish/update *kanban* staging locations
- 08   Generate *kanban* cards
- 09   Establish/maintain wiring diagrams

03A02—Supplier Selection
- 01   New supplier investigation
- 02   Submit/review request for quotes
- 03   Contact existing/potential suppliers
- 04   Supplier selection
- 05   Establish/maintain supplier information files
- 06   Contract and pricing negotiation
- 07   Establish/update purchase price standard cost file
- 08   Establish/maintain blanket purchase orders

03A03—Supplier Development
- 01   Capability study
- 02   Supplier survey
- 03   Perform initial sample part inspection
- 04   Verify supplier process capability
- 05   Prepare receiving inspection plan
- 06   Award supplier certification
- 07   Develop quality status reports
- 08   Develop supplier quality improvement plans

uating activity sequence, redundancy, and waste.
- Third, the activity network allows the manager to assess the resource consequences of various decision scenarios. For example, one of the decisions in the supplier development process segment in Exhibit 12 is a branch (C) to inquire whether a new supplier is selected.

All these considerations have repercussions on activities and, thus, on resources. The nature of the cost dynamics of various decisions becomes more resolute as the manager uses the activity network to simulate alternative decision paths.

Cost driver activity patterns

When building activity networks, an important distinction must be made between two different types of routine activity patterns that emerge within organizational structures. The first type is the customary activity patterns associated with normal operating conditions, which are triggered by steady-state inputs on a repetitive basis. The second type of activity pattern is routine events that do not represent steady-state operating conditions. These cost drivers represent contingencies to respond to circumstances that occur by exception, such as machine breakdowns, raw material stock-outs, engineering change orders, or customer returns. Any contingency that reflects a perturbation in the steady-state nature of a process is defined as a negative cost driver. Cost driver events trigger activity patterns. Frequently, these activity patterns cut across the steady-state processes of the organization. For example, the purchasing-related activity of "contract negotiations" is routinely performed during the product development cycle. However, this activity may also be required as the result of an unscheduled engineering change order that entails a modification of supplier part specifications. As a general rule, in situations where individual activities are shared by both types of activity patterns, the steady-state patterns are used to configure the process segments.

An example of an event-dependent activity pattern is shown in Exhibit 14. In this case, the cost driver event is triggered by the number of *kanban* (which is Japanese for "card") containers not equaling the number of *kanbans*. This event creates an expedited situation that flows off logic junction C within the 03E1 process segment (receiving, storage, and handling) at the top of Exhibit 14. The activities that are triggered by this event cut across the steady-state process segments, as shown. This activity network can be used to demonstrate the cost of these perturbing events. Moreover, a cost per event can be determined and used as a basis for modeling the spending reduction that can be achieved by reducing the incidence of this cost driver. The projected spending reduction could be deter-

mined (in much the same way as discussed previously) through rolling the activity reductions back up into the resource categories where the organization is staffed. These resource savings would be actual reductions in spending emanating from reduced or redeployed headcount (and other resources) that are presently necessary to support the cost driver event. In this way, the objectives of *kaizen* (a continuous improvement) and activity-based management become mutually self-supporting.

In summary, the key benefit of constructing event-dependent activity networks is the ability to identify the cost of performing exceptions, both in terms of their sustained cost over time and in terms of the cost of each occurrence. These costs are significant and inhibit continuous improvement, because they represent the cost of variation in the process.

Summary

This article provides a description of an ABC framework that can be used to support process analysis, product costing, and pro forma cost simulation. Exhibit 15 illustrates the framework. The cost flow down to the product is accomplished via allocation techniques that incorporate multiple product attributes. The architecture provides, additionally, a hierarchy of process information that can be used to budget and plan process performance. Pro forma assessment of the spending impact due to activity changes on resource categories requires a completely different analysis. Such analyses begin by developing the short-term cost behavior patterns for each resource category and specifying the engineering functional relationship between the activity and resource category. From this information, the economic consequences from various simulations can be determined.

A tension exists between advocates of accounting simplicity and advocates of cost management. The checkered history of cost accounting has caused many to abandon variance reporting and other traditional cost control techniques on the grounds that they are not useful metrics in promoting continuous improvement. Those in the simplicity camp argue for visual control and use of physical measures for evaluating performance and im-

Exhibit 14. *Example of a Cost Driver Activity Pattern* (*Delivery Quantity Does Not Equal Number of* Kanbans)

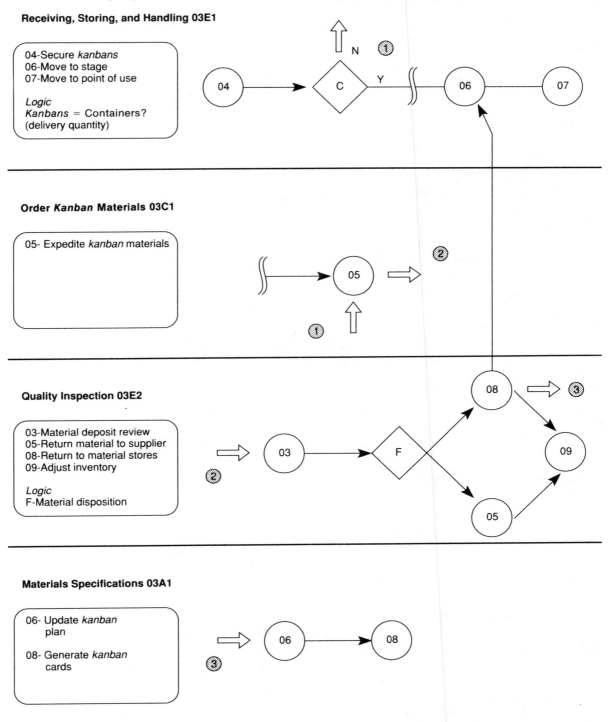

Receiving, Storing, and Handling 03E1

04-Secure *kanbans*
06-Move to stage
07-Move to point of use

Logic
Kanbans = Containers?
(delivery quantity)

Order *Kanban* Materials 03C1

05- Expedite *kanban* materials

Quality Inspection 03E2

03-Material deposit review
05-Return material to supplier
08-Return to material stores
09-Adjust inventory

Logic
F-Material disposition

Materials Specifications 03A1

06- Update *kanban* plan

08- Generate *kanban* cards

Exhibit 15. *Cost Allocation vs. Cost Estimation Schema*

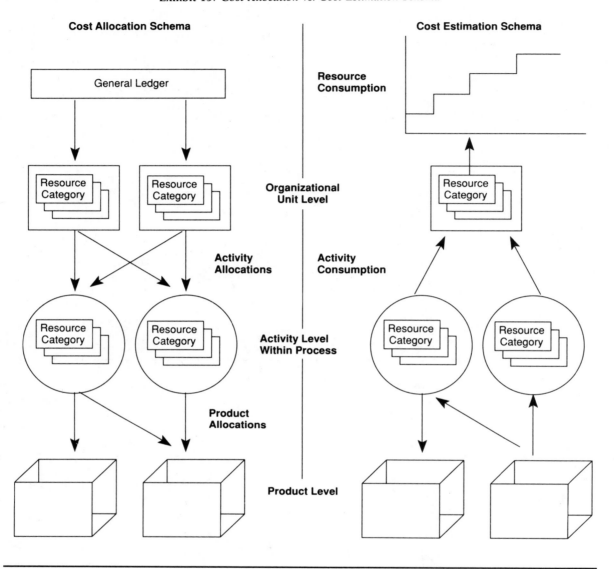

provement. We agree with respect to streamlining bill of material structures and widening transaction gates for simplified inventory valuation.

However, the abandonment of cost management is a different issue; we cannot afford to throw the baby out with the bathwater. Simplicity may have served well in environments in which the opportunities for waste reduction have been obvious, but it may not serve as well when the operating questions become much more subtle.

A review of cost management practices in

Japan and Europe would seem to indicate that the simplicity (zero accounting) option is not universally shared. Indeed, Japanese cost management practices indicate a rigorous approach designed to promote cost reduction and to identify hidden cost savings at the very lowest levels of the organization.

The framework offered in this article is not simple. Indeed, this framework is likely unworkable except in an advanced manufacturing environment. The degree of activity complexity in a traditional process flow or large batch environment is probably so tangled as to make our approach difficult to apply. Within cellular and other mature environments, however, ABC management tools are likely to be welcomed as opportunities for improvement become less obvious. ▲

Notes

1. For example, see Robin Cooper, "Cost Classification in Unit-Based and Activity-Based Manufacturing Cost Systems," *Journal of Cost Management* (Fall 1990): 4–14.
2. This is our reading of some of the concerns raised by G.J. Beaujon and V.R. Singhal in "Understanding the Activity Costs in an Activity-Based Cost System," *Journal of Cost Management* (Spring 1990): 51–72.
3. See Y. Monden and M. Sakurai, *Japanese Management Accounting: A World Class Approach to Profit Management,* (Cambridge, Massachusetts: Productivity Press, 1990).
4. R. Cooper and R.S. Kaplan, "Profit Priorities for Activity-Based Costing," *Harvard Business Review* (May–June 1991): 130–135.
5. Additional discussion of this topic is contained in James M. Reeve, "Cost Management in Continuous Process Environments," *Handbook of Cost Management* ed. Barry J. Brinker, Chap. C3 (New York: Warren, Gorham & Lamont, 1991).

Using Activity-Based Management Systems in Aerospace and Defense Companies

Lewis J. Soloway

This column synthesizes the experiences that aerospace and defense contractors and subcontractors have had with activity-based management (ABM) systems, which—despite roadblocks—can work for government contractors. The column considers ABM in the context of the Cost Management Systems (CMS) program of Computer Aided Manufacturing-International (CAM-I). CAM-I has led efforts to address the changes required in traditional cost accounting systems to support the growing use of advanced manufacturing technologies. Note that the Defense Contract Audit Agency (DCAA) has been an active observer of the CMS program and considers it an appropriate forum for government and industry to discuss changes to cost accounting systems.

The outlook for most aerospace and defense (A&D) contractors and subcontractors is not good. According to the Center for Strategic and International Studies, nearly 70 percent out of the almost 120,000 A&D firms operating in 1982 had left the industry or gone bankrupt by 1987.[1]

One result is that the surviving companies are employing a broad array of strategies to cope with today's defense contracting environment. A&D companies appear to be employing four basic strategies:

1. *Continue emphasis on defense business* (e.g., E-Systems, Loral, Northrop, General Dynamics, Logicon, MA-COM);
2. *Maintain current business mix* (e.g., Boeing, McDonnell Douglas, Martin Marietta, Raytheon, Rockwell, Gen Corp.);
3. *Actively diversify* (e.g., TRW, Hughes, Lockheed, Watkins-Johnson); and
4. *Divest defense businesses* (e.g., Ford, Honeywell, Goodyear, Eaton, Singer, Gould).

Competitive cost structure essential

These and other A&D contractors have learned that technical superiority is not enough: A competitive cost structure is essential, and a company's infrastructure must be compatible with market requirements.

Consider, for example, the experience of one A&D contractor that sought to leverage its military technology into the commercial market. Initially, the company was able to penetrate the market. To meet this new threat, commercial competitors quickly responded with lower prices and faster delivery. The A&D contractor also lowered prices, but its cost system indicated that marshalling the resources needed to compete was expensive—staying in the market at these lower prices was unprofitable.

The contractor's cost system assumed that all overhead costs would be increased incrementally by the fully loaded burden rate as the new resources were added. The cost system gave no good picture of what the true cost flows would be when resources were shifted to support the commercial market entry. The cost system also failed to identify processes that could be streamlined to keep costs down. As a result, the contractor eventually abandoned the business.

The poor outcome experienced by this contractor illustrates the need that A&D managers have for information that they can use to structure the organization and to determine its costs. Many—including the Defense Contract Audit Agency (DCAA)—believe that an activity-based management (ABM) system can provide this information.

Exhibit 1. *CAM-I Expanded ABC model*

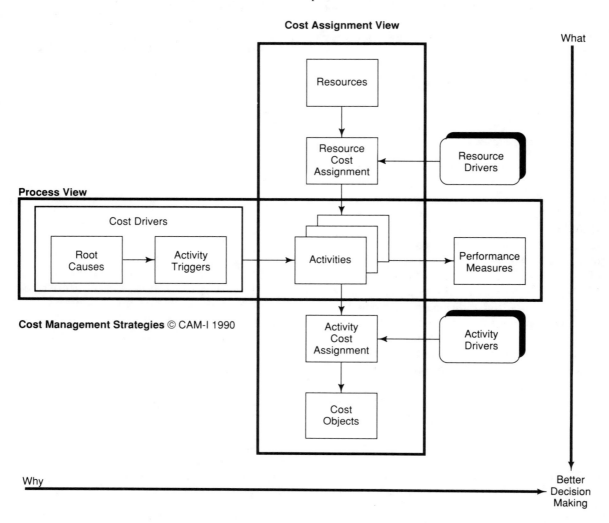

ABM concepts

The foundation of an ABM is that *resources* are consumed by *activities* and that *activities* are, in turn, consumed by *cost objects*.[2] See Exhibit 1.

Resource. A *resource* is an economic element that is applied or directed to the performance of activities.[3] Labor, materials, and departmental expenses, such as travel and office supplies, are examples of resources used in the performance of activities.

Activity. An *activity* can be thought of as work performed within an organization or as an aggregation of actions performed within an organization.[4] Examples include such broad-based activities as *purchasing, product design,* and *receiving inspection.* Activities, however, can be defined at a more detailed level. In relation to the above examples, more detailed activities can be considered, such as *correcting problems with accounts payable, product design—structural,* or *receiving—electrical test.* The level of detail of the activities (i.e., the number of activities included) depends on the complexity of the organization and the specifics of the ABM analysis being performed.

Cost object. A *cost object* is any customer, product, service, contract, project, or other work unit for which a separate measurement of cost is desired.[5] The choice of cost object, like the choice of activity, depends on the

Exhibit 2. *Product View Example—QA Organization*

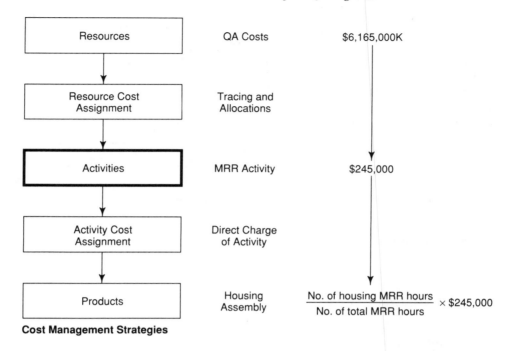

Cost Management Strategies

Resources	QA Costs	$6,165,000K
Resource Cost Assignment	Tracing and Allocations	
Activities	MRR Activity	$245,000
Activity Cost Assignment	Direct Charge of Activity	
Products	Housing Assembly	$\dfrac{\text{No. of housing MRR hours}}{\text{No. of total MRR hours}} \times \$245{,}000$

specific analysis being performed. If product profitability is paramount, then the cost object should be specific products or product lines. If customer profitability is the important issue, then the cost object should be the specific customers in question.

Cost assignment view. This chain of resources to activities to cost objects is called the *cost assignment view*. Cost assignment is the tracing (or allocation) of resources to activities or cost objects.[6]

Exhibit 2 illustrates the cost assignment view by showing resource costs being traced to products in a hypothetical quality assurance (QA) organization. The total QA resource costs of $6,165,000 include salaries, fringe benefits, office supplies, travel, and other overhead. These costs are consumed by a number of activities, one of which is the material reject review (MRR) activity, with a cost of $245,000.

The MRR activity consists of examining discrepant material, determining its cause, making a disposition, and filling out the paperwork. The cost of the activity can be traced to specific products, customers, or contracts. In this example, the MRR activity is traced to the product "housing assembly" based on the number of hours charged to the product relative to all products that are part of the MRR activity.

The process view. Exhibit 1 shows the activity-based costing (ABC) model developed by Computer Aided Manufacturing-International (CAM-I) as the vertical dimension, but it also shows another view as the horizontal dimension. This *process view* of the model illustrates how cost drivers trigger activities and how activities can be tracked through performance measures. A *cost driver* is any factor, decision, or event that effects a change in the cost of an activity. A cost driver can be the immediate initiator of the activity (i.e., an *activity trigger*) or it can be the earliest trigger in a chain of triggers, the *root cause*.

Multiple cost drivers can be associated with an activity. A *performance measure* is an indicator of the work performed and the results achieved in an activity, process, or organizational unit.[7] Performance measures may be financial or nonfinancial.

Exhibit 3. *Process View Example—QA Organization*

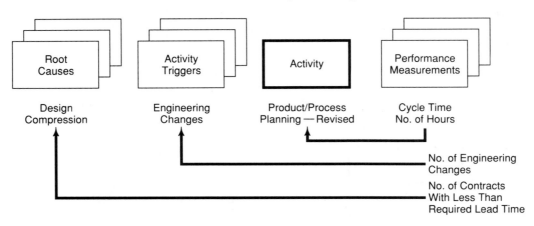

Cost Management Strategies

A *business process* is a series of activities that are linked to perform a specific objective.[8] An example of a business process is configuration management. The configuration management process begins at product development in engineering with the "as-designed" configuration, includes manufacturing planning and production with the "as-planned" and "as-built" configurations, and extends to customer support and field operations with "as-delivered" and "as-maintained" configurations. As this example shows, processes cross organizational boundaries.

The cross-functional aspects are especially important because many decisions in an organization affect the activities performed by people in other parts of the organization. Many impacts of a decision are unknown and are not intended by the decision maker. For example, an engineer who decides to make a design change to reduce product cost sets off a series of activities in the configuration management, materials management, procurement, and production planning processes, the cost of which may far exceed the expected design savings.

Exhibit 3 shows the power of the process view. The example used is the activity "product/process planning—revised," which is part of the configuration management business process. In this activity, manufacturing engineers revise the operations instructions used to produce specific products. The operations instructions change because of an engineering change (the activity trigger). The ultimate reason (root cause) why this occurred was because changes were required in a design after a salesman accepted an order in less than normal lead time (design compression). To meet the promised delivery date, the engineer had to make the changes that would allow manufacturing to purchase materials, fabricate the parts, and assemble the product in the reduced time available (other activities affected by the root cause).

Multidimensional model

The cost assignment and process views together form the multidimensional model of a business shown in Exhibit 4. It is a model with flexible boundaries, because it can include organizational functions, activities or processes, and cost objects (including contracts). Exhibit 4 also compares the single cost dimension of a traditional cost system with the combined process and product dimensions of an ABM system.

Although a traditional cost system presents data on the resources expended, it does not tell management why or how the resources were expended. An ABM system, by contrast, answers the questions by tracing the resource costs to activities, then reporting relevant information on an activity basis. The activi-

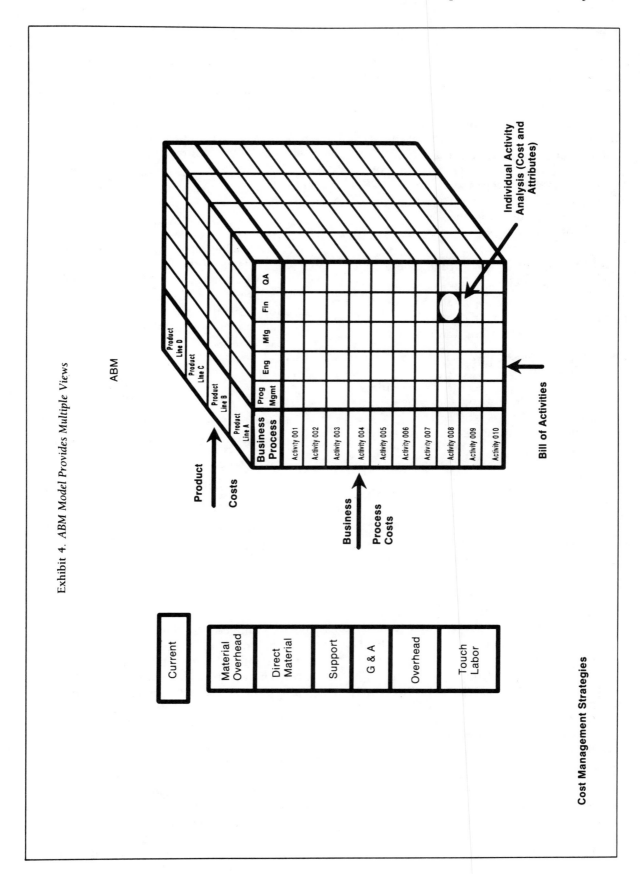

Exhibit 4. *ABM Model Provides Multiple Views*

ties can also be directly related to cost objects. Each activity is analyzed to determine how it can be assigned to the cost object in question, such as a product or contract. Contractors find the multidimensional capability of an ABM beneficial. It gives them the means to support cross-functional, world-class manufacturing initiatives such as total quality management (TQM), continuous improvement, and concurrent engineering. Managers can address their contractual and cross-functional issues within a cost framework that links financial information with operational information.

Multidimensional view promotes effective cost management

The multidimensional view promotes effective cost management by analyzing several important questions, including the following:

- What activities do we perform, and what do they cost?
- What drives the need for the activities?
- Are the activities value-added or redundant?
- What business processes are the activities a part of?
- How do product costs change under an ABM system?
- What product lines or contracts do the activities support?
- What other cost objects do the activities affect?
- How can the activities be improved or eliminated?

The objective of analyzing these questions is to provide a framework (i.e., a multidimensional model of the business) that can focus management on taking effective action. It provides an activity infrastructure that serves as the basis for a variety of analyses, depending on the decisions that need to be made. These analyses can identify all the activities associated with each decision, thus providing an understanding of the impacts of different decisions. Decisions that can be addressed have to do with the following:

- Production line rationalization;
- New performance measures;
- Plant restructuring;
- Cost reduction;
- Quality improvements;

- Customer service focus;
- Pricing and estimating strategies;
- Impact of complexity;
- Operations initiatives;
- New capital investment;
- Facility rationalization; and
- TQM.

Issues for A&D contractors

The A&D working group of CAM-I's Cost Management Systems (CMS) program has identified areas of special concern associated with the use of ABM systems.

Defective pricing and estimating. The first concern relates to the fact that current cost systems are oriented toward regulatory reporting rather than the need that managers have for cost information for decision making. The federal government's Cost Accounting Standards (CAS) require contractors to

---

Cost Accounting Standards (CAS) require contractors to use only one cost system for pricing and costing. The government argues that if a contractor uses only one system, the price that the government pays to the contractor will relate directly to the costs incurred.

---

use only one cost system for pricing and costing. The government argues that if a contractor uses only one system, the price that the government pays to the contractor will relate directly to the costs incurred. Moreover, costs will be treated the same way each time they occur (that is, consistency will result).

If a stand-alone ABM system is used in addition to a contractor's existing cost system, contractors fear that they will be charged with defective pricing and estimating. If, for instance, a contractor's existing cost system used a single burden rate for multiple sites, while the ABM system used different rates for different sites, the contractor would be in violation of the "consistency" requirements. Likewise, if a make-versus-buy decision is based on an ABM system that generated costs different from those generated by an existing cost system—i.e., the system according to which contract pricing was developed—the contractor would be in violation of the "consistency" requirement.

Cost impact studies. The second area of concern is the risk associated with submitting a cost impact study (CIS) for government approval of a contractor's use of an ABM system to replace the current cost system.[9] Contractors feel at risk of government charges because an ABM system will most likely change how overhead costs are allocated to products and contracts.

As a result of the changes, some contracts will appear to be overcosted while others will be undercosted. If the contractor performs only government work, the risk is usually mitigated (in theory, at least), because the CIS negotiation process with the DCAA is designed to be "cost-neutral" over all the contracts affected. (In actuality, A&D contractors privately say that DCAA negotiators do not maintain a "cost-neutral" stand.)

The risk goes up considerably if the contractor uses the same cost system for both government and commercial business. If the company's commercial business has been overcosted under the traditional cost system, the higher costs that might be allocated to government contracts under the ABM system approach will, generally, not be recoverable. The concept of cost-neutrality applies only to the government portion of the business.

To improve communication with the DCAA and heighten auditor understanding of what a contractor is trying to accomplish, the DCAA recommends that contractors that plan to adopt an ABM system should include the administrative contracting officer (ACO) and the DCAA auditors as part of the ABM project and the CIS from the beginning. Contractors that have already initiated pilot ABM system projects concur with this recommendation.

Disclosure. The third area of concern is that of *disclosure*. If an ABM system is used for management decision making and for making cross-functional improvements, but not for product or contract costing (i.e., the ABM system is used only to obtain the Process View of costing shown in Exhibit 1), the contractor might feel open to charges of noncompliance with standards and regulations. The fear is that the DCAA might argue that the process costs might also be used somehow to determine contract costs. The DCAA would then want to conduct another audit to determine if the contractor purposely kept cost information from the government, then seek redress by reducing payments to the contractor.

If a stand-alone ABM system is used in addition to a contractor's existing cost system, contractors fear that they will be charged with defective pricing and estimating.

Regulations. The last area of concern identified by the CAM-I CMS A&D working group is the lack of consistency within and between the many *regulations and mandated government programs.* Ultimately, this is the basis for the three preceding concerns. Management routinely points to the following regulations and programs as examples:

- Cost Accounting Standards (CAS), Defense Acquisition Regulations (DAR), and Federal Acquisition Regulations (FAR);
- Cost/schedule control system criteria (C/SCSC);
- Mil-Std-1567A (work measurement);
- Mil-Std-9858A (cost of quality); and
- Total quality management (TQM).

Each of these programs has its own requirements to meet and puts additional stress on the business. Some of them dictate how to account for costs (e.g., the CAS and the Military Standards) and the others mandate improvement of contractor performance (e.g., TQM).

Each regulation and program requires a separate audit by government agencies. To jaded industry veterans, the use of an ABM system could be viewed as just another opportunity for an audit.

Auditing regulatory compliance

The process of auditing regulatory compliance is always fraught with frustrations. Interpretation of the regulations can be inconsistent within the DCAA itself and also among the various government agencies. Conflicts between the regulations also cause problems. For example, elements of Mil-Std-1567A can be counterproductive to TQM continuous improvement.

These regulatory conflicts should not deter the initiation of ABM systems projects. ABM systems hold the best hope for alleviating some of the concerns of management, because they use both financial and operational information in an integrated manner. The regulations and mandated programs do not use integrated systems.

DCAA. It should be noted that the DCAA has been one of the biggest promoters of ABM. The DCAA recognizes that ABM will better address the change in the flow of costs to contracts caused by technological advancements on the factory floor. For instance, the DCAA recognizes that in an automated environment, machine hours often provide a more appropriate way of tracing overhead costs to a work order than do direct labor hours. In general, therefore, the DCAA should be receptive to such cost accounting change proposals.

The Accounting Policy Division of the DCAA conducted a research study in 1989[10] with the following three objectives in mind:

1. To determine if U.S. government defense contractors are implementing technological advances;
2. To learn if contractors' accounting systems are keeping pace with technological changes; and
3. If not, to determine whether the failure of accounting systems to keep pace with technological changes had an adverse impact on the government.

Several important conclusions were reached:

- Contractors have accomplished substantial technological advancements on the factory floor.

- Technological changes can change the flow of costs, which raises questions of potential problems with allocations and cost inequities.
- Current audit guidance and tools provide a good mechanism for identifying change and do not need to be modified.
- Auditor awareness of the issues needs to be heightened to help auditors understand the technological changes that are occurring on the factory floor and the implications for cost accounting systems.

Two overall conclusions can be drawn from this study. First, the DCAA recognizes that cost accounting systems have not kept up with technological changes, and the DCAA expects contractors to make changes. Second, the DCAA recognizes the need for the cost accounting systems of contractors to move toward the broader concept of ABM systems, and the DCAA is willing to be a part of this change.

The DCAA has spent much time and money understanding ABM by observing the proceedings at CAM-I CMS meetings, surveying contractors, participating in contractors' pilot ABM projects, and training auditors in preparation for implementation of ABM systems.

Unfortunately, the very fact that the DCAA is a promoter of ABM is cause for suspicion on the part of some managers. Contractors can fall into the trap of thinking that ABM could become another government-mandated program (like C/SCSC) that is designed to "help the company manage its contracts." There have been instances where contractors have not initiated ABM systems despite (or, perhaps, because of) their ACO's enthusiastic support of the projects.

A&D industry pilot project results

The list of A&D companies that have explored ABM is small relative to the number of commercial companies that have experimented with ABM. A&D companies in the CAM-I CMS program that have at least explored, if not initiated, pilot ABM system projects include Boeing, General Dynamics, Harris, Hughes, McDonnell-Douglas, Northrop, and Westinghouse.

Westinghouse Electronics. Westinghouse Electronics conducted a well-publicized study under the Department of Defense's Industrial Modernization Incentive Program (IMIP) to develop an advanced cost management system (ACMS) that incorporated many CAM-I concepts. This project also examined differences between the commercial and A&D approaches to cost management, examined barriers within the A&D industry, and postulated what the cost system of the future might look like.

The ACMS project found that current A&D cost systems focus on the *control of costs*. This contrasts with the commercial emphasis on the *reduction of costs*. The Westinghouse researchers found this to be a key philosophical difference between cost accounting and cost management. The barriers to change within the industry were similar to those mentioned previously.

The researchers viewed it, though somewhat philosophically, as needing a change in the cost management mind-set if the industry is

---

The cost system gave no good picture of what the true cost flows would be when resources were shifted to support the commercial market entry.

---

to achieve its objectives and benefit from the advantages of a new cost management system. They pointed to three primary items:

1. Direct labor can no longer be the sole basis for costing products;
2. The focus must be on reducing or containing *significant* costs (as opposed to only *direct* costs);
3. The system must help manage product cost reduction cost-effectively, not just report costs against budget.

The system that Westinghouse Electronics designed was structured to recognize that the cost information needed depends on the questions being asked. The researchers explicitly recognized the importance of time when they broke down these questions into the following four categories:

1. *Long-term decisions*
   - Strategic planning
   - Product life cycle planning
   - Capital expenditure planning
   - Trend reporting (cost/revenue, product, productivity)
2. *Cost containment*
   - Planned versus actual results
   - Function/activity costs
   - Product cost reduction analysis
   - Utilization/efficiency
   - Make-versus-buy analysis
3. *Product costing and pricing*
   - Material costs
   - Labor/machine conversion costs
   - Indirect conversion costs
   - Product cost tracking
   - Escalation/adjustments
4. *Inventory valuation and other concerns*
   - Material distribution
   - Labor/support cost distributions
   - Cost of production/sales
   - Cost recovery
   - Progress billing

An examination of these categories and their elements shows that the emphasis that drove the design was the reporting of information to facilitate decision making.

Westinghouse Electronics ultimately developed a software simulation model to provide a "proof of concept" for the ACMS design. Although the ACMS design was not implemented at Westinghouse because of its breadth of scope and generalized form, specific elements of the system have been implemented by both Westinghouse and others.

Other pilot projects

Of the other ABM pilot projects initiated by contractors, none have yet led to any significant modifications of a contractor's traditional cost accounting system. The one that has progressed the farthest was the ABM project at Hughes Ground Systems Group (GSG).

Hughes Ground Systems Group. The Hughes pilot was conducted in the GSG's Etched Circuitry Department, which fabricates printed wiring boards (PWBs). As a result of the pilot, a number of accounting system changes were proposed to the DCAA, including the following:

- Replacement of one overhead rate with multiple rates. (In CAM-I CMS terms, this is called *tracing,* which uses observable measures of consumption to assign resource costs to activities and then to cost objects);[11]
- Dissolution of direct charging pools;
- Charging of direct labor to an activity center rather than to a work order;
- Bidding cost by activity center buildups (instead of having a cost structure based on direct labor and material, with overhead rates allocated based on the labor and material costs, the ABM cost structure would be based on rates developed for each activity center and applied according to the usage by product of each activity center);
- Establishment of acceptable methods for updating cost assignment factors (to be in compliance with CAS 406);
- Temporary incurrence of cost on a basis different from bid, which violates CAS 401 (at point of transition from the old cost accounting system to the ABM system, the contracts in progress that were awarded based on bids submitted under the old system will be in violation of CAS 401; the DCAA will work with the GSG to solve problems associated with this situation).

The DCAA has been a participant in developing these recommended changes, and most of the changes have been accepted.

Hughes GSG cites good relations with local DCAA employees as a key to success. The GSG has actively informed, educated, and involved DCAA auditors throughout the life of the project. The DCAA auditors have been made part of the team and have developed a clear understanding along with the GSG team of where the project is proceeding. As a result, the local DCAA auditors have not impeded the testing; instead, they have worked alongside the GSG. The DCAA members of the team have made recommendations to the group that have been incorporated, such as reducing the number of activity pools in the etched area. In the process, they have determined where the test points of the system need to be for auditing purposes.

The GSG is currently running the ABM system with the proposed accounting changes in parallel with the traditional cost accounting system. Managers have benefited from the information provided by the ABM system. Just having the process view of operations leads to improvement (e.g., in material handling and cost of quality). Understanding the cost assignment view has provided better information for make-versus-buy decisions.

The GSG has initiated several more pilot projects. Most focus on the process view approach for improvement purposes. A few others are oriented to the cost assignment (or ABC) view to help develop a strategy for incorporating the ABM system changes into the cost accounting system.

One change that has been incorporated into the accounting system is the creation of several individual activity pools where a single overhead charge was formerly used. The results have been encouraging, though management does not understand that this is an application of ABM principles. The individual pools have provided visibility for the divisional executives to focus on reducing the costs charged to their programs. The visibility of the individual pools has caused dialogue between the divisional executives and the group managers responsible for the pools. As a result, the pool costs are going down. This behavior never happened before the accounting change, even though the divisional executives had been charged for the costs in the past. All that has changed is the new visibility; the divisional executives have a new understanding that they can control the costs associated with these corporate allocations, which is just the kind of behavior that ABM promotes!

Boeing Aerospace. Another ABM system project was conducted at Boeing Aerospace in the printed circuit board (PCB) operations facility. The operating environment is different from that at Hughes GSG because, at Boeing's facility, PCBs are fabricated for both military and commercial purposes.

The Boeing project generated information on product costing (approximately 1,200 products) and also earned more management attention from the cross-functional, process view. The major benefits apparently came from an understanding of the cost of quality (prevention, appraisal, and failure costs). The project had quick results (fourteen weeks).

The results have encouraged management to expand the project. Although product costing analyses will continue, the emphasis will continue to be on the process view to identify improvement opportunities.

ABM projects at other contractors have shown similar results. The major goal ahead is to incorporate the elements of ABM into the current cost accounting systems.

Conclusion

ABM systems provide better insight into operations process improvements, management decision making, and product and contract costing, as each of the pilot projects has proven. Over the long term, contractors that implement ABM systems will improve their competitive positions relative to others in the industry.

To accelerate the implementation process and to get more contractors and subcontractors involved, however, cultural barriers of dealing with the DCAA need to be overcome. Strategies must be developed for successfully managing change and alleviating risk.

One approach that may lead contractors to successful ABM system implementations starts by first addressing the process view. Contractors can use the activity analysis to focus on process improvements, thus generating immediate cost reductions. As this occurs, management incentives should be changed to encourage the realignment of short-term management thinking to the long-term success of the company.

After gaining experience with the process view and activity analysis, a contractor can then study the effects of the cost assignment view. Emphasis should be placed on understanding the impact on product and contract costing to alleviate the risks and fears. The local DCAA auditors should be brought into the project, educated, and made part of the team. Contractors should progressively increase the number of overhead rates traced and assigned to products and contracts.

This step-by-step approach avoids potential conflicts with the DCAA at the initiation of an ABM project by using activity analysis for process improvement. It avoids the product-related cost issues that occur with changes to the contractor's cost system. This allows time to work through the cultural barriers and manage change. Even if the cultural barriers prove too great to change the cost system, activity analysis can continue to be used and provide benefit for process improvements. ▲

Notes
1. Ralph Verbadian, *The Los Angeles Times*, 1990.
2. Norm Raffish & Peter B.B. Turney, eds., *The CAM-I Glossary of Activity-Based Management* (Arlington, Tex.: CAM-I 1991), app. B.
3. *Id.* at 10.
4. *Id.* at 1.
5. *Id.* at 5.
6. *Id.* at 6.
7. *Id.* at 9.
8. *Id.*
9. A CIS is required for any change to the current cost accounting system that would affect product cost calculations.
10. The DCAA issued two documents—a study report on cost accounting for technological modernization (90-PAD-10, dated Jan. 17, 1990), and a case study addressing the effect of technological change on a contractor's accounting system (90-PAD-29, dated Feb. 2, 1990).
11. Raffish & Turney, *The CAM-I Glossary*, at 12.

Activity-Based Management for Service, Not-for-Profit, and Governmental Organizations

John Antos

The original focus of activity-based costing (ABC) was the manufacturing sector of our economy, but the broader concept of activity-based management (or ABM) can help service organizations of all kinds—service companies, not-for-profit institutions, and governmental entities. This article discusses applications of ABM to medical malpractice insurance and to oil production in Alaska. It shows how the federal government has applied ABM to reimbursements to states for the processing of food stamp claims and social security disability claims. Financial institutions can use ABM to assign overhead costs to their various departments. The accounts receivable department of a hospital has used ABM to derive a bill of activities for patient services. A company that launders uniforms is applying ABM to its laundering and delivery operations. Finally, a large voluntary health and welfare organization has created a bill of activities for fund-raising activities to determine which of the activities are profitable.

Research about activity-based costing (ABC) was originally directed toward the manufacturing sector of our economy, but the wider concept of activity-based management (ABM) applies equally well to service, not-for-profit, and governmental organizations.

The service sector is less homogeneous than the manufacturing sector, which may explain why service organizations have been slow to adopt ABM. Manufacturing companies tend to perform many of the same types of activities in similar ways, but there is little similarity between the activities of an insurance firm, a hospital, a bank, a retail store, a not-for-profit organization, and a governmental department.

The aim of this article is to show service organizations how ABM can work for them. Since all organizations have activities, the challenge is to apply the concepts of ABM to the vast array of service organizations that exist. Although the organizational size and scope of operations differs in the examples discussed in this article, each organization has used ABM to help understand and improve its operations.

ABM applied to medical malpractice insurance

In the 1970s, a serious medical malpractice insurance crisis occurred; medical malpractice awards were running much higher than ever before. Malpractice insurers had not anticipated such large awards when they had set the premiums charged for medical malpractice insurance. Ultimately, only one insurance company continued to write certain types of hospital malpractice insurance.

As a service to members, the American Medical Association (AMA) and the American Hospital Association (AHA) hired Marsh & McLennan, a large insurance broker, to review the problem. At that time, hospital malpractice insurance was priced based on patient days. That is, a malpractice insurance rate per patient day was set for each area of the United States. An estimated premium was set by multiplying the rate per patient day times the estimated patient days. After the policy period was over, the exact patient days were known, at which time adjustments could be made to the total premium.

ABM was used to look at the cost of this insurance service in another way. The AHA was asked to collect information from a sample of hospitals—small, large, and teaching hospitals. In particular, information was requested about the *activities* that the hospitals engaged in (though the term "activities" was not used in this way at that time). Specifically, the information of interest concerned activities that might affect the risk of a malpractice claim.

Hospitals were thus asked for the number of normal vs. Caesarean deliveries, liver transplants, neural surgeries, spinal taps, cardiology-related surgeries, orthopedic surgeries, eye surgeries, and so forth. The hospitals were also asked about emergency room activities, because emergency rooms are high-pressure areas that deal with everything from the common cold to gunshot wounds and emergency deliveries (which can be high malpractice risks).

Different risks posed by different types of activities in different settings. One assumption of the study was that teaching hospitals would encounter more difficult cases than other hospitals, and it followed that more difficult cases posed greater risk of malpractice claims. Another consideration was whether the number of times an activity is performed could affect the risk connected with that activity. For example, if a rural doctor performs a spinal tap only four times a year, his lack of experience could cause greater risk to his patients than would occur in the case of a doctor who performed spinal taps on a daily basis. It was also assumed that medical activities in big cities posed greater malpractice risk than activities performed in rural areas, because people from big cities were assumed to be more likely to sue for malpractice.

This information about the various activities and how often they were performed made it possible to develop a crude computerized system for rating hospitals in terms of malpractice risk based on the type of activities they performed (e.g., type of surgeries and other hospital ailments). As can be imagined, the limited information made it difficult to determine malpractice insurance rates. Nonetheless, this activity rating approach seemed preferable to rating malpractice insurance based on patient days.

A malpractice insurance cost per medical procedure (activity) was calculated. For example,

a system was developed that would charge a certain amount for heart surgeries and another amount for deliveries. No attempt was made to differentiate between knee, hip, or shoulder surgeries, between single vs. multiple deliveries, or between fixed vs. variable costs for each activity. The point was simply to get started with a system that (crude though it may have been) would prove superior to rating risk based on patient days.

Note that the ABM approach to rating medical malpractice can be compared to a manufacturing company that uses direct labor or machine hours to allocate overhead, for patient days might well be considered the hospital malpractice insurance equivalent of direct labor. Although the ABM system was not particularly sophisticated, the AHA considered the initial results it produced more accurate than the old rating system based on patient days. This points out the importance in a service organization of *getting started* with ABM and not worrying too much about total accuracy from the start: Accuracy will improve with time.

Overcharges and undercharges for malpractice insurance. The initial results indicated that some hospitals were being charged too much for malpractice insurance while others were being charged too little. Even though the initial system was not very sophisticated, the AHA concluded that a malpractice insurance system based on activities was more representative of risk than a system that used patient days.

A similar approach was developed for the AMA to rate risk of malpractice for different classes of doctors and surgeons. For example, the AMA assumed that the highest-risk surgeons were obstetricians, neurologists, and cardiologists. In rating surgeons, it was important to determine not only the *number* of surgeries performed, but also the *type* of surgeries performed and state in which the surgeries were performed. Physicians in relatively urban states like California and Florida were charged more than physicians in relatively rural states like North Dakota and Washington—a procedure that followed from the large malpractice awards in states with large urban populations.

The work done on malpractice insurance for the AHA and AMA fits squarely into the ABM model, because activities relating to malpractice insurance were identified. The volume of the activity measure (e.g., the number of surgeries) was determined to calculate an activity cost per unit of activity measure. The unit activity cost was multiplied by each hospital's volume for that activity to derive a total cost per activity (e.g., per type of procedure). The various activity costs were then added to derive a total product cost.

In this case, the total product cost was the total cost of malpractice insurance for a particular hospital. Thus, the ABM model explains well what was accomplished. ABM also helped improve the rating system based on feedback from the AHA.

ABM in oil exploration and production

ABM was also used in 1991 at an oil exploration and production company on the North Slope of Alaska. When a well is dug, several types of activities are required to study a well and improve operations. One activity, called "E-line," involves sending equipment down a wire to determine the condition of well pipe and of the oil-producing formation. Another activity involves "perforating" or "shooting" the pipe. ("Shooting" the pipe is similar to putting a shotgun down a well and discharging the gun.) A third activity occurs when an oil-producing formation becomes clogged with sediment that slows the flow of oil into the pipe. When this occurs, the production company or an oil service company has to "fracture" the well, which means pumping a special mixture down the pipe and pushing it into the area where the oil is currently flowing. This allows the oil to flow faster and easier.

If a production company uses an oil field service company to perform these activities, the production company can budget by the expected number of the various types of oil well services (i.e., activities) required. The services required in the beginning phases of production may differ from the services needed toward the end of production. Based on the game plan for producing the well, the history of the field, and the available budget, the company can budget the number of each type of oil field activity required (e.g., E-lines, perforations, and frac jobs). Although the cost of each type of activity varies depending

on the depth, formation, size, and nature of the oil formation, an average cost per activity can be developed for a specific field. The number of times each activity is performed is multiplied by an average cost per activity to derive a total cost for that type of oil field activity. Taken together, these activities make a bill of activities for oil field production.

Bills of activities. Much as a manufacturing company develops a bill of activities for a product, an oil production company can build a bill of activities for a particular oil field. A bill of activities for the North Slope of Alaska has higher costs per unit of activity for most activities than an oil field in the lower 48 states because of the cold, snow, and higher wage rates in Alaska, though many of the activities would be the same regardless of the location.

This oil company was already budgeting by activities for its oil field services and was comparing actual activity levels and activity unit costs to budgeted amounts.

Applying ABM to oil field water treatment facilities. Another example of applying ABM in a producing oil field is for water treatment facilities. A water treatment facility treats water for drinking, though another important reason for having a water treatment facility in an oil field is to treat water that is injected into an oil formation. Untreated water has elements that can affect both the oil formation and the pipes through which the oil flows. In Alaska, moreover, since the water treatment facility was so far from base camp, the workers actually ate and slept in the water treatment facility. Major activities performed at an Alaskan water treatment facility might therefore include the following:

- Desalinization of water;
- Deoxygenation of water;
- Chlorination of water;
- Catering food for workers; and
- Providing living quarters for workers.

It might be argued that these are really groups of activities. For example, some would say that the activity of providing living quarters is really a group of activities including:

- Cleaning of rooms;
- Maintenance of rooms; and
- Washing of laundry.

At this particular oil company, however, it was felt that the activity should be called "providing living quarters." If needed, the activity could later be disaggregated into more activity groups as management deemed appropriate.

The following activity measures were chosen for the activities:

Activity	Activity Measure
Desalt water	Gallons of salt water processed
Deoxygenate water	Barrels processed
Chlorinate water	Barrels processed
Provide living quarters	Occupants
Cater food	Persons fed

This approach gave the group a new way to look at the operations. Previously they had viewed their budget and operating performance in the traditional way by considering salaries, supplies, fringe benefits, and occupancy costs. By using activities, however, their financial statements became easier to understand and more useful.

Better insight for budgeting. ABM provided management better insight for budgeting and controlling costs. As the seasons changed, so did the processing requirements. For example, construction occurred in the summer, which meant that less water was treated then. If a field required more treated water, people could see the cost per gallon to treat the water (i.e., rather than simply total supplies vs. budgeted supplies). If the incoming water quality changed (as it did) or if the desired outgoing quality changed, the cost per gallon processed could be changed and the rest of the budget (or financial statements based on activities) left alone.

The company identified the resource drivers that cause cost to increase or decrease. For chlorination, for example, cost drivers included:

- Cost of materials;
- Bacteria levels;
- EPA requirements;
- Weather;
- Age of equipment;
- Preventive and unscheduled maintenance;
- Training of employees;

- Fish going into intake tanks; and
- Water input and output quality.

Itemizing these resource drivers gave the company insight into what drives the use of more or less resources. The company could thus focus on ways to eliminate or reduce the cost of the activities. For example, to eliminate some costs, the company could use screens to prevent fish from being introduced into intake tanks; to reduce other costs, it could increase preventive maintenance to decrease unscheduled breakdowns.

As an oil field matures (i.e., as the production volume *decreases*), the amount of water treated *increases* because more water is needed to replace the oil that has been pumped out of the ground. Therefore, to budget water treatment based on production volume would not make any sense. Budgeting based on activities helps managers of the water treatment facilities understand the operation better and find ways to reduce costs.

Non-value-added activities. In defining non-value-added activities, the oil production company listed the following:

- Cleaning dumpings of halon fire extinguishers that occur because of false alarms;
- Drilling a hole incorrectly (thus necessitating additional oil field services);
- Engaging in litigation because of spills and violations;
- Reworking wells because the field is being produced poorly;
- Handling accidents; and
- Failing to build housing or production facilities correctly.

Armed with this list of non-value-added activities, the company could create both cross-functional and intradepartmental teams to find creative ways to improve operations.

It can thus be seen how the principles of ABM apply to an oil production company. ABM has as much usefulness and applicability to a producing oil field as to manufacturing, though ABM must be applied in a slightly different way.

Use of ABM by the federal government

The federal government has applied ABM to certain reimbursements made to the states. Traditionally, for example, a state has been reimbursed for processing entitlement claims for food stamps and social security disability. Reimbursements were based on some form of costs incurred for time and material (e.g., for staff wages, supplies, and costs for travel).

To improve productivity, the federal government has calculated an activity cost—a cost per claim processed. This cost is computed for the various states to compare performance from state to state. One budgeting manager in a state department of human services has raised the question whether the federal government might not profitably shift processing to those states that have a lower cost for the activity of processing claims. The states might well be better off if only the more effective states processed claims for food stamps and social security disability. Doing this would undoubtedly be a political hot potato, so states might approach the problem as the city of Dallas did with a similar problem. The city of Dallas, which was considering privatizing garbage collection, put its garbage collection activities up for bid but allowed the city's existing garbage collection work force to make a bid for the contract. Ultimately, the city's existing employees won the contract, but only after they had increased their productivity in collecting garbage by almost 25 percent.

Federal government turns away from time and material basis of reimbursement. The federal government decided to change from the traditional approach (i.e., reimbursing for the processing of food stamp claims based on time and materials) because of the differing productivity rates between the states.

In the future, the federal government will reimburse states for food stamp programs on the basis of so much per claim processed. Thus, if a state agency is inefficient and spends more than the federal government's reimbursement rate, that will end up paying more of the program's administrative costs. As a result, states will be forced to analyze waste and inefficiency through activity analyses (including analyses of non-value-added activities).

Benchmarking with other states. The states will need to benchmark themselves against other states. They will have to share informa-

tion with other states to determine ways to improve their processes and productivity to reduce costs. Only by identifying the various activities and resource drivers, then tracking the cost of the activities will they be able to improve their results.

ABM in a computer programming and systems integration firm

ABM has also been used successfully by a computer programming and integration firm. This firm wanted to use ABM to become more competitive in bidding for government contracts. With the fall of communism, the world seems like a safer place, which has led to a general downsizing of the defense industry. As a result, defense contractors have scrambled to get additional business in the nondefense arena (including nondefense federal contracts, state contracts, and also commercial business).

At this firm, costs of defense contracts in this company had always been allocated as follows: All direct labor and sometimes fringe benefits were gathered into a pool, then direct materials were added. Direct materials could be computer supplies, computers, and any other supplies connected with the job. Travel and the expense of relocating employees was another category that might be added to direct materials or else shown separately. At the beginning of the year, an estimate was made of divisional overhead and total direct labor. An overhead rate was developed based on direct labor. (In some ways, this sounds like the practice of manufacturing companies.) Then an estimate was made of total corporate and group overhead for the year. This was divided by an estimate of total cost input (i.e., the sum of direct labor, direct materials, and division overhead) to calculate a single combined corporate and group overhead rate.

How best to apply overhead? Given the changes in the business environment, the question now arises: Is this the most meaningful way for applying overhead? Does this method show what is *driving* the cost, or is it just a *convenient* way to allocate cost?

Public Law 91-379 requires that defense contractors file a "Disclosure Statement." Parts II–IV of this statement disclose how a company charges direct materials, labor, and indirect costs, and Part V shows how depreciation is treated.

Under depreciation method, it is interesting to note that the "unit of production" method is one choice, other listed choices being "useful life," "replacement experience," and "engineering estimate." Thus, the Disclosure Statement allows depreciation to be assigned based on methods other than the mere lapse of time, which means that the capital cost of an asset can be spread more equitably over the units produced by that capital asset than would be the case if the cost of capital were assigned arbitrarily using a time-based method.

By listing the "unit of production" method as an acceptable method, the government implies that units of production may be a guess at best, because even government contracts get canceled or increased. Some might fear that using estimates in this way would make a company an easy target for auditors from the Defense Contract Audit Agency (DCAA). However, if this approach more accurately reflects the use of the capital asset, then depreciation should be assigned based on units of production over an estimate life rather than time-based depreciation based on some tax life.

Tracing overhead items directly to contracts. Many corporate and divisional overhead costs can be traced directly to a contract rather than simply allocated as part of overhead. In government contracts, various contracts require different types of reports and different report frequencies. Some administrative officers require only quarterly or semiannual reports, while others require monthly reports. Similarly, some contracts require detailed reports, while sumary reports can be presented for other contracts.

The activities' "design special reports" and "run special reports" could be traced directly to a contract rather than simply being added to divisional overhead and allocated. Activities in accounting departments such as "prepare special reports" or "prepare billing" could be traced to contracts on the basis of usage depending on the type of accounting service provided.

Similarly, divisional or group human resource activities could be traced to particular con-

tracts on a cost-per-hire basis. The activity "administer benefits" could be traced to each person on a cost-per-person basis. Payroll department costs could be traced to each person on a cost-per-person or a cost-per-check basis. The activity "administer employee relocation" could also be traced to specific contracts based on a cost per employee relocated.

The activity "review quality" could be traced to contracts on a cost-per-review basis. Quality planning costs of the quality department could be allocated to the activity "review quality." Similarly, the activity "train for quality" could be allocated as a secondary activity to the primary activities for each department.

Fringe benefits. Although some companies include vacation, holiday, sick pay, pension, FICA, FUTA, workers compensation, unemployment, and severance pay as a divisional overhead item, more accurate costs can be obtained if these benefits are traced directly to the related direct labor charges.

It is important in a service organization to get started with ABM and not worry too much about total accuracy from the start: Accuracy will improve with time.

This company found that some contracts have more turnover, sick pay, or pensions than other contracts, which means that a direct tracing of these costs may prove useful for pricing as well as costing. Similarly, bonuses should be traced directly to the people who receive the bonuses instead of being added to a general divisional overhead pool. A company might want to trace a portion of a bonus to various contracts to show employees how their work on various contracts affected their bonuses. This would be useful not only from a costing standpoint, but also from a motivational standpoint to match rewards with results.

Facility rent and depreciation. Facility rent or depreciation can be traced according to actual usage of the facilities. Thus, if direct labor employees use a certain amount of space on average, they would be charged a fully loaded facility rate (i.e., a rate that includes the costs of rent, electricity, property taxes, building insurance, and janitorial services). Divisional overhead personnel would be charged a divisional facility rate that would be included in the rate they use in charging their work to the various projects and contracts.

Common sense. It is important to use common sense. In one experience with a defense contractor, managers in one department were asked to charge their time according to each job they worked on, though some managers worked on up to 30 different contracts in a single day. Whether it makes sense to use a time sheet in such a situation must be decided by each company. After using time sheets for a year, this company went back to use of a simple overhead rate based on direct labor. Another government contractor in the computer programming and systems integration field, however, uses "time sheet checks," which resemble surprise inspections in the army: An employee does not want to get caught with a time sheet that is not up to date.

Contract administration and planning. Contract administration can be traced to contracts based on the type and number of reports issued. Marketing efforts can be traced to contracts based on a combination of time and travel. Thus, there might be a cost of so much per hour of marketing time plus any direct expenses (e.g., travel expenses, printing, or graphics).

Since planning affects the whole company, planning efforts might be charged according to the type of plans created, the level of detail of each plan, and the amount of time spent in planning for each division and group.

Since many divisions have managers that are actively involved in the contracts, at least a portion of their time and cost can be directly traced to each contract. The balance of their time—and that of their secretaries—could be allocated to the contracts in their division. These are what have been called *secondary activities.*[1] Secondary activities may make up only a small portion of the total cost of running a department. They are allocated to the various primary activities in the department based on the percentage of total primary activity costs that each activity represents. In a labor-intensive department, the major factor of production would be labor costs. In other departments (e.g., for computer operations), the major factor of production might be computer run time.

FAR (Federal Acquisition Regulations) 31.200 discusses specific unallowable costs, including the following:

- Alcoholic beverages;
- Contributions;
- Disputes between prime contractors and subcontractors;
- Hospitality suites;
- Travel in excess of federal travel regulations; and
- Insurance on the correction of product defects.

Although these items are unallowable, the cost accounting standards (CAS) still require that they be traced if possible to cost objectives and then identified as unallowable.

Carrying cost for unbilled work. An item that has not been billed yet can be very important to the value of all work that has been performed. Costs may not be billed, for example, if a contract requires some type of holdback (e.g., a 10 percent holdback) or if the contractor has not yet achieved a specific milestone. In either case, these unbilled costs are similar to a manufacturing company's work-in-process and finished inventory. Until the milestone is completed or the contract finished, the company has carrying costs connected with these unbilled costs. This carrying cost could be charged internally to various contracts to get a better handle on contract profitability.

How banks can use ABM

Banks, too, can apply ABM in assigning overhead costs to their various departments. For a bank to assign service department costs based on revenue or fee income makes the assignment easy and auditable. The question, however, is whether doing so gives management meaningful information for decision making.

Consider, for example, the security component of bank overhead. In most banks, security expenses come in several forms, including:

- Security guards;
- Safes;
- Fireproof file cabinets;
- Security windows; and
- Outside security services.

If these expenses were to be applied based on some type of fee and interest income basis, the teller departments would be undercharged for security services, while mortgage and auto loan departments would be overcharged.

For example, one of the main reasons for having security guards in a bank is to prevent robberies. Thus, a Dallas bank that became one of only two noncash banks in the country (and thus had no security guards) found that its security expenses were substantially lower than they would have been if the bank had chosen to handle cash transactions. The size and nature of its safe and other required security measures were substantially less than would have been the case had the bank handled cash. According to a senior executive of this cashless bank, security charges for a bank should be charged mainly to the teller-deposit and check-cashing departments of the bank rather than included in overall overhead. Little should be charged to the mortgage, auto loan, or business loan departments.

High turnover of tellers. Another common problem in banks is the high turnover of tellers. One financial institution used ABM to analyze its teller department. The tellers identified the following activities:

- Handle deposits;
- Record withdrawals;
- Balance the cash drawer;
- Answer customer inquiries; and
- Handle money orders.

The financial institution estimated the cost per unit for each of these activities. The results indicated (as might be guessed) that, based on the average number of transactions and the customer fees charged, some types of savings and checking accounts were under-costed while others were overcosted.

This financial institution analyzed the cost to hire and train tellers, taking into consider-ation the impact that having high teller turn-over rates had on customer service and revenue. As a result, the financial institution is currently reassessing:

- Wages;
- Training;
- Use of part-time vs. full-time tellers; and
- Supervisory support needed by tellers.

Initially, the financial institution thought it would be cheaper to hire part-time rather than full-time employees on the grounds that part-time employees received a lower wage rate and did not receive medical insurance premiums, holiday pay, or vacations. Now, however, the financial institution has been forced to reconsider, because although part-time employees earn a lower wage rate, they also tend to be less loyal and dedicated. Since part-time employees learn less about the business and also have higher turnover rates than full-time employees, the financial institution ended up having to spend more time and money hiring and training new part-time tellers.

If the financial institution had used ABM, the cost of the hiring and training process would have been more apparent. The company would have understood much quicker that the part-time tellers probably cost more given the costs of lost business, training, and hiring costs.

Using ABM in a hospital to develop a patient's bill of activities

The accounts receivable department of a hospital in Dallas has used ABM to calculate its own department's portion of a typical patient's bill of activities. Note that, except for patients who pay their deductibles and a few patients who pay cash, most patient bills are paid by third-party insurance companies or by government programs such as Medicare and Medicaid.

In looking at the payment component of total patient cost, the accounting department looked at the main activities performed in the accounts receivable department, including:

- Mail processing;
- Lockbox processing;
- Medicare and Medicaid processing;
- Deposit preparation;

- Research;
- Copying; and
- Cashier activities.

Then the accounting department looked at the employee time associated with each activity. For example, two employees might spend part of their time checking for errors in the processing of checks handled by the bank's lockbox activities. An estimate of the time the two employees spend checking lockbox tapes for errors might show that one employee spends about ten minutes per batch while another employee spends about fifteen minutes per batch. If the two employees perform similar analyses to detect lockbox errors, the hospital can use ABM for comparative analyses of employees. Thus, the hospital can compare activity performance over time to determine a standard in terms of time and dollars.

Note that it is appropriate to analyze the performance of an activity in terms of time so that comparisons can be made without the distortions that are introduced by changing payroll rates. However, the dollar impact of certain activities needs to be determined to decide if an activity analysis is appropriate (or at least a high priority) for a given activity. A goal for continuous improvement could be set by employees and a variety of techniques used to lower the time and cost of the activity while improving quality. The hospital computed time per batch for mail processing and lockbox processing. A comparison of processing times was made and a benchmark time was set. Thus, activity analysis was used as a way to improve performance.

Activity maps. The accounting department prepared an activity map to show the activities and the alternatives in the hospital's accounts receivable department. For lockbox processing, the alternatives were:

- Receive bank reports over modem rather than on tape;
- Receive bank receipts electronically rather than on paper; or
- Have patients mail payments directly to the hospital rather than to lockboxes.

An activity map resembles a form of zero-based budgeting, because it forces someone to think through the alternative ways of per-

forming a function, business process, or activity. The goal is to eliminate the activity (if it is non-value-added) or to find a more effective way of accomplishing the objective.

Some of the cost drivers connected with the activity "lockbox processing" were:

- Length of time the hospital had worked with a particular bank;
- Bank's experience in meeting the needs of hospital;
- Skill, training, and experience of particular bank employees that work with the hospital;
- Number of bank receipts;
- Number of patients;
- Skill, training, and experience of hospital employees who check for lockbox processing errors;
- Length of bank tape; and
- Experience of insurance payers in providing the proper information.

The department reviewed a number of activity measures, including:

- Number of batches;
- Number of copies made; and
- Number of entries on a batch report.

The accounting department decided to use "number of entries on batch reports." This decision resembles the decision that purchasing departments in manufacturing companies must make about whether to use number of purchase orders or number of purchase order lines as an activity measure. There is no right or wrong answer: Each situation must be analyzed to determine what makes sense.

Other activities that were too small (in terms of time and cost) to break out separately were allocated to the primary activities based on the number of transactions for each department. A transaction for lockbox processing would be different from a transaction for Medicare or Medicaid, because lockbox processing involves separate checks for each patient whereas Medicare and Medicaid do not have individual checks. Another way to allocate other costs would be based on the total cost of each activity before the "other" category.

Two categories of cost per patient. Finally, accounting derived two categories of cost per patient for the accounts receivable department. One category was for Medicare or Medicaid patients; the other was for patients whose bill would be paid by insurance companies. These costs would be incorporated into a bill of activities for patient service. Here is a simple example:

Example: Patient Bill of Activities

Activity	Units	Cost/Unit
Admit patient	1	$xx
Prepare room	1	$xx
Feed patient	9	$xx
Prepare patient for surgery	1	$xx
Discharge patient	1	$xx
Receive payment	1	$xx
Total		$xxx

Use of ABM in a laundry company

Another application of ABM occurred recently in a company that launders uniforms for corporate clients such as service stations, manufacturing facilities, and restaurants. This is a highly competitive industry with many small local competitors, which prompted the company discussed here to implement a total quality management (TQM) program.

Here are some of the activities that a driver of a laundry truck might perform:

- Load truck;
- Deliver clean laundry;
- Sell additional business;
- Collect money;
- Measure customer's new employees so they can be fitted for uniforms;
- Handle disputes; and
- Make second trips for forgotten or lost clean uniforms.

Cost drivers connected with the activity "collect money" include:

- Number of accounts that are C.O.D.;
- Experience of driver;
- Nature of customers;
- Confidence of customer in driver's accuracy and integrity;
- Size of order;
- Whether invoice billing amount has changed since last delivery;
- Past errors;
- Special charges;
- Same services but more or less of those services;
- Whether delivery occurs on the regular delivery day;
- Partial or complete delivery; and
- Length of time doing business with a particular customer.

Note that these cost drivers have to do with the normal weekly collection of money for a week's laundry rather than collections of delinquent accounts.

The activity measure for "collect money" would be "cost per customer collected." By obtaining this "cost per customer collected," the company can determine if the activity "collect money" is the best use of the driver's time. The company may find, for example, that it is expensive for drivers to wait while a customer finds someone to sign a check. If so, the company might be better off sending invoices and thus using the driver's time more productively (e.g., for selling new accounts, selling additional items to old accounts, or selling to new departments in the current accounts). Thus, ABM makes certain costs more visible to management.

The same approach could be applied to other activities to determine a bill of activities for not only the driver's activities, but for the company as a whole.

ABM in a not-for-profit setting

The last example of the use of ABM occurs in the not-for-profit sector at a large voluntary health and welfare organization whose mission was to prevent birth defects. This organization conducted fund-raising activities such as walks, charity balls, and mothers' marches. At this organization, the "profitability" of fund-raising events was evaluated by creating a bill of activities for each fund-raising event.

Historically, voluntary health and welfare organizations have kept their books on a not-for-profit basis, which means that there is no equity, just fund balances. In a way, therefore, such organizations already calculate some activity costs. For example, an organization might show the following activities on its financial statements:

- Professional education;
- Community service;
- Research grants;
- Fund-raising; and
- Administration.

Often, a time study is conducted for one week of each month (which assumes that the week is fairly typical). Then, the results are extrapolated for the month. Costs for items like printing costs and educational supplies are charged directly to the various activities, as are travel and entertainment costs. Most other costs (including occupancy costs and telephone expenses), however, are charged to activities such as those listed above on the same basis as salaries. Thus, for example, if an employee spends 50 percent of his time on the activity "provide community service," then 50 percent of related salary, occupancy costs, and telephone expenses would be charged to the activity "provide community service."

This organization's interest in the profitability of its many fund-raising events is analogous to a commercial company's interest in the profitability of various product lines. The organization had previously done little to analyze the profitability of fund-raising events because historically it had had only two major fund-raisers. Over the years, however, many new fund-raising events were introduced to supplement the two major fund-raisers. As competition for charitable contributions has increased over the years and as money has become tougher to raise, the organization needed to know which of its many fund-raising events were actually worthwhile.

This organization ultimately concluded that some fund-raising events were not profitable. A program was initiated to review the various fund-raising events and either improve or delete those that were found to be unprofitable. The organization has determined that it can use ABM to help determine which fund-raising events justify the time and expense of directors, paid staffers, contributors, and volunteers.

Some chapters of the organization use spreadsheets to determine the profitability of each event. The spreadsheets calculate the expenses and staff time connected with a particular fund-raising event. These spreadsheets trace natural expense categories (e.g., staff

wages, travel, supplies, and occupancy costs) to individual fund-raising events (activities). In this way, the organization can calculate a cost per particular fund-raising activity. (As a first approach to the problem, the organization chose to consider each fund-raising event as an activity.)

Valuing time spent by volunteers. The next step is to value the time spent by volunteers. There are different levels of volunteers—from an event director, to someone who manages the collection of money, to someone who calls merchants for donations, to the volunteers who solicit donations. Each is a limited resource with limited time, money, and energy to contribute to charitable events. Since the organization needs to maximize the profitability of each event, it ultimately needs to assign a value to volunteers' time, then trace those costs to fund-raising activities along with all other costs.

Conclusion

An entire article could be written about each of these organizations. This article attempts to illustrate the use of ABM in various service organizations and thus to show how the principles of ABM apply even outside the manufacturing environment. Manufacturing is much more homogeneous than service organizations, and the carryover between companies is thus much greater in manufacturing than in service settings. Nonetheless, experience with service companies shows that ABM applies equally well in service, not-for-profit, and governmental settings. ▲

Notes:
1. Jim Brimson, *Activity Accounting* (New York: John Wiley & Sons 1991), 54.

CHAPTER B8

Activity-Based Management: An Australian Perspective

Stewart Lamond

Activity-based management (ABM) is becoming a major force in management accounting in Australia, even though most companies are only using parts of ABM so far and so have not yet realized all the benefits that ABM can bring. This article discusses the use of ABM at three Australian companies—Parke Davis, ICI Film Products, and Comalco Rolled Products. It shows how ABM is helping these companies measure performance from both a financial and an operating standpoint, how they determine the "true" costs and profitability of products and services, and how they identify and then control the factors that drive costs.

I n Australia, as in the rest of the world, both manufacturing and service businesses are experiencing fundamental changes in the way they operate. Examples of these changes include:

- Globalization of markets, products, and businesses;
- Increased consumer focus on quality;
- Greater price sensitivity;
- Deregulation; and
- The technological explosion.

While this transformation of the business environment has been happening, the stock markets have continued to press for short-term profits, which has (in turn) increased pressure on management at all levels.

Companies today have many questions to which they need answers, though usually they must seek answers from increasingly moribund traditional cost systems. These questions include the following:

- How do our profits and our cost structures measure up to our competition?

- Are we located correctly to source our labor and materials and to serve our customers at minimum cost?
- What impact will changes in our processes have on the bottom line?
- How can we reduce ever-increasing overhead costs?
- How can we eliminate waste?

Against this background of an increasingly dynamic business environment, technical innovation, and pressure to make crucial, prompt and accurate financial decisions, leading Australian businesses are seeking to:

- Measure performance from both a financial and an operating standpoint;
- Determine the "true" costs and profitability of products and services;
- Identify the factors that drive costs and how to control them;
- Isolate the current level of waste and redundant activities;
- Ensure that major decisions are based on wider business issues, not just costs and payback; and
- Assess the value to be derived from overhead.

Activity-based management

Australian businesses have found that their current management accounting and costing practices do not do a good job of answering these questions. Activity-based management (ABM) is now attracting much attention as a remedy. It has now gone past the theorizing stage in seminars and workshops, for it has now been implemented in a number of major businesses and institutions.

A number of leading-edge companies have undertaken activity-based costing (ABC) exercises, all with positive results. In most cases, however, the exercise has been regarded as an isolated event; the process has not become embedded into the organization. All the companies whose experience with ABC is outlined below started out by looking at product costs only; they were seeking ways to allocate overhead better.

Only one of the companies (the rolled aluminum products manufacturer) has graduated into full-fledged ABM. This company now is managed in operational areas on a day-to-day basis by the physical cost drivers that are used for the ABM system. The company uses ABM to identify where to improve itself next. The ABM system measures the success of the company's time-based management (TBM) and total quality management (TQM) programs.

Parke Davis

This major pharmaceutical manufacturer is characterized by a strong emphasis on cost control and profit growth, with an extensive and varied product range and long product life cycles. The selling prices of many of the company's products are controlled by the government rather than being market-driven. The overall cost structure of the company is (approximately) as follows:

- 60 percent direct material cost;
- 7 percent direct labor cost; and
- 33 percent overhead cost.

Parke Davis was driven by a number of factors to implement ABC, including:

- A need to match the company's excellent manufacturing facility with an up-to-date and pertinent cost management system (i.e., the finance function had not kept up with the operational areas);
- The increasing overhead component of the company's cost structure;
- Arbitrary overhead allocations, which resulted in cross-subsidization of products;
- A lack of confidence by production and marketing employees in the company's existing cost accounting system; and
- Initiatives such as TQM being hampered by misleading cost information.

Objectives of the ABM program. To overcome these factors, the objectives of the ABM initiative at Parke Davis were to:

- Reduce overhead expenses by categorizing activities as value-add vs. non-value-add;
- Provide more relevant product costs to support pricing decisions;
- Improve management reporting and control;
- Improve product quality and service through better support for TQM initiatives.

The results and benefits from this ABM program implementation have been mixed since only some of these objectives have been achieved to date. Tangible savings have been limited so far, though the continuing use of key performance indicators used in the cost analysis should lead to future cost savings and to improved quality and service.

Better investment decisions (as a result of more accurate product costs) have been attributed to the use of ABM. Better resource utilization has also been achieved, because ABM has made managers and staff much more aware of the non-value-added concept and the need to contain costs.

Better investment decisions (as a result of more accurate product costs) have been attributed to the use of ABM. Better resource utilization has also been achieved, because ABM has made managers and staff much more aware of the non-value-added concept and the need to contain costs.

Parke Davis can see the scope for widening this cultural change in management thinking. Only then will it be possible to de-emphasize the costing element of ABM and to focus more on the broader issues of continuous improvement. The operations people remain keen to set up ABM as a continuous process; they are collaborating with their financial colleagues to establish ABM permanently.

ICI Film Products

This major manufacturer and marketer of plastic-based film products faced declining confidence in its existing product cost systems. The company was attracted to ABC as a means of setting up more believable management reports; margin analysis reports were providing results that differed significantly from the monthly financial statements.

Operations managers felt that certain product lines were performing poorly, yet the financials continued to show these products in a favorable light. The sales and marketing departments had even established their own "satellite" cost systems for lack of confidence in the company's existing product costing system.

Finally, new manufacturing technologies demanded better performance measuring systems than those offered by traditional costing systems, which placed little importance on the physical information needed to run the company (e.g., production cycle times, plant reliability, and order processing times).

ICI's company policy was to remain at the forefront of professional accounting developments. When the concept of ABC caught the imagination of top management, ICI decided to set up a pilot ABC project at one of its sites before implementing it throughout the whole organization. The objectives of the pilot implementation were to:

- Provide fast-track results to identify the key problem areas ("let's get it vaguely right rather than precisely wrong");
- Install a flexible system for periodic "what-if" analyses; and
- Support the measurement of continuous improvements emanating from the company's TQM program.

The pilot site implementation was successful, for the most part, and has provided a sound basis for implementing ABC in the rest of the company. Clear and measurable benefits have come from using ABC to quantify product costs in a way that managers in all functions can agree is valid. While there is a perception and understanding that ABC can assist with ICI's TQM program, that development has yet to come. The ABC process will now be widened into a fully-fledged ABM program so that it can better complement ICI's TQM and similar initiatives.

Comalco Rolled Products

A major manufacturer of rolled aluminum products, Comalco introduced ABC because:

- Its current product costing system was administratively difficult and costly to maintain. It lacked credibility and drove decisions that were contrary to the new manufacturing strategy.
- It wanted to make decisions about product strategy but knew that the data from traditional cost systems were suspect.
- It had embarked on a program of continuous improvement and needed integrated operational and financial management information to ensure that success was being achieved.

Comalco's initial objective was to provide believable product costs. Management had continually questioned the contribution being made by one of its smaller product groups but could not be sure that it was a financial problem. Operationally, however, this product group caused havoc in scheduling the factory and achieving a production process with minimal variability.

Comalco's initial objective was to provide believable product costs. Management had continually questioned the contribution being made by one of its smaller product groups but could not be sure that it was a financial problem.

By the time Comalco had carried out many of the key steps in an ABM product cost analysis, however, it became clear that ABM gave the company a way to measure its management TBM program. Comalco saw how performance measures such as product throughput time, delivery performance, customer service, rejected product, and inventory days could be set at each level of management and enhanced with financial performance measures.

Exhibit 1. *Comalco Rolled Products Management Information Project*

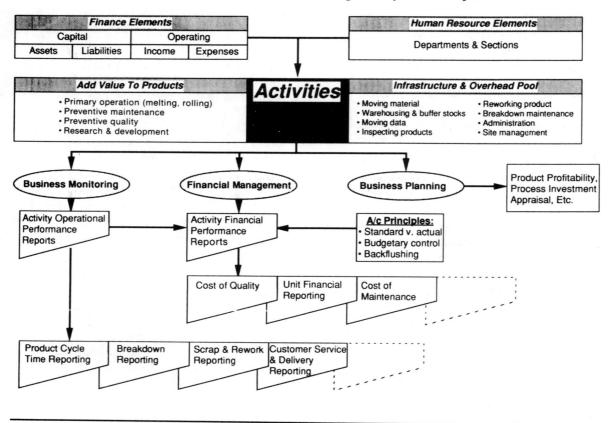

An early decision in Comalco's TBM journey had been to turn off its traditional costing system. Although some physical data associated with this system continued to be collected and applied in monitoring the TBM efforts, the myriad of costing reports previously produced were not missed, and much time and effort was saved.

Activity analysis. Comalco's activity analysis, which is the first major task in any ABM effort, led to a greater understanding of the company's processes, particularly those that crossed organizational units and were thus subject to organizational infighting. Managers made surprising efforts to identify (or perhaps justify) very detailed activities—often they were, in reality, merely tasks—so the project team worked hard to cut about half of the activities that the managers originally offered. The good thing about this work was that it pointed clearly to many areas of un-

derutilized resources, and thus to resources that could be reallocated or disposed of without any detailed financial analysis.

Recasting costs into the activity framework. Comalco, like the other companies described in this article, found that much work was required to recast costs into the activity framework (see Exhibit 1). This work was even more onerous than performing the activity analysis and the determination of each activity's cost drivers. To ensure that the chart of accounts would be able to capture activity costs in the future (and thus be able to be used to monitor costs continuously on an ABM basis), Comalco changed its chart of accounts. Now it routinely captures costs on both an activity *and* responsibility (i.e., organizational) basis (as opposed to capturing costs on just a responsibility basis).

The activity costs are now downloaded directly into ABM software. This saves much effort and time, because the accounting area no longer has to recast costs into an activity structure and manually key them into the ABM software. Cost driver statistics are captured by Comalco's operational database, which is set up to monitor continuous improvements in the TBM program and to allow Comalco to benchmark its operational performance. The statistics are also fed directly into the ABM software, which makes production of product cost reports and value analysis reporting on business processes straightforward. (The operational database was already capturing all the cost driver statistics used by the ABM software. Downloading from the general ledger and the operational database can occur monthly or even more often.) Exhibit 1 illustrates the overall ABM system.

One of the major benefits that ABM has achieved at Comalco is the elimination of the troublesome product group that initiated the exercise in the first place. This occurred because financial data from the new ABM system—which no one questioned—showed conclusively that the product group was unprofitable.

Summing up

As these examples show, ABM is becoming a major force in management accounting in Australia—even though most companies are only using parts of ABM so far and, consequently, have not yet realized all the benefits that ABM can bring.

Management accounting in the 1990s (whether in Australia or in any other country) will have the following characteristics:

- *Expansion beyond its traditional role of inventory valuation and responsibility accounting.* Increased emphasis will be placed on using activity analysis to cut product costs and set motivational goals for achievement; less emphasis will be placed on measuring performance against internally engineered standards.

- *A focus on cost drivers to identify and eliminate non-value-added costs.* More attention than ever will be needed to identify the causes of costs to reduce or eliminate them.
- *More relevant allocation methods will be used—methods that relate more closely to the activity, or driver, leading to the specific cost.*
- *Entrepreneurship will increase as quality, responsiveness, and cost of internal value-added services are pitted against the market for similar services.* Combined with cutting out non-value-added activities, this will do much to halt "overhead creep."
- *Systems will become simpler.* Companies will simplify their basic processes to reduce costs and minimize non-value-added activities. Accounting systems, in particular, will be simplified; unnecessary allocations and reallocations will cease as managers realize that success and profit stems from working together, not from finding ways of passing the buck elsewhere.
- *Management accounting systems will be specifically tailored to each organization.* Cost drivers vary from site to site depending on strategies, culture, and organizational structures. It will seldom be possible to lift an ABM system from one site to another.
- *Direct labor tracking and reporting will decline as the capital component in costs increases, as labor becomes more multiskilled and flexible, and as the cost of labor reporting exceeds the benefit to be gained.* This should help break down the barriers between management and the shop floor and thus help organizations make better use of the knowledge, ideas, and skills of their work forces. ▲

PART C

Advanced Manufacturing Techniques (JIT, CIM, etc.)

Management Accounting in a Just-in-Time Environment

Mark C. DeLuzio

A company that adopts just-in-time (JIT) manufacturing must undergo radical operating and cultural changes. One of the most important areas that must change is the management accounting system. Many JIT programs have been disbanded because of the accounting function's inability to adequately reflect critical performance factors. In particular, traditional accounting measurements often fail to measure those things that are crucial in a JIT factory, and traditional performance factors often promote dysfunctional behavior in a JIT environment. This article explains how traditional accounting systems conflict with JIT and suggests ways to improve management accounting systems and bring them into harmony with JIT.

I t is impossible to ignore the changes occurring in U.S. industry today. We have finally begun to recognize that we compete in a worldwide market. We are also coming to the realization that we can no longer manipulate profits simply by increasing our selling price. More and more, we are finding that selling prices are being established by a competitive marketplace. The only remaining variable to the profit equation is cost.

Many companies now realize that profitability is gained or lost depending on what happens on the factory floor. As important as efficiency and cost-effectiveness are, however, being able to compete in a time-based manner is often even more important. Meeting customer requirements with quality products in a timely—yet profitable—manner is nothing less than a matter of survival. To achieve this goal, many companies are turning to Japanese manufacturing concepts, as set forth by Eiji Toyoda and Taiichi Ohno. These concepts can be collectively labeled just-in-time (JIT).

Adopting JIT

When a firm adopts JIT techniques, the entire organization goes through a rapid and drastic change. JIT is not just a manufacturing project that leaves the rest of the organization unscathed; rather, the entire organization must undergo operating and cultural changes. For a JIT program to succeed, it must have the enthusiastic support of upper management. Indeed, senior management must be the driving force behind JIT.

In implementing JIT, one of the most important areas for change is the management accounting system. Again, however, it is critical that senior management understand and support the changes required. Unfortunately, many management accountants themselves cannot understand why their traditional systems must change in a JIT environment. They reason that their systems have been tested by time, and thus do not need to be changed. This attitude is dangerous, however, because the accounting function can be the difference between a successful JIT program and one that fails.

Many JIT programs have been disbanded because of the accounting function's inability to adequately reflect critical performance factors. Traditional accounting measurements often fail to measure those things that are crucial in a JIT factory. In fact, traditional performance factors often promote dysfunctional behavior in a JIT environment.

Traditional management accounting systems

Traditional management accounting systems were established to serve the needs of outside customers such as the IRS or the SEC (and, sometimes, those guys at corporate). As long as regulatory or statutory requirements (generally accepted accounting principles, IRS,

SEC) were met, the accounting system was judged to be adequate.

Outside auditors required that stringent controls be placed on an organization. The more controls, the easier it was for an auditor to render an unqualified opinion of the financial position of a company. As accounting systems evolved, the accounting function took on the role of watchdog—a role that is still prevalent today in many U.S. industries.

Accountants may have done a good job of satisfying outside customers' needs. They often failed, however, to recognize that an important internal customer was being neglected—namely, the manufacturing people, who usually got whatever scraps were left over from the Ivory Tower accounting systems. As a general rule, accountants thought they knew what was good for the manufacturing group. (Although other internal customers are equally important, this article focuses especially on the needs of the manufacturing group.) On further inspection, however, we find that management accounting systems were developed with management accountants in mind. Many systems and controls have been imposed on manufacturing to give the accountants a better sense of control. Here are some examples:

- Accountants needed a way to track manufacturing costs, so the manufacturing group was directed to use discrete work orders. Non-value-added activities (e.g., labor recording and inventory movement transactions) were performed to support this system.
- For control purposes, accountants required that inventory be locked in a controlled stockroom. Inventory was kept out of the sight of management and therefore never became an issue. The mere existence of a stockroom acknowledged that an undetermined level of waste was acceptable. Room always existed for excess inventory.
- Management accounting systems required that tooling be kept in a centralized tool crib (which is wasteful for many of the same reasons a stockroom is).

As painful as these controls were, the accounting profession then attempted to use the output from these systems to measure the performance of the manufacturing group.

These measurements were developed to satisfy the needs of the accountants. Even if the information provided any value to the manufacturing group, it was rarely, if ever, timely. Corrective action was always after the fact.

What a management accounting system should do

Management accountants in a JIT environment should concern themselves with helping the manufacturing group, rather than being a roadblock. The first step is education. Management accountants must first learn as much as they can about JIT manufacturing techniques. Without at least a basic understanding of the JIT philosophy, management accountants have little hope of understanding why management accounting systems must change.

Next, the management accountants must make an objective evaluation of the management accounting system currently in place by answering the following questions:

- Who uses the information provided by the management accounting system?
- Why are particular types of data required?
- What would happen if a specific type of information were no longer provided?
- Does anyone ask for a particular type of data, or is the information simply imposed on others?
- Are decisions being made based on the information provided?
- What decisions are being made?
- Does the information support company goals, or does it support dysfunctional behavior?
- Does the information help the manufacturing group?
- Do we collect information that tells us something we already know?
- Would other measures be more helpful to the manufacturing group to monitor its performance (whether nonfinancial measures or financial measures)?
- Do the performance measures reflect continuous improvement trends?
- Is the information timely?

Changes to a management accounting system in a JIT environment do not happen overnight. As an organization changes, its management accounting system should reflect and complement the new organizational changes.

As JIT is implemented, changes in a management accounting system should evolve in a commonsense manner. One thing, however, is for certain: Management accountants should be prepared to eventually throw away many of the principles basic to the traditional management accounting system. Without this understanding, change will never occur. Management accountants who persist in trying to maintain traditional systems can find themselves in a role that is viewed as non-value-added. Many accountants simply cannot understand why traditional management accounting systems are not longer needed. They insist on forcing their traditional systems and controls on those who are trying to operate in a JIT environment, which is why some accountants get labeled as uncooperative and impediments to progress. Even worse, an unwilling management accountant has the potential to drive a JIT system to its knees. Many accountants do not realize that they have this power, but the demise of many JIT programs can be attributed to an unwillingness to change on the part of the management accountants.

How JIT affects a management accounting system

The discussion that follows focuses on the many changes that must occur in a management accounting system when a company converts to a JIT environment. Many (if not all) of these changes to a management accounting system cannot occur unless the organization changes. These changes cannot happen overnight; rather, there must be a transition. Eventually, the changes should lead to a significant reduction in the accounting staff, because as the organization becomes streamlined, information becomes easier to collect. In addition, many traditional accounting tasks (e.g., labor accounting, variance analysis, detailed inventory accounting, and scrap valuation) can be eliminated. The following sections look at several of these new approaches.

Impact of JIT organization on overhead costing structure. A manufacturing firm that embarks on a JIT program must refocus its

attention on the factory floor. The manufacturing group becomes one of the most important "internal customers" of the organization. Service groups treat the requirements of the manufacturing group with greater respect and diligence. Due to their increased customer focus, service and business support groups are held more accountable for their results than they were in the past.

This new attention to the factory floor has a direct impact on the overhead structure of an organization. In a traditional manufacturing company, the manufacturing group is supported by functional departments that were previously presumed to be a part of the manufacturing organization. These centralized groups, however, were structured in such a way that they really were not a part of the manufacturing organization. They were, in fact, territorial in nature; their interests and goals were not always congruent with those of the production people. Examples of these support groups include:

- Purchasing;
- Production control;
- Manufacturing engineering;
- Industrial engineering; and
- Quality control.

Decentralization. In a JIT environment, with this new focus on the factory floor, the services of support groups must be redeployed directly to the JIT cells. The main advantage is the enhanced focus on the requirements of the manufacturing group. In fact, the cells (or group of cells) take on the form of a factory within a factory. For example, a cell may be assigned a purchasing agent, a production control clerk, a quality engineer, and a manufacturing engineer. These individuals are strictly dedicated to the needs of their particular cell. The production manager for the group thus has enhanced control and responsibility over his operations—he controls his own destiny. Those that have been redeployed gain a greater sense of ownership than they had when they were part of a centralized (and less accountable) functional group. Problem detection and resolution is also enhanced. Feedback about shop floor problems is immediate in this decentralized environment because of the reliance on visual controls and this new sense of ownership.

Note, however, that the decentralization of support groups occurs gradually over time. An organization must be fairly well along in its JIT implementation before it can accommodate this type of organizational change.

Product costing and overhead application. The main implications of JIT for management accounting systems arise in the area of product costing and overhead allocations. In a traditional manufacturing environment, overhead is applied utilizing a frequently arbitrary allocation base. For example, total overhead, which includes centralized support costs, is lumped into a single cost pool and allocated based on direct labor hours, machine hours, square footage, or some other allocation methodology. The resulting overhead rate is then applied to individual products for product costing purposes. The effect of this allocation is a severe distortion of product costs.

In a JIT environment, by contrast, many support costs that were previously centralized in a traditional setting are directly associated with a manufacturing cell. Because of this direct association, costs can be traced directly to the particular products made in each cell. Product costing thus becomes more accurate than ever before. Note, however, that the driving force behind these changes in overhead allocations occurs not because of changes in the accounting system, but because of changes in the organizational structure brought about by JIT.

One of the most significant impacts that JIT has on an organization is the effect it has on overhead costs. If a firm employs all the tools of JIT, the improvements and elimination of waste will drive overhead costs down. Many accountants would like to give their accounting systems the credit for overhead reduction; such claims have been made for activity-based costing, for example. It should be realized, however, that overhead reductions should occur simply as a by-product of adopting JIT.

Product costing in a JIT environment

As mentioned, JIT forces overhead costs closer to the cell level, making overhead costs more closely associated with particular products. Product costing, therefore, becomes more accurate because fewer overhead allocations are required.

In a JIT environment, new definitions of overhead costs are needed, as follows:

Cell costs. Cell costs are those overhead costs that can reasonably be traced directly to a cell. Included in this cost pool are:

- Cell management salaries (including production control, quality assurance, purchasing, and manufacturing engineering);
- Labor costs;
- Tooling;
- Supplies;
- Equipment depreciation; and
- Travel cost.

Note that both fixed and variable costs (as conventionally defined) are included in this pool.

Support costs. Support costs are those costs that are not directly traceable to a cell. These costs should be allocated to the particular cells to which they apply. Included in this cost pool are:

- Centralized support costs;
- Plantwide heat treating;
- General maintenance;
- Plant depreciation;
- Taxes;
- Insurance; and
- Centralized manufacturing management.

Note that most costs can be traced to a particular cell. Detailed data collection systems should not be devised simply for the sake of cost allocations, however, unless these costs are significant as a percentage of total costs. For example, a heat treating department may service a given number of cells, but it might well prove to be wasteful to track costs based on the various products going through heat treating. Instead, heat treating might best be considered a support department whose costs are allocated only to those cells that receive the benefits of heat treating.

The key point is that the pool of support costs goes down as JIT is implemented, so fewer dollars have to be allocated. In a JIT environment, support costs are easier to allocate because of a simplified shop floor layout. Exhibit 1 shows typical cell costs and support costs as a percentage of total overhead in a traditional environment, compared with corresponding percentages in a JIT environment.

Exhibit 1. *Overhead Cost Analysis: Traditional vs. JIT Environments*

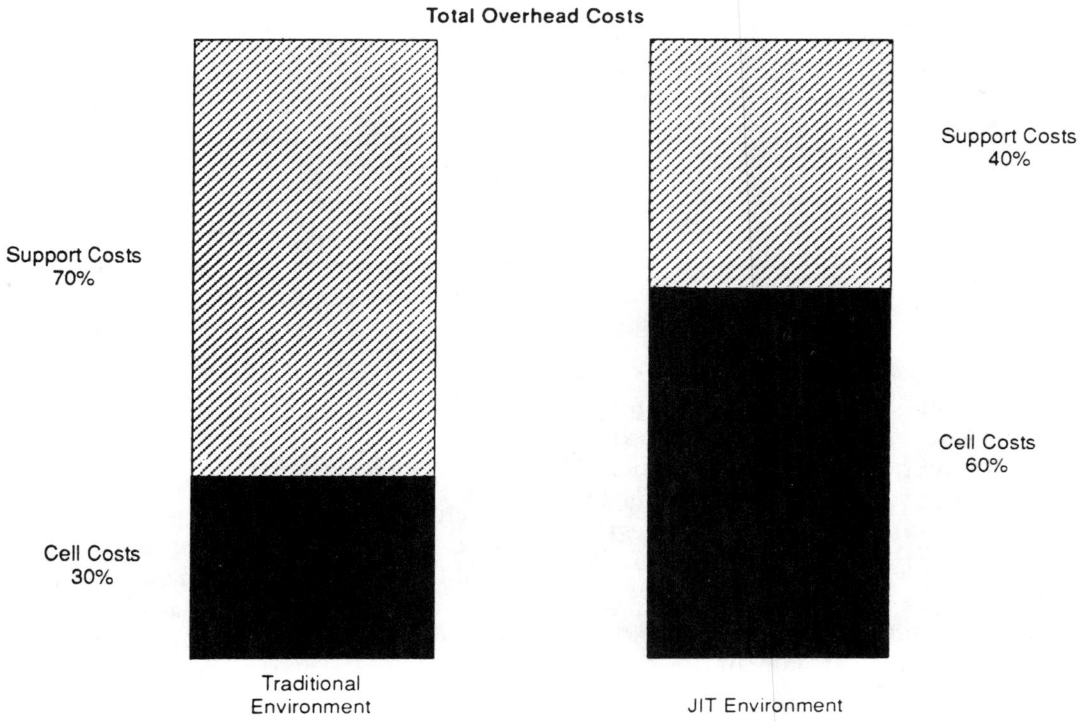

Total Overhead Costs

Once costs are classified as cell or support costs, they must be applied to the product level. In a cell that produces relatively homogeneous products, costing could be done on a per-unit basis. Given the data in Exhibit 2, for example, note that the overhead cost of $4 per unit could actually be broken down into a cell cost rate of $3 and a support cost rate of $1.

Exhibit 2 illustrates product costing when homogeneous units are produced in a cell. However, a cell might produce items that are dissimilar in terms of resources required in production. In that case, similar products could be grouped into product categories. These groups of products could be assigned an equivalent unit factor for use in applying the overhead rate. Exhibit 3, for example, illustrates a product with a factor of 1.00. It would be costed at $4.08 per unit, whereas a product with an equivalent unit factor of 1.3 would be costed at $5.30 per unit.

Another method for assigning overhead costs to products involves the use of a product's *takt* time based on standard work calculations. (See the sidebar, "Standard Work Concepts," for an explanation of *takt* time and standard work.) Exhibit 4 shows an example for a cell that makes two products.

While no one costing method will apply to all situations, it is reasonable to expect that changing overhead structures in a JIT environment will lead to more accurate product costing.

Inventory management in a JIT environment

In a traditional manufacturing company, the use of shop orders to control the production process is a common practice. Materials, labor, and applied overhead are charged to these orders as actual expenses. When a product is completed, the shop order is credited for the standard cost of the part or product manufactured. Any difference between the actual costs and the standard cost is recorded as a closed order variance.

The use of shop orders as a control device simply does not work. The large volume of

Exhibit 2. *Product Costing Example:*
Homogeneous Units

Cell Costs Budgeted	$1,500,000
Support Costs Budgeted	500,000
Total Overhead Costs	$2,000,000
Budgeted Units of Production	500,000
Overhead Cost per Unit	$4.00

- Support Costs Are Allocated to Each Cell
- Although Allocations Are Required, Costs Are Easier to Assign Because of Cell Layout

shop orders make it impossible to have any control or visibility over what is happening on the shop floor. Analyzing a closed order variance each month is equally impractical, and closed order variances are rarely timely. The use of shop orders involves countless inventory transactions that add no value to the product.

A typical production flow of a manufactured part in a traditional environment, for example, might involve the following steps:

- Raw materials are purchased and received into a centralized stockroom;
- Several shop orders are generated to produce the various subassemblies required for the finished part;
- Raw materials are issued to the first shop order to produce subassembly A;
- Subassembly A is completed and transferred to the stock room. The shop order is closed out;
- Subassembly A, along with other required raw materials, are issued to a new shop order to produce subassembly B;
- Subassembly B is completed and transferred to the stock room. The shop order is closed out;
- Subassembly B, along with other required raw materials, are issued to a new shop order to produce subassembly C;
- Subassembly C is completed and transferred to the stock room, then the shop order is closed out;
- etc.

Note that each shop order represents batch production. Parts are also stored in batches. Exposure to obsolescence and larger write-offs due to defects is greatly enhanced. The product also has a significant travel time within the shop. This non-value-added movement of inventory also affects the lead time for getting a product to a customer. When parts are made in batch, it is impossible to ascertain if particular parts are in fact required for a specific customer. It is also difficult to determine the status of a particular customer order.

Production in a JIT environment

A JIT environment handles the production of a part in an entirely different way. Parts are made one at a time (one-piece flow). A part is taken from its raw material state and processed through to its finished stage of completion. The use of shop orders is unnecessary. Production is scheduled at the cell level. Since parts are produced one at a time, wasteful inventory handling is eliminated. The use of stockrooms is curtailed and should eventually be eliminated in a JIT environment, which has important overhead implications. Through agreements with suppliers, raw materials are delivered and stored directly at the point of use. Parts are controlled at the cell level, using visual control techniques. Once a product is produced, it gets shipped directly to a customer instead of to a stockroom.

Backflushing. Since parts are not stored and physically transported throughout the shop in a JIT factory, it is reasonable to expect that inventory control costs should be significantly reduced. The use of backflushing aids in this process.

Backflushing is a means of relieving the stocking locations of raw materials consumed in production, based on the most current configuration of the bill of material for a particular assembly. Shipping transactions of a finished product to customers triggers the deduction of all related raw material components from the appropriate cell inventory balances throughout the shop. During the initial stages of a JIT program, it may be necessary to backflush within a cell rather than throughout the whole shop. Eventually, shopwide backflushing can be implemented once inventory levels are reduced and confidence with backflushing is gained.

Inventory valuation. Although the use of visual control should be encouraged, inventory

Exhibit 3. *Product Costing Example: Assigning Overhead Based on Equivalent Units*

- Parts Produced in a Cell May Not Be Homogeneous in Terms of Resources Required
- Parts Should Be Grouped into Categories
- Assign Equivalent Unit Factors to These Parts

Category	EU Factor	Units	Ext EU's	Cost/Unit
Head	1.00	100,000	100,000	$4.08
Body	1.30	300,000	390,000	$5.30
		400,000	490,000	

Total Costs $2,000,000
Cost per Equivalent Unit $4.08

Exhibit 4. *Product Costing Example: Assigning Overhead Based on* Takt *Time*

Product	Takt Time	Volume	Ext Takt Time
A	60 SEC	200,000	12,000,000 SEC
B	45 SEC	300,000	13,500,000 SEC
		Total *Takt* Time	25,500,000 SEC
		Total Cell & Support Costs	$2,000,000
		Cost Factor	$.0784

Product A: $.0784 × 60 SEC = $4.704
Product B: $.0784 × 45 SEC = $3.528

valuation is nevertheless an issue in a JIT environment. Without a secured stockroom, there should be more reliance placed on cycle counting to maintain appropriate inventory accuracy levels. A shop that institutes one-piece flow has little overhead cost in work-in-process. In this situation, the use of backflushing will pose few problems for inventory valuation. However, if a shop is still in a batch environment, the use of shopwide backflushing will understate the value of work-in-process. Intermediate backflushing may then be appropriate to capture the overhead costs that remain in inventory (i.e., work-in-process).

Lower inventories. Although lower inventories is a desirable goal, a word of caution should be issued. First, lowering inventories means that a company will produce less than it sells during the period of inventory decline. This will generate significant unfavorable absorption variances. If absorption variances are used in the management control process, there will be pressure to keep inventory at constant or increasing levels. This is clearly dysfunctional to the goal of lower inventories.

Second, by lowering inventory, JIT is often blamed for causing problems that never existed before. When a firm has a high level of inventory, many problems are hidden. For example, production inefficiencies are not perceived as a problem, because customer orders can be shipped from high inventories on hand. When inventories are lowered, however, problems are likely to delay the shipping of products to customers. The problems become more pressing and must be corrected immediately. Note however, that JIT is not to blame. The problems existed all along; they only became apparent and urgent when inventories were reduced.

Nonfinancial measures in a JIT environment

As previously noted, many financial measures can lead management to the wrong conclusions about performance. Although many financial measures are valuable, a host of nonfinancial measures are also useful when

Exhibit 5. *Nonfinancial Measures in a JIT Environment*

- Units Produced Per Man Hour
  —World Class—2% Improvement/Month
- Customer Service Trends
  —Percent Past Due/Fill Rate
- Days Inventory on Hand
- Quality Rejects
  —Pareto Analysis
- Scrap Units/Dollars
- Employee Suggestions
- *Kaizen* Results
- Daily Production Status
- Purchasing Measurements
  —Supplier Performance

---

tracking continuous improvement trends (see Exhibit 5 and the explanation discussed to follow). These nonfinancial measures should be posted prominently within the appropriate cell.

Units produced per man hour. Units produced per man hour is a productivity measure that is calculated by dividing total good units produced by total shop hours. Note that total shop hours are used (both direct and indirect in the traditional sense) to calculate the productivity measure. By using total shop hours, a company recognizes that productivity gains are possible in all areas of labor. Units per man hour should be tracked to a continuous improvement goal. World-class Japanese companies can be benchmarked by using a goal of 2 percent improvement per month (27 percent compounded improvement per year). This goal may seem unreasonable at the beginning, but once standard work concepts and other JIT tools are mastered, improvements will take place.

Customer service trends. Customer service trend lines, such as percent past due or order-fill rate, can be useful to gauge the level of customer service provided.

Days inventory on hand. Inventory trend data serves as a barometer to tell if a company's other programs are working. Inventory should come down as a by-product of implementing JIT.

Quality rejects. Pareto analysis of quality rejects provides useful information about problem areas within a cell. Trends indicate if improvement in terms of reducing quality rejects is being achieved.

Scrap units/dollars. Scrap reduction should be significant when the practice of one-piece flow becomes institutionalized. Trend data helps identify improvements.

Employee suggestions. The number of employee suggestions is a good indicator of how well a work force is committed to making improvements. The posting of improvement figures will promote friendly competition between cells. *Kaizen* (i.e., continuous improvement) must come from all levels of the organization. The best consultants, it has been pointed out, are those who do the job.

Kaizen *results*. *Kaizen* results should be posted so that improvement projects can be reviewed by anyone in the organization. A good format is to show present *kaizen* projects, future *kaizen* projects, and past projects just completed. Posting of *kaizen* results will encourage employees to participate in *kaizen* projects.

Daily production results. An ongoing electronic display board can be used to show the current production status. To be effective, the display should show the total units required for the day, current units produced, and the amount ahead or behind schedule as of any given moment. The display should use the *takt* time for the cell to determine units over or under the daily schedule.

Purchasing measurements. When a company looks at evaluating the purchasing function in a JIT environment, attributes other than purchase price variance must be used to measure performance. Since there is a focus in JIT on reducing the supplier base and establishing long-term commitments, items such as on-time delivery, quality, and concurrent design play a much more important role. Competitive bidding is inconsistent with the fostering of long-term relationships.

Summary

A company that implements JIT must also make changes to its management accounting system. There is no magic formula about

Standard Work Concepts

A great Japanese consultant once said that to fully understand just-in-time (JIT), a person must first understand standard work, which is one of the most comprehensive and powerful tools found in JIT.

The underlying principle of standard work is that every process must have a standard procedure. Standard work defines the interaction of man and machine. A *standard operation* is the combination of man and machines to carry out production in the most efficient way. Once a procedure is standardized, those who perform it can do so in the same manner as anyone else. That is, no variation occurs in the process.

There are many benefits to be gained from standard work. Once a procedure is standardized, for example, the procedure serves as the foundation for all future improvements to the process. Without standardization, there is no effective way to improve a process because too much variation occurs—it's like trying to hit a moving target. Another benefit of standard work is its value in managing a production process. Scheduling and manning requirements become easier to manage because standard work calculations clearly indicate manning and machine capacity.

The final result of standard work is a significant reduction in labor. Its real worth, however, comes from the steps that produce the final result. Specifically, a company learns to distinguish what is value-added from what is non-value-added, and also what is normal from what is abnormal. These are the elements that truly drive overhead cost reductions.

Components of standard work

The three components of standard work are:

1. *Takt* time;
2. Work procedures (work sequence); and
3. Standard work-in-process.

A discussion of each component follows.

Takt time

Takt is a Japanese word that means "baton"—as in the baton that a drum major uses to set the beat for others to follow. *Takt* time is the beat a factory should follow; it is the most fundamental element of standard work. *Takt* time is defined as follows:

$$\textit{Takt time} = \frac{\text{Time available per shift}}{\text{Sold units}}$$

In this equation, *time available* recognizes productive time available for making a product. This could be expressed in minutes or seconds. *Sold units* reinforce the concept of making only what is needed. No overproduction occurs, because units produced are driven by demand.

A JIT cell that makes a product with a *takt* time of 75 seconds must complete one unit every 75 seconds. In other words, one finished unit must come off the end of the line (or cell) every 75 seconds. If the product cannot be made within the required *takt* time, customer requirements are not met. Note that *takt* time is *customer driven*. If an operator has more than 75 seconds of work to do within a given cycle, the cell will not be able to meet the required *takt* time. Note that each operator's cycle time must be at or slightly below the *takt* time to meet customer demand.

Work procedures (work sequence)

The term *work procedures* refers to the order in which an operator performs work—for example, the order in which an operator brings material, loads it on a machine, then unloads the piece afterward.

A work procedure must define every detail as clearly as possible. There should be no room left for second guessing. If a work procedure is not clear, each operator may perform a task differently. Even the same operator may deviate from cycle to cycle. With well-defined work procedures, a worker will make higher-quality parts with less variation.

Note that an operator sequence may or may not be the same as the process sequence. In a standard operation, it is possible for an operator to start with the first operation in the cell, then move immediately to the last operation in the cell, while other cell members complete the remaining operations. In standard work, the concern is with the operator, not the process flow.

Standard work-in-process

The term *standard work-in-process* refers to parts left on a machine so that an operator can continue to the next operation. Every machine will have at least one piece of standard work-in-process.

what to change or when. As the business changes, however, the necessity to change the management accounting system should become evident.

There are certain risks, however. In a JIT implementation, the profit and loss statement based on traditional accounting approaches will suffer. For example, as inventory is reduced, unfavorable absorption variances will initially distort the true cost of production. Additional expense will also be incurred for rearrangement and plant cleanup. This negative P&L impact could lead to the demise of the JIT program if management does not fully understand and support the adoption of JIT. This is where management accountants earn their pay. They must explain the difference between the negative "accounting" effects incurred during a JIT implementation and the true operational results.

As JIT is implemented, it becomes clear that traditional accounting systems come in conflict with JIT. There is no one best solution to this problem, but understanding the necessity for changes to a company's systems is the first step on the road to *kaizen*. The goal is to improve these systems and bring them into harmony with JIT. A company that truly believes in *kaizen* necessarily accepts that its systems will never be perfect. But the pursuit of perfection should motivate us to change rather than to maintain the status quo. ▲

The ABC/JIT Costing Continuum

John B. MacArthur

Many companies are striving to be competitive in the global marketplace. Just-in-time (JIT) manufacturing and activity-based costing (ABC) are two important innovations of recent years to help companies attain world-class status. This article argues that, although JIT and ABC have common elements (in particular, the analysis of activities), they are basically alternative approaches to dealing with some of the problems that complex, multiproduct companies face by having to operate in highly competitive markets.

Activity-based costing (ABC) and just-in-time (JIT) manufacturing are complementary to a degree. The search for cost drivers under ABC, for example, should lead to the identification of non-value-added activities that can be reduced or even eliminated, and much the same thing happens under JIT production and JIT purchasing systems. However, ABC was originally designed to improve the accuracy of product costing;[1] the identification of non-value-added activities is an almost incidental—albeit important—side benefit. By contrast, JIT was conceived as a method for eliminating all forms of wasteful activity in an organization.[2]

JIT is best suited for the manufacture of "closely related standardized products" in which homogeneity (rather than heterogeneity) is a dominant characteristic of the output.[3] The implementation of JIT manufacturing in such production environments should reduce the need for complex ABC systems with multiple cost drivers to allocate indirect costs. Indeed, JIT or backflush costing systems that support JIT purchasing and production tend to be far less complex than even traditional costing systems.[4] In a full-blown JIT purchasing and production environment, therefore, an intricate ABC system might well be considered a redundant, non-value-added activity that should be considered a candidate for elimination.

Similar objectives

Both JIT and ABC are intended to help organizations become more globally competitive. JIT is a strategic response to increased competitive pressure by the manufacturing and purchasing functions, whereas ABC is an accounting contribution to the cause. In fact, one of the side benefits of ABC is that it enables accountants and production personnel to communicate on a common wavelength because of its emphasis on identifying and costing production activities (and, often, marketing and administrative activities as well). Managers who are not accountants recognize the strategic usefulness of this cost information, because they face fierce competition. This feature of ABC may be particularly useful during the early stages of implementing JIT in an organization. An ABC pilot cost driver study could be conducted as part of the JIT start-up phase even if its usefulness may ultimately be short-lived.

Increasing indirect costs

In their own ways, JIT and ABC both respond to the allocation problem caused by the increasing proportion of indirect costs to total production costs. In general, indirect costs have increased in past decades as a proportion of the total costs of businesses because of the increased use of sophisticated technology and because of systematic reductions in direct labor costs. Indirect costs have also increased because of the many support services needed to cope with the increased complexity of multiproduct companies.

Exhibit 1. *Comparison of JIT and ABC Approaches to the Modern Manufacturing Environment*

JIT	ABC
• Reduce complexity through dedicated product work cells, standardization of parts and components, and reduction or elimination of inventory and other non-value-added activities.	• Reduction or elimination of non-value-added activities as they are identified.
• Reorganize service activities as direct to work cells, thereby reducing the significance of indirect cost allocation.	• Allocate increasingly significant indirect costs using proper cost drivers.
• Use simplified "backflush" costing.	• Use complex ABC costing.
• Use standard costs to support bidding and pricing.	• Use accurate ABC costs to guide bidding and pricing.

The JIT solution

The JIT solution is to group more of the production, sales, and administration functions by product lines so that they become direct costs of particular work cells. In addition, service work (including repair and maintenance, quality control inspection, and routine paperwork) are undertaken by the work cell of each product line rather than by separate service departments that formerly formed part of the overhead costs of production.

For many companies that adopt JIT, it would not be cost-beneficial to allocate the lesser amounts of the remaining common, unallocated costs to the product lines by means of sophisticated ABC allocation bases. In addition, the homogeneity within each product line permits each such cost object to allocate its costs to individual products using such simple bases as process hours, flow-through time, material value, and individual cost per unit.[5] In essence, therefore, JIT eliminates the problem of increasing overhead costs through the reorganization of operations, one result of which is to classify more costs as direct, at least at the product line level.

The ABC solution

ABC is, in a sense, a designed response to the increasing significance of indirect costs and the concomitant decreasing importance of direct labor costs. ABC also responds to the increasing complexity of multiproduct companies. For such companies, simple volume-based allocation methods no longer provide sufficiently accurate product costs to guide managers in setting prices and in other strategic decision making. With the increasing availability of computer power in the 1980s, more sophisticated ABC costing systems were designed to overcome the allocation problems caused by simplistic traditional cost systems. For example, Robin Cooper described the ABC systems of six manufacturing companies that use unit-level (e.g., machine hours), batch-level (e.g., setup hours), product-level (e.g., number of shipments made), and facility-level (e.g., dollars/value added) cost drivers to assign indirect costs to products.[6] The ABC systems of the six companies replaced their conventional cost systems that used unit-level allocation bases only (typically, direct labor). The ABC response to the allocation dilemma was, therefore, to increase the complexity of cost accounting, whereas the JIT solution involves the simplification of operations, which thereby eliminates the problem of inaccurate allocations.

Activity analysis for different reasons

The JIT and ABC philosophies both require the analysis of production and other operational activities, but the reasons for doing the analyses differ. JIT aims to simplify and standardize value-added activities and to reorganize production and purchasing units to eliminate wasteful activities (e.g., setup time and moving time). The establishment of work cells based on product lines can be viewed as the creation of minifactories within greater factories. The purpose of having work cells is to convert a complex, multiproduct environment into various simpler subunits based on product lines. These minifactories are akin to the manufacturing companies more typical at the turn of the century for which traditional costing systems were originally designed.

On the other hand, the purpose of identifying operational activities under ABC is to more accurately determine the causes of the organization's costs. This facilitates more accurate allocation of costs in a multiproduct environment where products receive different amounts of attention. Activities are the basic cost objectives,[7] and the cost of resources they consume can be allocated to products by means of appropriate activity drivers that measure the products' consumption of the activities. In addition, any wasteful activities that are identified can be handled as under a JIT system.

Conclusion

Many companies are striving to be competitive in the global marketplace. JIT and ABC are two important innovations of recent years to help companies attain world-class status. JIT and ABC have some common elements, such as the analysis of activities, but they are basically alternative approaches to dealing with some of the problems encountered by complex, multiproduct companies that operate in highly competitive markets. Two major difficulties that are both addressed by the use of JIT and ABC are:

1. The identification of the true cost of products or services; and
2. The need to run cost-efficient operations.

Exhibit 1 provides a summary comparison of the contrasting ways that JIT and ABC help address these problems in the modern manufacturing environment.

Companies with relatively homogeneous products or product groupings can choose

between JIT and ABC. However, companies that operate at the heterogeneous end of the product continuum may not be able to implement full-blown JIT purchasing and production systems. ABC may be a cost-beneficial way to help such companies become world-class competitors in the global marketplace. ▲

Notes
1. See, e.g., "John Deere Component Works (A)," *Harvard Business School Case 9-187-07* (Rev. 11/87) and "John Deere Component Works (B)," *Harvard Business School Case 9-187-08* (Rev. 11/87). These cases describe a pioneer ABC study that was prompted by the need to improve the accuracy of product costing to improve competitive bidding.
2. See, e.g., George Foster and Charles T. Horngren, "Cost Accounting and Cost Management in a JIT Environment," in *Emerging Practices in Cost Management*, ed. Barry J. Brinker (Boston: Warren, Gorham & Lamont, 1990): 200.
3. Charles T. Horngren and G. Foster, *Cost Accounting: A Managerial Emphasis*, 6th ed. (Englewood Cliffs, N.J.: Prentice-Hall, 1987): 583–584.
4. See examples of cost accounting in a JIT environment in Charles T. Horngren and George Foster, "JIT: Cost Accounting and Cost Management Issues," *Management Accounting* (September 1987): 19–25, and a detailed description of the Harley-Davidson backflush costing system in William T. Turk, "Management Accounting Revitalized: The Harley-Davidson Experience," *Journal of Cost Management* (Winter 1990): 28–39.
5. These allocation bases were considered by Harley-Davidson, as outlined in William T. Turk, "Management Accounting Revitalized: The Harley-Davidson Experience" *Journal of Cost Management* (Winter 1990): 36.
6. Robin Cooper, "Cost Classification in Unit-Based and Activity-Based Manufacturing Cost Systems," *Journal of Cost Management* (Fall 1990): 4–14.
7. See the description of activities as the fundamental cost objects or cost objectives in an ABC system in Charles T. Horngren and George Foster, *Cost Accounting: A Managerial Emphasis*, 7th ed., (Englewood Cliffs, N.J.: Prentice-Hall, 1991): 150–158.

The Effect of JIT on Management Accounting

Dan W. Swenson and Judith Cassidy

Many large manufacturers in the fabrication and assembly industries have implemented innovative manufacturing systems, notably just-in-time (JIT) manufacturing. This article reports the results of a survey about the adoption of JIT by U.S. manufacturing firms, including the use of material requirements planning (MRP) before and after adoption of JIT. Moreover, since a successful conversion to JIT requires cooperation between the production and management accounting functions, this article discusses how innovative manufacturing systems affect the role of management accountants.

In recent years, many manufacturers have adopted innovative manufacturing systems. Enthusiasts claim that implementing a just-in-time (JIT) manufacturing system leads to better quality, less inventory, and shorter product lead times, all at a lower cost.[1] Quality becomes an important concern in a JIT plant because of the disruptive effects of quality problems on a production line. Therefore, such quality-awareness programs as statistical process control (SPC) are often employed in conjunction with JIT to help eliminate product defects and the associated costs of scrap, rework, inspection, and customer returns.

Benefits of JIT and effect on management accounting

JIT manufacturing leads to reduced raw material and work-in-process (WIP) inventories. As vendors become approved as JIT suppliers, raw material requirements are minimized through smaller and more frequent deliveries. JIT also emphasizes reduction in setup time,

which makes the economical introduction of smaller lot sizes possible. This results in less WIP inventory. Faster setups and less WIP shortens the manufacturing cycle time. Thus, a JIT manufacturer becomes more responsive to customer needs by shortening product lead times.

A successful conversion to JIT requires cooperation between the production and management accounting functions. Unfortunately, management accountants are sometimes viewed as impediments to the adoption of innovative manufacturing techniques.

For example, as responsiveness to customers becomes more important, traditional accounting measures of efficiency and utilization become irrelevant to supporting internal business decisions.[2] Emphasis on efficiency and machine utilization, for example, encourages the building of inventory beyond what is needed to fill current customer orders. Management accountants therefore need to design accounting systems that monitor both financial measures (e.g., cost of quality) and nonfinancial measures (e.g., setup time, throughput, and vendor performance).

How successfully have U.S. manufacturers implemented innovative manufacturing techniques like JIT? And how have these new systems affected the role of the management accountant? The survey discussed in this article addresses these questions.

Description of survey

To evaluate how innovative manufacturing systems have worked, a sample of twenty-two U.S. manufacturing plants was selected from the *Directory of Corporate Affiliations*.[3] The twenty-two firms included:

- Eleven machinery firms;
- Seven transportation firms;
- Two computer firms; and
- Two consumer products firms.

Exhibit 1 shows the survey questionnaire. In addition, interviews were conducted to expand on respondents' answers to the written questions. The interviews helped avoid misunderstandings and also cleared up any questions the respondents had.

Summary results

The firms (which were interviewed in the summer of 1990) began converting to JIT manufacturing about four years before the survey was conducted (see Exhibit 2). The average firm had converted 63 percent of its plant operations and inventory systems to JIT at the time of the survey.

Nineteen of the twenty-two firms, or 86 percent, used material requirements planning (MRP) before implementing JIT. After converting to JIT, all except one of the firms (95 percent) used MRP. The one firm that discontinued MRP went exclusively to a *kanban* system. ("Kanban" is a Japanese word that means "display" or "instruction card." In a factory setting, a *kanban* is a card that describes a part number, a quantity of parts, where parts are from, where the parts are to be delivered, and the like.)

Sixty-four percent of the firms (fourteen out of twenty-two) required no changes (two) or only minor changes (twelve) to their materials planning and control software following adoption of JIT. Similarly, 64 percent also reported either no change (one) or less complex (thirteen) materials planning and control information requirements.

Cost accounting and performance measurement systems. As Exhibit 2 shows, the cost accounting systems that the firms used varied from job order costing to process costing. Two of the firms used a hybrid of the two types of cost systems. Eight companies converted from job order to process costing after implementing JIT. Seventy-three percent (sixteen) of the firms reported having less complex accounting information requirements following the adoption of JIT.

The firms' performance measurement systems recorded scrap and rework reductions of 44 percent, setup reductions of 47 percent, and inventory reductions of 46 percent after implementing JIT. Seventy-seven percent (seventeen) of the firms reported having less complex performance measurement systems after adopting JIT.

Plant operations and inventory systems. As Exhibit 3 shows, the assembly firms had been using JIT only slightly longer than the fabrication firms. Yet each of the eight assembly plants converted an average of 81 percent of their operations to JIT. This compares with a 51 percent conversion to JIT by each of the fourteen fabricating plants. Thus, the assemblers converted to JIT much more rapidly than the fabricators.

Analysis of the data shows a statistically significant difference between the fabricators and assemblers based on how quickly they converted to JIT. The differences are significant at an alpha of .05, using the Student t-test statistic.

Comparison between assembly and fabrication

Traditionally, JIT techniques have been applied to high-speed repetitive manufacturing. Repetitive processes adapt well to JIT manufacturing because of predictable process times and parts movements that can be synchronized for continuous flow. Assembly operations generally fit this description.[4] Furthermore, assembly lines generally have minimal machine setup requirements. Synchronized, continuous production processes, when combined with small lot sizes, results in minimal WIP inventory, which is a necessary condition for JIT.

Fabrication generally involves more complex production processes and longer machine setups than assembly. Yet processes that require fabrication vary considerably in their manufacturing patterns. At one extreme are job shops, which receive only unique orders and thus have unpredictable manufacturing patterns. Such job shop operations receive limited benefits from JIT. However, many job shops have some repetitive business that can be separated from unique orders. Equipment dedicated to particular tasks helps eliminate unproductive setups.

Exhibit 1. *Survey Questionnaire*

1. When did your facility first begin implementing just-in-time (JIT) manufacturing techniques?
   Year _____ Month _____

2. How close are you to completing the conversion to JIT in your facility? _____ %

3. Prior to implementing JIT, did your firm use materials requirement planning (MRP)? YES _____ NO _____

4. Is your firm currently using MRP with JIT? YES _____ NO _____

5. To what extent did you have to modify your materials planning and control applications software to implement JIT?
   _____ No modifications
   _____ Minor modifications
   _____ Major modifications
   _____ Required a totally new software package to support JIT
   _____ Not applicable, we do not use materials planning and control software

6. How do your current information requirements compare with your information requirements prior to JIT for each of the following systems:

	Much Less Complex					Much More Complex
Production planning	1	2	3	4	5	6
Production control	1	2	3	4	5	6
Performance measurement	1	2	3	4	5	6

7. How do the record-keeping requirements for your present cost accounting system compare with your record-keeping requirements before JIT?

Much Less Complex					Much More Complex
1	2	3	4	5	6

8. After implementing JIT, some firms eliminate accounting transactions that record the transfer of raw materials to work-in-process. Instead, raw materials are distinguished from work-in-process by periodic physical inventory counts. Has your firm eliminated accounting transactions that record the transfer of raw materials to work in process?
   YES _____ NO _____

9. Indicate the cost accounting system in use at your firm.

	Before JIT	After JIT
Job order	_____	_____
Process	_____	_____
Other (specify)	_____	_____

10. Which of the following performance measures were (are) monitored by your firm? (Check all that apply)

	Before JIT	After JIT
Vendor performance		
Quality	_____	_____
On-time deliveries	_____	_____
Scrap	_____	_____
Rework	_____	_____
Setup times	_____	_____
Labor efficiency	_____	_____
Equipment downtime	_____	_____
Machine utilization	_____	_____

11. How many of your vendors are meeting your requirements for JIT deliveries? _____ %

12. How much have scrap rates been reduced since implementing JIT? _____ %

13. How much has rework time been reduced since implementing JIT? _____ %

14. How much have machine setup times been reduced since you began implementing JIT? _____ %

15. Have you implemented statistical process control in your production facility? YES _____ NO _____

16. How much have you been able to reduce your inventory levels?

Raw materials _____ %   Work in process _____ %
Finished goods _____ %

Exhibit 2. *Interview Summaries*

Mean number of years sampled firms have used JIT	4
Mean percent of operations converted to JIT	63%
Percent of firms using MRP before JIT	86%
Percent of firms currently using MRP along with JIT	95%

Firms with modifications to materials planning and control software following the implementation of JIT:

No change	2
Minor modifications	12
Major modifications	3
New package	5

Complexity of materials planning and control information requirements following the implementation of JIT:

No change	1
Less complex	13
More complex	8

Types of cost accounting systems in use:

	Before JIT	After JIT
Job order	14	6
Process	4	12
A hybrid system	2	2

Complexity of cost accounting system following the implementation of JIT:

Less complex	16
More complex	6

Mean percent of vendors meeting JIT requirements	67%
Mean reduction in scrap and rework following JIT	44%
Mean reduction in setup following JIT	47%
Mean reduction in total inventory following JIT	46%

Complexity of performance measurement system following the implementation of JIT:

Less complex	17
More complex	5

Even if demand for a particular product is insufficient to dedicate equipment to its fabrication, groups of dissimilar equipment in manufacturing cells can often be dedicated to making families of parts that require the same manufacturing sequence.[5] The cycle time for producing small lots of parts in a cell of closely spaced machines is much shorter than for large batches that must move around the factory. A corresponding reduction in WIP inventory follows.

Thus, more creativity is often required to implement JIT for job shops that have fabrication requirements. The added complexity will slow JIT implementations in job shops compared with implementations in pure assembly operations.

The JIT/MRP partnership

Historically, manufacturers have used MRP as an inventory planning and control device. Once firms begin converting to JIT manufacturing, does this mean that MRP is displaced by another system, such as *kanban*? Exhibit 2 shows that more firms use MRP after adopting JIT (95 percent) than before JIT (86 percent).

This supports Karmarkar's belief that "most advanced manufacturing companies find that they require a hybrid of shop floor control systems—tailored systems, including innovative pull systems like kanban, as well as time-tested, computer-driven push systems like MRP."[6]

Exhibit 3. *Breakdown of Firms (Assemblers vs. Fabricators)*

	Assemblers	Fabricators
Number of firms	8	14
Years experience with JIT	4.5	4.3
Percent of operations* converted to JIT	81%	51%

* The difference between the assemblers and fabricators concerning number of operations converted to JIT is significant at an alpha of .05, using the Student t-test statistic.

MRP is a system that schedules purchased and in-house manufactured components and subassemblies as they are needed in each phase of the production process. MRP begins with end-item demand, then "explodes" the entire manufacturing operation into discrete component parts. It schedules purchase orders based on delivery dates and subassemblies based on manufacturing time requirements. Once MRP determines when purchased parts and subassemblies will become available, final assembly can be scheduled.

Extrapolating from projected demand. MRP's strength lies in its ability to project the following:

- External demand;
- The time it takes to meet demand; and
- The materials needed.

MRP coordinates material planning and purchasing. It also monitors a plant's ability to meet the production demand schedule. A fully integrated MRP system is considered a "push" system, because the computer schedules what and how much to produce at each work center throughout the plant. Production is initiated when material from an upstream work center is pushed to the next work center downstream. The downstream worker will generally continue to process parts as long as they are supplied.

Push vs. pull. The point at which MRP releases work orders is where many JIT firms depart from MRP. Instead of pushing work through, the work centers operate using a "pull" system, such as *kanban*. A pull system differs from a push system in that machine operators do not produce according to a schedule and material availability. Instead, production does not begin until parts are needed by a downstream operator. A downstream operator "pulls" the parts from an upstream supplier by use of a signal. *Kanban,* for example, is a card system that is used to signal when parts are needed. Once parts are taken, or pulled, by a downstream operator, an upstream supplier produces enough material to replace what was taken. Thus, WIP inventory cannot accumulate over a specified level.

A pull system differs from a push system in that machine operators do not produce according to a schedule and material availability. Instead, production does not begin until parts are needed by a downstream operator.

Cost management systems

One fundamental goal of JIT is simplification—simplification not only of manufacturing processes, but also simplified recordkeeping. To that end, several authors[7] have proposed techniques for eliminating certain accounting transactions. A "backflush" cost accounting system, for example, eliminates transactions to record the movement of raw materials to WIP. In a backflush system, movements of inventory are not reported until finished goods are produced (or, in some cases, actually sold). WIP inventory is updated only after taking a physical count of inventory on the shop floor.

Two moves toward simplification became apparent from the interviews. Eight of the twenty-two firms eliminated accounting transactions for the movement of raw material to WIP after implementing JIT. The eight firms further reduced record-keeping requirements by changing from job order to process costing (see Exhibit 2). As might be expected, 73 percent (sixteen) reported having a less complex cost accounting system following adoption of JIT.

Traditional cost accounting

A backflush cost accounting system may eliminate inventory transactions used for external reporting, but it does little to help internal management improve its decision making. Thus, traditional cost accounting systems often fail to provide managers accurate and timely information to promote operational control.

Management accountants should take a broader view of their role. The Institute of Management Accountants and Computer Aided Manufacturing-International[8] advocate using the term "cost management system" rather than the term "cost accounting system"; simply accounting for cost does not imply an ability to influence results. While both concepts recognize the need to identify and accumulate inventory values, cost management requires that financial managers identify performance measures that affect activity costs. Managers can then use these measures to focus on where improvements are necessary.

Management accountants should take an active role in identifying and monitoring critical performance measures, particularly nonfinancial performance measures. Otherwise, the accounting function cannot help provide effective operational control.

Inventory valuation and operational control are two separate functions, with different data base requirements. Thus, as Kaplan argues,[9] more than one cost system is needed.

Operational control systems

Because of the shortcomings of traditional standard cost systems, some production managers have created their own performance measurement systems.[10] Their aim is to better address the issues of customer satisfaction, flexibility, and productivity. These performance measurement systems are generally designed outside the world of management accounting. Significant problems can develop, however, if the performance measurement systems that are used in a company do not agree. For example, a production manager who successfully implements a JIT work cell

and witnesses dramatic improvements in quality, cycle time, and WIP inventory may nonetheless get blamed for poor financial performance because of large volume variances and underabsorbed overhead.

A management accountant must recognize the need for an operational control system that provides manufacturing managers accurate, timely feedback about performance. Cost information plays only a minor role in this function. Nonfinancial performance measures are the heart of an operational control system. The interviews revealed that only one firm did not measure vendor quality and on-time performance. Without exception, all the firms measured scrap and rework. Furthermore, twelve firms had significant setup requirements, and they measured setup costs as well.

Management accounting systems need to focus on cost drivers that have a significant impact on manufacturing costs. As one plant

---

One fundamental goal of JIT is simplification—simplification not only of manufacturing processes, but also simplified recordkeeping.

---

manager commented, "the cost accounting system is next in line to be overhauled." This plant manager made this comment because the performance measures in the accounting system did not correspond with the measures that he felt were important to operational control.

Performance improvements

Every firm reported improved performance after converting to JIT (see Exhibit 2). Specifically, scrap and rework went down by an average of 44 percent. Average machine setup time declined 47 percent, and total inventory fell by an average of 46 percent.

Effective quality control programs are critical to the success of JIT. An important characteristic of JIT production is that once defective parts are discovered, production comes to a halt until the cause of the problem is discovered and corrected. Parts cannot be produced downstream after the limited WIP is exhausted. Production upstream also stops since there is no "pull" from the producer of the defective part. Instead, the entire production line focuses on determining the cause of the problem, then correcting it. With the attention of the entire production line focused on the problem, workers are no longer tempted to apply the "quick fix" mentality. The operator is more likely to focus on continuous improvement to prevent problems from occurring in the first place, thus preventing the unwelcome attention that arises from shutting down the production line.

Effective quality controls also help minimize WIP inventory, because large WIP inventories are not needed to buffer the plant from disruptions caused by poor quality. If an operator discovers a defect from a previous operation and the defect is addressed immediately, only a few parts are at risk of being scrapped. But if a large buffer of WIP inventory exists, and parts from the previous operation prove to be defective, many more parts must be scrapped.

Scrap and rework. As Exhibit 2 shows, scrap and rework went down by an average of 44 percent after adoption of JIT. Generally, the firms implemented a formal quality control program before attempting JIT production. All the firms implemented SPC before JIT was adopted or in conjunction with the adoption of JIT. Without excellent quality, WIP inventory buffers are difficult to reduce because of the line stoppages that occur when defective parts are discovered.

Exhibit 4 shows a positive correlation between the percent of manufacturing operations converted to JIT and the amount of scrap and rework reduction. As more plant operations are converted to JIT, a decline in scrap and rework occurs.

Cost of quality programs

Development of a formal cost of quality program is an excellent way for management accountants to help manufacturing management. A cost of quality program divides quality costs into four categories:
1. External failure costs;
2. Internal failure costs;

Exhibit 4. *Correlation Coefficients*

	Percent of Plant Operations Converted to JIT
Percent reduction in scrap and rework	.52*
Percent reduction in setup time	.52*
Percent reduction in total inventory	.48*

Interpretation: Firms with more manufacturing operations converted to JIT are able to reduce scrap, rework, setup time, and inventory more than other firms.

	Percent of Vendors That Qualify as JIT Suppliers
Percent reduction in raw materials inventory	.85**

Interpretation: Firms with more vendors who qualify as JIT suppliers are able to reduce raw materials more than other firms.

	Percent Reduction in Scrap and Rework
Percent reduction in work-in-process inventory	.69**

Interpretation: Firms with less scrap and rework are able to reduce WIP more than other firms.

* Significant at alpha = .05.
** Significant at alpha = .01.
Note: These numbers refer to correlation coefficients. For example, .00 would indicate no correlation; 1.00 would indicate perfect correlation. The first correlation coefficient (.52) refers to the correlation between the percent of plant operations converted to JIT, and the percent reduction in scrap and rework. In this Exhibit all correlation coefficients are statistically significant.

3. Appraisal or detection costs; and
4. Prevention costs.
External and internal failure costs are the most difficult to measure, yet they are the most costly. External failure costs occur when defective products are sold to consumers, which leads to warranty adjustments, returned goods, and customer ill-will. Internal failure costs are the result of scrap, rework, and the resulting down time.

Appraisal activities are meant to limit exposure to product failure. Most appraisal costs have to do with receiving and WIP inspection procedures. Finally, prevention includes a broad category of activities whose purpose is to limit the occurrence of all other quality-related costs. Quality engineering, quality training, and SPC activities are examples of prevention costs.

JIT emphasizes the need to shift quality control activities toward prevention. Firms often find that resources invested in prevention are more than offset by reductions in appraisal, internal failure, and external failure costs. The ultimate goal is to invest adequate resources in a prevention program to eliminate the need for product inspections and to reduce product failures to a negligible level (e.g., a few parts per million).

Setup reduction

Exhibit 2 shows that the average time required for machine setups fell by 47 percent (the decreases in the firms ranged from 3 percent to 90 percent). Setup reductions are more important to fabricating operations than they are for assembly. Seventy-seven percent of the fabricators reported that setup labor is an important component of direct labor and that setup reduction is a necessary element in WIP inventory reduction. Once setup time is reduced, a firm can reduce lot sizes and thus lower WIP throughout the plant. Exhibit 4 shows a positive relationship between the percent of operations converted to JIT and the reduction in setup time.

Only one assembly plant reported that reductions in machine setup times are important. The other assembly operations either have minor setup requirements or have machines that are dedicated to the same repetitive processes. The only exception was a make-to-order assembly plant that reduced setup time by 90 percent. In addition to reducing direct labor, a make-to-order environment can use setup reduction and smaller lot sizes as a competitive weapon by reducing customer lead time. Setup time is an important nonfinancial performance measure that management accountants should recognize.

Inventory reduction

As Exhibit 2 shows, total inventories fell an average of 46 percent among the manufacturers surveyed. As Exhibit 4 shows, there was a positive correlation between the percent of

operations converted to JIT and reductions in inventory.

Raw materials

A breakdown of inventory into raw materials and WIP highlights other significant relationships. As Exhibit 4 shows, a strong, positive correlation exists between the percent of vendors that qualify as JIT suppliers and the reduction in raw materials inventory. As more vendors begin to ship JIT, fewer raw materials need to be warehoused.

Reductions in raw materials often involve cost trade-offs. Having less raw material frees up working capital and warehouse space; it can also reduce material handling, especially if vendors deliver directly to the production line. These savings may be offset, however, by the additional freight costs of more frequent deliveries and vendor charges for maintaining more inventory at their warehouse.

Work-in-process

A significant relationship was also found between scrap and rework improvements and WIP inventory. As quality improves, WIP inventory buffers can be reduced. Thus, as expected (see Exhibit 4), a positive correlation was found between reductions in scrap and rework, and reductions in WIP inventory.

As WIP declines, parts move through a plant in less time. With less work in the pipeline, changeovers to new products also occur more quickly. Thus, a manufacturer becomes more responsive to the customer by reducing product lead times. Large WIP inventories create an environment in which the actual time spent working on a product represents a small percentage (perhaps as little as 5 percent) of the production cycle's length.[11] During most of the cycle, the product is being inspected, being moved by material handlers, waiting to be processed in the job queue, or being stored in the stock room as a raw material or a subassembly. Through the elimination of non-value-added activities (i.e., activities not devoted to actually working on a product), a firm can reduce inventory and cycle times, thus becoming more responsive to customers.

Once again, management accountants can provide production managers information to help with operational control. In addition to monitoring such financial performance indicators as inventory levels, accountants can help monitor such important nonfinancial measures as throughput and on-time deliveries.

Conclusion

U.S. manufacturers are responding to the changing demands of the competitive marketplace. This survey shows that improvements in manufacturing effectiveness have been made in the areas of quality, inventory reduction, and customer responsiveness.

Many respondents mentioned the need for continuous improvement. Continuous improvement applies to the accounting function as well as to the manufacturing function. Management accountants must take an active role in the implementation of innovative manufacturing systems; otherwise, the accounting function will be an impediment to innovation. An effective cost management system must help management accountants become key players in the drive for continuous improvement. ▲

Reprinted from *Journal of Cost Management*, Spring 1993, pp. 39–47. Copyright © 1993 by

Notes
1. See R.D. McIlhattan, "The Path to Total Cost Management," *Journal of Cost Management* (Summer 1987): 5–10, and R.A. Howell and S.R. Soucy, "Operating Controls in the New Manufacturing Environment," *Management Accounting* (Oct. 1987): 25–31.
2. K. Cross and R. Lynch, "Accounting for Competitive Performance," *Journal of Cost Management* (Spring 1989): 20–28.
3. *Directory of Corporate Affiliations* (Wilmette, Ill.: National Register Publishing Company, Inc., 1990).
4. U. Karmarkar, "Getting Control of Just-In-Time," *Harv. Bus. Rev.* (Sept.-Oct. 1989): 122–131.
5. R. Walleigh, "Getting Things Done," *Harv. Bus. Rev.* (Mar.-Apr. 1986): 38–54.
6. Karmarkar, "Getting Control of Just-In-Time": 122–131.
7. See C. Horngren and G. Foster, *Cost Accounting: A Managerial Emphasis* (Englewood Cliffs, N.J.: Prentice-Hall, 1991): 627, and H.J. Johansson, "Preparing for Accounting System Changes," *Management Accounting* (July 1990): 37–41.
8. C. Berliner and J.A. Brimson, eds., *Cost Management for Today's Advanced Manufacturing* (Boston: Harvard Business School Press, 1988): Ch. 1.
9. R.S. Kaplan, "One Cost System Isn't Enough," *Harv. Bus. Rev.* (Jan.-Feb. 1988): 61–66.
10. C.J. McNair, R.L. Lynch, and K.F. Cross, "Do Financial and Nonfinancial Performance Measures Have to Agree?," *Management Accounting* (Nov. 1990): 28–36.
11. "The Path to Total Cost Management": 5–10, and R. Walleigh, "Getting Things Done," *Harv. Bus. Rev.* (Mar.-Apr. 1986): 38–54.

Activity-Based Costing in Cellular Manufacturing Systems

Dileep G. Dhavale

This article presents an activity-based costing model based on process characteristics of cellular manufacturing systems. The model reflects typical relationships between parameters of a cellular manufacturing system. The article provides rationales behind different components of the model so that users can modify the model to represent any cellular manufacturing environment. Finally, the article discusses an actual application of the model at a Fortune 200 company.

To receive the most benefits from new manufacturing, engineering, and management concepts, users must adopt the philosophy of *group technology*. Simply stated, group technology entails solving problems by:

1. Identifying differentiating characteristics in a set of elements;
2. Forming subsets of the elements that exhibit similar characteristics; and
3. Exploiting similarities within a subset to obtain a solution.

Even though this idea of concentrating on commonality within a group may appear unsophisticated, impressive results have been obtained.[1]

Group technology has many different facets, much of which is beyond the scope of this article.[2] Nonetheless, one facet of group technology—the grouping of products or parts with similar processing requirements—forms the basis for developing cells in cellular manufacturing systems. After a brief description of cellular manufacturing, this article investigates activity-based costing (ABC) in such a system.

Cellular manufacturing

Cellular manufacturing is an innovative production method that can help solve the problems caused by the inherent inefficiencies of batch production. These inefficiencies result from the operational characteristics of the type of factories that are used to manufacture products in batches—job shops. The following sections explain job shops and then define cellular manufacturing.

Job shops. A job shop makes many different products whose mix and demands are, for the most part, unknown until orders are actually received. A job shop must thus maintain a variety of general-purpose machines, which are usually physically segregated into departments, according to their functions. But this mode of operation creates enormous scheduling difficulties, because process planners must first determine the least-cost method for processing a given batch, then the appropriate machine routing, based on machine capacities and prior loading.

Sometimes costly substitute machines may have to be used at bottlenecks. These scheduling problems create delays. Indeed, it is estimated that some 90 percent of throughput time is spent waiting in queues for machines to become available.[3] As each machine completes a batch, it must be prepared for the next batch by (for example) changing tooling, fixtures, and dies. Such setups are time consuming and costly, and they reduce productive time. Job shops also expend considerable effort in transporting batches between departments according to machine routings. Cellular manufacturing overcomes these problems and provides many other benefits that result in enhanced efficiency and cost savings.

Definition of cellular manufacturing. Application of the group technology principle to a job shop environment suggests that parts with similar machining requirements should be grouped together and manufactured together. Such groupings are known as *part families*.

Since products in a part family have similar machining requirements, they can be manufactured sequentially without much setup change, and their flow is generally unidirectional. When machines required to manufacture a part family are physically laid out in the appropriate sequence as a production line, a *cell* is formed. A *cellular manufacturing system* consists of several such cells that manufacture a range of part families.

Classifying manufactured parts. Several steps are necessary to transform a job shop operation into a cellular manufacturing operation. The first step involves application of a classification scheme to all manufactured parts.

A classification scheme consists of assigning an alphanumeric code for each part. The character values in the code are determined by properties of a part. These properties may include such factors as:

- Material used;
- Shape;
- Size;
- Finish; and
- Tolerance.

Commercially marketed schemes are available, and others have been developed by universities and professional associations.[4]

Many benefits accrue immediately from the classification and coding of parts. Some of these benefits include:

- Improved design retrieval;
- Elimination of duplicate design;
- Standardization of parts;
- Identification of inconsistent manufacturing processes;
- Lower estimating costs;
- Standardization of process for a family of parts;
- Analysis of the capacity of existing machine tools;
- Improved product mix; and
- Better knowledge of the requirements of new machines.[5]

These benefits are made possible by a computer's ability to retrieve, manipulate, sort, group, identify, and organize the part codes in any fashion desired.

Process planning. The next step in transforming a job shop operation into a cellular manufacturing operation is process planning, which involves analyzing the processing requirements of each part to determine which machines should perform the job.[6]

Once the processing requirements are known, each part can be grouped into families based on similarities. Several methods, which differ in terms of the criteria and assumptions used to detect similarities, have been devised to group parts into families.[7]

Identifying machines needed. The last step involved in transforming a job shop into cellular manufacturing is identifying the machines needed to process part families and determining their optimal configurations. Production lines can then be formed such that each line (i.e., a cell) manufactures a part family.

Since only similar parts are manufactured in a cell, setup times are dramatically reduced by designing tooling and fixtures appropriate for the whole part family. The setup efficiency and production efficiency can be further enhanced by purchasing special-purpose machine tools. The insignificant time required to change production from one part to the other makes efficient manufacturing of very small batches economical.

Reduction in setup effort. This reduction in setup effort is the crucial requirement of the new manufacturing concepts, such as flexible manufacturing system, computer-aided manufacturing, and the just-in-time philosophy.[8] Products can thus be manufactured only in the quantities needed and when they are needed, one result of which is the virtual elimination of work-in-process and finished goods inventories. In other words, the full benefits of computer-aided manufacturing systems cannot be achieved without implementing the group technology philosophy to create manufacturing cells.

Other benefits of cellular manufacturing include the following:

- Sizable reductions in transportation costs of parts within the shop because the parts no longer have to be taken from a machine in one department to a machine in some other department for processing;
- Improved quality and reduction in scrap because of the expertise developed by workers who produce similar parts;
- Drastically reduced throughput times, which lead to superior on-time performance; and
- Uncomplicated scheduling of parts.

Scope of the model

The model that this article develops determines manufacturing costs incurred in the production of parts in cellular manufacturing using ABC and generally accepted accounting principles (GAAP). Thus, the inventory and cost of goods sold valuations from this model are acceptable for external reporting purposes. Adherence to GAAP makes users far more likely to accept this method.

It should be noted, however, that this model may not always provide the best decision-making tool possible in all circumstances because it ignores opportunity costs, which are useful in portraying decision alternatives and their impact. Opportunity costs of unused capacity, idle machines, defective parts, and suboptimal routings due to bottlenecks have all been used in operations research models for cellular manufacturing.[9] Including opportunity costs in product costs would violate GAAP, because opportunity costs are not based on actual transactions.

Types of cellular manufacturing systems.
Cellular manufacturing systems differ considerably in practice, depending on such factors as:

- Types of products manufactured;
- Degree of automation achieved in cells;
- Degree of adherence to the group technology philosophy;
- Deviations from preferred processes due to lack of machine capacity; and
- Mix of cellular manufacturing and job shop routing.

Modifications to the model developed here will probably be necessary before it can be applied. These modifications could be in the form of eliminating, adding, or combining resource or activity drivers, cost pools, or activity centers. Other modifications could include changing some cost flows to represent the operating conditions at the site in question.

The complexity of an ABC system depends on such factors as the number of resource or activity drivers and cost pools. The complexity increases in direct proportion to product and process diversity of a manufacturing operation. In cellular manufacturing, however, similarities in products processed in a cell and the operational simplicity of the system make it easier to form homogeneous cost pools, which help reduce the complexity of an ABC system.

An ABC cellular manufacturing model

The model developed here does not assume that the factory converts completely to cells (i.e., a pure cellular manufacturing environment) but allows for the coexistence of cells and a job shop (i.e., a mixed cellular manufacturing environment).

Most companies that have converted from a job shop toward cellular manufacturing indicate that the change is gradual. Product families are switched over as cells are formed either by relocating or dedicating the required machines. Even after the conversion is complete, many companies continue to maintain a job shop (albeit on a much smaller scale), because some parts cannot be categorized into families and thus must continue being made the old-fashioned way. A job shop also maintains flexibility by providing alternate routings for bottleneck machines in the cells. Consequently, the model given here assumes several cells and a job shop.

Unidirectional routing. The preferred routing of batches in a cell is unidirectional, but the model presented in this article does not restrict routing to one sequence. Many companies operate following the principle of cellular manufacturing, but without physically rearranging machines into separate cells. This avoids the cost of a new layout of machines, but transportation costs, supervisory costs, and the like are higher than they would be if the layout were improved. The model allows for these variations.

Exhibit 1 shows a schematic diagram of a mixed cellular manufacturing system that includes many cells (three of which are shown) and a job shop. Even though the exhibit shows physically separated cells with unidirectional parts flow, the model (as just described) represents a more general situation.

Exhibit 2 shows a schematic diagram of the proposed ABC model for a mixed cellular manufacturing. The first column shows fifteen different manufacturing overhead resources used in the production of parts. As the resources are used, their costs are allocated to the units (the last column) through intermediate resource and activity drivers and pools. These resource and activity drivers and pools were identified after a thorough study of the operational aspects of group technology and cellular manufacturing, and based on visits to companies that use these techniques. The objective of this study was to develop a detailed yet general model that can be modified or simplified to fit any cellular manufacturing site.

Capital outlays vs. recurring expenses. The resources shown in Exhibit 2 are identified as either *capital* (C) outlays or *recurring* (R) expenses. Of the two resource drivers shown, both are used for creating cost pools for machines. Capital outlay costs are allocated by either resource or activity drivers based on expected activity levels over the economic life of an asset. To allocate recurring expenses, on the other hand, expected activity levels for one-year periods are used. By keeping these costs separate, a clearer causal relationship is shown between the activities and the drivers, and the model is simpler to understand and operate. This is analogous to not mixing cost of an asset and its routine maintenance expense.

Activity centers. Activity centers play an important role in cost control, because resources costs are first pooled at each activity center. This pooling of costs gives managers data for planning and controlling activities and for measuring the performance of the activity centers.

An activity center may have one or more cost pools. For example, the activity center "each machine" has two cost pools: one collects capital outlays and the other recurring expenses. "Each cell" and "each part" are activity centers with one cost pool each. The cost pool "each cell" collects recurring expenses, whereas the cost pool "each part" collects only capital outlays.

Three cost pools are called *central pools*. In a pure cellular manufacturing environment in which machines have been reconfigured into cells, the central pools will not exist; instead, the activity center "each cell" will have additional cost pools. For the purpose of applying the model, the job shop is viewed as an additional cell. Thus, if a site has four cells and a job shop, computations will be based on five cells.

Activity drivers. Activity drivers are used to allocate costs from cost pools to a batch of parts based on the consumption of resources by that batch at each activity center. Each cost pool has exactly one activity driver associated with it. Seven cost pools are shown in Exhibit 2 but only five activity drivers, because the activity driver "direct materials cost for a batch" is shared by three pools. Once the manufacturing cost per batch is known, the calculation of unit costs is straightforward.

In the following sections, rationales and relationships between the model components and costs flows are explained, so that users may determine any modifications needed for particular cellular manufacturing operations.

Resources

This section explains the fifteen resources listed in the left-hand column of Exhibit 2.

1. Machine and its dedicated tools. This cost includes the purchase cost of a machine and all other costs necessary to get the machine ready for production (e.g., cost of tools and fixtures developed for that machine). In other words, this is the historical cost of the asset as shown on the balance sheet. Each machine is treated as an activity center, and a cost pool A (see Exhibit 2) is created for that machine, and to which this amount is added. As explained earlier, the small letters C and R that characterize each resource and cost pool stand for capital outlay or recurring expenditure, respectively. Cost pools contain only

Exhibit 1. *Schematic Diagram of a Mixed Cellular Manufacturing System*

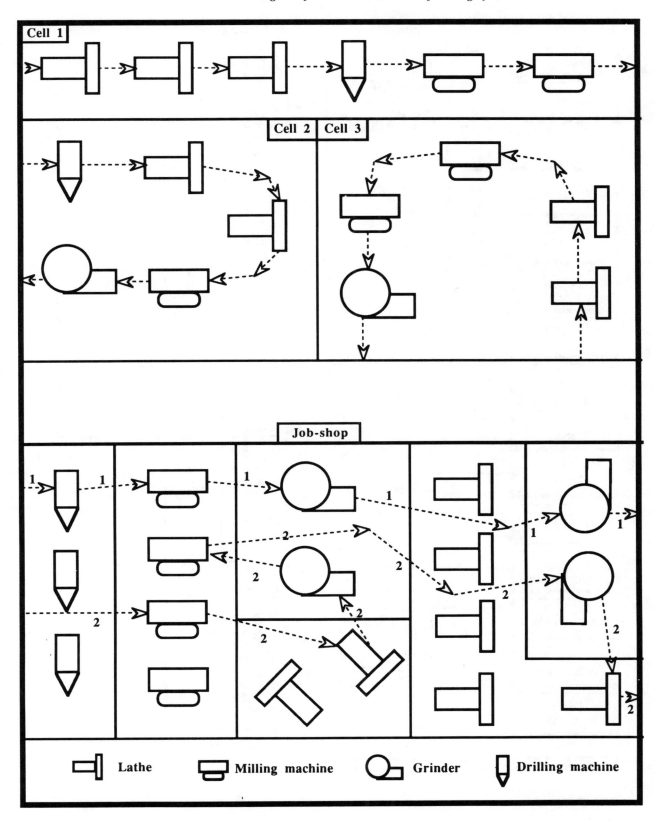

Exhibit 2. *Schematic Diagram of Activity-Based Costing in a Mixed Cellular Manufacturing System*

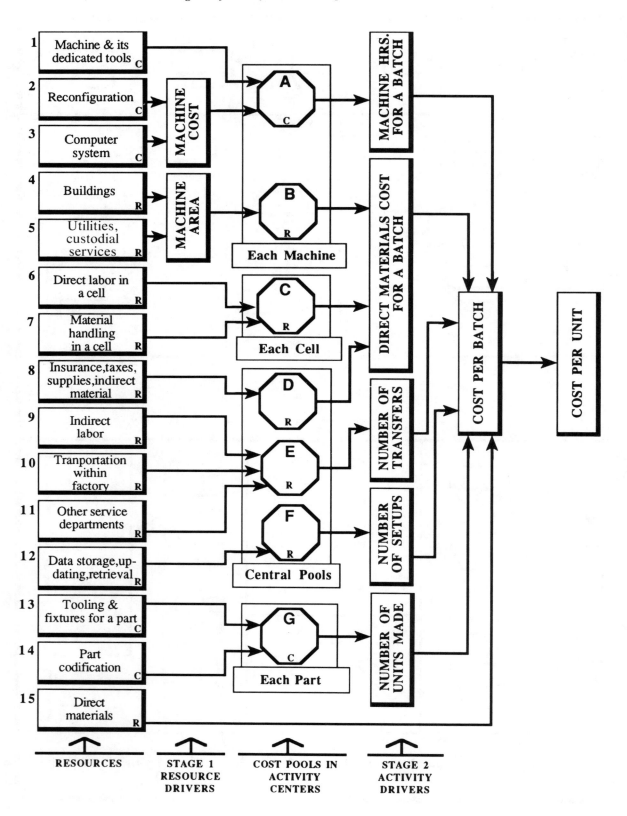

pure capital outlays or only recurring expenditure, never a mixture of the two.

2. *Reconfiguration.* Reconfiguration costs are incurred when existing machines are moved to form cells; included are all costs incurred in getting a machine ready for production at the new location. New machines purchased to be put directly into cells would not incur this cost.

If the cost of moving each machine can be determined, that cost can be directly added to cost pool A. In the absence of such information, the total reconfiguration cost may be allocated to cost pool A in proportion to the historical cost of the machines that were moved. Since this cost can be substantial, some companies opt for a system in which machines are dedicated to a part family but are left scattered throughout the factory instead of being reconfigured into a physical cell. Any savings obtained by such "reconfigurations," however, are nullified by the substantially higher transportation costs incurred, and by the decrease in manufacturing efficiency because of the lack of automation and the higher demands made on labor and supervision.

A reconfigured cell works like a miniassembly line (i.e., a part starts at one end and is completed when it leaves the last machine in the cell). An automatic material handling system may be used to transfer parts efficiently from one machine to the next in the cell. The capital outlays for automatic material handling equipment should be included in reconfiguration cost. Resource 7, Automatic Material Handing in a Cell, is the recurring cost of that system, which is discussed later.

3. *Computer system.* To obtain the maximum advantage from group technology, a computer system is needed to store and manipulate information about part families. This information is useful in design as well as manufacturing phases of the operation.

Computer costs are assigned to cost pool A in proportion to the costs of machines used in a cellular manufacturing. The rationale behind this allocation method is that the computer is an essential part of the machines. Hence (just as in the case of dedicated tools and fixtures of the machines) computer cost should be borne by the machines in proportion to their costs.

4. *Buildings.* Building rent or depreciation expense is allocated to each machine based on its floor work area and is added to cost pool "B," which is also formed for each machine. Hence, each machine has two cost pools, A and B.

5. *Utilities, custodial services.* Costs of utilities and custodial services are also allocated to each machine (based on its floor work area) and added to cost pool B. Although this allocation basis is quite logical for heating and cooling expenses and for custodial services, electrical power consumption may not be exactly proportional to machine areas. Ideally, a meter is used to measure the energy consumption of each machine; the actual expense can then be added directly to the cost pool rather than allocated using a resource driver. If meters are not used, and if none of the machines are intensive energy consumers (e.g., a furnace for heat treatment), the area of a machine is probably a good surrogate for its consumption of energy.

6. *Direct labor in a cell.* Direct labor used to play a dominant role in manufacturing. With increased automation, however, manufacturing has become far less labor intensive. In electronics manufacturing, direct labor costs are reportedly as low as 3 percent.[10] For fully automated flexible manufacturing systems, the range is from 5 percent to 10 percent.[11]

Because of automation, an operator can often look after several machines in a cell that may be working on different batches. This makes it difficult for the operator to allocate his time to batches with any objectivity. Consequently, since direct labor is no longer a prime cost, it becomes difficult to trace direct labor to batches.

Since direct labor constitutes a small percentage of total cost and is difficult to allocate properly, it has been suggested that direct labor cost often should no longer be considered a major component of manufacturing costs. Consequently, its use as an activity driver should be limited to situations where it can be measured accurately and its costs can be allocated in proportion to production volume.[12]

The model explained in this article does not treat direct labor as a major cost category: It is not separately pooled, and it is not directly traced to batches. Instead, the direct labor cost in a cell is collected in cost pool C, which is later allocated to batches. If a user finds it necessary to trace direct labor costs to batches, it can be done simply by bypassing the pool C and adding the cost directly to a batch, as is done in the case of resource 15, direct material cost.

7. Material handling in a cell. As described earlier, the capital outlays of material handling equipment are added to reconfiguration cost; only recurring expenses are dealt with here. Recurring expenses are added to cost pool C, which is formed at each cell as an activity center along with direct labor cost in that cell.

8. Insurance, property taxes, supplies, indirect materials. Insurance and property taxes are based on the value of the assets. Consequently, the related costs can easily be traced to those assets and hence to the cells where the assets reside. The other resources, supplies and indirect materials, are also used within cells. Thus, in a pure cellular manufacturing system, all costs in this pool are traceable to individual cells. In a mixed system, however, supplies and indirect materials are difficult to trace to products in a job shop, so a separate cost pool becomes necessary to correctly allocate these costs.

Insurance, property taxes, supplies, and indirect materials are pooled together because these cost components, even though characteristically different, are homogeneous as far as their proportional consumption by various products is concerned. If a manager wants more details about any of the cost components, additional cost pools may have to be formed.

9. Indirect labor. Indirect labor is used all over the factory, in the cells as well as in the job shop. Its use is not uniform. Usually, a job shop consumes more indirect labor compared to a cell. The indirect labor is accumulated in a pool E.

10. Transportation within the factory. The transportation costs discussed here are not the automatic transportation costs within a cell, which were discussed earlier. Rather, the transportation costs within the factory include the costs of transporting raw materials to, and finished goods from, the cells and the job shop, as well as transportation of parts within the job shop.

One of the incentives for switching to cellular manufacturing from a job shop operation is the reduction of these transportation costs. The job shop section of the mixed cellular manufacturing will tend to consume a great deal of this resource compared to all the cells put together. This cost is accumulated in a central cost pool E.

11. Other service departments. The support of several service departments in cellular manufacturing is essential to the smooth functioning of the manufacturing system. These departments include:

- Maintenance;
- Process Planning;
- Manufacturing and Industrial Engineering; and
- Plant Accounting and Administration.

While computer systems, utilities, custodial services, material handling, and transportation are handled separately, all other service departments are grouped together here. The cost of these departments, which can be substantial, is accumulated in cost pool E, along with the costs of the two previous resources.

12. Data storage, updating, retrieval. A computer system is an important component of cellular manufacturing; without a computer system, data retrieval, manipulation, storage, sorting, grouping, and organizing cannot be done. This data handling capability is necessary for:

- Designing new parts;
- Modifying old parts;
- Scheduling parts in proper cells;
- Avoiding duplication of design efforts; and
- Standardizing manufacturing.

The recurring cost of storing, maintaining, and updating these data sets and software is accumulated in a separate cost pool F.

13. Tooling and fixtures for a part. There are two types of tooling and fixtures. The first type, the machine dedicated, is attached to a machine as long as the machine continues to be a member of a cell. These attachments are designed for the part family. The other type of tooling and fixtures is designed specifically for a part and is attached to the machine when that part is being made. This cost is added to cost pool *G* at activity center "each part."

14. Part codification. Parts must be represented in alphanumeric code which forms the database that is used in grouping parts into families, in computer-aided manufacturing and design (CAD and CAM), and in computer-aided process planning. The cost incurred in analyzing a part so that it can be coded is added to the cost pool *G*.

Instead of actually measuring the cost for each part that was coded, the total coding cost may be divided by the number of parts coded to obtain this figure.

15. Direct materials cost. The cost of direct materials for each batch is determined from requisitions from inventories and supplies. Since this cost is directly available for each batch, no intermediate cost pools or activity drivers are necessary. Since direct material cost can be measured with great accuracy (i.e., with no allocations or measurement errors), it has a desirable property of a good activity driver, so it is used as such.

Activity drivers

Activity drivers play a crucial role in allocating pooled costs to batches of parts. Ideally, an activity driver should reflect the actual use of a resource by the batches. In practice, however, it is not always possible to identify an appropriate activity driver because the relationship between it and resource use may be indirect, spurious, or nonlinear. Moreover, an activity driver should be easily and accurately measurable. Errors in measurement are serious and will be magnified when allocations are performed.

Five activity drivers are identified in Exhibit 2 based on an analysis of manufacturing operations in cellular manufacturing systems. Each is discussed below.

1. Machine hours for a batch. The activity driver "machine hours for a batch" is used to allocate cost pool *A*, which contains capital outlay costs associated mainly with machines. In a traditional setting, capital costs of this kind are depreciated using the straight-line method. Since machine usage is not uniform over the life of a machine, the straight-line method does not provide accurate product costing data. A machine that is new is used more often because of its newer technology, higher productivity, lower breakdown rates, and higher-quality output. Therefore, the units produced early in a machine's life are subsidized by those produced later. But if depreciation is based on actual use of a machine—e.g., based on machine hours used in manufacturing a batch—more accurate costing is achieved.

2. Direct materials cost for a batch. The activity driver "direct materials cost for a batch" is the only activity driver that is partly based on the volume of production; it is used to allocate the costs in cost pools *B*, *C*, and *D* to the batches.

The parts manufactured in a cell require similar processing and are made from the same, or similar, raw materials. Hence, the higher the weight of a part, the more demand placed on resources required to complete the processing. Consequently, the weight of a part can be used as an activity driver.

If the raw material used for all parts in a family is the same, the cost of the raw material (which would be proportional to the weight of a part) could be used as an activity driver. Under certain conditions, direct materials cost can be the single most important volume-related activity driver in cellular manufacturing and can appropriately be used as a base to develop a flexible budgeting system.[13] When one automotive parts factory switched its operation to cellular manufacturing, the weight of parts was used as an activity driver.[14] The weight of a part or the cost of raw materials can thus be appropriate activity drivers for cellular manufacturing.

3. Number of transfers. The cost pool *E* consists of cost accumulations from three resources. Each resource is examined separately in the following to explain its use with "number of transfers" as the activity driver.

Almost all indirect labor (resource 9) can be traced in cellular manufacturing environments to cells, because it is used within one of the cells. Indirect labor for a cell can thus be included with the direct labor of that cell, because no clear distinction exists between the two. In other words, in a pure cellular manufacturing environment, all labor (i.e., both direct and indirect labor) could be used instead of direct labor as resource 6. In the mixed model shown in Exhibit 2, however, indirect labor continues to be separately identified.

Transportation within the factory (resource 10), which occurs predominantly in the job shop, does not include material handling within a cell. In a pure cellular manufacturing operation, this resource would not be distinguishable from material handling in a cell (resource 7) and would be added to it.

Other service department costs (resource 11) in a traditional facility are indirect costs, but in a mixed cellular manufacturing environment, many of the costs become direct costs with respect to the activity centers where the cost pools are formed. For example, utilities and custodial service costs are accumulated for each machine. In a mixed cellular manufacturing environment, costs of process planning and scheduling, plant accounting, and plant engineering departments continue to be indirect. In a pure model, on the other hand, most of these costs are direct to cells and are thus accumulated there (see Exhibit 3).

The three resources discussed previously—indirect labor (resource 9), transportation within the factory (resource 10), and other service departments (resource 11)—are consumed at a greater rate in a job shop than in a cell, because they are consumed every time a job moves from one machine to the next machine in its routing sequence. In a cell, only when a job is started and removed from the cell does the resource consumption take place.

The activity driver "number of transfers" correctly reflects the consumption of these resources. It is defined as the number of times a job is transferred from one machine to the next until completion. These transfers include the transfer of raw material to the first machine in a sequence and the transfer of finished goods from the last machine to a warehouse. Thus, the number of transfers equals the number of machines used in the

processing plus one. For a cell, this number is always two because a cell is considered one machine for this purpose.

4. *Number of setups.* Every time a part is produced in a cell or in the job shop, information about it (e.g., raw materials needed and the processing sequence) must be provided before the setup can be performed. Consequently, the number of setups is used as an activity driver for allocating costs of data storage, updating data, and retrieving data—i.e., the operating costs of the computer system. Note, however, that the capacity-related cost, which is a fixed cost, is accumulated in cost pool A.

The number of setups for a batch in a job shop equals the number of machines needed to process the job, since each machine in the routing sequence must be set up with appropriate tools, dies, and fixtures. The number of setups for a part manufactured in a cell, however, is always one, because machines in the cell are always set up to manufacture that part family (although additional minor setups may be required for some parts).

The two activity drivers "number of setups" and "number of transfers" as they are defined here, are perfectly correlated, since

$$\text{Number of transfers} = \text{Number of setups} + 1.$$

Either one of the activity drivers can be substituted for the other; thus, one fewer activity driver may be used. The activity driver that is easier to track or measure accurately should be selected.

5. *Number of units made.* Cost pool G, which is created for each part, accumulates costs incurred specifically for each particular part. These costs include the cost of tooling and fixtures (resource 13) needed to manufacture each part, and also the part codification costs (resource 14). These costs are allocated based on the number of units of each part expected to be manufactured over its life span.

Cost per batch and unit cost

Activity drivers provide the cost per batch based on the actual values of the five activity drivers for each batch. Cost per unit is obtained by simply dividing the cost per batch by the number of units in that batch.

Exhibit 3. *Schematic Diagram of Activity-Based Costing in a Pure Cellular Manufacturing System*

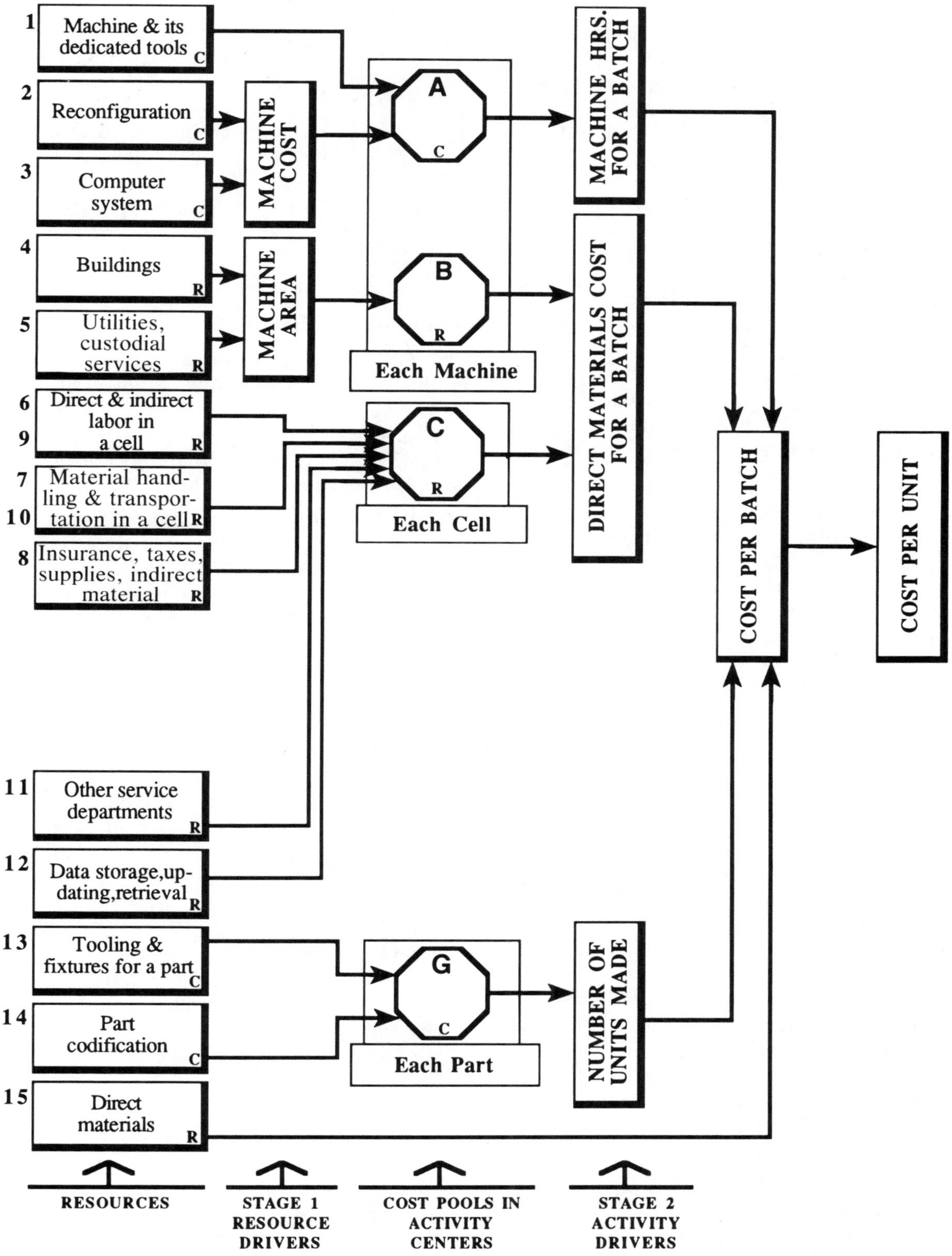

Simplifying the model. Considerable simplicity in the model could be achieved if there were no job shop. The three central cost pools (i.e., cost pools D, E, and F) that were created to account for operational differences between a job shop and the cells would no longer be needed. Resource 8 could thus be traced directly to each cell and accumulated in cost pool C instead of cost pool D. Exhibit 3 provides a schematic diagram of such a cellular manufacturing system.

As mentioned, indirect labor (resource 9) can be traced to each cell; since the distinction between direct and indirect labor disappears, both are accumulated in cost pool C. Transportation within the factory (resource 10), which is movement of batches in the job shop, also disappears. The transportation of raw material to the cells and finished goods from the cell is thus included with resource 7, material handling in a cell.

Most other service department costs (resource 11) can be directly traced to the cells once the job shop is removed. Those that cannot be traced can be allocated to cells equally if the cells have about equal activity. If not, the costs can be allocated in proportion to the number of different parts manufactured in a cell, because demand for services (e.g., accounting and process planning) is based on the number of different parts made in each cell. The same reasoning described also applies to resource 12, data storage, updating, and retrieval; its cost is added to cost pool C.

To summarize, in a pure cellular manufacturing operation, resource 9 is not considered separately. Cost pools D, E, and F are added to cost pool C. Moreover, two activity drivers, "number of transfers" and "number of setups," are no longer used. As Exhibit 3 shows, four cost pools and three activity drivers remain. With the removal of central pools, cost pools are now formed at the cells or on lower levels—namely, at machines and parts. This kind of detailed tracing provides a manager with accurate data for product costing.

In a pure cellular manufacturing environment, the direct materials cost for a batch becomes the dominant activity driver. As Exhibit 3 shows, it is used for nine out of fourteen resources. Direct materials cost is a volume-related activity driver for production within each cell. Further simplification is possible if parts in a family are similar in terms of design or shape as well as manufacturing process. In that case, a high correlation exists between the weight of the part (hence its cost) and the amount of machining required. Under such circumstances, the activity driver "machine hours for a batch" can be replaced by the activity driver "direct materials cost for a batch." The only other non-volume-related activity driver under these circumstances would be the number of units made in a batch.

Application of the model

The model developed in this article must be modified to reflect local operating conditions. To exemplify this procedure, a firm that uses a cellular manufacturing system was chosen—EG&G, Inc., a Fortune 200 company with sales of over $2.5 billion.

EG&G has several business segments that specialize in different types of manufacturing. The division that was contacted, EG&G Sealol, is in Warwick, Rhode Island, and is well known for its early adoption of cellular manufacturing (in 1980). At that time, the machines were not reconfigured into physical cells. The reconfiguration, which took place in 1990, has greatly improved overall efficiency and also created additional working space.

EG&G Sealol has five major product lines. Each product line is treated as a separate department. Each product line has between four and six product families, which thus determines the number of cells. A job shop and tool room are considered together as a cell. The flow of jobs in the cells is not unidirectional. Although, EG&G Sealol currently does not use an explicit ABC system, many elements of its costing system are based on a careful analysis of activity drivers.

The managers most closely associated with EG&G Sealol's cost accounting system were provided detailed information about the model explained in this article. After presentation and discussion of the model, the managers were asked to modify the model to reflect their operating environment. After further discussion, the managers arrived at the modified version of the model shown in

Exhibit 4. Their reasons for changes are discussed in the following.

Operating conditions that affect how ABC is applied. As mentioned earlier, each plant or firm has unique operating conditions that affect how the general ABC model explained so far would be modified.

EG&G Sealol is a defense contractor. It manufactures military and civilian products in the same departments and often in the same cell. The Department of Defense requires that product costing procedures be described in detail, submitted for review, and approved before they are used. The model described next is modified to fit within currently approved procedures. Any deviation from an approved procedure would necessitate EG&G Sealol's performing a cumbersome cost impact study to indicate how the product costs under the new method differ from the product costs under the old method.

The two main requirements of the existing approved costing method dictated how the normative ABC model explained earlier would be modified. First, the department-wide cost pools that are currently being used must continue. The advantage of this is that it avoids having to allocate costs to the departments, because many support department costs are either direct as far as the department is concerned (i.e., because the support department employees are assigned to the departments), or they can be traced to the departments based on actual usage. The direct cost to the departments obviates the need for first-stage allocation procedures, which must be approved by the Department of Defense. The modified ABC model therefore uses cost pools at the department levels. Second, the approved procedures require that direct labor be used as the allocation base. Use of a different activity driver would require a lengthy and time-consuming cost impact analysis statement; moreover, use of a different activity driver would probably be forbidden in any case. The modified ABC model shown in Exhibit 4 therefore uses direct labor dollars as the activity driver.

These requirements make the modified ABC model less accurate than what could be achieved with data currently available to the company. Nonetheless, this provides a good

example of how exogenous considerations often play an important role in the selection of activity drivers and cost pools. Given a choice, a company probably would use a cost pool at the level of each cell, rather than at the level of each department.

Each department has one product line. The definition of a product line is based on marketing considerations, rather than considerations about manufacturing similarities. As a result, product families within a product line may have significantly different processing requirements. Having cost pools at each cell would avoid the product diversity within departments and related costing problems. The disadvantage of cost pools at each cell is that there would be fewer direct costs to cells and that additional resource drivers would be needed to allocate costs to cells from the resources. A more serious problem is the use of direct labor cost (which constitutes only about 14 percent of the total manufacturing costs) as the activity driver for each department. The problems associated with using direct labor as an activity driver also appear to exist at the company. EG&G Sealol's managers were aware of these problems and expressed a willingness to change from direct labor dollars to other activity drivers.

Other possible modifications. Some other interesting modifications to the model are as follows. The job shop and the tool room at EG&G Sealol were small enough to have an insignificant impact on costs in other cells. For practical purposes, therefore, EG&G Sealol has a pure cellular manufacturing.

Reconfiguration costs. A portion of the cost of reconfiguration was treated as an R&D expense and was charged to income in the period when the reconfiguration occurred. The capitalization of reconfiguration cost (as suggested in the normative model) would have increased the cost of the items manufactured after the reconfiguration. The remaining portion of the reconfiguration cost was charged to the parent corporation, which had agreed to this charge-back in order to support this attempt of EG&G Sealol to improve its manufacturing efficiency.

Depreciation, tooling, and fixtures. The depreciation expense of the computer system is

Exhibit 4. *Schematic Diagram of A Modified Activity-Based Costing System for Cellular Manufacturing at EG&G Sealol*

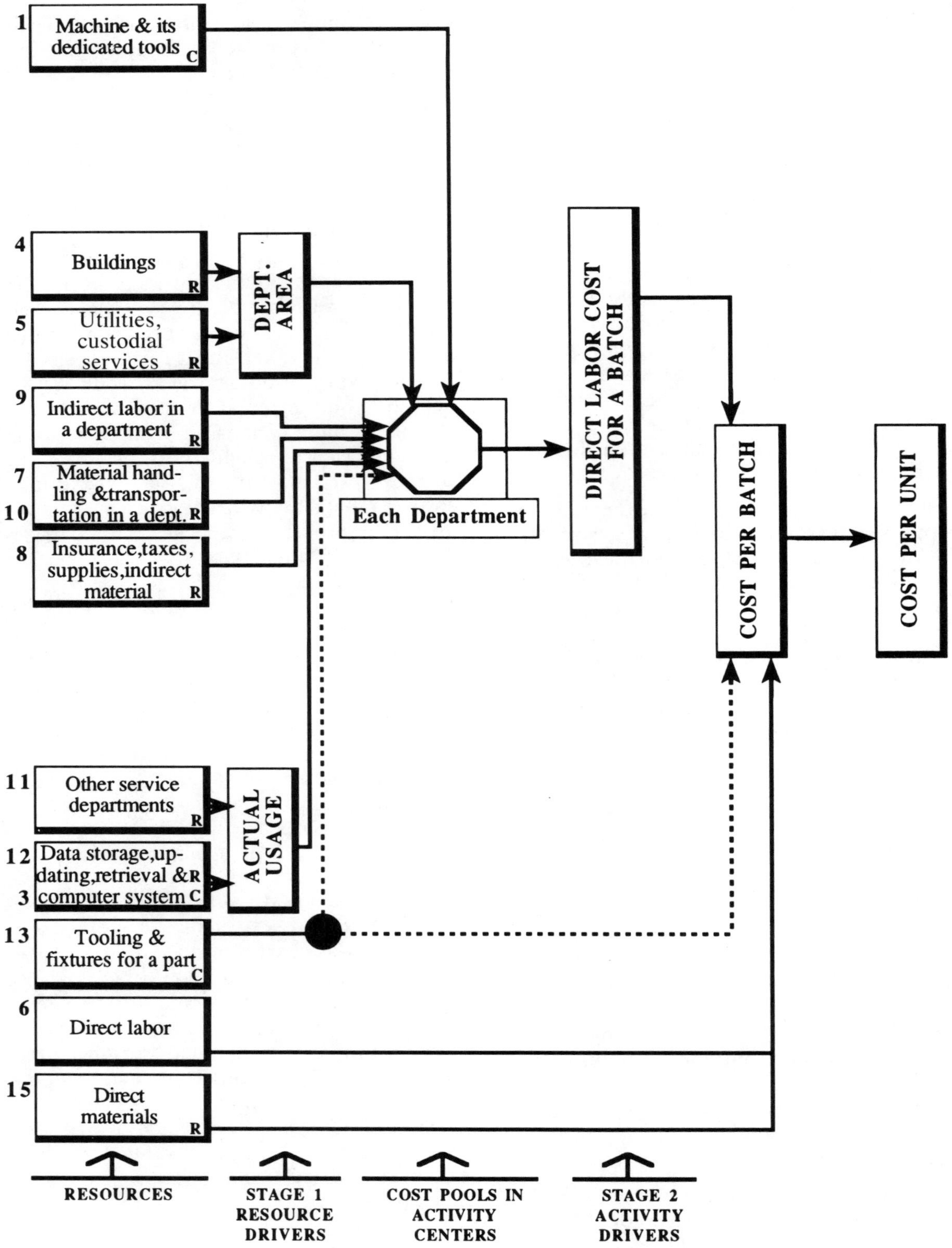

not differentiated from its recurring expenses and is charged to the other departments based on usage.

The cost of tooling and fixtures for a part (resource 13) also receives an interesting treatment. Specifically, the cost of tooling and fixtures of a routinely manufactured part is charged to the department in which the part is made, but a one-time-only order is charged for its tooling and fixture expenses.

Part codification costs are not separately tracked. Instead, the costs are included with other service department costs and are allocated when the supporting department costs are allocated (i.e., they are included with resource 11).

In a sense, EG&G Sealol is not a run-of-the mill manufacturer. It specializes in various types of high-precision seals for submarines and aircraft pumps. Many simplifications obtained in its modified costing system (compare Exhibits 2 and 4) are a result of the basic similarities between its products and the requirement that direct labor be used as the activity driver. In a more diversified product environment, the modified model would probably not be as simple.

Conclusion

The normative ABC model presented in this article should be viewed as a prototype model and a framework from which to start developing a company's own model. Each cellular manufacturing shop will have its own unique operating environment in terms (for example) of:

- Processes involved;
- Product mix and changes;
- Output volumes;
- Externally enforced requirements (e.g., government regulations); and
- Internally enforced requirements (e.g., availability of data, budget restrictions on reconfigurations, and buying new equipment to form cells).

Users must modify the normative model explained here to reflect their own operating environments. ▲

Notes

1. N.L. Hyer and U. Wemmerlov, "Group Technology and Productivity," *Harv. Bus. Rev.* (July-Aug. 1984): 140–149.
2. For more information about group technology, see C.C. Gallagher, and W.A. Knight, *Group Technology* (London, U.K.: Butterworths, 1973); see also M.P. Groover, *Automation, Production Systems and Computer-Integrated Manufacturing* (Englewood Cliffs, N.J.: Prentice Hall, 1987).
3. J.B. Young, "Understanding Shop Lead Times," *Proceedings of the 22nd Annual Conference of the American Production and Inventory Control Society* (1979): 177–179.
4. See, for example, H. Opitz and H.P. Wiendahl, "Group Technology and Manufacturing Systems for Small and Medium Quantity Production," *International Journal of Production Research* (Vol. 9, No. 1, 1971): 181–203; see also Robert N. Stauffer, "The Rewards of Classification and Coding," *Manufacturing Engineering* (May 1979): 48–52.
5. D.T. Desai, "How One Firm Put a Group Technology Parts Classification System into Operation," *Industrial Engineering* (Nov. 1981): 78–81.
6. For further information on computer-aided process planning, see L. Alting and H. Zhang, "Computer Aided Process Planning: The State-of-the-Art Survey," *International Journal of Production Research* (Vol. 27, No. 4, 1989): 553–585.
7. R.G. Askin and S.P. Subramanian, "A Cost-Based Heuristic for Group Technology Configuration," *International Journal of Production Research* (Vol. 25, No. 1, 1987): 101–113; see also A.J. Vakharia, "Methods of Cell Formation in Group Technology: A Framework for Evaluation," *Journal of Operations Management* (Vol. 6, No. 3, May 1986): 257–271.
8. D.G. Dhavale, "A Manufacturing Cost Model for Computer-Integrated Manufacturing Systems," *International Journal of Operations and Production Management* (Vol. 10, No. 8, 1990): 5–18.
9. Askin and Subramanian, "A Cost-Based Heuristic for Group Technology Configuration," 101–113.
10. Rick Hunt, Linda Garrett, and Mike G. Merz, "Direct Labor Costs Not Always Relevant at H-P," *Management Accounting* (USA) (Feb. 1985): 58–62.
11. D.G. Dhavale, "Product Costing in Flexible Manufacturing Systems," *Journal of Management Accounting Research* (Vol. 1, No. 1, 1989): 66–88.
12. George Foster and Charles T. Horngren, "Flexible Manufacturing Systems: Cost Management and Cost Accounting Implications," *Journal of Cost Management* (Fall 1988): 16–24; see also "Product Costing in Flexible Manufacturing Systems," 66–88.
13. D.G. Dhavale, J. Sounderpandian, "Flexible Budgets for Cellular Manufacturing Systems," Forthcoming in *Abacus* (Vol. 29, No. 1, 1993): 75–89.
14. A. Phillips and D.E. Collins, "How Borg-Warner Made the Transition from Pile Accounting to JIT," *Management Accounting* (USA) (Oct. 1990): 32–35.

Synchronous Manufacturing: New Methods, New Mind-Set

William K. Beckett and Khiem Dang

Synchronous manufacturing is a strategy to help meet customer requirements. It requires making the right part to the right specifications at the right time. By releasing only the exact amount of material needed to fill orders and establishing a strict priority for working on parts, a company can virtually eliminate opportunities for work on the wrong parts. The article explains Pratt & Whitney's experience with synchronous manufacturing, including the cultural change that was required throughout the organization.

Manufacturing departments challenged with meeting customer demands are finding that they need to bring the entire company in step with their efforts to achieve meaningful results.

On average, it takes a Pratt & Whitney Canada customer six months to build an airplane. Historically, it takes the company 9 to 12 months to build the engine that goes in it. Not surprisingly, as airplane manufacturers shortened their lead time, they pressured P&W Canada to bring its lead time in line with theirs.

To respond to these demands, P&W Canada is synchronizing its manufacturing operation. This effort is creating an awareness that cultural change is needed throughout the organization. For the company to live up to customers' expectations, that change must be successful.

Yet customer demand for faster delivery is only one factor driving the need for change. Other factors must be addressed, such as the shift in market demand. The company used to make a large volume of only a few types of engines; however, customers now demand a wide variety of models and options, which results in smaller quantities per engine model. Combined with the increasing complexity of models and options, customers' expectations of quality are also much higher and much more stringent.

These shifts have increased the pressure to create a flexible and reliable manufacturing process. All of these demands for faster delivery, more options, and better quality have caused the company to reevaluate its entire manufacturing strategy.

In the old manufacturing culture, the strategy was to combine batches for long production runs; setups were avoided. Inventory was not viewed as an important cost contributor. It was not a major concern if large amounts of inventory sat around for months; however, the company was concerned if a worker or a machine was idle. But these attitudes are misleading and in addition, they contribute to long manufacturing lead times.

In September 1990, P&W Canada set out to change these attitudes by changing its manufacturing culture. It began a pilot program to introduce synchronous manufacturing concepts to one of its key operations, manufacturing line 4770. These concepts focused on processing material as quickly as possible, based on customer orders. Large work-in-process (WIP) inventories and long production runs were avoided in favor of small WIP inventories and short, strategically planned production runs.

The company established a goal of cutting lead time and inventory by 50% while increasing on-time deliveries to a level of 100%. Between September 1990 and June 1991, using synchronous manufacturing techniques, line 4770 was able to increase on-time deliveries from 40% to 60%—a 50% improvement. During the same nine-month period, inventory and lead times were cut 25% and 38% respectively.

The company had found a manufacturing philosophy with the potential to help it meet new and more demanding customer requirements. To continue making improvements, however, P&W Canada would have to champion cultural changes throughout the organization.

It is hard to overstate how broad a change must occur for an organization to implement a new manufacturing strategy effectively. As line 4770 strove to improve delivery and quality while reducing inventory and lead times, the old manufacturing culture came into conflict with the new emerging culture in many areas.

It helps to understand that conflict will occur and that conflict is healthy. Nonetheless, the established ways must yield to new ways of thinking if the organization is to succeed in serving customers better.

New manufacturing measures

One aspect of the old culture targeted for change is the area of performance measures. Old measures (e.g., hours produced and efficiency) must be replaced by measures that are more appropriate for today's world. In a synchronous manufacturing environment, those new measures are throughput (defined as revenue generated by sales), inventory, and operating expenses.

Adopting these new measures affects many areas within the organization, including senior management, finance, purchasing, and marketing. All of these departments need to understand and endorse synchronous concepts, because their cooperation is vital to maximize the ability of these concepts to improve customer service.

In today's manufacturing environment, it is critical that managers and workers be judged on how well they satisfy customer demands rather than on how well they maintain labor efficiency at specific operations. During the 50 years before the 1970s, demand exceeded capacity for North American manufacturers. Everything that was produced was sold. Therefore, the way to make money was to

reduce cost. The primary strategy for reducing costs was to increase labor efficiency.

The situation today is quite different. The market has become much more competitive, and customers are demanding many more options. Requirements for success have changed dramatically. Lead time is now a significant competitive factor.

Synchronous manufacturing measures (e.g., throughput, inventory, and operating expenses) enable managers to run their operations as a business while paying daily attention to customer service and the bottom

> *"Synchronous measures have a global and external focus. They are, in fact, true manufacturing productivity measures."*

line. Synchronous measures have a global and external focus. They are, in fact, true manufacturing productivity measures; therefore, they help managers make better decisions.

Because standard cost accounting measures focus on internal, local efficiencies, they encourage local optimization, which, though appearing to be appropriate for a specific area, is often counterproductive for the manufacturing operation as a whole. When a manufacturing operation focuses on local efficiencies, it usually opts for long production runs, big batches, and minimal setups. These actions produce high efficiencies; unfortunately, they also produce long lead times, late shipments, and an expediting mentality. In the long run, targeting high, local efficiencies is an extremely ineffective way to run a manufacturing operation.

The old measures, with their focus on internal and local issues, undermine a manufacturer's ability to meet delivery requirements and customer demands. In addition, the old measures focus on direct labor, which usually makes up less than 10% of total manufacturing costs.

Under such a system, a company can't determine whether its manufacturing operation is making money. On the other hand, synchronous manufacturing measures, with their global focus, provide managers with a better technique for tracking and improving their manufacturing operation.

Perhaps one of the most serious shortcomings of the old measures is that manufacturing managers find it impossible to make effective decisions based on standard cost accounting techniques. With synchronous manufacturing, however, fundamental manufacturing elements (e.g., throughput, inventory, and operating expenses) are measured. This allows managers to make decisions much more easily.

If there is one major step that an organization can take to ensure the strategic success of its improvement program, it is to relegate outdated efficiency measures to a secondary role in decision making. When a manufacturing operation frees itself from such measures and institutes global measures that reflect bottom-line results, it can effect lasting changes in methods that will ensure its competitive position.

New methods for quality

Synchronous manufacturing is a strategy that helps P&W Canada meet customer requirements. It helps the company make the right part to the right specifications at the right time. By releasing only the exact amount of material needed to fill orders and establishing a strict priority for working on parts, P&W Canada has virtually eliminated the opportunities for operators to work on the wrong part.

To facilitate a fast, smooth change in this area of the company's manufacturing culture, numerous training sessions were held to shift workers' focus from outdated efficiency measures to meeting customer requirements. Workers were educated about the importance of sticking to the production schedule, doing all necessary setups, concentrating on quality, and striving to work on the right part at the right time.

To make sure that everyone works on the right part at the right time, workers are required to make a high-quality part the first time. To achieve this objective, each operator is now held accountable for quality. But along with this responsibility, operators are given the authority to shut down an operation if for any reason they cannot make a part that meets quality standards.

As the company strove to improve delivery and quality while reducing inventory, one of the first things it did was reduce its fixed planned lead times. Lead time is often viewed as a cushion, and it is commonly and erroneously thought that the longer the planned lead time, the better. Lead time, however, is actually a self-fulfilling prophecy: the longer the planned lead time, the more WIP there will be and the longer it will take to get parts processed.

As fixed planned lead times were reduced, batch sizes were also cut. These smaller batch sizes resulted in shorter lead times and reduced WIP inventory; this in turn allowed

---

"Operators are given the authority to shut down an operation if for any reason they cannot make a part that meets quality standards."

---

the company to respond to customer requirements much more quickly. But more important, smaller batch sizes resulted in improved quality.

With reduced batch sizes, if there were a problem there would be fewer parts with deviations and less time would have elapsed from the time the problem occurred. Therefore, people could still remember the source of the problem, which allows appropriate corrective action to be taken.

Smaller batch sizes also meant doing more setups, which required that the company improve its setups. P&W Canada rethought the way it did setups. Major gains were made after the company revised setup procedures and reorganized work areas, ensuring the availability of tooling and fixtures (devices to hold parts in place during machining) at the right time. But as the organization strives to further reduce batch sizes, the number of setups multiplies rapidly. This points to the need for innovative tooling and fixtures to further help improve setups.

After nine months of experience, it was clear that synchronous manufacturing techniques were transforming the company's culture. Instead of a complex, often chaotic environment characterized by the chasing of parts and chronic frustration, managers now had new tools to simplify the process.

Synchronous manufacturing is not simply another JIT approach. It offers specific advantages over JIT to help an operation meet delivery schedules. First, JIT logistical systems (e.g., *kanban*) have limited applicability—essentially, they are used in repetitive industries; otherwise, the level of inventory

---

"Synchronous manufacturing is not simply another JIT approach. It offers specific advantages over JIT to help an operation meet delivery schedules."

---

required would be too large. Synchronous manufacturing, on the other hand, can be applied successfully in any manufacturing environment.

Next, disruptions would adversely affect current deliveries under a *kanban* system. Synchronous manufacturing, however, exploits a fundamental insight into the critical role that constraints play in a manufacturing environment. It gives managers a way to minimize the impact of inevitable disruptions by providing a technique for strategically positioning buffers throughout the line. This approach ensures the smooth, uninterrupted flow of material through the process under all circumstances.

Furthermore, synchronous techniques are designed to help ensure that the process of continuous improvement is focused on the critical constraints, so the company is always getting the maximum return for its efforts, Conversely, under the JIT approach, improvement opportunities are addressed systemwide

and are not necessarily focused on areas in which the greatest payoff is possible.

In addition, a long and difficult process is required to implement a JIT/*kanban* system. Synchronous manufacturing, on the other hand, offers the techniques needed to improve and show progress relatively quickly. These concepts, with their emphasis on pinpointing the constraints in a process, allow P&W Canada to meet production schedules with a high degree of predictability while reducing inventory and lead times.

As the company changes and improves its manufacturing measures and methods, the collective mind-set of the organization is changing as well. The culture of a large manufacturing operation exists in the collective mind-set of everyone in that organization. Changing this mind-set is a requirement for effectively implementing a new manufacturing strategy, especially one that results in improved customer service.

The company's mind-set has been formed through years of being measured a certain way and devising methods to perform well against those measures. As the global manufacturing environment changes, however, those methods are becoming obsolete, and the old performance measures are becoming counter-productive.

For many production supervisors who have worked at P&W Canada for decades, it was traumatic to see batch sizes cut in half and lead times significantly reduced. For almost everyone, it was unnerving to see the piles of inventory—the company's security blanket for so many years—dwindle so quickly.

Mind-set change is difficult; it takes time to achieve. With education and direct experience with positive results, however, people are adapting. Everyone at P&W Canada is witnessing this strategy at work: the company is watching a culture change before its eyes. ▲

Reprinted from *Journal of Business Strategy*, January/February 1992, pp. 53–56. Copyright © 1992 by Warren Gorham Lamont, a division of Research Institute of America Inc. All rights reserved. Used by permission.

Flexible Manufacturing Systems: Implementing an Automated Factory

Mohsen Attaran

Flexible manufacturing systems can lead to shorter setup times, faster response to changes in demand, lower inventories, and higher machine utilization. Other goals of flexible manufacturing include improved quality, consistency, and performance. Strategically, improved flexibility can make it possible to produce low-volume products at competitive costs. This article discusses the economic benefits that a manufacturer can expect from a flexible manufacturing system, the prerequisites for successful implementations, and specific applications at several U.S. companies that use flexible manufacturing technology.

Flexible manufacturing technology enables production systems that are capable of creating a wide product variety at prices that approach those of mass production. American manufacturers that employ flexible manufacturing systems report that machine setup times are getting shorter, responses to changes in demand are becoming faster, inventories are dropping, and machine use is increasing. Quality, consistency, and performance are improving as well.

Significantly improved flexibility in the factory has many strategic advantages including the production of low volumes at competitive costs. Within their envelope of capability, FMSs can produce varied products with almost the same speed and efficiency as in the manufacture of identical products. This enhanced flexibility permits manufacturers to make a far broader product line, simplifies style changes, and may stimulate new product design. Faster throughput from the better use of all machines, shorter machine setups, and automatic material handling all allow FMS users to respond rapidly to changes in market demand. In addition, an FMS enables manufacturers to proliferate product designs to enter into market segments that are not economically feasible for competitors using traditional technologies.

This article discusses the economic benefits that a manufacturer can expect from a flexible manufacturing system, the prerequisites for successful implementation of such a system, and the FMS applications of some American companies that are capitalizing on the advantages of flexible manufacturing technology.

Applications in the U.S.

Although pioneered in the United States, flexible manufacturing systems were not implemented in American companies until fairly recently. By 1986, American manufacturers, following the influence of the Japanese, had installed more than 50 FMSs at a cost of about $200 million. The following sections describe some of the American manufacturers that have capitalized on the advantages of flexible manufacturing to achieve required standards of flexibility, quality, cost, and delivery.

Deere & Co. At its $1.5 billion complex in Waterloo IA, Deere's FMS is capable of producing 5,000 variations on 10 basic tractors. Customers can select the parts they want on their tractors and the FMS produces them to order. For almost a decade, Deere has been hailed as a pioneer of this manufacturing revolution. Its flexible manufacturing system has realized all of the cost reductions and productivity improvements that the company had aimed for since its decision to implement the system.

Allen-Bradley Co. At its 45,000-square-foot facility in Milwaukee, Allen-Bradley is using an FMS to build electric motor starters and contact devices for the world market. The company implemented the new technology when it switched its product line from electromechanical to solid-state technology in 1979. The FMS has reduced direct labor costs to 1.5% of total sales dollars, down from 15% 10 years earlier.

General Electric Co. GE has installed FMS technology in several of its plants. At GE's Erie PA locomotive plant, an FMS has reduced the time required to make locomotive motor frames from 16 days to just 15 hours. In GE's Somersworth NH plant, an FMS can be programmed to make up to 2,000 variations on 40 basic models of electric meters.

Cincinnati Milacron, Inc. In 1982, Cincinnati Milacron decided to install an FMS in its plastics machinery division (PMD), which produces plastic injection-molding equipment. PMD is recognized as one of the most important segments of the corporation, yet its lead time for producing the injection-molding machines was approximately twice the established norm. By 1985, however, the flexible manufacturing system had resulted in PMD sales that constituted 26% of the corporation's total, up from 15% in a three-year period.

Increased machine use, inventory reductions, shorter lead time, and shorter machine setup time have resulted in higher profitability. Cincinnati Milacron is saving 25% in both direct and indirect labor costs. The biggest contribution of the FMS has been as a catalyst for change within the entire company. The installation of the FMS not only forced better management practices, but increased the visibility of those areas that needed the attention of management.

Vought Aero Products Co. A superb example of how an FMS can outperform conventional systems is provided by Vought Aero Products Co., a subcontractor to Rockwell International Corp. The plant's 19 employees including maintenance staff are running a $10.1 million, eight-machine FMS through three shifts to build 568 parts for the B-1B bomber. This is compared with the estimated 72 workers and 24 machines that would be required to produce the same output using a conventional system. The plant is operating in 40,000 square feet of floor space, in contrast with the 120,000 square feet that a conventional system would need. The implementation of the FMS has allowed the company to go from being a subcontractor on government projects to being nearly a prime contractor. Vought's strategy is to have the manufacturing technology in place that will allow the company to bid on any piece of subcontract work and win, no matter what the work requires. Vought's management views flexible automation as a strategic weapon for enhancing the company's competitive position.

Intelligent body assembly: Japanese automakers

Japanese auto manufacturers are increasing the flexibility of production lines to handle a mix of models and options and to permit easy changeover. Efficiency is achieved through variety rather than repetition. This enhanced flexibility lets the car manufacturer create a broader product line; it also stimulates new product design, accommodates style change, and makes efficient processing on small production runs feasible.

Nissan Motor Co.'s Zama No. 2 assembly line is one of the most highly automated in Japan, with 97% of the 3,000 to 4,000 welds per car done by robot. Thirty-five robot arms hold the main parts of a Nissan Sentra body in virtually perfect alignment, and 16 others weld the spots together in 62 places. Within 45 seconds, the four-door sedan body moves along the assembly line and a computer automatically readjusts the bank of robots to assemble the next item on the line, a hatchback. After the computer does its work again, the robots assemble the body of a stationwagon. Down the line, each body will be painted a different color and receive different parts, all determined by computer command.

The new intelligent body assembly at Nissan's Zama plant is the first in the world to use computer-programmable robots instead of fixed jigs for aligning a car's main body parts, including floor, roof, and side panels. As a result, one assembly line can handle up to four models and eight body types at once. Lengthy and expensive retooling of jigs and production machines for model changes typically results in extensive downtimes for production lines.

With a flexible body-assembly system, many changes can be made by modifying the computer program. The system greatly reduces the time and cost of model changes—for example, the retooling costs for a new model are cut in half. The computer program can also be taken to another plant and production can begin in three months; previously it took 10 to 11 months to transfer production. The system now used in Nissan's plants at Zama and Tochigi will be introduced at two other Japanese plants and at Nissan's U.S. factory in Smyrna TN.

Other Japanese car manufacturers have also introduced a high degree of flexibility in their production facilities. Toyota makes Supra, Lexus, and Soarer models on the same line in its Tahara plant. Honda produces Accords and Integras on a single line at its Suzuka plant.

The evolution of FMS

Automation is not new in the manufacturing environment; numerical control machines have been around since the 1950s. A computer program guided the production of a tape containing the instructions for numerical control machines, which automatically cut, bore, milled, and performed other operations as instructed. More sophisticated technology developments have permitted the application of robotics in manufacturing. Robots are programmable, multifunctional machines capable of moving materials, often with many degrees of freedom, as well as performing repetitive tasks. Robots are flexible; they eliminate the need for operators and they provide consistent quality.

Various types of materials-handling systems have been used in manufacturing since the 1920s. New developments in data processing technology have led to the application of automated, guided vehicles to large, complex facilities. These trackless, self-propelled vehicles are automatically routed and provide a flexible means of moving parts over random routes within a factory. Automatic storage and retrieval systems are used to locate and retrieve needed components. Automatic storage and retrieval systems can be integrated with the new automated factory without altering the basic mechanism by upgrading the FMS computer controller.

The introduction of robotics and computer-controlled materials-handling equipment into the manufacturing process has permitted the linkage of these standalone machines into a complex FMS. An FMS uses information technology to integrate computer-controlled machine tools (which consist of numerical control machines), robotics, materials-handling systems, and a system-level controller to form a highly automated and flexible system.

Significantly improved flexibility in the factory enables the production of low volumes at competitive costs.

Keys to successful implementation

The central core of an FMS is the manufacturing information system that contains all product- and process-related data. This system captures and stores relevant information necessary for the production of different parts. The integration of the different components of an FMS, computer-aided design and manufacturing (CAM/CAM) systems, robotics, and materials-handling systems depends on a carefully designed system of information flow. A properly designed manufacturing information system provides the FMS with the necessary information structure for the efficient conduct of the manufacturing activities, including the development, evaluation, testing, and production of a variety of products.

The adoption of an FMS depends upon the initial implementation of a manufacturing information system. Active participation by the IS manager greatly facilitates the integration of such an information system.

In addition to reviewing current manufacturing information systems, IS management must work with senior management to investigate changes in plant layout, equipment requirements, accounting and costing functions, as well as workers' attitudes. The following sections list the prerequisites to the successful implementation of an FMS.

Review the current manufacturing information system. It is the responsibility of the IS manager to facilitate this function. The IS manager needs to evaluate the manufacturing information system to identify and rank opportunities and to develop the specific objectives that guide the implementation of the FMS.

One assembly line can handle up to four models and eight body types at once.

Evaluate the company's current position. Senior management and IS management must determine and evaluate current practices in terms of the company's business goals and the competitive environment. A careful analysis of the needs and priorities of the company is part of this evaluation process.

Establish a desired outcome. The company must identify what it hopes to achieve from the implementation of an FMS. The benefits might range from increased productivity to improved quality of the workplace. The list of improvements expected from automation should be consistent with overall corporate goals and strategies.

Conduct a cost-benefit analysis. New technology is highly capital intensive. Capital budgeting procedures should be enhanced to incorporate the intangible benefits generated from flexibility, improved efficiency, and higher productivity to justify the high capital investment in FMS technologies.

Formulate long-run objectives. The implementation of new technologies is a long-term decision. Instant results cannot be expected.

Long-term plans should provide room for technological change and expansion.

Encourage worker involvement. Senior and IS management must explain the reason for changes to those employees whose jobs will be affected. It is important that employees be informed and made a part of the planning process to improve their perception of the changes.

The integration challenge. Linking the different IT components of an FMS poses a serious technological problem. Although the computers, robots, and sophisticated machines exist, the necessary systems software and common data bases to control and link the equipment are not yet sufficiently developed.

Another serious problem is the lack of expert knowledge in the field—both managerial and technical. Senior management must ensure that its suppliers will provide extensive assistance with the design and modification of hardware and software. In addition, senior management should develop a comprehensible master plan and implement it one step at a time. Improvements should be made in steps, rather than in one quantum leap.

Technical planning

The technical problems of implementing an FMS are often underestimated. Proper planning enables senior and IS management to take the steps necessary to minimize the chances of failure. To ensure a successful implementation of the FMS, IS managers can take the following actions:

☐ Obtain a clear understanding of the new technologies involved. One method is to talk to others who have implemented FMS technologies. IS managers can get accurate cost and operating information through suppliers, competitors, and professional organizations that will make it possible to determine how the new technologies can satisfy the existing needs of the organization.

☐ Form a multidisciplined project team to bring all the necessary technical skills and experience to the FMS project. Outside assistance may be needed to ensure objectivity.

☐ Select qualified vendors who will provide the essential hardware and software support.

☐ Formulate a training program to ascertain what level of training is required by employees who will be involved in the supervision and operation of the new technology.

☐ Monitor the initial performance of the FMS and maintain a basis for evaluating feedback.

☐ Assign adequate resources to support and maintain the technology after installation.

Because implementation of flexible manufacturing systems has not yet been reduced to a simple set of textbook rules and procedures, there are no detailed guidelines for manufacturers to follow. Yet meticulous planning enables a company's management to take the steps necessary to minimize the impact of possible pitfalls.

Conclusion

Increased national and international competition in manufacturing has stimulated the adoption of new technologies such as flexible manufacturing systems in the U.S. Those companies that fail to focus on the demands and opportunities presented by technological improvement are risking their continued profitability and long-term survival. The many challenges facing American manufacturers today indicate that technology management is a critical strategic issue. Successful design and implementation of new technology requires the close integration and coordination of variables ranging from technical issues to human and managerial ones.

Senior management must recognize the internal and external benefits and costs of new technology in the automated factory. Management must assess the technology's compatibility with the company's goals, as well as determine the company's financial ability to support an FMS project. Automation must be viewed as a manufacturing project with long-term objectives that encompass all aspects of the production facility. The involvement of the IS department and other employees in the planning as well as the installation process is critical to reduce resistance and skepticism. ▲

Accounting for Intangibles in Integrated Manufacturing

Robert Putrus

Manufacturers can view computer-integrated manufacturing (CIM) as strategic support for their critical business success factors, not as a point solution justified through cash flow analysis. CIM's tangible benefits, such as inventory savings and less scrap, are easily quantified by standard accounting techniques. Most CIM benefits, such as faster introduction of new products, are intangible and can advance manufacturers' strategic business objectives. The author's nonfinancial justification method, based on the analytical hierarchy process (AHP), helps rank CIM benefits and risks by prompting users to build decision models that reflect corporate business goals, define and weight justification criteria, and compare manufacturing options to reach CIM investment decisions.

The global market for manufactured products demands greater manufacturing flexibility, improved quality, and faster product delivery. CIM could be a common denominator for addressing these competitive challenges.

Financial justification methods, however, cannot readily account for CIM technology. Manufacturers have difficulty justifying flexible CIM, which is more than just automation. CIM should be viewed as strategic support for manufacturers' critical success factors, not as a point solution with tactical dimension justified exclusively through cash flow analysis.

Modeling CIM

The model in Exhibit 1 is a basis for CIM justification, characterizing CIM behavior in terms of risk, benefits (tangible and intangible), and time (short- and long-term).

CIM is considered high-risk because it requires a substantial investment, and CIM knowledge and experience is limited. If CIM implementation is managed improperly, particularly with respect to risk management, the expected level of integration cannot be met, leaving a manufacturer in a vulnerable competitive position. Executives should view their companies' structures as open systems whose key elements can be influenced by conditions or events outside the system. A major CIM program represents a transformation in the nature of a manufacturing enterprise because it creates a system with a high degree of coherence among its elements.

CIM's tangible benefits are easily recognized and quantified by current accounting techniques. They are geared to classic product costing (e.g., labor, material, and overhead) and include:

- Inventory savings in work in process (WIP), raw material, and finished goods.
- Less scrap and rework because of improved quality.
- Reduction in warranty expenses because of higher-quality products.

Most CIM benefits are intangible, however, and cannot be quantified by traditional evaluation, even though they have a great effect on a company's strategic objectives. Intangible benefits include:

- Faster introduction of new products and product delivery, leading to increased customer satisfaction and market share.
- Improved quality of work life and increased employee satisfaction through automation of hazardous jobs.
- Increased learning and experience by continually challenging employees.
- Flexibility in accommodating design changes.

Exhibit 1. *CIM's Benefits and Risks Are Functions of Time*

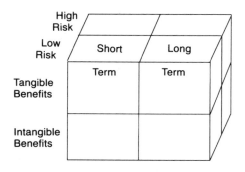

Time is a key variable in the CIM model because the associated risk can vary in different time periods. Risk can be great in a CIM project's first and second year (the short term), then decline because of experience gained and removal of cultural barriers. Risk may increase again in the long term as a result of the uncertainty of the market or evolving CIM technology.

CIM's chances for success increase with time. CIM has a longer useful life than traditional point solution projects, which can look attractive in the short run, but eventually incur greater risk while yielding fewer benefits. These projects may satisfy tactical goals but not necessarily supplement corporate strategic objectives. Most managers agree that CIM's benefits are more recognizable as time passes and anticipated risks are reduced as experience is gained.

Performance-based justification

It seems clear that future financial justifications for automation will be based less on the functions of individual technologies and more on their support for business performance (see Exhibit 2).

Some new justification techniques are based on modification of existing ones, and others on nonaccounting criteria. CIM implementation is a strategic business decision, not an accounting decision. Detailed information on strategic projects (e.g., CIM) is probably unavailable, although their effect is well known. For classic accounting techniques to be valid and reliable, detailed information must be available.

Because CIM's benefits increase as time passes, the dynamics of CIM benefits and risk should be viewed with respect to time. It is also important to quantify the relative value of total benefits to total risk of CIM projects without time as a factor. It is then necessary to adjust the dynamic behavior of either the benefits or risk in regard to time.

The nonfinancial justification method proposed in this article is based on the AHP technique, which develops a matrix of paired comparisons for each element of the parent hierarchy (see inset).

A company's business plan matrix should encompass all the functions in the company, from the executive levels to the shop floor, and integrate these functions. The matrix consists of four major levels:

- The strategic, which is planned, executed, and monitored by top management.
- Critical success factors, which are planned, executed, and monitored by top staff management.
- The functional, which is planned, executed, and monitored by staff and line management.

Exhibit 2. *CIM Financial Justification Based on Business Contribution*

Mission	┌──── Competitiveness of the Enterprise ────┐		
Objectives	Profit Level	Market Share	Sales Growth
Critical Success Factors	Reduced Lead Time	Improved Quality	Reduced Cost
Functions	Engineering	Manufacturing	Production
Selections	Short-Term Risks and Benefits	Medium-Term Risks and Benefits	Long-Term Risks and Benefits

Exhibit 3. *The Analytical Hierarchy Process: Comparing Factors to Establish Priorities*

AHP starts by refining a complex problem into smaller elements. It then organizes the elements into sets of homogeneous clusters, which are subdivided into more detailed sets until the lower levels of the hierarchy are established. This structure represents the total view of the system (e.g., company) being studied.

AHP helps its users deal with complex problems (e.g., CIM justifications) by representing a manufacturing company in hierarchical form and identifying the major elements within each level, depending on the level of detail required (see Exhibit 2).

The number and type of elements within each level in the hierarchy depend on the company's business and marketing environment. (Exhibit 2 represents a generic manufacturing enterprise; other AHP models may differ.) The beauty of AHP is that manufacturing managers can build their own models with specific elements and priorities.

Defining the manufacturing strategy at different levels forces management to look closely at the effect of its decisions on its company's business performance.

AHP compares each element in each level with each other element in the next highest level. Pairwise comparisons are repeated with every element in each level, starting from the top level and continuing down to the lowest level of the hierarchy.

AHP helps establish priorities by asking users to judge pairwise comparisons of the element sets in each level in the hierarchy structure with respect to each of the elements in the next higher level.

• Measurement criteria, which are proposed and executed by line management.

The strategic level represents a company's fundamental business objectives (e.g., profit level, market share, and demand on resources). Critical success factors include reduced lead time, improved product quality, increased flexibility, and better work life. These are important measures according to the experiences of five companies now using computer-aided manufacturing, integrating

existing systems, and implementing new integrated systems. Critical success factors are the intangibles that traditional accounting techniques are unable to deal with. AHP considers these intangibles relative to a company's strategic goals and functional areas.

Critical success factors support attainment of a company's strategic goals and help ensure its successful competitive performance. Different industries have different critical success factors, which are time dependent and should be adjusted as the market changes.

The functional level is organized into engineering design (e.g., computer-aided design/computer-aided manufacturing [CAD/CAM], group technology, computer-aided process planning [CAPP], simulation), manufacturing engineering (e.g., CAM, NC development, tool management, plant maintenance, capacity planning), and production (e.g., shop floor, Just In Time [JIT], quality control, materials handling, flexible machining systems).

How to justify

Step 1. Build an enterprise hierarchy defining each of the hierarchy's levels, all of which depend on the business plan matrix.

Step 2. Using AHP techniques, construct the weighting factors of each element in every level, except the selection level.

Step 3. Define the company's selection level as follows:

- Use total benefits and risk as the two alternatives for measuring the total percentage of benefits versus total percentage of risk in applying CIM projects.
- Construct the weighting factors of these alternatives with respect to each element in the next-highest functional level.
- Combine the alternative matrices with respect to the weighting factors of each element (in each level) until final ranking of each alternative is calculated in the highest level of the manufacturer's corporate structure.

Step 4. Repeat step 3 using the benefits of CIM as a function of short term (one to two years), medium term (two to five years), and long term (more than five years).

Step 5. Repeat step 3 using the risk of CIM as a function of short term (one to two years), medium term (two to five years), and long term (beyond five years).

Step 6. Calculate the ratio of total benefits to total risk values by dividing the final ranking of total benefits by the total risk percentage calculated in step 3.

Step 7. Adjust the final ranking of short-, medium-, and long-term risk calculated in step 5 by the constant calculated in step 6.

Step 8. Calculate the ratios of short-, medium-, and long-term benefits to risk by dividing the final ranking of step 4 by the results of step 7. This calculation produces three different ratios, each representing different time intervals. A ratio greater than one means the benefits of the CIM project outweigh the risk of CIM for that term. A ratio less than one means the risk outweighs the benefits for that term.

Financial versus nonfinancial justification

In an example of justifying a flexible manufacturing cell in Company XYZ, the cell comprises computerized numerical control (CNC) equipment, a quality control check machine, a conveying system, and a cell controller. The cell's products are more price sensitive than quality sensitive. This assumption should be remembered during the process of AHP pairwise comparison for any two elements.

AHP is applied to the entire enterprise to justify the flexible manufacturing cell. The calculation represents two selections: total benefits and total risk. Company XYZ's business goals are assumed to be based on part type and sale price of the product, where the product is price sensitive.

Detailed information is not required when using AHP to justify advanced technology projects. AHP quantifies the intangible in an indirect way.

Manufacturers adopting CIM should examine the dynamic behavior of those benefits and risks as a function of time intervals (i.e., short-,

medium-, and long-term). Greater benefits and less risk are associated with CIM as more experience is gained.

Calculation of benefit dynamics for the flexible manufacturing cell is shown in Exhibit 3, using the AHP representation. The final ranking of the short-, medium-, and long-term benefits is 0.09, 0.26, and 0.65 respectively. The same procedure applied to benefits dynamics is applied on the risk dynamics of the cell.

Intangibles are the critical business success factors, including product quality, that traditional accounting techniques are unable to deal with.

Following CIM justification (step 7), short-, medium-, and long-term risk are adjusted by the factor 3.54, calculated by dividing total benefits by total risk (0.78/0.22). Adjusted risk as a function of the benefits is calculated as follows:

$$\left.\begin{array}{c} 0.70 \\ 0.20 \\ 0.10 \end{array}\right\} \div 3.54 = \left\{\begin{array}{c} 0.20 \\ 0.06 \\ 0.03 \end{array}\right.$$

The following ratios are percentages of CIM's total benefits to total risk for different time intervals:

Short-term ratio: 0.09/0.20 =   0.45
Medium-term ratio: 0.26/0.06 =   4.33
Long-term ratio: 0.65/0.03 = 21.67

Benefits are far greater than the risk as time passes in the CIM environment, compared with the short- and medium-term ratios, 0.45 and 4.33 respectively. Benefits outweigh risks in adopting and implementing CIM projects.

Using this scale, the user assesses the dominance of each element with respect to the elements in the next higher level. The user determines dominance factors (on a scale of 1 to 9) of every matrix.

The user determines the off-diagonal relationship in one half of each matrix. If the matrix is built of n elements, the number of pairwise comparisons to be made is $n(n - 1)/2$. Reciprocals are

Exhibit 4. *Calculating CIM Benefit Dynamics*

Maximize Competitiveness of the Enterprise

Overall Ranking for:

Short-Term Benefits (STB)	0.09
Medium-Term Benefits (MTB)	0.26
Long-Term Benefits (LTB)	0.65

Objectives	Profit Level (PL)	Market Share (MS)	Sales Growth (SG)
	(0.60)	(0.11)	(0.29)
STB	0.09	0.09	0.09
MTB	0.26	0.26	0.25
LTB	0.65	0.65	0.66

	LT	IQ	RC	LT	IQ	RC	LT	IQ	RC
	.28	.09	.63	.20	.07	.73	.42	.16	.42
STB		0.08			0.10			0.09	
MTB		0.22			0.27			0.27	
LTB		0.70			0.63			0.64	

Critical Success Factors	Lead Time (LT)	Improved Quality (IQ)	Reduced Cost (RC)

	E	M	P	E	M	P	E	M	P
	.08	.63	.29	.23	.10	.67	.08	.29	.63

Functions	Engineering (E)	Manufacturing (M)	Production (P)
STB	0.08	0.06	0.11
MTB	0.19	0.19	0.31
LTB	0.73	0.75	0.58

placed in the transposed positions. Exhibit 4 illustrates one pairwise comparison matrix for part of the manufacturing enterprise hierarchy shown in Exhibit 2. This matrix has nine entries (i.e., cells) to fill. Three are already committed to 1s. Three of the remaining six are reciprocals. This leaves three judgments to make. If, verified by the formula $n(n-1)/2$, a matrix has $n \times n$ dimensions on a 3×3 matrix, which has 9 entries, the number of elements to fill is $3(3-1)/2$. A matrix of 6×6 dimensions has 36 entries, and the number of entries to fill is $6(6-1)/2$, or 15.

This step is vital to AHP because it provides the framework for data collection and analysis.

Calculating priorities

The matrix of comparisons with respect to increased market share is a function of a manufacturer's three critical success factors (i.e., reduced lead time, improved quality, and reduced cost). In the matrix shown in Exhibit 4, cell (2,1) has a value of 4. This means that the evaluator views improved quality as outperforming reduced lead time; the degree of dominance 4 means improved quality is between weak importance and strong importance compared with reduced lead time.

Cell (3,1) implies that reduced cost is relatively important compared with reduced lead time. And cell (3,2) implies that reduced cost is between equal importance and weak importance, compared with improved quality.

Calculating relative weights

The criterion weight for this matrix is calculated using a commonly used approximation procedure, taking the geometric average of the entries in each row (2). The next step is to normalize these averages to obtain a vector of priorities whose elements add up to 1. Each value represents the evaluation/weight of the row's selection/criterion. Normalizing requires summing the elements of geometric mean and dividing by that sum. Extracting normalized weights is repeated for each of the linkages of the hierarchy in Exhibit 2, after developing the pairwise comparisons.

After this process is extended to the entire hi-

Exhibit 5. *Matrix of Pairwise Comparisons*

Increased Market Share	1 Reduced Lead Time	2 Improved Quality	3 Reduced Cost	
1 Reduced Lead Time	1	$1/4$	$1/5$	← Reciprocals of Entries Below the Diagonal
2 Improved Quality	4	1	$1/2$	
3 Reduced Cost	5	2	1	

Judgments of an Evaluator
(2 vs 1, 3 vs 1, 2 vs 3)

---

erarchy, the normalized weights in the lower level (selection A, B, C) should be combined with the relevant weight of the elements in the next higher level (e.g., engineering, manufacturing, and production). This upward-moving process continues through the whole hierarchy until final ranking of selections A, B, C is calculated.

A new structure

This method depends greatly on the experience and discretion of corporate management. Detailed information is not required to carry out the justification process. Management can make great use of this process by determining CIM's contribution to business objectives. This justification process also helps ensure that management has a consistent understanding of company business objectives and provides a communication tool, as well as a structure for CIM justification. ▲

PART D

Competitive Environment and Change Management

The Shape of Twenty-First Century Global Manufacturing

Joel D. Goldhar and David Lei

Time is a strategic resource. Fast-response manufacturing has therefore become an important tool in the fight for global market share. Its ingredients include responsiveness, flexibility, customized orders, timely delivery, and limitless product designs. As this article explains, to be competitive in the future, U.S. manufacturers must streamline management layers, cut inventory, and reduce production time. Suppliers and customers must be sought from around the globe and linked through networks that help engender long-term cooperation.

As we approach the twenty-first century, U.S. manufacturers have begun to realize the critical importance of time as a strategie resource to compete globally. In the next century, the organization of design and manufacturing activities will differ radically from even the most "modern" methods and organizational formats used today.

Consider how a diversified U.S. manufacturer of cellular telephones, circuit boards, and memory chips is utilizing fast-response manufacturing as the latest weapon in the fight for global market share: Sales representatives in the field enter a customized order into a hand-held computer that is directly linked to an automated factory some 1,500 miles away for delivery in a few days. The order is processed immediately within the factory's sophisticated information network and database without disrupting any batch already in production, with no downtime needed for changeover.

Meanwhile, product design teams at both headquarters and a Far Eastern subsidiary 4,000 miles away are finetuning the specifications for the next product generation. Using fax and satellite transmission, they finish the design for on-line production in a matter of days. Computer-aided design (CAD) workstations and information networks link up the company's designers with its manufacturing engineers and suppliers, making it possible to conceive, produce, and sell a totally new product in days and hours, rather than months and weeks.

The shape of global manufacturing in the next ten years will come to resemble much of the preceding scenario across a wide array of industries in every corner of the globe. Networks and multifunctional work teams are speedily replacing the layers of management and long chains of command found in older factories.

We are already witnessing the evolution of fast-response organizations to order prescription eyewear or to process photographic film—all in less than an hour. Digital information technologies are consolidating once-disparate industries and making them more related, as computer chips, microprocessors, and fiber optics are now found in consumer electronics, office equipment, cars, and appliances.

Just as important, these same information technologies are revolutionizing factories where design and manufacturing teams will be much more closely linked to suppliers and customers in any part of the world. These are the ingredients of fast-response, global manufacturing that will determine tomorrow's winners in the fight for survival.

Fast-response, global manufacturing

Even now, the competitive environment is undergoing a massive upheaval in which these events are becoming commonplace:

- Increasing fragmentation and volatility of consumer buying patterns that demand the highest quality goods in the shortest possible time;
- Faster diffusion of the latest advances in science and technology that can transform industries, production methods, and product designs in days, rather than years;
- The spawning of new "learning" organizations from every part of the globe that can design, produce, and innovate faster than ever before; and
- An enormous propagation in the number of different technologies and skills required from companies to compete across different industries and products.

We are now in a global competitive environment in which flexibility, responsiveness, and low-cost/low-volume manufacturing skills will determine the sustainability of competitive advantage.

"Fast-response organizations can make prescription eyewear or process photographic film in less than an hour."

The strategic picture is clear: Today's manufacturers must not only deal with such conventional dilemmas as outsourcing or in-house production, joint venturing or going it alone, and high product variety or standardized designs; they must also manage that most precious of all resource: *time*.

In short, fast-response, global manufacturing demands nothing less than a complete break with yesterday's operating procedures, organizational methods, and attitudes to survive. Time has become the paramount competitive resource as today's innovations become tomorrow's commodities seemingly overnight.

Corporate success in fast-response, time-driven manufacturing requires management to understand and master a broad range of new concepts and skills for competitive suc-

cess. Three distinct features of fast-response, global manufacturing are:

- Computer-integrated manufacturing (CIM);
- Strategic alliances and networks with suppliers around the world; and
- Transforming manufacturing as a service.

Computer-integrated manufacturing

CIM brings the latest advances in telecommunications, computers, and materials-handling technologies into the factory. By linking up smart, multimission tools with computerized inventory control in one integrated platform, CIM offers unparalleled flexibility to produce a growing variety of different product configurations.

Compared with traditional manufacturing technologies which emphasize standardized product designs, economies of scale, centralized planning and control, and slow change-over, the new CIM-based factory thrives under conditions of multiple product designs, small batch orders, decentralized authority, and fast turnaround.

The essence of CIM's power is to erase the traditional manufacturing constraints of quality vs. variety and cost vs. volume. Therefore, the system can accommodate even radical changes in product mix in a short time. Examples of how CIM has helped many leading manufacturers solidify their global market positions include the following:

- Allen-Bradley can produce over 750 variations of industrial controls in a single factory, making "goods flow like water."
- Ingersoll Milling Machine Company uses a CIM system that can produce 25,000 different part designs, mostly in lots of one, and many one-of-a-kind designs to support its world dominance in the global market for specialized production machinery.
- Panasonic Bicycle Company of Japan is able to turn out over 11 million variations of bicycle designs according to each customer's body height, size, and color preferences—all without any downtime in the factory.
- General Electric has introduced CIM-based manufacturing techniques to vastly improve productivity across such diverse products as locomotives, dishwashers, and circuit breaker boxes. Its Major Appliance Group

is regaining domestic market share even in the face of rising foreign competition.

Within the factory, the vital source of CIM's success depends on a new way to organize work. Traditionally, manufacturers have functioned in an environment in which designers and manufacturing engineers never talked to each other, even when working on the same product.

Today, companies such as IBM, Allen-Bradley, Hewlett-Packard, Chaparral Steel, and General Electric are trying to remove such barriers to link up all operational activities into one cohesive unit—the heart of which is the versatile, multifunctional team.

Even at such mammoth global firms as General Motors, Ford, Sony, Honda, and Xerox, the team approach links designers with engineers and marketers to speed up communications and information flow. These efforts are already paying off: Production time at General Electric, Fujitsu-Fanuc, Matsushita, and Boeing is increasingly measured in hours and days, rather than months.

Strategic networks to capture global suppliers

Fast-response manufacturers reinforce their competitive advantage by aggressively searching for and linking up with suppliers around the world. Global supply strategies consist of two primary vehicles: strategic alliances, and information-based networks with long-term vendors to specialize value-adding activities.

At IBM, Mitsubishi, DuPont, and NEC, strategic alliances with suppliers help slash the amount of paper and wasted time involved in product design and production. For example, IBM uses a series of alliances with Japanese suppliers to fill out its product line; Seiko Epson produces several key components for IBM's Proprinter, while Canon produces the color printer used in many of IBM's desktop publishing and printing systems.

Within the auto industry, each of the Big Three U.S. manufacturers has an extensive series of supply alliances with their Japanese counterparts (e.g., GM-Isuzu, Ford-Mazada, Ford-Nissan, and Chrysler-Mitsubishi) that involve co-designing and co-producing small cars under such labels as GM's Geo and

Sprint, Ford's Escort line, and Chrysler's Dodge Colt. These alliance platforms enhance each partner's competitive strengths and give the opportunity for both to learn from one another.

Long-term vendor agreements between supplier and manufacturer are vital to successful time-based competition. Information networks that tie in a supplier's CAD/CAM system with that of a manufacturer are making great strides in cutting down the elapsed time in traditional product innovation.

In addition, two-way CAD networks complement just-in-time (JIT) inventory management systems that are already the hallmark of the successful fast-response manufacturers. For example, Xerox has adopted a JIT "network" that eliminates the long weeks before inventory from a supplier arrives at a plant. Ford goes a step further: It often allows its most trusted vendors direct access to many of its CAD-based workstations to speed up design turnaround for tools, dyes, jigs, and auto parts.

"AT&T is targeting a carefully designed set of customer niches."

Product specs and designs flow back and forth between vendor and manufacturer, while electronic order entry expedites the JIT delivery of parts and finished goods.

The companies that exemplify the artful combination of flexible CAD/CAM networks and JIT inventory controls are Yamazaki Mazak and Okuma of Japan. Both firms lead the world in producing sophisticated, computer-based factory machinery for any customer in the world; delivery time for complete installation of a custom-designed machine cell is often less than two months.

Manufacturing as a service in the twenty-first century

The final impact of fast-response, global manufacturing is to transform successful manufacturers into providers of *customer service* as well as goods. All of the dimensions of fast-response manufacturing—responsiveness, flexibility, custom orders, timely delivery, and limitless product designs—are the dominant characteristics of today's service businesses.

One excellent example of how a U.S. firm is blending a manufacturing and service strategy across numerous market niches is that of AT&T. Instead of competing head-on with such industry giants as IBM and Fujitsu, AT&T is targeting a carefully designed set of customer niches (e.g., Firestone, American Airlines, Xerox, and the federal government) where it can excel in such competencies as integration services, local area networks, software, and office automation equipment—all of which can be customized to individual needs.

First, AT&T moved aggressively to upgrade its UNIX software operating system with partner Sun Microsystems in order to link all of the incompatible forms of UNIX sold before.

Second, AT&T is investing considerable sums into a modern, computer-based plant to manufacture a wide range of personal computers to deliver the "hardware" of its system offerings.

Third, the company has formed a series of global supply alliances with Intel, NEC, Mitsubishi Electric, N.V. Philips, and other leading global companies to further upgrade each new generation of product and component designs for its own use.

Fourth, it is planning to build a series of sales partnerships in Europe to gain better access to local distribution for enhancing customer responsiveness, delivery, and service.

As the PC itself is fast becoming a commodity, AT&T is shifting its focus to designing custom software and computer chips that expand the individual capability of local area networks and office integration. Thus, AT&T is able to parry and riposte competitors' moves across a wide range of product and service offerings.

In the future, such industries as automobiles, consumer electronics, food processing, computer chips, and office equipment face the simultaneous challenge and opportunity to redefine themselves as providers of both custom-manufactured goods *and* customer services.

The next step in the evolution of fast-response, global manufacturing will be the direct tie-in of manufacturers with suppliers and customers of all sizes to take advantage of new technologies, ideas, and innovations no matter where they originate.

The successful competitor of the late 1990s and the early twenty-first century will no longer be the firm that relies exclusively on big size, large market shares, and a resource-intensive approach to corporate and business strategy.

Instead, the agile and nimble twenty-first century competitor will rely on time-based innovations to compete across a wide series of global market niches that are constantly changing.

Tomorrow's competitors will not exhibit the high walls separating manufacturing from design and marketing found today; rather, they will aim to compress all of their key-value adding activities into a service delivery system that focuses on customized, made-to-order offerings and timely delivery.

Already we can attest to the arrival of this new competitor: Okuma and Mazak in machine tools; Krups in small and modular kitchen appliances; Black and Decker in household gadgets and appliances; Microsoft in computer software design; and Federal Express in transportation services.

Note that all of these firms are relatively new and have essentially created their own market niches based on using fast-response information or manufacturing techniques, as well as putting customer service first.

Across the Pacific, these trends are even more stark: Japanese producers such as Sony and Hitachi can develop new television formats and technologies in one third the time of U.S. manufacturers; Toyota, Nissan, and Honda are able to outdesign and produce entire new lines of luxury automobiles faster than their U.S. or European counterparts; Fujitsu and Hitachi are starting to give IBM a run for its money in its critical mainframe computer business.

Preparing for the twenty-first century

The implications of fast-response manufacturing are clear: Five-year-old innovations that guided a company's conventional wisdom or best practice could well become obsolete tomorrow. Firms must base their manufacturing strategies on the assumption that *everyone, everywhere* will have access to the same underlying elements, including hardware, software, and technologies. Any new competitive advantage must come from *how* these elements are used and, more important, how *fast* they are assimilated into the system. The most critical steps U.S. manufacturers must take within the factory entail:

- Massive streamlining in management layers that get in the way of building design, engineering, and marketing teams.
- Streamlining inventory, production time, and factory work-in-process that militate against fast-response and time-based competition.
- Aggressively search for suppliers and customers around the globe, no matter how far, and
- Linking up the firm with its key suppliers and customers through *networks* that engender long-term cooperation.

Although U.S. companies such as Xerox, General Electric, Ford, IBM, and Black and

Decker have made tremendous strides, many other firms have only just begun to realize the decisive but ephemeral advantages of time.

As even the most modern technologies become available to anyone with a telephone, fax machine, or photocopier, stand-alone strategies will not be sufficient. A firm must use strategies that nurture distinct, core competencies in manufacturing.

Technology itself will no longer be the only key that unlocks future sources of fast-response competitive success. Now, time is the only real resource that all firms have. It is also equally available to everyone; all that matters is how one uses it. ▲

Rebuilding U.S. Manufacturing Industries for Sustainable Performance Acceleration

Arun Maira

Many U.S. manufacturing organizations need rapid improvement in their cost and quality performance. They need to build the foundation for continuous improvement in areas that are vital for their longer-term competitive position. The dilemma, of course, is how to effectively integrate top-down direction, based on the corporate strategy, with bottom-up, voluntary actions. Clearly, implementation of corporate strategy through effective operations management requires an integrated approach to business process engineering and employee empowerment.

To improve its international competitiveness, U.S. manufacturing companies have two major objectives in the 1990s:

1. Improve manufacturing operations; and
2. Integrate top-down "business process engineering" with bottom-up "employee empowerment."

Many companies may, however, have insufficient resources for completing these tasks successfully. Since the 1970s, manufacturing has not been an attractive profession for the brightest young Americans: The glamour and money in strategy and finance have distracted them.

A number of consulting firms have begun to fill the gap with resources for the overhaul of U.S. manufacturing organizations. However, they are divided into two camps:

1. Firms that specialize in cost reduction (some of which are now moving into business process engineering); and

2. Training-oriented firms that address employee empowerment concerns (many of them under the total quality banner).

An effective integration of these approaches is required for sustained improvement in performance.

Having good strategies and implementing them

Successful firms have good strategies and, just as important, the ability to implement them effectively. In international competition (and especially against Asian competitors), the weakness of U.S. manufacturing firms lies perhaps more in their inability to implement strategy through effective manufacturing management than in their lack of a good strategy. Thus, U.S. firms that are leaders in developing new technologies often lose markets to competitors who implement technology more effectively in their products and manufacturing processes.

The focus of "strategy" is shifting in the United States from *where* to compete to with *what* to compete. The major input for strategic decisions so far has been an analysis of the marketplace. Such an analysis leads to a choice of businesses or product lines in which to invest (and from which to withdraw when a competitive advantage no longer exists).

Essentially, a CEO needs to answer four questions:

1. What "competencies" or "capabilities" does the company have? (What, for example, are the ingredients of these competencies or capabilities, and what are the formulas for blending them?)

2. How can these competencies or capabilities be developed as quickly as possible?
3. How does a company determine which competencies or capabilities to build?
4. If a company has more than one competency or capability, where should they be deployed to enlarge the firm's revenues and income?

Within the blurring definitions of operational improvement and strategy development, the first two are operational issues, the latter, strategic concerns. The more critical need for the U.S. manufacturing industry is to find answers to the first two questions. Only if these two questions can be satisfactorily answered is it really worthwhile to address the other two.

Accelerating the rate of improvement

On the surface, firms compete based on quality and time in their products and processes. Beneath the surface, the real competition is on the rate at which they improve. Therefore, the process that must be of utmost concern to a CEO is improving the competencies or capabilities that matter—the process for giving a firm "acceleration" to overtake the competition.

Even the strongest and best firms are vulnerable. Twenty-five years ago, the quality of Toyota's low-priced small cars barely met standards in the U.S. market. Now, Toyota's Lexus has a credible, quality image in the high-priced European luxury car market. Although U.S. and European manufacturers

have continued to improve over the years, Toyota has improved much faster (see Exhibit 1). The Europeans are concerned; they want to keep the Japanese out of their markets to give themselves time to catch up. But if the Japanese keep improving faster than the Europeans, protection will ultimately not help, as U.S. auto manufacturers should have learned by now.

Implementing lean production

"Lean production" enable Toyota and Honda to get ahead of their U.S. and European competitors. An excellent description of the power of lean production is given in *The Machine That Changed the World,* a book that describes the findings of a multimillion-dollar, worldwide benchmarking study of automobile producers conducted at the Massachusetts Institute of Technology.[1]

Experience shows that the concepts of lean production apply even outside the auto industry. Two characteristics of lean production organizations stand out:

1. Good processes; and
2. Involvement of the doers (i.e., those who actually work in a business process) in process improvement.

Large business processes, such as product development and production, are more effective in "lean" organizations. They work faster, have less wasted effort, and deliver better quality output. Also, the doers participate actively in designing and improving these processes. Engineering, manufacturing, marketing, and suppliers work much more closely in product development in lean organizations, as do assemblers, their foremen, and quality engineers in production.

Becoming lean rapidly

The challenge for many U.S. organizations is to become lean rapidly: to catch up and then stay ahead of the competition. The question is how should this be accomplished? *The Machine That Changed the World* describes how lean organizations function. It alludes to some of the things Japanese organizations did on their way to becoming lean. But these steps were taken over a period of at least twenty years. Benchmarking and following in the footsteps of the Japanese may relegate U.S. manufacturing to a never-ending game of

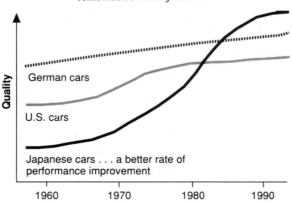

Exhibit 1. *Faster Rate of Improvement of Japanese Automobile Manufacturer*

Quality

German cars

U.S. cars

Japanese cars . . . a better rate of performance improvement

1960   1970   1980   1990

catch-up. Benchmarking can be a catalyst, but not an instruction manual.

Nonetheless, there are two essentials of lean organizations:

1. Systematic process redesign; and
2. Participatively managed change.

These subjects are discussed in more detail in the following sections.

Systematic process redesign

Sound operations management, which is essential in translating strategy and new technology into results, is based on well-conceived *business* processes. Note the emphasis here on *business* processes to distinguish them from narrow, technical processes such as machining, stamping, and steel rolling. For example, Henry Ford's mass-production process made it possible to produce cars at a cost that was so low that it substantially increased the market for cars. This strategy effectively pulled the rug out from under Ford's competitors.

Since the design of good business processes is essential to a firm's success, process design work is generally assigned to the best-trained minds in the firm. This has led to the growth of industrial engineering and centralized management information systems functions over the past several decades. But these top-down modes of process design have a serious limitation: The doers do not participate adequately in the creation of the process. When the doers are not actively involved in design of a business process—perhaps because they are insufficiently trained in process creation—they cannot be expected to make continuous improvements to the process after it is implemented. (If they were expected to make improvements, the assumption would be that they could improve on the work of those who supposedly know much more than they do.)

Participatively managed change

The failure of the top-down, directive mode of process design and improvement to provide satisfying roles for the operating members of the organization has led to the "empowerment" movement. Empowerment is appropriate in democratic societies, where it is believed that individuals must have a voice in the management of their surroundings and

that their actions should, as much as possible, be voluntary. Empowerment is considered more effective than coercion from above because voluntary action is generally expected to be more committed than involuntary action.

The problem with empowerment is that the voluntary actions of individuals and empowered groups, even those with the best of intentions, often are not tied into the organization's strategic goals. Even if incremental improvements are achieved and employees feel more satisfied than they did in a directed, hierarchical organization, the thought that arises in many a chief executive officer's mind is, "If only we could channel all this energy and enthusiasm more purposefully, we could surely get results much faster."

The dilemma, of course, is how to effectively integrate top-down direction, based on the corporate strategy, with bottom-up, voluntary actions. Clearly, implementation of corporate strategy through effective operations management requires an integrated approach to business process engineering and employee empowerment.

Business process engineering

As Exhibit 2 illustrates, business process engineering is carried out, broadly, in three stages:

1. The organizational paradigm is examined and a description of the overall process is aligned with strategy.
2. Roles of organizational functions or units in various parts of the process are analyzed.
3. The tasks of individuals (or teams) within these organizational functions or units are defined.

Each of these stages has problems whose solutions require the involvement of process doers.

At the first stage, we need to creatively rethink the process paradigm, which, to be implementable, must have the active participation of key organization members. At the second stage, where we deal with bundles of tasks assigned to different organizational functions or units, we encounter the problems of organizational chimneys and interunit power-sharing and politics. The breakthrough of these barriers is facilitated by interfunc-

Exhibit 2. *Business Process Engineering*

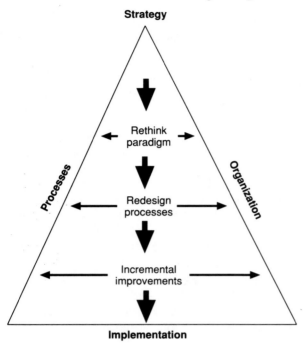

tional and interdepartmental task forces working on process redesign.

At the third stage in the definition of individuals' tasks, we have seen the need for the doers to take more responsibility for defining their tasks. This enables the doers' experience to be built into the tasks, giving the doers a greater understanding of what they will do and a greater sense of commitment.

An integrated approach

For effective operations redesign, it is necessary to integrate logical, top-down process engineering with more open, participative employee involvement at each of the three stages. A problem with combining these two approaches is the different mindsets required. *Processes* are a series of steps, each logically leading to the next one. Process engineers like to be fully in charge of process development so that they can ensure the completeness and sufficiency of the process to meet objectives that are set beforehand.

Empowerment, however, is based on handing over responsibility to many other people, with faith that their decisions—which are continuously emerging—will create the best

system. The outcomes of their decisions cannot be predicted in advance, nor is it easy to ensure that they will fit together and optimize the whole. Hence, practitioners of the process engineering approach to operations improvement tend to consider the empowerment/total quality management (TQM) practitioners as flaky, while the latter view the former as too mechanical!

Engineering business processes vs. bottom-up culture change

Since consultants label their approaches creatively, it is important to determine the philosophy of the approach and not merely go by the label. The choice is essentially as follows: Companies can have consultants (or internal experts) who can "engineer" business processes, or they can have consultants (or internal champions) who foster bottom-up "culture" change programs to empower employees.

It is very tempting to call on the former when defined results are required rapidly, and these consultants can deliver them, as did industrial engineers in mass production. Many process engineering consultants are now filling the role that internal industrial engineering staff filled when U.S. manufacturing organizations had strong internal departments to which they were able to attract the best engineering and management talent in the country. However, the paradigm of improvement and change is unaltered and will lead to the same outcomes: quick, "engineered" change, with inadequate buy-in from the operating staff and, hence, limited follow-on improvement. Operating employees see these process engineers much as industrial engineers of yore were seen: as tools of top management that may serve some overall corporate purpose, but at the cost of jobs and the freedom of operating staff.

Empowerment and TQM consultants. The empowerment- and training-oriented total quality management consultants also show some early results, but of a different type. They give an organization a sauna bath that opens the pores and gives a refreshing feeling. That is a good step toward health, no matter what game one plays. But to win, one also needs to develop skills and a game plan

Exhibit 3. *High Performance Businesses: An Integrated Improvement Approach*

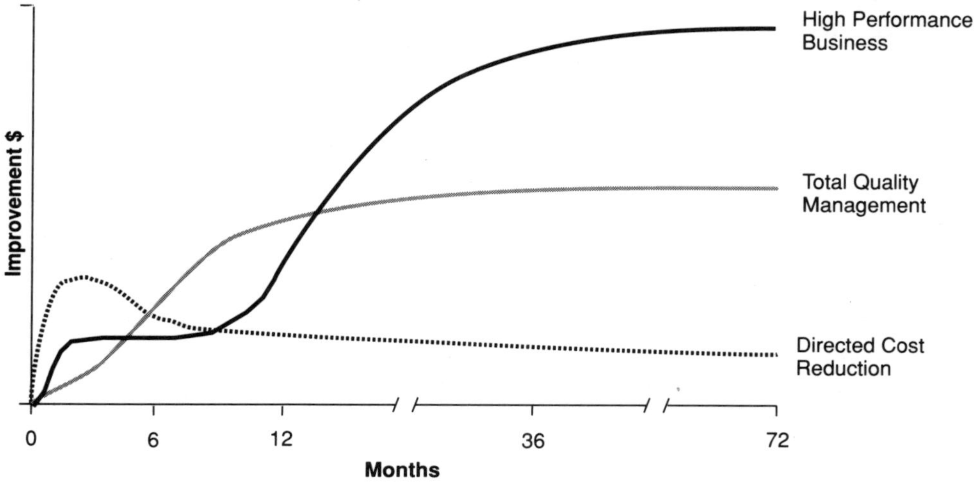

High Performance Business—an integrated improvement approach
Total Quality Management—bottom-up, inside-out approaches
Direct Cost Reduction—top-down, outside-in approaches

specifically related to the game and the chosen strategy. Generally, these consultants are inadequate for this larger role. They can be the team's physical health instructor, but not the coach.

There is catching up to do, and the need to stay ahead thereafter. What many U.S. manufacturing organizations need is rapid improvement in their costs and quality performance. But while doing this, they need to build the foundation for continuous improvement in areas that are vital for their longer-term competitive position. While immediate cost reduction is often essential, continuous improvement must be ensured. While taking action should not be delayed, the root cause of problems must be determined first. Sustainable acceleration of performance requires a blend of an analytical, top-down approach with more open, bottom-up employee involvement.

The ability to effectively integrate these seemingly contradictory approaches in a manufacturing improvement program is not yet easy to find. Having a framework for such an approach is a prerequisite to developing persons and organizations with this integrated ability, which is vital for improving the competitiveness of U.S. manufacturing. The "high perfor-

mance business" approach (see Exhibit 3) is a holistic framework of organizational concepts and methodologies for process improvement. In a company that uses the high performance business approach, change is brought about by involving top management, employees, and unions in determining priorities, then effecting the desired changes. Generally, the result is early and large gains (e.g., well-targeted cost reductions) and continuous improvement as achieved in well-managed TQM programs. The high performance business framework is emerging as a powerful approach for overhauling U.S. manufacturing firms and putting them on the path to sustainable performance acceleration. ▲

Reprinted from *Journal of Cost Management*, Spring 1993, pp. 68–72. Copyright © 1993 by Warren Gorham Lamont, a division of Research Institute of America Inc. All rights reserved. Used by permission.

Notes
1. James P. Womack, Daniel T. Jones, and Daniel Roos (New York: Rawson Associates, 1990).

Fast Forward: The Challenges Facing Controllers in a Global Market

C.J. McNair and Ronald Teichman

To succeed in an increasingly global marketplace, companies must outperform competitors on more than just cost. Since each change in an organization ultimately has financial implications, management must ensure that every activity is performed as efficiently as possible. Constant efforts should be made to eliminate waste and improve quality. For these goals to be accomplished, a change must occur in the way that business is accounted for. This article explains the steps companies should follow to transform their accounting systems into flexible databases of management information. This involves—among other steps—recasting accounting information as one part of a flexible relational database and maintaining a strategic focus.

"Go around asking a lot of damn fool questions and taking chances. Only through curiosity can we discover opportunities, and only by gambling can we take advantage of them."
—Clarence Birdseye

Global competition is redefining the playing field for companies and the managers in them. These changes are being reflected in a heightened concern for meeting, and exceeding, customer needs in order to a competitive edge. Customers, it would seem, are no longer satisfied with a high-quality product at a high price, delivered in six months or longer. Instead, they want high quality, reasonable cost, and rapid delivery. And, should any unplanned problems or needs arise, they expect their suppliers to be responsive, quickly meeting these new demands.

To succeed in this demanding global marketplace, a company has to outperform its competition on more than just cost. Competition on many fronts means that management must ensure that every activity is performed with an eye toward eliminating waste and improving quality. Responding to these challenges, companies are adopting new technologies, processes, and management techniques to encourage every employee to participate in the improvement effort. Additionally, technological breakthroughs, ever the impetus for change, are accelerating products through life cycles at increasing rates. The result is a turbulent and challenging corporate landscape.

Such a major change in the way business is conducted requires a corresponding change in the way that business is accounted for. The challenge facing controllers today is to understand how each of these changes in the way companies do business affects financial performance. To understand these issues, controllers must move beyond their traditional roles, becoming proactive members of the management team. Changing the types, and purposes, of information accumulated and generated on an ongoing basis is the starting point.

A path of change

Radical changes began taking place in American manufacturing in the early 1980s. Major industries became less and less competitive against foreign competition, most noticeably the Japanese. What was so difficult to understand was the reason for their success, and our decline. How could the Japanese, who had to overcome distance and natural re-

Table 1. *Continuous Improvement Tools*

Tool	"Waste" Targeted for Elimination
Just-in-time manufacturing (e.g., cellular manufacturing)	"Move" and "quene" time
Kanban	Buffer inventories (e.g., work-in-process)
Total quality management	Defects and rework
Total preventive maintenance	Unscheduled machine downtime
Flexible manufacturing systems	Set-up
Employee involvement	Failure to recognize, and employ, individual problem-solving skills and knowledge
Design for manufacturability	Engineering change notices; modifications caused by faulty design

source barriers, beat America at the manufacturing game?

The answer to this quandary did not emerge quickly. At first, it seemed that the heart of the issue was better quality control techniques, such as quality circles. American companies flocked to quality seminars (and still do), hoping to find the magic key that would unlock the door to competitive success.

The Japanese, though, were concerned about more than the quality of a final product. They relentlessly pursued continuous improvement in all areas of their companies. As Table 1 suggests, it is this pursuit of continuous improvement that lies at the heart of the Japanese management system. Each management tool noted is focused on eliminating waste somewhere in the organization.

However, looking across the list of items targeted for elimination, it is interesting to note that none of these "costs" are normally collected, analyzed, or reported by the accounting system. While the level of inventories may be recorded on the balance sheet, the dollars saved by reducing them (e.g., carrying costs) are not.

The impact on the competitive environment of "continuous improvement" driven companies was significant. Companies could no longer succeed by competing on only one product dimension, such as cost. Instead, companies began competing on multiple dimensions at once. A competitive edge today comes from being the best performer in terms of cost, quality, delivery, and responsiveness to customer requests.

These changes have created a demand for information that is flexible, responsive to ongoing changes in the organization, multidimensional, focused on decision support and forward-looking. The direct implications for controllers are that the traditional focus on historical product cost data needs to be reexamined. To support strategic and operational decision making, information has to arrive before the decision is made.

In fact, accounting scorecards are only the starting point for developing a system of cost estimates that tie to the activities that cause them. Historical cost numbers are the result of taking action; focusing on them will not change the past. They do provide some signal about potential future costs, but they must be examined in light of changing global market conditions.

The general ledger actually becomes a constraint on the accounting system when the focus is turned toward decision making and the future. Its highly structured, historical orientation, bundled with a burdensome system of reporting and disclosure regulations that makes even the most avid accountant groan, places artificial time and structure boundaries on the information available. Given that management, the controller's customer, requires flexible, responsive information to support decision making, then these restrictions need to be understood and addressed.

Contingent costing: dollars that make sense

Reviewing the list of recent criticisms leveled at management accounting (e.g., irrelevance, lacking timeliness, and distortion of performance reports), it seems that accounting needs to become contingent, horizontal as well as vertical in orientation, flexible, and integrated with other performance measurements. Contingent costing means that different cost systems are developed as new information demands arise: It is the embodiment of "different costs for different purposes" you learned by rote in your accounting program.

These flexible information structures are needed to ensure that changing conditions inside the company can be rapidly mirrored in the accounting system. Accomplishing this means that data must be collected and stored in database form. The data must include operational as well as financial measures and reflect the flow of activities as well as the structured reporting hierarchy underlying traditional accounting reports. The result is a relational database of costed activities that management can call upon to analyze any type of decision, to project the cost of various design alternatives for a product, and to provide the basis for control of ongoing efforts.

At the heart of the changes needed to create a value-adding accounting system is the need to focus on decision support as the starting point in designing a cost system. The structure, and complexity, of the cost management system must match the organization, as suggested by Lou Jones of Caterpillar, Inc.:

> "A good cost system should mirror the manufacturing process and the related support processes. The cost system quantifies these processes, product by product. The more complex and inconsistent these processes are the more complex the cost system becomes. In other words, the complexity of the manufacturing operations drives the complexity of the cost system."

Designing a cost system means that the controller understands the actual work flows of the organization and has encapsulated them in the system's structure. The operative word is "design"—transforming accounting to a value-added decision support tool requires an active design effort; the cost system needed to support Caterpillar won't fit Citibank. Each company is unique in the way it processes its work, the bundle of products and services it provides, and the objectives it pursues. The cost management system, therefore, has to be

designed to match the unique characteristics of each company.

Once the company has developed the cost management database, the second aspect of "contingent costing" becomes important: the use of different cost constructions for different decisions. The database sits, quivering, waiting for a question or problem to address. As each decision arises, the database is queried to obtain the relevant pieces of information, summarize them, and create a tailored report for the manager making the decision.

In an evolutionary sense, then, contingent cost management systems provide different cost constructions for different activity structures, different decisions, and different points in time. The unifying focus is the need to provide information to support strategic and operational decision making.

Figure 1 suggests how this database operates. Information from the general ledger, the shop floor control system, and other information sources in the company, are fed into a relational database system that can move flexibly from one data set to the next, pulling those pieces of data needed from each. If the decision context changes, so does the data required. This is no problem; it simply means that the database is queried once again.

This is not a system of the future. The technology exists today to create the relational database using existing information sources within the company. Companies such as Frito Lay and Caterpillar are using these integrated databases to provide real-time information to their management. Using simple data input systems, such as bar coding and other forms of magnetic data imaging, continuous flows of actual results from the field are fed into the database, providing instant updates to the system itself. Management can access this information to drive changes to prices in a specific region of the country in response to changes in a competitor's marketing plan, for example.

What about the auditors?

All discussions about changing accounting systems eventually raise a large question. The overriding concern is responding to the auditor's requests that financial information be maintained, and summarized, in conformance

Figure 1. *The Solution*

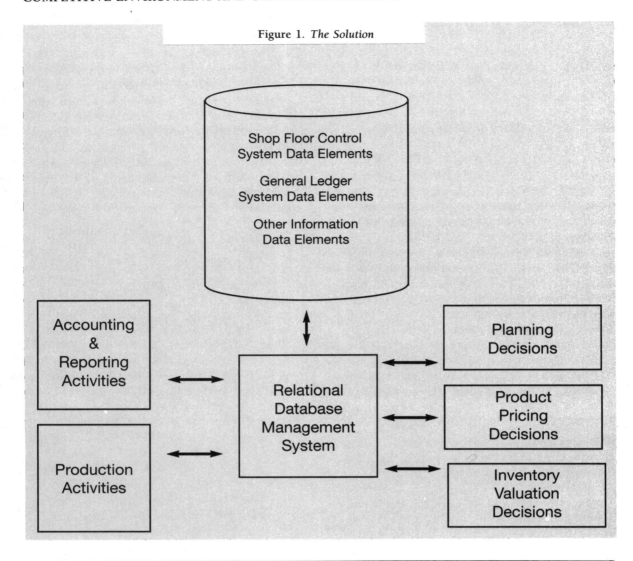

with generally accepted accounting practices (GAAP). Often this need to conform takes on a life of its own, become the end, or objective, of the controller's tasks rather than simply one stopping point along the way.

There is little doubt that a company, to remain economically viable, must consistently receive a favorable audit opinion. The auditors, though, don't say that management can't maintain internal information for decision support. Their request is simply for full absorption product costing information, and a trackable audit trail for all primary financial transactions. The first item, full absorption product costing, is actually a "no brainer." Any reasonable inventory valuation technique will be accepted, as long as all the dollars

spent in production end up attached to some product. The auditors don't care which one, really.

Management does, though. The real focus in performing product costing exercises, then, is ensuring management of a relative degree of accuracy for setting prices, making make-versus-buy decisions, and for developing strategic plans for product line and market segments. These demands for information are much more exacting, and much more critical for organizational survival, than supplying the required documentation for the auditor. In fact, the required financial reports and product cost numbers can be treated as one of the many uses of the relational database information.

Everyone gains when the integrity, flexibility, and usefulness of accounting data are improved. Auditors can more closely examine the reasons for changes in financial position from one year to the next. Managers obtain a value-adding tool for understanding where problems are and identifying solutions for them. Controllers, though, gain the most of all, as they replace the "bean counter" image with that of a proactive, informed, valuable member of the management team.

Opportunities, not threats

The changes occurring in the field have been perceived by some controllers as a threat to their existence in corporate America. In reality, the future never looked brighter. Companies faced with intense global competition must know that their decisions are based on sound numbers, whether operational or financial in nature. Even more critical is the need to understand how changes in the way work is done affects the firm's economic performance. The economic imperative has not gone away—it has intensified as customers come to expect more in terms of quality and service, at a lower cost.

The final question is, how do we transform accounting into this flexible database of management information? The steps are:
1. Recast accounting information as one part of a flexible relational database.
2. Develop a strategic focus.
3. Walk around and become reacquainted with the people and processes in your company.
4. Learn about the new tools and opportunities available in the field, don't resist them.
5. Get involved with the changes occurring in your company.

These may sound more like prescriptions than steps, but the first critical step is changing the accounting mindset itself. The controller can create and maintain the information management needs, but he or she must first understand what is required, and why. Accounting for accounting's sake is not the goal; adding the value to the organization is.

The key is to keep an eye on the horizon, to always look forward, not back. The past is a good starting point for understanding the causal relationship between costs and activities, but it is not the final destination: the customer is. Meeting customer expectations means that every manager, in every area of the organization, must understand their role in the value chain that connects the company to the marketplace.

As companies transform in response to demands from the global market, the need for relevant, reliable information will continue to grow. Every change made in the organization will have financial implications at some point in time. Understanding these relationships and exploiting them will be the key to competitive survival. ▲

Turbo Marketing Through Time Compression

Philip Kotler and Paul J. Stonich

A host of advantages will flow to companies that learn to make and deliver goods and services faster than their competitors. However, four key questions must be answered to determine if a "turbo" marketing approach is suitable for any given company. Specifically (as this article explains), these questions turn on: the size and attractiveness of the market; the feasibility of shortening cycle times; the ongoing costs of following the new marketing strategy; and whether competitors will be able to match the company's reductions in cycle time.

In the 1990s, companies will need to master a new set of skills if they hope to compete successfully in the marketplace. With marketing battlefields constantly changing, only those companies that grasp these changes early enough to exploit them will prosper, leaving in the dust their tradition-bound competitors who stick with obsolete strategies.

In the first wave of competitive marketing, successful companies discovered ways to make goods cheaper. Henry Ford did everything possible to reduce the cost of manufacturing automobiles in order to expand the market for Ford cars. His obsession with cost reduction catapulted Ford Motor Company into the number-one position in a burgeoning automobile market.

Second-wave companies worked on designing their products to be different from those of their competitors. General Motors applied this strategic principle to the limit. Instead of standardizing its cars to keep costs down, GM differentiated its cars by features, styles, branding, and price points. Not surprisingly, it stole away the number-one spot from Ford.

Third-wave companies learned to make products better. Japanese manufacturers led the quality revolution by applying the management principles of total quality improvement. Toyota, Honda, and other Japanese companies paid close attention to the needs of customers as well as to feedback from them to continually improve the quality of their products. These quality-oriented companies won increasing sales in their markets.

In the 1990s, fourth-wave companies will be those that learn to make and deliver goods and services faster than their competitors. These "turbo marketers" will have the competitive edge. Eyelab and Federal Express are two examples of fourth-wave companies.

☐ Eyelab sought to reduce the long waiting time (normally one week) required to deliver custom-finished eyeglasses to consumers. It did this by transferring manufacturing from a single, centrally located laboratory to mini-laboratories at each of its retail outlets. Today, every Eyelab store has lenses, frames, grinding equipment, and technicians who are able to provide customers with eyeglasses within one hour.

This transfer of production from a single large factory to individual retail outlets is being implemented in a growing number of businesses ranging from film processing to snack foods (e.g., Mrs. Fields, where cookies are baked on the premises as needed).

☐ The huge success of Federal Express is the result of Fred Smith's recognizing the importance that households and businesses place on fast and reliable delivery services. Smith implemented a brilliantly conceived hub-and-spoke system that enables Federal Express's U.S. operation to guarantee that letters and small packages picked up before 5:00 P.M. one day will be delivered anywhere in the United States before 11:00 A.M. the following day. The company's record of on-time delivery— well over 95%—is so much faster than the normal delivery time that the U.S. Postal Service admits that Federal Express users are willing to pay 25 to 40 times more for this service.

"Market research is a useful tool for identifying what segments of what markets place a particular value on cycle time reduction."

Time compression, one of the major new avenues for attaining competitive advantage, has its roots in today's changing society. Consumers value time more than their parents did just one generation ago. The growth of two-income families, with their increased job and social responsibilities and the generally faster pace of life, has created a large consumer base that is willing to pay a premium for timeliness.

In addition, by using improved management techniques, such as total quality management, improved information and communications technology, job enrichment programs, flatter organizations, etc., companies have been able to speed up their performance. In many instances, this ability to provide goods faster has also stimulated demand.

Finally, time compression has increased in importance as the traditional sources of competitive advantage (i.e., cost, differentiation, service, and quality) have been more fully exploited; its potential as a competitive tie-breaker has been increasingly recognized.

Time-based strategies

Will a time-compression strategy help every company? Executives need to consider four questions to determine whether a turbo marketing approach will benefit a particular busi-

ness. If all the answers are positive, a company can gain considerable advantage by transforming itself into a turbo marketer.

1. Is there a sufficiently large and attractive time-sensitive market? A time-compression strategy makes sense only when significant numbers of customers value time compression enough to pay a premium price or increase their purchases. The economic equation depends heavily on the relative degree of time sensitivity.

In some markets, time sensitivity is overwhelming. This is the case in the medical market, where surgeons and injured patients need immediate access to hospital operating facilities. In financial markets, stock traders and foreign exchange dealers need up-to-the-moment information.

In other markets, however, only a fraction of the buyers may be time impatient. Buyers often vary greatly in terms of their tolerance of waiting time.

Consider the reactions of different customers upon hearing that there will be a one-hour wait to be seated at a fine restaurant: Some will wait, others will leave, and still others will slip a $10 bill to the headwaiter in hopes of being seated sooner.

Some customers will refuse to wait. Either they lack patience or high-quality food is not that important to them; possibly, waiting might make them late for the theater. For a busy attorney, waiting time may represent lost money; for a sales representative, it may be an inconvenience that leads to a lost opportunity for calling on a key account.

Market research is a useful tool for identifying what segments of what markets place a particular value on cycle time reduction. The small-package delivery service, which in recent years has grown into a significant industry, is one example of a market in which a large number of consumers is willing to pay a high premium for overnight delivery service—or even same-day delivery.

Focus groups and surveys are useful tools for determining how many people want or demand more than standard first-, second-, or third-class delivery, and how much they are willing to pay for it. Sometimes an entire market may value time compression. For example, one digital switch manufacturer has used market research to plot its performance in terms of quality, price, and delivery time against the performance of its major competitor, as well as customer needs.

Research revealed that the company's products and those of the competition were meeting customer needs similarly and satisfactorily in terms of quality and price; the only significant difference was in delivery time. Thus, the manufacturer's management recognized that if the organization were able to cut delivery time and still meet customer quality and cost expectations, it would be well on its way to dramatically improving its competitive position.

Of course, achieving faster cycle time is one thing; getting customers to pay for it is another. "Paying for it" means increasing volume and/or paying a premium price. So the question becomes, even when there is a significant number of time-sensitive buyers in a market, will they pay more for the speedier delivery of a product or service? And if the answer is yes, how much more will they pay?

Consider the advent of faster film development services. Suppose the normal waiting period is two days. How much of a premium will consumers pay to have film developed in one day? Half a day? One hour? Clearly, the premium will vary among buyers with different levels of impatience. As Federal Express has proven, impatient customers are willing to pay substantially more for cycle time reduction.

2. Is it feasible to shorten cycle time? Once a company has examined the demand side and has estimated the size of the time-sensitive market and the price premium or volume increase, it can turn to the supply side and ask:

- What implementation effort will be required, how long will it take, and at what investment cost?
- How much time can be taken out of the cycle?
- Will the investment pay off?

Reducing cycle time sometimes requires developing new technologies; more often it requires reorganizing work routines so that many activities, beginning with sales and ending with delivery and setup, can be shortened. Typically, companies work hard to reduce manufacturing time, so that it is the areas outside manufacturing where additional opportunity for reducing time should be sought.

Cycle time can be reduced in three ways. First, the time used by each individual functional area can be cut. Second, activities can be combined so that they can be accomplished simultaneously. Third, a step can be eliminated entirely. Consider these three examples:

☐ To reduce mortgage approval time, Citicorp Mortgage cuts the interval between initial customer contact and the beginning of credit analysis by sending the mortgage application to the prospective borrower by overnight delivery. The service person then calls the customer, helps him or her to fill out the necessary forms over the telephone, and reminds the customer to return the completed forms in the prepaid overnight envelope supplied by Citicorp Mortgage. Thus, the major first step is accomplished in three days rather than the usual week or more required when traditional methods are used.

☐ Sears and Levi Strauss have linked themselves electronically so that Sears' retail sales are recorded and transmitted to Levi Strauss, and the order for more product is entered daily. Thus, the steps are accomplished virtually simultaneously rather than sequentially.

☐ Technology can often be used to eliminate a step entirely. One equipment manufacturer changed its design so that a new product could be shipped and literally plugged in and used by its industrial customers. Prior to the change, technical representatives were required to wire the product and test it on site.

Shortening the cycle

In general, three principles can be applied to reduce cycle time: reorganize the work; organize and reward to encourage time compression; and lead the cycle time reduction effort aggressively.

Reorganizing the work requires a clear understanding of the current work flow and the way information is used and by whom. The analyst can use flowcharts, critical path analyses, documentation reviews, and other tools and techniques to determine how work is performed, how it might be accomplished better and faster, and what work activities fail to add as much value as cost.

The company must view not only its own internal work activities in a systems perspective, but also the work performed by its suppliers and distributors. Companies such as Ford, Xerox, and Hewlett-Packard have reduced the number of their suppliers and tied the remaining ones much closer to them through electronic interchange systems, message systems, etc.

"One equipment manufacturer changed its design so that a new product could be shipped and literally plugged in and used by its industrial customers."

Organizing and rewarding are additional methods to encourage time compression. The organizational structures of short cycle time companies share several common characteristics. First, these structures tend to be relatively flat. By eliminating layers for approvals and decision making, time-based firms escape the bureaucratic delays so prevalent in large organizations.

Second, organizational structures are usually designed around a product/market focus. This helps the organization keep its eye on the customer and reduces the time-consuming problem of negotiating resources from functional organizations.

Third, these organizations use small work teams composed of multifunctional players to carry out the work. By creating and empowering small teams, they remove another roadblock to timeliness.

In addition, turbo marketers organize their data to compress cycle time. Information, whether computer-generated, handwritten, or verbally communicated, plays a vital role in helping organizations better manage time. Timely feedback from the sales force, distributors, and customers; rapid feedback to suppliers; and continuous communication across the organization all help reduce process time. However, too much information—or unnecessary information, forms, and procedures—can be counterproductive.

A final characteristic of fast cycle time companies is that they emphasize timeliness in their measurement and reward systems. They keep records of completion times and set high improvement targets; awards and recognition are given to reinforce desired behaviors.

For a firm that embarks on a time-compression strategy, *aggressive leadership* is equally important. Often a firm's culture needs to be changed before cycle times can be shortened. Leaders need to understand the current culture and behaviors and what new behaviors are necessary for success. They must formulate a vision, communicate it, gain commitment to it, change attitudes, and use champions to power the change.

The driving force that energizes the implementation process is commitment. To elicit commitment and secure buy-in, leaders must be skilled in:

- Indicating how a time-based strategy will benefit the company and the individual contributors.
- Gathering and exchanging views with employees and involving them in key activities and decisions.
- Communicating to share information, to elicit the views of others, and to provide positive feedback to reinforce others' contributions.
- Providing support through resource allocation and training and influencing others to integrate their priorities with the broader time-based vision.

For time-based strategies to be implemented successfully, everyone in the organization must believe that the leader's vision and strategy for achieving that vision can work; everyone must also share that vision, understand that the goal of becoming time-based includes every individual in the company, and see the benefits that a time-based organization offers each of them as individuals.

The implementation effort and cost required to reduce cycle time will be substantial. Typi-

Exhibit 1. *Five Companies That Reduced Cycle Time*

		Cycle Time	
Company	Product	Before	After
Matsushita	Washing machines	360 hours	2 hours
GE	Circuit breakers	3 weeks	3 days
Brunswick	Fishing reels	3 weeks	1 week
Otis Elevator	Freeing stuck elevators	2 hours	0.5 hour
Square D	Electrical equipment	18 weeks	4 weeks

cally, a cycle time reduction effort requires a minimum of 12 to 24 months of sustained effort and a continuing commitment thereafter. The effort will be large but the payoff can be great. Exhibit 1 gives examples of companies that have reduced cycle time by 50% or more.

3. *What are the ongoing costs of following a turbo marketing strategy?* Obviously, the implementation costs need to be weighed against the potential benefits of providing increased value to the customer through reduced cycle time. But what about the ongoing costs of being a turbo marketer?

Some critics suggest that speedups often result in reduced product quality and/or increased costs. The alleged trade-offs have been expressed in various ways:

- If a company speeds up, its costs will rise and its quality will fall.
- If a company improves its quality, its costs will rise and it will take more time to produce high quality.
- If a company reduces its costs, its quality will suffer and its speed will be slowed down.

This conventional wisdom is incorrect. Time, quality, and cost are generally consistent with one another. Many companies have reported that the steps taken to improve quality have resulted in lower costs and faster production.

For example, in the mid-1980s, Northern Telecom decided that it needed to reduce costs substantially in order to maintain a competitive edge. A company task force defined cycle time reduction as the single most important goal of the effort. By 1990, Northern Telecom had succeeded in reducing cycle time by 50% or more; at the same time, qual-

ity (as measured by customer satisfaction) had soared and costs had been reduced significantly.

The techniques used to take cycle time out of a system are, in fact, first cousins to continuous improvement/total quality management techniques. So it is not surprising that both timeliness and quality can be improved simultaneously while costs fall.

Cycle time shortening and quality enhancement can reduce costs for two reasons. First, overall efficiency improves because costly rework is reduced, useless administrative tasks are limited, and lower inventory levels are required. Second, high-quality, time-based companies attract new customers. A growing customer base and volume expansion generally lead to lower unit costs as overhead expenses are absorbed by more units.

4. *Can competitors easily match the company's cycle time reduction?* Even if competitors catch up, companies that are the fastest first achieve an initial advantage. They establish a time gap and win brand loyalty, market share, and an attractive cost position. In some industries, they are able to sustain their lead.

Toyota's success in reducing automobile development time from five years to three years has left U.S. car manufacturers still trying to catch up. Although Ford has been working to reduce its development time to four years, and then to three years, by the time it reaches this goal Toyota will likely have reduced its development time still further. Leaders never rest.

In other industries, such as those involving high technology, the time advantage may be less sustainable. In 1985, Motorola spent three years developing a new model cellular phone. Today, the development cycle takes only 15 months; Motorola's goal is to reduce this time to just six months.

But even though the development cycle is shrinking rapidly for Motorola, competitors clearly understand the time game and are hoping to leapfrog Motorola's advances. In industries where technological breakthroughs can quickly erase the time gap, being fastest first does not necessarily lead to a sustainable advantage.

However, much depends on creating a culture that is innovative, nimble, and quick. Companies must couple the so-called soft aspects of management with efforts to achieve measurable time-based results.

3M, for example, is famous for its ability to quickly bring new products and product extensions to market. A large percentage of 3M's sales are derived from new products. Some of this success has been driven by 3M's measurement and rewards system, and the way the company is organized. But much of it is also the result of an innovative, nimble, and time-conscious corporate culture—one that values new ideas, new products, and new approaches, and one that places emphasis on making things happen quickly.

One should carefully consider the value of using a turbo marketing strategy by examining the market size of the time-sensitive segment and the price premium that it will pay, the feasibility and cost of shortening cycle time, and the sustainability of this advantage. Timeliness can offer a strong competitive advantage to companies in almost every industry. The 1990s will not only be about who can produce goods cheaper, different, or better, but this decade will also favor those who can produce them faster. ▲

Reprinted from *Journal of Business Strategy,* September/October 1991, pp. 24–29. Copyright © 1991 by Warren Gorham Lamont, a division of Research Institute of America Inc. All rights reserved. Used by permission.

How a Controller Communicates the Change to ABC

Steven M. Hronec

Change is inevitably painful. Consequently, *how* a new cost system is implemented matters just as much as *what* it is supposed to accomplish. Any company that plans to implement a productivity program or a new cost management system (such as activity-based costing) must plan in order to make the transition as smooth as possible. The proven approach explained in this article involves, first, identifying the barriers to change, then minimizing or overcoming those barriers with such change management techniques as creating an awareness of the barriers, consensus building, team building, and creating a success story.

Picture this scenario. Your CEO asks some very hard questions: What's the true cost of our products? How do we know if our company is making progress toward our strategic goals? Can we manage—or, better yet, reduce—overhead and focus on speed-to-market at the same time?

The answers take the form of a new cost/ performance management system.

As the controller—the keeper of performance measures—you have a vested interest in the new system, which uses both financial and nonfinancial measures to focus everyone in the organization on the continuous improvement of performance, cost, and quality. You have been asked to help implement it.

You're behind the project 100%, but you predict that there will be implementation pitfalls. After all, your current cost/performance measurement system is imbedded deeply in your company's culture. Not only is it the primary

performance system, it is also the primary communication vehicle.

Even though the new system is in your company's best interests, there are bound to be barriers to any changes. How can you minimize their impact?

A pro-active plan eases the pain

Change is good and change is natural, but change is also inevitably painful. A company planning to implement a new cost management system or productivity program should pro-actively plan to make the transition as smooth and as positive as possible.

Experience with thousands of companies shows that there is a proven approach to change management. Phase One of the implementation plan involves identifying the four barriers to change. Don't read that as a directive to look for problems or be negative; it simply means facing facts. People are often uncomfortable with change, and success often hinges on how well a company diffuses resistance up front. Phase Two involves minimizing or overcoming the four barriers with five change management techniques.

Understanding the barriers to change

Even though there may be general agreement concerning the need for change, be aware of the four levels of resistance: individual, organizational, cultural, and environmental. The "difficulty factor" increases from one level to the next (i.e., change is easiest at the individual level and hardest at the environmental level).

Individual barriers. People resist a new cost management system for various reasons:

- They believe the status quo is satisfactory.
- They perceive a need for change, but fear of the unknown breeds resistance.
- They fear a loss of status, because a new cost management system triggers a change in reporting relationships and a reassessment of individual positions in the organization.
- They will suffer a bruised ego, because a new system implies that there is a better way to do the job that they've been doing.
- They fear a lack of needed skills will leave them out of the new system: fear of obsolescence prompts considerable resistance.
- They contend that the new system won't be credible (i.e., they won't have control over the new measures, nor will the new system give a reliable picture of what they do).

Organizational barriers. The organizational issues are more complex and far-reaching. Management levels are affected, since productivity improvements often require a flattening of the organizational chart. If management isn't behind the new system, it can't be implemented effectively.

Similar to individuals resisting any decrease of their status, departmental conflicts of interest can inhibit change. As a new cost management system takes a cross-functional "process view"—judging the effectiveness of a whole process, not just its parts—departmental lines justly are blurred or eliminated. No longer can the individual succeed without cooperation across traditional company boundaries.

Finally, if a company has a conventional top-down structure, the hierarchy is typically strong and the decision-making is nonparticipatory. The threat here is, again, that management won't get behind the change and won't apply new concepts to its own work habits. Unfortunately, leaders often perceive that *others*, not themselves, have to change.

Cultural barriers. One step up from how a company is organized is how it conducts business. An organization's traditional values are hard to buck and can make a big difference in how smoothly and quickly a new cost management can be put in place.

Changes proposed only from an outside source have less likelihood of acceptance than those generated, at least in part, internally. Management especially might assume that

outsiders don't "understand our business." The right advisors solicit and even insist on employee input and help generate "buy-in" throughout the company.

Expectations play an important role in creating cultural barriers. If a conservative organization historically has penalized risk-taking, for example, the implementation will be stymied by a lack of innovative spirit. The culture is set against change; there are no rewards for trying.

A precedent of too much change can be just as bad. A project-of-the-month mentality, bred from a history of false starts and unfinished projects, creates cynicism. When told of a new cost management system, people can take a "wait and see" attitude, assuming that this project, too, will fade away.

Environmental barriers. Although the hardest to get around, environmental walls can be accommodated. The regulatory environment might require the continued practice of some "old" cost management techniques, especially in regard to keeping score. Generally accepted accounting principles, the Securities and Exchange Commission, and the Internal Revenue Service have specific reporting and documentation requirements. You still must "get the numbers."

Changing the performance measurements means changing the job descriptions, and that often triggers resistance from unions and other employee groups. Criteria for compensation and promotion, for example, have to continue to meet standards of fairness and equity. Careful negotiations are essential in this situation.

Overcoming barriers: strategies for success

First wisdom, then action. With the wisdom of knowing the four barriers, you can attack them with five management techniques.

1. Create an awareness of the barriers. Communicate, communicate, communicate. This doesn't mean telling everyone everything all the time; it does mean putting into action a consistent, comprehensive intracompany communication system.

The barriers to change have to be discussed openly. You'll never get 100% buy-in, and there is nearly always a drop in attitude and productivity before a new system is complete.

Exhibit 1. *Change Readiness Survey*

Is Your Company Ready for Change?

Before planning specific strategies to overcome barriers to change, management needs to assess the organization's readiness. Ask key people these questions:

- To what extent is there a perceived need for the information provided by new cost management systems? (Specify the type of information to be generated.)
- On whom can you count for support? (These people will become the change agents in the project.)
- What resources would help build consensus and cross-functional teams?
- What elements in the current cost accounting and performance measurement systems could be used to ease the transition to the new system? (You might not have to discard the old system entirely.)

After you receive the answers, call a few of the participants and ask them to elaborate on their responses. Finally, be sure to tell participants that their opinions are valuable. Information gathered by this *Change Readiness Survey* gives management a good foundation for effective implementation strategies.

But people are more receptive to change if they perceive that management is interested in their needs. Regular, short meetings or the systematic asking of employees for their reactions and input helps break down the barriers.

A *Change Readiness Survey* (see exhibit) can get a company's project started on the right foot. Such a tool helps management understand everyone's perceptions and expectations. Then, as the project progresses, it's important that the implementers keep their eyes open for new barriers and deal with them promptly.

2. Management first. "Actions speak louder than words" is never more true than when you're trying to implement change. If management does not apply the new measure-ments to its own performance, lower levels in the organization won't either.

Management has to "practice what it preaches" by supporting the project 100%. Attending and conducting training sessions, for example, is an effective way to make support visible.

3. Consensus building. Because everyone has to be involved in the project, participation at all levels should be encouraged during each step of the cost management system project, including in the developing of recommendations and the making of decisions about implementation strategies. Different techniques, such as focus groups or quality circles, can act as change levers, drawing together the diverse groups to move them toward a common goal.

At each step, commitment is gained by providing checkpoints and asking people for feedback. Remember, be prepared to hear bad news as well as good. When you get input, use it or explain why you didn't. Again, clear and consistent communication at all levels is vital, if for no other reason than to identify where management support is needed most.

Consensus comes as you create a desire for change. The new performance measurements have to be positioned as an essential foundation for the future. Management should sell the benefits of change by pointing out new opportunities; change efforts should be celebrated and rewarded.

4. Team building. While consensus building moves up and down an organization, team building moves across it. Departmental segmentation prevents "process-driven" performance measures.

Different functions, such as engineering, marketing, and accounting, have to work together with unprecedented levels of cooperation. Strategies, goals, rewards, and budgets should cross traditional departmental barriers.

5. Create a success story. Success doesn't happen; it's created. Because "nothing succeeds like success," the best way to illustrate the benefits of change and to overcome anxieties is to create a success story.

When choosing a division, plant, or department to pilot the new system, pick an area that has strong leadership, a reasonable size and scope of operations (make sure it's not a "no brainer"), high visibility, and enthusiasm for the project.

Once the pilot proves the benefits, management should publicize the results, bringing the implementation full circle to communication for greater awareness throughout the whole organization.

"How" matters as much as "what"

Every company is different, and so is every cost/performance system. To be right for your company, performance measures have to be tied closely to long-term, market-driven strategies.

Without effective, aggressive implementation, a new cost management system is no more than words on paper. How a system is implemented matters just as much as what it hopes to achieve.

The simple change-management techniques described here, applied consistently and coherently, can help assure success. ▲

Change Management as a Platform for Activity-Based Management

Roger Beynon

People do not instinctively resist ideas; rather, they resist change. Any major culture-changing initiative like activity-based management (ABM) can thus lead to problems. Probably no one opposes getting more accurate, more timely, and more useful cost information, yet many employees get defensive when they are confronted with the introduction of ABM. The methodology for change toward ABM proposed in this article is founded on the premise that "belief determines behavior." Ignoring the force of people's reactions to change dramatically reduces the chances that an implementation of ABM will succeed.

L‍ast year we asked members of the quality roundtable at a major airline the following question: "When was the last time you met someone who was *against* the idea of better quality?" Members of the audience looked at one another with puzzlement, given the apparent absurdity of the question: "Never," was the unanimous reply.

"Then why," we continued, "do so many companies encounter resistance when they embark on quality programs?"

The only response to this question was silence—as it was for questions about resistance to safety programs, environmental programs, or any other program that could be considered a mainline corporate initiative.

Resistance to change

In much the same vein, there is probably no one who opposes getting more accurate, more timely, and more useful cost information. So why do so many employees get defensive when they are confronted with the introduction of activity-based management (ABM)?

The answer, so far as we can surmise, is that people do not instinctively resist ideas; rather, they resist change.

Companies that introduce any initiative with signficant implications for corporate culture are well advised to recognize the existence of change as a separate force on the psyche of a work force. To ignore the impact of people's reaction to change is to build a mistake into a process, thus breaking one of the basic principles of modern thinking about quality and (as a result) dramatically reducing the chances that an initiative will succeed.

The search for a methodology

Acceptance of this premise leads to a search for a methodology for effective change management. This section describes several methodologies that have been proposed.

Dr. Kenneth Blanchard (of "One-minute Manager" fame) offers a program designed around the following four-phase sequence:

1. Denial;
2. Bargaining;
3. Anger; and
4. Acceptance.

This theory, however, was originally developed to explain the behavior patterns of addicts: Even in companies dense with what IBM calls "tree-huggers," few workers can appropriately be described as clinically *addicted* to their processes. Consequently, the theory has limited applicability in everyday work environments.

Understanding motivation, planning, and communication. The field of organizational development has linked successful change management to an understanding of motivation. As if to add weight to this contention, a bewildering array of motivational theories exists, but there is no coherent synthesis that could be used as a blueprint for effectively managing the change process.

Other texts stress the importance of planning and communication. While this is sound advice, a vast new consulting industry has arisen to help jump-start stalled quality programs, many of which were planned and communicated as if they contained truths carved in stone on Mt. Sinai. Planning and communication, no matter how meticulously carried out, are not enough.

Indeed, we have yet to discover a proven, practical methodology available for effectively managing change. As a result, we were forced to develop our own methodology by working with—and learning from—our clients and our mistakes. What we have developed has grown from rapid, repeated trial and error in doing whatever it takes to make an initiative take hold and take off. Trainers might call it a methodology; manufacturers might call it a process; accountants might call it a system. Whatever you call it, try it: It seems to work.

Theoretical underpinnings

The starting point of our methodology is the premise that "belief determines behavior." This is based on the "ABC" principle that the American psychologist Albert Ellis developed, where:

- A stands for *activating event*;
- B stands for *belief system*; and
- C stands for *consequent behavior*.

Ellis maintains that identical activating events will produce widely differing consequent behavior depending on the individual belief system that filters the event. For our purposes, let's define a belief as "an opinion held to be true."

A simple example serves to illustrate the principle. Senators who voted on the recent nomination of Clarence Thomas for the Supreme Court experienced (at one level) the same activating event (i.e., the testimonies of the witnesses) yet demonstrated differing consequent behaviors (i.e., either a yea or nay vote) because of their differing belief systems (in this instance, literally whether they believed Clarence Thomas or Anita Hill).

Exhibit 1. *The Behavioral Cycle*

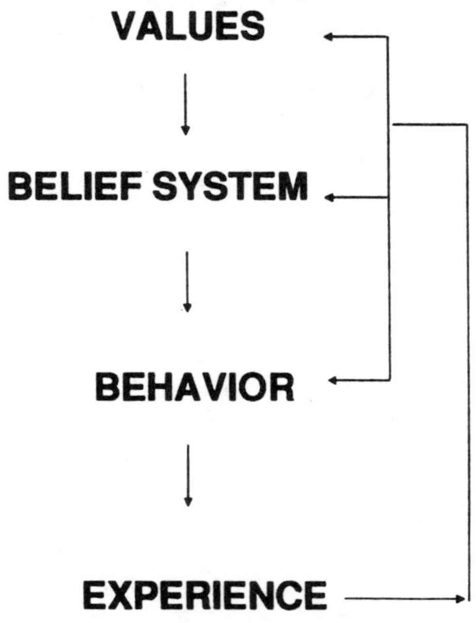

Theory X vs. Theory Y. In a business context, management styled on Theory X is essentially a set of behaviors based on the implicit belief that man is inherently lazy and corrupt. Theory Y-styled management is behavior predicated on the (again implicit) belief that man is inherently good and hard working. If we accept for the moment that belief determines behavior, what, we should ask, determines belief? The following model attempts to depict in simple terms what is a complex set of interrelationships. We are suggesting that there is a cause-and-effect hierarchy in operation. Our values (which are expressed as something we believe *in*) give us our belief system (which is expressed by saying we believe *that* . . .). Our belief system leads to our *behavior*, which in turn results in *experiences* that constantly loop back to modify one or more of the three previous components (see Exhibit 1).

Let's look at how the model might work in the context of a corporation.

- *Value*: XYZ Corporation and its employees believe *in* openness and honesty in all interactions.
- *Belief system*: Since an employee of XYZ should believe *that* it pays to be open and honest in every aspect of his work, his behavior should be consistent with that belief.

Exhibit 2. *Beliefs Model*

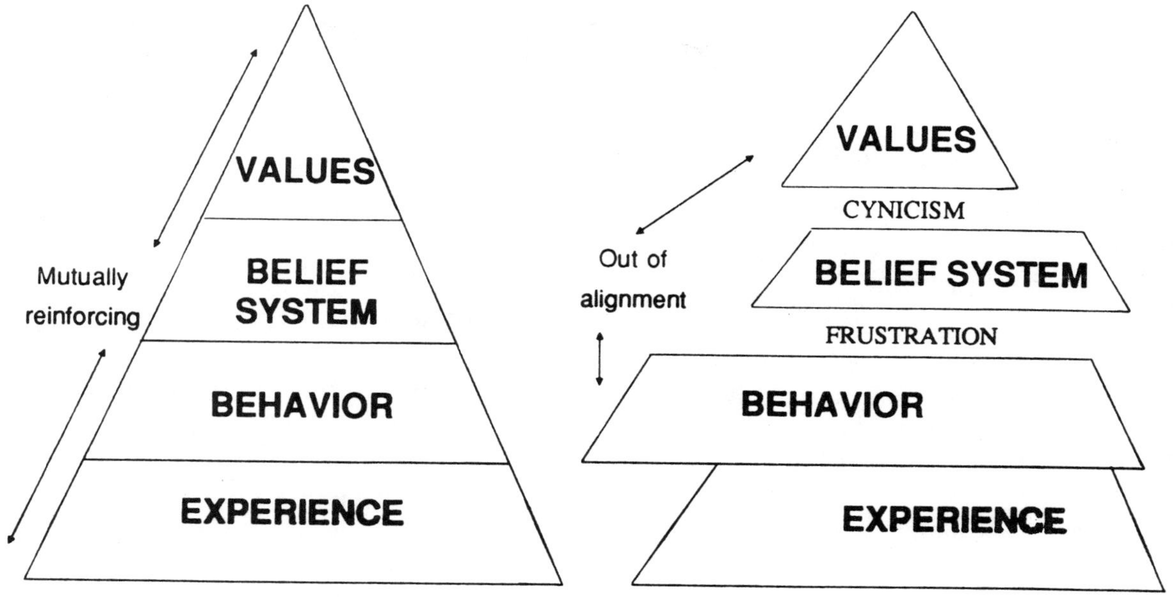

- *Behavior*: Assume, for example that an employee fails to submit a report on time—perhaps because the process within which he works allows several bosses to set conflicting priorities—but then owns up by taking responsibility for the late report. The employee's resulting experience should (assuming that the corporation lives up to its own values) be as shown next.
- *Experience*: The boss accepts the employee's apology, appreciates his candor, and helps correct the process so that opportunities for the problem will not recur.

Note, however, that if the corporation does *not* live up to its values, the effect on the employee's belief system can be dramatic. What if the employee makes a mistake and owns up to it, then promptly gets demoted?

At the corporate level, the prescribed value system has not been modified—the posters still proclaim it—but the employee (and all his peers) will undergo a radically modified belief. The new belief holds that if you cannot get a report out *on* time, then you'd better have a darned good excuse *in* time.

Changed beliefs affect productivity. The behavior and time of employees who hold de-

fensive beliefs of this sort will be less productive than that of their counterparts in an organization in which values, beliefs, behavior, and experience are consistent and mutually reinforcing. Breaks or contradictions between a belief system and the behavior or experience components of the model produce *frustration* in employees. A contradiction between values and beliefs produces *cynicism*, which, from a management perspective, is a far more systemic problem to tackle than frustration.

From one perspective, then, the role of management (as shown in Exhibit 2) is to realign the various components of a belief model and to counter or preempt anything that would force them out of alignment. In practical terms, any major culture-changing initiative has the potential to cause misalignment. Since ABM represents a powerful force for change, therefore, it has the potential to cause significant misalignments.

Distinguishing between model and actual beliefs

For methodological purposes, our next step is to distinguish between the beliefs a company strives to attain and the actual (or operating) beliefs at work in the minds of its employees. The response to an ABM initiative will be determined by the operating beliefs at play, *not* the model beliefs that management would like to see in place.

"We believe in our people." Let's assume, for example, that one of the values espoused by a company is as follows: "We believe in our people." An appropriate model belief derived from the value might be: "We believe that our people will conduct themselves responsibly with a minimum of supervision." Behavior consistent with that might be that employees use discretion in how much time they spend on personal telephone calls. Employees would therefore experience a minimum of management surveillance.

But what if—in the pursuit of greater cost control—management were to introduce an automatic telephone monitoring system, which confronts employees with hard, cold feedback about their telephone habits? The model belief would be superseded by an operating belief that might be as follows: "We believe that when management says it is introducing a new tool, what they really mean is that they have found a new weapon to use against us."

> *Management styled on Theory X is essentially a set of behaviors based on the implicit belief that man is inherently lazy and corrupt.*

If this were an active operating belief in *your* company, how would your employees react to the introduction of ABM, which is described as a powerful new business tool? That's right—they would be cynical!

Operating beliefs are usually invisible. Probably the most difficult aspect of predicting and managing the response of employees is that operating beliefs are generally invisible. We can actually *see* the values that are supposedly in place in a corporation, because the values are usually published or displayed. We

can also *see* the behavior and resulting experience through our own observations and because of the efficiency of the corporate grapevine. But we cannot readily see what is inside people's heads.

Yet if operating beliefs *do* determine the response of employees to the introduction of ABM, then implementations of ABM will be far easier if management makes those operating beliefs visible.

Observations on change

The next step in the methodology is to recognize that ABM represents change. To create a picture of employees' operating beliefs, therefore, we need to understand:

- The key characteristics of change and
- The response mechanisms of the individual to change.

Both are discussed in the sections below.

Characteristics of change

1. *It is a fact of life.* Although this assertion may seem obvious, resistance to change is a far more common reaction than acceptance of change and accommodation to change. People routinely refuse to accept the inevitability of change and the necessity of adaptability.

2. *It is a matter of individual perception.* Stated in another way, "one man's meat is another man's poison." This observation is crucial to effective change management, because it implies sensitivity to a range of possible reactions and to the dangers of anticipating a uniform response from a group.

3. *It is necessary for growth.* In a business world in which growth is essential for survival, change is a prerequisite for growth. The business press is awash with stories of corporations suffering from the consequences of a reluctance to change; Robert Stempel of GM bears witness to the fact every day.

4. *It is not necessarily good.* Imagine, if you will, what it would be like to live with no memory: The task of having to relearn everything every day would be the same as living with perpetual change. We would have no assumptions to act on, for we would have no memory to validate the

assumptions. Everything would always be new. We must therefore be sensitive to the amount of change in our own and other people's lives. There is a continuum between no change and constant, total change; we must be aware of our position between these two extremes.

5. *It is always connected to the past.* Nothing is totally new; everything grows out of something. Even the most radical innovation or departure has roots, no matter how deep and well-hidden. We can understand our present and our future only in terms of our past.

6. *It is always both an internal and an external condition.* Change that comes because of an external stimulus (such as a sharp turn in the economy) affects all of us. But even change that occurs first to only one individual (because, for example, of a religious experience), ends up affecting others as well. Interaction and reaction between the world and any individual are constant.

Response mechanisms of the individual

The characteristics of change listed above form a structural framework for our individual response mechanisms. Six such mechanisms are listed below, though there may well be many more.

1. We tend to see ourselves either as agents or victims of change. Self-professed *change agents* are few and far between. Most employees tend to see themselves as *victims* of forces over which they have little or no influence. Ironically, victims exert great influence over the fate of change initiatives, because, collectively, they embody the inertia that suffocates improvement.

2. We accept or resist change according to how it affects the meaning of our life. This has been the most valuable insight we have come across. While the phrase "meaning of life" may sound grandiose, its components are actually simple elements. The foremost element may be our individual sense of identity, which may change significantly over time.

One member of our company, for example, used to take his sense of identity largely from his academic credentials, his list of publications, and his intellectual accomplishments—

but that was before he got married. He now maintains that his identity comes almost exclusively from his ability to be a good father, husband, and provider. Any significant change in his work environment is evaluated primarily in the context of his parental identity. If change for this colleague were to arrive in the form of a new client far from our office, our colleague would consider the extra travel a serious threat to his identity; the travel would mean being away from his family for extended periods, and he believes that time is the most precious resource a family can share.

Any major culture-changing initiative has the potential to cause misalignment. Since ABM represents a powerful force for change, therefore, it has the potential to cause significant misalignments.

Now think of a cost accountant whose sense of identity is grounded in his professional status. He has invested years in learning a certain way of doing things and has been recognized for his ability to work in the conventional system. When an important problem-solving exercise has come along, management has traditionally asked that this man be assigned the task because of his investigative skills. His whole value to the company is defined by the quality of his contribution to the company's conventional cost accounting system. *Then along comes ABM.*

Will the company value this cost accountant's skills as highly as before? Will others look to him for help and guidance? Will management pay him the same respect as in the past? Will he even be needed in the new system? Will they give him a chance to learn the new system and to develop new skills? How will he react to being the student again, after all these years as the teacher? Will he be ridiculed as a dinosaur? What will he tell his wife and children and friends?

Exhibit 3. *Conventional Management Planning*

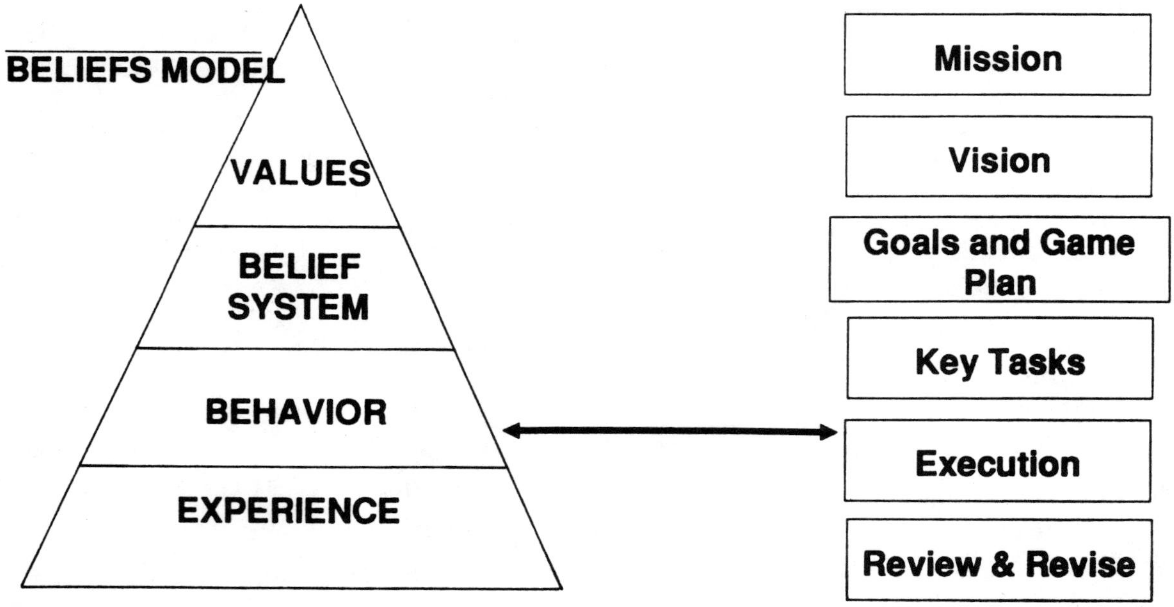

BELIEFS MODEL

VALUES

BELIEF SYSTEM

BEHAVIOR

EXPERIENCE

Mission

Vision

Goals and Game Plan

Key Tasks

Execution

Review & Revise

The operating beliefs through which ABM is filtered in this person's mind are both rational and irrational. From a change management perspective, both are real, because both determine the person's response.

3. We seek equilibrium between our values and our lives. We tend to gravitate toward companies or groups that share our basic values and attitudes and away from those that do not. This is probably less true in times of rampant job insecurity (such as now), but the general proposition does appear to be valid.

4. We change most readily if we develop a "habit of growth." The goal-setters among us—those who constantly strive to be "the best that they can be," the disciples of continuous improvement—accept change as a constant and feel substantially less threatened by it than those of us who can be considered either "contented" or "risk-averse."

5. We resist giving up one set of certainties for an uncertainty. This idea is traditionally expressed by saying "better the devil you know than the devil you don't know," a saying that reflects our reluctance to embark on a journey without a clear idea of our destina-

tion and a cast-iron rationale for traveling in the first place.

6. We worry about the "fairness" of change. One of the more frightening aspects of change is its ever-accelerating pace. The buggy whip industry did, indeed, die out in the United States around the turn of the century, but not nearly as fast as the U.S. VCR industry died in the 1970s. The increasing pace of change causes us to fear that we will not be able to adapt fast enough; we may fear that management will not have the patience (or resources) to see us through our new learning curve.

None of these observations have any scientific basis; they are empirical conclusions drawn eclectically from our work with companies that have committed themselves to the gargantuan task of changing their cultures. We use the observations as interpretive and analytical tools. They should prove useful if they are applied in the following approach to implementing or refining an ABM strategy.

Implementation

Exhibit 3 depicts the point at which conventional management practice plugs into the beliefs model. An effective ABM implementation calls for the coordinated design of both elements of the exhibit, as indicated in the ten key actions listed below. Also, see Exhibit 4 for an illustration of the interplay between values, model beliefs, and operating beliefs.

Key actions

1. Assemble the team responsible for an ABM implementation and have that team develop its own beliefs model for the company.
2. Identify and break out the model beliefs most relevant to the implementation of ABM.
3. Build a corresponding list of operating beliefs to reflect the attitudes and prejudices at play in the work force.
4. Identify which of those operating beliefs are likely to impede the introduction of ABM and which are likely to facilitate it.
5. Put together an implementation plan using conventional project planning steps, but adapt the design so that it maximizes the value of those operating beliefs that facilitate the adoption of ABM. Also address—do not skirt—those operating beliefs that impede the adoption of ABM.
6. Include as "success criteria" any goals that reflect success in razing the barriers.
7. Design a system to measure how well you succeed in reducing barriers to acceptance of ABM—that is, how good a job you are doing of managing people's responses and fears. We suggest making these "softer" measurements visible, so that everyone can see the progress being made. (We have found this openness to be more constructive than dangerous, and an excellent monitoring and feedback mechanism).
8. Constantly review progress and revise your game plan accordingly.
9. As you review progress, think of change management as an engine that is perpetually in gear; use events as tools to tune the engine's performance.

Exhibit 4. *Value—"We believe in frugality"*

Model Beliefs	Operating Beliefs
1. We believe that only the low cost producers will survive in our industry.	1. We believe that "low-cost producer" is "management speak" for wage cuts and freezes.
2. We believe that working for the lowest cost producer will mean greater job security.	2. We believe that working for the lowest-cost producer means a stagnant standard of living.
3. We believe that only through ABM will we be able to achieve low cost producer status.	3. We believe that ABM could certainly identify where waste exists in our company.
4. We believe that ABM will help us secure our future.	4. We believe that management will use ABM only to identify waste at lower levels of the company.

10. Explore and articulate your own responses to change and use the insight to manage better those with whom you work.

Conclusion

Successful implementations of ABM require a shift in management perspective. If a company can manage to position ABM in the wider context of continuous change—rather than addressing change as a secondary issue in the wider context of an ABM implementation—it will significantly improve its prospects for success. Without that fundamental shift, management's twin battles with dinosaurs (i.e., those who cannot see the need for change) and dragons (i.e., those who fight change with every breath) will continue . . . unchanged. ▲

Reprinted from *Journal of Cost Management*, Summer 1992, pp. 22–28. Copyright © 1992 by Warren Gorham Lamont, a division of Research Institute of America Inc. All rights reserved. Used by permission.

PART *E*

Customer-Supplier Relationships: Supply Chain

Measuring the Cost of Ownership

Lawrence P. Carr and Christopher D. Ittner

Suppliers play a significant role in a firm's achievement of a just-in-time (JIT) production process and the realization of a successful total quality control (TQC) program. Factors controlled or influenced by suppliers (e.g., on-time delivery, quality of materials, and lead times) are critical for JIT and TQC. Yet many cost accounting systems continue to motivate managers to select suppliers based solely on quoted price. Recognizing that material price represents only a fraction of the cost of doing business with suppliers, a growing number of companies are now measuring both purchasing department and supplier performance based on the *total cost of ownership*. This article discusses cost of ownership and provides examples of cost of ownership systems.

To achieve world-class manufacturing goals, companies must build and maintain partnerships with those suppliers that offer the best overall value. A strong linkage between companies and their suppliers is a prerequisite for high quality, manufacturing flexibility, and responsiveness to changing customer demands. In practice, however, supplier value is all too often defined solely in terms of quoted price, which ignores the significant costs associated with ordering, expediting, receiving, inspecting, and using purchased parts and materials. These added costs of ownership are ignored for many reasons, but mainly because of the shortcomings of traditional accounting systems and the performance measures that flow from them.[1]

Typical cost structures

The need to maximize the value received from purchased goods and materials is easy to understand given the cost structures found in many companies. Purchased materials, components, and subassemblies frequently represent in excess of 70 percent of manufacturing expenses.[2]

The costs of acquiring and using the component can also be significant. Philip Crosby, for example, estimates that 50 percent of a firm's nonconformance costs are caused by the extra work involved in disposing of, repairing, scrapping, or reworking defective purchased materials. These nonconformance costs also include costly schedule changes and downtime caused by nonconforming supplies and materials.[3] When all these factors are taken into account, supplier linkages have a greater effect on total cost than the manufacturing process itself.

Traditional manufacturing cost systems, however, track only the purchase price associated with a particular part number or supplier; they bury the costs of ordering, expediting, receiving, inspecting, and using purchased goods in factory overhead accounts or general manufacturing expenses. By obscuring these additional costs, accounting systems encourage purchasing managers to select the lowest bidders to avoid unfavorable purchase-price variances, even though the lowest bids may not represent the best overall value in terms of cost, quality, and delivery. At the same time, management loses valuable information for evaluating supplier performance.

Companies that have embraced just-in-time (JIT) manufacturing and total quality control (TQC) realize that suppliers should not be chosen based solely on quoted price. Instead, long-term relationships with suppliers must be developed to reduce the *total cost of ownership*,[4] which includes not only the purchase price but also the following:

Exhibit 1. *Examples of the "True" Cost of Ownership*

Texas Instruments Study

Integrated Circuits		**Connectors**	
(Texas Instruments)		(Electronics Manufacturer)	
Purchase price	$2.50	Purchase price	$ 0.55
Overhead:		Overhead:	
Inspection		Inspection	
Warehousing		Warehousing	
Insurance		Insurance	
Handling		Handling	
Transportation		Transportation	
Purchasing		Purchasing	
Overhead total	0.45	Overhead total	0.45
Price + overhead	2.95	Price + overhead	$ 1.00
Testing	$0.22	Testing	2.00
	$3.17		$ 3.00
OEM warranty	0.53	Defect replacement	15.00
End user's maintenance	1.06	Final test replacement	42.00
Cost of ownership	$4.76	Field replacement	40.00
		Cost of ownership	$100.00

Source: *Electronic Purchasing* (July 1988).

- *The costs of purchasing,* including the costs of ordering, freight, and incoming quality control;
- *The costs of holding,* including the costs of storage, insurance, obsolescence and the cost of money;
- *The costs of poor quality,* including the costs of rejection, re-receiving, scrap, rework, repackaging, downtime, and warranties; and
- *The costs of delivery failure,* including the costs of expediting, premium transportation, downtime, and lost sales owing to late deliveries, and also holding and administrative costs related to early deliveries.

As Exhibit 1 shows, these additional costs of ownership can be significant; indeed, they may actually exceed the purchase price. Texas Instruments, for example, found that the cost of an integrated circuit increased from $2.50 to $2.95 after the costs of purchasing and holding were factored into the total cost of ownership. But if the same integrated circuit was of poor quality, the total cost of ownership rose to $4.76 because of the additional costs of burn-in, rework, and warranty claims.

More dramatically, a study by another electronics manufacturer found that purchasing and holding costs increased the total cost of ownership for an electrical connector from $0.55 to $3. If a defective connector was not identified until the product reached the field, the total cost of ownership rose to $100—more than 180 times the original purchase price.

Measurement systems

Recognizing the significant role that suppliers play in achieving world-class manufacturing performance, a growing number of companies are beginning to consider the cost of ownership when selecting and evaluating suppliers.

The following examples illustrate a representative sample of techniques that companies use to measure and evaluate the cost of ownership. These examples provide useful starting points for developing systems to measure the strength of supplier partnerships and the performance of purchasing departments.

Northrop

Northrop Aircraft Division (NAD) tracks elements of the cost of ownership through its cost-based Supplier Performance Rating System (SPRS). SPRS grew out of a 1985 study that revealed that more than 50 percent of the more than 100,000 production receipts during the previous year had paperwork or hardware discrepancies or did not meet delivery schedules. NAD's management was extremely concerned about the soaring administrative costs, which were conservatively estimated at $5 million–$10 million annually. They needed to resolve these nonconformances. The obvious need for better quality and on-time delivery prompted the material and quality assurance functions to jointly sponsor the development of a system to identify and fix responsibility for quality and delivery problems. The resulting SPRS program serves to motivate both NAD buyers and its suppliers to improve quality and delivery performance, recognize and reward supplier excellence, and reduce excess costs.

The SPRS system measures the added administrative costs that NAD incurs to resolve suppliers' hardware, paperwork, and delivery deficiencies. As Exhibit 2 shows, each type of nonconformance "event" is assigned a standard cost based on industrial engineering studies of the hours required to resolve the problem. For each event, the number of occurrences during the previous quarter is multiplied by the associated standard cost to obtain the total cost of nonconformance. A supplier performance index (SPI) is then calculated as follows:

$$SPI = \frac{\text{Nonconformance costs} + \text{purchase price}}{\text{Purchase price}}$$

where

purchase price is the total invoiced costs of goods purchased from that supplier during the rating period.

Exhibit 3 illustrates the method used to calculate the supplier rating.

The SPRS output provides the basis for NAD's Key Plan Award for superior supplier

Exhibit 2. *NAD's Nonconformance Cost Standards*

Nonconformance Event	Standard Hours to Correct	Standard Costs (hrs. × $50)
Documentation	3	$150.00
Material review board	12	600.00
Return to supplier	6	300.00
Rework	15	750.00
Undershipment	7	350.00
Overshipment	2	100.00
Late delivery	10	500.00

Note: Standard hours and costs have been disguised.

Exhibit 3. *Example of NAD Rating Calculation*

Purchase cost	$250,000

Nonconformance costs:
Return to supplier (2 units @ $300 each)	$ 600	
Undershipment (5 shipments @ $350 each)	1,750	
Late delivery (3 shipments @ $500 each)	1,500	
Total nonconformance costs		$ 3,850

$$\text{Supplier rating} = \frac{(\$3,850 + \$250,000)}{\$250,000} = 1.015$$

performance and assists in identifying which suppliers need help in meeting quality and delivery standards. More important, the sharing of the SPRS output with suppliers helps strengthen the linkage with suppliers by focusing attention on the mutual benefits that NAD and its suppliers can gain from improved performance.

Choosing suppliers. The SPRS rating also serves as a bid multiplier for purposes of selecting suppliers; it is used to determine the "true" cost of purchasing from a given supplier. To illustrate, consider the following competitive bid:

	Supplier A	Supplier B
Quoted price/unit	$100	$105
× SPI	1.1	1.0
Total cost/unit	$110	$105

Based solely on quoted price, Supplier A is the low-cost vendor. However, after factoring in past quality and delivery performance as measured by the SPRS, Supplier B provides the better overall value.

Though the SPRS system currently considers only quality and delivery performance, NAD is developing a common rating system that will also incorporate the following quantifiable rating parameters:

• Technical and manufacturing capabilities;
• Security; and
• Financial strength.

Texas Instruments

Much like Northrop's SPRS system, the supplier rating system used by Texas Instruments (TI) incorporates quality and delivery factors into the vendor selection process. Based on studies of the additional costs incurred in dealing with supplier deficiencies, TI has developed an SPI that is derived from the following formula:

$$SPI = 1 + (1.3 \times \text{lot reject rate}) + (1.3 \times \text{weighted poor delivery}),$$

with delivery performance weighted according to the graph shown in Exhibit 4. (Note: TI arrived at the factor of 1.3 for the lot reject rates and weighted poor delivery by conducting industrial engineering studies.)

For example, a supplier whose deliveries are, on average, five days late receives a weighted delivery score of 0.10. Assuming a 5 percent lot reject rate, the supplier's SPI is computed as follows:

$$SPI = 1 + (1.3 \times 5\%) + (1.3 \times 0.10) = 1.195$$

The quoted price is subsequently multiplied by the SPI to determine the total cost of ownership.

Initial studies of supplier performance revealed that the average TI supplier had a lot reject rate of 6.7 percent and a weighted poor delivery score of 0.15. The SPI of 1.28 implied by these figures indicated that TI was spending 28 percent more than the quoted price to purchase goods and materials. Using cost of ownership information to pinpoint opportunities, TI has since implemented a variety of supplier improvement and vendor consolidation initiatives to eliminate the quality and delivery deficiencies that drive these costs.

McDonnell Douglas

The cost-based supplier rating system that McDonnell Douglas (MD)[5] has developed considers four factors in determining the added cost of supplier quality deficiencies:

1. The part type;
2. The nature of the problem;
3. Where the problem occurred; and
4. What MD did with the part.

After reviewing the number of hours required to resolve a sample of rejection notices, MD has developed the "lost-hour" matrix shown in Exhibit 5. For each factor noted, the added cost to resolve the problem has been identified as being either high, medium, or low.

Supplier linkages may have a greater effect on total cost than the manufacturing process itself.

For example, problems with electrical or functional commodities are considerably more expensive to resolve than problems with raw materials. Similarly, it is cheaper for MD to scrap a part and seek credit from the supplier than to return the part to the vendor, because the latter option requires performing extra paperwork and preparation of the part for shipment back to the supplier. Based on combinations of the factors in the lost-hour matrix shown in Exhibit 5, MD has developed average costs per $1,000 worth of business. These averages are used to assign costs to each type of rejection. Ratings are then calculated based on the following formula:

$$\text{Rating} = \frac{\text{Total dollars lost}}{\text{Accounts payable}}$$

Suppliers with a rating of $2 per $1,000 or less are considered excellent. Suppliers with ratings in the category of from $2.01 to $5 per $1,000 are considered acceptable. Suppliers with a quality rating in excess of $5 per $1,000 are considered to have a quality system that requires immediate attention and improvement.

Exhibit 4. *Texas Instruments Delivery Weighting Factors*

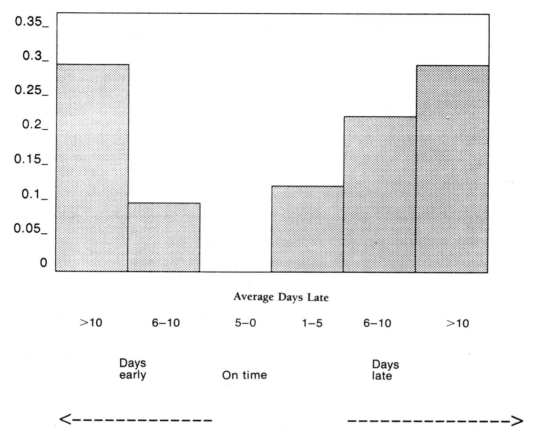

Delivery Weighting Factors

SPI = 1 + [1.3 × lot reject rate] + [1.3 × weighted poor delivery]

Black & Decker

A plant owned by Black & Decker in Spennymoor, England, has integrated the cost of ownership concept into its activity-based costing (ABC) system. Spennymoor produces more than 10 million power tools per year, with material representing approximately 70 percent of its cost structure.

In developing the ABC system, Spennymoor sought to encourage the plant's JIT and quality initiatives while also promoting vendor development. The solution was to allocate material-related overhead based on supplier performance.

Supplier ratings are first determined through multifunctional rankings that incorporate such factors as quality, delivery, flexibility, and customer service. Each department that

Exhibit 5. *McDonnell Douglas (MD) "Cost of Lost Hours" Matrix*

Cost	Commodity	Nature of Problem	Location of Problem	Disposition
High	Electrical Functional	Functional failures	Customer Flight Line	Rework at MD
Medium	Paints and chemicals Outside production	Tooling errors Planning errors	Assembly	Return to vendor
Low	Raw material Stock items Mockup supplies	Appearance items Safety wires, keys, and pins	Fabrication Receiving	Accept as is Scrap (charge supplier for cost)

Source: Eugene Baker, "Counting Costs: Another Approach to Supplier Rating," *Quality Progress* (Nov. 1984): 67.

---

has dealings with a supplier participates in this stage to assess the overall performance of the supplier base. As one Spennymoor manager noted, "You can be dealing with the best company in the world in terms of quality, customer service, and flexibility, but if they can't get their invoices right, you're going to have trouble doing business with them. So finance has an input into it as well." After reviewing and debating the results from the multifunctional rankings, overall supplier ratings of 0 to 100 are determined. Suppliers that receive ratings of 85 or better are considered excellent.

The supplier rating scheme serves as the basis for Spennymoor's ABC system. A series of material-related overhead rates have been developed based on the resources consumed by suppliers at various levels of performance. Poor suppliers, for example, are significantly more expensive than excellent suppliers. Consequently, the poorer performers are allocated a larger share of overhead. The results have been twofold. First, manually assembled units have been found to be less expensive than previously believed after factoring in differences in cost of ownership. Second, and perhaps more importantly, the information has highlighted problem areas and identified opportunities to reduce overhead costs.

Beyond failure costs

As these examples show, most of the cost of ownership systems that we have encountered focus on supplier quality and delivery deficiencies. But significant opportunities also exist to reduce the costs of purchasing and holding materials and components.

Electronic data interchange (EDI), for example, reduces order placement costs and facilitates invoice payments. Vendor certification allows superior suppliers to ship directly to stock, thus eliminating incoming inspection costs. JIT delivery reduces inventory holding costs and obsolescence while increasing flexibility. Systems contracting allows companies to place a single yearly purchase order, which reduces the paperwork needed for subsequent draws against the order.

Exhibit 6 shows an example of the cost of ownership report that Digital Equipment Corporation (DEC) uses to capture some of these elements.[6] In addition to measuring the costs of quality and delivery deficiencies, the report also tracks the expenses associated with vendor surveys and qualifications, approval of samples, incoming inspection and lab tests, and order placement. By incorporating these factors into cost of ownership analyses, companies are in a better position to determine which suppliers offer the best overall value.

Exhibit 6. *Digital Equipment Corporation Supplier Rating System*

Supplier Quality Rating

FROM: _____ TO: _____

Quality Cost Factors	Vendor "A"	Vendor "B"	Vendor "C"
Cost of Defect Prevention:			
Vendor survey Cost for qualifications Approval of samples Specification revision			
Cost of Defect Detection:			
Incoming inspection Lab test cost			
Cost of Defect Correction:			
Additional inspection Processing of rejects Manufacturing losses Cost of complaints Loss of sales			
Total cost of quality assurance			
Total value of purchases			
Quality cost ratio $= \dfrac{\text{Total cost of quality assurance}}{\text{Total value of purchases}} \times 100$			

Supplier Delivery Rating

FROM: _____ TO: _____

Availability/Acquisition Cost Factors	Vendor "A"	Vendor "B"	Vendor "C"
Cost of Acquisition/Availability:			
Follow-up and expediting expenses Telephone and telegraph expenses Plant visitation expenses Manufacturing losses owing to vendor delinquency			
Total acquisition/availability cost:	$ 4,000	$ 2,500	$ 2,600
Total value of purchases:	$80,000	$65,000	$91,000
Acquisition/availability cost ratio	5%	3.8%	2.86%

Source: Narenda S. Patel, "Source Surveillance and Vendor Evaluation Plan," in *Quality Costs: Ideas and Applications,* A. Grimm, ed. (Milwaukee, Wis.: American Society for Quality Control 1987).

Realized benefits

Companies that have embraced the concept of total cost of ownership have realized significant benefits. For example, on-time delivery of Northrop suppliers improved 20 percent in the first year of the SPRS system. Similarly, LTV Vought, which uses a cost of ownership system similar to Northrop's, saw lost dollars owing to supplier deficiencies fall from $2.09 per $1,000 purchased to $0.80.

The improvements generated by cost of own-ership systems are due in large part to the improved communications between buyers and sellers that the systems foster. While this communication typically concerns ways in which the buyer can help the supplier improve performance, the benefit can run both ways. During the initial pilot run of the SPRS system, Northrop found that many supplier problems arose because NAD buyers failed to communicate specification and delivery changes effectively to suppliers. As a result, NAD's procedures were modified to ensure

Exhibit 7. *Digital Equipment Corporation Vendor Service Rating*

Characteristics of Vendor	Vendor		
Excellent = 5 points; Average = 4 points; Below average = 2 points	A	B	C

1. *Personnel Capabilities:*
  a. Caliber and availability of sales and technical personnel.
  b. Is management progressive?
  c. Technical knowledge of supervision.
  d. Cooperation on changes and problems.
  e. Technical field service availability.
  f. Labor relations.			

2. *Facilities Capabilities:*
  a. Capability for anticipated volume.
  b. Latest technology and equipment.
  c. Excess production capacity.
  d. Geographical location.
  e. Financial capacity to stand behind product failures.
  f. Investing capital in the organization?			

3. *R&D Capabilities:*
  a. New product development.
  b. Alerting for future needs?
  c. Does the vendor update the buyer with the latest techniques?			

4. *Product Service Capability:*
  a. Offers emergency assistance?
  b. Does vendor provide consultation for potential troubles?
  c. What type of warranty is furnished?
  d. Is the vendor willing to accept responsibility?
  e. What is the vendor's record for reliability in past dealings?			

Total service points			

Source: Narenda S. Patel, "Source Surveillance and Vendor Evaluation Plan," in *Quality Costs: Ideas and Applications*, A. Grimm, ed. (Milwaukee, Wis.: American Society for Quality Control 1987).

that changes were communicated to suppliers in a clearer and more timely manner. As this example clearly illustrates, partnerships involve two parties, and reduced cost of ownership requires adjustments on both sides.

Caveats

Though cost of ownership measurement can be a useful tool for assessing supplier value, it is not a panacea. Many important factors in source selection (e.g., assistance in product development and cost reduction efforts) are difficult to quantify and may require many subjective judgments when assessing overall value. As Exhibit 7 shows, for example, DEC uses subjective evaluations to rate supplier service on four dimensions:

1. Personnel capabilities;
2. Facilities capabilities;
3. R&D capabilities; and
4. Product service capabilities.

A composite rating based on a weighted average of the cost of ownership index and the supplier service index is then developed to determine overall supplier value. Although subjective evaluations such as these may be required to capture less quantifiable factors, caution should be taken to avoid introducing substantial bias into the resulting performance measure.

Rating new and infrequent suppliers. Problems may also arise when rating new suppliers. A common solution is to apply the average rating for the commodity group to new suppliers until enough information is available to rate new suppliers based on their records.

Exhibit 8. *Rockwell International "Q-Factor" Lot Size Adjustment*

Rockwell measures supplier performance using a Supplier Performance Index (SPI) that is similar to Northrop's SPRS measure except for the multiplication of nonconformance costs by a "Q factor." The Q factor is a lot-size normalization obtained by dividing the average lot value for an individual supplier by the average lot value for all suppliers of that commodity.

Supplier A
(10 lots @ $100 each)

SPI Without Q

$$SPI = \frac{1,000 + 500}{1,000} = 1.50$$

$$Q = \frac{100}{1,467} = 0.68$$

SPI With Q

$$SPI = \frac{1,000 + \{500\,(0.068)\}}{1,000} = 1.03$$

Supplier B
(10 lots @ $10,000 each)

SPI Without Q

$$SPI = \frac{100,000 + 500}{100,000} = 1.005$$

$$Q = \frac{10,000}{1,467} = 6.817$$

SPI With Q

$$SPI = \frac{100,000 + \{500\,(6.817)\}}{1,000} = 1.03$$

Source: Thomas Stundza, "Can Supplier Rating Be Standardized?" *Purchasing* (Nov. 8, 1990): 63.

Another potential issue concerns infrequent suppliers, which can be severely penalized for one bad lot. Similarly, suppliers of small lot sizes can also be penalized severely if the lot they supply has even one defect. Rockwell International has developed what it calls the "Q factor" to control for lot size when developing supplier ratings.[7] As Exhibit 8 shows, the Q factor is determined by dividing the average lot value for an individual supplier by the average lot value for all suppliers of that commodity. By multiplying nonconformance costs by the Q factor, Rockwell places suppliers of small lot sizes on an equal footing with suppliers that deliver in larger lot sizes.

Misuse of cost of ownership information.
Potentially more troublesome than the technical issues noted above is the possibility for the misuse of cost of ownership information. To achieve world-class manufacturing status, companies must replace traditional adversarial supplier relations with true partnerships. Unfortunately, many firms have in the past used cost-based supplier rating systems to hammer suppliers into cost reductions, thereby creating what Roy Shapiro of the Harvard Business School calls "the new adversarial relationship." The true value in cost of ownership measurement lies in helping suppliers reach their full potential in the part-

nership between buyers and their suppliers rather than serving as a club for extracting concessions.

Required changes in performance measures.
Traditional accounting systems typically measure purchasing department performance based on purchase-price variance. Consequently, purchasing managers are motivated to select the lowest price supplier to avoid unfavorable variances, even though the supplier may not represent the best value in terms of total cost of ownership. If the performance measurement system does not reflect the total cost of ownership, the purchasing department is likely to continue emphasizing quoted price when evaluating bids. Companies must therefore modify their internal performance measurement systems to realize the full benefit and richness of a cost of ownership program.

Summary

Regardless of the methodology used, cost of ownership systems can enhance the performance of purchasing departments and suppliers by providing information about the best overall value of materials and components. Performance problems can thus be corrected before they get out of control. Low-performing suppliers can be eliminated, and opportunities for overhead reductions can be highlighted. To achieve the full benefit, however, cost of ownership information should be used in conjunction with the development of true partnerships between buyers and their suppliers.

The innovative cost of ownership systems discussed in this article have proven valuable in providing information for improved decision making and performance measurement. As the purchasing shifts from being a clerical function to being a strategic business operation, the criteria for measuring the performance of purchasing departments must also shift away from efficiency measures and purchase-price variances toward effectiveness measures that consider not just cost, but also delivery, quality, flexibility, and service. Cost of ownership measures provide a means for capturing these factors comprehensively and objectively.

Cost of ownership systems also provide critical supplier evaluation data—information that is normally masked by traditional cost accounting systems. Both accounting and nonaccounting data are readily available in most companies to make measurement of the performance of purchasing departments and suppliers more relevant and useful. Unfortunately, the information is frequently spread throughout the organization, which makes it difficult to obtain in a timely manner. Cost of

ownership measurement provides a way to draw this disparate information together so that it can be used readily and meaningfully.

With decisions about suppliers becoming increasingly important, cost of ownership measurements can provide a valuable tool for evaluating and promoting supplier partnerships, which are rapidly becoming a necessary ingredient for competitive success. ▲

Notes
1. Louis J. DeRose, "Negotiate for Value," *Purchasing World* (Sept. 1990): 12.
2. H.T. Johnson & R.S. Kaplan, *Relevance Lost* (Boston, Mass.: Harvard Business School Press 1987): 183–187.
3. D. Smock, "How to Stem the Tide of Shoddy Materials," *Purchasing* (May 13, 1982): 51–57.
4. R.S. Kaplan & A.A. Atkinson, *Advanced Management Accounting* (Englewood Cliffs, N.J.: Prentice-Hall 1989): 377.
5. The discussion of Douglas Aircraft is based on the article by Eugene M. Baker, "Counting Costs: Another Approach to Supplier Rating," *Quality Progress* (Nov. 1984): 67–69.
6. Narenda S. Patel, "Source Surveillance and Vendor Evaluation Plan," in Andrew F. Grimm, ed., *Quality Costs: Ideas and Applications* (Milwaukee, Wis.: American Society for Quality Control 1987): 285–296.
7. Thomas Stundza, "Can Supplier Rating Be Standardized?" *Purchasing* (Nov. 8, 1990): 63.

Overcome the Barriers to Superior Customer Service

A. Lynn Daniel

Numerous barriers inhibit companies from implementing an effective customer service strategy. These include a focus on internal information rather than on the needs of clients and the perception that customers are a means to an end rather than a vital business asset that should be managed for the long run. This article gives practical steps that companies and managers have taken to overcome these barriers.

Managers talk a lot about customer service. They tout this service in advertisements and brochures and are quick to tell customers how responsive their organizations are. Customer service strategies are prominent in strategic plans. Evidence strongly shows that having superior quality products and service pays off in profitability.

The Profit Impact of Marketing Strategy (PIMS) model of the Strategic Planning Institute shows a strong correlation between a business's profitability and the perceived quality of its products and services. On the basis of the experience of more than 3,000 businesses in the data base, return on investment more than doubles when the quality of the product and service provided are high.

The December 1987 issue of *Fortune* magazine highlights leading customer service companies in several industries. In almost all cases, these companies grew much faster than the industry in which they competed and were generally more profitable than others in the industry.[1]

Yet there is a wide gulf between the talk and the service that customers receive. For example.

☐ Customer complaints are up. The Technical Assistance Research Programs Institute of Washington DC finds that "the service operations of many companies are fielding over twice as many complaints today as they did in the 1970s. . . . Buyers, whether consumers or corporations, are demanding more of sellers and too often aren't getting it."

☐ The Yankelovich Monitor, an annual survey of consumers, reports that among seven service industries, only supermarkets have improved the perceived quality of their service in recent years. The perceived quality of restaurant, hotel, and department store service remained the same, whereas the perceived service quality of banks, airlines, and cable TV operators all dropped.

The effects of poor customer service are dramatic. The US Office of Consumer Affairs reports that 90% of dissatisfied customers will not buy again. Moreover, a dissatisfied customer will tell at least nine other people of the unpleasant experience.

If superior customer service pays off and poor customer service is so damaging, why don't more organizations concentrate on providing superior service to gain a competitive edge? The short answer is that having superior service is difficult. The complete answer is found by looking at the organizational barriers that inhibit the production of truly superior customer service. These include the following:

• Companies focus on internal information and pay too little attention to information about the external environment. Such companies change to meet their own needs rather than those of customers.

- Managers view the customer primarily as a means to an end and not as a vital business asset to be managed for the long run.
- There is an unwillingness to provide first-line employees with the authority and power to solve customer problems.
- Managers and investors lack the patience to successfully execute a superior customer service strategy.

Mark Fuller of the Monitor Group, an international consulting firm, notes that approximately 88% of the information systems in one Fortune 10 company exist to provide internal information. According to Fuller, this is characteristic of other companies as well, both large and small.

Much of the explanation for this internal focus is found in the relatively slow rate of product and market innovation and change that took place in the 1970s. There was less need to listen to customers or to pay attention to the external environment. But today, companies must look carefully and continuously at the external environment. If management fails to do this, it can miss customer changes vital to keeping a company in sync with its customers' needs.

Staying in sync with these needs is fundamental to providing high-quality service. Staying in touch with customers and overcoming this focus on internal information means taking steps to firmly place the customer squarely in the view of company employees and managers.

A customer-centered strategic planning process

Focusing on the external environment requires an organization to have a truly customer-centered strategic planning process that examines real customer needs. The strategic plan is based on customer needs. A customer-centered strategic planning process assumes that market share is built one satisfied customer at a time.

For example, in one company that designs and installs environmental control systems, management makes its customer needs tangible by starting the strategic planning process with a key customer review. This review examines the sales and profit generated by each customer and identifies major problems or successes with them. Managers review lost orders and pay particular attention to reasons for losing the orders. They also define the apparent strategy of each key customer to assess their own company's long-term strength and to determine the amount of resources to devote to each customer. This company has an outstanding track record for building market share, improving profits, and keeping its customers satisfied.

Though the firm in this example operates in the industrial market, where the number of customers is small, the principle of making

> *"Focusing on the external environment requires an organization to have a truly customer-centered strategic planning process that examines real customer needs."*

customers real is still appropriate and possible even with larger numbers of customers. Managers in consumer products companies need to see and talk to customers to find out why they buy the product, how they use it, and what they like and dislike about it.

Putting the customer at the center of the strategic planning process means that the customer must be in a continuous change cycle with the business. What customers say and do is fed back into the planning process, and the organization changes as a result of this information (see Exhibit 1).

Making the customer a part of the continuous change cycle means that there is active communication with the customer at all levels in the organization. The CEO and other members of senior management are in contact with customers to make certain that they are hearing and understanding what customers are saying. Sales reports, formal market research, and other internal information are part of their information network.

Such information, however, is one-way, from the customer to management, and it often

Exhibit 1. *Continuous Change Cycle*

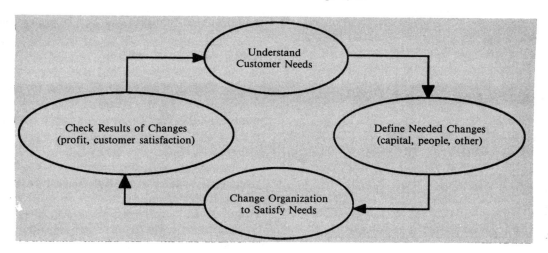

gets filtered as it comes through the organization. Senior managers should have direct, fact-to-face contact with customers to see firsthand how well the company delivers its product and how it serves the customer. This also provides senior managers with up-to-date, firsthand knowledge regarding the products or services.

For example, MCI Communications Corp. has institutionalized senior management contact with customers. Senior executives have customer accounts, and these accounts are intended to lead to long-term relationships.[2]

Those in such functions as finance, personnel, and management information systems also must have regular communication with customers. In one company, the personnel department decided to start a regular customer visitation program. As a result of these customer visits, the department was able to design an improved hourly employee recruiting program for one operation. This program reduced turnover among field installation crews, reduced costs, and improved the quality of the final installation.

Responding to specific customer comments and problems provides opportunities for managers to communicate with customers and see firsthand how organizations need to change.

Customer comments, either those about specific problems or those that are more general, provide a company with a great opportunity to solve a problem and get information in the process.

For example, one company, which introduced an industrial filter product, sold a unit to a key customer. After a few weeks of operation, the unit failed. The customer was upset because the failure stopped production. The company responded by sending a new filter and installing it within 24 hours. Even more important, managers discovered that the filter failure resulted from an incomplete maintenance manual. The general manager, who was in the middle of solving the customer's problem, promptly corrected the manual, ensuring that similar failures would not occur with future customers.

Customer information that comes from comments and problems may be (and often is) at odds with conventional wisdom or what managers are saying. Such contradictions are useful because more questions are asked and therefore more attention is paid to what is really happening with customers. Bringing these contradictions to the surface helps an organization understand what is really happening in the external environment and what the business must do about it.

Exhibit 2. *Typical Customer/Company Interface*

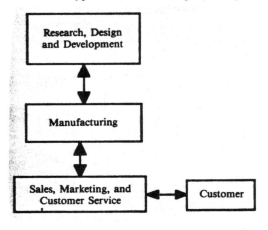

Only a means to an end

In too many businesses, the customer is viewed only as a way to achieve a sales goal and not as a vital, long-term business asset. Getting an organization to see the customer as an asset first involves a significant change in management attitudes. Senior management must see the customer as an asset to be nurtured and cared for over time. There are some specific steps management can take to implant this view in a company.

Create a win-win relationship with the customer. The customer/company relationship must be defined as a two-way or win-win relationship. Establishing this type of relationship starts by having products and services that are designed and manufactured to meet customer needs. This means that customers are involved in the design and manufacturing processes early on so that the product or service will ultimately satisfy their needs.

Typically, the customer sees the product only when it is ready for sale. As shown in Exhibit 2, customer contact is exclusively with the sales, marketing, or customer service function responsible for selling and servicing the product. If it is not designed or manufactured to meet customer needs, it is up to the sales, marketing, and service people to "make it work." Given the distance from the customer to the design and manufacturing people, it is often difficult to get important information back to them.

To have superior service, the products and services sold by a company must satisfy customer needs. To fully understand these needs, customers must be involved through the design, development, and manufacturing stages (see Exhibit 3). In this way, the final product or service is much more likely to satisfy customer needs when it reaches the market.

Involving customers is not that difficult. Process Systems, Inc., a Charlotte NC manufacturer of electronic instrumentation equipment, is particularly committed to involving customers in its design and development process. Customers review product designs and suggest improvements early in the design process. In addition to design improvements, customers make marketing suggestions that help later on when the product is introduced. This close customer involvement helped the company introduce a meter in a short time.

When a product or service is designed and manufactured with input from customers, the resulting product or service is more likely to meet customer needs. The sales, marketing, and customer service people do not have to persuade a customer to change to accommodate a new product—it was designed and built with the customer's needs clearly in mind. A secondary benefit of involving customers in the development process is that they acquire a feeling of ownership of the product that can ultimately help a new product's success.

Exhibit 3. *Desired Customer/Company Interface*

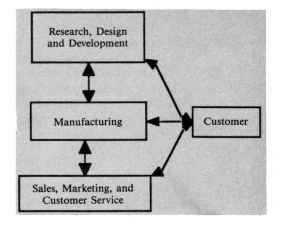

Focus attention on retaining customers. Too often, new customers become the Holy Grail for management. Existing customers are taken for granted, become dissatisfied, and defect. Pressures to find new customers then increase, creating an unprofitable cycle. If the customer is to be a real asset, management must focus the organization toward retaining customers.

Frederick F. Reichheld and W. Earl Sasser determined the amount of profit a customer generates over time for several industries. In one industry (industrial laundries), the longer the customer remained a customer, the greater the profit that customer generated. Why are long-term customers more profitable? They tend to buy more, have lower operating costs, and create additional profit through referrals.[3]

Manage the customer relationship, not customer profitability. Management pressure, force, coercion, or encouragement cannot create a profitable customer. A customer's profitability is a measure of just how much of a win-win relationship exists between the customer and the company.

Managing the customer/company relationship involves several facets. First, managers must choose customers that are potentially profitable. Customers have varying needs, and a company cannot serve all customers equally well.

In the bulk transport market, some customers are sensitive to the appearance of the equipment hauling their products. They view the trucking company as an extension of their customer service and distribution functions, so the appearance of the drivers and the equipment is as valued as consistent service. These customers are also willing to pay slightly higher rates to have new equipment and well-groomed drivers.

Other customers are much less concerned about equipment and driver appearance but want the lowest possible rates. The trucking company with new equipment and the best-trained and best-groomed drivers may be unable to profitably serve this latter market segment.

Another important facet of managing the customer/company relationship is knowing just how profitable (or unprofitable) customers are. Having inadequate or unavailable customer profitability information is a real weakness in too many companies. Profitability information may show only gross margin dollars generated from a customer and ignore many of the transactions costs (e.g., receivables and inventory levels, number of invoices, and special handling needs). In the industrial market, having complete customer profitability information is critical, because the customer base is sometimes so small that just a few unprofitable customers make an entire company unprofitable.

"If a company is to have a superior customer service strategy, employees must have the needed responsibility and authority to satisfy customers."

One company, a supplier of commercial photographic services, sought to do business with any customer no matter the customer's order size. Individual order sizes ranged from $500 to more than $10,000. The company had customer profitability information to the gross margin level that showed that even the $500 order was profitable. However, a transaction analysis showed that the amount of overhead costs associated with handling a $500 order and a $10,000 order were virtually the same (approximately $250).

With a gross margin of 35%, the company was losing $75 on each $500 order. Not surprisingly, the company was losing money. Management decided to focus on the segment of the market with larger, more professionally demanding customers.

A final facet to managing the customer/company relationship is constantly monitoring customer profitability and refining and segmenting the customer base. Customers' needs change over time, as does a company's ability to serve these needs. A profitable customer one year may not be so the next.

The power to solve problems

In too many companies, first-line employees with the most frequent customer contact and the greatest opportunity to satisfy customers often lack the power to do so. If a company is to have a superior customer service strategy, employees must have the needed responsibility and authority to satisfy customers for two primary reasons. First, it removes a crutch that is often used to justify poor customer response: "I need to check with the boss." Second, it invigorates an organization's employees. It is a clear vote of confidence in employees when management says, "You have the responsibility and the power to solve the customers' problems. We expect you to solve them. No one gets in trouble for trying to solve customer problems."

Remember that selection and training are prerequisites. There is a concern that if first-line employees are given too much responsibility and power, mistakes will happen and "too much will be given away." This is a valid concern if attention is not given to proper employee selection and training. Those employees who are able to balance the sometimes conflicting demands of customer and company must be placed in customer service positions.

Employees should also be trained to handle difficult customer service problems. They should be given broad exposure to how products are manufactured so they know how to answer specific customer questions. Good performance should be rewarded, financially and by personal recognition. Poor performance should be identified and corrected by training.

Reduce middle manager resistance. Giving employees the responsibility and authority to make decisions and solve problems causes some managers discomfort. After all, what is the manager to do if not make decisions? Companies with high-quality service know this and therefore usually have the minimum number of middle managers.

Make investments that enhance service. In high-quality service companies, management makes capital investments that enhance the ability to serve customers. Consider Lands' End, the Wisconsin-based direct-mail company. From a customer perspective, this company has an excellent information system. It provides customer service representatives with accurate inventory information, which means they can tell customers if a requested product is in stock and when it will ship. Lands' End chose an information system with its customers clearly in mind.

A company's competitive position and its profitability should improve as a result of providing superior customer service, but it will not occur immediately. An organization must first change its collective behavior, and customers must experience the change, generally more than once, to believe it. Real improvements in customer service happen, but they are not immediately reflected in an improved bottom line.

Companies often try to implement a superior customer service strategy without specific and quantifiable improvement objectives. Steps to implement the strategy are taken, which generally consumes a lot of time and resources. After a while, managers become uncertain about what is being accomplished because no clear objectives were established from the outset. They lose patience, the effort loses steam, and it is finally scrapped.

Specific, quantifiable improvement objectives are more realistic. For example, in the case of a trucking company, a quantifiable improvement objective was to reduce bill entry errors. By reducing these errors, customers would receive a more accurate bill and receivables would decline, because accurate freight bills are processed faster and payments are not delayed.

Superior customer service is a potent competitive strategy. Product difference along cost and quality dimensions are narrowing as worldwide engineering and manufacturing capabilities improve. Consider the success that Lexus is having against Mercedes-Benz, BMW, and others. Lexus is competing on price and quality dimensions, but high-quality customer service is an integral part of the strategic mix.

Superior customer service creates a significant hurdle for the competition to overcome. Companies that are successful will stand out, creating a significant competitive advantage and erecting a major barrier to new competitors. Recall how difficult it was for competitors to enter the US mainframe computer market during the 1970s and early 1980s: they ran smack into IBM. A major part of IBM's competitive advantage at that time, and still today, is superior customer service.

Superior customer service is a competitive advantage that is defensible over time. Good customer service usually engenders customer loyalty, making it more difficult for competitors to entice customers away. Moreover, the main ingredient for outstanding customer service is dedicated and motivated employees throughout the organization. A competitor can't hire away one or two employees and steal a competitive advantage, as would be the case with a key design engineer, manufacturing manager, or marketing person.

The internal barriers that get in the way of creating superior customer service are present in most companies, but these can be overcome. It is not technically difficult to do, nor does it require huge capital outlays; it does require change. Policies and procedures, systems, and long-held practices may have to be revised. More important, attitudes must change, particularly those of senior managers. They must be committed to and passionate about creating superior customer service.

Creating superior service is not a one-shot strategy. It is an ongoing process of improvement in which the senior managers are constantly communicating their commitment and passion for service to every employee in the company. Each employee must eventually come to see that satisfying the customer is the single most important aspect of his or her job. ▲

Notes
1. B. Uttal, "Companies That Serve You Best," *Fortune* (December 7, 1987), pp. 98–116.
2. "MCI's IS Leader Is Customer Focused," *Datamation*, International Edition (June 1, 1990), pp. 101–107.
3. F.F. Reichheld and W.E. Sasser, Jr., "Zero Defections: Quality Comes to Services," *Harvard Business Review* (September/October 1990), pp. 105–111.

Satisfy Your Internal Customers

Bruce Pfau, Denis Detzel, and Andrew Geller

Companies must ensure that all customers are satisfied—both within and outside the firm. Usually only comparatively few employees of a company serve external customers, but all employees supply products and services to their coworkers—their internal customers. Like external customers, these internal customers need to receive the best in quality and service. A lack of close attention to internal supplier-customer relationships can jeopardize external customer satisfaction. As this article explains, to genuinely improve internal customer satisfaction, organizations need to know who their internal customers are, to understand their needs, and to measure the extent to which these needs are being met.

How important is providing quality service to internal customers? Simply put, it is critical. Consider the following example.

A junior investment banker spent six months working on a major project that hinged on data derived from hundreds of calculations completed by another team in the company. A few days before a client presentation, one of the senior partners on the project discovered an inconsistency in the data and asked him to check it out.

He found that a mistake had been made in an early calculation. It was a small error—except that it had been compounded in hundreds of subsequent calculations. It took a lot of energy and many staff hours to get those calculations redone in time, but the project was completed and the presentation went smoothly.

What he later learned was that his own team's original mistake occurred because of a typographical error in material that had been provided by an individual in yet another internal group. When the consultant told that individual's manager of the problems the error had caused, the manager's response was telling: If only he had known how important the project was, he would have had the figures triple-checked.

In the end, though, the banker was grateful to that typo—and to that candid supplier of information. He was fortunate to have learned so early in his career that when an internal relationship between a customer and a supplier is weak, it can cause problems in supplier-customer relations right up the line.

From then on, he was sure to clearly communicate his needs, expectations, and objectives for a job whenever he enlisted the service of an internal supplier. And he is just as certain that this type of communication has helped him to avert countless eleventh-hour problems.

Striving for customer satisfaction has traditionally been the keystone of success in business. Efficient, top-quality service sends the message every customer wants to hear: "It's our pleasure to serve you."

Although most employees know that putting their best face forward to external customers is one of the basic tenets of quality service, only a small fraction of an organization's employees may directly serve external customers. However, almost all employees supply products and services to their coworkers—their internal customers—who also need to receive the best in quality and service.

A company's ability to meet its external customer needs depends directly on how well it satisfies the needs of these internal customers. Lack of close attention to the internal supplier-customer relationship not only can jeopardize external satisfaction but also can call into question the added value provided by most staff and operations support functions.

In the past, many organizations have failed to view internal staff functions as vital elements of customer service. However, a subtle but crucial realization is emerging today: Service and quality must be built from within the organization. Employees increasingly are looking to obtain resources quickly and at a top-quality level so that they can service other internal customers in the best possible way.

"Many organizations have failed to view internal staff functions as vital elements of customer service."

A growing number of companies are implementing service and quality improvement programs that enhance their own employees' knowledge and skills, boosting internal customer satisfaction and loyalty. These programs also encourage units to approach innovation, productivity improvement, or cost control much in the same way as outside vendors do: as an integral part of their daily work.

In more and more organizations, the results are already evident: strengthening relationships with internal customers improves relations with external ones. External customer satisfaction is really the outcome of excellent teamwork and close, cooperative relationships among various departments and people within the organization.

However, the flip side of this issue is just as telling: a company that delivers excellent service externally but lags in internal service reveals a serious gap in quality that is linked to wasted time, extra quality control costs, and wasted dollars that translate directly to the bottom line.

Renewed focus on internal service can enhance a unit's strategic value to the organiza-

tion. Because today's organizations are more cost-conscious than ever before, many companies want their internal units to be competitive with the services and prices of outside suppliers.

Internal service focus

Adopting an internal service focus does not happen overnight; the transformation is an evolutionary process that can gradually gain momentum. At the same time, building service and quality from within an organization requires creating an entrepreneurial climate, one that promotes close communication within the organization and encourages constant evaluation and improvement of the quality of service within each department.

The process may even involve restructuring or implementing a new organizational design, launching the organization into a more horizontal, decentralized structure, and increasing the number of employees reporting to each manager. This new type of structure typically pushes more decision making into the hands of individual line workers, with management taking on a guiding, rather than a controlling, role.

Companies can begin to adopt an internal service focus by helping their employees in internal-supplier functions identify just who their customers are. Critical to this process are:

- Recognizing each and every internal customer.
- Understanding their internal customers' needs and expectations.
- Understanding the extent to which their internal customers' needs are being met.

Getting to know what the customer really needs depends on careful communication between the two groups. Many times, there are important differences between what the internal customer wants and expects and what the internal supply is actually providing.

For example, a supplier might be striving for accuracy in preparing data when the customer needs only a rough working estimate and a quick turn-around. Another supplier might think that the customer requires speed when, instead, accuracy is called for (even if it takes another week to prepare the project).

To begin to stimulate an internal service focus that really gets at those needs, organizations often conduct an internal survey, whose purpose is to determine how the various supplier units within an organization respond to each other's requests and requirements. This process first surveys the supplier's customers—what they expect, what they would like to ideally receive from suppliers, and their satisfaction with the supplier's performance.

The supplier's staff is also surveyed to determine what people inside the units think about the service they are rendering and about their customers' satisfaction. By doing this, the company can compare the gaps in perception and get both of the partners talking together about improving the quality of their relationship.

The survey can also expand a company's overall perspective by helping the organization understand more clearly how employees feel about how they are recognized and rewarded, how committed they are to their work and to their workplace, and the extent to which the organization itself nurtures teamwork and support.

Satisfaction barometer

Early this year, the Hay Group conducted a pilot study of about 50 corporate MIS departments and 25 purchasing departments of industrial, financial, and service companies to identify the specific organizational factors that contribute to high internal customer satisfaction. By surveying the actual internal customers of each of these departments, Hay was able to identify those MIS or purchasing units that rated high and low on customer satisfaction.

At the same time, Hay also surveyed the staff of the supplier departments themselves—both the high- and low-rated units—to determine the organizational characteristics that typified those units.

The MIS and purchasing departments that ranked high on quality internal service were those that received better specifications from their suppliers (e.g., user specifications for MIS or accurate sales forecasts for purchasing units). Staffing depth and consistency were other key factors.

Turnover in the high-satisfaction group was half that of the low-satisfaction group; in both MIS and purchasing, the highly rated units experienced less employee rotation, and fewer staff members were promoted into those units from other areas of the company. MIS departments ranking higher in internal satisfaction had a higher ratio of professional and total staff to total company employees as well as better technical backup.

The study also suggested that internal service quality is related to financial and operational control. Highly ranked MIS departments had the authority to set their own project priorities and could directly fund projects and service without imposing direct user charges.

"Strengthening relationships with internal customers improves relations with external ones."

Perhaps even more important to quality service in such departments was an effective day-to-day flow of informal communications with internal customers. This was found to be much more valuable than exclusive reliance on formal communications, such as newsletters or one-shot interview studies.

Although a pilot effort, this study highlighted several areas that seem critical to quality internal service (e.g., having well-defined lines of accountability and authority). Internal customers need to clearly and directly specify their needs to get the quality service they want; internal units providing those services need to have the decision-making authority to address those needs.

Survey respondents also indicated that responsiveness was a crucial factor. Suppliers that took the time to identify and explain deviations in meeting deadlines or specifications were more appreciated than those that provided flawless but rote delivery of the project.

Effective management of human resources plays a pivotal role in internal user satisfaction as well. A stable staff, minimal turnover, and little reliance on external resources are all tied to top-quality internal service.

To get another picture of employee expectations of internal service, Hay asked about 45 units—including human resources, purchasing, MIS, customer service, and manufacturing—in 10 companies to rate the quality of the services received from the various departments within their organizations. A preliminary profile was developed of characteristics associated with high-performing units throughout an organization.

The primary factor distinguishing service units that provide superior service was management style. Managers in outstanding departments actually did things differently—and this appeared to influence employees' commitment to quality and their views of the entire organization. Leaders of highly ranked units tended to:

- Involve their people in a formal planning process, with clear and realistic goals.
- Create a unit structure that encourages people to get involved in decision-making processes and gives them the information they need to make effective and timely decisions.
- Emphasize working with other people and units in the organization and breaking down barriers.
- Communicate clearly, encourage constructive criticism and open discussion of conflicts, and solve problems quickly.
- Insist on high-performance standards, hold people accountable for achieving performance objectives, and reward superior performance.
- Create challenging opportunities and a sense of personal satisfaction.

The change process

What can companies do to change the way individuals work that will enhance internal customer relationships? Shaping a culture that stresses and successfully drives internal customer satisfaction requires a number of steps.

The organization first needs to address basic employee needs. Traditional employee relations provisions (e.g., job security, pay competitiveness, adequacy of benefits, labor relations, safety, and fair, respectful treatment) must meet reasonable standards. If these basic needs are not met, it is unlikely that employees will be committed to focusing on satisfaction.

Human, physical, and technological resources must also be adequate. Staff levels and capabilities must be commensurate with the work load, turnover rates must be manageable, and training must be effective. In addition, technological resources should be state-of-the-art for the industry, with customer and supplier accessible to one another, information systems in place to do the job, and tools, parts, and supplies adequate to the tasks being performed.

Companies can spotlight internal customer service as a priority in several ways. For example, employees must really be empowered to value and contribute to internal customer service; they must be allowed to innovate without fear and to challenge the conventional wisdom.

"Many companies want internal units to be competitive with the services and prices of outside suppliers.

In addition, participative decision making will heighten ownership and realism of plans and objectives; employee involvement in decisions will increase awareness of competing departmental objectives. When workers feel confident that their problems will be addressed and their talents will be fully utilized, internal service goals will be seen as credible—and feasible.

Finally, when managers and employees are held accountable for correcting service problems, the internal customer focus must be appropriately rewarded (e.g., annual incentives, merit increases, spot bonuses, and recognition programs).

Internal customer satisfaction can be rigorously monitored both formally and informally by involving customers in developing assessment tools, comparing customer assessments to supplier assessments, and actually using customer satisfaction data to involve customers in resolving problems.

An internal reorientation

Some companies may choose to revise and revamp the structures and functions of the entire organization to truly reflect and encourage an internal customer orientation. The rebuilding can begin by establishing competency-based models that emphasize selecting and developing customer-focused employees.

Information systems can be restructured to encourage internal suppliers to obtain adequate market information, describing just who their customers are, what their requirements consist of, what their customers use the supplier's products for, and what criteria a customer uses to gauge its own success or failure.

"The primary factor distinguishing service units that provide superior service was management style."

Opportunities for communication between internal suppliers and customers must be timely, and channels must stay open so that units do not have to rely exclusively on formal communications vehicles. In this regard, supplier accessibility and responsiveness are vital.

Because conflicting objectives and performance measures often result from unclear organizational priorities, companies must communicate their overall objectives clearly; this allows internal suppliers and customers to align their departmental goals accordingly. Alignment usually involves decision making on the part of senior management—defining who is the supplier and who is the customer.

Leadership of internal supplier and customer units should be checked for compatibility. Personal or political conflict between senior managers of customer and supplier functions can disrupt productive relations between units and stymie efforts to achieve customer service goals.

More and more organizations are learning that the internal customer focus is too important to ignore. To genuinely improve internal customer satisfaction, organizations need to know who their internal customers are, understand their needs, and measure the extent to which these needs are being met.

Within the organization itself, other changes need to be implemented. An organization develops and maintains its culture as a direct result of its strategy, structure, processes, and employees; all of these systems are related to internal service.

Only tangible alterations to these facets of organizational culture can help turn internal rhetoric into real action. But in doing so, a company can tap new sources of productivity and profit. ▲

Designing a Customer Retention Plan

Glenn DeSouza

What is your company's customer retention rate? How many customers are price defectors? Have you identified barriers that prevent customers from switching to a competitor? According to a recent study, customer retention has a more powerful effect on profits than market share, scale economies, and other variables that are commonly associated with competitive advantage. This article outlines four steps a company should consider in designing a customer retention strategy. These steps integrate concepts from marketing and quality management and apply them to the challenge of keeping customers.

Nothing may seem more obvious than the need to keep customers coming back. Yet, customer retention is either overlooked or devalued when it comes to strategy development. Any marketing manager can provide you with a market share estimate, but ask for the customer retention rate and you may well get a blank stare.

Buck Rodgers, who headed worldwide marketing for IBM as the company's sales grew from $10 billion to $50 billion, speaks forcefully about the importance of customer retention in his book, *The IBM Way:* "It seems to me," observes Rodgers, "that most companies are a lot better at prospecting for new customers than maintaining their customer list. As far as I'm concerned, customer maintenance is imperative to doing business. . . . Someone once said I behaved as if every IBM customer were on the verge of leaving and that I'd do anything to keep them from bolting."

It pays to be obsessive about retaining customers. A cost study of service companies by Bain & Co. found that customer retention has a more powerful effect on profits than market share, scale economies, and other variables that are commonly associated with competitive advantage. More specifically, Bain found that companies that reduce customer defections by 5% can boost profits from 25% to 85%.[1]

As customer retention goes up, marketing costs go down. Moreover, loyal customers frequently bring in new business. The role of the customer as sales-person is especially important in the case of complex products. Buying a telecommunications system that will be at the heart of a business is a major risk. Prospects are filled with worries: Will the dealer provide prompt service? Can the system be expanded later? Will the dealer go out of business? To get reliable answers, prospects tend to rely on friends and colleagues rather than on salespersons or brochures.

The true cost of losing a customer is the amount that person could have spent while involved in a business relationship with the company over a life-time. The bitter and enduring memories created by a bad buying experience are illustrated by the problems currently facing Detroit.

In 1980, according to a J.D. Power and Associates survey, the owners of General Motors, Ford, and Chrysler automobiles recorded three times the number of problems with cars 90 days out of the showroom than did owners of Japanese automobiles. By 1990, US manufacturers had trimmed the quality gap to 25%. Yet, during the same decade, the Japanese market share rose eight points.[2]

A plan to foil defectors

Here are four steps that a company should consider in designing a successful customer retention strategy. These steps integrate concepts from marketing and quality management and apply them to the challenge of keeping customers.

Measure customer retention. In sports, even in individual events like the long jump, it is essential to keep score. Without measurement, there is no impetus to do better, no records to break. It's the same in business. Nothing is real unless it gets measured.

If customer retention is not measured, it will not be managed. Fortunately, it is easy to calculate measures of customer retention, since only internal file data is required for the calculations.

"If customer retention is not measured, it will not be managed."

The crude retention rate measures the absolute percentage of customers that are retained. If the number of customers drops from 500 to 475, the crude rate is 95%. The crude rate treats every customer loss as equivalent. The weighted retention rate resolves this problem by weighting customers by the amount they buy. If the 25 defecting customers had unit purchases that were double the average, the weighted rate is 90%.

If customers source from multiple vendors, high retention rates can mask a problem. For example, when an airline decided to split an order between Boeing 767s and Airbus Industrie A-300s, Boeing retained a customer, but on a shared basis. To reflect multiple sourcing, a customer penetration index must be calculated by evaluating whether sales to retained customers are growing as fast as market-unit sales. The differences reflect changes in customer penetration.

Interview former customers. Many companies write off customers who are definitely lost; this is a mistake. One can learn a great deal by talking to former customers, either directly or through a consultant. There is no need to guess why customers leave when you can ask them. The information they provide is likely to be more specific and actionable than usual market research.

Customers defect for various reasons, and not all of them are preventable. Some defections result from forces that are external to the business. Other defections can be prevented if corrective actions are taken or new strategies are adopted. Consider these six types of defectors.

☐ **Price defectors** are customers who switch to a low-priced competitor. For example, low price was the sole attraction of People Express, the discount airline started by Donald Burr in 1981. Passengers could fly between Boston and New York (Newark NJ, actually) for about half the fare charged on the Eastern shuttle. Bargains like this were compellingly attractive to tourists, students, and other discretionary travelers. By 1984, People had become the fastest-growing airline in the history of aviation.

☐ **Product defectors** are customers who switch to a competitor that offers a superior product. A customer who is lost because of price can be "bought back," but it is almost impossible to get a customer back who has switched to a competitor that is perceived as offering a better product.

☐ **Service defectors** are customers who leave because of poor service. For example, within a few years, customers of People Express began to leave because of poor service, which included lost bags, scrambled reservations, over-booking, and delayed flights. The exodus accelerated once the major carriers used their computer systems to selectively match People's low prices (e.g., American Airlines offered an Ultimate Saver Fave).

By 1986, the party was over for People Express. Declining load factors and negative cash flows forced a sellout to Continental Airlines. In an ironic footnote, Donald Burr was again working for his odd boss, Frank Lorenzo, a man he had called Darth Vader.

☐ **Market defectors** are customers who are lost, but not to a competitor. The customer may go out of business or move out of the market area. During the early 1980s, for example, companies that sold equipment to oil drillers and explorers lost many of their customers when oil prices dropped sharply and customers filed for bankruptcy.

☐ **Technological defectors** are customers who convert to a product offered by companies from outside the industry. During the 1980s, Wang Lab's customers converted en masse from dedicated word processors to multipurpose personal computers. Wang could have prevented these defections, but only by embracing the new technology. Wang did eventually introduce a personal computer, but never marketed it with any seriousness. It was too little and too late.

☐ **Organizational defectors** are customers who are lost because of internal or external political considerations. For example, Boeing frequently runs into political problems when selling to state-owned airlines in the developing world. Boeing claims that many of these airlines buy Airbus equipment because they are told that the aid they receive from European governments may be contingent on their willingness to buy from Airbus.

Analyze complaint and service data. It is natural to regard complaints as a nuisance and an irritant—an unpleasant side effect of doing business. However, complaint data can be a gold mine for the analyst who wants to identify problems that cause customer defections. After all, for every customer who complains, there are possibly 10 others who did not voice their complaints. Listening and acting on these grievances can help retain not only the customers who complain, but, more important, those who did not.

The introduction of toll-free complaint lines has increased the amount of complaint data available for analysis. In 1977, Procter & Gamble became the first company to print a toll-free telephone number on all its packages. Doing this did not reduce the volume of mail P&G received, and the net result was an increase in the number of customer contacts. To enable a meaningful statistical analysis, complaints must be classified by problem, product model, product year, and dealer; the product's registration number should also be noted.

Complaint data must be statistically analyzed. The analysis must go beyond the computation of means and variances. Individual elements must be plotted to identify patterns in the data as well as elements that lie outside the normal expected range. Without statistical methods, attempts to improve a process are hit or miss.

As emphasized by W. Edwards Deming, most problems result from systemic factors such as faulty design, poor supervision, and machines out of order. Complaint analysis may reveal that a particular model or factory account for a disproportionate share of complaints. This indicates that the problem is systemic and can be eliminated by management action.

Some systemic problems can be eliminated by product redesign. For example, Polaroid has used complaint information to make its cameras easy to use. On an early model, Polaroid received thousands of calls about torn pictures; customers could not pull the film out without tearing the prints. In the next model, Polaroid built in an automatic ejection feature for the film.

Polaroid also received calls complaining that the camera did not work. When callers were asked if they had checked the battery, most replied that they did not know the camera contained a battery. To handle this problem, Polaroid decided to locate the battery in the film pack so that the battery was changed along with the pack.[3]

The need for complaint analysis has been recognized by the judges of the Malcolm Baldridge National Quality Award. Baldridge Award judges not only examine whether contestants resolve complaints promptly, but also how they analyze complaints and translate the findings into improvements.

Service data can be helpful in trying to understand why customers defect. In particular, if certain service problems keep recurring, this suggests that the cause is systemic. Some products, such as an automobile, need routine and emergency service if they are to operate at peak efficiency. For other products, service may be as simple as teaching customers how to use the product.

For example, software firms have set up pay-for-service lines where registered customers can receive advice on how to resolve a particular problem or perform a particular application. The callers are often sophisticated users of the software who have a problem that their colleagues are unable to answer. By analyzing the calls, a company can identify attractive new features or insert helpful suggestions into its user manual.

Service data differs from complaint data. The complainer is an aggrieved individual, with a problem that may be trivial or extreme. The person who needs service is a customer with a standard, technical problem that demands and gets actual attention. Because service data differs from complaint data, its analysis may offer new insights into systemic problems.

Complaint and service data is inherently useful; if such data is not being used, this suggests poor statistical analysis or reporting.

"A good retention strategy should identify barriers that will prevent a customer from switching to a competitor, even one perceived as offering a better product at a lower price."

Few companies use statistics effectively, a point made by Deming in his book *Quality, Productivity, and Competitive Position.* To quote him: "No resource in any company is scarcer than statistical knowledge and ability. No source of knowledge can contribute more to quality, productivity, and competitive position."

In the context of reporting complaint data, the most common mistake made is to prepare a single, multipurpose report. Senior managers will not read a thick report; they will find most of the information irrelevant. A series of reports must be prepared and at least one of them should highlight possible, corrective actions.

Identify switching barrier. A company that limits itself to analyzing defections and complaints is back-filling—identifying problems that need to be corrected. But a good retention strategy must move beyond problem resolution. It should identify barriers that will

prevent a customer from switching to a competitor, even one who is perceived as offering a better product at a lower price.

Lotus Development Corp., for example, sells against competitors that offer software that is cheaper and in some ways more technically advanced. Yet Lotus still dominates the market. There is a Lotus infrastructure consisting of millions of users, scores of applications and macros, and many special-purpose user groups. Hidden costs associated with a switch from Lotus far exceed the direct savings realized by buying the cheaper software.

To identify switching barriers, look outside your own industry for the best demonstrated practices. If you borrow a practice that is farthest afield from your own industry, your chances of surprising the competition are better. A borrowed practice will, of course, need to be modified to fit your customer's needs.

Electronic data interchange (EDI) is a technological example of a switching barrier. Department stores have traditionally been the most fickle of buyers. In the past, they would readily grant shelf space to a new vendor with a trendy look or a big price discount, but less so today.

Vendors with an EDI link enjoy a protected status. Under EDI, the store and vendor share data. The vendor can look at a terminal, see how many items have sold at the department store, and ship more product. The result is that the department store carries minimal inventory. The reward—a newfound loyalty to the vendor.

"Strategic bundling can also create a barrier to defections."

Strategic bundling can also create a barrier to defections. A bundle is a group of products or services offered as a single cost-saving and convenient package. A banking bundle, for example, includes checking and savings accounts, a credit card, a preapproved auto loan, and a special cash flow statement. A customer who buys a bundle is less likely to defect if someone offers a better deal on one of the items in the bundle.

Paradoxically, the ultimate barrier to competition may be a new twist on that old standby—accounting management. Many companies use the Willy Loman approach, where Willy deals with the buyer or some other middle manager.

This relationship is placed in jeopardy if Willy moves on to greener pastures or alienates the contact at the account. In the new model, a team approach is used to forge a bond that lasts no matter which person on the sales force is the key contact in the relationship.

The account team may be headed by the CEO.[4] Typically, CEO efforts are limited to talking with fellow CEOs to forge company-wide programs. But the involvement can go beyond the ceremonial.

At Xerox, CEO Paul Allaire personally handles six of the copier company's largest accounts. At Bose Corp., founder Amar Bose gets directly involved in opening markets. He visits Japan at least twice a year, which may explain in part why Bose is one of the largest sellers of high-performance loudspeakers in Japan.

Team account management is an all-hands-on proposition. Even the clerical staff should get involved. Nothing can be more frustrating to a customer than a conflict with an anonymous clerk at the billing or shipping department.

I recently surveyed two corporate subsidiaries, both of which were using identical service systems. Yet customers rated one subsidiary higher. The reason was the person who managed customer service at the better subsidiary. She had been with the company for 20 years and was on a first-name basis with customers, many of whom she had met at trade shows.

To companies that are financially strapped, installing a free terminal in a customer's office or sending a clerical supervisor to a trade show may seem like an unwarranted extravagance. However, creating switching barriers requires a willingness to spend, to experiment, and to break with industry tradition. To the extent that customer retention actually improves, the expenditures are a justifiable investment. There are few things that are more closely associated with superior business performance than a high rate of customer retention. ▲

Notes
1. F.F. Reichheld and W.E. Sasser, Jr., "Zero Defections: Quality Comes to Services," *Harvard Business Review* (Sept.–Oct. 1990), p. 106.
2. "A New Era for Auto Quality," *Business Week* (Oct. 22, 1990), p. 85.
3. J. Goodman, *Summary of White House Complaint Handling Study,* Technical Assistance Research Programs (Washington DC 1981), p. 12.
4. See "Chief Executives Are Increasingly Chief Salesmen," *Wall Street Journal*, Aug. 6, 1991.

Improved Customer Service: Measuring the Payoff

Harvey N. Shycon

Will enhanced levels of service automatically lead to greater sales and profits? According to a recent survey, the answer is a resounding yes. The survey shows that regardless of industry, improved service quality results in a consistent pattern of increased market share and revenues. The quality of a company's service can cause it to gain or lose as much as 10 percent in sales revenues. Service affects sales directly by enhancing the reliability of product availability as well as indirectly by increasing a buyer's preference for (and loyalty to) a supplier.

Managers have always known that better service increases sales and market share—up to a point. But how much added sales and revenues do you get for how much added service? And how do you link service levels with profit levels?

Accepting the importance of improved customer service does not require a leap of faith. It can be documented in solid financial terms.

Arthur D. Little has discovered a basic truth concerning service quality, one that is found in every industry it has studied: improved service quality results in a consistent pattern of increased market share and revenues. That pattern is shown in Exhibit 1.

The firm's studies indicate that the quality of a company's service can cause it to gain or lose as much as 10% in sales revenues. Service affects sales in two ways:

- Directly, by enhancing the reliability of product availability.
- Indirectly, by increasing a buyer's preference for and loyalty to a supplier that provides reliable service with fewer problems.

The challenge is to determine the specific elements of improved service that can improve revenues and market share. A company can then formulate a marketing program that emphasizes these elements while reasonably containing the cost of service elements to which the customer is indifferent.

Over the past dozen years, Arthur D. Little conducted an annual survey to determine the relative importance of product quality, service quality, and value to customers. The customers surveyed are generally purchasing agents or buyers for distributors or retailers. They are knowledgeable about the purchasing process as well as the products and services they buy.

The surveys have helped to identify approximately 60 elements that these buyers consider important, elements that can affect sales and profitability in any given market and product category. They include breadth of product line, order fill rate, lead time, consistent on-time delivery, accuracy, quality of the response to emergency customer requirements, responsiveness of sales personnel, and presence in the market in addition to product quality and price.

During this 12-year survey period, the relative importance of some of these factors has changed significantly. When Arthur D. Little began the surveys, the quality of the product and its performance ranked first, price was second, and service was third. In the past three to four years, however, although product quality has remained the most important factor, service now ranks above price in importance. Customers are telling the firm that they are willing to pay a reasonable price for the value added by service.

Exhibit 1. *The Impact of Service on Sales*

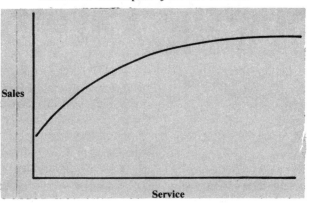

Quantifying the value of service

Improved service frequently carries a cost. To determine its true value, management must quantify the potential payoff for improving service. A manufacturer or distributor should measure the benefits in increased sales or in increased price that it can achieve by providing the customer with the proper mix of services. In other words, the seller must determine how much added revenue, and the attendant contribution to profits, a company can expect to gain for how much added service.

The firm has developed a method for making this determination during the course of a study it did for a large national food product company (which in this article will be called Butterfield Farm Foods, Inc.). Butterfield enjoyed a 38% market share nationally, whereas its principal competitor had a 35% share. Clearly, the competition was keen.

With one of its major customers (a large regional chain), Butterfield had 41% market share, whereas the competitor had only 32%. The firm found that for this customer, Butterfield had a special four-times-a-week delivery schedule, in contrast to the twice-a-week schedule it provided most of its other customers.

The increased delivery frequency reduced the inventory the customer needed to carry, increased turnover, improved freshness, and eliminated the need for store personnel to restock the shelves. The more frequent sched-

ule meant reduced cost and higher value for the retailer.

For the manufacturer, although the more frequent delivery schedule required somewhat lower volumes of safety stock, it meant a higher cost of service. But the total cost of service to both manufacturer and retailer combined was lower than it had been. Thus, the manufacturer and retailer negotiated a somewhat higher price for the manufacturer.

The result was increased profits for both. In addition, Butterfield's gain of three share points translated into an 8% increase in sales volume and nearly double that in profit improvement.

However, this connection between service and profits was evident for only one customer. The critical questions for Butterfield were:

- Would this pattern hold true across a range of customers and markets?
- Would other improvements in service yield similar benefits?

To answer these questions, the firm had to determine the value to the customer of specific service elements that Butterfield provided. Those service elements were compared with the service packages that major competitors provided (each of which included product quality, service, and price). It was then determined how the customer split the purchases among several suppliers. Finally, it was determined how the customer valued the total service package and the level of service it was willing to pay for.

In this case, the retailer clearly valued the more frequent delivery enough to pay a slightly higher price for the total service package and to place more business with Butterfield. However, the firm did not know precisely how much value each element of the service package provided.

Here is the logic of the technique used for quantifying the elements of a service package. When the firm finds customer purchase behavior that differs from the norm and the investigation reveals, as in the Butterfield case, that one supplier provides different service quality over others, it is this service difference that may account for the unique purchasing behavior.

When a consistent pattern of these differences is found in service and purchasing behavior across a large number of customers, perhaps in different markets and under different competitive conditions, this may produce a cause-and-effect relationship.

"Finding statistically reliable relationships between quality service and purchasing patterns is difficult."

When extensive statistical analysis of data gathered from a large number of customers under different market conditions reveals a statistically reliable relationship between service quality and purchasing behavior, a valuable theorem has been established. This theorem can then be used, in mathematical terms, to project market response under a variety of conditions.

Although the logic may be straight-forward, finding statistically reliable relationships between quality service and purchasing patterns is difficult. Arthur D. Little has found that the technique that is most successful is regression analysis. In most cases, market share is the dependent variable.

The independent variables are the approximately 60 service elements (e.g., product

quality, price, presence in the market, and breadth of product line) on which the firm has gathered data through customer surveys. In virtually every case, 6 to 10 of these elements are critical to the success of a marketing program. However, these critical elements differ by industry, market, and company.

The variables determined to have significant impact on market share are regressed. They include such factors as the frequency of advertising and the frequency of sales force visits. The analysis reveals those elements that have a significant influence on market share. When competitors' service lags in those elements, management can establish a marketing program that features them.

Other analyses and techniques that relate service quality to sales and market share advantage include the following: perceptual mapping, conjoint analysis, discriminant analysis, cluster analysis, and factor analysis. Each is appropriate under certain circumstances, and each relates increases or decreases in market share to specific service quality and levels provided to various market segments.

In the Butterfield case, once the relationships between service levels and value were identified, the payoff was enormous. After the design and implementation of a total service package in all its markets, Butterfield gained two share points nationwide, for an additional $15.8 million in annual sales revenues and an additional $4.75 million in profit—a substantial return on the service investment.

A case study: service impact on market share

A West Coast manufacturer of athletic sportswear (which in this article will be called Prestige Athletic Sportswear, Inc.) sought to increase its market share. Prestige was third in its market with about a 10% share nationally. The two top competitors had about 32% and 28% of the market respectively, with approximately 50 other manufacturers sharing the remainder, none with more than 5%.

With its top two competitors sharing 60% of the market, Prestige was at a critical point in its history. The company's president felt that with aggressive marketing, it might gain on the leading two companies; if it took no action, however, it might fall into the cate-

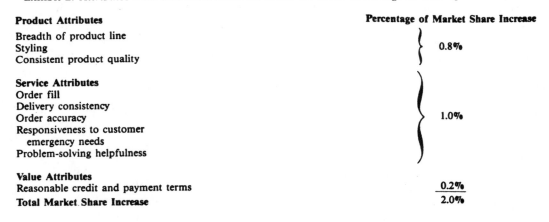

Exhibit 2. *Attributes That Command Increases in Market Share at Prestige Athletic Sportswear, Inc.*

Product Attributes	Percentage of Market Share Increase
Breadth of product line	
Styling	0.8%
Consistent product quality	
Service Attributes	
Order fill	
Delivery consistency	
Order accuracy	1.0%
Responsiveness to customer	
emergency needs	
Problem-solving helpfulness	
Value Attributes	
Reasonable credit and payment terms	0.2%
Total Market Share Increase	**2.0%**

gory of the also-rans. He felt that Prestige had to become aggressive to ensure a solid position as number three and perhaps to gain substantially on number two.

To mount his marketing campaign, the company's president needed to find the elements in his competitors' marketing programs that were not satisfying their customers' needs. First, however, he wanted to learn what the customers' needs were.

Once he identified the gaps in his competitors' marketing programs—elements important to customers but those not provided by the top two companies—he could formulate his own aggressive program to meet these needs and thereby gain market share.

To accomplish this, the following six-step program was implemented:
1. Documenting the market structure for athletic sportswear.
2. Identifying the specific segments that drive the market.
3. Identifying the service needs of each market segment by conducting a large-scale survey among buyers.
4. Analyzing the survey results to determine the critical service elements that could increase market share.
5. Quantifying the contribution each service element could make (i.e., how much added service gets how much added share).
6. Formulating the package of services needed to achieve the maximum service contribution.

A survey was conducted in which approximately 600 retailers were interviewed nationally. Those who were surveyed were divided among the segments that drive the market, which include sportswear chains, department stores, independent sportswear retailers, team suppliers, school athletic programs, and sporting goods chains.

The survey revealed a decided preference for doing business with quality service providers. It also identified the specific service elements to which market share was sensitive and the service levels that each major competitor provided.

Exhibit 2 lists the nine critical elements (of the more than 60 that were examined) that turned out to have a significant influence on market share. By excelling in these specific elements, Prestige would increase its market share to 12%, for an increase in revenues of approximately 20%.

It is clear from Arthur D. Little's experience in a broad range of industries—consumer, manufacturing, processing, and commodity—that customers are sensitive to quality service, in particular to specific, identifiable service elements. Customers respond with a greater volume of business to suppliers that provide these elements in proper measure. Market share may be more sensitive to service in some industries than in others, but this important relationship exists in all industries. And proportional increases are possible for companies starting at any market share level, low or high.

Exhibit 3. *The "Sweet Spot" (Service Level that Provides Maximum Difference Between Sales and Cost)*

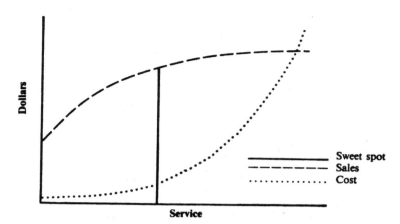

Those service elements to which the customer responds positively by placing increased orders can be identified. The service elements to which the customer does not respond can also be singled out. Management can reduce costs by minimizing investment in service attributes that customers do not consider critical.

The ability to quantify both the costs and the revenues associated with different levels of service allows for the design of service packages that optimize the return on investment by providing the best combination of quality elements that a company should provide its customers. As shown in Exhibit 3, this method can pinpoint the "sweet spot" at which the level of service provided will yield the highest possible profit. It also can identify the point at which additional investments in service will yield diminishing returns.

Finding the service sweet spot is critical for every service provider—whether manufacturer, distributor, or retailer—that wishes to increase its market share. ▲

A Guide to Global Sourcing

Mark L. Fagan

Global sourcing is rapidly becoming a prerequisite to competing in today's marketplace. A growing number of companies are purchasing materials and services from everywhere across the globe to obtain the right product at the right price at the right time. In addition to lower costs, other reasons for global sourcing include availability, uniqueness, and quality. This article explains how to capture the benefits of global sourcing while minimizing costs and risks.

As the lowering of trade barriers eases the flow of goods worldwide, business survival increasingly hinges on a company's ability to compete globally. Competitors from overseas are targeting previously secure domestic markets, while competitors at home are using overseas sources of supply as a basis for cost reduction and product and service innovation. Standing pat in traditional markets no longer ensures a firm the growth and profitability it needs to remain competitive.

Global sourcing is rapidly becoming a prerequisite to competing in today's marketplace. The question is not longer whether to go global—virtually all companies will be tapping resources globally within five years—but how to capture the strategic benefits of global sourcing while minimizing the costs and risks.

Traditionally, the most widely recognized benefit of global sourcing has been lower costs. Less-expensive labor, less-restrictive work rules, and lower land and facility costs have enticed companies to foreign suppliers; reduced product cost remains the main attraction for perhaps one third to one half of those companies currently pursuing global sourcing.

Tax advantages can reduce costs further. In addition to enjoying the favorable tax treatment a national may use to lure foreign companies, firms can also avoid some taxes outright. For example, processing a product in a free trade zone and then sending it out to the worldwide market eliminates inventory holding taxes.

However, lower costs are no longer the only benefit of global sourcing. For many firms, the payoff increasingly comes from the following:

☐ **Availability.** Some firms source globally primarily to strengthen the reliability of their supply. They look to worldwide markets to supplement their domestic sources or to meet an increase in product demand.

☐ **Uniqueness.** In other cases, a company simply cannot get the materials it needs from domestic sources. For example, most U.S. products using small motors are fitted with supplies from Asia because few other regions can produce small motors cost-effectively. Surveys by the tool and machining industries consistently show that their members source globally because the materials and services they need are not available at home. Similar patterns occur in other industries, where the technical specifications or capabilities of products manufactured overseas exceed those of domestic units.

☐ **Quality.** Quality is joining cost as a lure to overseas purchases. An analogy is only as far as the next Japanese auto. The Japanese first penetrated the U.S. car market with price advantages. Later, the focus shifted to a price/quality relationship.

High product quality, improved product availability, and lower costs will continue to spur conversions to global sourcing. But companies on the leading edge are already focusing on an even more fundamental factor: sustainable competitive advantage. The potential for a lasting advantage lies in three ways:

☐ **Technical supremacy.** Companies can gain technical supremacy by securing access to innovative technology developed overseas and locking out competitors from the technology base. This route to competitive advantage is already being aggressively pursued in the electronics industry.

☐ **Penetration of growth markets.** A toehold in a promising new market can be obtained by sourcing in that market. Toyota, for example, sources from the Pacific Rim not just to achieve lower costs but to enter markets with

---

"By adjusting product components to avoid local content restrictions and other trade barriers, the global sourcer can enter a lucrative protected market before its competitors."

---

restrictive quotas by increasing the local content component of its cars. By adjusting product components to avoid local content restrictions and other trade barriers, the global sourcer can enter a lucrative protected market before its competitors.

☐ **High speed.** The flexibility and global reach of a company's sourcing network are critical. Slow and unresponsive sourcing will undermine even the best just-in-time or quick response strategy. A well-established global sourcing program, on the other hand, can provide a strong foundation for a speed advantage.

The downside of global sourcing

In addition to the high costs of overseas travel and communication, brokers' and agents' fees must be paid. Using these agents is usually worth the cost—they provide the entry

to a foreign culture, they know the local rules and regulations, and they know how to get business done. But it's a nonissue with domestic sourcing.

Expenses for physical distribution also come under the direct cost category, accounting for the largest component of those costs. A product sourced in Malaysia but assembled in St. Louis incurs costs for transportation and delivery to the Malaysian port, carriage overseas, and transportation to St. Louis. The distribution charges may add 10 percent to 15 percent to the unit cost of a product.

Tallying the direct costs is straight-forward. Beyond these costs, however, lie indirect expenses that planners accustomed to domestic sources may overlook.

The most onerous of these costs is often the increased expense for inventory buffers. The buffer itself may add only 5 percent to 10 percent to unit costs, but mistakes in estimating the necessary buffer size can lead to greater penalties: excessive costs if the buffer is too large; product delivery difficulties and disgruntled customers if the buffer is too small.

Calibrating the optimum inventory size depends on accurately gauging lead times, which will differ significantly from the lead times common for domestic sources. Delivery of a domestically sourced product typically takes three to five days, perhaps a week to ten days if the product must be transported from the West Coast to the East Coast.

For products from South America, Africa, Europe, or Asia, the lead times are both longer (four, six, or eight weeks) and less certain. The weak transportation infrastructure in developing nations, such as China, hobbles attempts to standardize lead times and estimate delivery dates. Inventory buffers must compensate for such variability.

A second indirect cost, and one with a potentially higher financial impact than inventory buffers, stems from the need to rework products. Foreign-made products often require design changes and other reworking. For instance, the way overseas equipment performs may differ, the methods for measuring tolerances may vary, and agreement on tolerance and quality requirements may be difficult to obtain. The charges for such reworking could be minimal, but they may increase unit costs by as much as 35 percent.

Increased paperwork adds another increment to the indirect costs of global sourcing. Importing materials and services means filing forms, passing customs, and perhaps managing quotas and licenses. In addition, the purchase orders issued for an overseas procurement are more complex than those issued for domestically sourced goods. Every detail must be put on paper and in a language everyone understands.

A fourth set of indirect costs arise from cash flow issues. But issuance of the "currency of the deal" (the letter of credit) can precede by several weeks the actual availability of the product for use in manufacturing, reselling, or another activity. The cash required to back the letter of credit will be tied up during that period.

Finally, in addition to direct and indirect costs incurred by global sourcing, companies must assess the business risks involved. Going overseas reduces the control a firm exercises over its technology, and foreign countries generally provide fewer protections for products and technologies. For proprietary technology, the risk simply may be too great, regardless of the potential cost savings.

Exchange rate fluctuations are another business risk. Effective ways to handle this risk must be developed. Also critical are well-thought-out plans for handling political turmoil, resolving disputes with foreign vendors, and settling jurisdictional issues if claims or suits must be instituted.

Strategies for success

The costs and risks may sound daunting, but the benefits of global sourcing are too attractive to ignore. To capture these tactical and strategic benefits, firms must first develop clear goals. For some, the overall focus will be on minimizing labor costs. Others will seek an optimum blend of cost and distribution advantages. For still others, meeting technical specifications will be vital.

Approaches to global sourcing will also be influenced by industry conditions and a company's marketing position, but responses to those influences will differ. In the highly competitive apparel industry, for example, the jeans manufacturer Gitano, based in New York City, sources from dozens of underdeveloped nations where labor is relatively inexpensive. Gitano brings in the equipment, trains the workers, and supports the development of the necessary infrastructure. Once a country begins to attract other manufacturers, and labor rates begin to rise, Gitano looks for new opportunities.

Other apparel manufacturers, however, source from the Caribbean rather than from countries with lower costs, such as Thailand. The proximity of the Caribbean to the North American market, the skills of the region's laborers, and some U.S. tax incentives provide a blend of advantages preferred by those companies.

"An additional indirect cost, and one with a potentially higher financial impact than inventory buffers, stems from the need to rework products."

Another successful approach to global sourcing involves blending competitive advantages in the supplier's market with cost advantages in a domestic market. One U.S. machine-tool maker captured such an advantage by buying turning machinery (for milling steel) from an Asian car manufacturer.

The firm first looked to obtain cost and quality benefits. What it found, in addition, was a market with an increasing demand for highly engineered computer control products. The relationship gave the company exposure in the new market—an opening it quickly pursued.

An international computer company found another way to multiply the advantages of global sourcing. Using overseas suppliers for computer terminal components yielded some price advantages; however, the company sought an additional edge by negotiating prices on an FOB origin basis and then managing the inbound physical distribution itself. Controlling the distribution gave the company another 13 percent reduction in unit cost.

Extending this approach (to control the entire channel) proved rewarding for the Bose Corporation, a manufacturer of high-quality audio equipment. Bose, based in Framingham, Mass., sources almost entirely in the Pacific Rim. The company handles the complex logistics involved by focusing on the entire channel, from the vendor to the loading dock and all the way to the stateside manufacturing intake. Each link in the supply chain—vendor, customs broker, transportation company—is treated like a partner. As a result, Bose operates its sourcing as if it were a just-in-time cycle despite lead times of six to eight weeks.

"The Bose Corporation operates its sourcing as if it were a just-in-time cycle despite lead times of six to eight weeks."

Global guidelines

Implementation will be most effective if it occurs step by step. The initial stage in developing a global perspective will be a gradual introduction of nondomestic sources.

For example, to broaden a supplier base, companies that source primarily with domestic vendors can add foreign sources as secondary suppliers while retaining the major domestic vendors for base supplies. As the relationship with the secondary supplier improves (assuming cost benefits and other advantages are maintained), a company could increase its reliance on the foreign source and begin scouting additional locations. In this second phase, foreign suppliers eventually may move into lead supplier roles.

As the integration of foreign and domestic suppliers proceeds, the company pursuing a global sourcing strategy begins to acquire "too many" suppliers. At that point, the firm enters another phase of strategy planning: streamlining the vendor base. Streamlining involves more than just dropping suppliers from a master list; an effective strategy depends on ongoing evaluations of current suppliers to identify the optimal sources for each material or service purchased.

Perhaps products from East Germany or Poland won't meet specifications today. What about tomorrow? Tracking such opportunities and continually assessing potential suppliers are critical activities if global sourcing is to succeed.

Ongoing evaluation of new opportunities is just one of the elements of a successful global sourcing strategy. Foremost among the other key requirements is the capacity to think globally and the commitment to maintain that perspective. Thinking globally does not simply mean "overseas." While buying goods from Asia or Africa could well be the best option, ignoring choices closer to home is a mistake. The United States should not be overlooked as an option, and Canada and Mexico remain viable suppliers.

Other important hallmarks of effective international sourcing include the following:

☐ **Make a commitment from the top.** The commitment to global sourcing must begin at the top, and it must be sustained. A short-term focus negates the potential benefits of a global operation.

For example, Malaysia and Indonesia once lacked the technology and skills needed for production of footwear and apparel. But they acquired the technology and skills that were needed. Companies that once sourced from Korea and Taiwan are now beginning to take advantage of the lower-cost labor available in Malaysia and Indonesia.

An ongoing evaluation of potential sources would have been necessary to reveal this opportunity. Without management commitment and time, these new opportunities might be missed.

☐ **Examine total costs, not just direct costs.** Coupled with an ongoing evaluation of sources must be a commitment to assessing total costs. Looking at half a ledger could doom the effort to optimize sources. Furthermore, once direct and indirect costs have been calculated, a periodic review can reveal the need for a change.

That's what happened when Conair, an Edison, N.J.-based manufacturer of hair dryers and other small appliances, examined the total costs of its Pacific Rim sources. Although the company sourced almost exclusively from the Pacific Rim during the 1980s, lower labor and facility costs did not outweigh the indirect costs of using overseas suppliers. Conair now sources much of its product from Mexico.

☐ **Develop trust and respect.** Companies sourcing overseas must be willing to help their suppliers succeed, to appreciate cultural differences, and to deliver benefits to the local economy. Paying the training and equip-

---

"Perhaps products from East Germany or Poland won't meet specifications today. What about tomorrow?"

---

ment costs for operations in a developing country, for example, improves the skills of the work force, as the sponsoring firm gains competitive advantage from low-cost labor.

☐ **Use technologies that enhance control.** Especially valuable are technologies that improve communications and control. Electronic data interchange, among other benefits, can help purchasing agents meet changing demands for inventory and order fulfillment. As the flow of information increases, so does the company's control of its sources. New partnerships with brokers and third-party providers may result. Or a company can explore innovative logistics alternatives.

☐ **Develop ways to handle business risks.** The risk of losing proprietary technology can be offset by developing joint ventures. A joint venture integrates operations and profitability in ways that simple sourcing relationships cannot and cements the partner's interest in protecting the technology.

Risks from exchange rate fluctuations can be guarded against by quoting prices in dollars or by hedging the currency. During periods when the dollar is relatively stable, a dollar quote might be best. At other times, the company may prefer to buy yen or marks up front, to ensure a stable price upon delivery.

A related strategy is the purchase of a futures contract for yen or francs or another appropriate denomination. These hedging strategies are similar to practices common in manufacturing, where the necessary materials for production may be purchased at a known and established price for future use or purchased at the last moment to avoid carrying costs, depending on which strategy costs less.

The risks associated with political turmoil can be countered by a "revolution" strategy built around a contingency plan for local unrest. The backup plan might include multiple sourcing or development of sufficient inventory to compensate for uncertain supplies. The plan, rather than just a paper exercise, should be "ready to go" with alternative suppliers, alternative routes, etc.

Global sourcing is not a simple or easy solution to a company's sourcing needs. But business aiming to grow during the 1990s cannot ignore its potential. New markets and new competitors will challenge established businesses. Global sourcing offers one approach to meeting this challenge. ▲

Reprinted from *Journal of Business Strategy*, March/April 1991, pp. 21–25. Copyright © 1991 by Warren Gorham Lamont, a division of Research Institute of America Inc. All rights reserved. Used by permission.

PART F

Japanese Cost Management

Target Costing at Toyota

Takao Tanaka

Cost planning at Toyota is mainly an effort to reduce cost at the design stage. Using cost planning, Toyota sets goals for cost reduction, then seeks to achieve those goals through design changes. To correctly assess the gains made, the exact amount of cost reduction through design must be measured, excluding all other factors. At the profit-estimation stage, Toyota calculates differences between the new and current models, distributes portions of the cost-reduction goal to the design divisions, and then assesses the results. Profit targets for the life of the new model are also calculated as differences between estimates and targets. Setting goals and assessing the results based on cost differences between old and new models constitute the essence of budget control at Toyota. The idea behind it is that goals for each control unit should be clearly specified to ensure that the goals of the company are attained.

Major differences seem to exist between what Western and Japanese manufacturing executives expect from cost information and how they use it. A manager in Europe or the United States generally expects to use cost information to make decisions about pricing and investments,[1] while a Japanese manager expects to use cost information to control costs. While neither is blind to the other possible uses of cost information, this contrast points out a basic difference in priorities.

Japanese manufacturing companies have long recognized the importance of control over production costs as a component of profit control. Cost control, in concert with total quality control and a just-in-time manufacturing system, has contributed substantially to the production of high-quality, low-cost products in small lots.[2] Japanese companies have pursued *kaizen* (a Japanese word meaning continuous improvement) to reduce costs ("cost *kaizen*") as well as to improve productivity on the factory floor.[3] Cost *kaizen*, however, is becoming relatively less important at large companies that have good control systems, because *kaizen* efforts throughout a company inevitably lead to fewer opportunities to cut costs.

Better product planning and development

Managers are now becoming convinced that more opportunities for cost reduction can be found in product planning and development than in production.[4] When a new product is developed at leading Japanese manufacturers, development divisions are given cost targets, along with goals for product quality and performance. Effort at the planning and development stages to attain a cost target set by management is called target costing, which is carried out mainly by the design divisions.

Target costing, as it has developed in Japan, was invented by Toyota in 1965. Cost estimation plays a role in target costing, but the two differ in several ways. Estimating cost is not the only goal. Rather, target costing is used to bring the target cost and the estimated cost into line by better specification and design of the product. The ultimate goal is to enable a product to attain profit targets throughout its market life.

Although many major manufacturers in Japan use target costing, the system used at Toyota Motor Corporation is the oldest and technically the most advanced. This article, which is based on interviews with the chief engineer

Exhibit 1. *Schedule for Automobile Development and Production*

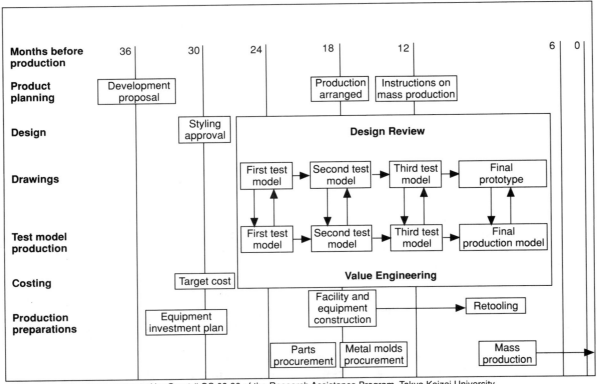

This research has been supported by Grant # CC 02-90 of the Research Assistance Program, Tokyo Keizai University.

and controller at Toyota, explains Toyota's pioneering target costing system.

Product planning

Automakers undertake two broad categories of product development: development of new types of automobiles, and full or minor changes to existing models. This article focuses mainly on the latter.

In Japan, passenger cars usually undergo full model changes every four years (although the time between full model changes may become longer in the future). A model change begins with a proposal for development of a new model. These plans are usually made by chief engineers. They are proposed and approved at what Toyota calls a "product-planning meeting." As Exhibit 1 shows, after a proposal is approved, development of the new model begins three years before the expected release of the new model.

The plans usually include:

- Specifications like size (length, width, wheelbase, and interior space), weight, mileage, engine (type, displacement, and maximum power), transmission (gear and moderation ratios), chassis (suspension and brake types) and body components;
- Development budget;
- Development schedule; and
- Retail price and sales targets.

The new model basically maintains the same product concept as its predecessor. The development plan may define some specifications for the new model, but styling is left unspecified; probably no more than a vague image is mentioned.

Most of the cost incurred in any model change is for prototyping; prototype costs increase in proportion to the number of test models built. When the Lexus (Toyota's high-end model) was developed, 400 test cars were needed, though only 300 test cars were needed for the three Celica models. The cost of producing a test car is usually twenty to thirty times the unit cost of a mass-production model.

In a model change, styling is usually approved about thirty months before the new model is released. Typically, three prototypes have been built and tested twelve months before mass production of the new model begins. This schedule is about the same for every model. It is often said that final specifications for a new model are set when the second prototype is made, about eighteen months before the release.

Retail prices and sales targets. Retail prices and sales targets are usually proposed by the sales divisions. A principle used in setting the retail price is that the price remains the same if there is no change from the previous model in function or value to the driver. Ideally, therefore, prices change in accordance with changes in product value.

Increases in retail price are decided by market recognition of additional value from new functions (e.g., four-wheel steering and active suspension in the 1990 Celicas) or better performance (e.g., higher horsepower or better fuel-efficiency). In short, the price comes first.

Formula for list price of a new model. The list price for a new car model can be described mathematically this way:

$$U = U_o + (f_1 + f_2 + \ldots + f_n) \qquad (1)$$

Where U = price of the new model
U_o = price of the existing model
f_1 = value of added functions as recognized by the market

Production volumes, on the other hand, are usually proposed by the sales division based on past sales, market trends, and the situations of competitors. The sales division proposes a figure that it considers safe compared with the current figure, often restraining optimism in favor of realistic goals.

The chief engineer usually makes the development plan for a new model. His boss, the director in charge of product planning, proposes the development plan for approval at the product-planning meeting. The chief engineer is equivalent in position to a general manager, and there are as many chief engineers as there are product lines. They have

authority and responsibility for development of their specific lines.

With the help of engineers in the design, test-production, and technical divisions, a chief engineer makes the development plan for the new model and then leads the development project. The engineers work with him on the project, but since they belong to different divisions, not all are under his supervision. There are probably only about a dozen people who report directly to him. In this sense, the chief engineer is more a project leader than a supervisor of development.

At the product-planning meeting, the technical vice-president convenes the ten or more directors in charge of the technical divisions (product-planning, design, and test production), production technology, sales, purchasing, and accounting. The meeting consists of subcommittees under the executive committee, which is organized according to function (such as production, quality assurance, sales, and costing), and entrusted with making the decisions.

When the marketing conditions are set, including a product plan, retail price, and production volume, the project moves on to cost planning.

Setting goals

At a cost-planning meeting (see the box "target cost" in Exhibit 1), a cost-planning goal is set, based on the product plan and the targets for retail price and production volume. Setting a cost-planning goal is equivalent to setting a profit target. At the working level, this means specifying a net cost that will allow a target profit, which is done by setting a cost goal at the design stage. The target profit is the expected profit from total sales of the product over its life, usually four years. The target cost is the unit cost on which the profit target is based. The unit cost, as described later, is calculated and shown in terms of desirable cost cuts made through cost planning.

The cost-planning goal, which occurs three years before the release of the new model, is set at a cost-planning meeting. This meeting includes directors in charge of technical divisions, production, sales, purchasing, accounting, and other divisions. The meeting is chaired by the senior vice-president in charge of accounting or finance.

Calculating target profit and target cost. How are target profit and target cost calculated? The lifetime target profit $\overline{P}_a$ for product A (e.g., the Celica) is calculated this way:

$$\overline{P}_a = \overline{S}_a \times P' \qquad (2)$$

Where $\overline{S}_a$ = target sales
P' = profit ratio of sales

The sales target $\overline{S}_a$ is set using the retail price and production volume decided at the product-planning meeting:

$$\overline{S}_a = \overline{U}_a \times \overline{Q}_a \qquad (3)$$

Where $\overline{U}_a$ = target retail price
$\overline{Q}_a$ = target production volume over product life

Target production volume $\overline{Q}_a$ is calculated based on the realistic production volume for the current model. Retail price, as mentioned earlier, is subject to change depending solely on market evaluation of added functions. This holds true over the entire life of the product (and is in contrast with the situation in the U.S. market). The sales profit ratio is set with reference to the long-term target profit ratio.

Estimated cost is calculated as the sum of all possible costs, and estimated profit is calculated from that figure. Estimated profit is usually less than the target profit. The difference between target profit and estimated profit is the amount to be cut from costs through cost planning. The cost-planning goal G is obtained as follows:

$$G = \overline{P}_a - P_a \qquad (4)$$

Where P_a = estimated profit
$\overline{P}_a > P_a$

Simple transformation creates this corollary:

$$\overline{P}_a = P_a + G \qquad (4')$$

The goal of cost planning is to determine the profit needed to achieve the profit target and the amount to be trimmed from cost through cost planning.

Estimated profit (P_a) is related to estimated cost, retail price, and production volume as follows:

$$P_a = (\overline{U}_a - \underline{C}_a)\overline{Q}_a \qquad (5)$$

Where $\underline{C}_a$ = estimated cost
$\overline{U}_a$ = target retail price
$\overline{Q}_a$ = target production volume

In the same way, $\overline{P}_a$ is obtained thus:

$$\overline{P}_a = (\overline{U}_a - \overline{C}_a)\overline{Q}_a \qquad (6)$$

Where $\overline{C}_a$ = target cost
$\underline{C}_a > \overline{C}_a$

Substituting Formulas 5 and 6 into Formula 4:

$$\begin{aligned} G &= (\overline{U}_a - \overline{C}_a)\overline{Q}_a - (\overline{U}_a - \underline{C}_a)\overline{Q}_a \\ &= (\underline{C}_a - \overline{C}_a)\overline{Q}_a \end{aligned} \qquad (7)$$

And, since the aim of cost planning is to bring the goal G to zero:

$$\underline{C}_a - \overline{C}_a = g \qquad (8)$$

The formula shows that the aim of cost planning is to bring the difference g between estimated cost and target cost to zero.

The lifetime target profit for the new model (which is based on the product plan, retail price, and production volume set at the product-planning meeting), and the target cost reduction to be made through cost planning to realize the target profit, are set as goals at the cost-planning meeting. The cost-planning process takes place for over two years under the leadership of the chief engineer.

Estimating differential costs

Now that the process of determining the cost-planning goal has been outlined, the next topic is a more detailed discussion of specific methods for estimating costs.

Rather than add together all the costs for a new model, Toyota's unique approach to cost planning is to sum the differences in cost between the new and current models. The advantages are several. With this method, cost planning can begin even before blueprints for the first test model are drawn. Estimating the total difference, instead of the total cost, tends to be less troublesome and more accurate, and it helps the related divisions understand cost fluctuations.

The estimated cost (C_{t+1}) of a new model can be described this way:

$$C_{t+1} = C_t + m \qquad (9)$$

Where C_t = cost of current model
m = change in cost due to design change

A full model change brings many differences in design; m is the sum of all changes:

$$m = m_1 + m_2 + \ldots + m_n \qquad (10)$$

Where m_i = difference in cost accompanying the design change for part i

Toyota added four-wheel steering to the new Celica model to help stabilize cornering. Another version will come with an active suspension, which monitors the road surface through sensors and electronically adjusts the hydraulic suspension. Minor changes include using stainless steel for the exhaust manifolds. The changes in cost accompanying these design changes will be m_1, m_2, ... m_n, and the sum of these differences—the total difference in cost for the new model—is m. Total estimated cost of the new model is obtained by adding m to the part of the current model's cost that will stay the same.

The significance of estimating differences, in addition to the advantages already mentioned, is that it helps clarify the cost-planning goal and show accurately how much is accomplished through cost planning. The main concern of cost planning is design of the new model. Its effectiveness is measured as the amount of cost-reduction through design. Therefore, other factors that affect cost, including wages and fluctuations in indirect costs incurred by related divisions, must be eliminated from cost planning. By fixing the cost of the current model and calculating differences between the current and new models, Toyota's system deals only with cost changes resulting from changes in design and production volume (i.e., without the influence of other factors).

Without actual drawings for the new model, the estimate often begins with just an idea. Since rough sketches provided by the design division are often the only sources of information, estimates are made under the leadership of the technology-management division rather than the accounting division. Since the people at the design and technology-management divisions have the latest information on the results of basic research, they are best qualified to estimate costs from the sketches. Applying the results of basic research to product design is helpful both for improving product performance and for attaining the cost-planning goal. Cost planning tests the company's design capabilities, because if the design for the new model is at the same technical level, the costs cannot change.

Equipment investment and depreciation

A full model change inevitably requires a large investment in equipment. The amount invested, figured in terms of depreciation, affects the cost of the new model. For this reason, an outline of equipment investment is often provided at the product-planning stage, but the budget for equipment investment is officially set at the cost-planning meeting after the product plan is approved.

Equipment investment can be divided roughly into two categories:
1. Investments in equipment needed to replace metal molds; and
2. Investments to add, expand, or improve other equipment and facilities.

When a new part or system is added (e.g., four-wheel steering), production lines must be built to make them. When production methods change because of a model change, the lines may also need to be changed. If a plant does not have enough capacity to make the new model, for example, expansion may be necessary.

Many automobile parts (e.g., presswork, sheet metal, plastics, and castings) are made using metal molds. A model change requires changes in many body and interior parts. This requires changes in the metal molds for those parts, both for in-house production and those rented to the part suppliers. These molds are costly to manufacture. Since they are integral parts of the production machinery, they are considered production equipment. As Exhibit 1 shows (see the box "metal molds procurement"), automakers place orders for new metal molds early in a model-change project.

The production-technology division makes the equipment-investment plan. Since this is an investment for the production of a new car, the budget itself is accepted without discussion about whether it is needed, though the specific proposed figures are not always accepted. The accounting division produces an adjusted plan based on the budget proposed by the production-technology division, taking into consideration the influence on cost of the new model and the balance between the budget and the company's total equipment investment. This plan is officially approved at the cost-planning meeting. A full model change usually requires tens of billions of yen for equipment investment, and hundreds of billions when development costs are included. The cost to develop a new model is not usually recognized as a cost difference. Nor is depreciation of existing equipment estimated as a cost difference, because it is already built into the cost of the current model.

Promoting cost planning

The purpose of cost planning is to determine the amount by which costs can be reduced through better design of the new model. The cost-planning goal g is distributed (g_1, g_2, ... g_n) to the divisions in charge of design for the new model.

$$g = g_1 + g_2 + \ldots + g_n \qquad (11)$$

Where g_i = cost planning goal for design division i

Each design division is responsible for reducing costs by g_i from the original estimate. The divisions in charge of design of the engine, body, chassis, drive train, electronics, and interior all share the responsibility to cut costs.

Distributing cost targets. It is impossible to attain a target cost by simply deciding to reduce costs uniformly by x percent for all divisions. The chief engineer distributes a portion of the goal to each related division. The amount distributed is based on precedent and experience. The chief engineer asks each division to work to attain its goal. Discussion continues with each division until both the division and the chief engineer are satisfied with the amount distributed.

Suppose, for example, that the engine division estimates a cost increase of C_e for the new model because the engine will be upgraded by 10hp. The chief engineer looks at the precedents for upgrading engines by 10hp, then asks the division to compromise on $\overline{C}_e$. After negotiation, the cost-planning goal for the engine design division (g_e) is therefore:

$$C_e - \overline{C}_e = g_e \qquad (12)$$

One division might be asked to reduce cost because a part will be smaller or lighter; another might be asked to maintain the same cost, despite a change in materials, because there will be no change in performance. In this way, the cost target is distributed to the divisions.

The cost-planning goal is usually distributed to all related divisions two years before the release of the new model, and after body styling is decided.

Design policy and cost

There are more opportunities for cost-reduction during product planning than actual development. These opportunities vary, depending on the specific stage of product planning. The turning point is when styling is determined and production of the first prototype is about to begin. Decisions before this point have more effect on cost than those after.

For example, the Celica line consists of three sister versions—the Celica, the Corona Exsiv, and the Carina ED. Toyota planned that the 1990 models would be mass-produced at the rate of 7,000–10,000 units per month. About 3,000 Celica units were designated for the Japanese market; the rest, more than twice that number, were for export.

The three versions look quite different, but they have much in common in the engine and chassis. Differentiating the versions while using as many common parts as possible is vitally important to the product lineup.

Determining components. Before going into details of design, the components for each car type must be decided. The number of different parts and the resulting total equipment investment change, depending on which parts are shared across the versions. Generally, mass-produced parts reduce cost, while small-lot parts raise cost. If the three versions share certain parts, cost can be calculated based on 30,000 units per month. If each uses certain parts specific to it, the cost will be calculated for 10,000 units. If parts are shared with other product lines, costs fluctuate accordingly.

Body styling can also have a major influence on cost. Some designs create complex part structures and lower tolerances, thus increasing the number of man-hours needed in production. For example, a current trend is to make the bumper look as if it is part of the body. The space between bumper and body has been reduced from several millimeters to less than a millimeter on recent models. This inevitably reduces part tolerances, thus pushing up costs. When a certain body style requires a cost increase, it is up to the chief engineer to decide by how much.

Value engineering

Once the cost-planning goals—the amounts of cost to be cut—are distributed to the design division, value engineering begins. The designers' top priority is to create high-quality, high-performance products that satisfy the customer. At the same time, they must attain their cost targets.

Each design division becomes responsible for attaining its respective goal. The specifics of parts, materials, and machining processes are left to their discretion.

Exceptions are made for large, especially costly parts. The chief engineer will sometimes specify cost-reduction targets for parts to the related divisions. As mentioned previously, when projecting profit, cost is calculated by estimating differences in cost between the current and new models. Since additional costs for each part (which can change subsequently) are estimated at this stage, the cost-reduction goals for expensive parts can be specified. For example, consider a part that is estimated to cost ¥3,000. If it is judged that a cost break on this particular part will contribute significantly to attaining the target goal for the entire model, the chief engineer may ask the related design division for a specific cost reduction, perhaps of ¥500.

The design divisions often organize value engineering meetings to help attain the cost goals. Since test parts are developed at about this time, value engineering can be done using parts from the prototypes. Three test models are usually made, which means that the cycle of drawings, part production, and value engineering is repeated three times over a period of about a year.

The design is complete when the performance and cost goals are attained. The final mass-production plan is then drawn.

Various value engineering methods. There are various methods for conducting value engineering. It generally starts with performance checks on the test parts. Designs are changed to give the parts a specific degree of performance, neither more nor less. Then discussion turns to possible ways to cut costs while maintaining performance. There are no formulas or manuals for value engineering, but there are areas where it is possible, including:

- Material specifications and consumption;
- Yield;
- Number of parts;
- Ease of work; and
- Man-hours.

For instance, fewer fasteners will be used if it is determined that a part uses too many. A design may be changed based on a projection that a change in shape would make production much easier. Special parts will be replaced with mass-produced parts if performance is the same. The painting method for certain parts will be altered as necessary. Cost savings of a yen here and a yen there eventually mount up. Even if the cost saved per design change is only ¥1, if a part undergoes ten such changes, ¥10 is saved. Concentrating effort on expensive parts and parts for which cost has increased markedly, sometimes works to expand the effect of value engineering.

Knowing the effect of design changes. Designers must know how design affects such things as material consumption, yield, machining methods, and line time. The best designers are of no use if they are not fully conversant with production techniques. Design engineers often lack hands-on production experience. They are therefore expected to work closely with the production divisions to build their personal funds of information.

Accurately gauging changes in cost following design modifications is the responsibility of people assigned to this job from the technology-management and accounting divisions (the cost-planning group). There are about fifty such people in the two divisions. Several are assigned to each product line in support of the design engineers.

These estimators provide designers with such information as the affect on cost of a change in the machining process and the cost per minute of machine time.

Cost estimators use a cost table to calculate unit prices for manufacturing.[5] Rather than the basic costs used for budget management, a cost table used for cost planning shows cost per production line, which is manufacturing costs broken down into direct labor costs and indirect line costs. In standard costing, shops or cost centers are groups of two or more lines.

Value engineering is not purely intellectual work that a design engineer can do at a desk, working from drawings. Instead, value engineering is based on effort to improve production on the shop floor. Value engineering is not effective if production is not sufficiently well organized.

From cost planning to mass production

Since the main concern of cost planning is design, cost planning is effectively finished when the project goes to the mass-production stage. Unless something unusual happens, companies rarely fail to attain their cost-planning goals. Follow-up studies are done for about a year after start-up to ensure that mass production is going forward at the planned cost.

The essential point is that target cost in cost planning and standard cost for mass production are treated as different standards with different functions. In cost planning, costs are estimated from the cost tables as the sum of the differences between the current and new models, though at that point the planners do not know on which lines production will be done.

Standard cost at the mass-production stage changes depending on specific production line conditions. For instance, production on lines working below capacity pushes costs up, while production on lines working at close to full capacity leads to the best cost-performance. At the cost-planing stage, it is difficult to imagine the details of line conditions for every part and thus accurately to reflect these conditions in cost estimates. At the mass-production stage, the lines that work best under the current circumstances are chosen for production of the new model. ("Best" in this context means at the optimum for the entire company, which is not always optimal for the new model.) Once the lines are chosen based on these criteria, the standard cost is calculated. The production division then begins its effort to maintain or even improve on the standard cost.

Conclusion

This brief discussion of cost planning at Toyota points out that cost planning is an effort to reduce cost at the design stage. Using cost planning, a company can set goals for cost reduction and seek to achieve those goals through design changes. To correctly assess the gains made, the exact amount of cost reduction through design must be measured, excluding all other factors. To this end, at the profit-estimation stage, Toyota calculates differences between the new and current models, distributes portions of the cost-reduction goal to the design divisions, and then assesses the results. Profit targets for the life of the new model are also calculated as differences between estimates and targets.

Setting goals and assessing the results based on cost differences between old and new models constitute the basic rule for budget control at Toyota. The idea behind it is that goals for each control unit should be clearly specified to ensure that the goals of the company are attained.

This basic principle of cost control is not always easy to follow through with. Toyota sticks to it closely in target costing and cost *kaizen*, its basic systems for management accounting. The cost goals for design are met through target costing, and those for mass production are attained using cost *kaizen*. Cost control like this, backed by the excellent production control represented by just-in-time manufacturing, makes Toyota remarkably efficient. ▲

Notes
1. Robin Cooper and Robert S. Kaplan, "Measure Costs Right: Make the Right Decision," *Harv. Bus. Rev.* (Sept.-Oct. 1988): 96–103; see also Robert S. Kaplan, "Measuring Manufacturing Performance," *The Accounting Review* (Oct. 1983): 686–705.
2. Yasuhiro Monden, "Total Cost Management System in Japanese Automobile Corporations," in Yasuhiro Monden and Michiharu Sakurai, eds., *Japanese Management Accounting* (Cambridge, Mass.: Productivity Press, 1989): 15–33.
3. Masaaki Imai, *Kaizen* (New York: McGraw-Hill Publishing Company, 1986).
4. Takao Makido, "Recent Trends in Japan's Cost Management Practices," in Yasuhiro Monden and Michiharu Sakurai, eds., *Japanese Management Accounting* (Cambridge, Mass.: Productivity Press, 1989): 3–13.
5. Takeo Yoshikawa, John Innes, and Falconer Mitchell, "Cost Tables: A Foundation of Japanese Cost Management," *Journal of Cost Management* (Fall 1990): 30–36.

Comparing U.S. and Japanese Companies: Implications for Management Accounting

James R. Martin, Wendi K. Schelb, Richard C. Snyder, and Jeffrey S. Sparling

Research reveals Japan's completely different attitude about work and about managing the activities that create value and competitive advantage. Much of this research is linked to the accounting and control systems that are taught and practiced in the United States. This article compares U.S. and Japanese workers and also management policies in an attempt to show how the observed differences are linked to the need for different management accounting and control systems. The article also shows how traditional U.S. management accounting and control techniques are becoming increasingly inadequate for today's newer concepts.

A substantial body of literature documents the decline in competitiveness of U.S. industry in recent years.[1] One of the major causes of this declining competitive position is that Japanese manufacturers have managed to produce higher-quality products with fewer workers and lower inventory levels than comparable U.S. firms. (There are other schools of thought on the causes of U.S. economic decline. One idea popular with U.S. industry is that macroeconomic policies and events in the United States caused the problem. For example, high interest rates and a tax system that inhibits investment may have played a part in the decline.)[2] In any case, the Japanese have continuously increased their market shares in a long list of industries. Today, the Japanese and Germans are global economic leaders that appear more worried about each other than about the United States.[3]

To determine how the Japanese have achieved such an enviable competitive position, many researchers have studied the Japanese people and Japanese management practices.[4] This research reveals that the Japanese have a completely different attitude toward work and managing the activities that create value and competitive advantage. Much of this research has a link to the accounting and control systems that are taught and practiced in the United States. Thus, the purpose of this article is to compare U.S. and Japanese workers and management policies in an attempt to show how the observed differences are linked to the need for different management accounting and control systems.

The article is divided into the following sections:

- Characteristics and attitudes of workers;
- Management attitudes and policies toward workers;
- Competitive focus of management and management policies;
- Management accounting and control; and
- How U.S. companies are becoming world-class competitors.

Taken together, the summary comparison of attitudes and management policies provided in these sections reveals two important messages:

1. To compete effectively in the global economy, U.S. companies must embrace the newer management concepts implemented by the Japanese; and
2. Traditional U.S. management accounting and control techniques are inconsistent

with these newer management concepts, and, must therefore change radically to avoid a serious conflict between accounting and the long-term survival of the organization.

Characteristics and attitudes of workers

Although it is somewhat presumptuous to generalize about the characteristics and attitudes of millions of people, some rather basic and important differences between Japanese and U.S. workers appear to exist.[5]

Concept of self. First, the Japanese concept of self is very different from the view common in the United States. In Japan, each person is believed to possess a unique spirit, soul, mind, and heart, but the concept of self is considered an impediment to growth. The Japanese establish identities that incorporate friends, relatives, and coworkers in an open way that allows them to share feelings and improve on weaknesses. A worker's relationship within a work group is very important psychologically.

By contrast, U.S. workers are for the most part individualistic; they strive to appear as self-sufficient as possible. For example, a U.S. worker—particularly a male—who cries for practically any reason is viewed as weak at best and perhaps emotionally unstable, whereas, the Japanese view crying as an indication that a worker is sincere in seeking ways to improve.

Nationalism and educational systems. The Japanese are also strongly nationalistic; indeed, they believe that they are superior to all other races. Although Americans also have a strong sense of national pride, there are many racial conflicts in the United States that reduce our ability to work together. The educational systems in the two countries also differ. While the Japanese have a rigorous system through high school, it is possible for a student in the United States to graduate from high school without being able to read and write adequately. These differences may have serious implications for U.S. firms that seek entry-level workers.[6]

Cooperation and conformism. Perhaps the fact that the Japanese are all from a single race and have an entirely different concept of self

explains why, at least to some extent, they appear to be more cooperative and willing to work together in teams. To maintain and strengthen relationships within work groups, Japanese workers spend considerable time socializing after work. Japanese children wear uniforms to school. This practice is continued with company uniforms later in life. This willingness to dress alike and act alike differs dramatically from the attitude of the typical U.S. worker, who is taught to be competitive and to engage in various political power plays (e.g., taking credit for accomplishments and attempting to achieve "star status").

Attitudes toward work. Japanese workers also appear to have more respect for authority than their U.S. counterparts and an entirely different attitude toward work. The Japanese apparently live to work and are willing to sacrifice their personal lives for the company. They are more tolerant of long hours and uncomfortable working conditions than U.S. workers. They frequently work when they are sick and decline vacation time in order to avoid reducing productivity. One family service day per week seems to be adequate time for family matters.

The Japanese apparently live to work and are willing to sacrifice their personal lives for the company. They are more tolerant of long hours and uncomfortable working conditions than U.S. workers.

U.S. workers are more inclined to work to live (i.e., for self-gratification). They have less self-discipline and less tolerance for discomfort. In addition, U.S. workers expect to spend more time with their families and to obtain perquisites that have been won in hard-fought confrontations between management and labor over the years. (This is not to imply that these expectations are unreasonable—only that they are different from the expectations of the typical Japanese worker.)

Crime and litter. The Japanese keep their cities and factories crime free and spotless; trash, graffiti, and cigarette butts are conspicuously absent. Each worker keeps his work station clean. Even taxi drivers wear white gloves and are unforgiving if a patron soils the cab. Crime rates in Japan are low compared with crime rates in the United States, where cities are notorious for crime and garbage.

Loyalty toward employers. Japanese workers are also more loyal to their employers than U.S. workers; in many cases, they are essentially married to their employers for life. U.S. workers, on the other hand, tend to be loyal to themselves and their families; they frequently "use" a company to gain enough experience to move to a better-paying position at another firm. Some of the differences described above are more important than others, but we believe that all these differences must be considered carefully in developing the high-involvement work force required in today's global economy.

Management attitudes and policies toward workers

Management attitudes toward workers and policies toward employees also appear conceptually different in the two countries. The differences discussed below have been reported in a variety of articles and books published over the last ten years.[7]

Suggestions. Japanese workers are expected to provide suggestions for improving their own operating efficiency as well as the overall productivity of the organization. The rationale for this expectation is that suggestions promote *continuous improvement (kaizen* in Japanese), which is the fundamental philosophy of Japanese management. (Continuous improvement is discussed in more detail later.)

Although suggestion systems are also used in the United States, employee suggestions are often viewed as a threat to management. U.S. employees who constantly recommend changes are likely to be considered troublemakers.

Employees as most important resource. Japanese managers seem to view employees as

their most important resource. To develop these resources to the fullest, the typical Japanese firm offers lifetime employment, promotions from within, considerable cross-training and job rotation, and frequently a no-layoff policy. In this way, the Japanese use human resources as a competitive weapon.

Employment in the United States, by contrast, is somewhat analogous to a revolving door. Workers are routinely laid off during economic downturns, and there often appears to be little commitment to training. The scientific management approach used in the United States is based on a system of specialization, which often means that each worker performs only a few repetitive tasks. In this approach, workers' skill levels become so low that virtually every worker becomes expendable. Neither management nor the workers

---

Japanese workers are expected to participate in decision making by consensus. The group attempts to come to a unanimous decision. Although the final decision is made by the group leader, all members of the group are expected to accept it as their own decision.

---

trust each other, so the process feeds on itself. U.S. managers appear to use a type of short-term leverage in the area of human resources. In other words, by scavenging trained workers from other firms, the scavenger company uses other firms' investments in human resources to achieve results.[8]

Incentive systems. The typical Japanese incentive system is quite different from U.S. incentive systems. The Japanese place considerable emphasis on employee recognition, including simple pats on the back, business cards for all workers, trophies, company pins, plaques, medals, group approval, and charts or *andon* boards (i.e., lighted displays) over work stations to show goals and achievements. Although in Japan there are some small cash awards for suggestions and employee profit-sharing systems, Japanese workers seem to respond well to psychological incentives. U.S. incentive systems, by contrast, are for the most part monetary systems based on salary increases, promotions, and bonuses.

Employee participation in decision making.
Japanese workers are expected to participate in decision making by consensus. The group attempts to come to a unanimous decision. Although the final decision is made by the group leader, all members of the group are expected to accept it as their own decision. Voting is not allowed, because a vote means that there are winners and losers. In the consensus system, by contrast, there are supposedly only winners.

U.S. workers do not participate in work-related decisions to the same extent as Japanese workers; often, they have no real input into decision making. Most work-related decisions are made by autocratic supervisors. When group or committee decisions are made, the democratic voting process prevails, which means that there are always both winners and losers.

Accessibility of managers. Another difference between Japanese and U.S. companies is the accessibility of managers to workers. In Japanese factories, managers tend to wear the same uniforms as line workers; they work in offices that are inside the factory and open to workers. U.S. managers above the supervisory level are generally inaccessible to workers and are perceived by workers as being aloof. They are often pictured as working in air-conditioned offices that are separated from the factory by long, infrequently used corridors.

Competitive focus of management and management policies

The overall focus of Japanese management concentrates on the firm's long-term competitive strategy, as opposed to U.S. managers, who appear to be more concerned with short-term financial performance.[9] This difference may be explained by the variations in reporting requirements in the two countries. For example, Japanese companies are not required to submit quarterly reports to stockholders.[10] However, there are other, more fundamental differences in the way the Japanese manage. In fact, the concept underlying the very foundation of Japanese management is substantially different from the traditional U.S. concept of management.

Continuous improvement vs. optimization.
Japanese management policies and techniques are grounded by the concept of *continuous improvement* or *kaizen.*[11] On the other hand, traditional U.S. management practices are derived from the concept of *optimization,* which grew out of the scientific management era of the early 1900s and developments in operations research in the 1950s.[12]

Understanding the differences between these two concepts is extremely important, because they have a pervasive influence on the design and implementation of every management policy, technique, performance measurement system, and decision. The fundamental difference is that management based on continuous improvement is dynamic (i.e., constantly seeking perfection by removing constraints), while the concept of optimization is static (i.e., intent is on finding the optimal solution given a set of constraints). The pervasive implications of these two conflicting approaches to management are discussed below.

Just-in-time. In the area of resource management, the Japanese use the "subconcept" (a term that is used here to emphasize that the concept underlying all other Japanese management concepts is continuous improvement) of just-enough-resources (JER), which is commonly referred to as just-in-time (JIT) with respect to inventory (the term in Japanese is *kamban* or *kanban,* which means "signboard"). The idea is to squeeze out three kinds of waste:

1. *Muda,* which represents waste caused by idle resources and unnecessary motions (e.g., looking for misplaced tools);
2. *Mura,* which is waste caused by the irregular or inconsistent use of a resource; and
3. *Muri,* which is waste caused by placing excessive demands on resources.[13]

In the JER approach, all resources are minimized, including inventory, workers, equipment, job classifications, and product parts and subassemblies.

Just-in-case. Traditional U.S. managers use an entirely different concept that some authors have referred to as just-in-case (JIC).[14] In the JIC approach to resource management, large amounts of slack resources are kept on hand to guard against contingencies such as late deliveries, poor quality, production bottlenecks, and fluctuations in demand. Of course, these concepts have important implications for the resources themselves. JER and JIT require highly skilled, highly dedicated, and cross-trained workers; they also require high-quality raw materials and well-maintained equipment. In the JIC environment, by contrast, high skill levels and high-quality materials and equipment are not as critical. For example, in the area of inventory and production lot sizes, the idea (according to the applicable subconcept of optimization) is to find the economic order quantity (EOQ) or batch size that will minimize the conflicting costs involved in the decision at hand (e.g., ordering and carrying costs, or setup and carrying costs).

Total quality control. To promote high quality, the Japanese use the subconcepts of total quality control (TQC), or zero defects, and quality at the source (*jidohka* in Japanese). *Jidohka* places emphasis on correcting problems when and where they occur. Implementing these quality concepts obviously requires dedicated workers. High quality requires close relationships with vendors to ensure that the firm receives defect-free raw materials. Similarly, it requires maintaining close relationships with customers to ensure that customers' specifications are met. The Japanese view this as a codestiny relationship with their vendors and customers. These partnerships provide linkages across the entire value chain that lead to fewer, more reliable vendors, and also to more frequent deliveries from vendors and to customers.[15]

U.S. firms have traditionally used multiple vendors and placed more emphasis on price variances and quantity discounts. Thus, quality has not received the highest priority. Determining the optimum level of quality has been the norm for U.S. firms. This is evident when one considers the traditional standard

cost systems so common in U.S. accounting textbooks and manufacturing practice. Although there appears to be a new emphasis on quality in the United States, the newer U.S. approach is still grounded in optimization theory. In this new approach, which has been referred to as the "optimal economic conformance model," prevention and appraisal costs are balanced against internal and external failure costs.[16] This is fundamentally different from the dynamic TQC approach advocated by W. Edwards Deming, in which a company cannot have too much quality.[17]

Investment justification and asset deployment. The continuous improvement concept also affects Japanese decisions about equipment acquisition and utilization. Many Japanese companies tend to design and carefully maintain their own equipment, with preventive maintenance centered at the operator level. Equipment parts are replaced before they break to prevent idle time (*muda*) from occurring during production runs. In-house equipment development also promotes innovation and allows the Japanese to maintain technological leadership.

U.S. firms, on the other hand, are somewhat more inclined to buy turn-key systems and to replace parts only when they break down. In Japanese JER or JIT systems, maintenance is mandatory, not a discretionary decision to be used for shifting costs from current to future periods. It is also important to note that buying production equipment from others is another form of leverage that provides certain short-term benefits to the purchaser because the buyer does not incur the costs of research and development. However, the disadvantage of this policy is the higher long-term risk of losing market share to the technological leaders. Buying technology off the shelf prevents a firm from competing on the basis of product differentiation or innovation, because competitors will have access to the same technology.[18]

Unions. Japanese unions also play an important part in supporting continuous improvement and its many related subconcepts. In Japan, unions are sponsored by the company; they are more an extension of management than a separate entity established to represent workers. A Japanese union typically works to promote teamwork by supporting a small number of job classifications, considerable cross-training, and a no-strike policy.

U.S. union policies conflict with JER and JIT by requiring a large number of job classifications that prohibit cross-training. U.S. unions have adversarial relationships with management and use strikes as a weapon for achieving higher wages and benefits for union members.

Focused production. Another way that Japanese and traditional U.S. management practices differ is in the area of production. The Japanese tend to build smaller, more focused plants in which work is performed in sequential order to remove inconsistencies (*mura*) according to program work sheets. The idea is to remove wasted or unnecessary motions to improve efficiency. U.S. plants, by contrast, tend to be larger and less focused; U.S. workers generally perform the work in the order of their preference.

Management accounting and control

According to Hiromoto,[19] Japanese accounting and control systems are subservient to corporate strategy; they are used to influence behavior. In the United States, on the other hand, accounting and control systems have been used mainly to inform management about the company's performance. In Japan, planning and control are based on a bottom-up approach through which workers and lower-level managers participate in developing goals and receive considerable feedback as the plans are implemented.[20]

In the United States, planning and control are based on a top-down approach. The financial budget is rolled down into the organization.[21] The view that the Japanese are highly committed to planning and feedback is supported by their almost fanatical use of a system called plan-do-check-action (PDCA). In this system (which is frequently used by quality control circles), the *plan* step includes identifying the problem and the underlying cause, plus developing a plan for the problem's solution. The *do* step involves a trial run to determine if the plan works. In the *check* step, the trial run is evaluated and revisions are made if necessary. The final *action* step is to implement the plan. The PDCA approach is a never-ending activity for the Japanese, who are meticulous about providing documentation for nearly every decision.[22]

Target costing. The Japanese compare actual costs to market-driven target costs. Target costs are established somewhere between standard costs and allowable costs, which are determined by subtracting a target profit margin from the target price. The target price is the price that would provide the company with a competitive edge in the market. This approach is dynamic, since the target costs are continuously reduced, both during and after the design stage, to promote continuous improvement.[23]

The traditional U.S. approach is to compare actual costs with flexible budgets based on engineering-driven standard costs. It is important to note that standard costs are based on the static optimization concept, in which standards are set based on the current plant and resource constraints. The emphasis is on achieving the internal standard rather than on continuously reducing costs to achieve the external goal.

Life-cycle costing. The Japanese also use a long-term life-cycle approach to product cost; they place substantial emphasis on nonfinancial performance measures such as quality, lead time, and flexibility. Some of the more specific measurements include:

- The average number of jobs mastered per employee;
- Average setup times;
- Number of line stops;
- Down time;
- Process times;
- Amount of inventory; and
- Number of customer complaints.

Johnson[24] reports on a Japanese firm that manages with twelve "charts on the wall," which are used to report on some of the measurements listed above. These measurements, according to Johnson, represent activities that affect the company's competitive position.

U.S. firms have traditionally placed more emphasis on short-term variances from standard costs, with considerable attention directed toward labor efficiency measurements. However, the standard cost approach to control has been criticized because traditional variances can motivate managers to act in ways that worsen, rather than improve, the company's competitive position.[25] Thus, the standard cost methodology appears to be inconsistent with the concept of continuous improvement.

Japanese investment justification decisions are based on a long-term perspective in which emphasis is placed on growth, increasing market share, flexibility, and customer needs. Decisions are made using the Namawashi approach, which includes more involvement by lower-level managers.[26] When compared with Japanese companies, U.S. companies seem to place more emphasis on the short-term financial effects of investment decisions and quick paybacks. Thus, traditional U.S. investment decision techniques have not adequately considered the intangible factors involved that affect the company's long-term competitive position.

The Japanese also appear to be in a better position to exploit interrelationships among business units to achieve or maintain a competitive advantage. A horizontal strategy that coordinates investment decisions across a large group of interrelated divisions may well produce greater corporate benefits in the long run than a series of independent investment decisions made at the unit level. Porter[27] lists eight reasons why a horizontal strategy may be the next source of competitive advantage for Japanese firms. Porter's list seems to emphasize one major point: The Japanese simply work together better than their U.S. competitors.

How U.S. firms are becoming world-class competitors

The previous comparison of U.S. and Japanese workers and of the management attitudes and policies of their respective companies paints a rather bleak picture of the current position of U.S. companies and of their potential in the global economy. However, it should be emphasized that the summary comparisons provided above are based on a great many generalizations that do not apply equally to all workers and companies.

Many U.S. companies began to develop a different strategic mind-set in the 1980s;

many now follow the concepts previously attributed to the Japanese. One of the most notable examples of the changes taking place in U.S. management practices is provided by the cost management systems (CMS) conceptual design document issued by Computer Aided Manufacturing-International (CAM-I).[28] According to Peter Drucker, CAM-I's influence has already "unleashed an intellectual revolution" and a "new economic philosophy."[29] The CAM-I publication embraces the overall concept of continuous improvement and most of the accompanying subconcepts, including JIT, TQC, life-cycle costing, and a portfolio approach to investment management.

The CMS conceptual design was developed by many people who are employed by CAM-I's sponsoring firms and organizations; their efforts continue to develop better cost management and performance systems. In fact, many of CAM-I's sponsoring firms appear in Schonberger's "honor roll" of eighty-four firms (or divisions of firms) that have achieved major improvements by using JIT concepts and related ideas.[30] Many other examples of the achievements of CAM-I sponsors have been provided in recent literature that documents major improvements in the companies' ability to compete in the global economy.[31]

Conclusion

Today, perhaps most of the attitudes and management techniques previously attributed to the Japanese should, more appropriately, be labeled "world class," rather than exclusively Japanese. An important implication of this change is that most of the traditional attitudes and policies attributed to U.S. firms should probably be labeled "non-world class."

There is some evidence that U.S. management concepts and accounting policies are changing (if slowly).[32] It seems clear that many U.S. companies are at least on the right track toward regaining the status of global competitors. It is also clear that accountants should play a major role in designing systems that support the new management concepts that are so critical for world-class competition. However, a grasp of the relationships between the new management concepts and the subservient accounting performance measurements is a prerequisite for this task. Without this understanding, it will be difficult for U.S. accountants to regain their own status as members of a world-class profession. ▲

Notes

1. See, e.g., R.H. Hayes & W.J. Abernathy "Managing Our Way to Economic Decline," *Harv. Bus. Rev.* 67–77 (July–Aug. 1980); R.J. Schonberger, *Japanese Manufacturing Techniques: Nine Hidden Lessons in Simplicity* (New York: The Free Press 1982); R.S. Kaplan, "Measuring Manufacturing Performance: A New Challenge for Managerial Accounting Research," *The Accounting Review* 686–704 (Oct. 1983): R.H. Hayes & S.C. Wheelwright, *Restoring Our Competitive Edge: Competing Through Manufacturing* (New York: John Wiley & Sons 1984); and R.H. Hayes, S.C. Wheelwright, & K.B. Clark, *Dynamic Manufacturing* (New York: The Free Press 1988).

2. See Hayes, Wheelwright, & Clark, *Dynamic Manufacturing.*

3. This somewhat disturbing revelation was provided by Lester Thurow, Dean of the MIT Sloan School of Management, in a presentation made at the Saturday luncheon of the American Accounting Association national meeting in Toronto, Canada, on Aug. 11, 1990.

4. For example, see J.M. Juran, "Japanese and Western Quality: A Contrast in Methods and Results," *Management Review* 27–45 (Nov. 1978): S.C. Wheelwright, "Japan—Where Operations Really Are Strategic," *Harv. Bus. Rev.* 67–74 (July–Aug. 1981); R.T. Pascale & A.G. Athos, *The Art of Japanese Management* (New York: Simon and Schuster 1981); H. Takeuchi, "Productivity: Learning From the Japanese," *California Management Review* 11–18 (Summer 1981); R.H. Hayes, "Why Japanese Factories Work," *Harv. Bus. Rev.* 57–66 (July–Aug. 1981); Schonberger, *Japanese Manufacturing Techniques: Nine Hidden Lessons in Simplicity;* R. Rehder and F. Ralston, "Total Quality Management: A Revolutionary Management Philosophy," *SAM Advanced Management Journal* 24–33 (1984); R.H. Hayes & K.B. Clark, "Explaining Observed Productivity Differentials Between Plants: Implications for Operations Research," *Interfaces* 3–14 (Nov.–Dec. 1985): G. Starling & O.W. Baskin, *Issues in Business and Society: Capitalism and Public Purpose* Chap. 6 (Boston: Kent Publishing Company 1985); J. Teresko, "Manufacturing in Japan Beyond the Stereotype," *Industry Week,* Sept. 4, 1989, at 35–70; T. Hiromoto, "Another Hidden Edge—Japanese Management Accounting," *Harv. Bus. Rev.* 22–25 (July–Aug. 1988): W.E. Reitsperger & S.J. Daniel, "Japan vs. Silicon Valley: Quality-Cost Tradeoff Philosophies," *Journal of International Business Studies* 289–301 (Second Quarter 1990); and J.J. Fucini & S. Fucini, *Working for the Japanese* (New York: The Free Press 1990).

5. Much of the material in this section is summarized from the references provided in note 4. The book by J.J. Fucini & S. Fucini, *Working for the Japanese,* was particularly helpful in providing insight into the way the Japanese think.

6. See B. Clinton "Teaching to Rebuild the Nation," *AAHE Bulletin* (May 1988); and K. Redd & W. Riddle, *CRS Report for Congress,* Congressional Research Service, Library of Congress, Nov. 1988.

7. See, e.g., Wheelwright, "Japan—Where Operations Really Are Strategic"; Pascale, *The Art of Japanese Management;* Takeuchi, "Productivity: Learning From the Japanese"; Schonberger, *Japanese Manufacturing Techniques: Nine Hidden Lessons in Simplicity;* Starling & Baskin, *Issues in Business and Society: Capitalism and Public Purpose;* Teresko, "Manufacturing in Japan Beyond the Stereotype"; Fucini & Fucini, *Working for the Japanese;* and R.J. Schonberger, *Building a Chain of Customers* (New York: The Free Press 1990).

8. This idea is developed by Hayes, Wheelwright, & Clark, in *Dynamic Manufacturing,* Chap. 1.

9. A fairly large body of literature supports this viewpoint. For example, see Hayes & Abernathy, "Managing Our Way to Economic Decline"; Kaplan "Measuring Manufacturing Performance"; Hayes & Wheelwright, *Restoring Our Competitive Edge;* H.T. Johnson & R.S. Kaplan, *Relevance Lost: The Rise and Fall of Management Accounting* (Boston: Harvard Business School Press 1987); Hayes, *Dynamic Manufacturing;* and Johnson; "Professors, Customers, and Value: Bringing A Global Perspective to Management Accounting Education," *Proceedings of the Third Annual Management Accounting Symposium* 7–20 (Sarasota, Fla.: American Accounting Symposium 1990).

10. See *Cost Management for Today's Advanced Manufacturing: The CAM-I Conceptual Design,* C. Berliner & J.A. Brimson, eds. (Boston: Harvard Business School Press 1988).

11. J.J. Fucini & S. Fucini, in *Working for the Japanese,* use the term *kaizen* frequently in describing the practices at the Japanese Mazda plant in Flat Rock, Michigan. Also see, Masaaki Imai, *Kaizen: The Key to Japan's Competitive Success* (New York: McGraw-Hill Publishing Co. 1986).

12. See Johnson & Kaplan, *Relevance Lost: The Rise and Fall of Management Accounting,* Chap. 3, for discussions of the scientific management era and optimization models developed by operations research in the 1950s and 1960s.

13. For further discussion of these terms and concepts, see Fucini & Fucini, *Working for the Japanese.*

14. See Schonberger, *Japanese Manufacturing Techniques: Nine Hidden Lessons in Simplicity.*

15. For a discussion of value chain analysis, see M.E. Porter, *Competitive Strategy* (New York, The Free Press 1980); M.E. Porter, *Competitive Advantage* (New York, The Free Press 1985); J.K. Shank, "Strategic Cost Management: New Wine, or Just New Bottles?" *Journal of Management Accounting Research* 47–65 (Fall 1989); and R.A. Howell, "Customer Profitability," *Management Accounting* 43–47 (Oct. 1990).

16. See W. Morse, "Measuring Quality Costs," *Cost and Management* 16–20 (July–Aug. 1983); H.P. Roth & W. Morse, "Let's Help Measure and Report Quality Costs," *Management Accounting* 50–53 (Aug. 1983); S.J. Daniel & W.D. Reitsperger, "Management Control Systems for Quality: An Empirical Comparison of the U.S. and Japanese Electronics Industries," unpublished paper presented at the American Accounting Association national meeting, Toronto, Canada, Aug. 1990.

17. W.E. Deming, *Quality, Productivity, and Competitive Position* (Cambridge, Mass.: MIT Center for Advanced Engineering Study 1982).

18. For a discussion of the various types of competitive strategy, see Porter, *Competitive Strategy* and *Competitive Advantage.*

19. Hiromoto, "Another Hidden Edge—Japanese Management Accounting."

20. Support for these ideas can be found in several articles. See, e.g., Hayes, Wheelwright, & Clark, *Dynamic Manufac-*

turing; and S.J. Daniel & W.D. Reitsperger, "Accounting for Inventory and Flexibility in Japanese and U.S. Electronics Manufacturing: Empirical Evidence," unpublished paper presented at the American Accounting Association national meeting, Toronto, Canada, Aug. 1990.

21. See H. Thomas Johnson, "Performance Management for Competitive Excellence," in *Measures for Manufacturing Excellence,* ed. R.S. Kaplan, Chap. 3 (Boston: Harvard Business School Press 1990).

22. For more discussion of the PDCA approach, see Fucini & Fucini, *Working for the Japanese,* Chap. 6; and also Imai, *Kaizen,* Chap. 3.

23. For further discussion of target costs, see Berliner & Brimson, eds., *Cost Management for Today's Advanced Manufacturing: The CAM-I Conceptual Design;* Hiromoto, "Another Hidden Edge—Japanese Management Accounting"; W.L. Ferrara, "More Questions Than Answers," *Management Accounting* 48–52 (Oct. 1990); and M. Sakurai, "Target Cost and How to Use It," *Journal of Cost Management* 39–50 (Summer 1989).

24. See Johnson, "Performance Measurement for Competitive Excellence."

25. For a discussion of the problems with standard cost measurements, see R.D. McIlhattan, "How Cost Measurement Systems Can Support the JIT Philosophy," *Management Accounting* 20–25 (Sept. 1987); G. Foster & C.T. Horngren," JIT: Cost Accounting and Cost Management Issues," *Management Accounting* 19–25 (Feb. 1987); R.A. Howell & S.R. Soucy, "Management Reporting in the New Manufacturing Environment," *Management Accounting* 22–29 (Feb. 1988): J. Lessner, "Performance Measurement in a Just-in-

Time Environment: Can Traditional Performance Measurements Still Be Used?" *Journal of Cost Management* 23–28 (Fall 1989); and R.S. Kaplan, "Limitations of Cost Accounting in Advanced Manufacturing Environments," in *Measures for Manufacturing Excellence,* ed. R.S. Kaplan, Chap. 1.

26. See Berliner & Brimson, *Cost Management for Today's Advanced Manufacturing: The CAM-I Conceptual Design,* Chap. 9.

27. See Porter, *Competitive Advantage,* at 414.

28. See Berliner & Brimson, *Cost Management for Today's Advanced Manufacturing: The CAM-I Conceptual Design.* Other notable examples include the Bold Step Research Series published by the Institute of Management Accountants (IMA), which include a variety of publications that deal with many of the key issues discussed in this article. See R.E. Bennett, J. Hendricks, D.E. Keyes, & E.J. Rudnicki, *Cost Accounting for Factory Automation* (Montvale, N.J.: IMA 1987); and C.J. McNair, W. Mosconi, & T. Norris, *Meeting the Technology Challenge: Cost Accounting in a JIT Environment* (Montvale, N.J.: IMA 1988).

29. See P.F. Drucker, "The Emerging Theory of Manufacturing," *Harv. Bus. Rev.* 94–102 (May–June 1990).

30. R.J. Schonberger, *World Class Manufacturing,* App. (New York: The Free Press 1986).

31. For example, see Hayes, Wheelwright, & Clark, *Dynamic Manufacturing;* and J.H. Sheridan, "America's Best Plants," *Industry Week,* Oct. 15, 1990, at 27–64.

32. J. Emore & J. Ness, "Advanced Cost Management: The Slow Pace of Change," *Journal of Cost Management* 36–45 (Winter 1991).

The Strategic Persistence of the Japanese Firm

Dominque V. Turpin

The importance of persistence in Japan can be illustrated by the responses of 3,600 Japanese who where asked "What is your favorite word in life?" The top three words were *effort, persistence,* and *thank you.* When Japanese managers determine that an industry or market is crucial, they spare no efforts to capture market share and, notwithstanding setbacks, are unlikely to give up. Often, this involves targeting particular companies, then trying to catch up with them. Companies that compete head-on with Japanese firms (especially in Japan) must therefore not give up easily and must be prepared to take the long-term view.

Why is Sony, despite its Betamax setback of the early 1980s, continually pushing its new 8-mm standard against the VHS format of archrivals JVC and Matsushita? Why did Shiseido, the major cosmetic company in Japan, persist in investing continuously in the United States and Europe since the 1970s despite years of accumulated losses? Why is a company like Kubota, a leading manufacturer of farm equipment, moving into computers and biotechnology with no time frame for success?

The answer to these questions is simple: whenever Japanese management feels that an industry or a market is going to be strategically crucial for the survival and the development of their company, they will launch an all-out effort to capture market share in those industries. Moreover, despite continuous setbacks, Japanese companies are unlikely to give up.

A typical example of Japanese persistence is illustrated by Minolta, the camera manufacturer. In 1975, Nikon had 26% of the Japanese market for 35-mm single-lens reflex cameras. It was the clear leader in the industry, ahead of Asahi (22%), Canon (18%), and Minolta (14%). Five years later, Canon, with a 41% market share, had emerged as the new leader.

In the meantime, the Japanese market for this type of camera was experiencing almost no growth. In 1980, Minolta's market share in Japan had dropped to 8% and in 1984 fell even farther to 4%. Had Minolta applied the theories taught in some Western business schools, it would probably have given up and left the camera industry. In fact, Minolta's management decided to persist; two years later, Minolta was back in the number-one position with a 26% market share. Today, the company is battling Canon for the number-one spot in the industry.

None of these companies ever gave up the idea of competing in what seemed to be a mature industry. At Canon, cameras account for less than 16% of corporate revenue (versus 72% for office equipment), yet the company has no intention of giving up the products that brought it so much prestige. Izumi Hara, an economist at the Industrial Bank of Japan, claims, "Japanese companies never quit any product area, so they do not lose technology—even if it means going to China to make black-and-white televisions."

Ingrained persistence

Is persistence another stereotyped value of the Japanese? Why should Japan be singled out as the country where persistence is so cherished? Persistence is not peculiar to Japan. For both historical and cultural reasons, however, persistence is probably stressed more in Japan than in most other countries.

Japanese leaders of the late 19th century recognized that Japan had to industrialize to avoid Western domination. Persistence (*gambare*) was closely linked with the idea of survival (*ikinokori*) and catching up (*oitsuki*) with Western powers. In strong contrast to the West, where the mercantile class had, over time, displaced the aristocracy, Japanese public policy deliberately bred social entrepreneurs from the samurai (i.e., military) class. Strongly influenced by its Confucian values of patience, loyalty, determination, and endurance, the samurai class was given the formal mission of establishing Japan in the modern industrial world.

"Persevere, endure, and don't give up are concepts integral to being Japanese."

Presented as a model of virtue for society, the former samurai were quickly emulated by the other Japanese, so that the Confucian value system can to penetrate all facets of Japanese society. "Survive and catch up with the West" and "Japanese spirit and Western technology" became the mottos of modern Japanese.

Today, persistence and the will to endure are instilled in Japanese children early in their lives along with the other Confucian values of hard work, acquiring skills and education, and not spending more money than necessary. To Benjamin Duke, author of *The Japanese School*, "Gambare: persevere, endure, don't give up! is integral to being Japanese."[1] As children learn to walk, they may well hear their mothers say *"Gambare,"* loosely translated as "Do your best" or "Don't give up." By the time children reach school age, the concept of persistence will be part of their daily life.

As children struggle to learn the 1,945 basic ideograms of the Japanese writing system, their spirit of persistence is constantly challenged and reinforced. The pressure to succeed in school is tough, and stress levels are high among students anxious to win access to a top university.

After graduation, the new employee merges with the rest of the group to form a team for whom *gambare* is a permanent slogan. In such plants as the Mazda Works in Hiroshima, children's drawings with *gambare* slogans can be seen on the walls, to remind their fathers to work hard and diligently. At Dentsu, the largest advertising firm in Japan, the company's working guidelines emphasize in every employee's agenda, "Once you begin a task, complete it. Never give up!"

Is the persistent Japanese company always successful? There are times when a company's persistent efforts may be eclipsed by an even more persistent competitor. Take the case of Yamaha's motorcycle business. In 1982, its president announced, "In one year, we shall be the leader in the domestic market, and in two years, we will be number one worldwide."

The president of Honda, which held the number-one position, was quick to answer: "As long as I am president of this company, we will surrender our leadership position to no one. . . . We will crush Yamaha." As a result of faster product introduction and aggressive marketing, Honda maintained and even reinforced its lead. Two years later, Yamaha was forced to admit defeat.

However much persistence is shown, failures can sometimes result. In the early 1970s, despite the oil crisis, Japan believed that it could be a major player in the aluminum industry. Even with heavy investment and persistence, Japanese companies were unable to compete with U.S. and Canadian firms. Japanese smelter production went down from 1,013 million metric tons to 256 million metric tons between 1975 and 1980, though imports grew from 339 million metric tons to 1,415 million metric tons during the same period.

Obviously, some Japanese companies are more persistent than others. For example, although RCA and Ampex pioneered the videorecorder and licensed their technology to leading Japanese companies (e.g., Toshiba), not all large U.S. and Japanese companies persisted in bringing this new technology to the public. Sony did persist and succeeded because of the unique culture for innovation fostered by its founders. JVC was also successful because of the persistence of its engineers, who continued working on the idea of a videotape recorder despite an official order from senior management to discontinue the project.

In the mid-1960s, the Japanese cosmetics leader Shiseido attempted to break into the U.S. market with the same products that it sold in Japan, high-quality makeup that Japanese women applied with ritual slowness. The products were launched in more than 800 stores, including Bloomingdale's and Saks Fifth Avenue.

The average U.S. consumer wanted practical, quick-application cosmetics, so Shiseido had to pull out of 600 stores and return to Japan. Beaten? Absolutely not. The experience taught Shiseido a lesson. Undaunted by this first failure, the company returned to the United States with a new product line designed for the U.S. consumer. Advertising costs were sacrificed in favor of in-store service and promotion.

Twenty years after its original fiasco, Shiseido became the most successful Japanese cosmetics company in the United States, outpacing such competitors as Kao and Kanebo. Similar problems were also experienced in Europe during the 1980s. After years of heavy investments in France, Shiseido finally broke even on a cumulative basis in 1990.

Persist and catch up

One critical tool used to persist successfully is the definition of a target company to catch up with. Some slogans as "Let's beat Xerox" at Canon, "Let's encircle Caterpillar" at Komatsu, "K-P-G" ("Let's kill Procter & Gamble") at Kao or "B-M-W" ("Beat Matsushita Whatever") at Sony have been typical of the catch-up attitude of many Japanese corporations.

Targets evolve over time, as can be seen in the automotive industry. When Toyota and Nissan tried to penetrate the U.S. market in the late 1950s, they had difficulty selling their cars. Volkswagen, at that time the most successful imported brand, was selected as the

company to catch up with. Nothing could stop Toyota and Nissan from catching up with their German rival.

By 1975, the two Japanese manufacturers were number one and number two in the U.S. imported car segment. GM and Ford became the next targets. Then, in the late 1980s, Mercedes and BMW were to become the prey for Toyota's Lexus, Nissan's Infiniti, and Honda's Acura lines. By continually emphasizing a new target rather than gloating over achieving the last one, Japanese firms underscore the value of persistently striving for improvement; they continually tap their cultural energy source instead of cultivating complacency.

Sony's commitment to its Betamax VCR standard is an example. Sony was reluctant to license its technology, preferring to retain its proprietary rights on Betamax. However, the VCR industry embraced the rival VHS format developed by JVC and Matsushita as the industry standard. Reluctantly, Sony abandoned Betamax.

But Sony has persisted in its efforts to set up a new and different industry standard with the 8-mm format. As 8 mm is gaining increasing market share in the camcorder industry (close to 80% today in Japan), Sony may have a chance to beat archrivals JVC and Matsushita in the long run, as demand increases for smaller and lighter 8-mm VCRs.

Sony's strategy is typical of an adaptive persistence. As suggested by Richard T. Pascale, "The Japanese don't use the term *strategy* to describe a crisp business definition or competitive plan. They think more in terms of *strategic accommodation* or *adaptive persistence,* underscoring their belief that corporate direction evolves from an incremental adjustment to unfolding events."[2]

Many Japanese managers are not completely at ease with the Western concept of strategy and typically view any single-minded strategy as a weakness. According to Pascale, they typically prefer the term "peripheral vision as the key to corporate survival over the long haul."

Many companies (e.g., Shiseido and Fuji Photo Films) have been willing to leverage their strong domestic profits by taking long-term financial losses overseas to build an adequate sales and distribution network. Unlike U.S. companies, Japanese firms do not have to worry about quarterly profits. Moreover, lifetime employment and the social responsibilities attached to it make it more difficult for a Japanese company to exit from a specific business area. These conditions obviously facilitate Japanese persistence and highlight the Western habit of abandoning low-margin commodity businesses for high-margin business opportunities.

Besides maintaining contact with emerging technologies, staying in low-profit businesses forces Japanese corporations to maintain contact with customers and maximizes Japanese strength at persistently developing continuous small improvements (*kaizen*) in products and processes. Persistence is not another secret of

---

"Non-Japanese firms can develop their own spirit of gambare *by setting corporate milestones and emphasizing a competitive focus the way the Japanese do."*

---

the mysterious East to explain the often stunning performance of Japanese companies. As illustrated by the VCR industry, some Japanese companies (e.g., Sony and JVC) are more persistent than others (e.g., Toshiba and Hitachi). Typically, the most persistent Japanese companies (as mentioned by the Japanese themselves) are those with a strong and constantly nurtured entrepreneurial culture (e.g., Sony, Honda, Sharp, and Suntory).

On the other hand, Japanese persistence should not be underestimated either. Persistence is very much a part of the Japanese culture, as is suggested by a survey conducted by the linguist Toshio Ishiwata. When asked, "What is your favorite word in life?" the top three words of 3,600 Japanese interviewed were *effort, persistence,* and *thank you*.

A survey conducted by the writer among 400 European executives showed that when asked the same question, they listed *love, family,* and *fun* as their favorite words. How long will it be before these three words appear at the

top of the Japanese list? Will the favorite Japanese words ever appear at the top of the European list? What may Westerners learn from Japanese persistence?

First, Western companies facing Japanese competition must recognize that Japanese corporations play by different rules; they must understand that persistence is an underlying factor of competitiveness in Japanese firms. If your company competes head-on with Japanese corporations, you had better take a long-term view and be prepared not to give up easily, because the Japanese will not. This advice should be stressed even more if your company competes in Japan.

Non-Japanese firms can develop their own spirit of *gambare* by setting corporate milestones and emphasizing a competitive focus the way the Japanese do. Typically, Japanese corporations measure competitiveness by emphasizing market share much more than Western companies do. Several Japanese executives interviewed stressed that spreading competitive market share positions throughout the whole organization, together with identifying a competitor to overtake, is key to mobilizing employees.

Finally, Western firms can become more persistent by being more modest about their own successes. As another Japanese executive put it, "Japanese firms may be more persistent than many of their Western competitors simply because many Western firms have become overconfident with time and have lost the notion of persistence." Rediscovering the humility that enables one to learn from others may be for us the real challenge of Japanese persistence. ▲

Notes
1. B. Duke, "The Japanese School: Lessons for Industrial America," Praeger Special Studies (New York: Praeger Scientific, 1986).
2. R.T. Pascale, "Perspectives on Strategy: The Real Story Behind Honda's Success," *California Management Review* 26 (Spring 1984).

Business Intelligence in Japan and Sweden: Lessons for the U.S.

Jan P. Herring

Business intelligence activities abroad are often more developed and more effective than in the United States. This article takes a brief look at the business intelligence efforts of Japanese and Swedish companies, including the various roles in business intelligence played by government and industry. In both countries, multinational companies systematically gather business intelligence globally; they use both employees and external sources of intelligence to create the advantage they need to outthink and outperform the competition.

Business intelligence (BI) activities have increased significantly in the U.S. over the past five years—but mainly at the practitioner's level. For various reasons, senior managers in U.S. companies have not adopted intelligence as a strategic management discipline. As a direct result, the use and effectiveness of BI operations in U.S. firms remain questionable. Until senior executives become more interested and involved in the use of BI, the competitiveness of U.S. companies will be limited by their inability to understand and outthink global competitors.

In contrast, BI activities in a number of foreign countries are more developed and effective, particularly the gathering of competitor intelligence and its use by multinational companies. Consider both Japan and Sweden:

☐ Japanese BI capabilities are well-developed within companies, benefiting both the companies and government programs, which in turn support their international competition.

☐ Sweden's activities are more subtle but comprehensive, ranging from university education to well-developed corporate BI programs that are supported by a worldwide collection network set up by the country's international banks and government efforts at both the national level and by embassies abroad.

Swedish companies' senior management appear to be more like their U.S. counterparts, in that they have been reluctant participants in their companies' BI operations; Japanese managers, however, become part of the process almost effortlessly, due to the nature of their companies' consensus-building process. As a result, Japanese companies make greater use of intelligence at all levels and in all business functions throughout the company (e.g., sales, product design, strategizing, and decision making).

This column provides a brief look at the composition and focus of these two countries' BI efforts. What follows is an examination of how the BI effort in each country has arrived at its current level and the role played by government and industry leaders in achieving this level of implementation. In addition, the column examines how these countries have learned to apply intelligence in the business sector.

Sweden: a world leader in developing BI capabilities

Contemporary BI activities in Sweden trace their roots to the Wallenberg banking enterprise at the beginning of the century. Marcus Wallenberg hired 22-year-old Rolf Jollin and assigned him to secretly gather information about the bank's prospective customers and various business enterprises. In 1903, Wallenberg sent him to the Crédit Lyonnaise Banque in Paris to learn how the French bank had developed and used its BI department.

Crédit Lyonnaise had close relationships with French government intelligence, and Wallenberg believed that such professional underpinnings would be valuable to the development of an effective intelligence program for his bank. Wallenberg's "intelligence officer" learned from this training and subsequently established a very effective program for gathering intelligence about prospective and existing customers and business activities. Wallenberg was well aware of the security factors involved in such an activity and called the operation the "Statistical Department" so as not to raise suspicions.

Today, the Swedish banking community is still the recognized leader in that country's development and application of BI. During the late 1970s, the banking community took an innovative step by organizing a BI research company called Upplysnigs Centralen (UC Research). The firm, which is supported by all major banks, is the equivalent of a combined Standard & Poor's and the TRW credit service. UC Research provides fee-based BI services for banks and their major customers, including data base services consisting of public and published information on companies and individuals; proactive intelligence gathering, using the participating banks' overseas offices to answer specific and time-urgent requests; and the use of some 3,000 business agents around the world who can be tapped for specific expertise or information.

Government influence in BI activities receives strong support; Swedish embassies abroad often provide direct intelligence support to Swedish companies. Government emphasis on intelligence for business became apparent during the mid-1970s when government intelligence operations began to emphasize economic and technological coverage, representing some 60% of the government's overall intelligence activities. The Swedish State Police and the Swedish Employees Association both show strong support for BI activities, providing advice and education on related subjects, including company security practices. A number of local consulting firms, as well as the consulting divisions of major firms, offer BI-related services and advice to Swedish companies.

A key to the advanced state of BI in Sweden is the support it receives from leading univer-sities such as the Stockholm School of Economics and the University of Lund, where full-time courses in BI are regularly taught. The Stockholm School of Economics is soon expected to graduate the world's first Ph.D. candidates in the field of BI.

The strong educational base for Swedish BI can be attributed to a single individual, Professor Stevan Dedijer, who found his way to Sweden from Yugoslavia through the U.S. He served in World War II as an OSS officer and afterwards as a scientific and intelligence adviser to a number of developing countries. Having worked with several intelligence services, as well as seeing the need that developing countries had for economic intelligence, Dedijer recognized the contribution that an organized intelligence effort could make to any economic enterprise, whether it was a country or a company.

"A key to the advanced state of BI in Sweden is the support it receives from leading universities, where full-time courses in BI are regularly taught."

Dedijer began teaching (and preaching) BI at the University of Lund during the early 1970s. He attracted a small following of ex-Swedish intelligence officers and business leaders, including one ex-Wallenberg Bank executive. Over the past 20 years, Dedijer has created not only a body of educational knowledge concerning intelligence and its application in the business world but has produced hundreds of well-trained intelligence officers for the Swedish business community.

Today, more than 500 Swedish firms in the banking, insurance, electronics, furniture, automotive, and defense industries actively engage in BI activities. At least 50 of Sweden's major companies, including L.M. Ericsson, Volvo, and ABB, have world-class BI organizations, often headed by one of Dedijer's graduates. These individuals run well-integrated intelligence departments with intelligence collection and analysis closely linked to corporate planning and operations. Companies make effective use of their own employees for intelligence collection and supplement this information with externally acquired intelligence using consulting firms, Swedish diplomats, and their banks' overseas foreign offices.

As well-developed as BI is in Sweden, Dedijer and a number of the company BI directors have lamented the fact that although senior executives appear to appreciate the value of intelligence, they do not always use it themselves as effectively or aggressively as they should.

Outlook: Over the next several years, particularly as Sweden becomes an active participant of the new Common Market, more Swedish companies will establish formal BI systems. Executive management education programs will be developed to overcome older management's reluctance to use BI; over time, more of the younger managers already trained will fully embrace BI as a contemporary management discipline. Swedish firms can be expected to increase their use of BI as the means of gaining competitive advantage in foreign markets, particularly the U.S., the European Community, and Japan.

Japan: the world leader in practicing BI

The Japanese have a well-earned reputation for being world leaders in the businesses in which they compete. Their business strengths are equally matched by the ability to gather and use BI, including competitor, customer, market, and technological intelligence.

From outsmarting their competitors on international bids to devising superior competitive strategies to identifying and sourcing foreign technology for their next-generation products, Japanese companies effectively use BI as a means of gaining competitive advantage over their rivals. Much of this advantage is due to the ability to collect—but not necessarily analyze—and use BI in a timely and effective manner companywide.

Ironically, as the amount of accessible international business information has grown almost exponentially over the past 30 years, Japanese companies and their government have continuously sought new ways to manage the information glut to sort out those key pieces of competitive and business intelligence. Initially, this took place through government-sponsored foreign information programs and continued with electronic data bases and information processing systems. Currently, however, many Japanese companies feel they are losing the battle to manage and use the ever-increasing amount of publicly available information generated by almost every country in the world.

"Today, almost all Japanese companies involved in international business and trade have their own intelligence unit."

This had led a number of Japanese business leaders to believe they need to find a more organized and systematic way of managing the BI process. This, in turn, has led Japanese companies to reach out to the American Society of Competitive Intelligence Professionals (SCIP) for both new ideas and as a stimulant for the development of more modern and powerful BI systems for Japanese firms.

Japanese companies' current BI practices have largely been developed since World War II, when the government recognized that Western technology would be needed to modernize its badly damaged industrial base. During the late 1950s, the government established two principal organizations to support the development of Japanese BI. In 1957, it created a joint venture, identified as the Scientific Information Center (SIC), to gather and disseminate information about Western industrial technology to Japan's private sector. Subsequently, the Ministry of International Trade and Industry (MITI) established the Japan External Trade Organization (JETRO) for the purpose of promoting Japanese exports. JETRO was given the added responsibility of collecting and disseminating foreign business information to Japanese firms. That mission included the responsibility for providing world-wide intelligence on how other nations run their businesses and economies.

Initially, because the firms had no foreign presence and little hard currency, much of the foreign business information was gathered by the government, with organizations such as the SIC providing the means for broadly disseminating that information throughout various Japanese industries. The dissemination of foreign business and technical information by the government caused many Japanese companies to set up their own intelligence departments to fully exploit this data.

By the early 1960s, essentially all large Japanese multinational companies had created their own dedicated intelligence units. A survey conducted in 1963 by MITI identified the most effective foreign intelligence collection mechanisms, ranging from the stationing of employees abroad as "listening" posts to the use of both domestic and foreign consulting services, including the use of their related trading firms for proactive intelligence collection.

"Mitsui's motto is 'Information is the lifeblood of the company.'"

It was during this period that a school, The Institute for Industrial Protection, was established by Tokyo to train intelligence agents and security officers for Japanese corporations. The school was headed by a former Japanese ambassador; it included a nine-person staff and a number of experienced intelligence officers. Among the first 50 students at the school were some promising executives in their late 20s, who, over the four-month course, were taught a wide range of intelligence collection, analysis, and security techniques.

Today, almost all Japanese companies involved in international business and trade have their own intelligence unit. Typically, it is located in the planning or research departments. Some 10 to 20 employees are assigned these responsibilities within company headquarters, but the responsibility for intelligence gathering is companywide, with almost every employee participating (from the president to the sales force). Intelligence collection and dissemination is a well-developed process at most Japanese firms. However, it is the ability—almost culturally inherent—for sharing intelligence that makes the use of BI in Japanese companies so effective.

Some of the larger companies, such as Mitsubishi Corporation and Nomura Securities, have established more comprehensive intelligence[1] activities in the form of think tanks, whose primary purpose is to study the total business environment in which the companies operate. These think tanks also sell their services to other companies, in addition to producing intelligence for themselves and, sometimes, for the Japanese government.

Most Japanese firms are part of a larger group called the Keiretsu, a family of mainly non-competing companies whose various business functions cover banking, insurance, manufacturing, transportation, and sales and trading. Intelligence gathered by the various members is traditionally shared with the trading company for broader use by all; the member bank often provides some of the more valuable intelligence.

Japanese trading companies' reputation for operating worldwide intelligence networks is well deserved. Mitsui Corporation's trading company is reputed to have had such an excellent global intelligence network before World War II that it was used by the government for military purposes. These trading companies have hundreds of offices abroad, often with thousands of employees. Their basic mission is to gather competitive and market intelligence on an ongoing basis and send it back to the Tokyo headquarter's intelligence clearinghouse.

Today, Japanese trading companies are more sensitive than ever to the importance of global information, and some have stated that their goal for the 21st century is to become "globally integrated information corporations." The future vision does not diverge much from their past: Mitsui Corporation's motto is "Information is the lifeblood of the company."

The collection and use of BI by Japanese firms is world-class. However, the analysis of the intelligence has been less developed and effective. Their ability to often collect the answer to an intelligence problem, such as their competitor's strategy or a description of the competitor's future product, has resulted in less emphasis being placed on the development of more creative intelligence assessment skills and techniques.

In fact, because so much intelligence can be collected directly, it has led to problems where Japanese companies have been tempted—as in the Hitachi-IBM industrial espionage case—to collect a competitor's proprietary information. This situation, however, is much more prevalent in Japan, as the recent Komatsu industrial spy scandal has revealed.

As competitor intelligence becomes more difficult to collect and as the amount of information that is publicly available grows through electronic data bases and public disclosure, the weaknesses in Japanese firms' intelligence analysis techniques are becoming more evident. The types of analysis that Japanese companies have concentrated on in the past have been mainly the examination and organization of large amounts of data to discern competitor trends and business strategies. However, in view of the increasing amounts of information and the complexity of available data, Japanese firms will have to place greater emphasis on more sophisticated intelligence analysis to reduce the large amounts of collected information and derive useful insights.

Japanese firms believe that although they have had an intelligence advantage over their foreign competitors in the past, they are currently falling behind, particularly in the areas of organized BI systems. They perceive that the U.S. effort to organize competitive intelligence professionals (i.e., SCIP) is providing American companies with enhanced intelligence collection and analysis capabilities. This, in turn, has resulted in a major effort on the part of a number of Japanese business leaders and company officials, led by a major Japanese trading firm, to enlist the assistance of SCIP in organizing and developing the competitive intelligence profession in Japan.

Outlook: The Japanese are very good at acquiring, assimilating, and improving upon foreign business practices, as their successful adaptation of American quality control theory proves. They will effectively adopt U.S. BI methods and techniques to enhance their companies' overall competitiveness—probably sooner than most American companies.

Lessons for U.S. management

The Swedish and Japanese efforts to create modern BI capabilities for their companies evolved through two entirely different processes. However, in both cases, the results have generally been the same: Transnational companies systematically gathering BI on a global basis, using both employees and external sources of intelligence to create the knowledge-based advantage needed by their companies to outthink and outperform the competition.

U.S. business leaders and government officials should learn three basic lessons from these best-in-class country examples:

1. American companies, particularly their senior managers, need to examine their contemporary need for BI and their current capabilities to produce it themselves. Unfortunately, few companies have dedicated the resources or created the necessary organizational capability to produce the kind of BI needed to compete in today's global business environment. Company executives will have to take the lead to see that their firms develop the appropriate capabilities and skills.

2. U.S. companies and government agencies need to work together to create the BI capabilities that firms need to compete in today's global marketplace. The government can provide timely and cogent business information on foreign developments that affect industrial structures and markets; scientific and technical intelligence that have both government and business interest; and developments in foreign government policies and regulatory processes that affect U.S. corporations' ability to compete. All this can be done legally and ethically. With some organized effort on the part of the federal government, it can be provided equitably to all interested U.S. firms. Government is capable of providing support, but the private sector will have to ask for it—otherwise the administration and Congress will not address the issue directly, fearing that each would accuse the other of interfering in the free market.

3. Finally, from the Swedish experience, professional education is necessary for both managers and practitioners. Unfortunately, U.S. universities and business schools currently are unprepared to provide it. Lester

Thurow, Dean of the Massachusetts Institute of Technology's Sloan School of Management, has lamented, "It should be noted that there are virtually no courses in business intelligence at American business schools. Sadly, that includes MIT." At present, there are only two or three full-time courses on the subject of competitive intelligence being offered at American universities.

Finally, U.S. companies will probably have to carry the brunt of the effort themselves. The federal government has been hesitant to take the lead. And universities, particularly business schools, are not known for being leaders in new business practices.

Therefore, unless business leaders take the initiative, in 2000 we will be talking about how, during the early 1990s, American corporations missed the opportunity to adapt modern BI practices to their international business activities, just like they missed Dem-

ing's message on statistical quality control during the early 1960s. Of greater concern, it is all too likely that the result will be the same: U.S. companies being outsmarted in the marketplace as a result of foreign competition using an American-developed business discipline more effectively than they have. ▲

Note
1. The Japanese word for intelligence, *joho*, has a broad meaning, including the collection and use of information for specific purposes. It is used by the Ministry of Foreign Affairs to identify its Intelligence Bureau and by trading companies to denote their international research departments.

PART G

Management Accounting Systems and Techniques

Designing and Implementing a New Cost Management System

John A. Miller

To remain competitive in world markets, companies must continually improve the performance of activities and business processes. Since improvement of processes and activities is fundamental to long-term survival, managers need relevant and timely feedback so that they can measure and judge the performance of activities. Since traditional financial and cost accounting systems do not produce the information that managers require, new cost management systems must be designed and implemented. These new cost management systems must be designed and implemented with two purposes in mind: (1) to gather financial and operating information that reflects the performance of activities; and (2) to supply management with relevant information to plan, manage, control, and direct the activities of the business in order to improve processes and products, eliminate waste, and execute business operations and strategies. This article discusses how to plan, design, and implement a new cost management system.

Since the early 1970s, dynamic factors have reshaped the competitive marketplace. More than ever before, companies must compete on a global basis and meet world-class standards in order to survive. As managers have learned, world-class competition requires a commitment to continuous improvement (*kaizen* in Japanese).

Many managers have embraced total quality management (TQM) and just-in-time (JIT) improvement efforts as the cornerstone for continuous improvement in their organizations. The ultimate goal of this shared philosophy of TQM, JIT, and other continuous improvement efforts is for companies to continually improve their processes and activities so that their companies can effectively and efficiently meet customer needs.

An organization's TQM and JIT efforts focus on improving quality, reducing cycle time, and providing increased customer satisfaction as the means for achieving the lowest overall business cost. Therefore, managers responsible for continuous improvement need information about quality, cycle time, and customer satisfaction in addition to cost information. Having this information enables managers to evaluate how well they manage and control all aspects of a business—from initial customer contact through final customer satisfaction. Relevant information to plan, direct, and manage an organization's activities and operations is essential. The development of a new cost management system (CMS) is the most efficient and activist response to this business need for information.

A new paradigm for cost management

Traditional cost management systems focus on managing cost by means of cost-based budgets, standards, variances, and measurements established at the departmental level. In this paradigm, organizations have a vertical orientation; the emphasis is on the *cost* part of cost management. Accountants design and implement systems and procedures that make it possible to manage and control cost.

But the new paradigm for cost management is focused on managing processes and activities. Cost and performance measurements for quality, cycle time, customer satisfaction, and productivity are established at the business process and activity levels. In this new paradigm, organizations have a *horizontal* orientation; the emphasis is on the *management* part of cost management. Accountants design and implement systems and procedures that make it possible to manage and control *activities*.

In the new paradigm, cost management is viewed within a philosophy of continuous improvement and defined using active verbs: to plan, manage, control, and direct the activities of a business to improve processes and products, eliminate waste, and execute business operations and strategies. The purpose of a CMS in this new paradigm is to provide management with relevant information needed to judge how well cost management efforts are working. Linking cost management with continuous improvement broadens the definition and interpretation of cost management and drives a change in an organization's mind-set from managing costs to managing activities as the focal point of cost management.

Traditional cost management systems do not accumulate or report the information that managers require under the new paradigm for cost management. Therefore, new systems, procedures, and methods must be designed and implemented to provide management with the information they require to manage the activities of the business.

Cost management system outputs

The driving force behind the new paradigm for cost management is a focus on the outputs of the CMS—information to manage and improve activities and processes of the business as the means to achieve reduced cost. Therefore, the CMS must provide information about:

- How well activities are being performed; and
- Whether improvement efforts are working.

Feedback under this new CMS is not limited to cost information, although cost is an important part of the new CMS.

Organizations that are designing and implementing a new CMS will find that there are five basic information outputs for the new CMS. These include:

1. The cost of activities and business processes;
2. The cost of non-value-added activities;
3. Product cost;
4. Performance measurement; and
5. Cost drivers.

These information outputs are discussed below.

The cost of activities and business processes

Activities are the processes or procedures that cause work to be performed in an organization. They are, in essence, aggregations of tasks (whether performed by people or machines) to satisfy the needs of customers (whether they are internal or external customers). *Processes* are a series of activities that are linked to perform a specific objective.

Activities and business processes represent the way that a company uses its resources. Competitors serving the same customers and having access to the same labor pools, ma-

---

The new paradigm for cost management is focused on managing processes and activities. Cost and performance measurements for quality, cycle time, customer satisfaction, and productivity are established at the business process and activity levels.

---

chinery, technology, and raw materials differentiate themselves on the basis of how well activities are executed. Even companies that dominate markets must continue to improve how they execute activities and design processes if they intend to remain dominant in the long term.

Since activities form the very core of what a business does, the basic output of a new CMS must be to provide management with relevant cost information about each significant activity. Cost information about what the business does—i.e., about its activities—is a fundamental information output of a new CMS.

The cost of non-value-added activities

Some activities add value to a product or service, while some do not. In a manufacturing operation, the cost and time associated with moving parts, waiting, rework, and scrap are often-cited examples of non-value-added activities. Rework and scrap are not limited to the factory floor. Many nonfactory floor activities include inefficiency, redundancy, and duplication.[1] Virtually every organization will acknowledge the existence of work that could be done more efficiently or that never should have been done at all.

A *non-value-added cost* is a cost that does not contribute to customer value or to the organization's needs. "Non-value-added cost" is often defined as "a cost or [an] activity that can be eliminated with no deterioration of product attributes (e.g., performance, functionality, quality, perceived value)."[2] A CMS that identifies the cost of non-value-added activities has enormous value to management. With this crucial information output, the CMS provides a focal point for cost improvement efforts.

Performance measurement

Measuring the performance of activities provides a scorecard to report how well improvement efforts are working. Performance measurement is an integral part of continous improvement. A key output of the new CMS is the measurement of performance at the activity and business process level.

A CMS assesses at least four elements when measuring the total performance of activities:

1. Productivity;
2. Quality;
3. Cycle time; and
4. Customer satisfaction.

Each of these information outputs has limited value when viewed independently, because in isolation none of them can fully measure performance or fully describe how well the company is doing. For example, high levels of productivity would not be meaningful if cycle times were increasing or customer service levels were dropping. Each of these four performance measurements must be considered in tandem when judging total activity performance. For some companies, a fifth performance measure of an activity—flexibility—may be useful.

Productivity

Estimating and monitoring productivity are among the most critical information outputs

that a new CMS can provide to management. Productivity can be defined as the physical output of an activity divided by the cost of resources consumed, thus expressed as a cost per unit of output. Productivity improves, therefore, when the cost per unit of output declines. This productivity calculation links the physical output of an activity to its cost, a linkage that is unique to the new paradigm for a CMS.

Quality

A manufacturing organization that turns to a new CMS must be concerned with quality. Quality has many meanings in the new manufacturing environment, but its meaning can be narrowed by the new CMS to conformance to specification for an activity. The new CMS can measure this information output by identifying, for example, errors per thousand units or percentage of material scrapped. The CMS can then provide a comparative analysis of the numbers needed to conform to the activity's specifications.

Quality is perhaps the clearest example of why the four elements of performance measurement must be analyzed in tandem. Poor conformance to specifications directly affects productivity, for example, in that it slows the manufacturing process. This same nonconformance also slows productivity and lengthens cycle time. Above all, quality as a performance measurement is one of the most useful information outputs that a new CMS can offer management in its goal of achieving the lowest product cost and at the same time meeting customer needs.

Cycle time

Cycle time is a measurement of how long it takes to complete an activity or a business process. The total cycle time to make a product or service and deliver it to the customer is the summation of the "nonoverlapped" cycle time for each of the activities necessary to produce and deliver a product or service to customers. Cycle time is a measurement of time expressed in hours, days, weeks, months, or years. Like the other performance measurements, reduced cycle time is predicated on improved productivity, increased quality, and customer satisfaction.

Customer satisfaction

Improved productivity, increased quality, and reduced cycle time are meaningless if customers are dissatisfied. Customer satisfaction is an important element to consider when measuring the overall performance of an activity. This performance measurement should be quantified and expressed at its source—*by the customer.* For example, overall customer satisfaction for a given activity might be expressed on a scale of 1 to 10, where a 1 rating is poor and a 10 rating is excellent.

All four performance measurements evaluated by a CMS—productivity, quality, cycle time, and customer satisfaction—are interdependent. Their relative ranking and importance, in relationship to measuring activity performance as a whole, are dependent on the specific activity, product or service, organization, industry, and customer. Organizations that

---

Linking cost management with continuous improvement broadens the definition and interpretation of cost management and drives a change in an organization's mind-set from managing costs to managing activities as the focal point of cost management.

---

are designing and implementing a new CMS must include in their plans an initial commitment to performance measurement activities. How each organization actually measures performance—and each organization may have a different strategy—matters less than making performance measurement a priority of the new CMS.

Product cost

Products and services are provided to markets and customers through various distribution channels; they consume resources at different rates and they require different levels of support. Accurate product cost information is vital for selecting the individual and

segmented markets where an organization competes and for pricing in those markets. Product cost information is a pivotal information output for the new CMS.

Product cost is the summation of all company resources consumed in creating, producing, designing, supporting, and delivering a product or service to a customer. New CMS product cost information encompasses cost beyond the factory floor, to identify the total product cost (i.e., including distribution and support costs) associated with a particular market, customer, or distribution channel. The new CMS can provide accurate cost information by linking the consumption of activities directly to those products or services that require the activity.

While product cost has strategic value, its operational value is limited to directing managers to those products that consume too many resources to be competitive in a particular market, product, or customer group. Operational improvements can only come from improving the processes and activities used to design, produce, and deliver the product or service to the customer, all activities that the new CMS can measure.

Cost drivers

The final output of a new CMS is cost driver information. A *cost driver* is any factor that causes a change in the total cost of an activity. It is, in short, the cause of cost. Understanding the causal relationship between an activity and its cost enables management to focus improvement efforts on the areas that will produce the best result.

For example, a business process for one company that provides a service to manufacturers that consists of collecting and processing product and demographic information about customers includes the activity of data entry—manually keypunching customer-supplied information into a database. Productivity in this company is measured as a cost per card or the cost per entry of a customer response. Improvement efforts that focused on making data entry clerks (the company's major cost) work better and faster, produced mixed results. A new CMS that the company adopted instituted a cost driver analysis. This analysis discovered that, more than any other

Exhibit 1. *XYZ Corporation*
Cost Management System Top Management Report
Business Process 1

Activities	Cost Effectiveness			Performance		Cost Drivers		Product/Service Profitability		
	Value-Added	Non-value-added	Total	Measure	Measurement	Measure	Volume	Product/ Service 1	Product/ Service 2	Product/ Service 3
Activity 1				Productivity Quality Cycle time Customer satisfaction						
Activity 2										
Activity 3										
.										
.										
.										
Activity N										

factor, the design of the card was the root of cost in data entry. Poorly designed cards that were difficult to read slowed the data entry operators. Armed with this output information from the new CMS, management focused its improvement efforts on the card design activity, and ultimately achieved performance improvements in the data entry activity.

As this example shows, by identifying and reporting cost drivers, a new CMS can direct management toward areas where improvement efforts will produce the best results. When cost drivers are quantifiable (e.g., number of parts causal to manufacturing overhead or number of feet traveled causal to factory logistics costs), improvement efforts that focus on reducing the numbers of parts or on decreasing the distance traveled can be measured.

The CMS outputs described above—the cost of activities and business processes, the cost of non-value-added activities, performance measurement, product cost, and cost drivers—all contribute to management's effort at continuous improvement of the manufacturing process. Exhibit 1 illustrates the format for a CMS top management report from *XYZ* Corporation for a specific business process. It depicts, in *XYZ*'s particular style, each of the basic CMS outputs.

Relationship between a cost management system and the financial and accounting systems

Financial information produced under generally accepted accounting principles (GAAP) is not useful for planning, managing, controlling, and directing activities, because it does not provide information on how well activities are executed. GAAP information is more useful to banks, investors, regulatory agencies, and taxing authorities than it is for managing activities. The accounting and cost accounting required to produce GAAP financial information have little relationship to a CMS that emphasizes activities; the systems have different purposes.

In addition to external reporting, accounting systems are used to pay bills, track money that customers owe, record the flow of inventory, monitor fixed assets, record depreciation, and ensure that obligations are recorded and paid. Cost accounting in this context picks up where accounting leaves off. The primary purpose of cost accounting is to determine product and inventory costs, set standard costs, and prepare variance reports.

Most traditional accounting and cost accounting systems do not produce the kind of information that management needs in order to oversee the activities of a business. The only relationship between a new CMS and traditional accounting systems is that cost information is an integral part of each system. A CMS serves different users. Accounting and cost accounting systems are typically not designed to provide the new CMS information that managements require, although much of the cost data for a new CMS comes from the existing accounting system. Therefore, a new CMS must be designed and implemented to provide the information that management needs to execute its commitment to continuous improvement.

Designing and implementing the new system are discussed in the following sections.

Designing a new system

The fundamental design objective for a new CMS is to create methods, procedures, and systems to collect and report financial and operational data about the activities of an organization. To meet this design objective, the outputs of a CMS must mirror the organization's activities and provide appropriate and meaningful information for management. Accurate information about the cost and performance of activities is the cornerstone of a new CMS.

Unfortunately, most organizations do not collect financial and operational data about their activities; many have never even defined activities. Therefore, before implementation can take place, significant resources must be devoted to defining activities and establishing methods, procedures, and systems to meet the fundamental design objective.

In addition to this fundamental design objective (i.e., the ability to collect data about activities), several other issues must be addressed in the design stage of a CMS, including:

- Defining the system's purpose and use;
- Linking the organization's operations and strategy;
- Establishing simplicity as an effective tool;
- Maintaining relevance of information for decision making;
- Applying benchmarking, best practices, and target costing;
- Determining the frequency of distribution (i.e., the collecting and reporting of information under the new CMS); and
- Examining hardware and software issues.

Each of these CMS design issues is discussed below.

Purpose and use. The design of a CMS is driven by management's definition of the purpose and use of the system. While managers who help design and implement a CMS are all focused on making sure that they receive information that they can use to improve performance, the specific information required varies from management team to management team, company to company, industry to industry, and customer base to customer base. Therefore, management must assume the responsibility early in the design stage for clearly setting the parameters for the purpose and use of the new CMS.

For example, a company that competes primarily on the basis of innovative new products (e.g., in the computer industry) might design the CMS to place additional emphasis on the cycle time of activities associated with new product development. A wholesale distributor, on the other hand, which competes in different market segments on the basis of availability or service, might design its CMS to emphasize the cost of resources (i.e., activities) consumed in the various distribution channels. Designing for purpose and use means continually asking how the output information from the CMS will be used and what decisions it will drive.

Linkage between operations and strategy. Activities represent what an organization does and encompass daily operations. Both of these elements bridge the gap between the organization's operations and its strategy. According to Michael Porter, strategy simply means developing sustainable competitive advantage by outperforming competitors over the long term in those areas that have value to customers.[3] The selection, execution, and improvement of activities are sources of competitive advantage, and the result of activities performed over a long period of time is, in essence, the execution of a strategy.

Some companies and industries compete primarily on the basis of cost. Others compete primarily on the basis of innovation, value, or product availability. Marketing, distribution, and manufacturing strategies differ between companies. Therefore, a CMS must be designed with these differences in mind. The key design point after the system's purpose and use are articulated is that a CMS is based on activities, and activities enable the designer to link operations—what the business does—to strategy.

Simplicity. Virtually all successful TQM and JIT improvement efforts have a common principle: Simplicity. A cornerstone of an effective CMS is the avoidance of complexity whenever possible. The simpler a procedure is, the easier it is to implement, and the greater support it provides management.

Designers of a new CMS can follow the lead of their manufacturing counterparts, the designers of machinery. Machinery designers have learned that complex designs lead to complex repair problems and difficult modifications. Complexity can come in little doses, as when using two different kinds of fasteners in a product when one kind would do the trick. Complexity adds cost, does not improve functionality, and must constantly be designed out of products and services.

There is no reason to believe that it may be different for designers of a new CMS. Designing a CMS with a high degree of complexity means that management will be giving up future flexibility and guaranteeing that modifications, improvements, and changes will be difficult and costly.

A basic rule to follow when designing a new CMS is as follows: If the users of the output of the CMS are unable to understand the system's basic features and functions, then the system is too complex.

Relevance. For a new CMS to be useful, its focus must be on the important aspects of the business, at a level relevant to improvement efforts and for decision making. A common mistake of CMS designers is to define activities at such a low level that they represent tasks, not activities.

Designing a CMS so that its information output is relevant to management decision making is predicated on up-front management feedback about its goals for the CMS. Once these goals are articulated, the CMS design team must write specifications that will deliver the information management needs in order to assess its goals.

The following rule of thumb can be helpful to designers when they are narrowing the specifications of a CMS to meet management's needs: At least 80 percent of business costs should be captured in a framework of no more than twelve business processes, each containing from five to ten critical and key activities. In this way, both simplicity of design and relevance of information are built into the design of the system.

Benchmarking, best practices, and target costing. A new CMS should be designed so that users can compare internal costs and performance measurements of activities with externally driven targets. Management can then set standards or highlight performance gaps for a particular activity or business process.

CMS designers should anticipate and plan to compare internal costs and measurements from a CMS with external standards and requirements. To do so, design specifications for the CMS should take into account such techniques as benchmarking, best practices, and target costing.

Frequency of distribution. The frequency of distribution—i.e., the collecting and reporting of information under the new CMS—is largely a function of the system's purpose and use. It would not be unusual to report cost and performance measurements on an hourly basis for some activities, yet on a quarterly basis for others. The reporting of activity performance on both an hourly and a quarterly basis could exist within the framework of a CMS, assuming that activity performance is measured and reported to line managers hourly and summarized in a quarterly report to top management.

A design team has a more straightforward task when creating specifications for the frequency of distribution of information under the new system. They can design the system with this simple fact in mind: Whether reported on an hourly or a quarterly basis, the activity is the same—only the period of performance varies.

Hardware and software issues. The key design point when examining hardware and software issues is whether to implement the CMS off-line through a stand-alone (or networked) personal computer or to integrate the system on-line as part of existing financial and operations systems. This decision is largely driven by how well existing reporting systems mirror the activities of the organization. Integration works best when the existing system reports cost information consistent with activities.

At least initially, most organizations would be better served if they implemented a new CMS on a stand-alone basis using activity-based software currently offered in the marketplace. This approach enables the CMS designers to gain hands-on experience and knowledge about activity management without committing the organization to a major change of systems. Later, after managers gain experience with the reporting of the new CMS, integrated systems can be designed.

Implementing the new system

Management commitment is a prerequisite to implementing a new CMS. This commitment is a deeper one than the mere commitment of resources typically associated with improving an existing CMS. This difference can be explained in terms of the change in management's mind-set—from managing cost to managing activities—that a new CMS demands. In addition, implementing a new CMS requires management's willingness to pursue a strategy for improving the activities of the business. Without improvement efforts to reduce or eliminate non-value-added activities and costs, the resources devoted to implementation of a new CMS would be wasted.

Once committed to a CMS implementation, management must address its three phases:

- *Phase 1*—consisting of the data gathering and analysis needed to develop the knowledge, structure, and methodology for collecting and reporting information about the organization's activities. The amount of effort and resources required for Phase 1 depends on how well existing financial, accounting, and operating systems mirror the organization's activities. Companies in the process industry may have accounting systems (process accounting) and operating systems that are already fairly well aligned with activities. In such companies, managing departments is, in essence, managing

activities. Most often, however, this situation will not be the case in Phase 1, which means that considerable effort will be required to rethink the business in terms of its activities;

- *Phase 2*—consisting of implementing the procedures, methods, and systems to routinely collect and report data and information about the organization's activities; and
- *Phase 3*—consisting of maintaining the CMS. This phase is ongoing and is required in order to continuously improve the CMS.

Phase 1. Data gathering and analysis

Most organizations have never defined activities, much less routinely collected financial and operational data about the cost and performance of activities. Therefore, in most CMS implementations, significant effort must be devoted in Phase 1 to defining, understanding, documenting, and analyzing activities.

Phase 1 is a data-gathering and analysis stage. It includes six general steps that are necessary to build a new CMS:

1. Specify activities;
2. Trace cost to each activity;
3. Determine value-added versus non-value-added activities and cost;
4. Determine output measures and volume;
5. Select the appropriate cost drivers; and
6. Trace costs to product cost objects.

The completion of these steps, each of which is discussed below, is a prerequisite to an ongoing CMS. Once completed, the Phase 1 implementation provides a snapshot of activities at a particular point in time and serves as the base of knowledge and information for ongoing reporting.

Specify activities. Specifying activities is the first and most important step. This involves defining what is important to the business. A significant amount of time must be spent on data gathering (including specifying cost and other information or factors about these activities).

Activities should be defined in a way that captures the most important aspects of the business—its core activities—but not at such a detailed level to represent tasks. Once defined, activities can be linked to major business processes.

Exhibit 2. *XYZ Corporation*
Traditional vs. Activity-Based Costing

Traditional

Department/Expense Type	Amount
☐ *Sales/service*	$ 8.4
• Expense types include salaries, travel and entertainment, and rent	
☐ *New product development*	0.8
• Expense types include prototypes, outside services, and depreciation	
☐ *Manufacturing*	14.8
• Expense types include direct labor, indirect labor, depreciation, and tooling	
☐ *Engineering*	4.2
• Expense type includes primarily salaries	
☐ *Finance and administration*	3.6
• Expense types include salaries, computer and office supplies, and professional services	
☐ *Project management/question and answer*	0.8
• Expense type includes primarily salaries	
☐ Total cost	$32.6

Activity-Based

Business Process/Activities	Amount
☐ *Determining that a customer need exists*	$ 5.2
• Activities include targeting accounts, making sales calls, and preparing sales materials	
☐ *Preparing and delivering bids and quotes*	2.7
• Activities include pricing determination, determining estimated costs, and preparing the quote to the customer	
☐ *Interpreting a customer order and creating the sales/engineering documentation necessary to execute the order*	3.9
• Activities include preparing bill materials, assigning part numbers, and preparing manufacturing blueprints	
☐ *Planning and securing the necessary resources so that the customer's requirements are met*	4.3
• Activities include preparing routers, N/C programming, and purchasing goods and services	
☐ *Manufacturing and assembling products to the customer's specifications*	10.8
• Activities include machining, welding, moving, and inspecting	
☐ *Delivering the product, service, and/or documentation to the customer*	2.4
• Activities include preparing of shipping documentation, performing billing and collection, and implementing installation	
☐ *Other business processes and activities to support, control, and guide operations*	3.3
• Activities include preparing budgets, preparing and processing financial information, and initiating research and development	
☐ Total cost	$32.6

Trace cost to each activity. The purpose of tracing cost to each activity is to determine the cost of the activities. This step involves recasting cost from a departmental and expense-type base to an activity base; in other words, cost is recast from what it was spent *on* to what it was spent *for*. Tracing cost in this way is a time-consuming and detailed activity that involves interviews, analyses, and inspections of detailed cost information. The results of this step must be documented and preserved, since the methodology for recasting cost is integral to the ongoing CMS reporting.

Caution must be exercised when employees are interviewed to determine how they spend their time on various activities. The way that people actually spend their time, after all, can often be quite different than the way they *think* that they spend it. This disparity of perception can be used to explain why, in more sophisticated cost reporting, for example, labor cost may be collected on the basis of time cards that indicate activities performed.

Exhibit 2 illustrates a report from a company (again, *XYZ* Corporation) that recast cost from a departmental base to a business-process and activity base. This company produces a highly engineered piece of capital equipment for the oil service industry. Significant activities that were part of the business process are indicated in parentheses. From this exhibit, it is readily apparent that *XYZ* looks completely different when viewed from an activity standpoint.

Determine value-added vs. non-value-added activities and cost. Once activities are specified and cost is determined, the next step requires determining whether an activity and its cost are value-added or non-value added. This judgment should be made within the context of a companywide and well-understood definition for the terms.

Making non-value-added cost visible is one of the biggest benefits of CMS, but also one of the most difficult to achieve. For one thing, although employees may acknowledge the existence of waste and inefficiency on a companywide basis, they may find it difficult to acknowledge waste and inefficiency in their own areas. Also, defining what is value-added versus what is non-value added can be problematic.

Definitions of value-added and non-value added are often confused and misunderstood. To some, non-value added means waste; to others, it might mean the cost of quality; and to still others, it might mean everything other than touch labor. The reporting of non-value-added activities and cost can quickly become a "people" issue, because no one wants to be labeled as performing non-value-added activities; such labeling can easily be considered a threat to job security.

To address these ambiguities, therefore, a new CMS should report the cost of non-value-added activities within a predetermined, specific definition for a particular company in a particular industry. The CMS should focus on the activity, not on the people who perform the activity. The reporting of value-added and non-value-added activities and cost should be used to encourage and direct employee efforts to those activities that have value to customers.

At a minimum, the new CMS should provide a companywide estimate for non-value-added costs based on published case studies or on reliable empirical data. Even this minimum amount of clarification and visibility of non-value-added costs enables management to focus on the enormous opportunity available to improve the organization.

Determine output measures and volume. The purpose of determining output measures and volume is to select appropriate measures to accurately reflect an activity's cost, quality, cycle time, and customer satisfaction performance. In some cases, the volume information for the most meaningful measurement may be difficult or costly to obtain. In these situations, it is appropriate to select a measurement where the volume information is more readily attainable.

Select the appropriate cost drivers. A cost driver is a factor that has a direct influence on the cost and performance of activities. Cost drivers should explain why an activity's costs increase or decrease. Cost drivers are valuable because they enable management to focus on the cause of cost.

Selecting appropriate cost drivers is a creative process in the sense that it goes beyond traditional analyses in its search for the underlying reasons for cost. Many companies assume that the cost driver for manufacturing overhead is direct labor: The more direct labor, the more overhead. Consequently, reducing direct labor should lead to lower overhead.

Experience shows, however, that manufacturing overhead in many companies is driven not by direct labor but by the number of transactions and by the level of complexity on the plant floor. Significant correlations have been found between the number of part numbers, the number of engineering change notices, and the number of transactions on the shop floor and the amount of overhead. Correlation exists because significant amounts of overhead are required to balance, account, execute, confirm, and keep track of the various part numbers, engineering change notices, and transactions. Knowledge and understanding of cost drivers in these cases enabled management to attack the cause of cost by reducing the number of part numbers, engineering change notices, and transactions. In those cases where volume can be associated with cost drivers (e.g., number of part numbers), measurements can be established to gauge improvement efforts.

Trace costs to product cost objects. The purpose of tracing costs to product or service cost objects is to determine the pattern by which products or services consume the activities of the business. This step involves the creation of a bill of activities that lists all the resources (activity outputs) consumed by a product or service in a particular market, for a particular customer, or for a specific distribution channel. Linking the cost of activities directly to the products and services that consume the activities is the basis of product cost under the new CMS.

Once the initial Phase 1 data gathering and analysis are completed, the result should be a well-understood and clearly defined structure in which to develop the systems and procedures necessary to support ongoing CMS reporting.

Phase 2. Implementing procedures, systems, and methods

Phase 2 is the stage when procedures, systems, and methods needed for ongoing reporting are implemented. This phase often involves creating procedures to collect data for the first time, as well as redirecting information and other data sources from existing sources to the CMS.

Phase 2 is a true "hands on" period in the organization. It requires extensive training of personnel in the use of the new CMS. Due dates and implementation schedules should be established, and the quality requirements expected of data entering the new CMS should be standardized.

Phase 3. Maintaining the cost management system

Phase 3, unlike Phases 1 and 2, is an ongoing stage in the implementation of a new CMS. Phase 3 is the stage when the CMS is maintained. The resources required for maintenance include feedback on those activities and costs associated with the ongoing data gathering and information reporting. Feedback is also required about the resources and efforts needed to update, improve, and maintain the quality of reported data.

Activities change over time. Since activities are the basis of a new CMS, the system must be updated to reflect those changes. If estimates are used, they should be replaced with actual data. CMS improvements can be made

by identifying more accurate performance measurements. New products will also have to be costed. In short, Phase 3 reflects the concepts of continuous improvement. For the CMS implementation to be successful, Phase 3 must involve continual reassessment and effort.

Key factors for success

The design and implementation stages for a new CMS can often be quite technical in nature. These stages, however, must be supported by an entire array of both technical and nontechnical factors for the ultimate installation of the CMS to meet management's goals.

The key factors often associated with a successful CMS installation include:

- A cross-functional team;
- The company's "best and brightest";
- An environment that promotes waste reduction without job loss; and
- An easy-to-succeed first project.

Each of these supporting factors is discussed below.

A cross-functional team. A new CMS is an across-the-board phenomenon in an organization. Thus, it will have broad-based and pervasive effects on all employees and work strategies. A CMS has its best chance for success when a cross-functional team is associated with it. The cross-functional team should be comprised of various disciplines within the organization. It should include not only a representative from the accounting department, but also representatives from all departments affected by the CMS (e.g., production, engineering, marketing).

The best and brightest. The members of the cross-functional team will have high visibility. Their personal credibility often will lend legitimacy to the activities in which they are involved, including the cross-functional team. Thus, for a CMS to be perceived as an organizational priority and an important enterprise, members of the cross-functional team must be well respected by employees and managers. Members of the team must have previously demonstrated an ability to be flexible, innovative, and forward-thinking.

Exhibit 3. *Typical Time Line for Installation*
(Phase I Steps)

Steps	Time	Results
0. Data gathering and analysis	(months 1–5)	Visibility, relevance, and direction
1. Specify activities	(month 1; month 2)	Visibility of key activities and processes
2. Trace cost to each activity	(months 1–2)	Cost of key processes and activities
3. Determine value-added versus non-value-added cost	(months 2–3)	Visibility of non-value-added cost and assessment of waste
4. Determine output measures and volume	(month 3–4)	Preliminary performance data
5. Select appropriate cost drivers and measures	(month 4)	Cost driver analysis
6. Trace cost to individual product cost object	(months 4–5)	Estimating and pricing data product line profitability target costing

Months: 1 2 3 4 5 6

The company's best and brightest should be encouraged to join the cross-functional team involved with the new CMS. The leadership qualities that they bring to the team lend instant credibility to the new CMS. Since these employees often have strong communication skills, they can be the best advocates for the organization's new system. In its early and "bumpy" stages, a CMS will often have to traffic off the goodwill and respect that other employees have for the team members.

An environment promoting waste reduction without job loss. If a CMS is perceived as a "witch hunt" that is designed to eliminate jobs or to determine which managers are inefficient, the effort is doomed to failure. All companies have waste. The best companies develop an environment in which employees constantly look for ways to eliminate waste and do so without the threat of losing their jobs.

It is in such an environment that a CMS installation will thrive. Employees can broaden the horizons of the CMS effort if they feel that their jobs are not threatened. Liberated by this job security, they can often provide management with the most relevant feedback—straight from the shop floor, where the results of the system have the most impact. A collegial work environment and job security are assets in any CMS installation effort. They create an open atmosphere—one that is ripe for change.

An easy first project. An easy first project is a tried-and-true approach for any new undertaking, but especially for a new CMS. Building confidence is important with any new enterprise. Thus, instead of selecting the most difficult activities and business processes of the organization around which to design and implement a new CMS, management should target an area where information is easy to access and where only two or three departments are involved.

The experience gleaned from a successful easy-to-succeed first project will breed confidence in the employees involved with the new CMS. Once they become less tentative, they will be more receptive about applying the new CMS to the more complicated and difficult aspects of the business. As the initial activities are defined in this "easy" project, concentration should be on continuous improvement and waste reduction as a means to promote and finance the ongoing CMS effort.

Installation time lines

Once the supporting key factors for success are identified and satisfied, management must set time lines for the CMS installation. As a rule of thumb, the early phases of a CMS effort should involve a five- to eight-person team that is assigned to the project on a full-time basis for a period of from four to six months, regardless of the size of the business.

The variable in establishing these time lines is *scope*. For very large organizations, the resources available and the time lines needed may enable the cross-functional team to examine only two or three major business processes and perhaps twenty-five to thirty activities per year. Smaller businesses may be able to complete the entire CMS installation within a six-month period. Management, along with the cross-functional team, must determine what is reasonable for the organization to achieve and within what time line.

Exhibit 3 illustrates a typical time line plan that reflects the six general steps of the Phase 1 implementation.

Continuous improvement for success

To remain competitive in world markets, managers must continually improve the performance of activities and business processes. No organization can rest on its past success or performance. Improvements to processes, activities, and products must be continuous and ongoing.

Since improvement of processes and activities is fundamental to long-term survival, managers need relevant and timely feedback to enable them to judge the performance of activities. Existing financial and cost accounting systems do not produce the information managers require. The answer is the design and implementation of a new CMS.

A new CMS must be designed and implemented with two purposes in mind:

1. To gather financial and operating information that reflects the performance of activities; and
2. To supply management with relevant information to plan, manage, control, and direct the activities of the business in order to improve processes and products, eliminate waste, and execute business operations and strategies.

Yet a CMS, by itself, produces no increase in productivity, no reduction in cost, no improvement in quality, no reduction in cycle time, and no increase in customer satisfaction. Its true benefit can be measured only in light of management's actions initiated based on information provided by the new CMS. Those actions should be directed toward continuously improving the organization's activities and business processes through better decision making. ▲

Notes
1. J.G. Miller and T.E. Vollman, "The Hidden Factory," *Harvard Business Review* (September–October 1985): 142–150.
2. C. Berliner and J.A. Brimson, eds., *Cost Management for Today's Advanced Manufacturing* (Boston: Harvard Business School Press, 1988): 242.
3. M.E. Porter, *Competitive Advantage* (New York: The Free Press, 1985): chap. 1.

Budgeting and Control of Discretionary Costs

Donald W. Ramey

The budgeting and control of discretionary costs provides formidable challenges to management accountants because of the relative uncertainty surrounding correct or optimal levels of these costs. Organizations should adopt formal plans for managing these costs based on efficiency and effectiveness. If formal measurement systems are not feasible or cost justified, other subjective methods may be better than current incremental approaches. Subjective approaches may also be used to complement formal measurement systems.

How much should we budget for research and development (R&D) and advertising next year? What level of corporate support should be given to the operating divisions for personnel services, legal, and accounting? Given the expected enrollment, how much should we spend on faculty salaries for the coming academic year?

Questions such as these pose difficult problems for managers and management accountants because the costs in question are generally discretionary. That is, spending levels are based on management judgement and negotiation rather than on cost analysis or engineering studies.

Predictable and discretionary costs

Let's call one group of costs reasonably predictable (RP) and contrast those costs with discretionary costs (DC). Many RP costs relate to production and distribution functions, especially in manufacturing. Some RP costs are budgeted as fixed because the levels are expected to be relatively constant for a given range of activity. For example, depreciation is based on known book values and given de-preciation methods. Other fixed RP costs are contractual, such as rent on facilities and insurance on property. Even supervisory salaries are predictable in many manufacturing settings if direct labor or machine hours are predictable, and if an efficient supervisory span of control has been established.

For variable costs to be predictable, three factors must be known with reasonable accuracy, as the following equation illustrates:

$$\text{Budgeted Cost (\$)} = \text{Input per unit of output (I)} \times \text{Price per unit of input (P)} \times \text{Output or activity (O)}$$

For example, assume that each unit of product X requires about six direct labor hours (I) and that direct labor is paid $20 per hour (P). If we expect output (O) of product X to be ten units during a given period, we would budget $1,200 for direct labor costs.

In many manufacturing processes, the level of inputs required per unit of output (I) is relatively stable in the short run. (In the long run, however, the production process can be redesigned, nonvalue-added activities can be eliminated, suppliers can be changed, and productivity can be enhanced through investment.) Material input is often determined by a product's design. Labor input is determined

---

Material input is often determined by a product's design. Labor input in determined largely by the design of the production process.

---

largely by the design of the production process. Since the production process is an ongoing, repetitive activity with a measurable output (O), labor input can thus be estimated from experience. Other predictable costs include utilities, supplies, indirect labor, and repairs and maintenance. If supervision is adequate and absent evidence to the contrary, it can be inferred that past inputs per unit of output approximate a relatively efficient level.

Required input per unit. For discretionary costs, the observed input per unit of output (I) may vary over a wide range, whether because the output is not standardized (e.g.,

> *For discretionary costs, the required input per unit of output may vary over a wide range, whether because the output is not standardized (e.g., customer service calls) or because the production process is variable (e.g., teaching).*

customer service calls) or because the production process is variable (e.g., teaching). In addition, the output or activity level (O) driving the costs may not be readily measurable if the output is information or some nonquanti-

> *The output or activity level driving the costs may not be readily measurable if the output is information or some nonquantifiable service.*

fiable service. Examples of discretionary costs include:

- Research and design;
- Engineering;
- Marketing;
- Corporate support functions such as accounting and personnel; and
- Most production costs in not-for-profit industries and government.

Surrogate measures. Suppose that a company wants to budget customer service expendi-

tures for handling user inquiries related to product support. To budget, the company should have a measure of the expected output from customer services. Presumably, the real output is units of service that are consumed by customers and that increase customers' satisfaction and product loyalty. It is difficult

> *Companies often use a surrogate measure for output, such as the number of inquiries handled.*

to quantify such measures of real output, however, so companies often use a surrogate measure for output, such as the number of inquiries handled. This surrogate measure is referred to here as an "activity" to distinguish it from a measure of real output. The term "output" is used in a generic sense and can refer to either an activity or a real output.

In using activity measures to budget, the company should assume that a stable relationship exists between the activity and the related real output, because budget variations should be based on changes in real output and the cost per unit of real output. Even if a stable relationship exists between real output and a surrogate measure, however, the company in this example must still determine how much input (I) to budget per complaint or inquiry. Inputs include direct labor time and hardware (computer and telephone) support. The level depends on such factors as the complexity and age of the product, buyer knowledge, desired response time, and competitors' service policies. Given the many variables, budgeted service costs are often determined based on management judgement and negotiation, rather than on an analysis of past costs and outputs or engineering studies.

The nature of budgeting and discretionary costs

In setting budget levels, a company must determine the resources a department or function should use to achieve its expected output. The budget should be based on *effectiveness* and *efficiency*, where effectiveness implies that the output (O) is consistent with organizational goals, and efficiency is based on using the fewest resources (I) for the given output. In the case of manufacturing, effectiveness in production would suggest timely output with minimum standards of quality for a given physical product.

For such a discretionary cost as customer service, the output should result in satisfied, loyal customers. Hence, effectiveness might be measured by the percentage of repeat customers or based on surveys in which customers rank how satisfied they are with customer service. If the measure of effectiveness is stable, we may presume a correlation between real output and the activity measure for budgeting purposes. Efficiency may be approximated by a measure such as cost per inquiry.

In a department that is producing output effectively and efficiently, forecasted increases in activity measures should lead to a higher budget. Conversely, if inefficiency or slack exists, real output and activity can be increased with the same budgeted costs by eliminating inefficiency.

A decline in an effectiveness measure should lead to reduced budgets for any given volume of activity because the decline means a decrease in real output relative to the activity measure. Conversely, budgets based on activity should be increased to reflect actual or expected increases in effectiveness.

Incremental budgeting. In practice, budgets for discretionary costs are often incremental. In other words, they reflect expected changes in input prices and levels of workload or activity. Unfortunately, incremental budgeting assures neither an effective nor an efficient use of resources.[1] It is quite possible to have higher levels of activity with little or no increase in real output. This is especially true if real output is difficult to measure, as is true in many not-for-profit organizations.

While there is no single method to ensure efficiency and effectiveness in budgeting discretionary costs, different approaches have been successful. An organization may wish to try one or a combination of these approaches, subject to the traditional cost-benefit criteria.

Approaches to the control of discretionary costs

The goal is to budget discretionary expenditures efficiently and effectively. Some approaches are subjective in nature, while others rely on formal measurement systems of effectiveness and efficiency. The subjective approaches—each of which is discussed next—include priority incremental budgeting, organizational design, and organizational culture.

Priority incremental budgeting. Under priority incremental budgeting, managers are asked which activities or tasks they would change if significant budgetary decreases (e.g., decreases of 10 percent to 20 percent) occurred. This exercise forces managers to prioritize and justify expenditures. Even when real output is difficult to measure, the presumption is that a manager can and will subjectively rank activities such that the greatest expected real output per dollar of expenditure is achieved. Managers are then encouraged to redeploy resources toward those activities with the highest priorities. One result should be an increase in real output per dollar of spending—in other words, a more efficient budget.

Organizational design. An organization may provide centralized staff services (such as accounting, personnel, legal, and data processing) to its operating divisions. It is generally agreed that, when it is feasible, users should be charged for the services they use, but what level of charges will promote effectiveness and efficiency for centralized services?

To the extent that the charges cover full actual costs of operations, central services have little incentive to be effective or efficient; the system may also promote empire building. One alternative is to allow operating managers to decentralize the service (e.g., operating divisions may use microcomputers rather than rely on a centralized data processing department). Operating managers may also be allowed to purchase services externally if they cannot negotiate reasonable charges for central services.[2]

A profit center manager has an incentive to purchase service inputs that generate the greatest real output per dollar of expenditure. Although subjectivity is involved, an operating manager is the best judge of whether central services are competitive with services offered elsewhere. Failure to provide a high-quality service at a competitive cost should reduce the demand and budget for central services and thus promote greater efficiency and effectiveness.

Organizational culture. The term "organizational culture" refers to a set of shared values and beliefs that influence people's behavior toward achieving organizational objectives. Some alternative characteristics of a culture are:

• Individual accomplishment versus being a team member;
• Innovation and risk-tasking versus stability;
• Results orientation versus following the rules; and
• Customer focus versus financial results.

New managers are often recruited and selected on the basis of personal characteristics similar to those of successful established managers. Once hired, managers receive formal orientation to the values and expected behaviors and are given role models (e.g., successful managers) to follow.

A manager is evaluated by whether he supports the culture as determined by his behavior and actions. Presumably, actions that support the culture will lead to the production of output (often unmeasurable) that will result in the achievement of organizational objectives.

Performance evaluations may be subjective through the use of peer groups or objective using such techniques as behaviorally anchored rating scales. For each significant dimension of a job, critical behaviors (effective and ineffective) are identified for the manager and evaluation is based on actual versus critical behaviors. For example, in auditing, job dimensions include technical knowledge, client relations, and teamwork. For technical knowledge, effective behavior may be reflected in continuing education, while ineffective behavior results from seeking help for problems that should be solved independently.

Culture is a useful control device where effectiveness measures are difficult to implement. This may occur in such functions as R&D and in not-for-profit organizations. For example, the real output of the R&D function for a software firm should be information that leads to commercially successful products. We may use lines of code written as a measure of activity, but is effectiveness measured by the number of copyrights, number of commercially successful products, or dollars of sales of new and upgraded products? All these measures are subject to a lagged relationship with activity and a measure like dollars of sales reflects the effectiveness of marketing as well as of R&D.

Similarly, patients processed may be used as a measure of activity for a drug rehabilitation program. Real output and effectiveness are measured by the number of cured patients, but what is a cured patient? Is it a patient cured for one year, or five years, or life? Even if we agree on a measure of effectiveness, there is a lag between activity and real output, and it may be impossible to obtain follow-up data to measure cured patients (e.g., because patients move away and cannot be traced).

Formal measurement systems

Companies that use formal measures of efficiency and effectiveness need a standard for judging whether a function is efficient and effective. A cross-sectional approach compares the measures at some point in time with measures for comparable organizations. This provides a gauge of relative efficiency and effectiveness. Cross-sectional information may be obtained from such sources as trade publications, professional associations, or consultants, such as J.D. Powers.

Suppose, for example, that a company wants to budget costs for personnel services. Activities of the personnel function include recruiting and staffing, training, and compensation design. Based on these activities, the company develops surrogate measures of output for such budgeting purposes as the number of vacancies filled, number of employees trained, or total number of employees. The use of these measures depends, however, on whether the personnel department is operating efficiently and effectively.

If we assume that, consistent with organizational objectives, the real output of a personnel department should be units of service resulting in highly motivated and loyal employees, then effectiveness could be reflected in ratios concerning retention or promotion of employees. These ratios measure the percentage of employees hired in a given year who are still employed or have been promoted. Each year a new ratio is calculated. Efficiency might be measured by the ratio of hiring costs to employees hired in a year, by personnel cost per employee, or by a nonfinancial measure, such as average time to fill a vacancy.

The cross-sectional approach attempts to infer whether efficiency and effectiveness are high relative to comparable organizations. If the personnel function is judged to be effective and efficient, changes in such activity measures as number of vacancies filled may be a fairly reliable basis for the budget.

In judging relative efficiency and effectiveness from cross-sectional data, a trade-off between the measures should be recognized. Since the measure of efficiency is based on activity rather than real output, a relatively high cost per hire ratio in our example may be associated with either a high or low effectiveness measure. If so, to the extent that the added resources used per hire result in more real output and effectiveness, the high cost per hire does not reflect inefficiency and waste. Only when a high cost per hire is associated with low effectiveness should we presume inefficiency in the budget.

Lack of data on effectiveness. In practice, use of cross-sectional measures is limited because of the unavailability of data on effectiveness (which is based on organization-specific goals) and problems with comparability of financial data.[3] In judging relative efficiency, a company must determine which personnel costs to include in costs per hire. There may

be some consistency between companies with respect to direct costs (e.g., advertising, travel and relocation, costs of personnel staff, and fees paid to agencies), but organizations differ about how they allocate indirect corporate or headquarters costs to personnel. Some organizations may choose to include only the costs of the personnel department, while other organizations may include costs incurred in other departments that support the personnel function (e.g., costs related to a tour of the facilities). Nonfinancial measures appear to be better suited to cross-section analysis.

Time-series analysis. An alternative to cross-sectional analysis is the time-series approach, which views measures of efficiency and effectiveness over time and shows trends in these measures rather than optimal levels.

Time series measures are unique to an organization and are generally useful in suggesting which direction the budget should take rather some optimal level. Exhibit 1 shows a simple numerical example to illustrate how time series measures of effectiveness and efficiency should affect budget negotiations for discretionary costs. Ideally, the personnel costs used in the analysis should reflect all the costs of providing the personnel function, including costs incurred in other departments that support personnel functions.[4] This in itself may necessitate a significant measurement project if departments have considerable functional interaction.

The costs in Exhibit 1 are variable costs of hiring (e.g., interviewing costs, outside recruiting fees, and relocation costs). Fixed and semifixed costs (e.g., facility costs, supervi-

Exhibit 1. *Time Series Measures of Effectiveness and Efficiency*

Case	(1) Efficiency	(2) Forecasted Activity	(3) = (1) × (2) Preliminary Budget	(4) Effectiveness	(5) = (2) × (4) Real Output	(6) = $166.67 × (5) Final Budget
Base	$100	1,000	$100,000	60%	600	$100,000
1	100	1,200	120,000	60	720	120,000
2	120	1,200	144,000	60	720	120,000
3	120	1,200	144,000	72	864	144,000
4	100	1,200	120,000	58	696	116,000
5	100	1,200	120,000	62	744	124,000

Legend: Efficiency is measured by the cost per hire: forecasted activity is number of hires in a year; effectiveness is the retention ratio.

Measures of Efficiency and Effectiveness

Function	Efficiency	Effectiveness
Customer service	Cost/inquiry	Customer satisfaction survey
R&D (software)	Cost/line of code	New product sales ($)
Personnel	Cost/hire	Retention ratio
Sales	Marketing cost/sales $	Sales ($)
Accounting	Cost/accounts processed	Error rate
Accounting, cost	Cost/No. of reports	User satisfaction survey
Production	Cost/unit produced	Error rate, on-time production
Teaching	Student/faculty ratio	Applicants per vacancy, job offers per student
Health care	Cost/patient treated	Successful treatments/total treatments

Note: in practice, multiple measures of effectiveness and efficiency may be required to judge performance in a discretionary cost center.

---

sion, and advertising) would be added to the variable costs for the complete budget.

Base Case. Absent cross-sectional or other data to the contrary, the initial assumption is that the personnel function is relatively efficient and effective. If recent costs per hire in column 1 of Exhibit 1 were $100 and no added costs per unit are anticipated for inputs, the preliminary budget for 1,000 hires would be $100,000, as shown in column 3.

Effectiveness, as measured by the retention ratio in column 4, attempts to measure the real output of the personnel function in terms of loyal employees hired or developed. The 60 percent retention ratio means that for every 1,000 hires, 600 remain with the organization for some specified time period. This translates to a real output of 600, as shown in column 5. The final budget in column 6 is based on the $166.67 cost per unit of real output ($100,000/600) multiplied by the level of real output (600).

Case 1. If the measure of effectiveness in Column 4 of Exhibit 1 remains unchanged at 60 percent, in case 1, it can be assumed that real output will vary directly with activity. A 20 percent increase in hires to 1,200 will thus be associated with 720 employees remaining with the organization. A 20 percent increase in the budget may be justified based on this change in real output.

Case 2. In case 2, it is assumed that the cost per unit of inputs associated with hiring in-

creases to $120 and that the activity level will be 1,200 hires for the year. The preliminary financial budget thus suggests a need for $144,000. (The usual rationale for an increased budget when "incremental" budgeting is used is that "our input costs are going up.") As column 6 shows, however, if the retention ratio in column 4 remains unchanged at 60 percent, the higher level of activity justifies a final budget of only $120,000.

But what about the increase in the cost of inputs to $120 per hire? Based on our earlier equation, the efficiency measure, cost per hire, is composed of two parts:

$$\text{cost per hire} = \text{inputs per unit of output (I)} \times \text{cost per unit of input (P)}.$$

The term (I) is often referred to as a measure of the productivity of inputs, such that a decrease in (I) means an increase in productivity. An increase in the cost per hire reflects increases in the cost of our inputs (P) related to hiring (advertising, wages and salaries, travel) with no equivalent increase in the productivity of the inputs (I).

If effectiveness in column 4 is expected to remain unchanged from the base case, more costs per hire are budgeted to produce the same real output in terms of satisfied, loyal employees. The added spending adds no value to the organization and reflects an inefficient use of resources. An exception may occur (as in the present case) if the measure of effectiveness ("employees staying three years") follows the budget with a lag. But prior increases in the cost per hire can be analyzed to determine the subsequent impact on effectiveness. This should provide a guide for current budget levels.

Case 3. In case 3, the increase in spending per hire from $100 to $120 results in an increase in the retention ratio to 72 percent. This means that for every 1,200 new hires, we expect 864 to remain with the organization. This would justify a budget of 864 × $166.67, or $144,000. "If we want to hire better people, we have to spend more money recruiting them," is simply saying that increased effectiveness as well as activity levels may justify greater spending.

Case 4. A decrease in the retention ration from 60 to 58 percent associated with a per hire of $100 could reflect a decline in the performance of the personnel group or factors outside their control, such as a reduction in the size or quality of the labor pool. A decline in performance should be associated with a reduction in budgeted resources to $116,000, whereas a shrinkage in the labor pool may necessitate increased spending per hire, if the organizational goal is a stable retention ratio.

Case 5. Where the hiring function exhibits rising effectiveness and performance, the productivity gains can be shared with the activity by increasing the budget to $103.33 per hire ($124,000/1,200 hires). This increased cost per hire should reflect higher wages and salaries for the personnel involved in the activity.

Summary

The budgeting and control of discretionary costs provides formidable challenges to management accountants, not only because of the large dollar volume of these costs, but also because of the relative uncertainty surrounding correct or optimal levels of these costs. An organization should adopt a formal plan to manage these costs based on efficiency and effectiveness. Where formal measurement systems are not feasible or cost justified, other subjective methods may be better than current incremental approaches. Subjective approaches may also be used to complement formal measurement systems. ▲

Notes
1. Problems associated with traditional budgeting are discussed in Thomas A. Stewart, "Why Budgets Are Bad For Business," *Fortune* (June 4, 1990): 179–180, 186, 188.
2. For example, see H. Thomas Johnson and Dennis A. Loewe, "How Weyerhaeuser Manages Corporate Overhead Costs," *Management Accounting* (August 1987): 20–26.
3. David W. Young addresses many of the conceptual issues in cross-section analysis in "Cost Accounting and Cost Comparisons: Methodological Issues and Their Policy and Management Implications," *Accounting Horizons* (March 1988) 67–76.
4. For an excellent discussion of cross-functional costs, see A.J. Nanni, Jeffrey Miller, and Thomas Vollman, "What Shall We Account For?" *Management Accounting* (January 1988) 42–28.

Functional Costing for Better Teamwork and Decision Support

J. Stanton McGroarty and Charles T. Horngren

The primary focus of a cost accounting system should be on decision support. This article describes *functional costing*, a cost-effective replacement for many traditional cost systems. A functional costing system relates costs to the functional groups and physical things that make up the operations world. Functional costing provides more intelligible reports and also provides modeling tools that aid predictions of how decisions affect income.

Management accountants and academics have searched for a better cost accounting system. They are motivated to find a better cost system because managers are tired of surprises from monthly operating results: Managers do not like making decisions without knowing what will happen to the bottom line.

A common thread that runs through all developments in cost accounting throughout this century is the attempt to link causes and effects. An example is the long-standing (and often ignored) warning by writers of cost accounting textbooks about being misled by product costs that are based on plantwide overhead rates. Managers want to know how their decisions (the causes) create costs (the effects).

Decision support

The primary focus of a cost accounting system should be on decision support. This article describes *functional costing*, a cost-effective replacement for many traditional systems. Functional costing is an ongoing, regular accounting system that ties cost accounting to the physical world it models. The system is called *functional costing* because it is more useful (functional) than typical cost accounting systems. A functional costing system relates costs to the functional groups and physical things that make up the operations world. Functional costing is a user-friendly operations tool, but it also has a look and feel that is familiar to financial people. Users of functional costing systems agree that functional costing provides more intelligible reports. Functional costing also provides modeling tools that aid predictions of how decisions affect income.

The term *functional costing* is not new, though it has had various meanings. In a book published in 1955, for example, *functional costing* was used to describe what is essentially *activity-based costing* for marketing costs.[1] Instead of *cost drivers,* however, the term *control factor units* was used. The book explicitly discusses cause-effect relationships, as exemplified in this passage: "*Control* is a word expressive of a current causative relationship between some variable quantum and the amount of dollar cost, between sales and commissions, etc."[2]

ABC vs. functional costing. Regardless of their labels, all variations of functional costing and activity-based costing (ABC) are essentially attempts to link causes and effects. All cost systems associate costs with operating management of the business. For example:

- Natural expense (traditional) systems use the natural accounts to tell users "where the checks went" for all expenditures.
- ABC systems tie costs to activities to provide clues about why the expenditures were incurred.

- Functional costing ties costs to the things that were bought, thus relating physical changes to operational changes.

Of the three types of systems, functional costing often has the greatest appeal for operating people. Why? Because it provides a straightforward tool for modeling the cost impact of decision alternatives and because it supports contribution margin cost analysis for pricing and performance measurement.

As described in this article, functional costing blends old and new cost accounting concepts in a workhorse system intended for daily use. For firms that need the detailed analysis of ABC, a cost-effective approach may be to install functional costing first. Then functional group costs can be used to perform activity matrix analysis as desired. Thus, for some companies, the procession might well be from natural expense systems to functional costing to ABC.

The first part of this article describes functional costing and the logic behind it. The second part is a case study that describes the implementation of functional costing at a Midwestern pump manufacturing company.

The functional costing system: Focus on communications and decision support

Flawed communications between operating managers and financial managers are commonplace. Operating managers and engineers concentrate primarily on physical measures like headcount, machines, yields, and setup time. Financial managers and accountants, on the other hand, concentrate primarily on financial measures such as budgets, accruals, and overhead. Financial measures are essential. They quantify in monetary terms the ultimate effects of operating decisions. Their usefulness is multiplied when the whole organization can interpret and use them.

Most companies allow a great linguistic and cultural gulf to separate operating managers from financial managers. Nowhere is this clearer than in U.S. manufacturing, where top managers are usually characterized as "numbers types" or "operations types," as if the two were mutually exclusive. Perhaps it is no coincidence that the Japanese, who cross-train executives in finance, marketing, and production, often beat Americans in the market-

place. Even though Japanese organizational structures and cost systems look much like ours, their decision making is usually far less parochial.

A useful cost reporting system focuses on:

- Bridging communications gaps between all business functions. The system's modeling and reporting capability should be readily understood throughout the organization.
- Supplying decision support so that managers can better judge the impact of their decisions on total financial results, particularly on income.
- Relating cost classifications to the cost objects (things) that managers can do something about, especially human resources (employee headcount) and purchased resources (materials, parts, and other tangible assets like floor space and equipment).

Perspective on functional costing. Although the term functional costing is not exhaustively descriptive, it characterizes the main thrust of the approach to cost classification described in this article. The emphasis is on tying the financial model to the "real" decisions that managers make about people and purchases. Functional costing has a heavy "physical" flavor that operations people easily relate to.

Most accounting systems are based on natural cost classifications; that is, they group costs under the account most easily identified with the check disbursed. The natural cost classifications often represent the initial formal record in an accounting system, but, as was noted long ago: " . . . the expenditures are not made merely to acquire specific goods or services but rather to achieve certain objectives through the performance of specific functions."[3] The use of natural accounts necessitates breaking up the cost of physical objects among various accounts. For instance, the cost of a production worker is typically split among "direct labor," "payroll taxes," "overtime premium," and several fringe benefit accounts.

For the purposes of operational decision support, it helps to shift the focus away from where a purchase was made (i.e., natural costs) toward what was bought (i.e., functional or physical costs). Why? Because things that are bought are key reasons for costs. This means that natural accounts such as "payroll taxes" and "shift premium" are most useful when linked directly to the employees for whom the expenditure is made. As Arjay Miller, former president of Ford Motor Company, has said, "All costs walk in on two feet." This comment may have been an exaggeration, but it is a quotation worth remembering.

The results of breaking up the cost of physical objects among various accounts may at first seem methodologically untidy since some natural accounts do, in fact, correspond to real things in the business. Nonetheless, users of functional costing find that the new account structure improves decision support dramatically, because costs are associated with the real things that cause them.

Three rules of functional costing

Functional costing employs three rules:

1. Use account names that are real—physical things or functions—and capture the complete cost of each thing on one line.
2. Group accounts in order of variability in relation to units produced.
3. Minimize allocations.

The resulting information can be compiled and manipulated much like traditional cost reporting. By making the connection between the financial and physical worlds without excluding all traditional accounting concepts, functional costing provides a usable tool that financial and operations managers can share. Modest retraining and investment in computer power are required. The sections that follow expand on these three rules.

Account names

Functional costing uses line items with names like "tooling," "material handling," and "production utilities," which requires that many of the so-called natural accounts be reclassified. For example, a traditional line item like "payroll taxes," which represents checks written to a few government agencies, must be directly linked to the many employees for whom these taxes are paid. Twenty years ago this might have been unreasonable, but today most accounting and database software packages can make these links automatically.

Exhibit 1. *First Rule—Use Account Names That Are "Real Things"*

Line Item	People Cost	Purchased Cost	Total
Production labor	XXX		XXX
Utilities		XXX	XXX
Tooling	XXX	XXX	XXXX
Maintenance	XXX	XXX	XXX
Selling	XXX	XXX	XXXX
Depreciation		XXX	XXX

Once this step is taken, no translation is necessary between operations and financial worlds. For instance, the cost of a toolmaker (including base pay, payroll taxes, insurance, and fringe benefits) is captured on a single line (Exhibit 1). Thus, the cost of a short-run decision to hire or lay off a worker becomes clearer.

A traditional system will often model the decision to add a toolmaker as follows:

- Indirect labor rises by the amount of the new employee's wages;
- Six or seven fringe benefit accounts will rise by the amounts of various taxes, insurance premiums, etc.;
- Plantwide overhead rates will rise; and
- If it is a standard cost system and the new toolmaker was not budgeted, an overhead absorption variance will be created.

By contrast, if tooling cost is captured on one line, there is only one change: Tooling cost rises by the total of the toolmaker's salary, payroll tax, and fringe benefit costs.

Some natural accounts like "equipment depreciation" or "production material" or "utilities" remain in the functional costing statement because they represent the major (physical) purchased items affected by decisions. This approach gives an intuitively readable statement that managers like. The resulting format is illustrated later in the case study.

Group accounts by variability

The second rule focuses on how various costs tend to behave. Although assorted factors may cause costs to fluctuate, the volume of units produced is usually the dominant fac-

Exhibit 2. *Second Rule—Group Costs in Order of Variability*

Functional Costing Statement				Span of Control
Line Item	People Cost	Purchased Cost	Total	
Production Material		XXX	XXX	} Cell
Production Labor	XXX		XXX	
Factory Support				
Tooling	XXX	XXX	XXX	} Plant
Maintenance	XXX	XXX	XXX	
Utilities		XXX	XXX	} Division
Material handling	XXX	XXX	XXX	
Equipment depreciation		XXX	XXX	} Corporation
Etc.	XXX	XXX	XXX	
Nonfactory				
Accounting	XXX	XXX	XXX	
Product engineering	XXX	XXX	XXX	
Building depreciation	XXX	XXX	XXX	
Etc.	XXX	XXX	XXX	
SG&A				
Selling	XXX	XXX	XXX	
Administration	XXX	XXX	XXX	
Total	XXX	XXX	XXX	

"Variable" ↑   "Fixed" ↓

Note: Grouping by variability helps show which costs are affected by a particular decision

tor. If factors other than volume are significant, the classifications must be more detailed. For example, material handling costs may vary with the number of loads moved, but not necessarily with the number of units moved. In such cases, material handling may not be a variable cost in relation to units produced. Better still, the plant should be reorganized to avoid most material handling.

Exhibit 2 illustrates the general idea, which is based on the contribution approach that has long been popular. The contribution approach essentially advocates distinguishing between variable and fixed costs. In this way, managers are better able to measure how various costs will affect their short-run and long-run decisions.

Of course, many costs may be either fixed or variable, depending on the time frame and other elements of a particular situation. For this reason, the classifications of cost behavior should range from unambiguously variable costs (e.g., production material), to medium-period fixed costs (e.g., production supervision), to long-run fixed costs (e.g., central-office data processing operations). Appropriate data analysis and discussions within a knowledgeable management team can usually lead to a consensus concerning how costs behave and how they should be regarded for purposes of any specific decision. This approach has always been helpful, but it has been rendered unworkable by traditional systems that mix the costs of people and purchased items over a variety of line items.

Determination of variability is made much easier by the first rule (as explained previously), because differences in variability are based on physical relationships. Some (physical) things must be paid for, regardless of whether any product is produced or not; these costs are less variable than things like production material, which is purchased only

Exhibit 3. *Third Rule—Minimize Allocation*

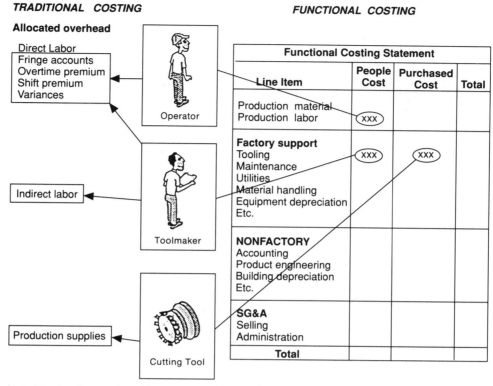

Note: Allocation disconnects cost from causes, making cost data useless for decision support

---

if production occurs. Relative variability in the physical world is easy to understand, so cost lines that link directly to physical things make it easier to determine cost variability.

Minimize allocations

Adherents of functional costing speak of three kinds of cost linking (see also Exhibit 3):

1. *Direct linking* is the specific identification of a cost with a given cost object in an economically feasible way. For example, a production worker's pay and fringe benefits are directly linked to production labor. The cost accounting literature often uses the term *direct costs* to describe direct linking and *indirect costs* to describe all other costs. (These costs are divided in functional costing as shown in the next two items.)
2. *Causal linking* is the linking of an indirect cost to a cost object on the basis of cause

and effect. For example, occupancy costs are often causally linked to departments in proportion to floor space occupied. Operating managers usually find causal linking credible.

3. *Residual linking* is the linking of an indirect cost to a cost object even though there is no strong causal relationship. For example, even though the plant manager's bonus may not be caused by a particular department or product, it is often arbitrarily linked with cost objects for purposes such as inventory valuation.

Most residual linking occurs with fixed costs, which are not caused by production of specific parts. (Of course, the definition of fixed costs is heavily dependent on a particular decision situation.) It is important to remember that, since residual linking uncouples a cost from its causes, residual costs are lost for purposes of decision making. This is the reason for minimizing residual linking.

As with traditional systems, second- and third-stage cost linkage is possible. For instance, the occupancy cost of the toolmaking department is typically encompassed in an hourly rate that is assigned to production departments on the basis of tool use. Similarly, consider the cost of floor space occupied by a building maintenance group. The cost of the occupied floor space is a part of building maintenance cost, which is encompassed in office and factory occupancy cost, and, in turn, is borne by production departments.

The main focus of cost accounting has often been inventory valuation. Any reasonable, consistent approach to cost linking can perform this task, but the resulting fully absorbed costs are not precise enough to support operating decisions. Unfortunately, that is how many managers use these costs. The third rule is designed to prevent this kind of misunderstanding. Wherever possible, costs should be directly or causally linked, rather than residually linked. By maintaining this connection between the physical and financial worlds, functional costing equips anyone who uses cost information to concentrate on the items that are affected by a particular decision—and to treat the rest as unaffected.

Case study: A functional costing system at work

Pump Company, a medium-sized pump manufacturer located in the Midwest, is a family-owned business with a fifty-year history of excellent engineering and high-quality products. The family has created a culture that breeds openness and teamwork, which eased the functional costing project considerably. Pump Company had reorganized much of its production into manufacturing cells: self-supervising work centers that produce complete products. The cell program was initiated because of a strategic decision—with no cost data to support it—to improve customer service. The financial impact of the program was unclear; the operational causes and the financial effects were murky.

During a cell project review, the company's president learned that the cell project had progressed to a point where 25 percent of his people produced 50 percent of his output in about 20 percent of his floor space. The cells had scored a major improvement in productivity, but no bottom-line relationship had emerged. The president called for financial help.

A multifunctional project team was formed. Team members were drawn from the accounting, manufacturing, manufacturing engineering, systems, and materials functions.

Developing a snapshot

The team began its investigation by recasting a year's costs into a functional costing statement. Exhibit 4 compares this "snapshot" statement with the traditional cost statement that preceded it. The traditional statement is dominated by a "natural" chart of accounts. In contrast, the functional costing statement is dominated by a "functional" classification that attempts to capture the cost of an operation-related item on one line. The team decided how to construct the new classification. Each cost line has a label that is significant to operations people, and each line shows people costs and purchased costs. The team also grouped costs in operationally relevant blocks:

- Production material;
- Production labor;
- Factory support;
- Occupancy;
- Nonfactory support; and
- Selling, general, and administrative (SG&A).

In accordance with the second rule, these blocks were arranged in order of variability, but they were also found to align with the responsibility spans of various plant management levels.

When the original statement was complete, the team reviewed the classifications to determine whether any specific cost control actions should be taken. Early results were promising. The first target that emerged was to reduce the costs of several expensive factory functions like material handling, expediting, and production supervision. The team then tried to identify factory changes that would make it possible to eliminate these functions. Complete cellularization of the factory was the obvious answer.

Exhibit 4. *Traditional vs. Functional Cost Statements*

Pump Company—Traditional Cost Statement

Cost Area	Cost	Percent Of Cost
Direct Cost		
Direct material	46,752	46.8
Direct labor	9,699	9.7
Indirect Cost		
Fringe benefits	3,846	3.8
Indirect labor	3,705	3.7
Payroll tax and insurance	3,471	3.5
Depreciation	3,274	3.3
Maintenance	1,881	1.9
Engineering	1,857	1.9
Production supplies	1,256	1.3
Tooling	1,054	1.1
Utilities	1,036	1.0
Factory supervision	988	1.0
Rentals	957	1.0
Quality assurance	932	0.9
Leasehold expense	660	0.7
Maintenance supplies	603	0.6
Office supplies	582	0.6
Data processing	474	0.5
Purchasing	470	0.5
Accounting and credit	437	0.4
Other production expenses	387	0.4
Real estate tax and insurance	294	0.3
Packaging material	233	0.2
Human resources	232	0.2
Waste disposal and environment	146	0.1
Sales, Gen'l. and Admin.		
Brokerage fees	3,656	3.7
Administration	2,751	2.8
Travel and entertainment	2,439	2.4
Sales	1,878	1.9
Public relations	1,767	1.8
Fleet car expense	1,046	1.0
Research and development	943	0.9
Marketing	294	0.3
Total	100,000	100.0

Pump Company—Functional Costing Statement

Cost Area	People Cost	Purchased Cost	Total Cost
Production Material			
Material		46,207	46,207
Freight in		545	545
Paint and process chemicals		401	401
Subtotal material		47,153	47,153
Production Labor			
Manufacturing	12,609		12,609
Subtotal production labor	12,609		12,609

Cost Area	People Cost	Purchased Cost	Total Cost
Factory Support			
Equipment depreciation		2,957	2,957
Tooling	1,408	1,053	2,461
Material handling	1,632	89	1,721
Factory supervision	1,285		1,285
Quality assurance	1,211	49	1,260
Equipment maintenance	768	484	1,252
Factory engineering	945		945
Shipping	933	233	1,166
Data processing	616	257	873
Production supplies		855	855
Expediting	844		844
Production utilities		700	700
Purchasing	611	12	623
Other production expenses		297	297
Waste disposal and environment	159	145	304
Subtotal production support	10,412	7,131	17,543
Occupancy Costs			
General expense		1,314	1,314
Building maintenance	1,366		1,366
Real estate tax and insurance		294	294
Janitorial	152	119	271
Subtotal occupancy	1,518	1,727	3,245
Nonfactory Support			
Product engineering	1,469		1,469
Accounting and credit	568	81	649
Human resources	302	183	485
Subtotal nonfactory	2,339	264	2,603
Sales, Gen'l. and Admin.			
Selling	2,442	6,096	8,538
Administration	1,510	3,593	5,103
Marketing	382	1,767	2,149
Research and development	495	562	1,057
Subtotal SG&A	4,829	12,018	16,847

	People Cost	Purchased Cost	Total Cost
Total cost	31,707	68,293	100,000

Note: The functional cost statement is a familiar looking presentation, but the data are new

Cellular manufacturing

Cellular manufacturing reduces the need for in-process inventory and, thus, working capital and floor space; it also improves quality by reducing inspection, scrap, and rework cost. The chief cost advantage of cellular manufacturing, however, comes from the elimination of non-value-adding activities that occur between production operations in a traditional plant. Product moves, storage activities, and some cleaning and inspection steps are partially or fully eliminated by cellularization. Consequently, material handling can be cut by as much as 90 percent, and in-house expediting is almost eliminated. However, these reductions have their greatest effect when *all* manufacturing is cellular. Until then, the material handling and expediting organizations are needed to support the remaining noncellular operations. Many costs behave in this "lumpy" manner. This lumpiness explained the company's failure to realize any significant bottom-line improvement from its first few manufacturing cells.

The team made a manufacturing plan that identified the number of production workers and supervisors needed to staff a fully cellular facility. The manufacturing labor figures made it easy to determine the cost impact of reductions in manufacturing headcount. The functional costing statement also identified the major cost impacts of expediters and material handling people and equipment. Therefore, it was easy to quantify the cost reduction potential of reducing the fork lift population to one truck per shift and eliminating in-house expediting.

A review of the other cost lines led to the discovery that, since about a third of the factory floor space would be vacated by the shift to cells, it would be possible to make rather than buy parts and thus reduce total costs. Knowing that some costs would not actually vanish because of cellularization, the team selected the term "unused resources" for all excess cost and produced the statement shown in Exhibit 5.

The company's president had been considering the construction of an additional facility. After reviewing the new cost statement, he scrapped the expansion plan and told his operations people to complete cellularization.

Functional costing helped in making this decision because it provided causal connections between proposed actions and financial impacts. Without functional costing, extracting this kind of information would have required a special study.

Linking costs to product lines

Given the decision to divide manufacturing into product cells, the team focused on costs by product line. Production material and cell labor were captured from the bill of material. Factory support costs were linked to products based on the cost drivers identified through discussions with the operating managers of the various functions. Occupancy costs were linked to products in proportion to the actual floor space covered by the product cell and its inventory.

In accordance with the third rule, nonfactory costs were causally linked as much as possible, with a few residual linkages remaining. Working with account lines that corresponded to functional groups, it was surprisingly easy to make these appropriate linkages:

- Product engineering was analyzed with an activity matrix and linked to the appropriate product lines.
- Accounting and credit were linked by the number of customer orders handled by each cell.
- Human resources was linked in accordance with employee headcount.
- SG&A departments were asked where they spend their time, and specific new product development and marketing programs were broken out and linked with the relevant products. The team agreed that the remaining SG&A costs would be linked in proportion to cost of goods sold—admittedly an arbitrary (residual) linkage.

This split permitted the team to produce a set of product-line functional costing statements, each having the same line items as the summary statement.

Product costing and inventory valuation

Product-line cost figures are needed for decisions concerning pricing, product mix, make-or-buy decisions, and inventory valuation. Exhibit 6 shows the pricing worksheet that the team generated for new products pro-

Exhibit 5. *Pump Company Cost Reduction Opportunity*

Cost Area	Current Production Cost	Cellular Production Cost	Unused Resources
Production Material			
Material	46,207	46,207	
Freight in	545	545	
Paint & process chemicals	401	401	
Subtotal material	47,153	47,153	
Production Labor			
Cell labor	12,609	8,839	3,770
Subtotal production labor	12,609	8,839	3,770
Factory Support			
Equipment depreciation	2,957	2,957	
Tooling	2,461	1,929	532
Material handling	1,721	248	1,473
Factory supervision	1,285	919	366
Quality assurance	1,260	1,260	
Equipment maintenance	1,252	1,252	
Factory engineering	945	945	
Shipping	1,166	1,166	
Data processing	873	873	
Production supplies	855	855	
Expediting	844	252	592
Production utilities	700	700	
Purchasing	623	623	
Other production expenses	297	246	51
Waste disposal & environment	304	252	52
Subtotal Prod. Support	17,543	14,477	3,066
Occupancy Costs			
General expense	1,314	1,043	271
Building maintenance	1,366	1,084	282
Real estate tax & insurance	294	233	61
Janitorial	271	215	56
Subtotal occupancy	3,245	2,575	670
Nonfactory Support			
Product engineering	1,469	1,469	
Accounting & credit	649	649	
Human resources	485	364	121
Subtotal nonfactory	2,603	2,482	121
Sales, Gen'l. and Admin.			
Selling	8,538	8,538	
Administration	5,103	5,103	
Marketing	2,149	2,149	
Research & development	1,057	1,057	
Subtotal SG&A	16,847	16,847	

	Current Production Cost	Cellular Production Cost	Unused Resources
Total cost before tax	100,000	92,373	7,627

Note: The team projected major cost reductions from cellular manufacturing. Secondary effects (e.g., in purchasing, quality control) were ignored at the planning stage

Exhibit 6. *Product Cost Worksheet*

Incremental Variable Costs:			
Production material	$65.00		
Production labor	15.00		
Additional factory support	3.00		
Incremental Production Costs		$83.00	
Marketing	$ 0		
Selling	0		
Engineering	0		
Working capital cost increase (decrease)*	3.50		
Incremental Non-Production Costs		3.50	
Incremental Product Costs			$ 86.50
Fixed Costs (normally linked):			
Factory support	$20.00		
Occupancy	1.00		
Fixed Manufacturing Costs		$21.00	
Nonfactory support	$ 3.50		
Marketing	1.00		
Selling	6.50		
Administration	4.50		
R&D	.50		
Fixed Nonmanufacturing Costs		16.00	
Total Fixed Product Costs			37.00
Full Product Cost			$123.50

* Impact of change in inventory and receivables
Note: Contribution margin logic shows incremental, fixed, and full product cost

---

duced in a cell. Contribution margin logic was used to design the worksheet:

- Production material, labor, and additional support (in this case an in-house plating operation) are straightforward computations, using the new account lines.
- The marketing, engineering, and sales lines depict amortization of estimated project costs over the expected volume of business throughout the product's life cycle.
- The cost effect of the working capital increase is based on the estimated increase in inventory and accounts receivable for the new product.
- Fixed costs that would be residually linked to a comparable amount of current production are included. This establishes the fully loaded break-even cost.

This approach provides the pricing committee with all the cost data needed for decisions to introduce a product at incremental cost, to price a niche product at a premium, or to maintain current levels of profitability on a routine order. A fully loaded cost number is generated, but the relative roles of variable and fixed costs are spotlighted.

As with pricing support, inventory valuation can be developed using the same model. A manufacturing cell can usually be modeled as a single operation, so the cost sheet would look similar to the pricing model. In more complex factories or when multiple passes through the cell are required, multiple sheets are used and the results are totaled.

The cellular manufacturing environment simplifies product line costing, as it does product line management, but the same logic can be applied to each manufacturing operation in a traditionally organized plant. The key is to include both non-value-adding operations (e.g., storage and material handling) and value-adding steps. In all cases, it is wise to have as many costs as feasible directly or causally linked to the related operations or parts.

Make-or-buy decisions

The same contribution margin logic applies to make-or-buy decisions. The first step is to

Exhibit 7. *Make or Buy?*

TRADITIONAL APPROACH				FUNCTIONAL COSTING			
Make		**Buy**		**Make**		**Buy**	
Materials	$10	Purchase price	$30	Materials	$10	Purchase price	$30
Labor	5	Freight in	2	Labor	5	Freight in	2
Overhead	20			Fixed costs	20	Fixed costs	20
Total Cost	$35	Total Price	$32	Total Cost	$35	Total Price	$52

TYPICAL DECISION ↓ BUY!	BEST DECISION ↓ MAKE!

Note: Functional costing systems point the make-or-buy decision in the right direction by using real operating costs directly from the financial statements

consider which costs will change depending on whether an item is made or purchased, then use only those costs to model the decision.

Exhibit 7 compares a small-scale make-or-buy review as it is often performed under full-absorption systems to a make-or-buy review using relevant cost analysis and functional costing. In the traditional scenario, the decision is made to buy the product, because $20 of overhead cost is considered related to the direct labor that goes into producing the part. In the functional costing scenario, the $20 is recognized as a fixed cost and treated the same whether the part is made or bought, so the "make" decision becomes obvious. (This approach is, of course, already used in contribution margin analysis by many companies.)

Larger-scale make-or-buy decisions (e.g., an automaker's decision whether to make or buy engines) require a more sweeping approach. Decisions on this scale could benefit greatly from construction of à functional costing statement for the whole business unit. Each line must be challenged, and before and after scenarios must be established to capture the cost impact of changes in, for example, floor space requirements, material control staffs, and data processing needs.

Fitting functional costing to the data processing system

Pump Company was scheduling its plants with a highly modified version of an old materials requirements planning (MRP) system. The move to cells eliminated the need for a

shop floor scheduling module, but the team members were concerned about the ability of the old system to support functional costing.

Exhibit 8 shows the result of the team's investigation. The data already collected for the order entry, inventory control, and manufacturing cost systems were adequate to support functional costing, but their reports were all "hard coded" (i.e., preprogrammed into the software). Although the reports could have been reprogrammed, the expense would have been high.

After a member of the team from data processing began working on a set of reports using a personal computer, a stroke of luck made the reports unnecessary. The accounting department had lost patience with its old general ledger package and was searching for a new one. The ability to generate flexible reports was added to the list of purchase criteria for the new general ledger package, so development of a PC-based translation tool was obviated.

Data used by the traditional system-supported functional costing and the new report generators provided the needed output. This is not surprising; generation of functional costing reports is within the capabilities of most current data processing systems. Occasionally a software upgrade or add-on report generator is required.

Functional costing and GAAP

Once the team had assembled the documentation to describe the new cost accounting system, they asked the firm's auditors to review

Exhibit 8. *Flow of Data for Product Line Statements*

Data	Processing	Reports

Production materials:
• Vendor invoices
• Bill of material

Direct labor:
• Payroll distribution

Payroll system

→ Direct Linking

Overhead:
• Inventory as expense
• Depreciation
• Invoices
• Salary
• Time cards (temp.)
• Fringe benefits

Accounts payable system
General ledger system

→ Causal Linking

Nonfactory support:
• Accounting
• Data processing
• Human resources
• Engineering

Sales, gen'l. and admin.

→ Causal and Residual Linking

Product Line Statements

Note: Functional costing uses existing data gathering and systems support

---

it and to rule on whether it could supply adequate tax data. Again, functional costing paid off through the use of a traditional balance sheet and report formats that were familiar to the auditors.

Their conclusion was that the output from the functional costing system would allow for much better tracing of costs to causes, resulting in much more precise inventory valuation. No new ground had to be plowed to fit the functional costing output to generally accepted accounting principles (GAAP).

Progress to date

The functional costing specification project began in early 1991 with an eight-week design phase (Exhibit 9). Since then, the team has loaded the functional costing report formats into the new general ledger package. The company is now using the reports for performance measurement and pricing support.

Largely because of insights gained during the functional costing project, Pump Corporation is now in the final stages of cellularizing its plant. New products are being developed to fill the soon-to-be-vacant floor space, and no new construction is planned.

Case summary

Functional costing contributed importantly to managing Pump Company's operations. The new system made it clear that cellular manufacturing made economic sense from the standpoints of both operating costs and capital conservation. It also helped solve a much longer-standing problem.

Like many mature businesses, Pump Company had a history of developing new products that later became commodities. When certain models became commodities, niche producers would cut prices on the high-volume products and capture the business, leaving only the high-engineering, low-volume portion of the market for Pump Company. Functional costing in a cellular manufacturing environment has shown Pump Company the extent to which the commodity

Exhibit 9. *Timing of Functional Costing Project*

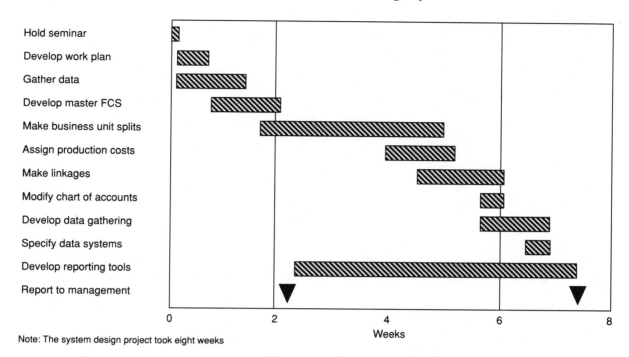

Note: The system design project took eight weeks

---

portion of its business had been subsidizing the special products, and Pump has repriced accordingly. Market response is still uncertain, but the sales people are optimistic.

Pump Company continues to discover new benefits of functional costing. Managers know better what their individual products cost to produce, so they are making wiser pricing decisions, and they have eliminated much non-value-adding work from their operations. But the most important development, according to the CEO, is that the teamwork between operations and financial people is producing better decisions than ever before.

Conclusion

A major attraction of functional costing is its cost-effectiveness and its adoption as an inte-

gral part of an ongoing, regular accounting system. Functional costing is a pragmatic crystallization of old and new cost accounting concepts. It helps span the communications gaps between financial and operating people, and frequently provides vastly improved information for wiser decision making. ▲

Reprinted from *Journal of Cost Management,* Winter 1993, pp. 24–36. Copyright © 1993 by Warren Gorham Lamont, a division of Research Institute of America Inc. All rights reserved. Used by permission.

Notes
1. For example, see D. Longman and M. Schiff, *Practical Distribution Cost Analysis* (Homewood, Ill.: Irwin, 1955): 110, 188, 348.
2. *Id.* at 167.
3. *Id.* at 70.

Is Anything Really Wrong With Cost Management?

P.L. Primrose

Advanced manufacturing techniques and just-in-time manufacturing can affect cost management systems in many ways. As this column points out, however, the problems that arise with traditional cost systems (especially about investment decisions) can often be attributed either to failings in the procedures companies use or to the application of cost information to decisions for which it was never intended. Most companies would do better to concentrate on how to apply existing principles correctly, rather than trying to develop new principles for measuring and controlling manufacturing costs.

There is an all-but-universal belief that the complexities of modern manufacturing—such as those brought about by the introduction of advanced manufacturing technology (AMT) or the need to work in a just-in-time (JIT) environment—mean that traditional cost management systems are inadequate and that new systems need to be developed.

Many examples from industry have been adduced to support this belief. However, a common feature of much of this literature is that the symptoms are described, but not the cause or the solution. As a result, many organizations have come to believe that they must develop an alternative to their existing cost management systems. They have sometimes tried to accomplish this without first clearly defining the problems that they have had with their old cost systems.

This column is based on work over the past five years with companies interested in introducing AMT. The work concentrated on defining *why* an existing cost management system seems to have problems rather than attempting to develop a new cost management system. In every case studied, the reasons why problems occurred could be identified. It was also possible in every case to show how the problems could be overcome by using existing cost management principles.

Investment appraisal

Many of the problems of costing start with investment justification. One of the biggest difficulties encountered is the need to correctly identify changes in cash flow. This occurs (at least in part) because some of the benefits of AMT are often considered intangible and—by implication—unquantifiable. But there is no such thing as an intangible benefit: Every benefit that can be identified can be redefined, quantified, and included in an investment appraisal. No benefit should ever be excluded on the grounds that it is intangible.

Quantifying every benefit is important because it overcomes the main excuse managers have for making investments without an evaluation. More importantly, if some benefits fail to be quantified, the project cannot be correctly reflected in the company's cost system. While all the costs of a project will be known and included in the cost system (because the bills have to be paid), major benefits are often reflected only as unplanned variances. However good a project may be, if benefits that exceed costs are not projected and planned in an initial evaluation, the project will invariably be shown as a financial failure.

JIT. The importance of correctly defining the objectives of an investment is illustrated in much of the literature about JIT. JIT is an operating philosophy based on the belief that it is necessary to make everything "just in

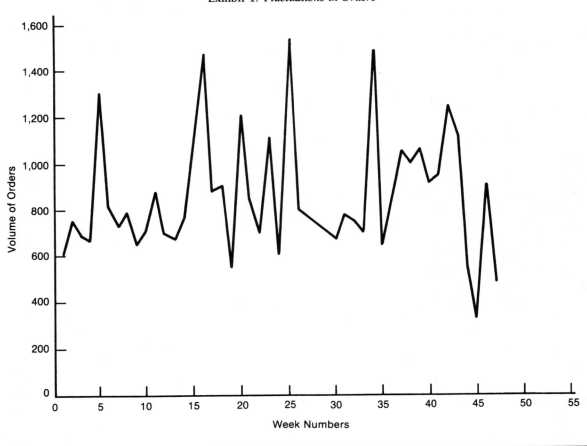

Exhibit 1. *Fluctuations in Orders*

time," while at the same time reducing inventory. The justification for JIT is often based on the platitude "just in time, not just in case."

Although the introduction of JIT in a company can lead to large expenditures of financial and management resources, the benefits of JIT are rarely quantified in advance, because the introduction of JIT is not normally considered an investment decision. As a result, the cost of introducing JIT is usually not evaluated.

Exhibit 1 shows how the volume of orders varied in one company. When manufacturing lead times are long, these fluctuations do not matter much. As the company attempts to reduce both lead times and inventory levels, however, at some point, the factory's output must be able to adapt rapidly to meet short-term changes in sales volume. At the same

time, an increase in productive capacity will be required, because the closer the factory response time becomes to the receipt of sales orders, the greater the company's required capacity.

In the past, the company in Exhibit 1 may have been able to meet customer demands with a capacity of 800 units. As lead times decrease, however, the company may need to increase its capacity to over 1,000 units. Keep in mind that there will also be periods when the factory output will drop well below the 800-unit level.

Although increased flexibility is sometimes cited as a benefit of JIT, in cases such as this, the increased flexibility is not itself a benefit. In fact, providing the increased flexibility represents a considerable cost. To provide the flexibility needed to cope with the reduced lead times associated with JIT, the company has to invest in additional capacity. Unless the expected benefits of JIT, such as increased sales, are forecasted, not only will it be difficult to justify any capital expenditure required (except as an act of faith), but the increased capacity will be reflected as an increase in standard costs.

Another company that attempted to introduce JIT invested considerable resources into reducing its manufacturing lead time from four weeks to one week. The company found that it had to continue to quote eight weeks delivery time to customers, because this was the only way the company could respond to fluctuations in product mix and sales volume without having a considerable increase in manufacturing capacity. In fact, the financial benefits that the company obtained were negligible.

Companies that have introduced JIT may have been aware of the costs involved, but their failure to define and quantify the benefits has led to the belief that cost management systems are somehow inadequate for dealing with the JIT environment. In reality, the problem is that no one has defined the objectives of JIT in quantifiable terms.

Replacement decisions

Only a small proportion of the extensive literature written about investment appraisal deals with practical applications. Even when practical examples are given, they are normally simplistic. For example, examples often consider the proposed investment in isolation (as happens in "green field site" projects). They rarely take into account the changes that will take place in the existing facilities.

In practice, most investment decisions are for the replacement of existing facilities. The replacement element may be obvious, such as the simple replacement of an old machine for a new one, or the replacement of drawing boards by computer-aided design (CAD). It may be less obvious in expansion situations where the investment in increased capacity is likely to involve the replacement of some of the existing equipment.

Evaluating replacement decisions is complex because the cash flows from an investment must be compared to cash flows that would occur if the investment were not made. If

there are many complex levels to be considered, it is important to start by evaluating the lowest-cost option, because many of the benefits may be obtained from that level of investment. Even if the most expensive option could be justified in comparison with the existing situation, the extra costs involved may not produce any significant additional benefits.

Evaluating the cheapest option

The procedure is first to evaluate the cheapest option, then to compare the additional costs against the additional benefits of the next cheapest option. Doing the evaluations this way identifies the most profitable investment and does not try to justify investment in the most complex technology possible (unless that also happens to be the most profitable choice). The following simplified example illustrates the process.

Example. A company has two old manual lathes that are in poor condition and used for two shifts. The choice is whether to replace them with two new manual lathes (which cost $20,000 each), a new computer numerical control (CNC) machine (which costs $80,000), or a flexible manufacturing module (or FMM, which costs $150,000). Each alternative has a life of ten years and equivalent capacity.

If the existing machines are not replaced, the annual maintenance cost would be $2,000 per machine. In addition, the annual cost of scrap would be $3,000 per machine.

Comparing investment in two manual machines with the alternative of doing nothing gives:

| | Investment in Two New Manual Lathes | | | |
	Year 0	Year 1	Year 2	Years 3 to 10
Capital cost	$(40,000)			
Savings		$10,000	$10,000	$10,000
Cash flows	$(40,000)	$10,000	$10,000	$10,000

This would give an internal rate of return (IRR) of 21.4 percent, so the investment would be justified.

Investing in CNC machines would cost $80,000, but would avoid the expenditure of $40,000 for manual machines. Since only two operators would be needed with the CNC machines (instead of four), the company would realize savings of $10,000 per operator each year. Since existing maintenance costs and scrap would be avoided by investing in manual machines, those costs cannot be claimed as additional savings for CNC. The cash flows are as follows:

Investment in Computer Numerical Control (CNC) Machines

	Year 0	Year 1	Year 2	Years 3 to 10
Capital cost	$(80,000)			
Capital avoided	40,000			
Savings		$20,000	$20,000	$20,000
Cash flows	$(40,000)	$20,000	$20,000	$20,000

This would give an IRR of 49 percent, so the additional investment would be justified.

Investing in FMM would cost $150,000, but would allow the company to avoid an expenditure of $80,000 on CNC machines. The FMM would only need one operator, which would thus yield an additional saving of $10,000 per year. The cash flows are as follows:

Investment in Flexible Manufacturing Module (FMM)

	Year 0	Year 1	Year 2	Years 3 to 10
Capital cost	$(150,000)			
Capital avoided	80,000			
Savings		$10,000	$10,000	$10,000
Cash flows	$(70,000)	$10,000	$10,000	$10,000

This would give an IRR of only 7 percent, so the additional investment would not be justified. Note, however, that if the first two stages are omitted, an evaluation of FMM against the existing situation would compare a capital cost of $150,000 against annual savings of $40,000, giving an IRR of 23.4 percent, which would suggest that an investment in FMM would be viable.

Subsequent and delayed projects

Normally, an implicit assumption of investing in AMT is that the project is the first of a series. At the end of a project's life, in other words, the assumption is that the AMT will be replaced by similar or better AMT. When technical innovations occur rapidly (which is usual in the early years of a new technology), additional savings should easily justify the second-generation replacement.

The problem perceived by many companies, however, is: What happens if the rate of innovation slows down and stops? Will potential savings be enough to justify the

replacement? To illustrate, consider a project with a life of five years that generates the following cash flows:

	Year 0	Years 1 to 5
Capital cost	$(10,000)	
Savings		$3,000

These cash flows give an IRR of 15.2 percent.

If it is assumed that, at the end of five years, the investment is replaced by another investment that is identical, the cash flows become:

	Year 0	Years 1 to 4	Year 5	Years 6 to 10
Capital cost	$(10,000)		$(10,000)	
Savings		$3,000	$3,000	$3,000

These cash flows also give an IRR of 15.2 percent.

At the end of a project's life, if the investment is not replaced by equivalent or better equipment, conditions will revert to those that existed when the original evaluation was made. If conditions were to revert to the original state, an evaluation would then produce a case for replacement as good as the one that existed at the time of the original investment.

Allowing for technical advances

The situation becomes more complicated if new technology is constantly being developed and is not yet available. The decision is whether to invest in currently available technology to obtain some benefits today versus delaying investment in the hope of obtaining larger benefits in the future.

When evaluating the alternatives, it is important to define the nature of the expected additional benefits, with both the additional costs that will be incurred and the additional benefits being quantified. It is also necessary to make an accurate assessment of the delay before the new technology will become available, including any allowance for commissioning new (possibly prototype) equipment, as compared with the time to install existing proven technology.

Assume, for example, that a company has a choice between investing $10,000 in available technology that will produce savings of $2,000 per year for ten years, or delaying investment for two years, at which time the cost will be $15,000, but the savings will be $4,000 per year, again for ten years. It would not be worth investing $10,000 now and then replacing it in two years at an additional cost of $15,000 to obtain the additional savings of $2,000 per year. The cash flows from investing now, compared with doing nothing, are as follows:

Cash Flows From Investing Now

	Year 0	Years 1 to 10
Capital	$(10,000)	
Savings		$2,000

These cash flows give an IRR of 15 percent.

The cash flows from investing in two years, again compared with doing nothing, are:

	Year 2	Years 3 to 12
Capital	$(15,000)	
Savings		$4,000

These cash flows give an IRR of 23.4 percent, which is a far better return than investing now in existing technology. Since the investments are not mutually exclusive, the evaluation in each case is done against the alternative of doing nothing rather than evaluating the two options against each other.

Machine utilization

Once the problems of investment appraisal are identified, a second set of problems appears. Specifically, how can investments be correctly reflected in the company's cost system? Disappointing financial results of using AMT in the past have usually resulted from a failure to reflect investments in AMT properly in cost systems.[1]

As part of the process of representing investments in cost systems, one of the factors that needs to be estimated is expected machine utilization. Many companies installed their cost systems at a time when capital costs were relatively low and direct labor was the largest cost. Since utilization levels were not considered critical, little attention was paid to them (even though utilization rates can vary between 1 and 168 hours per week).

Depreciation. With the advent of AMT, capital costs have been increasing. Now, depreciation is often a much larger element of standard costs than labor. If the level of utilization is incorrectly forecasted, the depreciation rate per hour will be wrong. For example, if depreciation is calculated on the basis of utilization of eighty hours per week, but the actual utilization is only eight hours, the depreciation value included in the rate per hour for the machine will be only 10 percent of its correct value.

If the forecasted utilization is wrong, the allocation of overhead other than depreciation will be only slightly inaccurate, because the machine involved is one of many to which overhead costs are allocated. If (in the example above) the other machines represent 1,000 hours of use per week, the error in estimating utilization of the one machine means that the overhead will be spread over 1,080 hours per week instead of 1,008. Thus, the percentage error will not be great unless the forecast for all the machines is similarly wrong.

Effect of machine utilization on cellular manufacturing

The effect that machine utilization can have on cost systems can be seen in companies that have introduced cellular manufacturing (CM). CM uses systems for coding components so that components can be classified into families that have similar machining characteristics. Cells of machines are then set up for each family.

In the 1960s (when much of the early work on CM was being done in Europe), few companies had numerically controlled (NC) machine tools, so the capital costs of the machines being put into cells were low. As a result, the low machine utilization rates associated with cells were not normally considered a problem that affected standard costs.

With the widespread introduction of computer numerical control (CNC) in the 1980s, the difficulty of creating CM cells has increased considerably. This has occurred not only because of the need to justify the cost of buying additional machines, but because the low utilization of expensive machines may increase standard costs.

The decision to set up CM cells must be evaluated so that (as with any other investment) the financial benefits are identified and quantified. Only by doing this will the potential increase in standard costs (caused by reduced utilization) be offset by the savings. If this is not done, the introduction of CM cells, however viable, will appear to show an increase in costs and be reported as a financial failure. As with AMT, much of the past perceived failure of CM may have been caused by failing to quantify the benefits—and thus include them—in the company's cost system.

JIT and machine utilization

One of the problems companies face in introducing JIT is the effect on machine utilization. Even when companies have a full order book (so that volume fluctuations are not a problem), changes in product mix will likely result in load fluctuations. For example, Exhibit 2 shows how (in a company with a long delivery time) the required capacity on the machining centers varied during a year when the company had a full order book.

Most batch manufacturing companies have "galloping bottlenecks": Since the workload on machines fluctuates, the bottlenecks keep moving around the factory.

Exhibit 3 shows how the capacity required on the lathes varied at the same time. Plotting the load on all the other machine groups showed similar fluctuations, but with very little correlation between the timing of the peaks and troughs. In practice, the company overcame the problems of load fluctuations through a combination of having queues of work at each load center and failing to meet delivery dates.

For a company to produce components just in time, it needs the ability to make the output on each group of machines fluctuate. Where, in the past, the capacity of machine groups would be based on average load, the requirement with JIT is for capacity to be based on peak load, but with output sometimes dropping well below average.

Providing this peak capacity is likely to require the purchase of additional machines (thus reducing the average utilization and increasing the depreciation rate per hour).

Only if the resulting financial benefits are identified and quantified can an increase in standard costs be prevented.

Optimized production technology

One technique developed for dealing with the problems of production control is optimized production technology (OPT). This technique is based on identifying production bottlenecks and scheduling work through them. (It is assumed that there is always surplus capacity on non-bottleneck machines.) Unfortunately, most batch manufacturing companies have "galloping bottlenecks." In other words, since the load on machines fluctuates (as Exhibits 2 and 3 illustrate), the bottlenecks keep moving around the factory.

Thus, a company may increase the capacity on today's bottleneck (for example, by resorting to overtime or subcontracting), only to find that the problem then moves to another group of machines. If the bottleneck that restricts production starts to become permanent, the company normally invests in extra production capacity. The goal is to ensure that average capacity is always greater than average sales requirements.

Standard costs

Most companies have an internal cost system that is used to ensure that all manufacturing costs are absorbed into the product's sales price. Cost information is widely available in many companies, because the information is used to monitor actual manufacturing costs against budgeted costs.

One result of this wide availability of cost information is that managers often use cost information for purposes for which it was never intended. In doing so, they fail to realize the implications of what they are doing. Many reported problems with cost systems are caused by this improper use of costs.

Single hourly labor rates

When early computerized cost systems were being developed, engineering companies were usually labor-intensive. Direct labor was often the largest single cost factor. As a result, cost systems were developed that divided costs to establish hourly labor rates. Since it is much easier to calculate standard costs if a single

Exhibit 2. *Fluctuations in Machining Center Work Load*

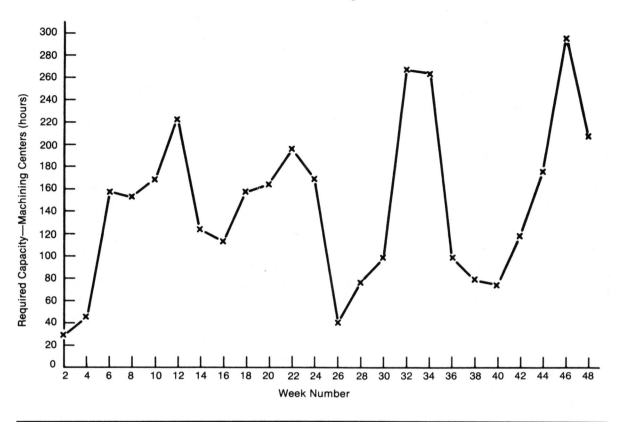

Exhibit 3. *Fluctuations in Lathe Work Load*

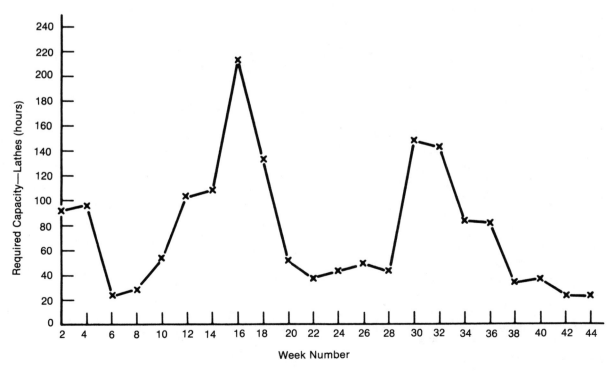

rate is used for all direct workers, many companies (including some large companies in the aerospace industry) still use a single hourly labor rate for all direct workers.

Having a single rate means that some workers—such as those in the assembly line, where capital costs are low—have their time costed at an excessively high rate. On the other hand, operators of expensive equipment have a rate that is too low.

Using a single cost rate means that manufacturing costs of complex products that require the use of expensive machinery are understated, while costs of simple products are overstated. Although companies often use market conditions to set their sales price, standard cost is also considered to ensure that products are not sold below the manufacturing cost. An apparently low standard cost of a complex product encourages a company to reduce its sales price, whereas the apparently high cost of simple products encourages the company to increase the sales price.

Customers buy products if the sales price is lower than the true manufacturing cost, because the price will tend to be lower than prices quoted by competitors. Customers will rarely buy products whose cost—and thus price—is overstated. The result of having a single cost rate is that, if the standard cost is reflected in the sales price, the company will find it much easier to sell complex products than simple ones, but the profit margin between manufacturing cost and selling price will be much smaller than the value that the cost system forecasts.

Companies in this situation find that the more complex their products are, the easier it appears to be to obtain sales. As a result, they continue to design products that are more and more complex, while the company continues to become less and less profitable.

Companies that use a single labor hour rate tend to subcontract simple operations (such as pillar drills or capstan lathes). They can easily find companies to produce at less than their standard cost rate, which is too high. Such companies also tend to take on subcontract work for their large expensive machines (such as multi-axis machining centers). Other companies are happy to pay a standard cost rate that is too low.

One cost rate for different types of machines

A similar problem arises in companies that use the same cost rate for several different types of machines. Engineers try to plan components for the machine that give the lowest standard cost for the component. For example, a component may take ten minutes on a manual lathe, but only three minutes on a CNC machine. If both machines have a rate of $30 per hour, using the CNC machine appears to reduce the cost from $5 to $1.50.

This leads to all components being planned for the (expensive) high-technology machines, which provide the shortest operation times without reflecting the high capital costs. As a result, the most expensive machines become overloaded, so pressure builds to invest in more expensive machines. If the procedures for investment appraisal are inadequate and do not identify what is happening, the company can end up making unnecessary and expensive investments.

Make vs. buy

Companies use standard costs for decisions about whether to make components in-house or to buy them outside, and for decisions about subcontracting work. Unfortunately, the use of standard cost data to compare make versus buy costs consistently biases the decision against in-house manufacturing.

For example, if a component can be bought for $90 each and its standard manufacturing cost in the company is calculated at $100, the obvious decision is to buy the component. However, a detailed cost breakdown may be:

	Make Costs	Buy Costs
Material cost	$20	
Variable costs	20	
Overhead allocation	60	$60
Bought-out cost		90
Total cost	$100	$150

The in-house overhead exists even if the component is purchased, so the $60 of overhead must be attributed to both alternatives. (Note that as the number of bought-out components increases, there may be some slight reduction in fixed overhead—for example, if the number of machine tools is reduced.)

Decisions that many companies have made in the past to concentrate on making complex components that require considerable technical expertise and to subcontract out all simpler components may have been made as a result of the incorrect use of standard cost data. Many of the engineers who are responsible for these make-versus-buy decisions are probably unaware of the difference between standard and variable cost. The accountants who do understand the difference may not be involved in the decisions.

Cost reduction projects

Standard costs based on hourly labor rates are still the most common way for companies to allocate costs to products. Engineers who use this data may wrongly conclude that cost reduction projects aimed at direct labor savings can be attractive.

For example, if labor cost is $5 per hour plus a 400 percent overhead allocation (i.e., a standard cost rate of $25 per hour), reducing labor would appear to save $25 per hour. In reality, however, the change may save only $5 per hour; the remainder represents overhead and depreciation, which remain unchanged.

Engineers have commonly used standard cost data to measure cost reduction projects. The use of standard costs has overemphasized the advantages of labor savings, so many companies have concentrated on reducing the size of their direct labor force. Often, this is done by increasing the number of indirect workers or by investing in AMT.

Downward spirals. One consequence has been that, as the number of direct workers has decreased, a higher proportion of costs become fixed overhead. This means that the ability of companies to reduce costs by reducing the labor force in response to cyclical downturns in business decreases. Thus, companies that invest in flexible manufacturing systems (FMS) can find that if sales volume decreases, utilization decreases and standard costs increase. The inevitable result may be an increase in selling prices, which starts a downward spiral for the company.

Even if a company uses discounted cash flow (DCF) techniques to evaluate investments in a capital plant, minor noncapital expenditures for which the investment decision is made at the plant level are often based on the use of standard cost data.

Example. To illustrate what happens in such cases, consider the case of a company in which the cost of labor is $5 per hour. Overhead and depreciation yield a standard cost rate of $25 per hour for the company's two CNC machines.

The company can invest in quick-change tooling to reduce setup times on two machines. For both machines, the cost of tooling

---

Much of the perceived failure of automated manufacturing technology in the past may have been caused by a failure to quantify the benefits of the new technology and include those benefits in the company's cost system.

---

would be $10,000, but on machine A, the savings would be four hours per week, while on machine B, it would be eight hours per week. The savings would be calculated as follows:

Machine A = 4 hours/week × 50 weeks × $25/hour
= $5,000/year
Machine B = 8 hours/week × 50 weeks × $25/hour
= $10,000/year

Tooling for machine B would therefore seem to be the best investment. However, closer examination may show that the existing setups on machine B do not produce any scrap or rework and that the machine is not operated at full potential capacity. The only savings from reducing setups would be a saving in labor costs.

On the other hand, assume that machine A is overloaded; surplus work would have to be subcontracted out at $25 per hour. Reducing setup times by 200 hours per year will reduce the subcontracted hours by 200. Since the hours worked by the machine and operator will remain unchanged, the savings are in subcontract costs, not in labor or machine costs. Only the work content changes. Therefore, the cash flow savings will be:

Machine A = 4 hours/week × 50 weeks × \$25/hour
      = \$5,000/year
Machine B = 8 hours/week × 50 weeks × \$5/hour
      = \$2,000/year

The use of standard cost data would have led to the wrong decision. Not only would the company have made an investment that was not financially viable, but by spending money on tooling for machine B, the company would have failed to spend for retooling machine A.

Conclusion

AMT and JIT can affect cost management systems in many ways. However, these problems can be attributed either to failings in the procedures that companies use or to the misuse of cost information—a typical example being the use of standard cost data, rather than variable cost data.

There is little evidence that anything is wrong with basic accounting principles. The problem is that companies have not updated their investment evaluation procedures to reflect how changes in technology change operations. With the benefit of hindsight, many of the supposed problems with cost systems disappear. Nonetheless, many companies continue making the same mistakes. Companies should stop trying to develop new principles for measuring and controlling manufacturing costs and should instead concentrate on how to apply existing principles correctly. ▲

Notes
1. See P.L. Primrose, "The Effect of AMT Investment on Costing Systems," *Journal of Cost Management* 27–30 (Summer 1988).

Accounting Innovations: A Cross-Sectional Survey of Manufacturing Firms

Forrest B. Green and Felix E. Amenkhienan

This column reports the results of a survey that was undertaken to learn what U.S. manufacturing firms are doing in terms of accounting innovations. The results show that, although changes are taking place, companies largely continue to rely on outmoded accounting methods, though the emphasis placed on the tracking of direct labor is gradually waning. There is an increasing acknowledgment of the need to use measures other than direct labor as bases for assigning costs to products and measuring productivity more accurately. Those firms that have embarked on programs of accounting innovation (e.g., activity-based costing) report that their competitive positions have improved. This can only serve to motivate others to realize that production accounting properly directed may well provide a vital competitive edge.

Changes in U.S. manufacturing over the last decade have been more dramatic than at any time in the past fifty years. Faced with intense global competition, advanced technologies, and enhanced consumer expectations, manufacturing firms have moved to adopt new philosophies and techniques, including just-in-time (JIT), total quality control (TQC), flexible manufacturing systems (FMS), computer-integrated manufacturing (CIM), and optimized production technologies (OPT). This apparent plethora of three-letter acronyms has been the result of genuine changes in manufacturing methodologies, management innovation, and technological application.

Because of these evolving manufacturing developments, management accounting methods have been scrutinized and criticized for not providing the kind of information needed to measure and support new production innovations. The literature on manufacturing initiatives not only criticizes conventional management accounting, but provides numerous examples of how distorted cost figures, traditional measures of efficiency, and inappropriate measures of performance actually frustrate manufacturing initiatives. This lack of compatibility between accounting and manufacturing has become known as the "productivity paradox." An article in *Business Week* that included a survey of U.S. business managers found that conventional accounting methods often led managers to shy away from promising innovations, to focus inordinate attention on reducing direct labor, to discontinue profitable product lines, to make poor pricing decisions, and to cripple long-term effectiveness by emphasizing short-term cost reductions.[1]

Background

Management accounting differs from compliance accounting, since its primary purpose is to provide managers with information designed to support and enhance decision making. In many respects, management accounting can and should be the most creative and adaptive of all accounting practices, because it is unconstrained by tax laws, financial regulations, and generally accepted accounting principles (GAAP). Too often, however, the necessity to accumulate data for financial reports dominates corporate accounting activity. Financial reports are clearly necessary and satisfy a portion of the information needed by managers, but these statements (and related reports using the same data) are confined to knowledge of what the firm has done in the past. They do not provide for the larger set of performance measures and opportunity figures required to assess new initiatives and chart future direction.[2]

Fortunately, the limitations of conventional accounting in advanced manufacturing environments have been recognized, and new accounting initiatives are being tried and tested.[3] Accounting methodologies with names like backflush costing, transaction accounting, and activity-based costing (ABC) have received considerable attention. Some firms are expanding their accounting databases beyond cost information to include such nonfinancial measures as manufacturing lead time, delivery performance, quality yield, space utilized, time required for setups, throughput, and extent of cross-training.[4] These nonfinancial measures add a new dimension to the accounting information system.

With so much attention being given to the need to revise manufacturing accounting, and given the widespread disenchantment with conventional accounting, many companies have begun to revise their management accounting practices. Cooper[5] discusses indepth the experiences of five manufacturers. Innes and Mitchell[6] describe the process of change in management accounting that occurred in seven selected electronics firms. A spokesperson for the Institute of Management Accountants, referring to a 1990 study by the research consortium Computer Aided Manufacturing-International (CAM-I), identified fifty U.S. firms that were in the process of implementing ABC, and that number has probably grown substantially.

The study discussed in this column was undertaken to survey chief production accounting managers in a cross section of plants and factories throughout the United States. The purpose of the study was to determine and identify innovations adopted in manufacturing accounting practices. The study is exploratory in nature; it does not purport to reflect the full extent of innovative manufacturing accounting practices.

Methodology

For the study, a questionnaire was developed and tested with the assistance of accounting managers in several manufacturing plants. Concurrently, a mailing list was developed to include manufacturing firms believed to be involved in advanced manufacturing technologies. A total of 610 firms were selected. The questionnaire was addressed to production accounting managers (by name in some instances) or controllers, who were requested to refer the document to the person most familiar with production accounting at the plant level. Due to the sensitive nature of information requested, and the level of detail sought, the anonymity of respondents was assured. Even so, a large response rate was not anticipated.

A total of 63 questionnaires were returned. A follow-up mailing to a randomized sample of nonrespondents brought the total number of returned questionnaires to 76, a response rate of 12.5 percent. Only two questionnaires were not usable; the remaining 74 were used in this analysis and reported in the results.

Survey results

The plants and factories surveyed ranged in size from fewer than 100 employees to more than 1,000. Annual revenue from the sale of manufactured products ranged from less than $10 million to more than $1 billion, with median revenues in the $50–$100 million dollar range. Eighty-one percent identified their business unit as a profit center.

Manufacturing processes covered the entire spectrum—from continuous processing to job shop, with the largest percentage (34 percent) identifying batch production as the predominant process. Most reported mixed unit volume, with 57 percent describing their product range as consisting of many product types. Some firms identified their operations as highly labor-intensive, while others were highly machine- or capital-intensive. Using means only, the aggregate breakdown is 44 percent labor-intensive and 56 percent machine- or capital-intensive. The sample distribution represents a relatively wide cross section of manufacturing capability.

Production accounting systems

Production accounting features, which were the focus of the survey, are revealing as well. Thirty-two percent of respondents described their production accounting system as being largely prescribed or designed at the corporate level, 36 percent at the group or division level, and 28 percent developed independently at the plant level. The accounting systems themselves ranged from product cost accounting systems (43 percent), job cost systems (28 percent), process cost systems (19 percent), and other systems described as transaction based, activity based, or something else (10 percent).

A major contention of advocates of accounting change is that direct labor accounts for a diminishing share of total product cost. This was confirmed by the survey, which identified direct labor to be as low as one percent and no higher than 25 percent of product cost. Taken as an aggregate measure, the mean percentage attributed to direct labor was 11 percent, material accounted for 57 percent, and overhead was 32 percent of total manufacturing cost.

While direct labor accounts for a lesser share of product cost, one of the trends in management accounting is the recognition that other functions normally treated as overhead may now be identified as direct costs. To examine this possibility, eighteen functions were listed on the questionnaire, with instructions to check the functions as either direct or indirect manufacturing costs. Respondents were asked to omit items not included in product cost. The results are displayed in Exhibit 1.

Predictably, almost all of the companies surveyed considered production labor and materials as direct costs. Of greater interest are the next six functions in Exhibit 1 (i.e., setups, packing, machine utilization, shipping, material handling, and quality control), which were treated as direct costs by one fourth to one half of the firms surveyed. Note that each of these functions involves the actual handling of the product (or its components) at some point in the process. The remaining ten functions listed in Exhibit 1 do not involve the handling of parts or products; they were not regarded as direct costs by the vast majority of the respondents.

Activities tracked by cost system

Respondents were asked to identify transactions or activities that their cost systems tracked. The results are presented in Exhibit 2, which shows that a significant percentage of the companies (more than 25 percent)

Exhibit 1. *Manufacturing Functions Regarded as Direct Cost, Indirect Cost, or Not Included in Product Cost*

Function	Percentage of Respondents (Rounded)		
	Direct Cost	Indirect Cost	Not Included
Production labor	99	0	1
Materials	96	3	1
Setups	50	45	5
Packing	41	47	12
Machine utilization	38	43	19
Shipping	35	62	23
Material handling	24	70	6
Quality control	23	73	4
Facilities	14	81	5
Maintenance	14	81	5
Engineering	8	68	24
Product design	5	59	36
Purchasing	4	86	10
Cost accounting	3	65	32
Research and development	3	58	39
Personnel services	1	70	29
Data processing	1	7	92
Marketing	0	62	38

tracked all but the last two activities listed (i.e., times product handled and product redesign). A much lower percentage identified the transactions or activities in Exhibit 2 as cost (or activity) drivers.

The level of detail captured by the tracking of these items ranges from low to high, with a surprisingly large percentage identifying costs associated with specific models and part numbers. The lowest level at which cost items were captured is indicated below:

Plant level	11%
Major product lines	13%
Specific product within product lines	22%
Particular models or part number within product lines	42%
Other (shop, work center, etc.)	12%

According to the literature, ABC systems achieve their improved accuracy over traditional, volume-based cost systems by using multiple cost (or activity) drivers and by applying overhead to products through the activities that are directly related to the costs.

Product costing under ABC encompasses more elements than the typical three elements

Exhibit 2. *Transactions or Activities Tracked Separately by Cost System and Identified as Cost Drivers*

Transaction or Activity	Percentage of Respondents (Rounded)	
	Tracked	Cost Driver
Materials consumed	95	61
Units produced	92	41
Production labor hours	91	65
Scrap or yield	73	20
Orders placed	55	5
Rework quantities	54	9
Part numbers used	47	7
Engineering change orders	46	11
Setup times	42	16
Machine time utilized	39	24
Quality control checks	36	7
Production cycle time	30	8
Schedule changes	28	5
Times product handled	15	7
Product redesign	9	8

Exhibit 3. *Questions Regarding Performance Measures and Comparisons With Percentage of Responses (Rounded)*

Question:	*Which of the following traditional measures of performance are maintained?*	
	Material variance	77%
	Labor variance	72
	Labor efficiency	65
	Machine utilization	22

Question:	*Which of the following nonfinancial measures of performance are maintained by your accounting system?*	
	Inventory turns	82%
	On-time delivery rates	41
	Production lead times	35
	Quality yield	32
	Throughput	32
	Time required for setups	26
	Space utilized	12
	Extent of cross training or new skills obtained	8
	Other	3

Question:	*For the purpose of measuring performance, which of the following are used for cost comparison?*	
	Material standards	68%
	Product cost standards	66
	Labor or job standards	61
	Costs obtained from prior accounting periods	54
	Target costs or improvement goals	35

used in traditional systems (i.e., direct materials, direct labor, and factory overhead). In order of percentage response, the following emerge as the most recognized activity drivers:

Production labor hours	65%
Materials consumed	61%
Units produced	41%
Machine time utilized	24%
Scrap or yield	20%
Setup times	16%

These represent only a small fraction of the possible activity drivers identified by Cooper and others. It may well be that activity drivers have not yet been fully understood and identified in most production cost accounting systems.

Performance measures

Performance measures are essential to a management accounting system, because they provide managers with a "scorecard" for purposes of evaluation. Here again, conventional accounting has been criticized for using outmoded performance measures and for force-fitting values derived solely from the financial database.

Several questions in this study addressed the use of performance measures; the results are presented in Exhibit 3. The traditional measures of labor productivity, variance, and efficiency, are maintained by 65 to 72 percent of respondents. The persistence of these measures is ironic, given that labor constitutes, on average, only 11 percent of the cost to manufacture. On the other hand, 77 percent of the respondents report using material variance, which is appropriate since material constitutes 57 percent of the cost to manufacture. Material productivity is now measured by a higher percentage of respondents than earlier surveys indicated. Machine utilization, however, is measured by a low percentage of the respondents (22 percent), a curious phenomenon in an age of capital-intensive, high-tech manufacturing.

Nonfinancial performance measures. Looking toward nonfinancial performance measures, inventory turns per year stand out as the primary measure maintained by most accounting systems. Other measures, such as production lead times, on-time delivery rates, quality yield, and throughput were maintained by the accounting systems of a third to a half of the respondents. Although the percentages are not high, several respondents noted that these measures may be maintained within the plant, but not as part of the accounting system. This may explain why such measures as quality and delivery performance—which are essential to today's manufacturing—reflected lower percentage responses than prior surveys, which did not limit responses to measures maintained by the accounting system. For instance, one study reported the use of product quality indicators and delivery performance measures at 83 percent and 75 percent respectively.[7]

Overreliance on standard costs. Another area in which conventional accounting has been criticized is overreliance on standard costs. The rigid application of standard costs (which

---

Management accounting methods have been criticized for not providing the kind of information needed to measure and support new production innovations.

---

play a big part in variance and efficiency measures) fails to recognize the value of continuous improvement, shorter lead times, reduced setups, and mixed model production—those qualitative factors that lead to improved customer service. In response to a question on performance measurement regarding values used for cost comparison, two thirds of the respondents identified product, material, and labor standards. About half identified costs obtained from prior accounting periods. Only one third use target costs or improvement goals.

While it would not be appropriate to abandon standards without an effective basis of comparison to replace them, the preferred trend toward greater use of target costs and improvement goals does not seem to be materializing.

Production accounting innovations

The survey indicated that most firms were making improvements to their accounting systems. Respondents generally acknowledged a recognition of the need to update existing systems for product costing in light of new competitive challenges.

Some noteworthy changes reported include the following:

- Reduced efforts to track direct labor;
- Increased numbers of overhead pools used;
- Expansion of cost variance analysis to include production variances;
- Installation of MRP II systems;
- Integration of production accounting with other areas (e.g., industrial engineering, materials management, and manufacturing management);
- Recognition of setup and rework costs as direct product costs;
- Activity driver accounting;
- Cycle counting;
- Process value analysis;
- Use of ABC; and
- Increased use of computers.

Although these changes fall short of the far-reaching innovations that seem to be indicated, it is particularly encouraging to note that 45 percent of the respondents reported having adopted ABC (at least to some degree) in their plants. The breakdown of ABC implementation is as follows:

Not at all	55%
Some	23%
About halfway	11%
Extensive	7%
Plantwide	4%

With these and other accounting changes taking place, it is prudent to examine benefits and problems resulting from production accounting innovations. Using a four-point scale, respondents were asked to identify the extent to which their organizations had benefited from a list of cost accounting innovations. The scale ranged from "no effect" (or "not applicable") to "definite effect." The major benefits listed (which averaged between "somewhat" and "definite") were as follows:

- Makes for better cost control;
- More useful to production and marketing;

- Provides more accurate information on profitability;
- Generates more timely information;
- More useful to accounting and finance;
- Provides information that improves company's competitive strategy; and
- Provides better and more appropriate performance measures.

Other benefits that received lower average ratings were as follows:

- Eliminates duplication;
- Reduces record keeping;
- Facilitates make-versus-buy decisions;
- Improves communication;
- Helps identify non-value-added activities;
- Proves more useful to engineering and product design;
- Aids in capital budgeting decisions; and
- Justifies new technology.

Among the problems experienced by firms, the only standouts were the following:

- Increased level of detail required;
- Increased paperwork;
- Activity drivers difficult to identify; and
- Inadequate support from top management.

These received average ratings, which indicates that they were somewhat of a problem. Overall, the benefits appeared to outweigh the problems experienced.

Accounting innovations and manufacturing competitiveness

A key intent of the survey was to obtain information about the responsiveness of cost management systems to shifts in the firms' competitive strategy. Accordingly, one question specifically requested respondents to describe how accounting innovations in their organizations had helped to improve competitive positions. Here is a summary of the responses from the firms that reported innovations:

- Better profit margin analysis;
- Better understanding of the structure of manufacturing costs;
- More success in bidding for cost reimbursement contracts;
- Better analysis of segment performance;
- Improved cost control;
- Reduced lead time for new product launches;

- Significant reduction in inventory holding costs; and
- More accurate product costing.

Those firms that had introduced or were experimenting with some form of innovation in cost management invariably indicated that their competitive position was enhanced as a result—an observation that should be gratifying to the advocates of accounting innovation.

Summary and implications

This survey undertook to explore the accounting innovations that U.S. manufacturing firms were adopting to compete in the new marketplace. While U.S. companies seemed to recognize the need to update their production accounting systems, the actual level of response (as indicated by aggregate survey results) is still somewhat disappointing. A significant lag still exists between innovations in manufacturing and innovations in management accounting. Although changes are taking place, firms, to a large extent, continue to rely on outmoded accounting methods.

A major contention of advocates of accounting change is that direct labor accounts for a diminishing share of total product cost. This was confirmed by the survey, which identified direct labor to be as low as 1 percent and no higher than 25 percent of product cost.

One encouraging development is that the emphasis placed on the tracking of direct labor is gradually waning. There is an increasing acknowledgement of the need to use other measures as bases for assigning costs to products and measuring productivity more accurately. In most organizations, direct labor costs are already under good control, but high indirect costs are having significant impact on production effectiveness. To the extent that these costs and their associated activities are identified, real improvements can be made. As noted earlier, those firms that have embarked on programs of accounting innovation (e.g., ABC) report that their competitive positions have improved. This can only serve to motivate others to realize that production accounting properly directed may well provide a vital competitive edge. ▲

Notes

1. O. Port, R. King, & W.J. Hampton, "The Productivity Paradox," *Business Week,* June 6, 1988, at 100–114.

2. D. Shadoan & R.R. Sharp, "Accountants and Economists Must Join Hands," *Business Forum* 16–19 (Summer 1990).

3. I.C. Magaziner & R.B. Reich, *Minding America's Business* (New York: Harcourt, Brace, Jovanovich Publishers 1982); H.T. Johnson & R.S. Kaplan, *Relevance Lost: The Rise and Fall of Management Accounting* (Boston: Harvard Business School Press 1987); C. Berliner & J.A. Brimson, eds., *Cost Management for Today's Advanced Manufacturing: The CAM-I Conceptual Design* (Boston: Harvard Business School Press 1988); and C.J. McNair & W. Mosconi, *Beyond the Bottom Line: Measuring World Class Performance* (Homewood, Ill.: Richard D. Irwin, Inc. 1989).

4. F.B. Green, F. Amenkhienan, & G. Johnson, "Performance Measures and JIT," *Management Accounting* 50–53 (Feb. 1991).

5. R. Cooper, "Cost Management Concepts and Principles: The Rise of Activity-Based Costing—Part One: What Is an Activity Based-Cost System?" *Journal of Cost Management* 45–54 (Summer 1988).

6. J. Innes & F. Mitchell, "The Process of Change in Management Accounting: Some Field Study Evidence," *Management Accounting Research* 3–19 (Mar. 1990).

7. R.A. Howell, J.D. Brown, S. Soucy, & A.H. Seed III, *Manufacturing Accounting in the New Manufacturing Environment* (Montvale, N.J.: National Association of Accountants 1987).

PART *H*

Performance Measurement

Performance Measurement: The Balanced Scorecard Approach

Lawrence S. Maisel

Companies should adopt a broad-based set of performance measures based on the concept of a balanced scorecard. The performance measures selected can—and must—support the management initiatives currently under way in many companies (e.g., total quality management and continuous improvement). The potential benefits to be derived from enhanced competitiveness and improved business performance will justify and encourage management to improve overall performance measurement systems and to adopt measures that are relevant to the businesses pursued, workers employed, and customers served.

L ast year, Business International published the results of an international survey of chief executive officers and other senior decision-makers.[1] These executives indicated that to be successful in the 1990s, their firms will need to strike a balance between efficiency and low product costs because of a marketplace characterized by constant change, intense competition, and more responsiveness to satisfying customer demands. Companies around the world have embarked on various initiatives to provide customer satisfaction and improve business performance. These initiatives—such as expanding product differentiation, improving customer service, introducing total quality, and pursuing continuous improvement—have become the cornerstones of corporate strategy.

As Exhibit 1 illustrates, the same executives reported that the key objectives of their organizations are now driven—and will be over the next three years—by the following five critical success factors:

1. Customer responsiveness;
2. Profitability;
3. Quality;
4. Innovation; and
5. Flexibility.

The majority of the firms surveyed have moved toward a more decentralized organizational structure and leadership style, and this movement is expected to increase significantly over the next several years. Corporate leaders believe that decentralization and employee empowerment improve a company's effectiveness and competitiveness, even though management is challenged by the difficult task of executing its strategic vision and building team cooperation among more autonomous business units.

Overemphasis on financial performance measures

In contrast to this strategic redirection that is taking place, many companies continue to maintain performance measurement systems that are heavily weighted toward financial measures (see Exhibit 2), which has had several notable adverse effects.

First, financial performance measures create barriers, often hidden, to executing strategies and achieving competitiveness and profitability. For example, to achieve improved manufacturing efficiency, an organization might be tempted to build excess inventories to avoid potential volume variances reported by traditional cost accounting systems. Similarly, to reduce headcount, and organization might use contract employees or outside vendors to comply with budgetary reductions on departmental payroll costs. To obtain lower material cost and to eliminate purchase price variances, an organization might select lower-priced suppliers.

Exhibit 1. *Key Objectives of Global Organizational Structure*

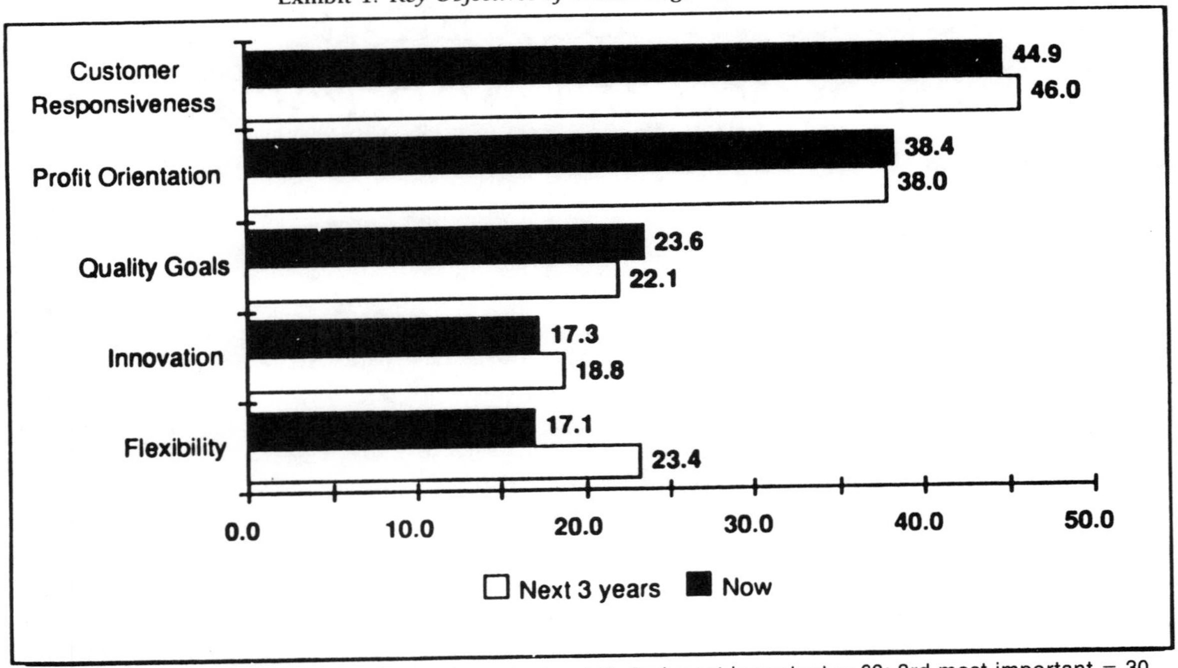

	Now	Next 3 years
Customer Responsiveness	44.9	46.0
Profit Orientation	38.4	38.0
Quality Goals	23.6	22.1
Innovation	17.3	18.8
Flexibility	17.1	23.4

☐ Next 3 years ■ Now

Values represent weighted averages: most important = 100; 2nd most important = 60; 3rd most important = 30.

Source: Business International Survey

Exhibit 2. *Performance Measurement Is Currently Heavily Weighted Toward Financial Measures*

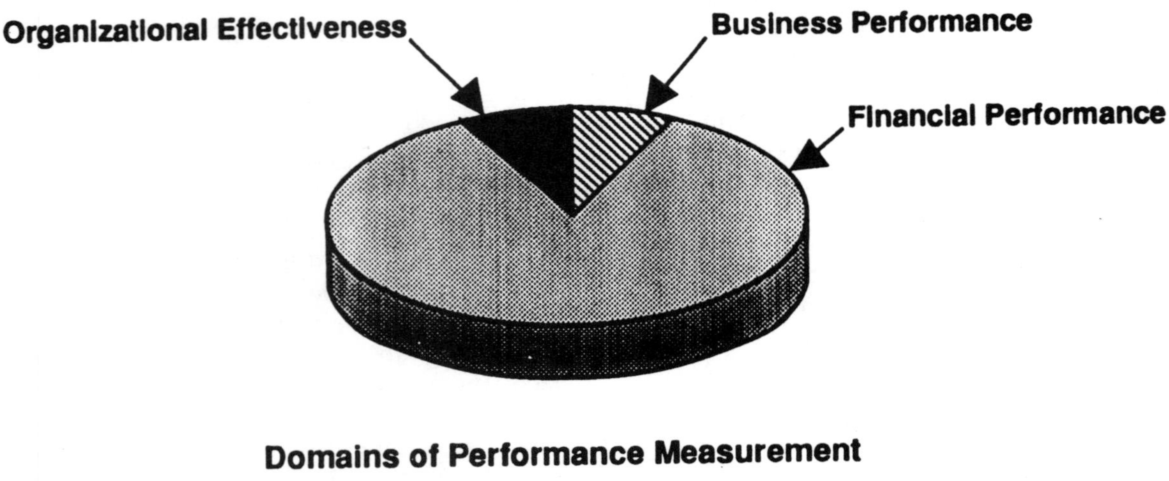

Organizational Effectiveness　　**Business Performance**

Financial Performance

Domains of Performance Measurement

Financial Performance	Business Performance	Organizational Effectiveness
• Sales growth and profitability • Product cost and margin • EPS • ROA • ROI	• Market share • Quality/Zero defects • Customer satisfaction • Marketing effectiveness • New product introduction • Productivity • Competitive benchmarking • Cycle times	• Internal environment and capabilities • People • Education/training • Corporate culture • External environment and capabilities

Exhibit 3. *Barriers to Executing Strategies and to Achieving Competitiveness and Profitability*

In each of these examples, the measures used to manage the business provided "false positive" signals of more effective operations and performance. These measures constitute barriers to executing strategies, for they encourage workers and managers alike to take actions that lead to favorable employee performance evaluations but that are detrimental to the business as a whole (see Exhibit 3).

Purchasing function's dilemma. To illustrate this point, consider the purchasing function and the dilemma that its employees face. The financial measurement system may hold them accountable for purchase price variances (a financial measure), while manufacturing is separately held accountable for quality measures (e.g., zero defects) and customer measures (e.g., on-time deliveries). If purchasing contracts with higher-price suppliers, its financial performance is unfavorable even though certain higher priced suppliers may provide higher-quality products or services or better delivery times than lower-cost suppliers.

More relevant measures

Recently, some companies have adopted more relevant performance measures for purchasing, such as cost of ownership. However, this approach is flawed, because no matter how

relevant one set of measures is to managing a business, the same measures often lack integration and consistency with other measures used in other functional areas of the company.

Consequently, companies must begin to transform their performance measurement systems to foster better linkage between strategies and measures. Companies need performance measures that provide meaningful feedback (i.e., measurement) about activities performed. In effect, the goal of a company's measurement process is to achieve a balance between several different dimensions and for these measures to be integrated with the strategies of the company.

The balanced scorecard approach

One approach now being used relies on the concept of a "balanced scorecard," which means that an organization must define key dimensions of performance for which discrete yet linked measures can be reported, as Exhibit 4 illustrates. For many companies, the measures would normally be related to one of the following categories or dimensions:

- Customers;
- Business processes;
- Human resources; and
- Finance.

Exhibit 4. *Driven by Strategies*

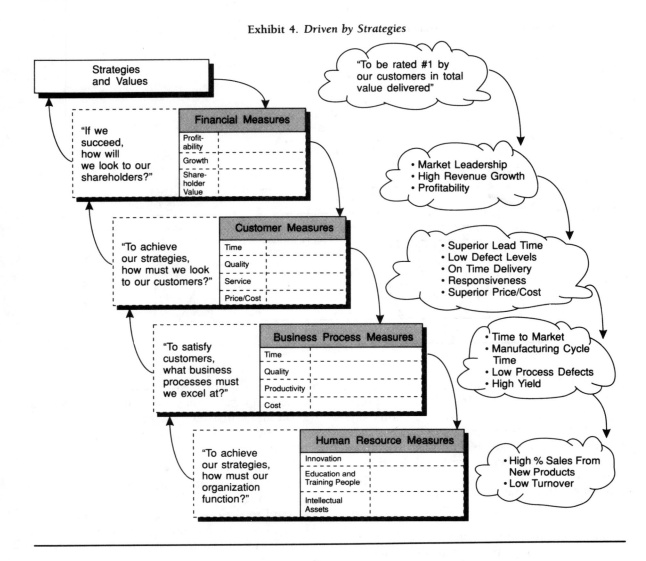

Within each of these dimensions, a company should select performance measures that enable the business to achieve its strategies and become more competitive. These performance measures vary from business to business. Many companies, however, have found those discussed below to be useful.

Customer measures

Since the creation of value begins with the customer, it is natural that performance measurement should start by viewing products or services through the eyes of the customer. To that end, customer measures can often be broken down into five attributes: time, quality, service, cost, and market share. Companies are now establishing measures to track these attributes. Examples are as follows:

- Time (in terms of the ability to meet customer requirements);
  —Product development cycle
  —Order to delivery cycle
  —Service cycle
- Quality (in terms of specifications as determined by the customer)
  —Product quality
  —Service quality
- Service (in terms of satisfying customer expectations)
  —Responsiveness
  —Customer satisfaction surveys
- Cost (in terms of competitive alternatives)
  —Price/value
  —Cost of ownership
- Market share (in terms of customer demand)

—Product/service mix
—Innovations and competency

Business processes measures

Traditional measurements typically focus on spending and output levels for activities performed by departments. This can often lead to fragmentation and suboptimization of performance at lower levels of the organization. This occurs in many instances because managers have traditionally focused on how *much* is spent rather than on the *resources required* to perform necessary activities. Such spending is only indirectly linked to specific activities that must be performed to operate the business.

One of the principal benefits of activity-based management (ABM), by contrast, is its ability to assign cost more directly to activities; ABM groups activities into business processes that cut across organizational or departmental structures. This perspective helps managers analyze the cost of activities and thus highlight opportunities for cost reductions.

Measuring spending instead of performance. A company that seeks to measure business performance using only ABM-assigned costs, however, will be making a serious error, because the company will continue to measure levels of spending without measuring what really matters—i.e., operational performance (such as time, quality, and productivity), which should be evaluated in terms of how, why, and for whom business processes are undertaken.

This more holistic view of performance measures (i.e., taking cost, time, quality, and productivity) creates a meaningful context for measuring rates of continuous improvement and evaluating investments in capital and technological resources used.

Human resources measures

Companies today must be able to establish an effective organizational structure by assembling employees who can perform value-adding activities for customers and also develop new products or services. In the context of the balanced scorecard, performance measures are needed so that management can gauge the effectiveness of its organization and the capabilities of its people.

Selecting these performance measures is by no means an easy task. It requires management to evaluate its current human resource practices in light of the changing business environment in which it competes. There are several essential factors that a company will find valuable as it seeks to establish relevant measures, including:

- Education and training;
- Internal rewards and recognitions;
- Morale and corporate culture;
- Core competencies;[2] and
- Innovation.

These factors, together with traditional elements of an effective human resources management program, will become an important basis for constructing this dimension of the balanced scorecard.

Financial measures

Within the balanced scorecard, financial measures remain an important dimension, for they help a company assess how well it is performing for its customers, shareholders, creditors, and other constituents. The issue that many financial executives grapple with involves determining the *focus* and *level of detail* of financial measures (as explained below).

Recent studies[3] have provided insight into the role of financial management within the organization, including helpful guidance to financial executives in selecting the focus and level of detail of financial measures that could be incorporated into the balanced scorecard approach.

Focus. In determining appropriate sets of financial measures to be reported, several elements are necessary, including the following:

- Deployment of assets;
- Profitability;
- Liquidity and capital structure; and
- Resource control.

Within each of these categories, financial measures must be established so that managers can effectively plan, control, and achieve the desired performance results. Exhibit 5 illustrates financial measures relating to these four areas.

Exhibit 5.

Area of Focus	Financial Measures
Deployment of assets	ROI ROE Shareholder value Inventory turns
Profitability	Sales Product customer profit- ability Gross margin Activity accounting
Liquidity and capital structure	Cash flow Debt/equity Debt service
Resource control	Financial statements Department expenses Activity accounting Cost of quality Value-added/non-value- added ratio

Level of detail. In determining the level of detail for these categories, the orientation of the financial function becomes quite significant. A study by the Financial Executives Research Foundation[4] notes the following three financial management orientations:

- *Competitive-team:* An orientation toward greater interaction with line managers and greater involvement in responding to external factors that affect the business.
- *Command-and-control:* An orientation toward maintaining effective internal control over resources owned by the company.
- *Conformance:* An orientation toward technical compliance with external rules and regulations and external accountabilities.

The level of detail for financial measures will incorporate aspects of each of these orientations. Most organizations, however, will evolve toward a dominant style that typically reflects the organization's business environment, overall management culture, and strategic direction. This dominant style has the greatest influence in shaping the level of detail, frequency, and complexity in capturing and reporting these financial measures.

Consequently, companies that are devoting significant resources to their current financial reporting practices must reassess these practices to determine whether the existing financial measures provide managers with useful information. All too often, financial measures are excessive and overburden managers with information that does not enable them to determine the adequacy of their strategies and actions. This was best characterized by the executive who said: "When I receive the financial reports, I'm either happy or upset, but rarely am I smarter."

Summary

This article describes a broad-based set of guidelines that can be used to select performance measures based on the concept of a balanced scorecard. The number and selection of specific measures, and the process and resources required to implement new or revised measures are compatible with many management initiatives currently under way in many companies (e.g., improving customer service, introducing total quality, and pursuing continuous improvement).

The management challenge, therefore, is for companies to integrate these initiatives into the way they measure performance. The potential benefits to be derived from enhanced competitiveness and improved business performance will justify and encourage management to improve overall performance measurement systems and to adopt performance measures that are relevant to the business pursued, workers employed, and customers served. ▲

Notes
1. "Winning in The New Global Marketplace: Strategic Redirection For the 1990's," Business International Corp., New York, NY (Oct. 1990).
2. C.K. Prahalad and Gary Hamel, "The Core Competencies of The Corporation," *Harvard Business Review* (May/June 1990): 79–91.
3. *Building Global Profitability and Competitiveness: The New Role of Finance* (New York, NY: Business International Corp. 1989); and Patrick J. Keating and Stephen F. Jablonsky, "Changing Roles of Financial Management" (Morristown, NJ: Financial Executives Research Foundation 1990), 49–53.
4. Keating and Jablonsky, "Changing Roles of Financial Management" (Morristown, NJ: Financial Executives and Research Foundation 1990), 49–53.

The New Math of Performance Measurement

Francis V. McCrory and Peter G. Gerstberger

How managers keep score should be aligned more closely with what is important to shareholders. Traditional accounting measures such as ROI are of little value to managers in measuring progress toward creating shareholder value. Although creating shareholder value and managing a business are two radically different activities, they can—and must—be reconciled. For this to happen, however, companies must rethink how the business is managed. This rethinking involves consideration of how and what we measure as performance, how performance is rewarded, and what is considered good and bad.

Executives, Take Your Risks" read the headline of a *New York Times* article.[1] The story opened with the following item:

Anothony Luiso, the International Multifoods Corp.'s chief executive, was due for a $100,000 raise last year. He not only turned it down but also told the board to hold back $100,000 of his bonus. In their place, he took $200,000 in stock options, exercisable in 10 years at $32.625 each, the price on the day the deal was signed.

"Executives should have enough at risk so that they spend a couple of sleepless nights over their decisions," Luiso said, "We should be in the same shoes as the shareholders."

Walking in the shareholders' moccasins has become a popular theme among senior executives and board members as they increasingly accept the idea that creating value for the shareholders is a business's primary objective. Achieving all other objectives with respect to various stakeholders becomes dependent on satisfying this primary one.

But talking about creating shareholder values versus actually *managing* a business to this objective are radically different activities. We

believe that these two activities can be reconciled. However, it will require a reorientation in how a business is managed: in how and what we measure as performance, in how performance is rewarded, and in what is considered to be good and bad.

For instance, growth (generally regarded as good) can dissipate shareholder value in some circumstances; specifically, growing a business that fails to generate a stream of discounted cash returns in excess of its risk-adjusted cost of capital does not benefit shareholders. And it does not matter whether this kind of growth is achieved internally through reinvestment or externally through acquisition. In fact, the record on corporate acquisitions strongly suggests that most have diminished value for shareholders, yet they remain a popular avenue for building larger and larger corporations.[2]

Translating this concept into practice is challenging for most CEOs and senior executives. However, the measurement system represents the place to start: how managers keep score should be aligned more closely with what is important to shareholders. And changing how performance is measured requires overt support from the board of directors, which must be willing to compensate senior management accordingly.

Therefore, performance measurement must change so that the shareholder value concept can be used as a guide by operating management in strategic and tactical decision making. Without this step, the shareholder value approach is in real danger of becoming an analytical exercise for the corporate staff rather than the new paradigm used to guide the organization toward achieving the corporate objective.

Exhibit 1. *du Pont Model*

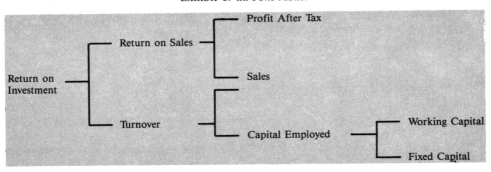

One reason why the approach has not penetrated into the operational arena is that managers at that level have not adopted the new math of risk-adjusted, discounted cash flow in their decision making. They continue to use the traditional, more familiar measures by which they have been evaluated. The traditional measurement system is the accounting system as reflected in the du Pont model and the return on investment (ROI) concept.

The traditional approach

The du Pont model and the emphasis on ROI represent the traditional approach. This model, initially developed by the du Pont Company during the 1920s, integrated operating statement and balance sheet concepts in a series of ratios culminating in ROI. Exhibit 1 portrays the familiar relationships in the model.

The ROI concept had such power and simplicity that it was ultimately adopted by all major U.S. corporations. Alternatives to ROI such as the residual income approach were considered but quickly dismissed.

By the 1950s, the du Pont model was, in effect, the management paradigm. Since then, corporate objectives have included an ROI target (hurdle rate), and portfolio, strategic, capital budgeting, and tactical decisions, as well as managers' compensation, have been based on ROI contribution.

The ratio is attractive because it is:

- A single number that reflects both operating and asset performance.
- A ratio that facilitates comparison among various business units and with other corporations.

- Generated directly from the traditional accounting system.

In addition, U.S. business managers are familiar with the du Pont approach. The measurement concept is deeply ingrained in the culture of most corporations and has become part of the day-to-day language. Everyone knows what a hurdle rate is and "making the numbers" has become shorthand for measuring business performance under the du Pont framework.

Unfortunately, the du Pont model and the ROI ratio are not entirely supportive of nor consistent with the shareholder value approach. The du Pont model is flawed by the inadequacies in the traditional system, which relies on ROI, are in the following areas:

- Inventory costing policy (FIFO accounting inflates income during periods of inflation).
- Depreciation policy (depreciation affects both income and investment).
- Capitalization policy (decisions on how to handle equipment leases affect both income and investment).
- Asset costing practices (original cost accounting understates investment during periods of inflation).

In addition, the calculation of ROI does not capture the very significant reinvestment activity critical to value.

A major limitation of the du Pont model can be traced to the use of accountancy profit and investment concepts that lend themselves to manipulation. Every executive has seen the year-end scramble to make the numbers look good—to defer expenses, to capitalize expenditures that should be expensed, to improperly take advantage of leases, to aggressively manage working capital so that target ratios will be met and bonuses maximized. These activities benefit the manager but not the shareholder. If we are truly concerned with creating shareholder value, the business must be viewed as an investment and focus must be placed on increasing the value of that investment.

The value of an investment is, of course, the future cash flow that it will generate—the cash flows associated with the business. The time value of that cash flow, as well as the risk associated with not achieving those flows, must also be recognized. Executives must explicitly recognize that some businesses are just riskier than others and investors will demand a risk-adjusted return on their investment. The "new math" incorporates these concepts.

The "new math"

A key principle of the shareholder value approach is that a business creates value when it meets or exceeds a cost of capital that correctly reflects its investment risk. Another important principle is that value is the sum of a stream of future cash flows discounted to the present. Thus, the du Pont model must be linked with an appropriate valuation model if it is to support the shareholder value approach.

Valuation models began appearing in the financial and economic literature during the late 1950s. Although a variety of specifications were developed, a cash flow model became the consensus by the 1980s.[3] The basic concept underlying the cash flow model is that the value of an investment is the sum of the future stream of cash flow that it can generate, discounted at an appropriate risk-adjusted discount rate. By focusing on cash flow, the model overcomes the inadequacies of the accounting system reflected in the ROI measure. Also, by using a present value approach, the model recognizes the time preference for money and the risk of an investment.

Since the cash flow stream represents potential return to both bondholders and shareholders, the model uses a cash flow without interest charges. The shareholder or equity value of the business is determined by subtracting the market value of debt from total value.

Essentially, the consensus valuation model[4] (Exhibit 2) has two major components: a discount rate and estimates of cash flow. Each of the components in Exhibit 2 are discussed and the key variables that determine or drive the value of an investment are identified.

☐ **Discount rate.** The appropriate discount rate for the valuation model is the weighted average cost of capital for the business.

$$\text{(Cost of Debt} \times \% \text{ Debt)} + \text{(Cost of Equity} \times \% \text{ Equity)}^5$$

Exhibit 2. *Valuation Model*

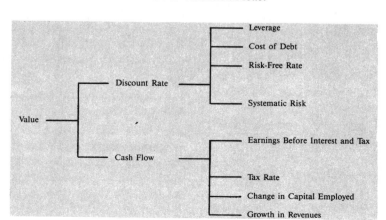

The percent of debt and equity is the target leverage for the business; the cost of debt is the after-tax yield on long-term (10-year) bonds for the business or a look-alike business; and the cost of equity is estimated with the capital asset pricing model (CAPM).

The CAPM is basically the sum of a risk-free rate for an investment (current yield on long-term Treasury bonds) plus the systematic risk for the business in question. Systematic risk is the risk that the cash flow stream of a particular business will be different from the cash flow stream of alternative equity investments.

The systematic risk for a publicly traded equity may be estimated from its beta coefficient (a statistic available for all traded equities). If the business in question is not publicly traded, it is best to use the beta of look-alike businesses that are publicly traded. The determinants or drivers of the discount rate are the target leverage for the business, cost of debt, risk-free rate, and systematic risk.

"We have all seen the year-end scramble to make the numbers look good. This benefits the manager but not the shareholder."

☐ **Cash flow.** The valuation model requires an estimate of the net cash flows for the expected life of the business. To be practical, this means discrete estimates of performance for the short term and a single estimate of the average performance for the long term. Although detailed estimates of operating statement and balance sheet accounts may be made, the information for the valuation model requires only an indication of baseline values and an estimate of the key determinants or drivers of cash flow.

The determinants or drivers, which may be stated in ratios similar to those of the du Pont model, are simply the ratio of earnings before interest and tax to sales (operating efficiency); tax rate; change in sales to capital employed ratio (capital productivity); and growth in revenue.

The operating efficiency driver may be specified in greater detail (e.g., cost of goods sold to sales, SG&A to sales, and research and development to sales). The capital productivity driver can also be specified in greater detail (e.g., change in accounts receivable to sales, change in inventory to sales, or change in working capital to sales).

The cash flow drivers are specified for each of the years considered short term (normally 5 years) and once for the long-term period (normally 20 years).

We believe that this valuation model is the appropriate instrument for measuring the value impact of a decision. It can be used in strategic planning, capital budgeting, and operational decision making. It requires using only eight variables, or drivers; four variables to determine the discount rate and four variables (for multiple periods) to determine cash flow. These drivers are hardly more complex than ROI and other du Pont ratios; however, they relate directly to shareholder value.

The valuation model is more complex than the du Pont model. However, it does capture the dynamics of risk, operating efficiency, capital productivity, growth, and time as they jointly affect shareholder value.

The "new math" at work

The theory sounds great, but how can managers begin implementing the changes that will result from the new math? How can corporations wean themselves from using familiar measures such as ROI in favor of these new metrics? Specifically, how will corporate management hold its business-unit managers accountable using the new math in place of traditional performance concepts?

Implementation requires more of a cultural than a systems change. The accounting and management information system can be easily modified to report value drivers and valuation levels. The challenge is to change management's focus from looking at ROI for a single period to the multiple value drivers over future periods.

Implementation requires a process that incorporates at least the following steps:

☐ **Commitment by the CEO and the senior management team.** There must be a firm and explicit commitment by the senior management team to the objective of creating shareholder value. Commitment means more than lip service, since it will have to be translated into instilling operating managers with values that they may have forgotten. It may require going as far as Anthony Luiso has in demonstrating his commitment to the concept. The board also has to buy in, which apparently has been the case at International Multifoods.

☐ **Education of business-unit managers.** Operating managers may have to be reminded (in the event that they have forgotten) that they work for the shareholders, whether the company is publicly traded or privately held. In the case of the latter, chances are that managers are reminded periodically of this reality by "owners" whom they see and interact with on a daily basis.

"The challenge is to change management's focus from looking at ROI for a single period to the multiple value drivers over future periods."

In public companies, operating managers can and do forget that they work for the shareholders. More important, operating managers must be made aware of how the elements of the business that they manage affect the value that accrues to shareholders. They must understand the new math and the rationale that drives it.

☐ **Baseline analysis.** Implementation requires that the corporate staff perform a baseline analysis for each and every business unit in the corporate portfolio. Specifically, a systematic risk factor (beta) will have to be assigned to each business based on finding look-alikes or peers for which this factor is available. The staff should also complete an analysis to determine which units are contributing to and/or detracting from shareholder value.

This analysis, coupled with business-unit strategic plans, sets the stage for a debate about the future role of each business in the corporate portfolio. The CEO, the CFO, and

senior corporate management will set the general guidelines for each unit and specify the role it expects each one to play. These guidelines provide the basis for revising strategic plans, if necessary, and for detailed budgeting.

☐ **Strategic planning and budgeting.** With the corporate guidelines as a basis, each unit prepares strategic plans and budgets. In planning and budgeting, operating-unit management pays close attention to the drivers of shareholder value under its control. A unit might be charged with maintaining value or with contributing a specific increment to value; the unit should outline how it plans to deliver the results in its formal budget submission.

Note that the delivery of value can be achieved by various combinations of numerical values in each of the drivers that management tries to control. In actual practice, only the cash-flow drivers and growth are under the manager's control because the discount rate applied to a business only changes as the risk-free rate changes (outside the manager's control) or as a particular business unit's industry changes (an infrequent event). Thus, managers need only concern themselves with balancing the cross-impact and mutual interdependence of pricing and operating efficiencies, capital productivity, and growth.

☐ **Performance measurement and reward.** The traditional accounting system can track the drivers, and the valuation model can be run to determine whether value is being created. It should be expected that compensation will be linked to managers' achieving the value contribution targets set by and for each of their respective units.

This article presents a brief overview of the major elements in an implementation program. The specifics, however, need to be developed on a case-by-case basis within the context of each organization's culture and heritage. The process for effecting the necessary reorientation becomes as important, if not more important, than any items in an implementation checklist.

The critical elements for success include having meaningful participation by management in defining their roles vis-à-vis the shareholders and buying into how value is created. In this regard, the first element—the commitment of the CEO to this approach—is probably the most critical one to ultimate success.

If the shareholder value approach is to penetrate operations and be used for strategic and tactical decision making, operating managers must begin using the valuation model. The challenge, of course, is having managers become as familiar and comfortable with the valuation variables or drivers as they are with the du Pont ROI concept.

This can be accomplished by incorporating the value drivers in the performance measurement system and making them an integral part of the business language in an organization. Furthermore, if business performance is measured by improvements in the value drivers and change in business value, and more important, if incentive compensation is coupled to these measures, managers will quickly learn the details of the valuation approach and concentrate on creating value for shareholders.

The change from ROI to value drivers would be a small step for operating managers and a major step for senior management toward achieving the full potential of the shareholder

value approach. Knowing that operating managers are driven by the same objectives as senior managers and shareholders may make those "sleepless nights" cited by Luiso a little more restful. ▲

Notes

1. *The New York Times,* Jan. 27, 1991, F25.
2. M. Porter, "From Competitive Advantage to Corporate Strategy," *Harvard Business Review* (May–June 1987), pp. 43–59.
3. Dividend and earnings models are widely used; however, a cash flow approach is clearly the consensus, particularly among academics and, more important, among a growing circle of investment analysts.
4. There are several implementations of the cash flow model with somewhat different specifications; however, the model discussed here is at a level of detail that masks those differences.
5. In theory, the leverage should be calculated on the market and not the book values of debt and equity. However, to link valuation to planning and performance measurement (including compensation), the traditional accounting system with book values must be accommodated.

Use of Nonfinancial Performance Measures[1]

Joseph Fisher

This article examines the implementation of nonfinancial measurement and control systems at several high-technology manufacturing plants. It traces the development of the nonfinancial systems from the environmental factors that precede the development of systems to the actual implementation of the nonfinancial control mechanism. The article also describes some of the benefits and negative consequences of these nonfinancial measurement systems.

Conventional reports about the financial performance of a business—whether they are internal reports (e.g., budget or variance reports) or external reports (e.g., income statements or cash flow reports)—are much like the scoreboard at a baseball game. A scoreboard tells a player whether he is winning or losing the game, but it tells him little about what he is doing right or wrong about the fundamentals of baseball. A player who tries to play baseball by watching the scoreboard will not be successful.

The "scoreboard" approach to performance measurement

Traditionally, a scoreboard approach has been an acceptable role for both internal and external financial reports. The role of accounting reports has generally been limited to providing periodic historical statements of financial performance, with little expectation that they can provide insights into the factors that cause that performance. Pursuing the analogy, we can say that traditional accounting records have served the function of a scoreboard. Success in baseball, however, is a function of hitting, fielding, and pitching, for these determine what goes on the scoreboard.

As competition in industry has intensified, managers have looked for new sources of information about the key factors that contribute to success and how they are measured. Many companies have looked to financial statements and standard cost systems for new insights, and to some extent these sources have yielded information. As managers know, however, financial measures reflect the results of past decisions, not the actionable steps needed for surviving in today's competitive environment.

The rise of nonfinancial measures

The recent rise of operational—i.e., nonfinancial—performance measures represents an attempt to reassert the primacy of operations over financial measures. By using nonfinancial measures, managers attempt to track progress on the actionable steps that lead to a company's success in the market. In this way, companies are trying to reemphasize that to get a hit, you have to watch the ball, not the scoreboard.

This article examines the use of nonfinancial measures at five high-technology manufacturers (most of them makers of semiconductors). On-site procedures consisted of documenting and analyzing the current accounting and control system. Each functional department head was interviewed to verify that the system was working as described. Interviewed employees were also asked about perceived strengths and weaknesses of the control system.

This article synthesizes the results from these interviews and describes the rise of nonfinancial measures as primary control mechanisms. The article reviews why these firms felt that their prior accounting systems did not cap-

Exhibit 1. *The Nonfinancial Implementation Process*

Phase 1	Phase 2	Phase 3	Phase 4	Phase 5	Phase 6
Company perceives a shock to its operating environment	→ Company concludes its current control system is deficient	→ Company attempts to define key success factors (KSF) that lead to competitive advantage	→ Company attempts to find quantifiable measures of KSF; many are nonfinancial	→ Implementation of new system	→ New outcomes -Positive -Negative

ture all measures that were important for success. The implementation and critical analysis of these new measures follows. Before starting this analysis, a brief overview of the process that firms followed in implementing a nonfinancial measurement system is presented.

The nonfinancial process: an overview

Each company that was studied went through the major steps shown in Exhibit 1.

Shock to operating environment. First, each company faced a perceived shock to its operating environment. This shock led management to conclude that current management practices did not lead to desired results. The shock may have been the company's termination as a supplier to a major client. In another case, the shock consisted of moving the company's plant to a new location. In one case, the shock was as subtle as the perception by management of increased competition. Whatever the shock was, it served as a catalyst that motivated management to find new ways of managing, measuring, and controlling the manufacturing process.

Old control system found inadequate. The second step consisted of concluding that the company's current control system (which was typically a variance system built on standard costs) was deficient. Rather than refining the current control system, therefore, a radically new method of control was needed. To overcome the perceived shortcomings of the control process, each company had to determine what factors might give it competitive advantage.

Defining key success factors. The third step, which consisted of defining potential key success factors, required an extensive commitment of time from senior managers to determine those factors and characteristics that would allow the firm to survive and thrive in its markets.

Finding objective, quantifiable performance measures. Once the key success factors were identified, the fourth step involved finding objective, quantifiable measures of these factors. The companies found that many of these measures did not require "dollarizing"; in other words, the measures were nonfinancial. For example, many measures of product quality do not require dollarizing and are nonfinancial. Many of the key success factors had no easy mappings to quantifiable measures. Assume, for example, that a firm determines that innovation is a key success factor: A business strategy of innovation does not lend itself easily to quantifiable measures that indicate success in attaining the strategy of innovation.

Implementation. After identifying the key success factors and quantifiable measures, the new control system was implemented. During this stage, the firms also attempted to find benchmarks for acceptable performance. This can be considered analogous to setting the standard in a standard cost system; however, the firms used innovative methodologies in defining these benchmarks.

Evaluating the new control systems. The last step the companies undertook was to evaluate the new measures along with the new control systems, which led to new outcomes, both positive and negative.

Deficiencies of traditional accounting systems

The companies that were studied all had complaints about traditional accounting systems that led them to the use of nonfinancial measurements. Most of this section examines weaknesses of controlling an organization using a standard cost system. Certain weaknesses are inherent in a standard cost system, while other deficiencies deal with implementation of standard cost systems.

Variances not actionable at the operating level. One of the major weaknesses was the perceived belief that a variance is not actionable at the operating level. The various departments of the plant had difficulty in interpreting a variance and tracing it to a specific problem. Since an unfavorable variance may have multiple causes, causality is often difficult to determine. Therefore, the actions needed to bring a variance under control are often not easily resolved.

A player who tries to play baseball by watching the scoreboard will not be successful.

Numbers too summarized and on too aggregate a level. Production managers seldom saw a direct connection between actions that they took on the factory floor and the numbers that they saw in monthly standard cost reports. One perceived cause of this problem was that the numbers were summarized on such an aggregate level that managers did not feel individually responsible for the variances. This led to frustration on the floor when the employees on the floor were controlled based on variances. As a result, variance reports were often ignored. As one production foreman noted, "You have to be an accountant to understand cost variances, and if you're an accountant, you're probably not on the factory floor where you can do something about them." One senior manager made the following statement: "In over forty years, I never learned to manage with standard costs."

Lack of actionability. For example, one firm calculated machine hour variances monthly.

A machine hour variance, however, occurs because of numerous activities that take place over the course of a month. While a variance may have indicated whether a machine was working efficiently or inefficiently (according to the standard cost system), the direct cause or solution was very difficult—if not impossible—to determine. The lack of actionability of a variance was a recurring theme in all the firms.

Overreliance on labor or machine hours. These problems were exacerbated when the cost accounting system relied excessively on volume-based allocation rules (i.e., labor or machine hours). Since traditional accounting systems send faulty signals about the cause of costs, reliance on the information that they generate resulted in dysfunctional activities. For example, relying on a cost system that allocates cost based on direct labor may lead managers to make decisions that assume that overhead will decrease in accordance with decreases in direct labor. This is not always the case, however: Overhead usually does not decrease to the degree suggested by a conventional cost accounting system. (At most of the firms visited, management was attempting to implement activity-based cost systems to deal with these problems.)

Dysfunctional activities. The goal of maximizing an individual variance may lead to dysfunctional activities for the firm as a whole. The maximization of any single variance may be detrimental to the firm's overall profitability. Consider the maximization of a price variance, for example: To maximize a favorable price variance, a purchasing department may purchase cheap, low-grade inputs. Low-grade materials, however, may cause manufacturing costs to increase because of quality problems caused by the low-quality inputs. Another example is found when standard costs include some elements of fixed costs. Standard cost systems show idle capacity as a negative variance, so managers may wrongheadedly manufacture products to decrease the unfavorable variance, even when the product is not needed.

Setting standards

Setting standards is a difficult and important step in a well-functioning standard cost system. The firms in this study competed in a complex, swiftly changing environment. Several manufactured computer chips, and faced very steep learning curves in a relatively short period of time.

Given a dynamic environment, the proper updating of standards was a difficult and costly process. Many managers argued that given the dynamic environments, the standards needed to be updated instantaneously. However, updating standards semiannually was the norm; updating weekly was considered prohibitively expensive. As a result, however, the standards that were used were considered constantly out-of-date on the manufacturing floor.

Conflicts with continuous improvement. Managers also argued that standards conflicted with the idea of continuous improvement. If standards were not carefully set, they had the effect of setting norms rather than motivating improvement. Workers may hesitate to perform to their maximum if they realize that the standard for upcoming periods may be revised upward by current results. In summary, observations from the factory floor led to the conclusion that the standard-setting process solidified the idea of norms rather than facilitated a philosophy of continuous improvement.

Lack of timely signals. The standard cost systems in the firms studied failed to provide timely signals. The typical standard cost system calculated variances on a monthly basis. At the end of each month, it would take at least two weeks for the accounting department to collect and dollarize the results and then return them to the manufacturing floor. By the time the results were disseminated, many people on the factory floor considered the information too old to be acted on. This phenomenon is especially noticeable in a dynamic environment where the manufacturing process and operating environment change rapidly.

It should be noted that the firms studied did not do away with their standard cost systems. Most of them still needed standard cost systems for GAAP reporting purposes. However, the companies stopped disseminating standard cost reports widely and little managerial

attention or control was placed on standard cost results.

Determining key success factors

The manufacturers of high-technology components in this study all found their market shares under attack, mostly from Japanese firms. They therefore were under pressure to find more effective manufacturing methods and better ways of controlling and measuring the effectiveness of their systems.

Increased competition caused the firms to reevaluate their success factors. Rather than relying on the signals that they received from their conventional control systems, management felt that a reevaluation of business strategy was required to determine the key success factors to compete successfully.

The business evaluation phase required large amounts of management time and attention. Typically, the firms determined what they considered essential to properly implementing their strategy. One firm went so far as to note that these key success factors, or imperatives, were essential for survival. These imperatives included:

- Customer satisfaction;
- Manufacturing excellence;
- Market leadership;
- Quality;
- Reliability;
- Responsiveness;
- Technological leadership; and
- Superior financial results.

Many of the key success factors were not based on cost considerations. Therefore, standard cost systems, with their heavily financial metric, were not considered adequate systems for controlling organizations.

Determining nonfinancial measures

Once the key success factors were identified, the next step involved finding accurate, timely measures of these key success factors, or imperatives. A few examples help illustrate the process of linking key success factors with quantifiable measures.

Measuring reliability. Several firms determined that reliability about promised delivery dates was an important aspect of competitive advantage. They found that a quantitative measure of on-time delivery was a nonfinancial measure that addressed this imperative. Therefore, the firms implemented control systems that tracked on-time delivery percentages. Even a measure of on-time delivery, however, needed to be fine-tuned. One company initially used the metric of the percentage of shipments delivered on time. Simple reliance on this measure motivated the plant to favor filling an order that was on time to one that was already late; in other words, under this metric, it was better to have one shipment very late and one on time than to have two moderately late shipments. Since the firm did not find this outcome desirable, they also added a chart for the aging of delinquencies.

Responsiveness to customers. Several firms identified responsiveness to customers as another important aspect of competitive advantage. One firm determined that the proper quantification of this key success factor was the lead time required to fill an order. Previously, the company tried using the number of new products introduced, but found this to be a difficult (i.e., poor) measure of responsiveness, because the number of new products did not strongly correlate with the time required to fill a customer's needs.

Quality. A key success factor identified by all the companies was quality. With the advent of just-in-time (JIT) manufacturing systems, the issue of product quality has increased in relevance. No longer can poor quality be buffered by large inventories. Most firms measure quality as a function of the outgoing quality rate. Other nonfinancial measures of quality included product yields and customer returns.

As noted by these examples, most of the nonfinancial measures were not directly based on cost considerations. These high-technology firms found that customers wanted a well-designed, functioning product delivered in a minimum amount of time. Cost considerations were perceived to have secondary importance. At a minimum, a standard cost systems—with its financial emphasis—resulted in unnecessary dollarizing steps.

Finding effective nonfinancial measures

Finding effective nonfinancial measures of key success factors is not a straightforward process. Many of these success factors are multifaceted, so several measures may be needed; in other words, there is rarely a one-to-one mapping between a key success factor and a quantifiable performance measure. To track the key success factor of quality, for example, a company may need to track outgoing quality rates, customer rejections, warranties, and even other potential measures.

It should be emphasized that the use of nonfinancial control systems does not make financial results unimportant. Rather, the firms in this study concluded that favorable financial outcomes would be a by-product of tracking the key success factors by means of nonfinancial controls. In other words, a by-product of control systems of this sort is superior financial results.

Control through nonfinancial measures

After each firm determined the nonfinancial measures to be used, the next decision was how to manage and control the organization using these measures. Two major issues faced the firms in this phase:

1. Determining acceptable performance in terms of the nonfinancial measures; and
2. Placing responsibility for the various nonfinancial measures.

The following sections address both of these issues.

Determining acceptable performance

The firms all had to determine what constituted effective performance. In a standard cost system, this step is analogous to determining the standard. However, the firms found the idea of setting a standard in the conventional sense unappealing for the reasons discussed in previous sections. Some examples in the sections that follow (which are meant to be illustrative rather than exhaustive) show which processes the firms used to categorize performance.

Stressing continuous improvement. Most firms stressed continuous improvement through the quantification of the learning curve. Once the learning curve was quantified, actual results were compared with results predicted from the learning curve. The firms concluded that tying the standard to the learning curve motivated the firm to improve continuously.

One company found that there was a direct relationship between the learning curve and the complexity of the organizational setting in which the problem was being addressed. Problems addressable within one organizational subunit (typically a department) tended to have short and steep learning curves. Problems that required coordination across the boundaries of organizational subunits but that were still addressable within one organization (e.g., multiple departments within a division) tended to have longer learning curves. Finally, problems that required cooperation and coordination across independent organizations (e.g., linkages between customers and suppliers) tended to have the longest and flattest learning curves.

One firm did not explicitly attempt to quantify the learning curve. This firm decided to base the standard on the actual outcome of the preceding reporting period. Current-period performance equal to the previous period's performance was unacceptable, because the new standard required improvement. Usually, progress was followed on a daily or weekly basis. The company's nonfinancial measures were plotted on graphs, with each graph showing continuous improvement as the goal.

Placing responsibility

Once the nonfinancial measures were determined and performance could be measured and evaluated, the firms had to determine how to control the organization through these nonfinancial measures. The issue was how to place responsibility for these measures at the plant (or management) level.

At one company, committees were organized for each of the key success factors and charged with determining how to implement them. For the committees to succeed, it was important to bring together people who were in a position to contribute to the identification of problems, underlying causes, and possible solutions.

The teams were typically staffed with several senior managers from the division and also

others who were familiar with the specific area. Frequently the teams would establish subcommittees to tackle a particular problem. After a team had been formed and its charter identified, the members began problem solving.

Problem solving. The first step in this process was the identification of the appropriate metric to use to measure performance. Once identified, team members collected data on that metric and analyzed the data to identify the sources of the failure. After the source was identified, possible corrective actions were listed and carefully considered. Several were tested before an acceptable action emerged. Once the "best solution" approach was determined, an implementation plan was developed and carried through. The process then began again. As mentioned, these teams were usually held to a target learning curve. Actual results were compared periodically to the targets, and teams were required to explain both positive and negative deviations.

Another firm delegated responsibility of the nonfinancial measures to the various departments within the plan. The firm attempted to match departmental responsibility for a nonfinancial measure with the department that had the major influence on that particular measure. Each department then tracked and was responsible for its assigned nonfinancial measure. For example:

- The manufacturing department was controlled based on manufacturing cycle times;
- The production planning department was controlled based on on-time delivery percentages and inventory levels; and
- The quality control department was controlled based on the rate of customer returns.

Strengths and weaknesses of the nonfinancial measures

The firms noted many strengths of the new measures as compared to using the standard cost system for control purposes. First, the nonfinancial measures were more directly traceable to the strategies (i.e., key success factors) of the firm. Management felt that progress on these measures directly affected the success of firm strategy. In addition, the measures did not require the dollarizing step.

Another perceived benefit was that the measures were actionable. One of the major complaints against a standard cost system was that the cause and cure of a given unfavorable variance was not always easily determinable. In contrast, nonfinancial measures were actionable at the plant level. For instance, a drop in quality was quickly determined using nonfinancial measures, so remedial steps could quickly be taken to solve the problem. As another example, consider the problem when a firm has a poor response time to customer orders. A typical standard cost system would not easily highlight this problem. However, the nonfinancial measures of on-time performance (and possibly cycle times) would directly address this issue.

Nonfinancial systems were also found to work well with high-technology manufacturing systems. The close coupling of manufacturing systems within an organization through manufacturing technologies such as JIT resulted in the increased importance of timely measures. Most firms argued that a nonfinancial measure could be calculated and returned to interested parties faster than a financial measure.

Role of controllers. The role of controllers changed in these firms. As noted previously, standard cost systems were not scrapped in the firms we visited. Therefore, the controller's office still calculated standard costs for purposes of GAAP, though standard cost reports were not typically disseminated beyond the controller's office.

The influence of controllers is likely to decrease if controllers no longer prepare control reports. In the firms in this study, the controller's (cost accounting) office never took an antagonistic stance against attempts to implement a nonfinancial control system. In some of the firms, the controller's office was actively involved—and even took a leading role—in the design and implementation of the new control system. At the other end of the specturm, the controller's office at one of the firms did not even participate in implementation of the new system; the change were designed and implemented solely by the manufacturing floor.

In those firms in which the controller was actively involved in the process, the controller's role changed significantly. Rather than being the source of control information, the controller's office was seen as a facilitator and an expert on the control and measurement process. The controller's office helped in determining the new measures and in measurement implementation issues.

Problems found with the nonfinancial measures

While the new measures were considered superior to the old methods of control, the nonfinancial system was not problem-free. One of the key difficulties of the nonfinancial system was the inability to dollarize the amount of improvement in the nonfinancial measurements. The tie betweem improvements in the nonfinancial measures and profits was unclear. Managers were not sure that their efforts were being rewarded with improvements in the bottom line.

A business strategy of innovation does not lend itself easily to quantifiable measures that indicate success in attaining the strategy of innovation.

For example, a dollarized quantification of decreasing cycle time was difficult (if not impossible) to do. The inability to quantify changes in terms of their effects on profits detracts from the impact of a nonfinancial system. Indeed, much of the uncertainty that exists about nonfinancial systems would dissipate if such a linkage were possible. This tie between nonfinancial and financial results would be very difficult to make with a traditional financial system. For example, one of the benefits of an excellent on-time performance record may be repeat business from the customer. Poor on-time performance may lead to decreased sales or to loss of customers. A typical financial accounting system may not explicitly pick up the opportunity cost of poor on-time performance. To tie nonfinancial measures to the bottom line, a financial measurement system would have to be modified. Items not included in traditional financial statements—opportunity costs, for example—would have to be quantified to make the tie-in explicit.

Going beyond the difficult tie between financial and nonfinancial measures, the measures may conflict in a short time horizon. For example, assume that a firm decides to purchase new machinery to decrease manufacturing cycle times. The expenses of this purchase are easily traced to the income statement. On the other hand, the increased revenues are difficult to tie to the decreased cycle times, so managers may perceive that this acquisition decreases net income. This tension is magnified when the division or plant is a profit center and upper management is controlled based on divisional profit.

Another example of this phenomenon is shipping behavior at the end of a period. At the end of a period, a plant may ship high-margin goods ahead of schedule at the expense of on-time delivery of lower-margin goods. This results in improved short-run financial performance, but an unfavorable on-time delivery performance. The financial results mask the fact that the late delivery of the goods will invariably decrease customer satisfaction, yet recognizing the profit now or next quarter may have no lasting effect on corporate performance.

Need for an overall theoretical framework. Another weakness of this implementation process is that without an overall theoretical framework, nonfinancial measures may conflict and make proper trade-offs difficult to determine. As a simple example, assume that the manufacturing department is controlled based on yields, while the quality assurance department is held responsible for customer returns. Rejections by quality assurance not only decrease customer returns, but also decrease yields. Therefore, a product that is borderline for rejection will probably lead to contention between these departments. As a further example, decreasing manufacturing cycle times at the exclusion of all other factors may be detrimental. For instance, the wrong products or lot sizes may be produced to lower cycle times.

Gaming. As with all measurement systems, "gaming" with nonfinancial measures may occur to optimize particular employees' per-

formance at the expense of optimal performance for the organization as a whole. The on-time delivery example given previously provides an example of this motivation to play games.

If the nonfinancial performance measure is the percentage of shipments delivered on time, there is an incentive for managers to sacrifice one late shipment for the sake of shipments that can be delivered on time. That is, on-time delivery performance looks better when nine shipments are shipped on time with one being shipped ten days late than when ten shipments are all delivered one day late. For the company as a whole, however, it may be better to deliver numerous shipments a little late rather than one shipment very late.

Conclusion

The rise of nonfinancial control systems occurs as companies attempt to become operations-driven, because many key success factors are not easily measured by the typical standard cost system. A nonfinancial control system attempts to address the actionable steps that lead to a company's success. However, as with any control system, a nonfinancial system cannot get rid of all dysfunctional behavior.

Nonfinancial systems are in their infancy; only now are they being designed and implemented in any number. Understanding the strengths, weaknesses, and trade-offs in nonfinancial systems requires development of an overall framework that explains these interrelationships. Much of the uncertainty that companies face in implementing nonfinancial systems will disappear once an accepted framework is developed. Certainly, a major missing link is a tie-in between nonfinancial performance measures and financial performance. ▲

Reprinted from *Journal of Cost Management,* Spring 1992, pp. 31–38. Copyright © 1992 by Warren Gorham Lamont, a division of Research Institute of America Inc. All rights reserved. Used by permission.

Notes
1. The author wishes to acknowledge the comments of Professor John Shank on previous drafts of this paper.

Performance Measurement for World Class Manufacturing

Brian H. Maskell

Traditional management and accounting systems are obstacles in the road to world class manufacturing. Companies can remove these obstacles by designing performance measures that reflect their companies' manufacturing strategies. New world class manufacturing performance measures relate directly to manufacturing strategy and are primarily nonfinancial in nature. The new performance measures must also be simple to use and must change over time as conditions change.

A primary problem facing many manufacturing companies today is that the traditional methods of performance measurement do not reflect those issues most important to a world class manufacturer. For example, traditional measures are largely expressed in financial terms, are derived from cost and management accounting systems, and are either irrelevant or misleading to the managers responsible for controlling the production and distribution of world class manufacturing.[1]

Analysts have completed considerable work in recent years examining the inadequacies of modern cost and management accounting techniques and suggesting new approaches to alleviate associated problems. They have developed a number of new performance measurement techniques. (For more on specific measures, see page H4-5.)

Although the new performance measures used by world class manufacturers vary considerably from one company to the next, seven common characteristics must exist for a system to be successful. For example, new world class manufacturing performance measures:

- directly relate to manufacturing strategy,
- primarily use nonfinancial performance techniques,
- vary between locations,
- change over time as company needs change,
- are simple and easy to use,
- provide fast feedback to operators and managers, and
- are intended to foster improvement rather than just monitoring. (See Figure 1.)

Relating to manufacturing strategy

A world class manufacturer will invariably have a clearly defined manufacturing strategy. Although the content of a strategy may differ from one company to another, the strategy will center around such issues as quality, reliability, short lead times, flexibility, or customer satisfaction. The chosen performance measures must directly measure the success or failure of the manufacturing strategy.

Two primary reasons exist for keeping the performance measures in line with the corporate manufacturing strategy. The first reason includes your need to know how well your company is achieving the goals laid out in its manufacturing strategy. You therefore should choose a small number of pertinent performance measures that enable company managers to constantly assess the manufacturing strategy's progress.

The second reason is that people tend to concentrate more on the things that are measured than on things that are not measured. For example, if you measure and report the results of an employee's work, that person will most likely be motivated to improve the quality of the items measured. In addition, the choice of performance measures can steer

Figure 1. *Performance Measurement Criteria*

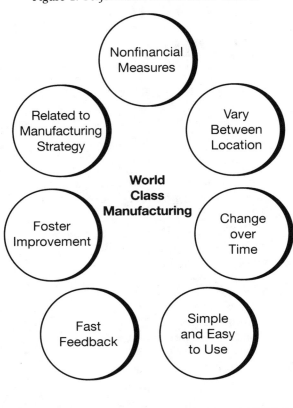

the direction of the company. Appropriately selected performance measures give a clear signal to company employees concerning senior management's top priorities.

Nonfinancial measures

In traditional manufacturing, financial results are of paramount importance in reporting corporate performance. In world class manufacturing, however, performance measures are usually the *only* measures the company's operational staff uses.

Relying on financial reports for operational performance measurement leads executives to assume that financial reports are valid and relevant to the control of the daily operations of a business. This assumption, however, is wrong. Not only are financial reports irrelevant to the daily operations of a business, they are often confusing and misleading. For example, traditional measures are not designed to address aspects of a company's business such as quality, inventory levels, employee participation, production synchro-

nization, on-time deliveries, and customer satisfaction. The performance measures used to control production plants and warehouses must be directly relevant and applicable to the jobs completed. Financial reports are relevant for external reporting in world class manufacturing (there is still a need to have the cost accounts and the financial accounts integrated and consistent); nonfinancial reports are more useful.

Measures vary between locations

The way businesses implement change in world class manufacturing usually varies considerably from one company to another—and from one location to another within the same company. Performance measures may differ significantly between locations because different aspects of WCM are more important in one location than another. Companies must recognize these differences when putting performance measurement systems in place.

Businesses cannot implement world class manufacturing techniques by merely setting policies and then expecting employees to put the policies into practice. Because the changes required for WCM are so radical from traditional manufacturing, each production plant needs to have at least one senior manager with "champion of change" vision, determination, and skill.

In addition, there are significant differences in needs of manufacturing plants. These differences derive from the kinds of products manufactured, the production processes required, the people employed within the plant, the age and suitability of the equipment, and a plant's existing strengths and weaknesses. Different methods of measuring performance therefore are needed to accommodate these differences of style, priorities, and need.

This approach runs counter to the tenets of traditional management accounting. For example, one of the most useful aspects of cost accounting techniques is that the same reports are used by everybody in the company. Having all departments use the same report provides a consistency that helps to simplify the comparison of one plant with another. In WCM, however, the control of the company focuses on the achievement of a range of strategic goals. These goals frequently vary from division to division and from plant to plant.

Figure 2. *Performance Measures and the Controller*

As corporate changes take place, the posture of corporate financial executives usually falls into one of two categories. Controllers either merely agree that changes should take place, or they actively sponsor, support, and become part of the change. Unfortunately, many controllers, while agreeing with the need for change, do not recognize the critical impact these changes should have on the financial control of the organization. Some controllers imagine that the company can be radically changed from the inside while retaining the same tried and trusted accounting and performance measurement systems. Nothing, however, can be further from the truth.

Many companies find themselves saddled with increasingly irrelevant accounting systems as they implement the techniques of world class manufacturing. Traditional management accounting is at best irrelevant to a world class manufacturer, and frequently is misleading and dangerous. In fact, it is common for the introduction of advanced manufacturing techniques to show poor short-term results when measured by the traditional methods. As a result, many companies hinder or halt these potentially beneficial changes because their success is measured by misleading criteria. Consequently, the financial control systems can become a wasteful burden leading the company in the wrong direction.

Measures change over time

The concept of continuous improvement is an important aspect of just-in-time and world class manufacturing. The idea is that nothing is ever perfect and no matter how much improvement is made, there is still room for more improvement. Throughout the implementation of a world class approach to manufacturing, and beyond, the company's priorities will change. The performance measurement system therefore must be flexible enough to accommodate these changes.

World class manufacturing is not a project that is started on one date and completed on another. Companies that are successful with world class manufacturing recognize that a cultural change is required in the way their businesses are run. There are no "quick fixes" here.

At the heart of WCM is the concept of continuous improvement. Continuous improvement consists of everyone in the company striving to improve their productivity and effectiveness, day in and day out. It is an atmosphere of consistent analysis and innovation. The journey to world class status is made up of thousands of small steps; each improvement opening the possibility to more improvement.

When a company introduces the ideas of world class manufacturing to a plant, the project team should concentrate on the specific aspects of WCM that are important at that time. Issues such as quality, customer service level, lead times, and inventory investment are often the highest priorities. A company must then establish performance measures to address these issues.

Once a company sees positive results from its introduction of WCM techniques with high-priority issues, it should switch the emphasis of the plant to other issues. Although the

> *Not only are financial reports irrelevant to the daily operations of a business, they are often confusing and misleading.*

original aspects are still important, improvement in these areas enables the company's managers to focus on new areas of improvement. Managers, however, should still continue to submit reports of summarized information on the previous issues. In this way, the company can monitor the old issues for continuing improvement and highlight any problems, while giving the new issues primary attention.

Simple and easy to use

In traditional manufacturing, many companies use complex techniques of performance measurement. These techniques often relate more than one aspect of performance and provide an index or ratio for measurement. Because many employees find these performance measurements difficult to understand, they are usually unsuccessful within world class manufacturing.

To monitor and motivate employees successfully, companies must ensure that employees clearly understand performance measurement reports. Employees must see the relevance of the measures to their jobs and to the company's manufacturing objectives.

A plain and simple measure of the most important elements of the business is better than subtle or complex measures. If a company measures an issue directly and presents the results in straightforward terms, employees tend to more easily understand these results. Consequently, the performance measure is more effective.

Traditional performance measurement techniques rely on the production of reports that are distributed to managers. These reports are usually produced weekly or monthly and contain a full analysis of the issues measured. In WCM, however, more immediate and direct methods of performance measurement are needed. Such methods include the use of charts, graphs, signals, and bulletin boards. It is common within world class manufacturing plants to see the results of performance measures posted continuously throughout the day on boards, charts, or graphs located adjacent to the production cells or lines.

Companies should express all performance measures in terms of what is done right, rather than to emphasize problems.

The advantage to this kind of presentation is that information is shown clearly, directly, and in a way all employees can understand. Direct reporting methods also can be useful motivators for shop-floor personnel. These employees, for example, can monitor their own performance on a continuous basis, while the company posts results for all to see.

Manual signals are useful when the information measured is simple. For example, colored lights are often used to indicate if a machine or cell is meeting quality standards. The light is green when all is well, orange when there is a problem requiring attention, and red when the operator has stopped the line because of a quality deviation.

Although it is not always feasible to use these direct display methods, they can be very powerful performance measurements in the day-to-day management of the production process.

Fast feedback

In most companies using traditional manufacturing, cost accounting reports are available weekly or monthly. These reports show the variances in such areas as material costs, material usage, labor productivity, labor rates, and overhead allocation. However, by the time the reports reach the employee, it is usually too late to do anything about a problem identified in them. Either the problem occurred so long ago that it is not possible to investigate the cause, or the plant already identified the problem and corrected it by other means.

With world class manufacturing, companies must detect and resolve problems as they occur. Companies cannot afford to wait several days while reports are produced. World class manufacturing emphasizes the elimination of anything that causes waste within the production process. For example, if companies give operators training and equipment to continuously monitor quality, rate of flow, and set-up times, these operators can detect and correct many problems on the spot. The purpose of any measurement of quality is to detect production deviations so that the root cause of a deviation can be eliminated.

In a traditional manufacturing environment, businesses overcome production problems by having additional safety stocks of components and subassemblies. Companies hold these safety stocks so that scrap materials or materials requiring rework do not hold up production. Because most traditional material planning and control systems allow the user to establish standard scrap quantities for components and assemblies, the system automatically calculates a need for additional supplies of material.

This approach is anathema to a world class manufacturer. To hold additional safety stock in lieu of future quality problems is the opposite of a just-in-time philosophy. In world class manufacturing, companies must keep inventory levels low. In fact, businesses should eliminate all inventory levels if possible. Fast feedback of quality deviations facilitates problem resolution, continuous improvement, and low inventory levels.

If a company must provide information in a printed report, these reports must be available as soon as possible. For example, a company can make a customer service report available daily, by shift, or as required. It is particularly useful if supervisors can request reports when needed rather than having to request performance reports via overnight computer runs.

Foster improvement

The last characteristic of performance measurement for world class manufacturing deals with employee motivation. Traditional performance measures are based primarily on monitoring employees' work; they are not targeted at providing information that will help employees improve their productivity. Selected performance measurements in world class manufacturing, however, must do more than merely monitor employees' work. Performance measures must clearly show where improvement was made and where more improvement is possible.

As a rule, companies should express all performance measures in terms of what is done right, rather than to emphasize problems. For example, it is better for a company to express production efficiency as a yield of good product rather than a reject rate. It is also better to show the percentage of orders that are shipped to customers on time, then to show the number of late orders. Although some of these approaches may seem cosmetic, they do betray an underlying corporate attitude—that everyone in the company must concentrate on getting better.

Companies must use performance measures in world class manufacturing nonpejoratively.

The measures themselves are, of course, impartial. The important issue is the way that employees and management interpret and use these measures. Using performance measurements in the traditional way is contrary to the objectives of world class manufacturing; using them in a way that encourages innovation and problem solving promotes continuous improvement.

Therefore, the controller of a company moving into world class manufacturing can either be an important agent of change, or an obstructive dinosaur holding the company back. As an agent of change, the controller can bring a significant balance and perspective that otherwise is unavailable to the manufacturing, design, and marketing people implementing the changes. To change corporate culture, support must come from the top of the organization. Financial management is therefore an essential piece of the picture. ▲

Notes
1. For the purpose of this article, world class manufacturing (WCM) describes the series of techniques and approaches introduced in recent years to enable western manufacturers to compete with the best Japanese and Pacific Rim manufacturers. Although world class manufacturing is a loosely defined term, it includes an emphasis on quality, a just-in-time approach to production scheduling, significant changes in the methods of managing people, and a concern for meeting the changing requirements of the customer.

PART I

Pricing

CHAPTER 11

Use Tactical Pricing to Uncover Hidden Profits

Robert A. Garda

Astute competitors are turning to the flip side of cost—price—for the next wave of performance enhancements. Contrary to the accepted wisdom, pricing often can be controlled and managed. Tactical pricing—the transaction-by-transaction control of pricing decisions—is one of the great unused profit levers available to management. Astute pricing tactics can yield nearly immediate and sustainable increases of 5 and even 10 percentage points in return on sales, without large price increases or significant lost sales volume.

Pricing is a bit like the weather. People complain about it; they worry about it; and in the end, they feel there is not much they can do about it. But unlike the weather, pricing can in fact be controlled. It can be managed. And it can be a powerful profit tool for business. Consider the following two examples:

☐ **Example 1.** The general manager of a $165-million electrical equipment manufacturer believed his sales force was leaving too much money on the table with its winning bids. The company tracked bids only on lost orders, which caused it to put downward pressure on prices. By analyzing successful bids, the general manager discovered that the company's average "winning" price quote was a full 7% below competition. Further, his research with key established customers revealed that, because of switching costs, it was necessary only to match the competitive bid to secure these orders.

A system to track all bids—both won and lost—and to encourage less aggressive price cutting with existing customers was implemented. The result one year later: a 5-per-

centage-point gain in return on sales and increased profits of $8 million annually.

☐ **Example 2.** Executives of a specialty chemical manufacturer disagreed over whether to target small-company customers for a sales push. While large customers brought in volume, smaller customers were believed to be more profitable because they paid higher invoice prices. However, sales were reported at the invoice level only, and the final "pocket price" paid by any given customer was not tracked.

It was discovered that despite higher invoice prices, smaller customers actually were paying a lower final "pocket price" because they were taking advantage of off-invoice incentives such as cash discounts, year-end rebates, free cases, and freight allowances—all intended for larger customers. (Exhibit 1 depicts the pocket price "waterfall" for the company.)

Armed with this information, management cut back on off-invoice programs. The effective average price to smaller customers was increased by 9% without changing list or invoice prices. And because of the strength of the sales organization, no large customers and only a few smaller customers were lost due to the changes.

These examples demonstrate that tactical pricing—the transaction-by-transaction control of pricing decisions—is one of the great unused profit levers available to management. Astute pricing tactics can yield nearly immediate and sustainable increases of 5 and even 10 percentage points in return on sales, without large price increases or significant lost sales volume.

Exhibit 1. *Pocket Price Waterfall*

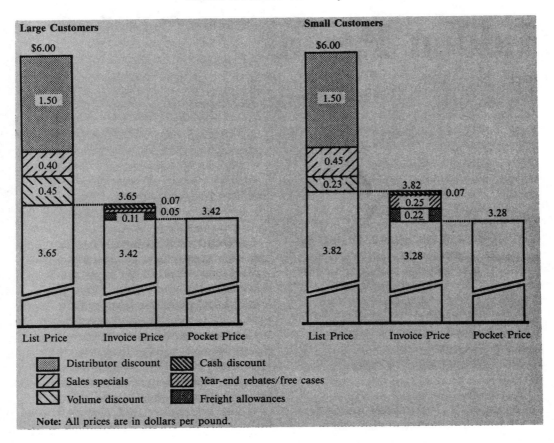

After nearly two decades of emphasizing cost reduction and productivity improvements as the means to increase profits, companies are reaching the point of diminishing returns. Many competitors, like the companies discussed in Examples 1 and 2, are turning to the flip side of cost—price—for the next wave of performance enhancement.

Tactical versus strategic pricing

Tactical pricing is the day-to-day management of pricing. In contrast, strategic pricing defines the company's longer-term price/value image in the market. Put another way, strategy is the grand battle plan designed to win the war over time, while tactical pricing is the guerrilla maneuvering that achieves the day's victory. And while strategic pricing decisions can net long-term competitive advantage, tactical pricing often yields a bigger immediate payoff.

Tactical pricing goes beyond traditional quantity and functional discounting to consider the unique customer-and order-specific costs of each transaction. Its goal: to optimize the frequently competing selling objectives of winning orders, maximizing order profitability, building long-term account potential, and assuming competitive positioning in the marketplace.

Tactical pricing can help a company:

- Shift the mix of orders toward more profitable products.
- Reduce the amount of money "left on the table" in winning situations.
- Gain share by selectively cutting price with specific customers—where doing so will not lead to a price war.
- Appear to exert upward pressure on industry prices in order to misdirect and confuse competitors.

Despite the potential profit impact, tactical pricing remains largely misunderstood, undermanaged, and virtually ignored in many companies.

For starters, poor pricing practices and missed opportunities are difficult to detect. As was true in Example 1, involving the electrical equipment manufacturer, few companies track competitive prices. They know their own "won" and "lost" bids, of course. But for wins, they generally do not know how much lower they were than competitors.

In losses, they may only know that their price was too high, without any specifics as to the competitive price range or significant non-price factors. Unfortunately, both scenarios promote downward price pressure and contribute to a constant, though vague, sense that the company's prices are too high.

Those companies that do track competitive bids usually track a composite of their own won and lost bids against the competitors' winning bids. This comparison always makes the competition appear to be lower in price. It is, in effect, comparing apples to oranges; the only relevant comparison is your "win" prices and the competitors' "win" prices—the true market price.

In addition, as was illustrated in Example 2, the specialty chemical company, few companies track "pocket price": the final cash-in-the-pocket price paid after all allowances, discounts, and deals. As a result, they have only a fuzzy picture of any one order's true profitability or where they really stand versus competitors' pricing.

Others believe that price is simply not manageable; they reason that price is set by the market at the point where supply and demand meet. However, the economic reality of nearly all markets is not a price point but a price band—a range of prices bid, accepted, and paid after all discounts and markdowns. The essence of tactical pricing is knowing where to price within the band in order to optimize a particular transaction.

Still others believe (erroneously, in many cases) that price differentiation among customers is illegal per se. They adhere to a printed price sheet and discount schedule for fear of FTC prosecution.

It is a little known fact that the Robinson-Patman Act dictates that price needs to be the same *only* for the same product sold to two customers who compete with each other. When these conditions do not exist, as would be the case in many industrial and business-to-business situations, pricing flexibility abounds.

Finally, the fact is that many companies have gotten along fine in the past with across-the-board price increases and have not had to worry about transaction pricing. Thanks to increased competition, changing market dynamics, and cost pressure, those days are gone.

"While strategic pricing decisions can net long-term competitive advantage, tactical pricing often yields a bigger immediate payoff."

The combined, bottom-line results of these myths, misunderstandings, and information gaps are large sums of money left on the table in winning bid situations, volume orders lost because of lack of selective price flexibility, and profit erosion caused by a weak product mix or inaccurate cost information.

Three key elements

Effective tactical pricing requires close attention to three principal elements: price level, timing, and method of communication.

☐ Determining price level—the target point within the price band for a given transaction—involves a clear understanding of where you stand, not just in relation to the competitors' quotes, but also in relation to such customer-specific characteristics as price visibility and price sensitivity.

Price visibility is the ability of a competitor to "see" your price "through" a given customer. A high-visibility customer is one who will make your price known to your competitors. High-visibility situations can be used to misdirect competitors about costs and pricing strategy.

In such a case, a company may want to price high, even if it occasionally means lost business, in order to give competitors the impression of upward price pressure. On the other hand, with a low-visibility customer, price can be selectively lowered to discreetly build volume.

Price sensitivity (the customer's sensitivity to variations in price) is also related to switching costs—the cost to the customer of obtaining a new supplier—and to the length and strength of the relationship between the customer and supplier. When price sensitivity is low, price should be set at, or even above, the competitive quote. Conversely, high sensitivity demands lower prices.

For example, a mechanical equipment supplier had a static share of a declining market and a pricing structure that was well known to competitors. Taking a fresh look at customers, management segmented the market on the basis of price sensitivity and visibility.

> *"High-visibility situations can be used to misdirect competitors about cost and pricing strategy."*

Prices were raised for selected high-visibility customers, giving competitors the impression of upward price pressure. At the same time, the company gained share with low-visibility/high-sensitivity customers by selectively cutting price.

For low-visibility/low-sensitivity customers, nonprice incentives such as engineering assistance were used to pick up additional volume. In six months, the company achieved a 4-percentage-point share gain overall while letting competitors lead a general 3% price increase.

☐ The timing of pricing changes can be nearly as important as the changes themselves. For example, a simple tactic of lagging competitors in announcing price increases can produce the perception among customers that you are the most customer-responsive supplier. The extent of the lag can also be important.

In one company, an independent survey of customers showed that the perception of being the most customer-responsive supplier was generated just as effectively by a six-week lag in following a competitor's price increase as by a six-month lag. A considerable amount of money would have been left on the table during the unnecessary four-and-one-half-month delay in announcing a price increase.

☐ Communicating pricing changes also has tactical ramifications. Even though deliberate advance communication to competitors concerning pricing changes is forbidden by law, competitors will closely monitor your price announcements. Publicizing a price increase is, therefore, generally desirable, provided care is taken to properly inform salespeople and customers in advance. It will position you in the eyes of competitors as the price leader.

The exception to the rule of publicizing price increases is the occasional customer. Routinely announcing price increases to infrequent customers will only tend to erode goodwill.

In contrast, price reductions that are widely announced can produce competitive retaliation and a downward price spiral. It is generally best to effect price cuts indirectly and to communicate cuts only through direct contact with customers by such methods as changes in terms of sale, reduced service charges, or revised discount schedules.

Unseen competitive edge

At its best, tactical pricing is invisible to competitors. While a company's overall strategy (to be positioned as the highest-value supplier in the market, for example) may be obvious to all competitors, tactical thrusts (e.g., low-visibility price cutting, off-list discounting, etc.) if effectively executed, should pass undetected.

With this in mind, companies that embrace tactical pricing sometimes completely do away with printed price lists and simply quote price directly on a case-by-case basis. While it may not be appropriate in all situations, the tactic never fails to create a good deal of uncertainty in the market, as competitors have much less to "shoot at" in gauging where to set prices.

Exhibit 2. *Information Needed for Pricing Decisions*

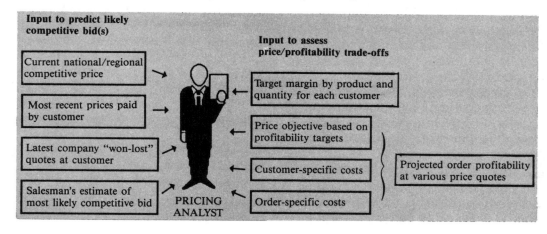

For example, an electrical components supplier, the share leader in its market, strictly adhered to a printed price list for its OEM customers, along with a predictable discount structure for large accounts. As a result, the number two competitor knew what prices to beat with key customers.

In a year-long targeted sales offensive, the number two company cut prices and gained five share points in direct take-aways because the leader was afraid to match the new, lower prices for fear of losing margins and because of the misguided fear of legal problems with differential pricing.

Finally, fed up with the share loss and the overall price decline and assured that differential pricing was not an issue given its customer base, the leader launched a three-part program. First, to protect existing OEM accounts, the leader linked its computers with customers' material requirements planning and order cycle systems; this provided a valuable service while effectively "building a wall" around these accounts by increasing switching costs.

Second, the leader attacked number two's largest account with sharp discounts, sending a strong message to the number two company about the consequences of a price war. While not winning over the customer, the leader's "shot across the bow" was clearly understood.

Third, to disguise its pricing and create confusion among all competitors, the leader took its price list off the market and began pricing each customer on its own merits.

The end result: The leader stopped the share erosion among its existing accounts and switched some of its competitors' customers for a regain of six share points.

The basic principles of tactical pricing are not strikingly new. However, until the advent of widespread computerization, controlling and tracking the myriad factors involved in every transaction was nearly impossible for a company of any significant size.

But computers can now provide the speed and detail-handling capability needed to allow product- and transaction-specific pricing decisions. Systems can be as simple as a single personal computer or as sophisticated as a massive international MIS. Whatever its form, the objective of such a system is to help a company forecast competitive pricing and set its own price according to price/profitability trade-offs. (Exhibit 2 depicts the data elements required for such a system.)

Pricing pitfalls

Tactical pricing does entail risks. Chief among these is the danger of proceeding without accurate, detailed information on true cost and profitability.

For example, an automotive components manufacturer based its pricing on the belief that small parts produced higher gross profit margins because of a greater price-to-materials markup (5 : 1 as compared with 3 : 1 for large parts). However, the manufacturing people complained that gross profit was not an accurate measure of product profitability because large parts absorbed more than their share of overhead.

They reasoned that an extruding machine generated more pounds of product per hour of capacity for large parts than it did for small parts; therefore, the large parts required less labor and overhead per pound.

Dissatisfied with overall profit performance, management agreed to reexamine its traditional gross margin costing philosophy. It discovered that taking into account the relatively greater machine time required for smaller, more complex parts produced a radically different cost profile. Variable contribution margin per machine hour became the new costing basis.

"A significant risk of tactical pricing is adopting the approach without first reorienting and, if necessary, retraining salespeople."

Comparison of the old and new costing systems for recent orders produced some shocking results. With the new costing method, management discovered that several orders that had been rejected due to below-target gross profit would have generated excellent returns under the variable-contribution-per-machine-hour system. With the new costing structure in place, profitability, now much more clearly understood on a product-by-product basis, increased dramatically.

A second significant risk of tactical pricing is adopting the approach without first reorienting and, if necessary, retraining salespeople. Traditional salesmanship stresses making the sale above nearly all else, with the result that significant sums of money may be left on the table in the bidding process.

Salespeople must have clear guidelines and decision rules to follow, as well as information that will enable them to set price to optimize the selling opportunity by taking into account profitability and volume objectives, order-specific costs, price visibility and sensitivity, and competitive positioning. In some cases, the sales incentive plan may need to be changed to reflect profit as well as volume objectives.

The importance of accurate cost information and appropriate decision rules is illustrated in the example of a component supplier that attempted to control the pricing process through clear distinctions in pricing authority but little else. Under the assumption that discounts are inversely related to gross profit levels, product managers were allowed to authorize prices up to 35% off list; marketing managers, 45% off list; and the general manager, 60% off list.

Sales were healthy, yet profitability was disappointing. Even though most individual orders met their profit targets, the overall gross profit objective of 40% was not being met.

Examining costs in more detail, management discovered that the gross profit measure did not depict the true profitability of its products; variable contribution margin was a better barometer. With hindsight, it was clear that well-intentioned decision rules had been subverted by inaccurate cost information.

For example, variable contribution margin costing revealed that, for some products, a 35% discount yielded only a 10% contribution margin; for others, a 60% discount yielded a 50% margin.

In effect, the combination of misleading cost information and discounting rules allowed the product manager to unknowingly authorize prices below the corporate profitability objective. On the other end of the spectrum, this obliged the general manager to get involved in relatively unimportant pricing decisions.

Given the new information, the decision rules were changed to a "cost up" profit orientation instead of a "price down" discount approach (i.e., pricing decisions were kicked upstairs for reasons of lower profits, not solely because of higher discounts).

Pricing remains a "black box" to many companies: misunderstood, undermanaged, and virtually ignored. As a result, many companies continue to leave large sums of money on the table with their winning bids, miss opportunities to secure profitable volume orders, inaccurately assess true profitability, and unknowingly telegraph cost structure and pricing tactics to competitors.

Astute tactical pricing offers a major, untapped opportunity for dramatic and sustainable profit improvement for both industrial product manufacturers and for consumer goods companies. Those companies that successfully embrace tactical pricing will be among the winners of the 1990s. ▲

CHAPTER 12

Predatory Pricing, the Price-Cost Test, and Activity-Based Costing

Bruce E. Committe and D. Jacque Grinnell

Federal antitrust laws make it unlawful to engage in practices that result in monopolies or that otherwise lessen competition. Predatory pricing is one practice that the courts have construed as monopolistic. To help determine which prices are predatory, courts have adopted a test that compares the price of a product or service to its "cost," but the courts have been unable to agree on which measure of cost to use. This article provides the legal background to the price-cost test controversy and explains why activity-based costing (ABC) provides an appropriate measure of cost for the price-cost test.

T he federal antitrust laws make it unlawful for companies engaged in interstate commerce to engage in practices that result (or tend to result) in monopolies or that otherwise lessen competition. Broad statutory language has allowed the courts wide discretion in deciding which practices are unlawful. Predatory pricing is one such practice, and it occurs when a company prices its products and services with the primary intent to reduce competition in the marketplace by eliminating competitors already present and by discouraging would-be competitors from choosing to compete.

The price/cost comparison

Distinguishing low prices that are predatory from low prices that are merely competitive has proved to be difficult. To help draw the line, courts have adopted a test that compares the price of a product or service to its "cost." When price is below "cost," courts are more likely to infer predation because they rarely find a valid business reason for companies to charge prices below cost.

The measure of cost used for the price-cost test is critical to any court decision. Courts have been unable to agree, however, about which measure of cost to use. This article provides the legal background to the price-cost test controversy and explains why activity-based costing (ABC) provides the appropriate methodology for measuring cost for the price-cost test.

U.S. antitrust statutes

The four U.S. antitrust statutes that are the source of the predatory pricing prohibition are:

1. The Sherman Act of 1890;
2. The Clayton Act of 1914;
3. The Robinson-Patman Act of 1936; and
4. The Federal Trade Commission Act of 1914.

Although the term "predatory pricing" does not appear in the language of any of these statutes, these statutes are the primary authoritative reference for all reasoning by the courts in the development of predatory pricing rules. (See accompanying box, "Federal Antitrust Statutes," for detailed explanations of these federal antitrust statutes.)

The four antitrust statutes taken as a whole contain two substantive and two jurisdictional provisions that are the foundation of the evolving predatory pricing doctrine and the related price-cost test.

The two substantive provisions are Section 2 of the Sherman Act and Section 2(a) of the Clayton Act as amended by the Robinson-Patman Act. Together these two provisions make it unlawful to:

• Monopolize;
• Attempt to monopolize; or

- Price discriminate when the effect is to lessen competition.

The two jurisdictional provisions are Section 4 of the Clayton Act and Section 5 of the Federal Trade Commission Act. These two provisions effectively give injured private parties and the Federal Trade Commission authority to civilly enforce the substantive provisions of the antitrust laws.

Monopolizing. Regarding "monopolizing" behavior, the U.S. appellate courts have stated that it consists of two elements:

(1) the *possession* of monopoly power in the relevant market and (2) the *willful* acquisition or maintenance of that power as distinguished from growth or development as a consequence of superior product, business acumen, or historic accident [emphasis added].[1]

Monopoly power is "the power to control prices or exclude competition in a relevant market."[2] Thus, the charge of "monopolizing" requires proof that either the defendant has willfully achieved a monopoly or (in the case of a natural monopoly or a monopoly not willfully achieved) that the defendant has exercised its monopoly power improperly. The price-cost relationship provides the courts with one method for determining whether acquisition or maintenance of monopoly power is willful.

Attempting to monopolize. Concerning "attempting to monopolize" behavior, the courts have stated that it consists of three elements:

(1) specific *intent* to control prices or destroy competition with respect to a part of commerce, (2) predatory or anticompetitive *conduct* directed to accomplishing the unlawful purpose, and (3) a *dangerous probability* of success [emphasis added].[3]

Thus, a successful charge of attempting to monopolize requires proof that, although the would-be monopolist has not already achieved a monopoly, a dangerous probability of achieving it exists. In this case, the courts look to price below cost as evidence of both intent and conduct.

Product price discrimination. Regarding "product price discrimination" behavior, the courts have stated that it occurs when a business charges different prices for the same

product at the same time to different customers without meeting one of the business purpose exceptions. This practice is unlawful, however, only when the different prices have a *reasonable probability* of lessening competition.

The courts have concluded that the "reasonable probability" standard required in price discrimination cases is lower than the "dangerous probability" standard required in attempting to monopolize cases. The cause of this lower standard is the use of the word "may" in the Robinson-Patman price discrimination statute (see accompanying box). Once again, the courts look to a price-cost test for evidence indicating that a reasonable probability of lessening competition exists.

Development of predatory pricing doctrine and the price-cost test

As noted earlier, the antitrust laws make no reference to predatory pricing, much less to a price-cost test or to an appropriate measure of cost for that test.

The authoritative development of antitrust predatory pricing doctrine has evolved in opinions of the Supreme Court and of the circuit courts of appeals. That is, the prohibition against predatory pricing is an interpretive rule of decision making that the courts have laid down to guide them in determining whether a violation of the broadly worded antimonopoly statutes has occurred. As part of the evolution, the courts have found the price-cost relationship to be useful in determining whether pricing behavior is predatory—and therefore monopolizing—in nature.

The "appropriate measure" of cost

After the courts began using the price-cost relationship in their predatory pricing decisions, Areeda and Turner turned to economic reasoning to conclude that the appropriate measure of cost for the price-cost test ought to be short-run marginal cost. Since they believed that short-run marginal cost would be a difficult measure to calculate, they concluded that the courts generally should use short-run average variable cost as a surrogate for short-run marginal cost.[4] They opined that courts should consider prices below the average variable cost to be predatory and prices above the average variable cost to be nonpredatory—but the courts have not universally accepted this proposal.

Most recently, in the 1990 case of *Atlantic Richfield v. USA Petroleum,*[5] the Supreme Court stated that it was unwilling to decide which measure of cost was most appropriate for the price-cost test or even to adopt the price-cost test as the sole factor in determining whether predatory pricing had occurred. Instead, the Supreme Court has chosen to permit the debate on predatory pricing and the price-cost test to continue in the appellate circuits. From future debate in and among the circuits, the Supreme Court hopes to find new ideas for use in developing well-reasoned predatory pricing guidelines and perhaps an appropriate measure of cost for the price-cost test.

A review of leading cases in each circuit suggests three perspectives that may be useful in formulating guidelines appropriate for making predatory pricing judgments and for choosing a cost measure for the price-cost test.

The "bright line test." The first of these three is the "bright line test" category, in which the courts rely solely on a price-cost test in answering the question of predatory pricing intent and conduct.[6]

In the First Circuit's *Barry Wright v. ITT Grinnell*[7] opinion, the court stated that predatory pricing decisions should be based on whether price is below incremental cost. In the Second Circuit's *Northern Telephone v. AT&T*[8] opinion, the court adopted Areeda and Turner's average variable cost as the appropriate predatory pricing benchmark. In the Seventh Circuit's *MCI Communications v. AT&T*[9] opinion, the court compared price with costs *caused* by a product or service (i.e., incremental cost) in reaching the predatory pricing decision.

The "other evidence" category. The second of the three categories is the "other evidence" category, in which the courts look not only to price-cost evidence but also to other evidence regarding the condition of the market in which the particular pricing decision has occurred.

In the Third Circuit's *O. Hommel v. Ferro*[10] opinion, the court relied soley on the price-cost test (using average variable cost) only when an independent analysis of the market revealed no trend toward monopolization. In the Fifth Circuit's *International Air Industries v. American Excelsior*[11] opinion, the court looked to the price below the average variable cost if the market was otherwise competitive and to the price below a short-run profit-maximizing price if barriers to market entry were great enough to enable the would-be predator later to reap the profits of predation. In the Tenth Circuit's *Pacific Engineering and Production Company of Nevada v. Kerr-McGee*[12] opinion, the court stated that factors other than the price-cost test may be determinative in deciding the ultimate predatory pricing issue, which (in this circuit) is whether pricing conduct is "anticompetitive."

The "burden shifting" category. The last of the three categories is the "burden shifting" category, in which the price-cost test is part of a three-tier model used to shift between opposing parties the burden of proving whether prices are predatory.

The Sixth Circuit in *D.E. Rodgers Associates v. Gardner-Denver,*[13] the Eleventh Circuit in *McGahee v. Northern Propane Gas,*[14] and the D.C. Circuit in *Southern Pacific Communications v. AT&T*[15] all adopted the Ninth Circuit's view expressed in *William Inglis v. ITT Continental Baking*[16] and *Transamerica Computer v. IBM.*[17]

The burden-shifting model works as follows: First, if the price is above the average total cost, either the defendant enjoys a nonrebuttable assumption that pricing did not occur with the required intent to prey on competitors or the plaintiff must prove with clear and convincing evidence that the defendant intended to prey on competitors.

Second, if the price is below the average total cost but above the average variable cost, the plaintiff must introduce other evidence to show that the defendant intended to prey on competitors; this evidence must be stronger the closer the price is to total cost.

Third, where the price is below the average variable cost, the defendant has the burden of proving by strong counterevidence that the defendant did not intend to prey on competitors.[18]

Role of product costing in the pricing decision

While the circuits vary in the weight that they give to the price-cost test in evaluating predatory pricing, all of them clearly consider the price-cost test important in deciding predatory pricing cases. It is also clear that the primary purpose of the price-cost test is to assist in determining the defendant's predatory intent and conduct. While the courts have been widely influenced by the Areeda and Turner analysis for inferring predatory intent and conduct, in the past decade the courts have increasingly questioned their approach.

Neoclassical economic theory. The basis for the Areeda and Turner price-cost test is neoclassical economic theory. As management accountants increasingly recognize, however, reliance on neoclassical theory as a foundation for cost analysis often represents the use of a good tool for the wrong purpose. This is becoming especially apparent in the area of product costing for decision-making purposes. As Kaplan states:

> "[T]here is an assumption that the organization's output can be captured by a one-dimensional measure. Thus, the economists' 'theory of the firm' (excepting some recent literature on economies of scope) is based on single-product firms. While this may be satisfactory for the kind of aggregate, market-based analysis that economists are really interested in, such a representation completely fails in understanding the cost structure of complex, multiproduct organizations."[19]

From an operational viewpoint, the neoclassical economic model has two particular limitations that prevent it from being a useful framework for predatory pricing analysis:

1. It does not adequately address the time horizon dimension of pricing decisions; and
2. It assumes an overly simplified model of the firm.

The model employs an analysis that defines costs as fixed or variable for a single-product firm operating within a short-run time period.

Time horizons. With respect to the time horizon limitation, Areeda and Turner opine that the relevant cost for the price-cost test should be the average variable cost, which they define as costs that vary with short-run changes in volume of output.

The traditional definition of short run is that period in which the firm's capacity does not change. Areeda and Turner do recognize that no single time period determines the short run or long run and that as the time period lengthens, more fixed costs become variable.

The concept of cost variability, as incorporated into the neoclassical model, is too elusive to use as a general guide for product pricing because the classification of costs as variable or fixed is time dependent. While the characterization of costs as variable or fixed (i.e., with respect to changes in volume of output) is useful for short-run cost control purposes, it is of limited use when making product-price decisions.

Distinguishing between short-run and long-run pricing decisions is critical to identifying those costs that are relevant to the decision. Horngren and Foster, for example, distinguish between these two categories as follows: Short-run pricing decisions (i.e., those with a time horizon of six months or less) are typified by one-time-only special orders that have no long-run implications. Long-run pricing decisions, on the other hand (i.e., those with a time horizon of one year or more), involve the pricing of products in markets in which sellers have discretion in setting their prices.[20]

Long-term pricing decisions should be based on an analysis of their long-term implications. Kaplan notes that most pricing decisions are long-term decisions that often focus on a period of three to five years.[21] Long-term incremental cost is the appropriate cost concept to employ in this context. In support of this view, surveys report widespread use of various "full cost" measures for guiding product pricing decisions.[22] Presumably, those using full cost to price products assume that full cost reflects long-run incremental cost.

The single-product limitation. With respect to the single-product limitation, the model on which the Areeda and Turner analysis rests is

Federal Antitrust Statutes

The Sherman Act of 1890. The Sherman Act, Section 2, makes guilty of a felony every person "who shall monopolize, or attempt to monopolize, or combine or conspire with any other persons to monopolize" interstate commerce. While criminal enforcement of the statute is the responsibility of the Department of Justice, the original act also provided a civil remedy to any person who could show that he suffered injuries by reason of anything forbidden by the act.

The Clayton Act of 1914. The Clayton Act, Section 4, supersedes and extends the civil law remedy provision of the Sherman Act by providing an all-inclusive cause of action to private parties that suffer injury by reason of anything forbidden by any of the antitrust statutes, not just the Sherman Act. The Clayton Act also grants persons, including the Federal Trade Commission and the U.S. Attorney General, the right to seek and obtain injunctions to stop monopolists and would-be monopolists from engaging in unlawful monopolistic practices.

The Robinson-Patman Act of 1936. The Robinson-Patman Act amends the Clayton Act by replacing Section 2 of the Clayton Act with new Sections 2(a) through 2(f). Section 2(a) makes it unlawful for any person engaged in interstate commerce:

> [T]o discriminate in price between different purchasers of commodities of like grade and quality . . . where the effect of such discrimination *may be* substantially to lessen competition or

tend to create a monopoly in any line of commerce, or to injure, destroy, or prevent competition with any person who either grants or knowingly receives the benefit of such discrimination or with customers of either of them [emphasis added].

The Act does provide exceptions to its price discrimination prohibition if:

- Cost differences in serving customers exist;
- Perishable or seasonable goods require timely disposition; or
- The reduction in price is for the purpose of meeting the low price of a competitor.

Also, the Act applies only to goods or commodities; it does not apply to services. Finally, the Act applies not only to sellers, but also to purchasers that induce or receive discriminatory prices from a seller.

The Federal Trade Commission Act of 1914. The Federal Trade Commission Act, Section 5, makes unlawful "unfair methods of competition in or affecting commerce." It empowers the Commission to prevent persons and business entities from using such unfair methods. Since the courts consider business practices that violate the antitrust laws to be unfair, Section 5 gives the Commission broad authority to civilly enforce all the antitrust laws, including the antimonopoly provisions of the Sherman Act and the price discrimination provisions of the Clayton Act as amended by the Robinson-Patman Act.

---

much too simple for today's multiproduct firms. As Kaplan and Atkinson point out, "recent research has revealed that the single product model . . . seriously misrepresents the economics of multiproduct firms."[23]

A difficult cost allocation problem exists for multiproduct firms that is absent for single-product firms. In the multiproduct setting, a concept of variability centered strictly on the volume of output is of limited use in determining product cost. Instead, a cost concept centered on the principle of *causation* should drive product cost measurements for use in setting prices.

Applicability of ABC

Making predatory pricing judgments requires a new cost paradigm that reflects a better understanding of the relationship of time to the pricing decision, addresses the multiproduct firm, and is operationally useful in determining which products cause which costs. Further, since predatory pricing strategies normally fall within the long-run category of pricing decisions, long-run incremental cost is the appropriate benchmark for the price-cost test. Fortunately, recent developments in product costing, as reflected by the emergence of activity-based costing (ABC) systems, provide a sound basis for assigning costs to products according to the principle of causation.

Assumptions and underpinnings of ABC. To understand ABC systems, it is helpful to view the business firm as an entity that is engaged in performing a series of activities (e.g., research and development, product design, manufacturing, marketing, distribution, and customer service) for the purpose of providing products (goods or services) to customers. In conducting these activities, the firm incurs costs. To accurately attribute these costs to products, it is necessary to determine the consumption of activities by individual products. Accordingly, ABC involves the process of identifying the significant activities within the firm, linking costs to these activities, and measuring the consumption of the activities by the various products. ABC may thus be defined as "a system that focuses on activities as the fundamental cost objects and uses the costs of these activities as building blocks for compiling the costs of other cost objects."[24]

Fundamentally, ABC is based on the notion that activities consume resources and products consume activities. Accordingly, product costing using ABC procedures involves a two-step allocation process in which costs are first allocated to activities and then the activity costs are allocated to products based on each product's demand for, or consumption of, the activities. ABC systems recognize that many types of overhead costs vary proportionally with measures of activity other than volume of product output. Some costs, for example, may vary with the number of production runs, raw material purchase orders, component parts in products, operations performed, inspections, customer orders, or other measures of activity not related to volume of output.

Conventional product costing systems assume that individual products (rather than activities) are the direct cause of costs. Accountants who use conventional costing methods typically assign overhead costs to products using allocation bases (e.g., labor hours, labor dollars, machine hours, and material dollars) that are proportional to the volume of units produced. While these conventional product costing systems may be adequate for the single-product firm that neoclassical economic theory describes, they are inadequate for today's complex, multiproduct firms. Indeed, these conventional cost accounting systems can lead to significant errors in attributing the consumption of resources to particular products and, consequently, to major inaccuracies in the assignment of costs to products.

Greater number and variety of allocation bases. In contrast to conventional product costing systems, ABC systems use a wider variety and greater number of allocation bases for assigning overhead costs to products. Some of these allocation bases may be proportional to the volume of output, while others are not. By using multiple allocation bases, accountants attain greater precision in assigning costs to products according to causation and resource consumption.[25]

ABC—with its focus on activities as the driving forces behind cost incurrence, and with a consideration of all costs in the value chain from research and development to customer service—provides the appropriate foundation for measuring long-run incremental costs and for linking them to the products responsible. ABC thus provides the means for breaking away from the simplistic distinction between variable and fixed costs based on volume of output; instead, when making and evaluating pricing decisions, the focus should be on causation as the fundamental cost concept. The major advantages of using ABC are that it captures the underlying economic conditions of the modern firm and it focuses attention on long-run cost causation rather than on short-run cost behavior.

Conclusion

Predatory pricing doctrine and the role of the price-cost test continue to evolve in the appellate courts. Of particular interest to management accountants are the developing views of the courts regarding the appropriate measure of cost for the price-cost test. While the short-run variable cost measure has gained favor in some circuits, there is growing evidence of dissatisfaction with that particular measure of cost.

Recent management accounting literature and management practice support the position that long-run incremental costs provide the proper base for making many, if not most, pricing decisions. Full-cost measures, as surrogates for long-run incremental costs, have long suffered from the stigma of inaccuracy and often have been viewed as arbitrary. Developments in ABC, however, show great promise in delivering more reliable measures of long-run incremental costs. By using multiple cost drivers, ABC attributes costs to the products and services that cause them.

Court opinions in several influential circuits have indicated the need to rely on a causation approach to cost measurement. Because ABC focuses on cost causation as the cornerstone of cost measurement, it provides the appropriate measure of cost for the price-cost test. To avoid significant adverse legal consequences, prices setters should become aware of the ABC methodology for measuring product costs. ▲

Notes
1. United States v. Grinnell, 384 U.S. 563, 570–571 (1966).
2. MCI Communications v. AT&T, 708 F.2d 1081, 1106 (7th Cir. 1983).
3. Chillicothe Sand & Gravel v. Martin Marietta, 615 F.2d 427, 430 (7th Cir. 1980).
4. P. Areeda & D.F. Turner, "Predatory Pricing and Related Practices Under Section 2 of the Sherman Act," *Harvard Law Review* 88: 697–733 (1975).
5. 58 U.S.L.W. 4547 (May 14, 1990) (No. 88-1668).
6. No standard-setting cases found in the Fourth and Eighth Circuits.
7. 724 F.2d 227 (1st Cir. 1983).
8. 651 F.2d 76 (2d Cir. 1981).
9. 708 F.2d 1081 (7th Cir. 1983).
10. 659 F.2d 340 (3d Cir. 1981).
11. 517 F.2d 714 (5th Cir. 1975).
12. 551 F.2d 790 (10th Cir. 1977).
13. 718 F.2d 1431 (6th Cir. 1983).
14. 898 F.2d 1487 (11th Cir. 1988).
15. 740 F.2d 980 (DC Cir. 1984).
16. 668 F.2d 1014 (9th Cir. 1981).
17. 698 F.2d 1377 (9th Cir. 1983).
18. Richard A. Posner, *Antitrust Law: An Economic Perspective,* (Chicago: The University of Chicago Press 1976): 188–192, presents an analytical framework similar to the three-tier model described here.
19. Robert S. Kaplan, "Contribution Margin Analysis: No Longer Relevant/Strategic Cost Management: The New Paradigm," *Journal of Management Accounting Research* (Fall 1990): 4.
20. Charles T. Horngren & George Foster, *Cost Accounting: A Managerial Emphasis* (Englewood Cliffs, N.J.: 7th ed., Prentice-Hall, Inc. 1991): 398.
21. Robert S. Kaplan, "Regaining Relevance," in *Cost Accounting, Robotics and the New Manufacturing Environment,* Robert Capettini & Donald K. Clancy, eds. (Sarasota, Fla.: American Accounting Association 1987): 7.27.
22. See, e.g., V. Govindarajan & Robert N. Anthony, "How Firms Use Cost Data in Pricing Decisions," *Management Accounting* (July 1983): 30–36; and Michael Cornick, William D. Cooper, & Susan B. Wilson, "How Do Companies Analyze Overhead?" *Management Accounting* (June 1988): 41–43.
23. Robert S. Kaplan & Anthony A. Atkinson, *Advanced Management Accounting* (Englewood Cliffs, N.J.: 2d ed., Prentice-Hall, Inc. 1989): 182.
24. Horngren & Foster, *Cost Accounting: A Managerial Emphasis,* at 150.
25. See Robin Cooper, "Cost Classification in Unit-Based and Activity-Based Manufacturing Cost Systems," *Journal of Cost Management* (Fall 1990): 4–14, for an excellent framework for designing an ABC system intended to produce accurate individual product cost information in a multiproduct firm setting.

CHAPTER 13

Making Transfer Pricing Work for Your Firm

Wayne G. Bremser and Michael P. Licata

Moving products and services between corporate divisions can be a headache. Having the right transfer pricing system in place, however, helps to guarantee smooth sailing and high profits. As this article explains, the organizational structure and strategy of a corporation should shape decisions about its transfer pricing environment, policies, and procedures.

The quality of a corporation's transfer pricing policies can make or break its ability to effectively and profitably control the movement of products between divisions within the firm. A company's transfer pricing policy determines the amounts charged by one internal organizational unit for a product or service provided to another internal organizational unit. Transfer prices are either cost-based, market-driven, or negotiated. Negotiated prices can be influenced by market-based and cost-based factors.

Developing pricing policies

The development of transfer pricing policies hinges on corporate level strategies as well as divisional level strategies. Highly decentralized firms with divisions that operate with considerable autonomy usually require different policies than more centralized firms where significant headquarters control prevails.

Fairness is also a critical element when designing a transfer pricing procedure. Policies perceived as fair by a company's divisions are likely to be a successful if implemented carefully. Once a transfer pricing strategy is in place, however, it requires continuous compliance monitoring to be effective.

Before developing a strategy, controllers must understand the impact of transfer prices on the firm's operation. For example, when divisions are autonomous, transfer pricing governs the sourcing decision. In this situation, division managers have the choice of buying the product from another internal division or buying it from an outside supplier. Market factors are usually very important in determining the sourcing decision.

If it must buy from an internal source, the procuring division views the transfer price as a cost that will ultimately affect the pricing of the final product. This, in turn, affects market share and other related factors including:

- cash management,
- production capacity,
- research and development,
- quality control, and
- state income taxes.

Transfer pricing environments

The organizational structure and strategy of a corporation should shape the decisions for its transfer pricing environment, policies, and procedures. Generally, only two basic transfer pricing environments exist—divisional autonomy and mandatory transfers.

Divisional autonomy. The degree of control held by headquarters or its ability to review various decisions is an important determinant of transfer pricing policies in divisional autonomies. A highly decentralized firm usually allows divisions sourcing autonomy. Here, market price governs the transfer. Because divisional profitability is typically a very important factor in measuring division managers' performance, the managers usually choose the source offering the lowest price for a product or service.

When internal sourcing is chosen, the transfer price is typically negotiated as a market-based price. While this price might differ from an outside supplier's, the outside market price and the costs of the supplying division will commonly be negotiating factors. Sometimes the procuring division will pay a higher price than that offered by an outside source for internal sourcing. This price, however, is usually offset by advantages from the supplying division that include quality assurance or supply reliability.

When divisional sourcing takes place in an autonomous environment there is also the possibility that the procuring division will buy from outside the firm. This can sometimes lower total corporate profits. Poor negotiating strategies by one division may cause the procuring division to seek outside sources. Another possibility is that the procuring division sees advantages to outside sourcing that the potential internal supplying division does not understand.

In many corporations, divisions can appeal to corporate headquarters to review the sourcing decisions. If corporate headquarters views internal sourcing as the best solution for the firm, it can apply dual pricing. In dual pricing, the procuring division pays the obtainable outside market price, but the sourcing division receives a higher price on its books.

A dual pricing policy can be problematic, however. In essence, dual pricing is a form of double counting that requires eliminations when headquarters prepares consolidated financial statements. With this double counting it is possible for both sourcing and procuring divisions to show a profit while the corporation as a whole is earning less of a profit or even suffering a loss. Thus a dual pricing policy could overemphasize divisional profitability at the expense of the big corporate profitability picture.

Mandatory transfers. When the sourcing division is acquired or established to carry out a corporate strategy of vertical integration, internal sourcing is mandatory. In this environment, the focus is only on determining the appropriate transfer price. The transfer price is some measure of cost, or a cost-plus mark-up, or a market price. To implement this vertical integration strategy, corporations can apply dual pricing.

Of the two basic environments, divisional autonomy and mandatory transfers, the mandatory internal transfer pricing situation poses the greatest challenge to a controller. Mandatory transfers require that a controller select and monitor a cost formula that best suits his organization's corporate strategy and structure. Various definitions make up the two primary categories of transfer pricing in this area—cost-based transfer pricing and market-based transfer pricing.

Cost-based transfer pricing

When cost-based transfer prices are used to account for mandatory sourcing transactions, controllers must determine what cost formula to implement. These cost formulas include full manufacturing cost, capital cost, manufacturing cost mark-ups, and activity based costing (ABC). Whatever cost definition is selected, however, cost measurement problems usually exist. It is, therefore, important to be as precise as possible in specifying cost definitions for transfer pricing policies.

Full manufacturing cost. Controllers who select full manufacturing cost as a transfer price usually work with both variable and fixed manufacturing costs. (Variable costs alone are usually unsatisfactory as a transfer price because fixed overhead is not covered by the supplying division.) When using full manufacturing cost, the transfer pricing process is basically a cost allocation procedure.

For example, during the annual budgeting process, the supplying division budgets a volume level over which to spread fixed manufacturing costs. To do this, the supplying division estimates the volume of business to be obtained from the procuring division. If the procuring division plans to buy a substantial portion of the supplying division's capacity, its potential influence over the supplying division's operations must be taken into consideration when designing the transfer pricing policy.

Controllers can base a full cost transfer price on actual or standard cost. If actual cost is used, however, controllers must ensure that the supplying division does not develop a lax attitude toward controlling cost, especially if it expects to pass costs on to the procuring division. This is an especially critical concern for controllers when the supplying division's product is sold only to procuring divisions and not to outside customers.

Controllers using a standard or budgeted cost may have better luck ensuring cost control. It is not always easy, however, to judge whether the standards used are realistic or attainable. To avoid unnecessary surprises, controllers should ensure that standards are negotiated at least once a year.

An example of a full manufacturing cost transfer price is shown in Table 1. In Panel A, the actual manufacturing cost is $49.80 and the standard cost is $46.36. Panel C compares the annual production volume for actual cost of 500,000 units to the annual production volume for the standard cost of 550,000 units. While actual fixed manufacturing costs are equal to the standard costs, a lower actual production volume causes the actual fixed manufacturing cost of $40.00 to be higher than the standard manufacturing cost of $36.36. This discrepancy raises the question of who gets charged with the unfavorable volume variance. A controller can determine the answer by turning to the company's transfer pricing policy.

When the transfer price is based on full manufacturing cost, the supplying division must look to outside sales to cover its selling and administrative costs, and to provide profits. At best, the selling division is breaking even on the internal sales. Another cost-based transfer pricing alternative, however, could allow for selling and administrative costs. Because some cost savings might exist for internal sales, controllers must question whether incremental selling and administrative costs should be measured for internal transactions. Alternatively, average costs could be used for internal transactions. Panel A shows that actual selling and administrative costs added $10 to total cost. Thus, $59.80 results for total actual cost compared to $55.82 for total standard cost.

Capital costs. Capital costs are another possible component of a cost-based transfer price. Many divisionalized firms charge division managers for using corporate capital. This is usually accomplished by applying a direct capital charge to the division for invested assets, reflecting a residual income approach to measuring divisional profits.

Table 1. *Cost-Based Transfer Pricing*

Panel A	**Actual**	**Standard**
Component part costs:		
Variable manufacturing:	$ 9.80	$10.00
Fixed manufacturing:	40.00	36.36
Total manufacturing	49.80	46.36
Variable selling & administrative	4.00	4.00
Direct fixed selling & administrative	6.00	5.45
	$10.00	$ 9.45
Total manufacturing and selling & administrative	59.80	55.81
Capital costs:		
Variable	2.00	2.00
Fixed	9.60	8.73
Total capital costs	11.60	10.73
Transfer price (economic costs)	$71.40	$66.54

Panel B		
Return on investment pricing:		
Desired return on investment		
Variable	1,500,000.00	1,650,000.00
Fixed	7,200,000.00	7,200,000.00
Total return	$8,700,000.00	$8,850,000.00
Total return per unit	17.40	16.09
Total manufacturing and S & A costs	59.80	55.81
Transfer price	$77.20	$71.90

Panel C		
Production volume— annual	500,000	550,000
Sales volume— annual	500,000	550,000
Fixed manufacturing—annual	20,000,000	20,000,000
Fixed selling & administrative	3,000,000	3,000,000
Traceable investment:		
Working capital	5,000,000	5,500,000
Fixed assets	24,000,000	24,000,000
	$29,000,000	$29,500,000
Cost of capital	20%	
Division's return on investment	30%	

An indirect way to charge division managers for using corporate capital is by implementing return on investment (ROI) performance objectives. For example, Panel C of Table 1 shows that the supplying division has a traceable investment in working capital and fixed assets. The working capital investment is variable because a higher level of activity requires more net working capital. In Panel C, the standard cost is $29,500,000, while the actual cost is $29,000,000. The lower level of actual activity therefore results in a proportionate decline in net working capital.

While the example shows a linear relationship, such a relationship does not necessarily exist. For example, applying the 20% cost of capital to the working capital investment of $5,000,000 results in a variable cost of $2.00 per unit. While the fixed capital cost in Panel A is $9.60 per unit for actual cost, the cost per unit for standard cost is lower ($8.73) due to the difference in volumes. The resulting transfer price of $71.40, which reflects capital costs, approximates what an economist would term the economic cost of manufacturing and distributing the product.

When the sourcing division is acquired or established to carry out a corporate strategy of vertical integration, internal sourcing is mandatory.

A strong case can be made for including the opportunity cost of capital for the working capital investment. The case for relating an opportunity cost to the fixed asset investment is less convincing. However, if the supplying division has established the productive capacity to produce units for the procuring division, the case becomes stronger. Including capital costs as a component of a cost-based transfer price allows the sourcing division to break even on internal sales dollars because it can cover the corporate charge for invested capital. Alternatively, in a ROI environment, the division earns the minimum rate.

Manufacturing cost mark-ups. Another cost-based transfer pricing alternative is to add a mark-up to manufacturing costs. This can be especially beneficial when the supplying division is recognized as a profit center. For example, a mark-up can be based on average mark-ups of sales prices to outsiders.

Another alternative is to calculate a mark-up using a return on investment pricing formula. For example, Panel B of Table 1 shows a desired return on investment of $8,700,000— using the 30% return on investment and the $29,000,000 traceable investment (Panel C). To achieve a total return of $8,700,000, divide by the 500,000 units. This translates into $17.40 per unit. By adding $17.40 to the manufacturing and selling and administrative costs, you get a transfer price of $77.20 (Panel B). This price is higher than the $71.40 standard price, which reflects the cost of capital. In this situation, it is assumed that the 30% return on investment reflects some specialized factors of the selling division, such as above-normal risk.

Other alternatives to cost-based transfer pricing also exist. When selecting an alternative, however, controllers must always ensure that the supplying divisions' cost accounting system measures costs reliably. For example, activity based costing (ABC) has recently developed as a popular cost-based transfer price alternative with firms trying to replace outdated, ineffective cost systems. Many of these companies charged high-volume products with too much overhead and low-volume, complex products with too little overhead. Using ABC, companies get a different profitability picture and learn to price products and product lines more realistically and logically.

Market-based transfer prices

Market-based transfer prices are appealing choices to account for mandatory sourcing transactions because they appear to reflect the realities of the marketplace. Market price, however, is not always readily determinable.

For example, it may be impossible to identify an external market for a customized component. Another possibility is that the supplier of this component product uses negotiated transaction prices rather than published prices. In this situation, although published prices are available, discounts are usually always negotiated for a particular order. There also may be a significant amount of cost involved in obtaining outside market prices. Usually the procuring division expends for this effort. The supplying division, however, may have some doubts about prices obtained.

Another consideration involved with market-based transfer prices is the movement toward just-in-time inventory management. Here the basic concept is that the procuring division has minimal inventory levels and the supplier delivers intermediate products as needed. In this type of arrangement, long-term contracts with suppliers are necessary. These contracts should be detailed and customized to each situation.

If an outside supplier knows that it is negotiating a just-in-time contract as a competitor to an internal source, the resulting market price might contain several biases. For example, although an outside supplier might provide a lower price than an internal source, it also might have compromised on service to the procuring division to justify that lower price.

Market prices must be adjusted for differences between outside sources and inside sources. Table 2 illustrates how market price should be analyzed. The standard terms are net amount due in ten days. Line C-1 shows the cost of capital is 20% for the firm, while line C-2 shows the annual purchase quantity for the procuring division is 260,000 units.

Multiplying the annual quantity purchased by the market price gives the total purchases of $18,200,000 on line C-3. Line C-4 shows $498,630 as the average accounts payable for this level of purchasing. In this situation, the outside supplier would finance these payables instead of the corporation's procuring division.

Using a 20% cost of capital, average accounts payable of $498,630 is translated into a financing cost of $99,726 (line C-5). Divide this by the annual volume of 260,000 units to get a financing cost of 38 cents per unit. If the procuring division buys the intermediate product from an outside source, it saves 38 cents per unit. The savings results because the company eliminates the inter-company transaction receivables and payables at corporate level. Since the procuring division is losing this accounts payable financing, it is fair to reduce the price by the amount of financing per unit.

Line D-1 shows the market price reduced for the financing cost from line C-6. Next, factor in a selling and administrative cost savings for the market price adjustment.

The supplying division might reduce selling and/or administrative costs because it is doing business inside rather than outside. As a result, this could decrease the transfer price. However, the procuring division also might save on selling and administrative costs. Savings here could reverse the above trend and increase the transfer price. These cost savings usually are difficult to measure and can be negotiating points between procuring division and suppliers.

Finally, there is a credit risk discount because the selling division does not have to worry about collecting its accounts receivable from the procuring division.

The numbers displayed in Table 2 prove that market-based transfer pricing is not a cut and dried proposition. To ensure a successful market-based transfer price policy, the company must define a formula for computing prices clearly. Controllers must ensure that formulas used are monitored carefully and that information on current market conditions is obtained in an efficient and objective fashion.

Table 2. *Market Price Analysis*

A. Market price per unit		$70.00
B. Terms are normally net 10 days		
C. Market price adjusted for 10 days float:		
1. Cost of capital		20%
2. Purchase quantity annually		260,000
3. Purchases		$18,200,000
4. Average accounts payable		
C3 × 10/365		$498,630
5. Accounts payable financing		
C1 × C4		$99,726
6. Per unit payables financing cost saving		
a. C5/C2		$ 0.38
b. Alternative calculation:		
A × C1 × 10/365		$ 0.38
D. Market price:		
1. Net of financing (A − C6)		$69.62
2. Selling & administrative cost saving		($ 0.50)
3. Subtotal		$69.12
4. Credit risk discount (D3 × 1%)		($ 0.69)
5. Adjusted market price		$68.43

Playing fair with pricing

No matter what type of transfer pricing environment or policy is designed and implemented, an overriding concern to its success is fairness. If division managers view the system as unfair, often they will try to circumvent or disable it. A significant responsibility for the controller is therefore to determine if a transfer pricing plan is fair to individual divisions while still being in the best interest of the corporation as a whole.

Implementing multiple measures of divisional performance can help reduce some competitive tension associated with transfer pricing. For example, suppose that a decentralized "*Fortune* 100" company acquires a supplier in Albany. Soon after, the company's Philadelphia-based division decides to contract for a service. Although the Philadelphia division can do the service itself in-house, it opens bidding to Albany and another division. Meanwhile, the company has already implemented a transfer pricing policy that requires Albany to get service contracts if at all possible. Although in the end Albany's price is higher than the other division's and the in-house cost, Albany gets the service contract. In this case, price for the service was only one measure of performance. The performance measure in Albany's favor is the corporation's adoption of a vertical integration strategy and appointment of Albany as the preferred servicer.

Differences in state income taxes are other factors to consider when designing a transfer pricing system for a company with divisions in several different states. For example, if a given state has favorable corporate income tax provisions, selling prices of sourcing divisions in this state may be higher than divisions from other states with fewer favorable tax provisions. This procedure makes the sourcing division look favorable on profit performance while reducing profits for its procuring divisions in other states with fewer favorable tax provisions. In reality, this sourcing division may be using the transfer pricing policy as a smokescreen to cover up production inefficiencies. Controllers must be wary of the significant ethical and legal problems such practices may pose to transfer pricing policies. ▲

PART J

Process Improvement and Reengineering

Process Value Analysis: The Missing Link in Cost Management

Michael R. Ostrenga and Frank R. Probst

Much of the existing literature on activity-based costing (ABC) shortcuts the necessary link between costing rates and operational cost drivers. The focus on activities in ABC is often restricted to improvements in product costs to the exclusion of process improvements and cost reductions. Process value analysis (PVA) is a methodology for reducing costs and improving processes by identifying resource consumption within a process and the underlying root causes of cost (i.e., cost drivers). The linkage between PVA and ABC is critical. Activities are the focal point of total cost management; they must be managed to gain and sustain a competitive advantage.

I n today's rapidly changing manufacturing environment, it has become increasingly difficult to answer the following three basic operating questions:

1. What do our products actually cost?
2. Why do they cost that much?
3. What can be done to reduce the cost?

Existing financial information systems continue to reflect a financial statement orientation. The emphasis continues to be on cost allocation and overhead absorption, when what we really need are:

- Relevant measures of product cost; and
- Techniques to better understand the sources of cost to facilitate cost reduction.

This article discusses an improved costing methodology called *process value analysis* (PVA) that addresses the three questions listed above. PVA gives a better understanding of cost behavior and the root causes of costs (i.e., cost drivers) than traditional cost-

ing techniques. PVA facilitates the improvement of processes and also the reduction of costs; it also serves as a foundation for more accurate product costs.

Activity-based costing (ABC; see accompanying box, "Definitions") has been widely advanced as a method for improved product costing. Experience shows, however, that ABC by itself may actually distort product costs. This distortion (which is described in the following sections) can be eliminated by integrating PVA with ABC.

What is ABC?

The objective of ABC is more accurate product costs. This objective is achieved by identifying the types and amounts of activities consumed by each product. Product costs are thus based on the cost of all activities consumed.

An activity cost is actually an overhead rate that is developed by assigning costs to activity pools, then dividing these cost pools by a quantifiable assignment base. Accurate product costs are developed by applying overhead to each product based on the consumption rate of each activity.

Shortcomings of current ABC methodologies

The primary limitation to the development of more accurate product costs is the determination of cost behavior. The important thing to remember is that cost is incurred at the process level, not at the product level. Understanding cost behavior requires identifying the causal relationship between the resources (i.e., the costs) consumed in a process and the underlying reason why the costs are incurred.

Identifying activity cost pools. The *first* area where conventional ABC falls short lies in the identification of activity cost pools. Many ABC methodologies force fit the definitions of activities from an existing dictionary of activities without ever analyzing the process. What may appear to be logical relationships between activities and costs often prove to be inadequate in practice.

Major activities need to be tied to the process in which they represent the significant resources in terms of cost and time. This ensures that proper recognition is given to those activities that increase value as well as to those that impede the work flow (i.e., non-value-added activities, or waste).

Definition of driver. The *second* limitation of ABC is the definition of the term "driver." Often no clear distinction is made between the root cause (i.e., the cost driver) of an activity and the activity driver that is used to assign cost to products (or to other possible cost objects, such as customers or regions).

The distinction is critical. To initiate process improvements, identifying the true root cause of a cost is essential. Otherwise, only symptoms are treated. In other words, the activity itself—rather than the cause of the activity—is attacked, so the cost tends to resurface elsewhere in the process.

A driver can be thought of as the root cause of an activity. This can be the fact, event, circumstance, or condition prevalent in the process that causes the activity. This activity driver can be operational, policy related, or environmental as it relates to the activity; it need not be a quantifiable basis of cost assignment.

The terms "stage-one driver" and "stage-two driver," which have been used in some literature about ABC, actually do not refer to drivers at all. Instead, they are methods of assigning cost from the general ledger to process pools and a measure of activity output consumed by products. A stage-one driver, in other words, is simply a resource driver, and a stage-two driver is simply an activity driver. Thus, for example, a stage-one driver is used to assign costs from a general ledger to a cost pool. For costing purposes, it is preferable to call a stage-one driver a "resource driver" and a stage-two driver an "activity driver." The

term "cost driver" should be reserved for references to the root cause or actual driver of a cost (see accompanying box, "Definitions").

This distinction can be illustrated by discussing a common activity driver—number of moves. While number of moves is a possible quantifiable base for applying cost to products, it is not necessarily a cost driver. Rather, the physical layout of a plant, a process imbalance, or a lack of standardization of parts may be the actual *driver* that *causes* the number of moves.

Definition of value-added vs. non-value-added. The *third* area where ABC falls short is in the definition of value-added and non-value-added activities. Some methodologies do not address the distinction at all. Others address it mainly from an operational improvement perspective without making the important distinction between the development of activity-based costs for process improvement and the proportion of non-value-added costs at the product level.

Selection of activity drivers. The *fourth* and final area where ABC falls short is in the selection of activity drivers. As pointed out previously, activity drivers may not be the true drivers of cost. Activity drivers should be tied (i.e., correlated) to the actual cost driver to properly reflect the behavior of costs.

For example, using material handling as a major activity might generate an activity-based cost related to the number of moves. While using the number of moves as an activity driver may be appropriate for part of a process, it may not necessarily be appropriate everywhere that material handling occurs.

Only by understanding cost behavior through PVA is it possible to make this determination. If material handling occurs mainly because of the number of parts, the number of parts issued to assembly might well be a more appropriate activity driver for material handling in subassembly and final assembly than number of moves.

In this case, the consumption factor at the product level would be the number of part numbers on the respective bills of materials. Conversely, the number of moves may be the appropriate activity driver for fabrication where pallets and batches are moved to the subsequent operations.

Process value analysis

As the experience of a Midwestern manufacturer of heavy equipment has recently demonstrated, the limitations of ABC can be overcome by integrating it with PVA. A useful linkage can be developed to reduce process costs and to provide more reliable product costs. After the PVA methodology is described, this linkage is illustrated by means of an extended example.

PVA is a methodology for reducing costs and improving processes. This is accomplished by identifying:

- Resource consumption within a process; and
- The underlying root causes of cost (i.e., cost drivers).

PVA starts with the premise that costs are incurred at the process level, which is where resources are consumed. The level of costs is determined by the configuration, complexity, flow design, flow flexibility, and similar attributes of a process. Process costs can be reduced by means of any of the following methods:

- Simplification;
- Reducing variation;
- Improvements in process layout;
- More compact design flows; and
- Synchronous processing.

With the exception of a pure product-focused work cell (i.e., one in which the production process and product flow are virtually identical), product routings follow diverse process paths. Each process has a series of inputs, transformation activities, and outputs through which a variety of products flow. Useful product costs and valid performance measures must reflect the diversity of activities consumed to support each part or product.

Accordingly, PVA provides:

- A framework for understanding cost behavior patterns;
- Support for the selection of activities within a process to which costs should be applied;
- Cycle time analysis;

- Identification of value-added versus non-value-added activities;
- Identification of operational cost drivers;
- Identification of opportunities for process improvements;
- Measurement base for continuous improvement efforts; and
- Foundation for improved product costing.

The use of PVA as a foundation for product costing generates cost information that reflects the physical environment, as the list above indicates. The dual focus on process and product costing offers the advantages listed below.

Process costing facilitates:

- Flexible budgeting to reflect changes in activities;
- Costing the effect of changes in the physical process or in activities;
- Investment justification; and
- Performance measurement.

The *product costing* perspective (which ABC offers in conjunction with PVA) supports:

- More accurate product costs;
- "Total costing" (including imputed interest and economic resources included in sales, general, and administrative expenses) rather than just manufacturing costing;
- Life cycle costing; and
- Target costing.

ABC: An extended example

The linkage between PVA and ABC can be demonstrated by using a series of examples from a study performed for the heavy equipment manufacturer mentioned previously.

The initial focus is on product costs, as Exhibit 1 shows. Product costs are developed from a bill of materials, a labor routing (i.e., a bill of labor), and an overhead rate based on direct labor. As Exhibit 1 shows, Product B is charged with twice the overhead of Product A because Product B consumes twice as much labor in terms of dollars.

This traditional approach does not differentiate between the various costs of activities actually consumed by each product. For example, the amount of scheduling, setup, material handling, and inspection actually consumed by Products A and B have no demonstrated relationship to the amount of direct

Exhibit 1. *Traditional Product Costing*

	Product A	Product B
Material	$300	$300
Direct labor	48	96
Overhead	144	288
Total	$482	$684

Source:
Material – Costed bill of material
Direct Labor – Process routing, standard labor
Overhead – 300% of direct labor

labor used by each product. Therefore, applying overhead on the basis of direct labor leads to distortions in the product costs.

Exhibit 2 illustrates the use of ABC to develop product costs. First, costing rates based on activity drivers are calculated for three processes: steel cutting, assembly, and material handling. Exhibit 2 identifies these activity-based rates and shows supporting activities, costs, and activity drivers.

In Exhibit 3, these cost rates are applied to Products A and B based on the activities consumed by each product. Specifically (as Exhibit 2 shows), the cost per work order is $200. This rate is used in Exhibit 3 to charge Product A with $2 of scheduling cost in the steel cutting operation based on 100 units of Product A per batch. The costs of conversion, inspection, and maintenance are likewise assigned to the products based on their activity drivers and volumes.

This use of activity drivers reduces the distortion in product cost shown in Exhibit 1 and goes a long way toward establishing useful product costs. As Exhibit 3 shows, Product B's ABC cost is $16 more ($595 − $579), or approximately 3 percent higher, than Product A's ABC cost. This compares to the 42 percent difference calculated under the traditional costing approach illustrated in Exhibit 1.

Improving the ABC methodology

Despite this improvement over traditional costing, the ABC methodology can itself be improved. First, note that the methodology

illustrated treats all material handling alike. As Exhibit 2 shows, a single cost pool is used to arrive at a cost of $42 per move. This $42 is then applied to material handling wherever it occurs, as shown in Exhibit 3.

A PVA study, however, showed that material handling was extensive in all processes. This finding necessitated identifying material handling costs within *each* process to give a more accurate picture of total process costs and the source of these costs.

After the PVA study, the cost charged to the material handling activity within each process was based on resource drivers of how many forklift trucks, automated guided vehicles,

---

PVA provides a framework for understanding cost behavior patterns and support for the selection of activities within a process to which costs should be applied.

---

cranes, and employees supported each process area. These resource drivers provided a logical assignment basis for developing the material handling cost pools. (Some ABC methodologies would call this a stage-one driver allocation. However, these factors are clearly not root cause "drivers" of the activities. Rather, the true cost drivers were related to process imbalance, machine downtime, stocking levels, and the like, all of which became the focus of PVA process improvement initiatives.)

Value-added vs. non-value-added. The typical ABC approach does not distinguish between value-added and non-value-added activities. While some methodologies do incorporate this distinction, without a PVA study to establish the process orientation and internal customer requirements, the selection may be more intuitive than real.

Selecting activity drivers. In this generic ABC example, the selection of activity drivers to be used in developing the rate for tracing costs

Exhibit 2. *Activity-Based Cost Rates*

Process	Activity	Cost	Activity Driver	Quantity	Activity Driver Rate
● Steel cutting	● Setup/scheduling	$200,000	No. of work orders	1,000	$ 200
	● Conversion[a]	100,000	No. of machine hours	5,000	20
	● Inspection	100,000	No. of setups	100	1,000
	● Maintenance	150,000	No. of machine hours	5,000	30
		$550,000			
● Assembly	● Changeover	$100,000	No. of scheduled batches	1,000	100
	● Conversion[a]	50,000	No. of parts	50,000	1
	● Inspection	125,000	No. of scheduled batches	1,000	125
	● Retrofit	75,000	No. of ECMs	500	150
		$350,000			
● Material handling	● Move material	500,000	No. of moves	12,000	42
		$1,400,000			

[a] Conversion cost = energy and machine depreciation.

Exhibit 3. *Activity-Based Product Costs*

				Product A			Product B		
A	B	C	D	E	F	G	H	I	J
Manufacturing Overhead	Batch-Related	Output Measure	Cost Rate	Output Measure Volume	Per Piece[a] Consumption of Batch[a]	(DxExF) Total	Output Measure Volume	Per Piece Consumption of Batch	(DxHxI) Total
● Steel cutting									
— Setup/scheduling	×	No. of work orders	$ 200	1.0	1/100	$ 2.00	1.0	1/100	$ 2.00
— Conversion	×	No. of machine hours	20	0.5		10.00	1.0		20.00
— Inspection	×	No. of setups	1,000	1.0	1/100	10.00	1.0	1/100	10.00
— Maintenance	×	No. of machine hours	30	0.5		15.00	1.0		30.00
● Assembly									
— Changeover	×	No. of setups	100	1.0	1/500	0.20	1.0	1/500	0.20
— Conversion	×	No. of parts	1	25.0		25.00	10.00		10.00
— Inspection	×	No. of scheduled batches	125	1.0	1/250	0.50	1.0	1/250	0.50
— Retrofit	×	No. of ECNs	150	1.0	1/500	0.30	1.0	1/500	0.30
● Material handling									
— Move material									
Steel sheets		No. of moves	42	3.0		126.00	2.0		84.00
Assembly		No. of moves	42	1.0		42.00	1.0		42.00
Subtotal						$231.00			$199.00
Direct material						300.00			300.00
Direct labor						48.00			96.00
Total						$579.00			$595.00

[a] That is, 100-piece work order with one piece consumption = 1/100; similarly, one engineering change notification (ECN) for a 500-piece work order with one piece consumption = 1/500.

Exhibit 4. *Summary of PVA Results*

Process	Major Activities	VA/NVA	Operational Activity Driver	Cycle Time/ Part	Time/ Shift	Process Activity Cost Pools
Steel cutting	● Product flow–related					
	—Material handling	NVA	Process layout	0.3		—Material handling
	—Queue	NVA	Process imbalance	3.4		—Conversion
	—Conversion	VA	Lineal inches	0.2		—Inspection
	—Inspection	NVA	No. of parts	0.1		—Maintenance
						—Setup/scheduling
	● Process-related					
	—Setup/scheduling	NVA	No. of work orders		0.5	
			No. of unscheduled changeovers		1.0	
	—Downtime	NVA	Machine reliability	___	0.5	
				4.0	1.5	

Cycle efficiency = 0.2/4 = 5%
Lost capacity per shift = 1.5/8 = 19%

Process	Major Activities	VA/NVA	Operational Activity Driver	Cycle Time/ Part	Time/ Shift	Process Activity Cost Pools
Assembly	● Product flow–related					
	—Material handling	NVA	No. of options, features	0.3		—Material handling
	—Conversion	VA	No. of parts assembled	0.3		—Conversion
	—Inspection	NVA	No. of units	0.5		—Inspection
	—Retrofit	NVA	Process specification	0.4		—Retrofit
						—Changeover
	● Process-related					
	—Changeover	NVA	No. of schedule changes	___	0.5	
				1.5	0.5	

Cycle efficiency = 0.3/1.5 = 20%
Lost capacity per shift = 0.5/8 = 6%

to products is generalized as the number of moves. In the PVA study, the activity driver selected for steel cutting was the number of moves. For assembly, it was the number of parts.

Exhibit 4 shows the results of PVA and identifies several important aspects of the process.

- The time spent adding value to the product was limited to 5 percent in steel cutting and 20 percent in assembly. Thus, 95 percent of the time in steel cutting and 80 percent of the time in assembly, non-value-added costs (e.g., for queue or storage time) were incurred, which inhibited the throughput velocity at which resources were converted to cash.
- Lost capacity on a per-shift basis amounted to almost 19 percent in cutting (1.0 hour

setup + 0.5 hour downtime) and 6 percent in assembly (0.5 hour changeover). Note that for product cycle time analysis, the product is in a state of queue while the process is tied up for setup or repair.

- The operational cost drivers identified represent root causes for use in planning operational improvements. These "true" cost drivers should not be confused with the term "cost drivers" as used in the past to describe a cost assignment base. These true operational cost drivers can, however, be used to support the selection of activity drivers for ABC.
- The process or activity pools were selected based on the significant activities defined in the activity analysis and cycle time analysis portion of PVA. The selections were supported by interviews with functional area

Exhibit 5. PVA/ABC Linkage

Process	Process/Activity	VA/NVA	Cost	Output Measure	Quantity	Cost per Output Measure
• Steel cutting	• Material handling	NVA	$300,000	No. of moves	10,000	$ 30
	• Setup/scheduling	NVA	200,000	No. of work orders	1,000	200
	• Conversion[a]	VA	100,000	No. of machine hours	5,000	20
	• Inspection	NVA	100,000	No. of setups	100	1,000
	• Maintenance	VA	150,000	No. of machine hours	5,000	30
			$850,000			
• Assembly	• Material handling	NVA	200,000	No. of parts	50,000	4
	• Changeover	NVA	100,000	No. of scheduled batches	1,000	100
	• Conversion[a]	VA	50,000	No. of parts	50,000	1
	• Inspection	NVA	125,000	No. of scheduled batches	1,000	125
	• Retrofit	NVA	75,000	No. of ECWNs	500	150
			$550,000			
			$1,400,000			

[a] Conversion Cost = energy and machine depreciation.

Exhibit 6. Integrated PVA/ABC Product Costs

A Manufacturing Overhead	B Batch-Related	C Output Measure	D Cost Rate	Product A — E Output Measure Volume	F Per Piece Consumption of Batch	Product A — G Extended VA	Cost NVA	Total	Product B — E Output Measure Volume	F Per Piece Consumption of Batch	G Extended VA	Cost NVA	Total
• Steel cutting													
—Setup/scheduling	×	No. of work orders	$200	1.0	1 100								
—Material handling	×	No. of moves	30	3.0			$ 2.00	$ 2.00	1.0	1 100		$ 2.00	$ 2.00
—Conversion		No. of machine hours	20	0.5			90.00	90.00	2.0			60.00	60.00
—Inspection	×	No. of setups	1000	1.0	1 100	$ 10.00		10.00	1.0		$ 20.00		20.00
—Maintenance		No. of machine hours	30	0.5			10.00	10.00	1.0	1 100		10.00	10.00
						15.00		15.00	1.0		30.00		30.00
• Assembly													
—Changeover	×	No. of setup batches	100	1.0	1 500								
—Material handling		No. of parts	4	25.0			0.20	0.20	1.0	1 500		0.20	0.20
—Conversion		No. of parts	1	25.0			100.00	100.00	10.0			40.00	40.00
—Inspection	×	No. of scheduled batches	125	1.0	1 250	25.00		25.00	10.0		10.00		10.00
—Retrofit	×	No. of ECNs	150	1.0	1 500		0.50	0.50	1.0	1 250		0.50	0.50
							0.30	0.30	1.0	1 500		0.30	0.30
Subtotal						$ 50.00	$203.00	$253.00			$ 60.00	$113.00	$173.00
Direct material						270.00	30.00	300.00			270.00	30.00	300.00
Direct labor						38.00	10.00	48.00			76.00	20.00	96.00
Total						$358.00	$243.00	$601.00			$406.00	$163.00	$569.00

Exhibit 7. Cost Comparison

Product		Traditional Costing	Conventional ABC	PVA/ABC VA	PVA/ABC NVA	PVA/ABC Total
A	Material	$300	$300	$270	$ 30	$300
	Labor	48	48	38	10	48
	Overhead	144	231	50	203	253
	Total	$482	$579	$358	$243	$601
B	Material	$300	$300	$270	$ 30	$300
	Labor	96	96	76	20	96
	Overhead	288	199	60	113	173
	Total	$684	$595	$406	$163	$569

representatives. The analysis revealed that a manageable number of activities could be defined for each process to provide a significantly improved cost perspective while keeping the level of complexity reasonable.

This example shows only two of the many processes analyzed. It should be noted that several activities were common among the processes analyzed. However, they were structured as specific activities within each process rather than as generic process pools. This treatment is because of the different operational cost drivers identified for certain activities depending on which process they supported.

Exhibit 4 shows the material handling example introduced earlier. Steel cutting is "driven" by the existing process layout. This layout caused more move frequencies to occur in order to overcome the lack of synchronization. Conversely, the driver of material handling in assembly was the complexity caused by numerous product options and features. This allowed for further differentiation in cost behavior and the selection of appropriate activity drivers.

Linking ABC with PVA

To link PVA with ABC, look at Exhibit 5, where the general process of material handling is *now* presented as a significant activity within each process. Here the activity driver used for material handling in the steel cutting process was the number of moves, but the activity driver used for the assembly process was the number of parts. This is the critical linkage of PVA information with ABC. The activity drivers selected are based on the insights gained from the operational cost drivers (and from the quantifiability and availability of data).

Exhibit 6 shows the calculation of costs for Products A and B using the PVA/ABC linkage. The extended cost in column G clearly identifies value-added and non-value-added cost components. The validity of the resulting product costs is based on the clear distinction between the cost driver and the activity driver. The specific drivers for each process in Exhibit 6 are as follows:

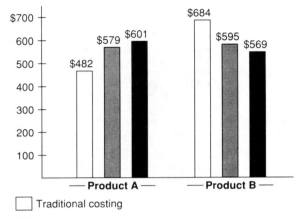

Exhibit 8. *Cost Comparison Graphs*

Traditional costing

Conventional activity-based product costing

Integrated PVA/ABC

Steel Cutting	Cost Driver	Activity Driver
Setup/scheduling	Product variety	No. of work orders
Material handling	Process layout	No. of moves
Conversion	Process time	No. of machine hours
Inspection	Poor tooling condition	No. of setups
Maintenance	Lack of preventative maintenance	No. of machine hours

Assembly		
Changeovers	End item configuration	No. of setup batches
Material handling	Product features/options	No. of parts
Conversion	Parts to assembly	No. of parts
Inspection	Product specifications	No. of scheduled batches
Retrofit	Lack of collaborative design	No. of emergency changes

Does this distinction make a difference? Exhibit 7 summarizes the calculation of product costs for Products A and B using the three approaches described. The different product costs under the three approaches is due primarily to the number of parts on the bill of material for Product A versus Product B (twenty-five versus ten). The marked differences in product cost are presented graphically in Exhibit 8. Since product costs are used extensively (e.g., for pricing support, promotions, sales mix decisions, and product profitability evaluations), an improved perspective on product costs will have important ramifications.

Other benefits of linking PVA/ABC

The benefits of the proposed linkage extend beyond more useful measures of product cost to process improvement and cost reduction opportunities.

Operational changes planned as a result of the improved awareness of cost behavior obtained from the integrated PVA/ABC initiatives for the company on which this case study was based include the following:

- Delivering material to point to use to reduce queue and storage;
- Instituting compact process layouts to reduce material handling requirements;
- Synchronizing process flow to reduce queue, material handling, lost material, and damage;
- Processing of mating parts sequentially to reduce handling, work-in-process levels, and matching;
- Improving preventive maintenance programs; and
- Focusing on setup reduction efforts.

Beyond the operational improvements prompted by PVA, the company now has the methodology and techniques in place to do the following:

- Better understand cost behavior;
- Provide a focused plan of cost reduction through operational improvement;
- Provide more accurate product costs;
- Make investment decisions by focusing on changes in processes and the impact on activity costs;
- Grow the business in a more profitable way; and
- Understand the cost of providing internal services to the company.

Much of the existing literature on ABC shortcuts the linkage between costing rates and operational cost drivers. Additionally, the focus on activities is restricted to improvement in product costs to the exclusion of process improvement and cost reduction. Accordingly, the emphasis should be on linking ABC with PVA.

As these examples suggest, the linking of ABC with PVA offers both operational and strategic advantages by providing a foundation for cost management. This linkage is illustrated in Exhibit 9.

Relevance found?

Observers of the manufacturing scene agree that cost accounting has not kept pace with technological innovation. The cost equation

Definitions

Activity 1. Work performed within an organization. 2. An aggregation of actions performed within an organization that is useful for purposes of activity-based costing.

Activity driver A measure of the frequency and intensity of the demands placed on activities by cost objects. An activity driver is used to assign costs to cost objects. It represents a line item on the bill of activities for a product or customer. An example is the number of part numbers, which is used to measure the consumption of material-related activities by each product, material type, or component. The number of customer orders measures the consumption of order-entry activities by each customer. Sometimes an activity driver is used as an indicator of the output of an activity, such as the number of purchase orders prepared by the purchasing activity.

Activity-based costing A methodology that measures the cost and performance of activities, resources, and cost objects. Resources are assigned to activities, then activities are assigned to cost objects based on their use. Activity-based costing recognizes the causal relationships of cost drivers to activities.

Cost driver Any factor that causes a change in the cost of an activity. For example, the quality of parts received by an activity (e.g., the percent that are defective) is a determining factor in the work required by that activity because the quality of parts received affects the resources required to perform the activity. An activity may have multiple cost drivers associated with it.

Process A series of activities that are linked to perform a specific objective. For example, the assembly of a television set or the paying of a bill or claim entails several linked activities.

Resource driver A measure of the quantity of resources consumed by an activity. An example of a resource driver is the percentage of total square feet occupied by an activity. This factor is used to allocate a portion of the cost of operating the facilities to the activity.

Source: "Glossary of Activity-Based Management," Norm Raffish & Peter B.B. Turney, eds., *Journal of Cost Management* 53–63 (Fall 1991).

Exhibit 9. *"The Linkage"*

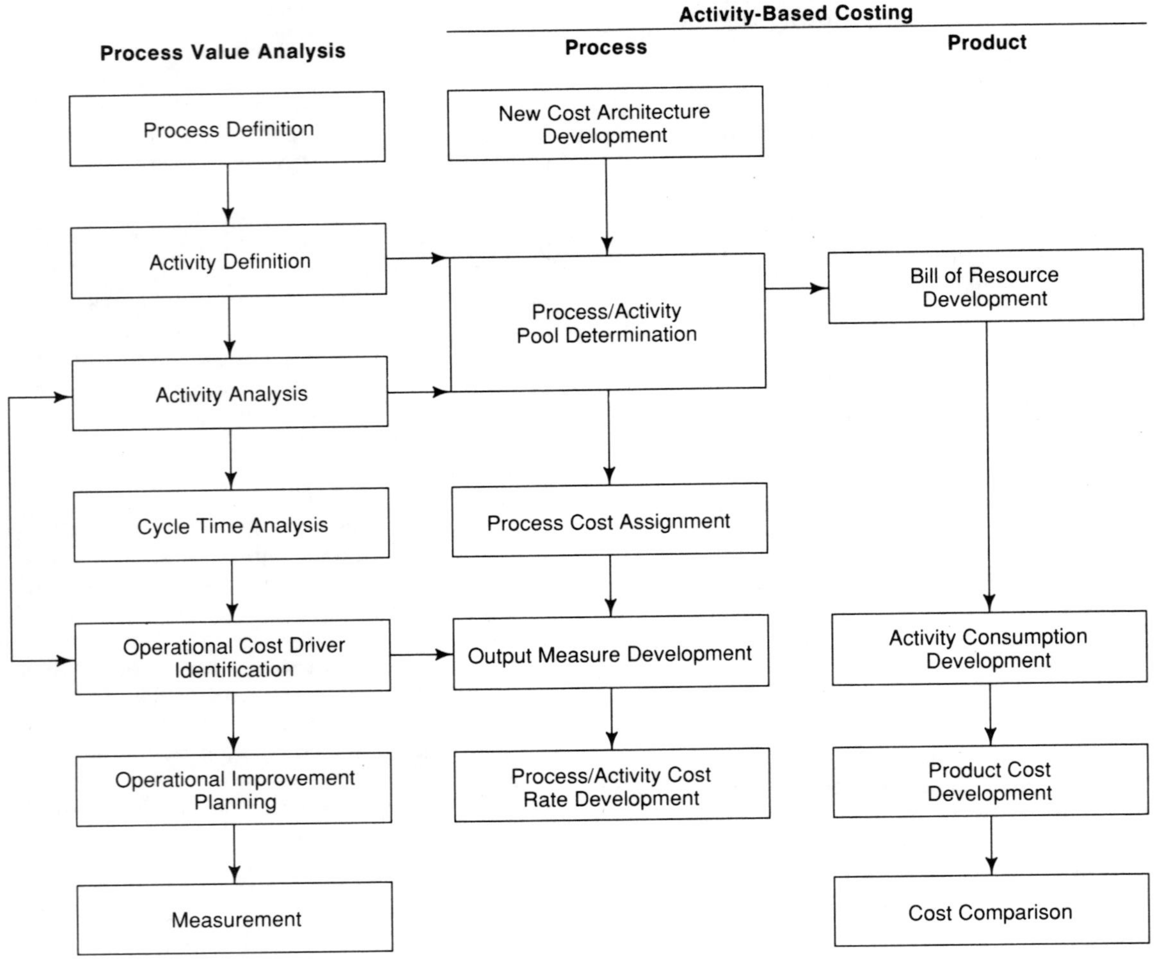

Activity-Based Costing

Process Value Analysis	Process	Product

```
Process Value Analysis          Process                    Product

┌──────────────────┐     ┌──────────────────┐
│ Process Definition│     │ New Cost          │
│                   │     │ Architecture      │
│                   │     │ Development       │
└────────┬──────────┘     └────────┬─────────┘
         │                         │
         ▼                         │
┌──────────────────┐              │         ┌──────────────────┐
│ Activity          │─────────┐    │         │ Bill of Resource │
│ Definition        │         │    ▼         │ Development      │
└────────┬──────────┘    ┌──────────────────┐└────────┬─────────┘
         │               │ Process/Activity │──►      │
         ▼               │ Pool             │         │
┌──────────────────┐     │ Determination    │         │
│ Activity Analysis │────►│                  │         │
└────────┬──────────┘     └────────┬─────────┘         │
         │                         │                   │
         ▼                         ▼                   │
┌──────────────────┐     ┌──────────────────┐         │
│ Cycle Time        │     │ Process Cost     │         │
│ Analysis          │     │ Assignment       │         │
└────────┬──────────┘     └────────┬─────────┘         ▼
         │                         │         ┌──────────────────┐
         ▼                         ▼         │ Activity         │
┌──────────────────┐     ┌──────────────────┐│ Consumption      │
│ Operational Cost  │────►│ Output Measure   ││ Development      │
│ Driver            │     │ Development      │└────────┬─────────┘
│ Identification    │     └────────┬─────────┘         │
└────────┬──────────┘              │                   ▼
         │                         ▼         ┌──────────────────┐
┌──────────────────┐     ┌──────────────────┐│ Product Cost     │
│ Operational       │     │ Process/Activity ││ Development      │
│ Improvement       │     │ Cost Rate        │└────────┬─────────┘
│ Planning          │     │ Development      │         │
└────────┬──────────┘     └──────────────────┘         ▼
         │                                   ┌──────────────────┐
         ▼                                   │ Cost Comparison  │
┌──────────────────┐                         └──────────────────┘
│ Measurement       │
└──────────────────┘
```

has changed, but the methodology for providing cost information has not changed correspondingly.

Efforts to reduce cost have been frustrated by attempts to manage cost at the product level. The measurement of product costs does increase the awareness of cost, but ABC is generally promoted in too narrow a scope. Activity-based product costs fail to identify *how* costs are incurred, *where* resources are consumed, and *what* the underlying cost behavior patterns are.

PVA establishes the foundation for understanding cost; it also sets the direction for cost reduction and process improvement. ABC should establish the relationship of cost to the activities performed within the process. This one-two punch provides the necessary linkage to employ the remaining tools of total cost management—investment justification, performance measurement, and responsibility accounting.

The linkage between PVA and ABC is critical. Activities are the focal point of total cost management; they must be managed to gain and sustain a competitive advantage. ▲

Reprinted from *Journal of Cost Management,* Fall 1992, pp. 4–13. Copyright © 1992 by Warren Gorham Lamont, a division of Research Institute of America Inc. All rights reserved. Used by permission.

Business Process Redesign: Key to Competitiveness

Robert O. Knorr

The issues that companies now face cross traditional functional boundaries. Successful manufacturers must focus on improvements that affect business across the entire value chain. A focus on the reengineering of business processes allows companies to deal with all the complex dimensions (including strategy, structure, process, technology, and culture) of the current competitive environment. None of these dimensions can be applied effectively in isolation. Each must be understood in terms of the interrelationships that exist throughout the entire value chain.

Before 1980, manufacturers operated in a relatively stable business environment. The bases of competition changed gradually. The physical aspects of the product (e.g., functionality and quality) dominated; delivery and customer service were largely set by standard business practices. The significant improvements that were made in manufacturing control through the application of technologies to factory floor scheduling can no longer provide a competitive weapon.

Since the mid-1980s, manufacturers have been increasingly squeezed by customers, competitors, and, in some cases, regulators. Specifically, there has been the consolidation of outlets and the growth of mega-chains, buying cooperatives, and others with purchasing clout.

In addition, the complexity of the market has grown and the increase in product proliferation has put tremendous pressure on manufacturers. Strong marketers have appeared in

a number of areas that U.S. companies once thought to be safe (e.g., dairy products and auto parts).

Manufacturers that are succeeding have had to redefine the relationships between both their suppliers and their distribution and retail networks. In some cases, customers have simply forced manufacturers into compliance. In other cases, manufacturers have effected change by developing true partnerships across the value chain, which include structuring mutually beneficial strategies for competing.

Nevertheless, manufacturers' accomplishments during the 1980s have been relatively simple compared to what is required today. Competitive measures that were considered innovative a short time ago are now the minimum commitment necessary to even enter a variety of industries. These commitments include what were once state-of-the-art advances in development cycles and retail-order turnaround.

The issues that firms must now face cross the traditional functional boundaries that used to define them. For example, order time to market—from customer request to customer receipt—is what counts in today's dynamic environment, not the time from manufacturing order to booking of finished goods. In addition, electronic data interchange, overnight transportation, and detailed consumer marketing information have made basic business relationships a major competitive factor. (Perhaps American managers can learn from the *keiretsu* after all?)

Tomorrow's successful manufacturers will take a broader approach then previous manufacturers and will focus on improvements that affect business across the whole value chain. The most successful manufacturers will look beyond the present business horizon to anticipate or influence environmental factors that are outside of the direct control of the enterprise. The market is demanding a new focus on continuous improvement, demands beyond efficiency and effectiveness.

Until recently, the overall improvement of a firm's competitive position has been addressed in a piecemeal fashion. Each new symptom was treated with a specially developed technique sponsored by the functional area of the firm that had direct responsibility for it.

> *"The reengineering of business processes must be a basic requirement for continuous improvement."*

For example, just-in-time (JIT) would be implemented by the production department to reduce work-in-process inventories and improve lead time. Material requirements planning would be used to improve scheduling efficiency and reduce raw material inventory. And advanced manufacturing techniques—including CAD, CAM, and CAE—would be promoted by engineering to reduce their costs and improve the development cycle. Even total quality management, representing an attempt to extend quality principles beyond the factory and integrate approaches across disciplines, has traditionally been applied to business functions in isolation.

This compartmentalized approach limits a company's ability to realize the gains promised by any of these tools. New techniques make it possible to look across the functional boundaries and treat the company as a whole. These techniques address all the dimensions of time and performance and the ability to translate them into new opportunities.

The focus is on understanding the key cost and performance drivers, by which time to delivery, delivery liability, the simplicity of doing business, flexibility of production, product quality, product cost, and customer

service are all examined in a holistic fashion when looking at the value chain.

For example, when examining the product, one needs to understand the total time it takes to develop a new product, how that product is differentiated, and what the options are for product use. The underlying complex set of issues of product design, technology, support, financing, distribution, promotion, and pricing must be examined as a whole.

Furthermore, by analyzing all the facets of a company's manufacturing operations—including the considerations of strategy, structure, process, technology, culture, and people—opportunities can be identified for continuous improvement in overall performance and competitive advantage.

On the basis of these issues, the reengineering of business processes must be a basic requirement for continuous improvement. Focusing on business processes allows one to deal with all of the complex dimensions of the previously mentioned issues and to apply the appropriate tools and techniques. In addition, no dimension of a firm's strategy, structure, processes, technology, or culture can be applied effectively in isolation. Each must understand the impact and interrelationships of the other vis-à-vis the value chain and the focus on business processes.

Business process redesign

The technique we have found useful in breaking down traditional organizational barriers is to look at a company in terms of broadly defined business processes and they to document both current and proposed processes in a logical, rather than an organizational, way. This is achieved by borrowing from the information technology and industrial engineering disciplines and by defining the common non-value-added activities across functional hierarchies.

Once defined, the processes to be examined in detail are chosen on the basis of the potential worth and possible amount of improvement, given a company's current processes and available skills and technology. The key factors are one's knowledge of the marketplace and prior experience, either directly with other firms or from competitive and benchmark analyses.

Looking at business processes from a logical rather than an organizational point of view allows for a broader perspective, beyond just viewing traditional organizational alignments. The following example describes an application in the area of order fulfillment.

A telecommunications equipment manufacturer recently implemented full JIT techniques in an attempt to reduce lead time to delivery. The program had been successful on the shop floor, but little improvement had been seen by customers.

"A company's strategy must focus on a vision of what can be achieved and on where improved capabilities can be leveraged in the market-place."

By looking at order fulfillment as a process, the entire flow was mapped out from customer request to customer receipt, and the company was able to show that only one-quarter of the total lead time was attributed to the shop floor. The remainder was taken up by order checking, reviewing pricing, reviewing and revising product configurations, checking credit, and recording the manufacturing order.

It became apparent that no single department could significantly reduce the lead time experienced by the customer. Only a divisionwide effort to redefine the company's procedures and eliminate bottlenecks could make the kind of difference needed to compete.

Another example shows that the product development process must be viewed as including marketing, engineering, and manufacturing. A large manufacturer of OEM automotive components found that the lead time that was sufficient in the past to develop a new technology was now causing the company to lose business to European competitors.

As a first step, the use of CAD/CAM tools was recommended to directly enhance development efficiency. The product realization process was then mapped out, and opportunities for marketing, manufacturing, service, and purchasing to get involved in the product development process right from the design stage were identified.

Our firm benchmarked design and products and also conducted a competitive assessment with customer and vendor analysis. International barriers to change (e.g., HR and cultural issues) were examined as well as process and technology issues. The result was to significantly reduce the time to market for a new generation of products. In addition, before redesign of the process, the firm's engineering department had exclusive control up to the final prototype. The new process required that the whole cycle be controlled by a multiskilled team.

In practical applications of process reengineering, we have sometimes found that the process in question depends on drivers in an area not usually associated with the process. For example, at a company that processes dairy products, we discovered that the costs associated with production greatly depended on adherence to schedule. By increasing the emphasis on sales forecasting and establishing a routine maintenance program to prevent equipment breakdowns, the company was able to improve costs and significantly reduce the order-cycle time.

Processes can also be controlled by elements of the value chain that are beyond the direct control of the firm. After a review of the market for a supplier of household textiles, it was found that the shipping date for a specific color and style was critical in the purchase decision. In reviewing the value chain for the industry, it became apparent that most of the delay in getting specific orders into the hands of the consumer occurred in the distributors' and retailers' organizations.

The key to a successful strategy was to get the cooperation of managers in the retail channel so that customer orders could be disseminated simultaneously throughout the value chain. The goal was to move the lead time from 16 weeks to five days, with an interim goal of four weeks.

A senior-level management team is often required to lead a process redesign. Seldom are there executives within an organization below the level of CEO who can manage a process across organizational lines and have the power and influence to push through changes in a coordinated way.

Firms have successfully established multidisciplinary project teams to provide overall direction. Before putting a team in place, however, consider these caveats. First, the team dynamic must be right. Second, the team must be vested with real authority and have the clear support of the company's top management. Finally, it is crucial to initially use an area that is open to change to pilot the team's improvements.

Although any business process can provide a company with competitive advantage, expertise in hands-on implementation is the critical factor in conceiving and setting the strategic vision for any business process or for the enterprise as a whole. Yet in most cases, we have found that existing strategies are formed outside the context of a company's ability to implement them. There is an inability to develop strategy because of a poor understanding of the implementation requirements.

A company must be looked at as a whole, and individual techniques must be applied to issues in a disciplined and orchestrated manner. There must be an understanding of the dynamics and interrelationships of the issues and tools. Taken in isolation, a company's manufacturing capabilities will never be enhanced and productivity gains never achieved.

A source for competitive advantage

Defining the current basis of competition and making incremental improvements is no longer a sufficient strategy in today's environment. Truly successful companies are contin-

uously redefining the bases. A company's strategy must focus on a vision of what can be achieved and where improved capabilities can be leveraged in the marketplace.

In the drive to use new capabilities to gain a competitive advantage, understanding and reengineering business processes gives strategic planners a wealth of new possibilities to explore. Furthermore, the holistic approach to business processes forces consideration of all relevant disciplines. A winning strategy can come from leveraging any area of the firm and can provide a company with a marketable differentiation.

The processes to apply this holistic approach should be selected through an understanding of the marketplace, using experience to determine which capabilities will lead to real competitive advantage. The support of senior management is also required to reap the benefits of reengineering processes, because only this level of management has the power to sponsor broad implementation.

When armed with an understanding of their underlying processes, firms can begin to align all of the dimensions—strategy, structure, process, technology, and culture—to exploit the newly designed processes and increase the pace of their continuous improvement. The whole will be greater than the sum of its parts. The company that understands this will achieve significant competitive advantage during the 1990s and beyond. ▲

Value Engineering: The High-Quality Solution to High Costs

Keki R. Bhote

Value engineering lets companies reexamine products and processes in a new way. The object of value engineering is to make items cheaper, either through material or labor reductions. This requires looking at the *function* of each item— i.e., what each part or item does—rather than what it is. The benefits of value engineering include significant reductions in procurement and manufacturing costs. Up-front investments are small and can lead to 10 : 1 returns on every dollar invested.

Jim Dowling, CEO of Livingstone Electronics, was not his hale and hearty self as he addressed members of his key staff. His face was drawn, his looks haggard, his voice almost a whisper. "I have bad news for you," he said with a deep sigh, "I have just been roughed up by our board of directors. They have complained that our profits are anemic; our return on investment is lower than a bank could offer; our market share is eroding. And to make matters worse, the Japanese are eating our lunch. I've been given one year to turn the tide.

"We must start with a major cost reduction effort. Our direct labor costs must be cut by at least 10% through a combination of layoffs and moving some lines offshore; our white-collar head-count should be cut an equal amount. We must impose a travel freeze, and all requisitions, even the ordering of pencils and pads, must be approved personally by your senior directors. The meeting is now open for discussion."

There was stunned silence. Jim's staff knew business was bad. But an ultimatum! With a drop-dead date! Finally, Cal, the controller, spoke up. He was an old-timer who was used to calling a spade a spade, "Jim, your diagnosis of the symptoms of our ailment is right on, but your cure is worse than the disease. Yours is the typical rearrangement of the deck chairs as the Titanic is sinking! This is what more than 90% of companies do when they are in trouble, and they end up on a downward spiral, spinning their way to extinction.

"There is a better way to turn this company around, a sure-fire way. First, we should concentrate on quality improvement. It is a known fact that companies with poor quality have poor profitability, poor return on investment, poor market share, poor productivity. Companies with high quality improve these business parameters—parameters that we

> *Fanatic Japanese dedication to value engineering is a major reason a Japanese car costs at least $1,000 less than an equivalent American car.*

worship—by factors of 2 : 1. Secondly, we should forget about direct labor, which constitutes only 5% of the sales dollar. Even if we can achieve a 10% cut in direct labor, profits can rise by a maximum of only 0.5%. Instead, let's attack material costs, which tie up 50% of our sales dollar. A 10% cut there can, in our weak state, double our profits."

Over a chorus of opposing voices, Cal continued: "All of you are probably wondering how to bell this cat. How do you improve quality and reduce cost at the same time? Isn't that an oxymoron? The answer is contained in a single discipline—value engineering!"

A veritable gold mine

Cal was right. The benefits of value engineering (V.E.) are legendary:

- An averaging reduction of 25% in procurement costs as well as manufacturing costs. Companies can achieve a minimum 10% reduction with ease, and 75% reductions are not uncommon.
- A 10 : 1 return on every dollar invested in V.E. (some companies have registered even 100 : 1 returns). Further, the amount of up-front investment required for such returns is modest.
- Improved customer satisfaction. V.E. is not just a cost-reduction or quality-improvement tool. Applied properly, it enhances all elements of customer satisfaction—reliability, service, performance, human engineering, safety, and delivery.
- Serendipity. By exploring new technology and materials, V.E. stumbles upon amazing discoveries that can reduce cost, improve quality, and enhance customer satisfaction.
- Higher employee morale. The basic building block of value engineering is an interdisciplinary team. The pursuit of value enhancement (cost reduction plus quality improvement) becomes a game. It's fun. It builds camaraderie among team members. Years after a V.E. project is finished, team members look upon the chase for dollar savings with affection and nostalgia.

Dawn and twilight

The value-engineering discipline originated in purchasing. Larry Miles, the founder of V.E., was head of General Electric's purchasing research department. During World War II, he was assigned the task of finding substitutes for scarce materials. He discovered, perhaps through serendipity, that the substitute materials were not only less expensive, but also superior in quality. A new star was born.

In the 1960s, the U.S. Department of Defense, especially under Defense Secretary Robert MacNamara, introduced value-engineering incentives, whereby defense contractors could submit ideas to reduce costs and improve quality. If approved, the savings on current contracts was shared, generally 50-50, with the supplier.

On follow-on contracts, the supplier received 10% of the savings, even if he was not awarded the follow-on contract. V.E. enjoyed this defense spotlight for 10 to 15 years. Gradually, however, the Department of Defense bureaucracy killed the goose that laid the golden egg. Its contract administrators did not want to be bothered with evaluating value-engineering ideas and negotiating payouts. Today, value engineering at the Department of Defense, while still on the books, seems to be headed for the Smithsonian Institution as a historic relic.

In value engineering, the challenge is to look at the function—what the part does, rather than what it is.

Japan steals a U.S. invention

Despite its brief reign at the Department of Defense, V.E. never even had a proper birth in commercial industry. A few progressive companies have used it to great advantage, but the great majority of U.S. companies have not even heard of V.E.

As one would expect, the Japanese were able to pick up, use, and milk to the fullest yet another technique invented in the U.S. The Japanese value engineer their products to death before the start of production. (It is at the design stage of a product where there is the greatest V.E. value for money spent.) This fanatic Japanese dedication to value engineering is a major reason why a Japanese car costs at least $1,000 less than an equivalent American car, even with the steep yen revaluation.

V.E. methodology

In traditional cost reduction, the design of the part or product is kept essentially the same. The object is to make the item cheaper, either with material or labor reduction. Often, "cheaper" results in lower quality and lower customer satisfaction. In V.E., the challenge is to look at the function—what the part does, rather than what it is. This function can be one of two types: basic functions that make the product work or supporting functions that sell the product. The next step is to research alternate ways to provide the function at lower cost and with better quality.

The tie clip example. A simple example illustrates the V.E. methodology. Let's say that a tie clip costs $2 to manufacture. Traditional cost reduction would maintain the integrity of the original design of the tie clip and concentrate on seeking less expensive materials or manufacturing processes. By contrast, V.E. examines the function and describes it in two words: *holds tie.* Then, it brings an interdisciplinary team together to research alternate and radically different ways to perform the function of holding a tie.

In the initial brainstorming or creative phase of V.E., all ideas—no matter how wild—are accepted as a starting point. In fact, it's been proven that the worth of the final idea is directly proportional to the number of brainstorming ideas generated. For the tie clip, a number of alternatives can surface during brainstorming:

- paper clip
- no tie clip
- no tie
- chewing gum
- velcro
- bow tie
- tuck in shirt
- paint on shirt
- tie loop

Even though some of the alternatives are frivolous, a few, such as a paper clip, cost a fraction of a cent—a savings of more than 200:1. Of course, the ornamental and prestige value of a paper clip would preclude it as a reasonable alternative. However, a tie loop is not only almost as inexpensive as a paper clip, it is also today's fashion. The tie clip has gone the way of the dodo bird! Of course, the first and supreme value engineering question should always be: "Can the function be eliminated altogether?"

The V.E. job plan. A more formal methodology, called the V.E. job plan, is outlined in Table 1 on page J3-4. It is a simple, but powerful, approach to solving any problem—be it in a product area, a service business, or any white-collar operation.

Value engineering and creativity. Albert Einstein once said that "imagination is much more important than knowledge." This spirit is captured in the most important aspect of V.E., its creativity. The V.E. team brainstorms creative, alternative ideas for better performance of both the basic and the supporting functions of a product, part, or process. Creativity, which also can be called deferred judgment, may be stimulated by a checklist of this type:

- Can the function itself be eliminated?
- Can the part or process step be eliminated or simplified?
- Can it be altered, minified, or magnified to perform multiple functions?
- Can all specifications be challenged and modified?
- Can lower cost processes or materials be used?
- Can a higher cost material be used that can simplify the design or production?
- Can tolerances, finishes, tests, or packaging be reduced in cost?
- Can quality/reliability be increased at no extra cost?
- Can other features, such as performance, service, delivery, human engineering, or safety, be improved to enhance customer satisfaction?

Many a V.E. effort is stalled, even torpedoed, if it is organized as a separate department or if an outside group is assigned the V.E. task.

The psychological factor

Many a V.E. effort is stalled, even torpedoed, if it is organized as a separate department or if an outside group is assigned the V.E. task. V.E. is sometimes called a second look at the design. If an outside team determines im-

Table 1. *The Value Engineering Job Plan*

Relationship of Value—Analysis/Value-Engineering Techniques

Job Plan	Functional Analysis	Key Techniques	V.E. Questions	Supporting Techniques
1. Information	Identify function and separate specifications Determine cost per functional relationship Define function Determine basic function	Use good human-relations techniques Get all the facts from the best sources Use accurate costs Employ cost visibility	What is it? What must it do? How much does it cost?	To be used as the problem dictates throughout all phases of job plan: 1) Spend company money as you would your own 2) Record everything 3) Employ good human relations techniques 4) Overcome roadblocks 5) Work on specifics, not generalities
2. Speculation		Think creatively Use industrial standards Blast and refine	What else will accomplish the function?	
3. Evaluation	Evaluate function	Put $ on and develop the main idea Use company services Use specialty vendors' materials, products, and processes Put $ on each tolerance Evaluate by comparison Use your judgment Overcome roadblocks	What will that cost?	
4. Planning		Work on specifics, not generalities		
5. Execution				
6. Report		Develop and use a V.E. proposal form, use good human relations techniques		

provements, the original design group feels that it is shown as incompetent, regardless of the purity of the team's motives.

Good value engineering is as much psychological as it is technical. It stands to reason that the original design group be made part of the solution rather than part of the problem. A team approach is the essence of good value engineering. Team members for product value engineering are drawn generally from purchasing, manufacturing, quality, accounting, and other disciplines as needed. But the team leader always should be drawn from the original design group, so that the effort can be looked upon as an improvement rather than as a slap at engineering.

An example illustrates this psychological aspect of V.E. In one Motorola division, Japanese competition required that product cost be reduced substantially. The task was given to the research department, a collection of high-powered talent, which made several recommendations to reduce costs. Then the proposal went to the development engineering group that had produced the original design. For a variety of reasons, not a single idea was accepted. The project was stopped cold in its tracks.

The division general manager then turned to this author, who was Director of Quality and Value Assurance for the division, to initiate a major value engineering effort. My first action was to establish six interdisciplinary teams to tackle various aspects of the product. I persuaded the chief engineer of the development group to be the overall captain, with several

Table 2. *Use of V.E. in Various Disciplines/Departments*

Discipline/Dept.	V.E. Methodology
Customers	• Value research: Determine the customer's strong "likes," strong "dislikes" and "neutrals." Reduce or eliminate the strong dislikes through redesign, etc. Advertise the strong likes. Value engineer the neutrals to reduce costs. Determine the cost of each retained function and provide that function at lower cost with higher customer satisfaction. • Combine V.E. with the new technique of Quality Function Deployment (Q.F.D.) to translate the voice of the customer into product, process, and material specifications.
Design	• Reduce part counts through V.E. challenges. • Standardize or at least commonalize parts, subassemblies, products. • Combine with the new technique of Group Technology (G.T.). • Combine with the powerful technique of Design of Experiments (D.O.E.) to reduce product variability and increase yield. • Combine with the powerful technique of Multiple Environment OverStress Testing (MEOST) to attain new heights of reliability.
Suppliers	• Consult with suppliers as the best source of V.E. ideas. • Ask the supplier to put a dollar value on every detailed requirement/specification. • Reduce the supplier base using the Pareto Principle. • Encourage the flow of V.E. ideas from suppliers with V.E. incentives and V.E. royalties—even if a particular supplier does not get the order. Pay for brains, not brawn.
Manufacturing	• Combine with the powerful technique of DOE to characterize and optimize key process. • Combine with the technique of Design for Manufacturability (DRM) to ease production and assembly. • Combine with work simplification (WS) to reduce direct labor and manufacturing overhead. • Combine with the technique of Poka Yoke to prevent worker errors. • Combine with the technique of Field Escape Control to anticipate and correct field fail users before they occur.
Service	• Use modular designs for ease of field repair. • Build-in diagnostics to facilitate fault detection. • Assure that designs are "user-repair" friendly. • Assure service logistics such as parts availability, exchange units, service speed, and accuracy to minimize customer dissatisfaction.
Accounting	• Determine value/cost ratio of every accounting report—based on feedback from accounting reports and from accounting's internal "customers." • Use V.E. principles to: reduce the cost of poor quality; allocate realistic overhead costs to projects; minimize bureaucratic systems and procedures; reduce inventories. • Monitor total savings associated with V.E. projects.
All White-Collar Operations	• Combine with cycle-time reduction techniques to reduce the cycle time associated with every step in any administrative process, reduce cost, and improve quality and next operation as customer (NOAC) satisfaction. • Reduce organizational "disconnects" and eliminate "white spaces."

---

of his engineering managers as team leaders for the six teams. A goal of roughly $1 million in cost reduction was targeted for each team—for a total of $6 million, representing an 18% reduction. As an added incentive, each team member was promised a color television set if the goal for that team was achieved.

The product generated unprecedented enthusiasm. The teams labored long and hard, often on their own time after regular hours and on Saturdays. At the end of six months, the total savings was $4.2 million. The accounting department audited and verified the savings as green dollars, not blue dollars. Even though the cost reduction was only 12%, against the goal of 18%, the division blocked the Japanese challenge. More important, morale became so high that the division went on to win several such "battles" against the Japanese.

Case study: the crystal filter

A more formal example in the product arena further demonstrates the power of value engineering. A crystal filter supplier quoted a complex 44 megahertz filter at a price of $73.50 per unit. Recognizing this cost as high, a V.E. team requested the supplier to identify those requirements or specifications with the highest costs. (A useful V.E. discipline is to put a dollar sign on every requirement, every tolerance, every test, etc.) The supplier pointed to two specific requirements where a relaxation of specifications could reduce the cost appreciably. The specifications for one requirement could not be eased. In fact, they were tightened during a one-day marathon session between the V.E. team and the supplier. But the other requirements could be reduced even beyond the supplier's recommendations.

With these concessions, the supplier was able to redesign the eight-section filter with just five sections. He also was able to reduce the cost of crystals by plating them differently. Tests were run with the new filter to assure that quality and reliability were not degraded. In fact, because the filter had fewer parts, the mean time between failures (MTBF) actually increased! The final cost: $27.00 per unit, almost a 3 : 1 cost reduction. Conventional negotiations to "squeeze" the supplier would not have achieved 10% of this savings.

Applications

A cardinal rule in value engineering is to challenge everything, question every rule, every procedure, every system, every assumption. Ask the question "Why?"; question the response with another why. Go five layers deep into such probing with five whys.

V.E.'s simple formula is:

- What is it (the part, product, or process)?
- What is its function?
- What is its cost?
- What else will provide the function less expensively, with better quality, and higher customer satisfaction?
- What will that cost?

This formula can be a road map to success in any discipline, in any department. Table 2 on page J3-5 lists how V.E. can be used in a number of such disciplines. In a sense, value engineering is an umbrella technique that encompasses several specific processes to improve customer satisfaction and reduce cost in any operation. It is beyond the scope of

> *A cardinal rule in value engineering is to challenge everything, question every rule, every procedure, every system, every assumption.*

this article to show how value engineering can aid each of the disciplines listed in Table 2. Nevertheless, the V.E. methodology considerably enhances the ultimate effectiveness of these disciplines.

A V.E. role for finance/accounting

Not only can value engineering be applied successfully in accounting, as shown in Table 2, but also the finance/accounting organization can play an important role in promoting and institutionalizing V.E. in a company.

- It can act as the goal champion for V.E., persuading a V.E.-illiterate management of its enormous potential for quality and profit improvement and customer satisfaction.
- It can be a role model by applying V.E. to clean its own house.
- It can act as a catalyst to assure the application of V.E. in all indirect labor operations, where productivity is abysmally low.

In the final analysis, the true mission of the finance/accounting organization is not to be numbers clerks merely collecting data and reporting on financial performance, but to act proactively in leading the way to profit and productivity improvement. Value engineering can light the way as few other tools can! ▲

Analyzing the Labor Efficiency Variance to Signal Process Engineering Problems[1]

Alan S. Levitan and Sidney J. Baxendale

The increase in automated manufacturing processes has changed the man-machine interaction from what it used to be in more labor-intensive manufacturing operations. Now it is common to find one employee who attends several automated machines. Since the efficiency with which process engineers configure the machines affects the efficiency of employees who tend machines, the traditional labor efficiency variance is no longer an appropriate measure of employee performance. The effectiveness of the machine configuration must be addressed. By introducing a standard relationship between human hours and machine hours, the traditional labor efficiency standard can be broken down into two parts: One part attributable to the efficiency of the machines and the other part attributable to the efficiency of employees. It would be incorrect to attribute the labor efficiency variance entirely to the employee. This suggested decomposition of the labor efficiency variance allows management to locate potential problems in machine utilization. These ideas have been implemented in a factory of the Colgate Palmolive Company. The results indicate that the decomposition of the traditional labor efficiency variance provides useful information for management.

This column proposes that the ratio of a machine tender's (i.e., an employee's) hours to the hours of the machine itself—captured in the form of a new labor variance—can signal potential process engineering problems.

Deficiencies of traditional cost accounting

Much has been written about the deficiencies of cost accounting for today's production methods. Charging that traditional accounting undermines production, one authority has urged companies to concentrate on total factor productivity, not just the productivity of labor.[2] The focus should be on quality, flexibility, and the efficient use of expensive information workers and capital. This contrasts with the emphasis on direct labor content that was prevalent when the traditional cost accounting model was derived.

Another commentator suggests focusing control systems on investment and inventory management, and establishing an equipment cost center that "rents" machinery to productive departments. The same commentator observes that burden rates, if based on direct labor, would approach infinity in automated factories. Control of labor and operating expense diminishes in importance when machine center managers have responsibility only for smooth operations.[3]

Other authorities have suggested that machine cost cards should be developed for each key machine to evaluate the cost effectiveness of each machine and to charge its cost to the products that are produced with the machine.[4] A new machine might reduce direct labor while increasing plant overhead. Since management must make incremental decisions and determine the sensitivity of costs to changes in volume, management might make various machines the cost centers of interest—i.e., machines become the central focus for the accumulation of costs.

Distinction between labor and machine efficiency

This article demonstrates a method of performance evaluation based on the division of the traditional labor efficiency variance into two variances that are more appropriate for an automated environment. These two new variances are:

- The *employee labor efficiency variance*; and
- The *machine efficiency variance*.

The traditional labor efficiency variance is broken down into an employee labor efficiency variance and a machine efficiency variance because the efficiency of the employee in an automated manufacturing environment has two different aspects. One aspect is directly related to the skill and industriousness of the employee; the other aspect is directly related to the state of readiness of the equipment. By recognizing each of these aspects in a separate variance, the management control system will be more likely to direct management's attention to the real source of problems (whether it is an employee or the configuration of machines).

Appropriate corrective actions

Directing management's attention to the real cause of problems is important because the appropriate corrective action that must be taken differs depending on the problem suggested by the two new variances. An unfavorable employee labor efficiency variance might suggest the need for additional training or better motivation for the employee. An unfavorable machine efficiency variance, on the other hand, might suggest the need for the process engineers to reconfigure how the machines relate to each other and to the employee.

In the example that follows, several estimates and relationships are established, as shown in Exhibits 1 and 2. A traditional labor efficiency variance is calculated in Exhibit 3 for a manufacturing department with three automated machines that are used sequentially to manufacture a single product. An employee labor efficiency variance and a machine efficiency variance are calculated for each of the three machines in the manufacturing department in Exhibits 4, 5, and 6. Exhibit 7 shows how the information in Exhibit 3 relates to the information in Exhibits 4, 5, and 6.

Dividing the traditional labor efficiency variance

To divide the traditional labor efficiency variance into the two new variances, process engineers must establish a standard ratio of employee labor hours to machine hours for each piece of equipment to arrive at the most efficient combination of humans and machines. These standard ratios can be established by time and motion studies or by analysis of actual experience. Exhibit 1 shows the standards set for each piece of equipment in Department A.

Exhibit 2 takes the information from Exhibit 1 and summarizes it in such a way that the traditional labor efficiency variance for the entire department may be calculated in Exhibit 3. Exhibit 2 shows that given the relationship between employee labor hours and machine hours shown in Exhibit 1, the predetermined standard employee labor hours per unit of product is 1.828125 hours.

One commentator asserts that in an automated factory, machine-based overhead rates should be used rather than labor-based rates.[5] This conclusion seems correct; the methodology shown here is perfectly consistent with any overhead application basis.

The employee used in this manufacturing department is paced by the state of readiness of the three machines that are being tended. Due to the machine-paced nature of the manufacturing environment, it is not useful to attribute the traditional labor efficiency variance entirely to the human machine employee. As Exhibit 3 shows, if the traditional labor efficiency variance were used to evaluate the employee, the labor efficiency variance would be $15,796 unfavorable.

Exhibit 1. *Department A*
Assumptions Used in Calculating Predetermined 19XX Employee Labor Overhead Rates

	Machine 1	Machine 2	Machine 3
Practical capacity in machine hours	8,000	7,500	7,000
Standard machine hours per unit of product	2.000	1.875	1.750
Standard ratio of employee labor hours to machine hours	0.250	0.125	0.625
Standard wage rate per employee hour	$15.00	$15.00	$15.00
Units of production at practical capacity	4,000	4,000	4,000

Exhibit 2. *Department A*
Calculation of Predetermined Employee Labor Overhead Rates for 19XX

Calculation Used for Traditional Labor Efficiency Variance

Machine	Machine Hour/Unit of Product		Standard Ratio of Employee Hours to Machine Hours		Employee Labor per Unit of Product
1	2.000	×	0.250	=	0.500000 hours
2	1.875	×	0.125	=	0.234375 hours
3	1.750	×	0.625	=	1.093750 hours

Standard employee labor hours per unit of product	1.828125 hours
Standard wage rate per employee labor hour	× $15.00
Standard employee labor rate per unit of product	$27.421875

Calculation Used for New Efficiency Variances

	Machine 1	Machine 2	Machine 3
Standard ratio of employee labor hours to machine hours	0.250	0.125	0.625
Standard wage rate	× $15	× $15	× $15
Employee labor rate per machine hour	$3.750	$1.875	$9.375

Exhibit 3. *19XX Performance Evaluation for Manager of Department A*
Employee Labor Efficiency Variance Calculation Only
(Traditional Method)

Units Produced = 3,800 units
Actual Labor Hours = 8,000 hours
Employee Labor Efficiency Variance Calculation
   3,800 units × 1.828125 standard hours per unit × $15/hour = $104,203.13
      Less: 8,000 actual employee hours × $15/hour = 120,000.00

     Unfavorable employee labor efficiency variance = $(15,796.87)

Exhibit 4. *Department A*
19XX Performance Evaluation for Machine 1

Actual Units Produced = 3,800
Actual Machine Hours for Machine 1 = 7,900
Actual Employee Labor Hours = 2,300

	Machine Employee Labor Charge	Required Employee Labor Cost	Allowed Employee Labor Cost	Favorable (Unfavorable) Efficiency Variance Employee Labor	Favorable (Unfavorable) Efficiency Variance Machine 1
2,300 hours × $15	$34,500.00			Required employee labor cost *less* machine employee labor charge	Allowed employee labor cost *less* required employee labor cost
7,900 hours × .25 × $15		$29,625.00			
3,800 units × 2.0 × .25 × $15			$28,500.00		
	$34,500.00	$29,625.00	$28,500.00	$(4,875.00)	$(1,125.00)

Exhibit 5. *Department A*
19XX Performance Evaluation for Machine 2

Actual Units Produced = 3,800
Actual Machine Hours for Machine 2 = 6,400
Actual Employee Labor Hours = 1,300

| | Machine Employee Labor Charge | Required Employee Labor Cost | Allowed Employee Labor Cost | Favorable (Unfavorable) Efficiency Variance | |
				Employee Labor	Machine 2
1,300 hours × $15	$19,500.00			Required employee labor cost *less* machine employee labor charge	Allowed employee labor cost *less* required employee labor cost
6,400 hours × .125 × $15		$12,000.00			
3,800 units × 1.875 × .125 × $15			$13,359.38		
	$19,500.00	$12,000.00	$13,359.38	$(7,500.00)	$1,359.38

Exhibit 6. *Department A*
19XX Performance Evaluation for Machine 3

Actual Units Produced = 3,800
Actual Machine Hours for Machine 3 = 7,300
Actual Employee Labor Hours = 4,400

| | Machine Employee Labor Charge | Required Employee Labor Cost | Allowed Employee Labor Cost | Favorable (Unfavorable) Efficiency Variance | |
				Employee Labor	Machine 3
4,400 hours × $15	$66,000.00			Required employee labor cost *less* machine employee labor charge	Allowed employee labor cost *less* required employee labor cost
7,300 hours × .625 × $15		$68,437.50			
3,800 units × 1.75 × .625 × $15			$62,343.75		
	$66,000.00	$68,437.50	$62,343.75	$2,437.50	$(6,093.75)

Exhibit 7. *Department A*
Reconciliation of Traditional With New Efficiency Variances

| | Favorable or (Unfavorable) Efficiency Variances | | |
	Employee Labor	Machine	Total (Exhibit 3)
Exhibit 4—Machine 1	$(4,875.00)	$(1,125.00)	$(6,000.00)
Exhibit 5—Machine 2	(7,500.00)	1,359.38	(6,140.62)
Exhibit 6—Machine 3	2,437.50	(6,093.75)	(3,656.25)
Total	$(9,937.50)	$(5,859.37)	$(15,796.87)

Calculation of the new efficiency variances

If the employee's performance is analyzed further, it can be seen that the employee worked more hours than were justified by the unit production because one or more of the machines did not synchronize properly with the other machines. This flaw in the use of the traditional labor efficiency variance in an automated manufacturing facility calls for a decomposition of the traditional labor efficiency variance into the two new efficiency variances.

These two new efficiency variances—employee labor efficiency variance and machine efficiency variance—are designed to help managers distinguish between the efficiency of an employee caused by factors that the employee is capable of controlling and the efficiency of the employee caused by the efficiency of the machines (which the employee cannot control).

In order to divide the traditional labor efficiency variance into the two new variances, however, it is necessary to estimate the relationship that *should* exist between machine hours and employee hours. This relationship, called the *ratio standard*, probably would be developed by process engineers. In manufacturing operations in which the pace is driven by machines, the ratio standard is a key number in analyzing how well or how poorly the employee maintained that pace, independent of the eventual output in units.

As Exhibit 1 shows, the ratio standard of employee labor hours to machine hours is 0.25 for Machine 1, 0.125 for Machine 2, and 0.625 for Machine 3. Thus, 100 percent of the human machine employee's time is allocated between the three machines he tends. The choice to allocate the total hours of one person over three machines tended is an attempt to keep the example simple. The use of three machines also makes it possible later to contrast three possible combinations of employee labor efficiency variance and machine efficiency variance—one combination for each of the three machines. In practice, as shown in the implementation described later, a group of machines could be tended by a crew of human machine employees, so that the ratio of employee labor hours to machine hours might be greater than 1 to 1.

Machine hours and employee hours

It is important to note that the two new efficiency variances discussed here require two other items of information in addition to the ratio standard for each machine in the machine cluster:

1. The actual number of machine hours each machine devotes to production in each accounting period; and
2. The actual number of hours the human machine employee devotes to each machine during the accounting period.

The first of these, the machine hours, is not difficult to determine; many automated machines have timing devices that enable accountants to determine the machine hours of operation. Similarly, the employee's hours devoted to each machine can be captured online by data collection terminals that are com-

> *These two new efficiency variances—employee labor efficiency variance and machine efficiency variance—are designed to help managers distinguish between the efficiency of an employee caused by factors that the employee is capable of controlling and the efficiency of the employee caused by the efficiency of the machines (which the employee cannot control).*

monly found at production workstations to collect labor hours worked in a job order costing system. Typically, the employee inserts a magnetically encoded plastic badge into a reader slot; the employee also may be prompted for additional information. Another more sophisticated collection method would be for each machine to electronically recognize the presence of a human machine employee within the machine's space and to record the duration of this presence on a permanent time record.

These three items of information associated with each machine—the ratio standard, the hours of machine operation, and the hours that the human machine employee devoted to each machine—when combined with the number of units produced during the accounting period, permit the preparation of the reports shown in Exhibits 4, 5, and 6, which illustrate the calculation of the employee labor efficiency variance and the machine efficiency variance for each of the three machines.

Machine 1

Exhibit 4 focuses on Machine 1 in Department A. It shows that the employee devoted 2,300 hours to Machine 1 in the year 19XX. That number of hours multiplied by a standard wage rate of $15 per hour yields machine employee labor charges of $34,500 associated with that machine. Considering that the machine operated 7,900 hours during the year, it is possible to conclude that 7,900 machine hours should have required 1,975 machine employee hours based on the ratio standard of 0.25 machine employee hours per machine hour. That 1,975 required machine employee hours (i.e., 7,900 hours × 0.25) times the standard wage rate of $15 per hour results in a required cost of $29,625. If the employee labor cost associated with Machine 1 is $34,500 and the required employee labor cost is $29,625, then the employee labor efficiency variance is an unfavorable $4,875. This variance tells us that the employee devoted more hours to the machine than were required, given the number of hours the machine operated and the ratio standard of employee labor hours to machine hours.

Machine efficiency variance. The machine efficiency variance, on the other hand, is designed to permit managers to assess the extent to which employee labor was under- or over-utilized because of machine efficiency or inefficiency. This variance will tend to signal an inefficient clustering of machines by isolating the extent to which a machine was responsible for wasting employee labor.

The required human machine employee labor hours (i.e., 1,975, as discussed above), when multiplied by the $15 standard wage rate per employee hour, gives us the required employee cost of $29,625. This amount, when compared with the allowed machine em-

ployee cost of $28,500, yields the machine efficiency variance. The allowed machine employee cost is calculated by multiplying the 3,800 units actually produced by the 2 standard machine hours per unit of product that the machine should have operated. Multiplying this number by the 0.25 standard ratio of human machine employee hours to machine hours for Machine 1 yields 1,900 allowed employee hours, given the number of units produced. Finally, this number multiplied by the $15 standard wage rate per hour yields the allowed machine employee cost ($28,500) used to calculate the machine efficiency variance.

The machine efficiency variance is important in highlighting the extent to which more or fewer employee hours were used, because, during the accounting period, more or fewer machine hours were used than were allowed by the process engineers for the quantity produced.

When overhead is applied based on machine hours, the machine efficiency variance will be of the same sign and proportional to the overhead efficiency variance. This is absolutely true when only one machine is used as an activity base, in which case the machine efficiency variance will be a function of the standard labor ratio, and the overhead efficiency variance will be a function of the standard overhead rate. If several machines are used, however, or if activity-based costing is being used, the variation in the relative magnitudes of the various rates preclude easy generalization.

Interpretation of the new efficiency variances

Exhibit 4 shows that Machine 1 had an unfavorable employee labor efficiency variance and also an unfavorable machine efficiency variance. Exhibit 7 shows that the total labor efficiency variance associated with Machine 1 was an unfavorable $6,000. Calculation of the two new variances above shows that $4,875 of the $6,000 unfavorable variance was caused by the employee devoting more hours to the machine than were required. The remaining $1,125 represents the unfavorable machine efficiency variance—i.e., the additional costs of employee labor occasioned by the machine's having been operated more hours than were allowed based on the number of units produced.

Both variances unfavorable. When the two efficiency variances are both unfavorable (as they are for Machine 1), one must consider the interaction effects. It is possible, for example, that the inefficiency of the employee might have contributed to the inefficiency of the machines. Alternatively, the inefficiency of the machine may have contributed to the inefficiency of the machine employee. It may be possible to gain an understanding of these underlying causes by examining both of the efficiency variances.

Management may take various steps to correct the underlying problems. If an unscheduled interruption occurs in the operation of

---

To divide the traditional labor efficiency variance into the two new variances, process engineers must establish a standard ratio of employee labor hours to machine hours for each piece of equipment to arrive at the most efficient combination of humans and machines.

---

the machines, for example, and if work rules permit, management may reduce the laborer's hours or reassign him to other duties during the interruption. In such a case, an unfavorable machine efficiency variance may occur, but there need not be an unfavorable employee labor efficiency variance. Unfortunately, the improper tending of machines is likely to result in an unfavorable machine efficiency variance, because no opportunity exists to reduce machine hour availability, and usually there is little ability to apply the otherwise idle machine hours for the production of other products.

Machine 2

Machine 2 (see Exhibit 5) illustrates a situation in which the total labor efficiency variance is an unfavorable $6,140 (see Exhibit 7).

Development of the two new variances previously described, however, reveals that the portion of the total variance that relates to the efficiency of the employee is really an unfavorable $7,500. This employee labor efficiency variance sends a strong signal that the human machine employee may need additional training to tend Machine 2. In addition, the machine efficiency variance for Machine 2 indicates that the efficient operation of the machine resulted in fewer required human machine employee hours than were allowed.

Machine 3

Machine 3 (see Exhibit 6) illustrates a situation in which the total labor efficiency variance is an unfavorable $3,656 (see Exhibit 7). Disaggregation of this variance, however, reveals that the portion relating to the efficiency of the human machine employee is really a favorable $2,437. This employee labor efficiency variance suggests that the employee is efficient in tending Machine 3. In contrast, the machine efficiency variance indicates that Machine 3 required excess employee labor because the machine required more operating hours than were allowed, given the number of units produced.

In this example, the traditional labor efficiency variance by itself is a misleading indicator of operational activity. Analysis of the two components of the total variance, however, provides valuable information. The unfavorable machine efficiency variance associated with Machine 3 may suggest that the machine was not operating properly or efficiently. If so, the solution may require action on the part of the process engineers rather than attention to the work methods of the employee.

In the new manufacturing environment, downtime becomes critical.[6] If the focus is kept on the ratio between machine hours and employee hours, problems with downtime become readily apparent to the management accountant.

An implementation

A field test of the value of dividing the traditional labor efficiency variance into its components was recently conducted at a factory of the Colgate Palmolive Company.

Exhibit 8. *Colgate Palmolive Liquid Filling Line*
Actual Data for the First 10 Months of the Year

Standard Ratio of Labor Hours to Machine Hours = 4 to 1
Standard Machine Hours per Unit of Product = 2.9091 per 1,000 units
Standard Hourly Wage Rate = $15.08

	Units	Machine Hours	Employee Labor Hours	Employee Labor Efficiency Variance	Machine Efficiency Variance	Total Variance
Jan.	50,478	165.5	374.00	$4,343	$(1,125)	$3,218
Feb.	31.943	100.3	214.00	2,823	(445)	2,378
Mar.	185,179	552.0	1,068.00	17,191	(802)	16,389
Apr.	212,274	713.8	1,495.75	20,501	(5,807)	14,693
May	48,390	160.0	364.00	4,162	(1,160)	3,002
June	82,436	232.0	536.50	5,904	471	6,375
July	36,208	104.0	283.00	2,006	80	2,086
Aug.	33,483	96.0	317.50	1,003	85	1,088
Sept.	31,560	96.0	328.50	837	(253)	584
Oct.	28,191	72.0	158.00	1,960	604	2,564
Total	740,142	2,291.6	5,139.25	$60,729	$(8,351)	$52,378

Exhibit 9. *Colgate Palmolive Liquid Filling Line*

Labor Efficiency Variance
First 10 Months of the Year

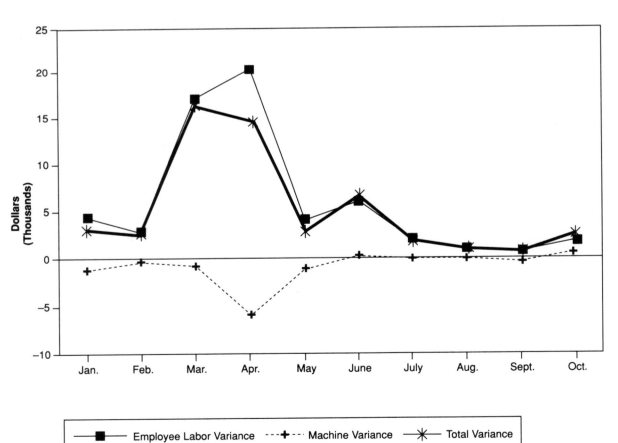

Exhibit 10. *Colgate Palmolive Liquid Filling Line*
Year-to-Date October 31, 19XX Performance Report

Actual Units Produced = 740,142 units
Actual Machine Hours = 2,291.6 machine hours
Actual Employee Labor Hours = 5,139.25 direct labor hours
Ratio Standard = 4 labor hours to 1 machine hour
Hourly Wage Rate = $15.08
Standard Machine Hours per Unit of Product = 2.9091 machine hours per 1,000 units

	Machine Employee Labor Charge	Required Employee Labor Cost	Allowed Employee Labor Cost	Favorable (Unfavorable) Efficiency Variance		
				Employee Labor	Machine	Total (Traditional)
5,139.25 hours × $15.08	$77,499.89			Required employee labor cost *less* machine employee labor charge	Allowed employee labor cost *less* required employee labor cost	Allowed employee labor cost *less* machine employee labor charge
2,291.6 hours × 4 × $15.08		$138,229.31				
740,142 units × .0029091 × 4 × $15.08			$129,877.83			
	$77,499.89	$138,229.31	$129,877.83	$60,729.42	$(8,351.48)	$52,377.94

An automated liquid filling line was used. Since this line had undergone an extensive overhaul two years previously, each machine was equipped with a programmable, real-time controller. The machine operators were classified as direct labor, worked as a team, and received the same rate of pay. Since machine hours, employee hours, and units were all budgeted, the data for the computations were readily available.

This field test (unlike the examples given previously) did not focus on individual machines in the automated process illustrated earlier. Instead, the field test focused on the entire process, because the company established its "ratio standard" for the entire process rather than for individual automated machines in the process.

Exhibit 8 shows the results for the first ten months of the year; the same data appear in the graph shown in Exhibit 9. The total labor efficiency variance for the period is a favorable $52,378. However, this masks a strongly favorable $60,729 employee labor efficiency variance and an unfavorable $8,351 machine efficiency variance (see Exhibit 10). On a monthly basis, the machine efficiency variance was unfavorable six times, with five of the unfavorable variances occurring in the first five months, which suggests an unfavorable use of machine hours, given the output

achieved, along with a lower than expected utilization of employee hours. The labor hours to machine hours ratio was certainly well below the established ratio standard of 4 to 1.

Bringing problems into focus

When the labor efficiency variance was divided into its components at the Colgate factory, potential problems that were previously concealed were brought into focus. Upon investigation, for example, several problems having to do with machine efficiency—problems that required the attention of process engineering—became evident.

One of these problems involved the design of the new bottle uncasing machine. Until the previous year, the bottle uncasing process had been performed manually in a labor-intensive operation. The unfavorable machine efficiency variance suggests that the transition from the manual operation to the automated operation may need additional attention from the process engineers. Anticipated reductions in machine employee hours may not have been fully realized yet, because the automatic bottle uncasing machine is not properly integrated into the automated process.

Another problem could be difficulties with the new electronic equipment on the line. Trouble-shooting problems with the programmable controllers require technical skills that the operators do not possess. Therefore, electricians must be used for situations that were previously remedied by simple mechanical adjustments. The additional time delays caused by the need to locate an electrician with the skills needed to correct the problem causes the direct laborers to remain idle for longer periods. This problem also requires the attention of process engineering. Problems of this sort with idle direct laborers caused by a nonfunctioning production line result in an unfavorable machine efficiency variance, even if the employee labor variance is favorable as a result of the heightened direct labor efficiency when the production line is operating.

In this field test, the decomposition of the variance proved valuable, because it focused management's attention on problems with the automated manufacturing environment. If only the traditional labor efficiency variance had been reported, the management accounting system would not have revealed these two process engineering problems. Had top managers focused only on the overwhelmingly favorable traditional labor efficiency variance, they would have concluded—wrongly, as it turns out—that operations on the automated liquid filling line were well controlled.

Conclusion

In an era in which automated machines with microprocessors and digital clocks can track machine time accurately and sensing devices can record labor time per machine reliably, a departure from the traditional view of labor

efficiency is warranted. This article demonstrates that use of a ratio standard of labor hours to machine hours for each major item of equipment permits a company to further analyze the traditional labor efficiency variance. Specifically, the traditional variance can be divided into an employee labor variance and a machine efficiency variance. This in-depth analysis has the advantage of isolating variances caused by the inefficient use of machines and also establishing a standard by which machine utilization can be evaluated. ▲

Notes

1. We wish to thank Ken Hynes for permitting us to implement our ideas at the Colgate Palmolive factory where he is the controller. We also appreciate the assistance of Jeff Dean, material planner—Soaps Division of the Colgate Palmolive Company, for his assistance in this effort.
2. The references in this paragraph are to Robert S. Kaplan, "Yesterday's Accounting Undermines Production," *Harvard Business Review* (July–August 1984): 95–101.
3. The references in this paragraph are to Allen H. Seed, III, "Cost Accounting in the Age of Robotics," *Management Accounting* (October 1984): 39–43.
4. Henry R. Schwarzbach & Richard G. Vangermeersch, "Why We Should Account for the Fourth Cost of Manufacturing," *Management Accounting* (July 1983): 24–28.
5. James A. Hendricks, "Applying Cost Accounting to Factory Automation," *Management Accounting* (December 1988): 24–30.
6. Robert A. Howell & Stephen R. Soucy, "Operating Controls in the New Manufacturing Environment," *Management Accounting* (October 1987): 25–31.

Moving Beyond Lean and Mean

Jewell G. Westerman and William A. Sherden

Slash-and-burn downsizings usually accomplish little over the long term because they ignore the fact that corporate resources are often inefficiently deployed. Traditional downsizings focus on superficial changes rather than addressing the sources of inefficiency. What is required instead is a comprehensive process for restructuring— one that addresses resource allocations, operating strategies, and work flows in a coordinated fashion. This article presents a six-step approach to realigning, eliminating, and reallocating resources to improve overall operations.

Over the past decade, more and more companies in every industry sector have embraced (by necessity if not by choice) the goal of becoming lower-cost producers. In most cases, their cost-reduction efforts have taken the form of organizational downsizing. For some, downsizing has meant spinning off both profitable and unprofitable business units in order to focus on core businesses. The more prevalent approach, however, has been across-the-board cuts in costs and staff.

This so-called slash and burn downsizing usually takes place as a last resort. The business climate turns bad, sales fail to meet expectations, and cost reduction becomes the overriding priority. In response, management initiates company-wide layoffs, blanket early-retirement enticements, or some other reactive staff-reduction program. Although the cuts often begin in overhead functions, they usually spread to more vital areas, such as business units and operational divisions.

Usually, very little is gained. No change is made in the way work is actually performed; as a result, head-count reductions prove fleeting. But even worse, as staffing in key functions is cut, employee morale and service quality drop precipitously. Large amounts of rework are often required, which sets off a surge in customer defections.

To solve this crisis, the company must quickly rehire staff to fill the holes it made in the organization. The firm often ends up with a higher-cost, lower-quality organization than it had before the downsizing began. This, in turn, leads to further restructurings—always with the same result.

The fundamental flaw in traditional downsizing strategies is that they focus on making superficial changes rather than addressing the sources of inefficiency throughout the organization. The problem is not that companies have too many employees; that's only a symptom. The real problem is that resources are inefficiently deployed—across businesses as well as within them. Cutting heads without addressing structural defects is merely a cosmetic solution and one doomed to fail.

What is required is a comprehensive process for organizational restructuring, one that addresses resource allocations, operating strategies, and work flows in a coordinated fashion. The goal is to create an organization that is not only lean but is also focused on providing high value to those customers that will be most profitable for the company to serve.

Such a process, as illustrated in Exhibit 1, requires managers to take a top-down view of the enterprise as a whole but it restructures

Exhibit 1. *A Comprehensive Approach to Restructuring*

Step 1	Step 2	Step 3	Step 4	Step 5	Step 6
Reorganize Around Business Lines	Evaluate Business Line Viability	Restructure Remaining Business Units	Optimize Business Unit Operations	Restructure Internal Suppliers	Managerial Restructuring

work from the bottom up to realign, eliminate, and reallocate resources in order to make the firm more competitive in its strongest businesses. The following discussion details this approach.

A six-step process

Step 1: Reorganize around business lines. The process starts by addressing the problem, occurring at the highest level, that afflicts most corporations and divisions: Many distinct businesses, which could stand alone, are yoked together organizationally. In this environment, work is fragmented among many different people and units, decision making is impeded by bureaucratic reviews and approvals, accountability for performance is limited, and resources are wasted on activities unrelated to the creation of value for either customers or shareholders.

For most companies, therefore, the first step is to restructure the organization into distinct business units that contain all the necessary components for independent operation. Such an organization may still require shared resources, such as distribution systems, but each unit should have a distinct mission and should control as many of the resources needed to achieve that mission as possible.

This initial restructuring will inevitably identify resources, functions, and positions that do not fit any of the business units and thus are probably no longer needed. The elimination of these functions lowers costs in a way that does not undermine competitive strengths. Moreover, it may actually help to reduce any needless interference and inefficiency that may have hindered the firm's performance.

As a case in point, a 4,000-member employee group within a major industrial products firm found that its costs to produce, sell, and distribute products were significantly higher than those of its competitors. It was losing customers simply because it could not compete profitably at industry-standard prices.

The company had tried to reorganize a number of times, but these attempts only further eroded employee morale and customer service; they produced no meaningful reduction in overall costs.

The company's problem was that it was restructuring an obsolete organization, one built around generic functions—administration, manufacturing, marketing, etc. When we began analyzing how work was actually being performed, we found that an enormous amount of time and money was being spent on activities that had nothing to do with serving the customer.

Many managers were making requests and installing processes that served themselves and their colleagues rather than customers. From outward appearances the units all seemed busy—but they were busy doing unnecessary jobs.

Ultimately, the company was reorganized into five business units (each responsible for one of the firm's five core products), and a separate centralized sales organization built around the company's major customer segments. The sales group's performance was measured by its success in increasing sales while maintaining profitable margins.

With this new structure, the company's operations staff, which focused on individual products, was empowered to achieve large gains in both productivity and quality; the sales staff could focus on the common needs of individual market segments, selling whichever combination of products was most appropriate for each given customer.

As a result, the company had better products, higher service quality, and a streamlined staff of 3,200 (rather than a bloated one of 4,000). It became profitable and generated the desired cash flow for the parent while also earning needed funds for research and development.

Step 2: Evaluate business line viability. Once individual business lines have been isolated, management should take a hard look at the future prospects of each line, deciding whether to build, fix, downsize, or exit. The analysis will often incorporate considerations of competitive position, market growth and attractiveness, investment requirements, and projected ROE.

With the elimination of unprofitable or marginally profitable business units, a second opportunity emerges to enhance profitability by removing the infrastructure and functions that had been required to run the exited businesses. The company's overall cost structure is reduced while its ability to grow its most profitable businesses is enhanced.

For example, the previously discussed industrial products group sold off one of its five business lines after further analysis revealed that it was peripheral to the company's core businesses and would remain at best only marginally profitable. The group's overall profit margin strengthened considerably as a result.

Step 3: Restructure remaining business units. Management should next seek opportunities to improve profits by restructuring the major functions of each ongoing business line. The first step in the restructuring process is to break out or de-average cost data by customer segment, product, distribution channel, region, and other relevant dimensions.

This action will often reveal to management that the 80/20 rule applies to its business: 20% of its customers are generally responsible for 80% of a business's problems. More importantly, it will reveal just who those customers are.

Armed with this de-averaged cost data, the firm will be empowered to pursue five restructuring opportunities:
1. Consolidating subscale business elements (products, functions, regional operations, etc.) in a way that improves productivity while maintaining or improving service, or both.
2. Repricing products and services by customer segment and distribution channel to enhance overall profitability and, where appropriate, discourage unprofitable purchases.
3. Pruning customers, products, channels, and regions that will remain unprofitable or marginally profitable even after repricing.
4. Eliminating or deemphasizing those activities that clearly do not contribute to customer value (or that if priced separately customers would not buy), including various services or product features that have proliferated under the false assumption that they were needed to stay competitive.
5. Eliminating or reducing the supporting organization elements that are no longer needed to manage the eliminated business elements.

Step 4: Optimize business unit operations. Once unprofitable elements are eliminated through restructuring, the firm will still have numerous cost-reduction opportunities related to inefficient process flows, redundancies and fragmented work, poor cross-functional handoffs, low-value activities that do no support outputs, excessive rework, and high employee and customer turnover.

The solution is to reengineer the firm's key processes on the basis of customers' values and expectations. The goal is to design the highest-value, lowest-cost processes with the necessary support systems to ensure smooth work flows and responsive customer service. In addition to streamlining operational flows by cutting out unnecessary steps, management should consider using the following tools for process improvement:

Benchmarking and Best Practices. For key elements of the process, the firm's performance should be benchmarked against standards set by competitors and other leading firms with analogous operations. Best practices can then be incorporated into the reengineered process.

Outscourcing. The firm should consider outsourcing subscale or highly specialized process functions that can be more efficiently performed by outside vendors.

Improve Employee Retention. Companies can reduce the resources wasted in employee recruitment and training by finding ways to retain and develop employees.

Once the processes have been reengineered to improve quality and productivity, the firm should consider developing a strategy for significantly improving customer retention. Many firms spend enormous sums on acquiring customers, but little on retaining them. As a result, profitability is needlessly undermined by customer turnover.

Step 5: Restructure internal suppliers. The database our firm has assembled from nearly 600 organizational analyses documents how companies allocate human resources among more than 300 work activities and how costs break down by function and activity. An analysis of this data reveals a steady shift away from core activities—those directly related to the production and distribution of goods and services for customers—to noncore activities, spanning everything from systems development to clerical support.

In the last half of the twentieth century, nonproduction work has supplanted production work as the major activity of business enterprises. At the close of the World War II, just as the United States was entering an era of unprecedented economic growth, three out of

---

"Business units should be allowed to deal with internal suppliers as they would with outside vendors."

---

every four working Americans had jobs directly related to creating and selling goods.

Today, only about 20% of the work force is directly involved in making, selling, or delivering products. Corporate allocations for support services now account for as much as 30% to 40% of a business unit's total ex-

penses, far exceeding their value to the unit's operations.

The solution to this problem is to allow business units to deal with internal suppliers as they would with outside vendors. Each business unit should be able to decide for itself which services it needs and where it will obtain them.

Once given this power, individual units will make a range of different decisions: scaling back on "purchases services," centralizing or decentralizing such services, outsourcing them to external firms, or establishing rigorous internal service contracts with cost, quality, and opt-out provisions. Implementing these decisions will inevitably lead to a restructuring of internal service providers. Thrust into a competitive environment, these providers will seek to enhance their efficiency and responsiveness in order to retain their previously captive internal customers.

Step 6: Managerial restructuring. Steps 1 through 5 will produce a very different organization—leaner, more focused, and requiring a new management structure to run it. This last step involves rationalizing the management structure within each business unit and

---

"Our analyses consistently reveal that true quality leaders also tend to be low-cost producers."

---

throughout the corporation as a whole, with the objective of reducing layers of management, broadening spans of control, and creating a flatter, more responsive organization focused on key activities.

Substantial cost savings typically result from this effort. A major oil company, for example, found that it had one manager for every 5.8 workers. By increasing the span of control to an average of only 7.6, it was able to save over $25 million.

Our firm's data base indicates that the average span of control for U.S. businesses, regardless of industry, is one manager for every 3.5 workers. So there are considerable opportuni-

Exhibit 2. *The Correlation Between Low Cost and High Quality Among Competitors in a Major Insurance Segment*

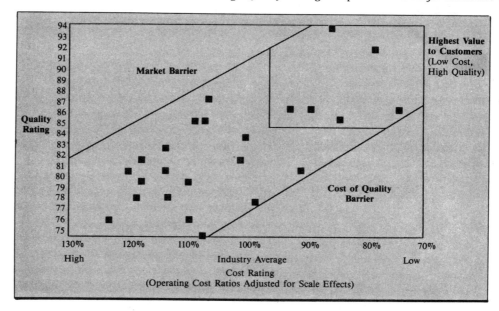

ties for profit enhancement in managerial restructuring.

Being a low-cost producer will be essential for an organization to maintain competitiveness in global markets; however, cost leadership alone is not enough. Dominant firms will also be quality leaders. Too often, low cost and high quality are viewed as two distinct and mutually exclusive market positionings, and many firms aspire to become a high-quality producer in order to mask their high cost structure.

Our analyses consistently reveal that true quality leaders also tend to be low-cost producers. (Exhibit 2 shows this relationship in a key segment of the insurance industry. The boxes indicate the cost/quality positionings of several companies.) They have achieved their dominant positions by focusing on high-profit customers and market segments and adapting

their operations and organizations to maximize customer value at the lowest cost.

Slash and burn downsizing will not propel a company into a high-value position. In fact, it will most likely end up diminishing the firm's performance in both cost and quality. Similarly, quality improvement programs are in themselves not enough, as competitive pressures typically derail such programs in high-cost firms. A more comprehensive approach to reorganization is the best route to becoming a more valuable firm to both customers and shareholders. ▲

The Return of High Performance to the U.S. Workplace

H. James Harrington

The real problems facing business today are the business processes and the systems that control them. Employees must work *within* the process. Improving work processes is thus the key to improving the quality of work life. Improving the business process should be the major strategy for improving the quality of work life in the 1990s. This, in turn, should set the stage for gains in the twenty-first century. If the proper strategies are used to change the business process, high quality and high performance will return to the U.S. workplace.

The single most important strategy for improving the quality of work life in the twenty-first century is reforming the business process itself. The inefficiency, bureaucracy, and complexity that have bogged down critical business activities, reducing productivity and competitiveness, have also greatly detracted from the satisfaction and pride that management and employees derive from their work.

In the 1990s, these failing business processes will come under frontal attack. If the proper strategies are chosen to redirect the business process, not only will high quality and high performance return to the U.S. workplace but the quality of work life in the year 2000 will be greatly improved.

Forecasting the future

How will work life change in the twenty-first century? If progress made in the past fifty years is any guide, this change will be revolutionary. Corporations with traditional bosses and a multitiered management structure will be replaced by a new kind of cooperative.

People will turn to these new cooperatives, not to find jobs but to buy business opportunities. These new cooperatives will be made up of thousands of partners, each competing to sell products or services to other members. Each partner will be a business unit; salaries will be replaced by profits, to be reinvested in new equipment and facilities depending on expected rate of return.

The work environment will be completely changed. Most work will be done at home. The structured starting and stopping times, the forty-hour week, will no longer exist. Instead, people will alter their schedules on a daily basis to meet the needs of their customers, making themselves available twenty-four hours a day, seven days a week.

Two trends will have a significant impact. These are the movement toward self-managed work teams and, most important, improvements in the business process itself: the conduct of all activities—from development to production, control, manufacturing, materials, quality, accounting, and so forth—that determine the environment employees and managers work in and are controlled by.

Self-managed work teams

Self-managed work teams are gaining popularity as a way to give employees more control over their jobs. Companies like Procter & Gamble are leading the way in this movement. Their success, as well as that of other companies, has stimulated a groundswell of pilot programs in companies around the world.

Most companies embark on the process of incorporating self-managed work teams with a small number of teams. As a first step, companies may allow each team to pick its own leader, selected on a rotating basis. Initially this individual will be responsible for the team's work assignments and associated paperwork.

"In three years, Globe Metallurgical had a 380 percent increase in productivity."

As time goes on, the team as a whole will assume additional responsibilities and accountability. This will include hiring and firing, setting job standards, appraising the performance of team members, budgeting, determining the salaries of team members, dividing bonus money, and deciding who will come into the team. As companies gain experience with these self-managed work teams and as employees gain competence and confidence in their business skills, the number of teams usually increases.

Experience has shown that these self-managed work teams have had a major, positive effect on both the quality of work life and the profitability of the organization in which this approach has been employed. Self-managed work teams improve productivity and quality, increase product ownership and pride, reduce cost and the need for overhead personnel, and boost employee morale.

Example

Globe Metallurgical, Inc., is a producer of ferroalloys and silicon metal. This company realized major improvements in quality, productivity, and cost as a direct result of empowering employees to manage themselves. Statistically and financially, there have been major improvements in the company's manufacturing process.

In three years, the organization had a 380 percent increase in productivity, and it is replacing Japanese suppliers in the United States and Asia. Not only that, but it has replaced Japanese companies supplying materials to Posco Steel in South Korea, beating out the Japanese in their own backyard.

At Globe Metallurgical, employees make many decisions previously restricted to upper management. When someone retires or leaves to go back to school (it is rare for someone to quit to go to another company), employees decide whether or not to replace that individual. In almost every instance, employees find some way to restructure the workload so that the person is not replaced by a new hire.

Often this is accomplished by reducing the workload in the department where the person served, or freeing up someone from another department to fill the gap. A very lucrative bonus system provides incentives for—and increases sensitivity to—reducing waste and improving quality.

Take Charles Marshall, for example, a furnace tapper at Globe Metallurgical. I spoke with him at his workstation. With the temperature almost 110°F and the air full of dust, he stood there in hard hat, eye shields, and mouth and nose filters, the sweat running down his dirt-covered face, his shirt full of holes burned when hot molten metal splattered on him. And yet he told me what a great place Globe is to work for and that he hopes he will never have to leave. He told me that he was really lucky to be working for such a fine management team. Is quality important to him? As he put it, "When we make a mistake, it really hurts on down the line, so we really have to strive to do our best—not just for our sake, to keep our jobs—but for the companies we supply metal to. We have to keep up with them."

I also spoke with Globe Metallurgical's "just in time" coordinator. He is responsible for telling the truck drivers where and when to dump their loads of coal, rock, etc. Because of the system he has worked out, the mountains of coal, rock, and other materials so common around a plant of this type are absent here.

In his spare time, he serves as a job training coordinator, working with the most experienced operators to assess how reassigned and new operators should be trained and evaluated. This job, which used to be handled by an overhead employee, is now being executed better, and in less time, by this hourly employee. He told me that he checks books out of the library in order to read up on training methods on his own time. He said that he wished he had more time to devote to training because it is important and he felt he was contributing a great deal to the company's success. Excited about his job? You bet!

These two men are typical of all the employees with whom I spoke at Globe Metallurgical. They work in an environment that they have every right to complain about. Instead, they are enthusiastic, challenged, and proud of themselves and their company.

"A company experienced a 40-to-1 return on money invested in improving the work process."

How does this affect the company's performance? Very favorably. As mentioned earlier, Globe Metallurgical's productivity increased 380 percent in three years. In the same three-year time frame, the company's share of the ductile iron market jumped from less than 5 percent to more than 50 percent. In two years, the number of returned products dropped from forty-four lots to zero. In all, the company experienced a 40-to-1 return on money invested in improving the work process. And the employees shared in the profits. In 1988, the average employee received a $5,000 profit-sharing bonus.

Is it any wonder that Globe Metallurgical was the first small company to win the Malcolm Baldridge Award (USA National Quality Award) and the first to win the Shingo Prize for manufacturing excellence? Should it come as a surprise that Globe Metallurgical continuously sets new records when companies like Ford and General Motors come to evaluate their quality systems?

Improving the business process

The realization that improving the work process is the key to improving the quality of work life is the single biggest breakthrough of the 1980s. But little attention has been given to how to go about it.

In contrast, a lot of attention has been focused on how to improve and control manufacturing processes. Papers abound on process qualification, process compatibility, statistical process control, operator certification, and failure analysis. But improving the manufacturing process has very little effect on the quality of work life when compared to improving business processes.

For one thing, everyone is affected by business processes, even companies that do not have manufacturing processes. For another, business processes have a greater impact on individual workers. In addition, most products' value-added costs are the result of the overhead and support activities that make up the business processes.

For these reasons, improving the business process should be the major strategy for improving the quality of work life in the 1990s and setting the stage for the gains that will be made in the twenty-first century.

Almost everything one does is a process. For example, inventory control and cost accounting are financial area businesses processes; inventory management and shipping are materials area business processes; and new product qualification and in-line process control are quality area business processes.

One of the first things that can be observed when assessing business processes is that, in most companies, these critical business activities are organized in such a way as to make them ineffective, cumbersome, and burdened with a high degree of bureaucracy. Oftentimes business processes flow horizontally, while companies are organized vertically.

The result is that the business processes become suboptimized, with a great deal of overlaps and voids. Suboptimization is encouraged, not discouraged. In fact, between 80 and 90 percent of one's time is spent performing repetitive activities that should (and can) be measured and controlled in much the same way that a manufacturing process is measured and controlled.

In any company, there are literally thousands of business processes going on every day. It is impossible to improve all of these processes at the same time. The best way to get the improvement process started is to form an executive team to prepare a list of business processes that must work superbly for the business to be successful.

Each of these business processes should be rated by the executive team as either "critical," "very important," or "important." The team should then evaluate each process on a scale of one to ten. A rating of one indicates no problems and a rating of ten indicates significant problems. The negative impact that problems in the process are having on the company's performance should also be noted.

By using this method of evaluation, the executive team can identify priority business processes and improve them.

The executive team's next step is to appoint a "process owner" for each priority process. Why? Because up to this point, no one has ever been responsible for making that business process work effectively and efficiently, and for ensuring that it is designed to adapt quickly to changing business needs.

The best way to accomplish this objective is to hold one person accountable for the performance of that process. Usually, this works best when the process owner is the individual who will benefit most from the improved efficiency of the process. Normally, this assignment will not be the process owner's sole job.

The process owner should be given the authority to gather people from all the different areas of the company involved in that process into a process improvement team. The team's objective is to maximize effectiveness, efficiency, and adaptability. It can do so through the following steps:

☐ **Define the beginning and ending.** The team's first task should be to define the starting and ending points of the process, customer requirements and expectations (effectiveness), and business requirements and measurements (efficiency).

☐ **Develop a block diagram.** It should then develop a block diagram, representing a quick overview of the activities that make up the process and how they fit together. (See Exhibit 1.) In order to do this, the team must have a complete understanding of the company's procedures, job descriptions, and training requirements.

☐ **Develop a flow diagram.** The team's initial block diagram should then be expanded upon and refined into a flow diagram, which should reveal more detailed information that allows for the identification of procedures requiring improvement. Frequently, two or three flow diagrams are developed to analyze the process from different perspectives. (See Exhibit 1.)

☐ **Follow work flow.** The team should next perform an activity walk-through, in which it follows the work flow documented in the flow chart from beginning to end, observing the process at the task level, comparing the actual product flow with the diagram, and refining the diagram accordingly.

☐ **Classify processes.** Each process should then be classified on a scale ranging from 1 to 6. (See Exhibit 2.) For example, if process management has not yet been applied, the process would be classified as belonging to Level 6.

☐ **Streamline processes.** The team should then strive to simplify the process by eliminating bureaucracy, duplication, and no-value-added activities; reducing processing time (focusing on those activities with long delays); standardizing activities; training and (if necessary) selecting personnel; and, where possible, computerizing/mechanizing routine activities to free up employees for more creative work.

☐ **Install control systems.** The process should then be documented in its new form and analyzed, after which process controls and feedback systems should be installed.

☐ **Continuously improve process.** The team should perform a new walk-through, continuously improving the process to keep it at Level 1.

☐ **Start over.** When the team thinks that everything is working as well as it can be, it should find the improvement to make and start the process over.

Looking ahead

The real problems facing business today are the business processes and the systems that control them. Employees must work *within*

Exhibit 1. *Types of Flow Charts*

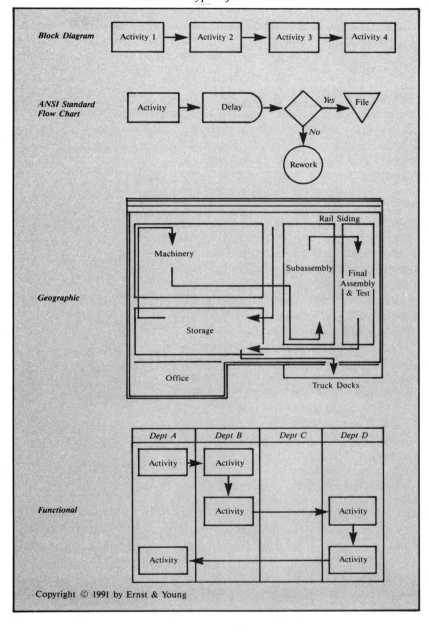

Copyright © 1991 by Ernst & Young

Exhibit 2. *How Each Process Can Be Classified*

Level	Status	Description
6	Unknown	Process status has not been determined.
5	Understood	Process design is understood, and operates according to prescribed documentation.
4	Effective	Process is systematically measured, streamlining has started, and end customer expectations are met.
3	Efficient	Process is streamlined, efficiency is improving.
2	Error-Free	Process is highly effective (error-free) and efficiency is close to being optimized.
1	World-Class	Process is world-class and continues to improve.

the process. It is up to management to work *on* the process, endeavoring to optimize effectiveness and efficiency through coordination of all business activities. That is the road to high-quality performance and to a superior quality of work life. ▲

Reprinted from *Journal of Business Strategy*, July/August 1991, pp. 23–27. Copyright © 1991 by Warren Gorham Lamont, a division of Research Institute of America Inc. All rights reserved. Used by permission.

PART *K*

Quality

A Customer's Definition of Quality

Thomas O. Miller

What's the best way to "get close to the customer?" As this article explains, the Norand Corporation has developed a customer feedback system that drives product design, sales, service, and support functions to ensure better responsiveness to customers. This customer service database gives Norand reliable, objective, and concrete information about market and customer trends. It also allows the company to track, understand, and respond to issues that are specific to individual customers.

Quality is defined by the customer. A technically perfect product that does not meet customer expectations will fail, regardless of its innovation or quality. The challenge is to determine what customers want and whether they are satisfied with the company, its products, and its service. This is where organizations involved in otherwise well-conceived quality programs can stumble badly.

Norand Corp., a manufacturer and marketer of portable computerized data collection systems and hand-held radio frequency terminals, with sales in 1991 of $100 million, has long prided itself on staying in touch with its domestic and international customers. It solicited input through customer meetings, periodic surveys, field visits, and sales reports. The results were carefully tabulated and tracked, and trends seemed gratifying: approximately 92% of all customers expressed positive comments.

Nevertheless, the costs of servicing customers were increasing and customer satisfaction ratings were decreasing: employees were working harder and the company was spending more, but the efforts were not effectively meeting customer concerns.

Norand's plight was not caused by a lack of effort or data. In the company's early years, Norand had stayed in regular contact with customers, which was easier then because it had a relatively small base of 150 accounts. When occasional complaints were recorded, the appropriate sales and service specialists aggressively addressed the problems and documented the actions to correct them. At regular meetings of equipment users, the company's sales, marketing, and customer service executives probed attendees for feedback on products and field support. In addition, the company accumulated more formal data through annual customer surveys conducted by an independent research firm.

As the company researched programs on quality and began developing its own quality process, however, it became apparent that such customer survey methods typically generate positive comments. In fact, the greater than 90% favorable ratings Norand turned up in its surveys were below what other companies were hearing from their customers on similar measures.

Closer analysis of the process further demonstrated that such data collection was not thorough, objective, or consistent enough. Company officials began to suspect that they were not hearing from a significant segment of customers and that the data was not received often enough to help provide real-time guidance on customer issues. Finally, there were concerns that what data existed was not shared widely enough to benefit all appropriate internal departments. As a result, the data was giving false readings on customer satisfaction, leading company executives to believe that customers were more satisfied with the company's performance than they really were.

In January 1990, Norand began to assemble elements of a comprehensive customer feedback system. The system was designed to develop a detailed pool of customer information to help drive product design, service, and support functions toward better customer responsiveness. In addition, this information could be used to augment the data needs of the company's new total quality commitment (TQC) processes. This effort aimed to develop the best, most comprehensive customer feedback system in the industry.

A formal feedback system

The company clearly defined the critical elements of this system. The most salient of these is the process of formal customer surveying. In March 1990, the company began using a research firm to conduct monthly in-depth telephone interviews with customers chosen at random. More than 1,000 interviews have been conducted, at a rate that has averaged 40 per month. Approximately 25% of the surveys contact customers who have had installations within the previous three months.

Customers are asked to describe their opinions of Norand products and systems, software, personnel, delivery performance, invoicing, service support, and overall company image. Customer comments are evaluated and tabulated into positive and negative comments in several specific categories.

The results of the surveys are compiled monthly and circulated. Although the report is confidential, it is distributed to a wide range of company executives representing management, engineering, marketing, sales, service, finance, and quality assurance. The report is online on each employee's terminal and specifically cites the customers who were surveyed and reflects their verbatim comments.

The original objective for the customer surveys was to develop data that could be helpful in spotting trends. However, Norand discovered that the surveys created an unanticipated challenge. These regular surveys provided an unprecedented opportunity for

customers to voice specific concerns (e.g., product malfunctions, billing problems, and software complaints). Once these concerns were communicated to the person conducting the survey, many customers expected that their complaints would be resolved.

But in establishing the survey and reporting system, no procedures were put in place to address specific calls for assistance. Weeks could elapse before the comments made to the surveyor found their way to company executives who were in a position to resolve the complaint. The issue surfaced when an angry customer surprised the company by calling to ask why it took so long to respond to the complaint he had made to the surveyor.

New procedures now require that specific customer complaints revealed in interviews be reported to Norand within five days. If the complaint is critical, the profile is sent to

---

"Specific customer complaints revealed in interviews are reported to the company within five days. If the complaint is critical, the profile is sent to Norand by fax."

Norand by fax. Company officials track these issues until they are resolved. As a result, the data collection process of the customer surveys, originally envisioned as a oneway communication channel, has evolved into another opportunity for Norand to respond to its customers.

Each quarter, monthly reports are statistically tabulated. This provides the company with a statistical view of trends over time. As these quarterly reports build up, they provide company officials with sound, reliable data on which to base a wide variety of decisions, including hardware and software designs, customer support programs, and quality improvement processes. The result is a data base that helps company officials determine key priority issues.

The customer surveys represent only one element of the company's customer data system. A second element is the customer profile data system. Extensive efforts have created a comprehensive data base that reflects customers' vital facts, including details about the customer that run the gamut from company name and address to sales history, service records, and credit information. The profile also shows how Norand rates on timely product shipments and order completions.

Another critical element in the customer feedback loop is the call monitoring and management system. This is a method of receiving, recording, and tracking customer complaints registered by telephone. This online, computerized system captures data by company and individual name and lists when and why the call was placed, the last action taken by the firm, and the present status of the issue. This online information is available to Norand customer support specialists and is updated every time the specialists take action. The online nature of this information provides for immediate tracking of customer calls, ready history of a particular complaint, and widespread accessibility to customer data. This information also serves a management role by allowing officials to assess how quickly problems are identified, acted on, and resolved.

The company is even assessing customer reactions to its sales presentations. Using the same independent research firm. Norand solicits information from companies to which it has made product presentations. With this feedback, Norand is gaining a better understanding of why contracts were won or lost. This information is also added to the customer feedback data base for evaluation and trend analysis.

Each of these elements exists to provide specific and valuable information vital to the company's overall quality program. In this case, however, the total is more than the sum of the individual parts, because the company compiles the separate data into a comprehensive customer data base that can be shared throughout the organization. As a result, company decision makers have free access to total customer information anywhere in the company.

The benefits are many. First, the firm is building a data base that provides a real-time assessment of customer opinion trends on the company, its products, and its services.

Month by month, the surveys combine to provide a source of objective, statistically valid data that can be extracted by numerous demographics (e.g., product, industry, customer group, and sales region).

Second, the customer surveys help augment contacts by Norand field sales and service representatives so solicit information on product and installation problems. Now that the company has provided for timely identification and tacking of problems presented to telephone surveyors, the customer survey system is serving a dual role in helping ensure customer satisfaction.

"In March 1990, the company began using a research firm to conduct monthly indepth telephone interviews with customers chosen at random."

Third, customers are reacting in an extremely positive way to the surveys. They appreciate being asked for their opinions and seem to view the survey as an objective way of communicating their input back to Norand.

A fourth benefit derived from the customer data base is its application for the company's TQC process. TQC focuses on tying together product quality, process improvement, and customer satisfaction. Employee teams are formed to develop improved methods of delivering products and services to customers. One of the key steps taken by the TQC team is gaining an objective and factual understanding of customer concerns. As a result, the data accumulated by the customer feedback system is helping to satisfy the information needs of the TQC teams.

Norand management has instituted a discipline on the TQC teams that prescribes a seven-step method for identifying, researching, and resolving product and process issues. One of the earliest steps requires the team to construct a current situational analysis based on information from customers. The customer feedback process is developing a rich data base from which TQC teams can draw.

As a result, teams can easily extract information that has been carefully and reliably developed. What's more, a single professional organization is responsible for surveying customers, rather than having various issue-specific TQC teams conducting uncontrolled surveys at random. The information generated by these interviews is readily available throughout the organization.

The system's twin benefits

The existing database allows the company to achieve two critical goals. First, it provides the firm with reliable, objective, and concrete information on market and customer trends. Because this information is developed monthly from existing customer lists, the data is current and far superior to data developed from the causal and anecdotal information formerly gathered during sales calls and cus-

---

"The customer feedback process allows the company to 'micromanage' its customers."

---

tomer meetings. The information is fresh and stays fresh, because new information is added monthly. The previous annual survey regimen allowed considerable time to pass between formal customer contacts—time too valuable to lose in the fast-changing electronic data collection industry in which Norand competes.

The second objective the firm has achieved is equally important. The customer feedback process allows the company to "micromanage" its customers. Trends identified by the customer surveys are extremely valuable. However, tabulation of the survey generally provides a statistical view of Norand customers; such statistics offer little in the way of help for specific customers. The combination of the customer profile data and the call management system gives the firm an online data base that enables company officials to

track, understand, and respond to issues that are specific to individual customers.

The ability to provide such micromanagement allows the company to be more efficient in addressing problems. As a result, customers may feel closer to the company because considerable information on each customer's product and installation history is readily available to Norand employees. With such information, Norand representatives can provide more tailored responses.

The company plans to add other data to its base. A competitor assessment survey will soon be included. The procedures used to survey current customers will be used to interview customers of competitive firms. This research will establish competitive benchmarks against which Norand can compare its performance.

Listening to customers requires much more than hosting meetings for product users, analyzing comments in sales reports, or even performing periodic formal surveys. Reliable customer feedback is produced through regular, carefully planned, and systematic effort.

In addition, just as photos in a newspaper are created from many individual dots, the picture of customer satisfaction required by the company must be produced from many different sources of information. That's why the firm is taking the time to combine individual "dots" of customer information that exist in the organization and pull the data together to form a picture. It is this picture—one that more clearly defines the customer's view of quality and company responsiveness—that will guide the company's planners as they work to achieve total customer satisfaction. ▲

Statistical Process Control That Minimizes Wasteful Production

Anita S. Hollander and Harold P. Roth

How much candy can be stuffed into a one-pound box? The search for a dependable management accounting system yielded activity-based costing (ABC), which helps provide data for analyzing the profitability of products and for making product-related production decisions. This article illustrates how statistical process control (SPC) can supplement ABC, focusing on a candy manufacturer's SPC-based investigation (supported by Lotus 1-2-3) of the amount of candy it was actually putting into its one-pound boxes. It turned out to be more than a pound, but now management knew how and when to adjust its packaging process to ship only the candy the customers were actually paying for.

For management accounting in multi-product, complex manufacturing environments, ABC-based costing provides better product costing data than volume-based cost systems. ABC-based systems identify costs with manufacturing activities, relating those costs to product's use of the activities. In most other cost systems, overhead costs are allocated to products on the basis of such volume-related factors as direct-labor hours, direct-labor dollars, or machine hours, so that volume-based systems report misleading cost data unless all overhead costs vary directly with the volume-related factor.

The problem with volume-based cost systems has been summarized as follows:

> When the quantity of volume-related input that a product consumes does not vary in direct proportion to the quantity of volume-unrelated input consumed, volume-based cost systems will report distorted product costs.[1]

Distorted data

Product costs are distorted because volume-based systems generally overstate the cost of high-volume products and understate the cost of low-volume products. Product-related decisions made by managers who use the cost data are likely to be less than ideal because they rely on distorted cost data.

In addition to product cost data, managers may want information about the activities associated with costs because costs can be reduced if the activities are reduced. Unlike volume-based systems, ABC can provide data for controlling activities and reducing costs; if the activities identified by ABC are cost drivers, controlling those activities helps control their costs. Managers who want to reduce costs through better activity control must understand the characteristics of the activities and the various types of activities that can occur.

Beaujon and Singhal modified a classification scheme developed by Robin Cooper to account for four levels of activities:[2]

- Unit—Incurred for each unit produced, these activities might involve processing time on machines or drilling holes to insert bolts. Materials and direct-labor usage would also be classified as unit-level activities because each unit requires materials and labor.

- Batch—Performed once for each batch or production run, these activities include setting up machinery for different products, moving batches of units to the next process, and inspecting samples from each batch to assure quality standards.

- Process—Related to a process rather than a unit or a batch, these activities include preventive maintenance and equipment repairs, supervision of workers engaged in the process, and cleaning and lighting the process area. They must be done for production to continue, but they are not incurred in direct proportion to the number of units or the number of batches produced.
- Plant—Necessary for operating a plant, these activities include building maintenance, plant security, public relations, and plant administration. As with process-level activities, plant-level activities are not incurred in direct proportion to the number of units or batches produced.

If move time between processes is a cost-driving activity, reducing the time should ultimately reduce costs. When using ABC data to help reduce costs, however, managers must thoroughly understand the activity before they decide what to do. With SPC, managers can learn about most unit-level and batch-level activities, which are performed repetitively and are measurable.

Natural variation

SPC is based on statistical theory that maintains there is some natural or random variation in repetitive processes and activities even when the process or activity is performed efficiently. Special events can also occur, however, causing orderly variation (e.g., a machine that is out of adjustment, an error made by a machine operator, damaged raw material or components, or a dull blade on a cutting machine).

SPC helps measure the parameters of an activity and assess when variability exceeds the random variation inherent in the activity (i.e., special events). When there is orderly variation, the activity is statistically out of control. The reason for the loss of control must be determined before the random variation in the activity can be reduced. If the move time for batches of a product is studied through SPC and the time contains orderly variation, the cause must be determined and eliminated before the appropriate managers can try to reduce the move time for all moves.

Control charts

SPC is implemented through control charts, which are graphic illustrations of data associated with an attribute or variable. Attribute data refers to such classifications as the number of products that conform or do not conform to specifications; variable data refers to measurements of such characteristics as length, weight, or strength. When SPC is used to analyze activities, many of the measurements are of variable data (e.g., measurements of move time, processing time, direct materials use, and setup time). SPC used to analyze an activity involves taking samples and plotting the characteristic measured on a control chart.

To determine if a sample shows orderly variation, the user compares the plotted point with upper and lower control limits. If the sample data falls between the limits, the variability is due to random fluctuations; if the point falls outside the control limits, further research is needed to determine the special cause. When an activity is in statistical control, the plotted points form a band around the average (i.e., mean) of the process somewhere between the upper and lower control limits.

Although a complete discussion of all the various types of control charts is beyond the scope of this article, the following discussion of charts for variables data outlines the basic SPC concepts.

For variable data obtained by sampling, there are two types of control charts—range (R) charts and average ($\overline{X}$, called X-bar) charts. R charts show the variability of the measurements within each sample; $\overline{X}$ charts show the average value for the sample. Because sample data is normally distributed (i.e., follows a bell-shaped curve), the descriptive statistics for the distribution and control limits for the R and $\overline{X}$ charts are derived from the statistical theory that underlies that distribution.

Out of control?

The first step in using SPC for variables data is to develop an R chart, which reveals whether the process is in control with respect to variability. If the range of measurements within a sample is too large, the process is unstable and out of control. If the R chart shows the process is in control, an $\overline{X}$

chart must be prepared to determine if the process is in control with respect to the average.

As noted, a value falling outside the control limits indicates a control problem. Although a runs test can also be used with control charts, it helps reveal whether trends in the data may indicate a control problem. For example, a gradual increase in the range or average for the samples may indicate a problem.

Although several software packages help develop control charts, spreadsheet software for personal computers provides a flexible and inexpensive way to implement SPC.[3] For example, a structured analysis and design methodology and Lotus 1-2-3, Version 2.01, helped develop the following example on an IBM PC.[4]

> **SPC is based on statistical theory that maintains there is natural variation in repetitive processes, even when they are performed efficiently.**

A manufacturer's application

A candy manufacturer that packages its products in one-pound boxes wants to use SPC to analyze a unit-level activity (e.g., direct-material usage), focusing on the quantity of candy actually packaged in each box. When developing control charts, the company selects five filled boxes every half hour and weighs the candy packaged inside. Exhibit 1 shows the data and corresponding spreadsheet information.

Because activities data can be recorded in a control system, the method presented here can be used when data is recorded in a source that is external to the spreadsheet. Downloading data from a mainframe or another operating environment requires creating an ASCII (i.e., a seven-bit generic computer code) file with a .prn filename extension. Data can then be input into the spreadsheet template through the File Import command. If it is necessary to edit the data once it is inside

the Lotus template, the Data Parse command must be used.

In this example, observation numbers are entered into column A of the spreadsheet through the Data Fill Command, and the weight of the candy in ounces is entered in column B. Columns A and B, cells 3 through 127 are named OBS# and DATA, respectively, through the Range Name Create command. As noted on the exhibits, other data in the spreadsheet is also given range names to facilitate development of graphs.

After the data is entered into the spreadsheet, the range for each sample is calculated to develop the R chart. That range is the difference between the highest and lowest value in each sample. For example, for sample number 1 (observations one to five), the highest value is 16.3 ounces and the lowest value is 15.8 ounces, representing a range of 0.5 ounces. The range for each sample is calculated in column D of the spreadsheet shown in Exhibit 2.

After the ranges for the samples are calculated, the average range ($\overline{R}$, called R-bar) is computed. The value 0.52 is the sum of cells D3 through D27 divided by 25 (i.e., the number of samples).

Exhibit 1. *Candy Manufacturer's Spreadsheet*

Spreadsheet Row	Spreadsheet Column	
	A	B
1	Observ.	Observ.
2	Number	Value
3	1	16.3
4	2	16.1
5	3	15.8
6	4	16.2
7	5	15.9
8	6	16.0
9	7	16.5
10	8	16.3
11	9	15.8
12	10	16.1
•	•	•
•	•	•
•	•	•
123	121	15.9
124	122	16.0
125	123	16.5
126	124	16.3
127	125	15.8

Range names:
OBS# A3.A127
DATA B3.B127

QUALITY

The control limits for the range shown in columns E and G of Exhibit 2 are 3-sigma control limits, or three standard deviations away from the mean of 0.52. The limits are calculated by multiplying the R-bar value by a factor available from statistical tables.[5] When the sample size is five, the lower control limit (LCL) factor is zero (0.52 × 0.0). For the upper control limit (UCL), the factor listed in the statistical tables is 2.11, giving a UCL of 1.10 (0.52 × 2.11). These UCL and LCL values for each sample, as well as the $\overline{R}$ value, are shown in columns E, F, and G of Exhibit 2 in order to graph the control limits and center line on the control chart.

One way to determine whether an activity's variability is in or out of control is to evaluate the numerical data (e.g., in Exhibit 2). (Another method—graphs—is described later in this article.) Column H of the spreadsheet in Exhibit 2 in-cludes range test values that indicate whether a range value falls outside the control limits. A zero in column H indicates that the R value is within the control limits. A value of one indicates that the R value is outside the limits. The range test value is computed through an if statement (e.g., for cell H3, the statement is @IF[D3<E3#OR#D3>G3,1,0]). Similar statements (with different cell addresses) are used for each line in column H. Because all values in column H are zero, the variability in the ranges is attributable to random fluctuations, and there is no evidence that the process is out of control.

Because the sample ranges are within the control limits, an X-bar chart can be prepared to determine whether the process is in control with respect to the average. X-bar refers to the mean value of the sample and is calculated by dividing the sum of the observations in each sample by the

Exhibit 2. Range Data

Spreadsheet Row	Spreadsheet Column					
	C	D	E	F	G	H
1	Sample	Sample	Range	Range	Range	Range
2	Number	Range	LCL	Average	UCL	Test
3	1	0.5	0	0.52	1.10	0
4	2	0.7	0	0.52	1.10	0
5	3	0.1	0	0.52	1.10	0
6	4	0.6	0	0.52	1.10	0
7	5	0.6	0	0.52	1.10	0
8	6	0.5	0	0.52	1.10	0
9	7	0.7	0	0.52	1.10	0
10	8	0.5	0	0.52	1.10	0
11	9	0.4	0	0.52	1.10	0
12	10	0.7	0	0.52	1.10	0
13	11	0.3	0	0.52	1.10	0
14	12	0.4	0	0.52	1.10	0
15	13	0.2	0	0.52	1.10	0
16	14	0.5	0	0.52	1.10	0
17	15	0.5	0	0.52	1.10	0
18	16	0.5	0	0.52	1.10	0
19	17	0.7	0	0.52	1.10	0
20	18	0.6	0	0.52	1.10	0
21	19	0.5	0	0.52	1.10	0
22	20	0.7	0	0.52	1.10	0
23	21	0.3	0	0.52	1.10	0
24	22	0.7	0	0.52	1.10	0
25	23	0.6	0	0.52	1.10	0
26	24	0.5	0	0.52	1.10	0
27	25	0.7	0	0.52	1.10	0

Range names:
SRANGE D3.D27
RLCL E3.E27
RAVE F3.F27
RUCL G3.G27
RTEST H3.H27

number of observations. For the first sample, X-bar is 16.06 [(16.3 + 16.1 + 15.8 + 16.2 + 15.9)/5]. Means for the samples are shown in column I of Exhibit 3. The average of the X-bars, $\overline{\overline{X}}$ (called X double bar) is 16.14.

Control limits for X-bar are calculated through $\overline{\overline{X}}$, $\overline{R}$, and a tabled factor, A2.[6] The upper control limit is $\overline{\overline{X}}$ + A2R, and the lower control limit is $\overline{\overline{X}}$ − A2R. For samples of size five, the tabled A2 value is 0.58. The UCL is 16.14 + (0.58 × 0.52) = 16.44, and the LCL is 16.14 − (0.58 × 0.52) = 15.84. The LCL is shown in column J of Exhibit 3; the UCL is shown in column L.

Column M of Exhibit 3 shows the results of the calculation that determines whether any X-bar values fall outside the control limits. As with the limits test for the range, a zero indicates that the value is within the limits, and a one indicates a value outside the limits. Because a one appears in column M for sample number 21, the process is

out of control with respect to the average and further investigation is needed to determine why the average of 16.46 for that sample is so large.

Graphs for visual representation

Although this procedure indicates whether R and X-bar are within the control limits, graphs provide a better visual representation of the process, revealing any trends in the data. The result could be early detection of a problem because a trend in R or X-bar may show up on a graph before a value exceeds the UCL or is less than the LCL.

To develop control charts for R and X-bar, the graph function is used to create keystroke macros. Specific instructions for developing the range chart are given in Exhibit 4; the R chart is shown in Exhibit 5.

Instructions for developing an X-bar graph are similar to those for the R graph; only the cell ad-

Exhibit 3. *Means Data*

Spreadsheet Row	Spreadsheet Column					
	C	I	J	K	L	M
1	Sample	Sample	Mean	Grand	Mean	Means
2	Number	Mean	LCL	Mean	UCL	Test
3	1	16.06	15.84	16.14	16.44	0
4	2	16.14	15.84	16.14	16.44	0
5	3	16.28	15.84	16.14	16.44	0
6	4	16.14	15.84	16.14	16.44	0
7	5	16.10	15.84	16.14	16.44	0
8	6	16.12	15.84	16.14	16.44	0
9	7	16.10	15.84	16.14	16.44	0
10	8	16.18	15.84	16.14	16.44	0
11	9	16.00	15.84	16.14	16.44	0
12	10	16.12	15.84	16.14	16.44	0
13	11	16.26	15.84	16.14	16.44	0
14	12	16.30	15.84	16.14	16.44	0
15	13	16.30	15.84	16.14	16.44	0
16	14	16.02	15.84	16.14	16.44	0
17	15	16.02	15.84	16.14	16.44	0
18	16	16.18	15.84	16.14	16.44	0
19	17	16.08	15.84	16.14	16.44	0
20	18	16.10	15.84	16.14	16.44	0
21	19	16.12	15.84	16.14	16.44	0
22	20	16.10	15.84	16.14	16.44	0
23	21	16.46	15.84	16.14	16.44	0
24	22	16.08	15.84	16.14	16.44	0
25	23	16.10	15.84	16.14	16.44	0
26	24	16.12	15.84	16.14	16.44	0
27	25	16.10	15.84	16.14	16.44	0

Range names:
SMEAN   I3.I27
MLCL   J3.J27
MAVE   K3.K27
MUCL   L3.L27
MTEST   M3.M27

Exhibit 4. *Commands for Creating an R Chart in LOTUS 1-2-3, Version 2.01*

User Input	Menu Item	Explanation
/G	Graph	Places user in graph function
R	Reset	Cancels graph settings
G	Graph	Cancels all graph settings
T	Type	Graph type (e.g., line, bar)
L	Line	Line graph
X	X axis	Labels along X axis
SAMPLE#¯		Sample numbers
A	A line	First line to be graphed
SRANGE¯		Graphs sample ranges
B	B line	Second line to be graphed
RLCL¯		Graphs lower control limit
C	C line	Third line to be graphed
RAVE¯		Graphs R-bar
D	D line	Fourth line to be graphed
RUCL¯		Graphs upper control limit
O	Options	Gives options menu
F	Format	Gives menu for formatting lines
A	A line	Options for formatting A line
B	Both	Graphs with both lines and symbols
B	B line	Options for formatting B line
L	Line	Graphs with line only
C	C line	Options for formatting C line
L	Line	Graphs with line only
D	D line	Options for formatting D line
L	Line	Graphs with line only
Q	Quit	Quits format menu
T	Titles	Gives title menu
F		First graph title
Range Chart¯		Titles graph Range Chart
T	Titles	Returns to title menu
X	X axis	Title for X axis
Sample No.¯		Titles X axis Sample No.
T	Titles	Returns to title menu
Y	Y axis	Title for Y axis
Range¯		Titles Y axis Range
D	Data labels	Gives labels for lines menu
B	B line	Label for B line
N14¯		Labels B line LCL = from cell N14
A	Above	Puts label above Y axis
C	C line	Label for C line
N15¯		Labels C line with mean from cell N15
L	Left	Puts label to left of Y axis
D	D line	Label for D line
N16¯		Labels D line UCL = from cell N16
B	Below	Puts label below Y axis
Q	Quit	Quits data labels menu
S	Scale	Provides scale menu for X axis
S	Skip	Sets interval on X axis
2¯		Skips every other X axis label
Q	Quit	Quit the Options submenu
N	Name	Graph names for saving inside worksheet
C	Create	Save graph settings to a graph name
RCHART¯		Graph is saved internally as RCHART
Q	Quit	Quits graph menu

NOTE: ¯(tilde) denotes carriage return

To maintain appropriate labels and spacing, cells N14.N16 include:

N14: +"   LCL = "&@STRING(E3,2)
N15: @STRING(F3,2)&"   "
N16: +"   UCL = "&@STRING(G3,2)

To view the graph after invoking the macro (or necessary keystrokes), use the Graph Name Use RCHART command, and press the ESC key when finished.

To save the graph to an external file for use with the Lotus PrintGraph option, issue the Graph Save command.

dresses, titles, and labels differ. The graphic output for the X-bar chart is shown in Exhibit 6. As expected from the values in columns H and M of the spreadsheet, only the X-bar value for sample number 21 is outside the control limits. The graphic representation reveals that fact more readily than does the tabular display of the data.

Sent to word processing

Exporting spreadsheet analyses to word processing documents makes the spreadsheet approach to SPC more flexible than file-oriented SPC software packages. In addition to graph output (through the Lotus Print Graph program), Lotus creates ASCII output that can be imported into word processing packages for inclusion in reports and documents. The print file command is used to save any portion of the spreadsheet template to an ASCII file, creating a text (.prn) file, which is external to the worksheet (.wk1) file.

The charts

The spreadsheet template created in this arti-

cle can be combined with observations from many manufacturing or administrative processes and activities. The File Import command can add the new raw data into a copy of the spreadsheet; then the F9 key can trigger the appropriate recalculations and invoke the graph macros.

This template can also be expanded to show updated activity information. After the initial data is collected and recorded, additional samples should be taken to continue monitoring the activity; the data for these samples can be added to columns A and B of the spreadsheet. If the original samples show an in-control activity, the initial means and control limits for X-bar and R can be used for the range and means tests of the additional samples. To prepare a control chart with more sample observations, the additional X-bars and Rs must be recorded in the appropriate columns of the spreadsheet and the range names updated to reflect the additional data and computations.

As with any business software, the template must be tested prior to implementation to guaran-

Exhibit 5. Range Chart

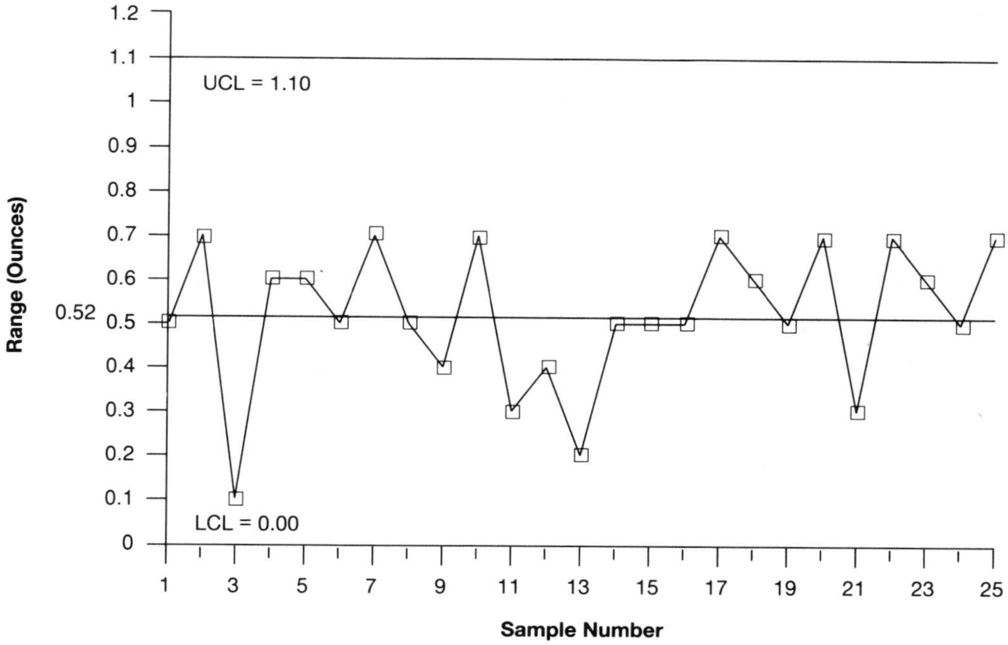

Notes:
LCL   Lower control limit
UCL   Upper control limit

tee valid logic, consistency, and desired outputs. In addition, the template must be documented properly by listing the programmer, revision dates, and a complete program narrative, which should include relevant variables, parameters, and assumptions, as well as an overview of template program processing. All macros should also be documented.

For multiple users

Macro menus are useful for enhancing basic spreadsheet templates to facilitate use by multiple or novice users. A keystroke or autoexec macro (i.e., a \o macro that executes as the worksheet file is retrieved) can be coded to branch to a macro menu. Menu choices include:

- Import data—For executing File Import and recalculating the template.
- View graphs—For creating graphs based on current observations and allowing users to view the desired graphs.
- Hardcopy print—For printing desired tem-

plate ranges through the print command options.
- ASCII Output—For saving desired ranges to a text (.prn) disk file through the Print File command options.
- Save Graph—For saving current graph settings to a (.pic) disk file through graph save.
- Quit—For stopping macro execution, allowing the user to stay inside the template.
- Exit—For exiting Lotus to DOS.

Control charts can help define the parameters of an activity to help maintain control over operations. Although these charts do not reveal precisely why an activity is out of control, they do provide visual representation of the activity that indicates whether the activity is unstable. Out of control points indicate orderly variability, whether the process must be investigated to determine the cause, and the appropriate countermeasures that can be taken.

Control charts may also indicate that management should modify the activity. In the candy manufacturer example, the average weight of the

Exhibit 6. X-Bar Chart

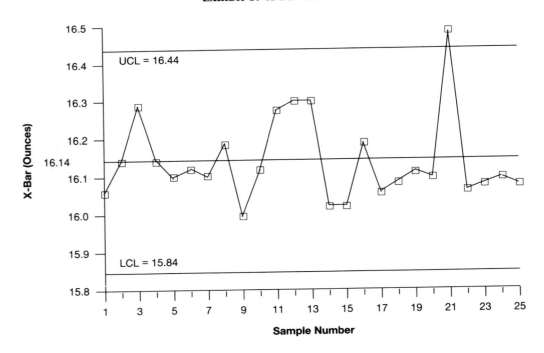

Notes:
LCL Lower control limit
UCL Upper control limit

candy packaged in the 25 samples is 16.14 ounces. Because the packaging standard calls for 16 ounces, costs are reduced if the average can be moved closer to the standard. If this fine tuning is attempted, however, the variability in the activity may also need to be reduced so that few or no boxes contain less than 16 ounces. Regardless of whether the variability or the weight is to be reduced, a change in the activity is needed because most of the variation is due to random fluctuations in the process. Searching for special events is not productive because they are not the cause of the excessive packaging.

Because control charts are easy to prepare and interpret, they can also be used to study the activities in many types and sizes of organizations. After the concepts behind SPC are understood, companies readily find other activities that can be analyzed and described through control charts.

Notes

1. Robin Cooper, "The Rise of Activity-Based Costing—Part One: What Is an Activity-Based Cost System?" *Journal of Cost Management for the Manufacturing Industry* (Summer 1988), p 53.
2. George J. Beaujon and Vinod R. Singhal, "Understanding the Activity Costs in an Activity-Based Cost System," *Journal of Cost Management for the Manufacturing Industry* (Spring 1990), pp 51–72.
3. See *Quality Progress* (March 1990) for an index and directory of software packages relating to quality concepts and SPC.
4. Boaz Ronen, Michael A. Palley, and Henry C. Lucus, Jr, "Spreadsheet Analysis and Design," *Communications of the ACM* (January 1989), pp 84–93.
5. Eugene L. Grant and Richard S. Leavenworth, *Statistical Quality Control,* 5th ed, (New York: McGraw-Hill, 1980) p 631.
6. Grant and Leavenworth.

Controlling Quality on a Multidimensional Level[1]

Thomas L. Albright and Harold P. Roth

As businesses strive to become world-class producers of goods and services, managers and financial staff need to expand their roles by becoming involved in measuring and evaluating the quality and performance of processes and activities. This article discusses statistical process control charts, which can help measure quality and performance in many situations. Although univariate control charts have been discussed in the cost management and accounting literature, the control chart concept is expanded here to include multivariate control charts, which provide a means for evaluating the system as a whole rather than individual parts. If an organization wants to maximize the quality of its activities, processes, and products, all managers, staff, and production workers need to understand the concepts of statistical process control.

Businesses that adopt total quality management need methods for evaluating and monitoring both production and administrative performance. Appropriate measures of quality and performance often depend on the specific process or activity under evaluation. The need for individualized performance measures suggests that each manager and employee must understand the underlying nature of the process for which he is responsible. Each person must also understand the various tools and techniques available for measuring and evaluating these processes. One tool that has become increasingly popular for evaluating the quality and performance of processes is the statistical process control (SPC) chart.

Statistical process control charts

SPC charts have become a popular quality management tool because they apply to many different types of situations. When SPC charts are maintained in real time, they provide an early warning signal about quality problems. The control charts that are usually illustrated and discussed in the cost management and managerial accounting literature[2] are generally for a single variable, even though many different variables may be measured for the same process.

Control charts that monitor one characteristic are called *univariate* (one-variable) charts. *Multivariate* (many-variable) charts track more than one characteristic simultaneously. When multiple variables are measured simultaneously, a single variable control chart may, under certain conditions, give misleading signals. The objective of this article is to show how a multivariate control chart can be applied to obtain additional, more useful, information about a process or activity when multiple characteristics are measured simultaneously.

Although many different types of SPC charts exist, they all have some similarities. In general, an SPC chart is a graph that shows the measurements of some characteristic of interest. The characteristic may be a quantitative variable (e.g., weight, length, or thickness) or it may be a qualitative attribute (e.g., whether a product is defective).

Control chart elements

Regardless of the type of chart or the characteristic, SPC charts typically possess the following elements:

- A center line, or process average, around which lie individual observations;
- Upper and lower control limits, which are typically placed at three standard deviations from the short-term process average;

- A horizontal axis that identifies the observations and preserves the time order of their collection; and
- A vertical axis that is scaled to the values of the observations.

SPC charts are used to identify points that differ from the process average and to discover shifts in the process. If the points on a control chart are randomly scattered around the center line and they fall within the upper and lower control limits, the process is considered to be in statistical control. An out-of-control condition is indicated if points fall outside the control limits or if *runs* exist in the data. (A run is a trend—i.e., a series of consecutive points above or below the center line.) By analyzing the conditions existing when an out-of-control signal occurs, an investigator attempts to discover the source of the variation and then determine a remedy.

SPC charts are appropriate for measuring and evaluating many different types of processes. Generally, they can be used in any repetitive situation where either a quantitative variable or qualitative attribute is measurable. Many manufacturing processes can be analyzed using SPC because:

- They are repetitive in nature; and
- Input-output relationships can be established.

However, SPC charts can also be used in other functional areas including:

- Accounting;
- Finance; and
- Marketing.[3]

Thus, managers in many different areas can use SPC analysis to evaluate the quality of their activities.

Uses of SPC analysis

Although SPC is only one quality management technique, it is so important that all managers and employees in a quality-oriented organization should understand its possible applications.

Generally, SPC can be used in three ways:
1. Helping control the quality of repetitive manufacturing processes;
2. Evaluating the performance of processes and activities; and

3. Measuring the quality of accounting and other administrative processes.

Use of SPC in repetitive manufacturing processes

As noted previously, SPC is appropriate for helping to control quality in many repetitive manufacturing processes. Because production employees and machine operators are often responsible for maintaining control charts for these processes, they need to understand how the control charts work and the statistical basis for the chart's validity. Others in the organization, such as managers and staff personnel, also need to understand the basics of control charts to better appreciate the quality control efforts of the production function.

Performance measures

When companies commit themselves to total quality management, nonfinancial measures of performance become more important. Many of these performance measures include quality and productivity for processes and activities.

A control chart can be used to help evaluate the nonfinancial performance of various processes and activities. Examples of processes and activities where control charts may be used include:

- Cycle time;
- Schedule attainment;
- Machine availability;
- Vendor lead time;
- On-time deliveries;
- Throughput time; and
- Defect rate.[4]

Since performance measurement often is part of the accounting function or some other staff function, employees in these areas need to understand control charts and how these charts can assist in performance evaluation.

Administrative and accounting processes

Many administrative processes also can be evaluated using control charts. All activities in these functional areas that are repetitive in nature would be appropriate candidates for SPC.

Examples of these repetitive activities in the finance and accounting areas include processing:

- Payroll;
- Accounts payable; and
- Accounts receivable.

If statistical control charts were used to evaluate these types of processes, personnel in these functional areas would gain a better understanding of the natural variability inherent in the processes and of how reducing this variability might result in more consistent services.

Although univariate control charts are appropriate for many of these applications, multivariate charts may also be needed. As illustrated in the remainder of this article, a multivariate control chart can provide additional information about a process that is not available from univariate control charts. This additional information may be needed to get the maximum benefits from the quality data.

Illustration of univariate chart

To illustrate a univariate SPC chart, an example for a material (pulp) used in manufacturing paperboard is developed. Monitoring the amount of raw material consumed in producing paperboard is necessary to control waste and to ensure that the material ratios are consistent with engineering standards. Thus, paperboard manufacturing provides many situations where SPC is useful.

In this example, twenty samples of pulp were collected. For each sample, four pulp specimens were weighed, then a sample average was calculated. The actual measurements and the average (mean) for each sample are shown in Exhibit 1. The grand mean reported on the last line is the average of all the observations in the twenty samples.

Exhibit 2 shows a control chart for the averages in Exhibit 1. (A range chart—which is not illustrated here—should also be developed for these data. Range charts are based on the variability in the sample rather than the average. They send an out-of-control signal if the variation within the sample is greater than expected.) The center line of Exhibit 2 is the grand mean of 934.25 pounds. The upper control limit (UCL) and the lower control limit (LCL) are the three-standard-deviation control limits that are calculated using statistical methodology.[5] As Exhibit 2 shows, the pulp usage seems to be

Exhibit 1. *Sample Data of Pulp Used*

Sample No.	Observation in Pounds				Sample Average
	1	2	3	4	
1	930	940	933	937	935
2	925	935	930	930	930
3	935	931	929	925	930
4	935	932	930	931	932
5	941	933	937	937	937
6	930	940	932	938	935
7	930	920	942	932	931
8	930	933	940	937	935
9	935	936	946	947	941
10	937	930	937	944	937
11	940	936	936	940	938
12	933	925	933	941	933
13	928	929	934	933	931
14	920	925	939	944	932
15	937	939	930	946	938
16	940	930	935	935	935
17	921	941	936	926	931
18	930	932	934	932	932
19	937	936	938	937	937
20	930	932	940	938	935
Grand Mean					934.25

in statistical control because all points fall within the control limits, and the points are randomly scattered above and below the center line.

Runs test. A runs test for the pulp data provides further evidence that the process is in a state of statistical control. When a run (or trend) occurs in the data, a process can be statistically out of control, even though no observations exceed the upper control limit or fall under the lower control limit. For example, based on the laws of probability, one would usually not expect eight sequential points to occur on one side of the center line unless a shift in the process average has occurred.[6] Since no runs of eight or more points appear in Exhibit 2, the "rule of eight" suggests that no shift in the process average has occurred.

Analyzing other characteristics. Other characteristics of this paperboard manufacturing process can also be analyzed and evaluated using SPC. For example, Exhibit 3 shows means data for two other ingredients, clay and chemicals, used in paperboard manufacturing. These data are plotted in control charts in Exhibits 4 and 5. Exhibit 4 is a control chart for the clay process, and Exhibit 5

Exhibit 2. *Univariate Control Chart Process: Pulp*

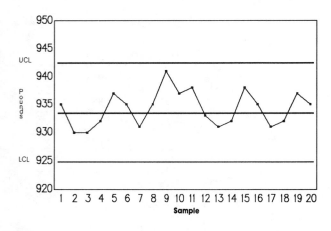

Exhibit 3. *Averages for Clay and Chemicals Usage*

Sample No.	Clay	Chemicals
1	55	36
2	53	34
3	53	34
4	55	35
5	56	37
6	53	34
7	51	33
8	53	37
9	49	36
10	56	34
11	58	36
12	55	35
13	52	33
14	53	34
15	56	37
16	54	37
17	50	33
18	52	34
19	55	40
20	53	37
Grand Means	53.6	35.3

for the chemicals process. While the clay process appears to be in a state of statistical control, the chemical process shown in Exhibit 5 appears to be out of control because the average for sample 19 exceeds the upper control limit.

Although sample 19 shows an out-of-control situation for chemicals usage, the univariate control charts suggest that none of the other data points indicate a problem. The problem with drawing this conclusion is that the data in the three charts are not independent. The reasons for the lack of independence are discussed next.

Correlated variables

Ryan[7] has noted the problem of monitoring a process using separate control charts for each variable of interest—namely, that erroneous signals are likely when the variables are highly correlated (i.e., a change in one variable is associated with a change in another variable). Variables are positively correlated if an increase (decrease) in one variable is associated with an increase (decrease) in another variable. (Negative correlations also may exist. For example, as the processing time for weekly payroll declines, the proportion of errors may increase.)

In the paperboard manufacturing example given previously, pulp, clay, and chemicals are not independent. An examination of the control charts in Exhibits 2, 4, and 5 suggests that the three variables are positively correlated—i.e., an increase in one ingredient (relative to the previous observation on the horizontal axis) is generally accompanied by an increase in the other two ingredients. Conversely, a reduction in one ingredient is generally associated with a reduction in the other two ingredients.

Statistical correlation tests. The statistical correlation test summarized in Exhibit 6 shows that the three ingredients are in fact significantly positively correlated.

Note that two values are provided for each variable in the correlation table. The upper number explains the relationship between two variables (identified by the row and column) in terms of a *correlation coefficient* that ranges from minus one to plus one. (Large positive correlation coefficients indicate greater correlation than small positive coefficients. Coefficients of less than zero indicate negative correlation.) The bottom number, which appears in brackets, is the *statistical significance* associated with the correlation coefficient.

For example, clay and pulp are positively correlated, as evidenced by a positive correlation coefficient of 0.7632. The significance

Exhibit 4. *Univariate Control Chart Process: Clay*

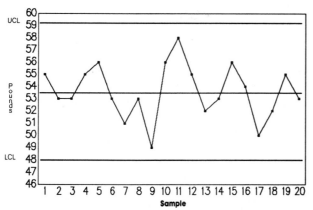

Exhibit 5. *Univariate Control Chart Process: Chemicals*

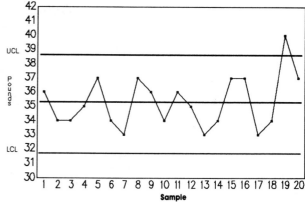

level states that the probability of obtaining a coefficient as large as 0.7632 would occur by chance only once in 10,000 times (0.0001) if pulp and clay were not correlated. As demonstrated in Exhibit 6, all the variables in this illustration are correlated at traditional significance levels of 0.05. Since the variables are highly correlated, the univariate SPC charts for this process may not be providing complete information about the state of statistical control for these processes.

The multivariate control chart

To obtain more complete information about the state of statistical control when two or more variables are measured simultaneously, a multivariate control chart should be used. The objective of a multivariate control chart is similar to that of a univariate control chart—i.e., to determine if the variation in a process is attributable to unusual influences.

A multivariate control chart monitors several variables simultaneously and sends an out-of-control signal when the relationship among the variables changes in an unexpected manner. For example, since the pulp and clay variables are positively correlated, increases in the usage of pulp should be associated with increases in the usage of clay. While this relationship is typical, exceptions can occur.

For example, if the pulp usage increases while the clay usage declines, something unexpected has happened. The unexpected

event should trigger an out-of-control signal in the multivariate control chart. The Hotelling's T^2 statistic for the observation in question (see the sidebar for an explanation of this statistic) would become very large relative to the other data points whose relationships were consistent with experience in the past.

Differences between multivariate and univariate charts

To understand and appreciate the multivariate control chart, it is useful to look at the differences between multivariate and univariate charts. The three main differences occur in:

1. Calculating the data point to be plotted on the chart;
2. Calculating the control limits; and
3. Investigating out-of-control points.

Exhibit 6. *Pearson Correlation Coefficients (Significance Levels)*

	Pulp	**Clay**	**Chemicals**
Pulp	1.0000	0.7632	0.6820
	(0.0000)	(0.0001)	(0.0013)
Clay		1.0000	0.4676
		(0.0000)	(0.0435)
Chemicals			1.0000
			(0.0000)

Mathematics of Multivariate Statistics

The mathematics of multivariate statistics are unavoidably more advanced than those of univariate statistics. An understanding of how to use a multivariate control chart, however, does not require understanding how to calculate the multivariate measure.

Statistical software is used to calculate each T^2 value (Hotelling's T^2) and produce the control chart by entering simple averages from a process into the program. This sidebar provides the supporting mathematical details for those who want to obtain a deeper understanding of how the T^2 statistic is calculated for use in multivariate control charts. Readers are referred to a statistics text, such as Neter, et al.,[1] for a review of matrix subtraction and multiplication.

Row and column vectors

Multivariate control charts evaluate many characteristics of interest simultaneously. Therefore, both a row vector (a row of numbers containing one value for each characteristic) and a column vector (a column of numbers containing one value for each characteristic) are required for the calculation.

For example, a row vector for the paperboard manufacturing example used in this article would contain three values, one each for pulp, clay, and chemicals. The column vector would contain the same three values. Hotelling's T^2 requires a row vector, a column vector, and an inverse of the variance-covariance matrix. The variance-covariance matrix, which explains the mathematical relationships existing among the data, contains the variances of each variable in the main diagonal positions (i.e., the northwest to southeast diagonal) and the covariances in the off-diagonal positions. Statgraphics software was used to calculate the variance-covariance matrix for the sample data set. To calculate Hotelling's T^2, the inverse of the variance-covariance matrix must be determined.

The inverse of the variance-covariance matrix can be calculated manually for a two-by-two or a three-by-three matrix. When matrices become larger as a result of using four or more different characteristics, a computer is needed to perform the calculations in a reasonable

time frame. Spreadsheet packages for personal computers can be used to invert matrices. For example, Versions 2.01 and higher of Lotus 1-2-3 have a matrix inversion function.

According to Neter et al.,[2] the definition of a three-by-three variance-covariance matrix is specified as follows:

$$B = \begin{bmatrix} a & b & c \\ d & e & f \\ g & h & k \end{bmatrix}$$

Statgraphics calculated the following variance-covariance matrix using the sample averages provided in the body of the paper.

$$B = \begin{bmatrix} 9.671 & 2.211 & 3.763 \\ 2.211 & 4.884 & 1.758 \\ 3.763 & 1.758 & 3.379 \end{bmatrix}$$

Hotelling's T^2 is based on the inverse of the variance-covariance matrix. Neter et al., define the inverse of a three-by-three variance-covariance matrix as follows:

$$B^{-1} = \begin{bmatrix} A & B & C \\ D & E & F \\ G & H & K \end{bmatrix}$$

where:

$$
\begin{aligned}
A &= (ek - fh)/Z \\
B &= -(bk - ch)/Z \\
C &= (bf - ce)/Z \\
D &= -(dk - fg)/Z \\
E &= (ak - cg)/Z \\
F &= -(af - cd)/Z \\
G &= (dh - eg)/Z \\
H &= -(ah - bg)/Z \\
K &= (ae - bd)/Z
\end{aligned}
$$

$$Z = a(ek - fh) - b(dk - fg) + c(dh - eg)$$

The inverse of the variance-covariance matrix becomes

$$
\begin{aligned}
B^{-1} &= \begin{bmatrix} A & B & C \\ D & E & F \\ G & H & K \end{bmatrix} \\
&= \begin{bmatrix} .183 & -.012 & -.198 \\ -.012 & .253 & -.118 \\ -.198 & -.118 & .578 \end{bmatrix}
\end{aligned}
$$

Hotelling's T^2, is calculated as follows:

$$T^2 = (\bar{x}^{(j)} - \bar{\bar{x}})' B^{-1} (\bar{x}^{(j)} - \bar{\bar{x}})$$

where:

j = subgroup (sample) number such as 1, 2, 3, 4, etc. Our data set contains twenty samples.

[1] J. Neter, W. Wasserman, and M. Kutner, *Applied Linear Statistical Models,* 2d ed. (Irwin, 1985): 185–196.

[2] J. Neter, W. Wasserman, and M. Kutner, *Applied Linear Statistical Models,* 2d ed. (Irwin, 1985): 185–196.

Mathematics of Multivariate Statistics (cont'd)

$\bar{x}$ = a vector (column) that contains the subgroup averages for each variable of interest. For example, for sample 1, the vector of averages for pulp, clay, and chemicals = [935 55 36].

$'$ = a transposition from a column vector to a row vector.

B^{-1} = the inverse of the pooled variance-co-variance matrix.

$\bar{\bar{x}}$ = the column, or vector, consisting of grand means. Each sample has an average (x-bar); the average of the sample averages is represented by x double-bar, the grand mean. As shown in Exhibits 1 and 3 the vector for grand means of pulp, clay, and chemicals = [934.25 53.6 35.3].

Using the data from Exhibits 1 and 3 the values for the row vector $(\bar{x}^{(j)} - \bar{\bar{x}})'$ and column vector $(\bar{x}^{(j)} - \bar{\bar{x}})$ are obtained as follows:

$$\begin{bmatrix} 935 - 934.25 \\ 55 - 53.60 \\ 36 - 35.30 \end{bmatrix}$$

= $\begin{bmatrix} .75 \\ \\ 1.40 \\ \\ .70 \end{bmatrix}$ Pulp: sample average − grand mean, sample 1
Clay: sample average − grand mean, sample 1
Chem: sample average − grand mean, sample 1

With the calculated values for the row vector, column vector, and inverse of the variance-covariance matrix, Hotelling's T^2 is obtained by matrix multiplication as follows:

T^2 for sample 1 =

$$[.75 \quad 1.40 \quad .70]\begin{bmatrix} .183 & -.012 & -.198 \\ -.012 & .253 & -.118 \\ -.198 & -.118 & .578 \end{bmatrix}\begin{bmatrix} .75 \\ 1.40 \\ .70 \end{bmatrix}$$

$= (.75(.183) + 1.4(-.012) + .7(-.198)).75 + (.75(-.012) + 1.4(.253) + .7(-.118))1.40 + (.75(-.198) + 1.4(-.118) + .7(.578)).70 = \underline{\underline{.42}}$

The T^2 of 0.42 for sample 1 is plotted on the multivariate control chart in Exhibit 7.

Each of these differences is briefly discussed before the multivariate chart is illustrated.

Calculating the data point to be plotted. As shown in Exhibits 2, 4, and 5, the points that are plotted on a univariate SPC chart for averages are the sample means. In a multivariate control chart based on samples, by contrast, the points that are plotted are a quadratic form of the means of the measurements in each sample. The quadratic form is determined using matrix algebra and is identified as Hotelling's T^2. (The sidebar provides a manual calculation to support the computer calculation of Hotelling's T^2 for sample number one.) Fortunately, computer programs are available for calculating these values and for constructing the control chart.[8]

Calculating the control limits. Another difference between multivariate and univariate charts occurs in the control limits. In a univariate chart for sample means, there is usually an upper and a lower control limit. In a multivariate chart, however, there is only an upper control limit, which considers such factors as the number of variables, level of desired confidence, and sample size. Once these parameters are identified, the software program calculates the upper control limit. A single control limit is used in a multivariate chart because of the manner in which the observations are calculated. For example, the Hotelling's T^2 becomes large when correlated variables move in an unexpected direction. The observer is, therefore, interested in detecting only large values of Hotelling's T^2. A small value indicates that variables moved together as expected, thus a lower control limit is not of interest.

Investigating out-of-control points. When a multivariate control chart provides an out-of-control signal, the investigator must first try to determine which characteristic (or characteristics) caused the process to be out of control. This, of course, is not necessary with a univariate chart since only one characteristic is plotted. To help in this determination, computer software may graph the characteris-

Exhibit 7. *Multivariate Control Chart Hotelling's T^2*

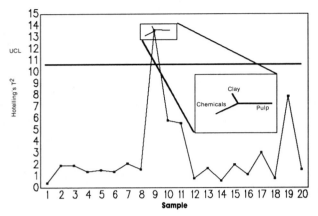

tics in the form of a *glyph,* which is a symbol with rays that show the relative value of each variable. The next example illustrates how a glyph may be used.

Example of a multivariate control chart

The data given previously in Exhibits 1 and 3 for the pulp, clay, and chemicals are used here to illustrate the multivariate control chart. Exhibit 7 is a multivariate control chart that combines data for the three variables. The data points are the calculated Hotelling's T^2 values for each sample. Notice there is no center line on the multivariate control chart; the solid line at the Hotelling's T^2 value of 10.7 is the upper control limit.

As Exhibit 7 shows, the value for sample 9 exceeds the upper control limit. Thus, the multivariate control chart provides a different signal from that of the univariate charts (see Exhibits 2, 4, and 5), in which all averages for sample 9 are within the control limits. An investigation is needed to determine what caused the out-of-control signal.

To determine the potential cause of the out-of-control signal, the software provides a glyph symbol rather than simply a dot. A glyph is illustrated for the out-of-control point in Exhibit 7. The three o'clock, seven o'clock, and eleven o'clock rays of the glyph represent pulp, chemicals, and clay, respectively. (The Statgraphics software package provides a legend to help interpret the glyphs.) The disproportionately small ray

representing the clay content and the disproportionately long ray representing pulp suggest that an imbalance in the relationship of clay and pulp has occurred. This imbalance is supported by an examination of the univariate charts for pulp (Exhibit 2) and clay (Exhibit 4). Specifically, in Exhibit 2, the pulp in sample 9 increased over sample 8, while in Exhibit 4 the clay decreased from sample 8 to sample 9. Additional investigation might show that some unusual event occurred that prevented the proper amount of clay from being added to the process.

Note that sample 19 does not produce an out-of-control signal in the multivariate chart in Exhibit 7, although Exhibit 5 suggests that an unusual event has occurred in the chemical process in sample 19. This anomaly is not detected by the multivariate chart because the variables moved in the same direction, as expected. Thus, although the chemical usage was so large that the univariate chart indicated an out-of-control situation, usage of the other two ingredients was in the same direction, and the plotted value fell below the control limit on the multivariate chart.

Multivariate charts complement univariate charts

As this example illustrates, univariate and multivariate charts should be used together because they complement each other. The univariate chart signals an out-of-control situation when the value for a specific variable falls outside the control limits. The multivariate chart provides an out-of-control signal when an imbalance exists among the variables. Therefore, when two or more variables are measured simultaneously for the same process or activity, the best and most comprehensive information comes from using the two types of charts in conjunction with each other.

Advantages of multivariate charts

Multivariate control charts may be needed when two or more variables are measured from the same sample. As noted previously, a multivariate chart provides an out-of-control signal when the variables move in a direction opposite from what is expected. While this condition might also be detected from a critical examination of the univariate charts, the multivariate chart indicates whether it is statistically significant. A multivariate chart is also easier to examine than three univariate charts simultaneously.

Another advantage of a multivariate control chart is that it can also detect differences in the *degree* of movement away from a process average. For example, consider several variables that are positively correlated, each with one observation moving upward from its process average. An out-of-control signal may be produced by the multivariate chart if all the variables move in the same direction but in varying degrees relative to their process average. Thus, the multivariate control chart may detect subtle changes in the relationships among the variables that would not be noticeable from individual univariate charts.

Evaluating the system as a whole. Multivariate charts also allow users to evaluate the system as a whole rather than as the sum of many individual parts. A multivariate chart thus provides a means for evaluating the control state of two or more variables simultaneously.

Note also that a multivariate chart requires no additional data if the data currently are accumulated for univariate control charts. With statistical software, little additional effort is required to produce a multivariate chart that combines the data.

Use of multivariate charts for administrative processes

Although the example in this article illustrates a multivariate chart for production activities, multivariate charts may also be appropriate for administrative and financial activities. For example, if accountants are using SPC to monitor the preparation of invoices, they may measure several such variables as preparation time, number of lines, and dollar amounts. Since these variables probably are correlated, it would be appropriate to use a multivariate chart to measure the relationships between the variables in addition to univariate charts for each variable.

Another example of an administrative process in which a multivariate chart would be appropriate is the receiving activity for parts and materials. An analysis of this activity

might include the number of different parts in the shipment, the size of the shipment, and the time to verify that the parts received are in agreement with the purchase order. If

---

A multivariate control chart monitors several variables simultaneously and sends an out-of-control signal when the relationship among the variables changes in an unexpected manner.

---

these three measures are correlated, a multivariate chart should be used to see if the process as a whole is in statistical control.

Summary

When used in conjunction with univariate charts, a multivariate control chart provides evidence about the state of statistical control within a process by considering several variables simultaneously. A univariate control chart that monitors only one characteristic of interest cannot evaluate the state of the system as a whole. Both types of charts are useful and assist in monitoring the quality of a process or activity.

Managers and staff who are involved in measuring quality and performance need to understand both univariate and multivariate control charts. A multivariate control chart allows them to evaluate the system as a whole in addition to the individual parts, which are monitored with univariate charts. A multivariate control chart may also provide additional information that can be used in reducing waste and improving quality, both of which are important goals of a world-class manufacturer. Organizations that seek to maximize the quality of their activities, processes, and products cannot ignore such quality tools as control charts. ▲

Notes

1. The authors wish to thank Mike Dugan, Bill Samson, James Schmidhammer, and Imogene Posey for their helpful comments and suggestions.

2. See, for example, C.T. Horngren and G. Foster, *Cost Accounting,* 7th ed. (Prentice-Hall, 1991): 841–842; R.S. Kaplan, *Advanced Management Accounting* (Prentice-Hall, 1982): 330–332; E.B. Deakin and M.W. Maher, *Cost Accounting,* 3d ed., (Irwin, 1991): 975–978; and L.K. Anderson and D.K. Clancy, *Cost Accounting* (Irwin, 1991): 820–825.

3. Using SPC to evaluate processes and activities in these areas is discussed in J. Reeve and J. Philpot, "Applications of Statistical Process Control for Financial Management," *Journal of Cost Management,* (Fall 1988): 33–40; R. Walter, M. Higgins, and H. Roth, "Applications of Control Charts," *The CPA Journal* (Apr. 1990): 90–93, 95; and J. Duarte, "Statistical Process Control in Marketing and Finance," *CMA Magazine* (May 1991): 20–23.

4. Reeve and Philpot, "Applications of Statistical Process," 37.

5. The critical values and equations for calculating the control limits appear in most industrial statistics books. For example, see E. Grant and R. Leavenworth, *Statistical Quality Control,* 5th ed. (McGraw-Hill Book Company, 1980): 631. A source in the accounting literature is M. Hirsch, *Advanced Management Accounting* (PWS-Kent Publishing Company, 1988): 344.

6. Other runs tests also can be performed. These tests include but are not limited to (1) six points in a row that are steadily increasing or decreasing or (2) fourteen points in a row alternating up and down. These rules are not based on sample size but on the laws of probability. Regardless of the number of observations, one would not expect to find points exhibiting behavior such as this if the process were affected only by random variation. For more information on runs tests, see Grant and Leavenworth, *Statistical Quality Control:* 91–92.

7. T. Ryan, *Statistical Methods for Quality Improvement* (New York: John Wiley and Sons, 1989): 215.

8. The statistical software package used for this article was Statgraphics Statistical Graphics System, Version 5.0, licensed by STSC, Inc. and Statistical Graphics Corporation.

Determining Optimal Quality Costs by Considering Cost of Lost Sales

Cynthia D. Heagy

This article addresses a critical managerial function—the analysis and control of quality costs. In particular, the article examines the traditional quality cost model (which categorizes quality costs as prevention, appraisal, and failure costs), then suggests how to make the model more meaningful by incorporating the cost of lost sales as a component of failure costs. Doing this increases the optimum quality cost.

We manage by the numbers, we judge by the numbers—and we lose by the numbers.[1] This sentiment is expressed often as managers are compelled to reconsider the usefulness of financial statement numbers for internal decision making. Some cost-accounting experts suggest that traditional cost systems are irrelevant to managing in today's business environment, which is characterized by advanced manufacturing technology and global competition. Outdated systems and financial models lead to suboptimal decisions, ranging from which products to add or drop to which managers to reward.

This article addresses one of the critical managerial functions that can benefit from more relevant managerial thought—the analysis and control of quality costs. The article reconsiders the traditional quality cost model and suggests how to make the model more meaningful for today's business environment. These suggestions incorporate the cost of lost sales into the model and place the optimal cost of quality (as determined by the model) in proper perspective. The article first describes quality costs and the quality cost model, then demonstrates how the cost of lost sales affects the optimal cost level. The article concludes with a discussion of the correct use of the cost model.

Description of quality costs

The major categories of quality costs are prevention, appraisal, and failure costs. Because the costs are interrelated, the trick for management is to determine how much to spend on one category to balance out the amount spent on the others. The costs have a hierarchical order. Thus, slack in prevention costs causes more to be spent on appraisal. Similarly, slack in prevention and appraisal causes more to be spent on failure costs. Each cost category is described below.

Prevention costs. It is generally most cost-effective never to build defective units in the first place. The purpose of prevention costs, therefore, is to improve quality by preventing defects from occurring. Expenditures in this category ensure that firms "do it right the first time." Prevention includes costs for research and development, machinery, technology, and educational programs.

Appraisal costs. The purpose of appraisal costs is to control quality by reducing the number of defective products that are released to customers. Appraisal costs (which include the inspection costs of the quality control department as well as the equipment and premises necessary for inspections) are sometimes called "monitoring" or "inspection" costs. Expenditures for appraisal costs compensate for the ineffectiveness of expenditures for prevention. Once a defective product is produced, the goal is to catch it at the plant.

Exhibit 1. *Components of Quality Costs*

Prevention Costs
- Product research and design
- Quality engineering
- Quality circles
- Quality education and training
- Supervision of prevention activities
- Pilot studies
- Systems development and implementation
- Process controls
- Technical support provided to vendors
- Auditing the effectiveness of the quality system

Appraisal Costs
- Supplies used in testing and inspection
- Test and inspection of incoming materials
- Component inspection and testing
- Review of sales orders for accuracy
- In-process inspection
- Final product inspection and testing
- Field inspection at customer site prior to final release of product
- Reliability testing
- Supervision of appraisal activities
- Plant utilities in inspection area
- Depreciation of test equipment
- Internal audits of inventory

Internal Failure Costs
- Net cost of scrap
- Net cost of spoilage
- Disposal of defective product
- Rework labor and overhead
- Reinspection of reworked product
- Retest of reworked product
- Downtime due to quality problems
- Net opportunity cost of products classified as "seconds"
- Data reentered due to input errors
- Defect cause analysis and investigation
- Revision of in-house computer programs due to software errors
- Adjusting entries necessitated by quality problems

External Failure Costs
- Cost of responding to customer complaints
- Investigation of customer claims on warranty
- Warranty repairs and replacements
- Out-of-warranty repairs and replacements
- Product recalls
- Product liability
- Returns and allowances due to quality problems
- Opportunity cost of lost sales due to bad quality reputation

Source: Adapted from Wayne J. Morse, Harold P. Roth, and Kay M. Poston, *Measuring, Planning, and Controlling Quality Costs* (Montvale, N.J.: National Association of Accountants, 1987).

The appraisal process usually requires a certain degree of statistical sophistication to use sampling techniques that will identify defective products. Although appraisal techniques reduce the number of defective products discovered by customers, these techniques do not eliminate the need to rework defective products.

Failure costs. Failure costs have no purpose: They are the result of insufficient or ineffective spending in the prevention and appraisal categories. Failure costs are thus a classic example of non-value-added costs.

There are two kinds of failure costs:

- *Internal failure costs.* These costs are associated with products that fail to meet quality standards, and thus result in manufacturing losses. Internal failure costs primarily involve costs of reworking defective units discovered by appraisal techniques.
- *External failure costs.* These costs are incurred because inferior-quality products are shipped to customers. They include warranty repairs and the opportunity cost of lost sales because of customer dissatisfaction.

Exhibit 1 provides a list of typical quality costs by category.

Traditional model of quality costs

The traditional model of quality costs shown in Exhibit 2 illustrates the relationships between the components of quality costs and shows the optimum total quality costs. The horizontal axis of the graph in Exhibit 2 represents the level of quality assurance, ranging from 0 percent quality assurance (i.e., 100 percent of all units produced are defective) to 100 percent quality assurance (i.e., zero units produced are defective). The vertical axis of the graph represents the amount spent on the various components of quality costs.

Note that all components of prevention and appraisal costs are represented on one curve. (Although it is probable that the more a company spends on prevention costs, the less it has to spend on appraisal costs, this article does not delve into that relationship. The current trend is to emphasize prevention

Exhibit 2. *Traditional Model of Optimum Quality Costs*

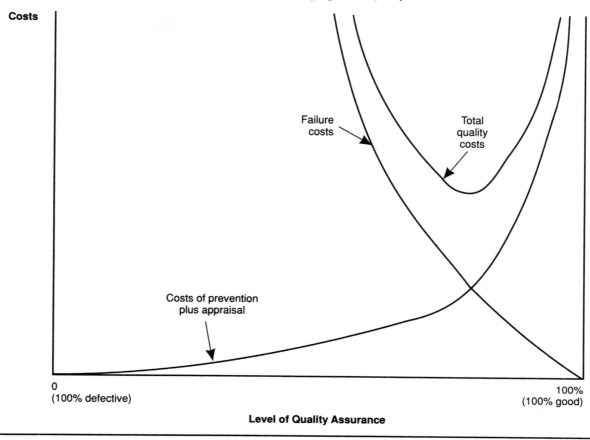

Costs

Failure costs

Total quality costs

Costs of prevention plus appraisal

0
(100% defective)

100%
(100% good)

Level of Quality Assurance

costs rather than appraisal costs.) Formerly, the conventional wisdom was to improve the production process to detect potential problems before they resulted in off-quality products. Today, the emphasis is increasingly on "robust quality." The notion of robust quality belongs to Genichi Taguchi, a Japanese consultant who recommends that instead of constantly adjusting production equipment to assure consistent quality, a product should be designed to achieve high quality despite fluctuations in the production process.[2]

Expenditures on prevention or appraisal have the same relationship with the level of quality assurance. As the curves in Exhibit 2 show, changes in prevention and appraisal costs directly affect the level of quality assurance. Note, however, that the level of quality assurance and failure costs are inversely related. Thus, as the level of quality assurance increases (decreases), failure costs decrease (increase). (Note that internal failure and

external failure costs are also combined into one curve.)

Total quality cost curve. The total quality cost curve in Exhibit 2 is the sum of prevention and appraisal costs plus failure costs. According to the traditional quality cost model, the optimum amount to spend on quality costs is determined by the point of minimum total quality costs. This minimum total quality cost is the lowest point on the total cost curve, i.e., where $1 of prevention and appraisal costs equals $1 of failure costs.

To the left of the optimum, prevention and appraisal costs go down but failure costs go up, with failure costs going up faster than prevention and appraisal costs go down. Therefore, at any level of quality assurance to the left of the minimum total quality cost point, for every $1 spent on prevention and appraisal, more than $1 is spent on failure costs.

To the right of the optimum, prevention and appraisal costs go up but failure costs go down, with prevention and appraisal costs going up faster than failure costs go down. Therefore, at any level of quality assurance to the right of the minimum total quality cost point, for every $1 spent on prevention and appraisal costs, less than $1 is saved on failure costs.

This model is widely accepted as a method for analyzing quality cost relationships—as evidenced by the many versions of it reproduced in textbooks on operations research and in articles and monographs about quality control.[3] A similar version of the model has been copyrighted by the American Society for Quality Control, Inc.[4]

Applying the quality cost model

Unfortunately, the traditional model is not appropriate for today's business environment unless the cost of lost sales is included in external failure costs. Because of the pervasive emphasis on quality, today's cost systems are designed to track many of the costs listed in Exhibit 1. However, even though these quality costs are incorporated into the quality cost decision model, the cost of lost sales is usually ignored because it is difficult to quantify. As a result, the quality cost model may be classed with those cost systems that Robert Kaplan calls "stagnant" because they are designed primarily to support the preparation of external financial statements based on recorded, historical transactions.[5]

The traditional model for managing quality costs by determining the optimum quality cost point still has merit, but the model must be improved by making it recognize all relevant costs. Ignoring the cost of lost sales because the information is unavailable from historical transactions can lead to poor decisions about how much to spend on the various components of quality costs.

Measuring cost of lost sales

Although the cost of lost sales is difficult to quantify, it can—and should—be estimated. Market research should provide a point of departure for producing a reasonably good estimate of the cost of lost sales. For example, a firm's sales force knows its customers

and the effects of losing customers because of poor quality. Also, trends in a firm's market share lost to competitors can be analyzed. Based on the findings of market research, a projection can be made of future loss of contribution margin. This amount can then be discounted to its present value. Making estimates like this is not so radical. After all, future cash flows are estimated in evaluating capital budgeting decisions. Quality cost expenditures certainly can be regarded as a long-term investment decision.

Optimum quality costs ignoring cost of lost sales

The effect of failing to recognize the cost of lost sales in the quality cost model can be demonstrated best by comparing the optimum costs (i.e., the lowest point on the total quality cost curve) when the cost of lost sales is *not* included in failure costs to the optimum costs when the cost of lost sales *is* included in failure costs. In other words, "optimum quality costs ignoring cost of lost sales" include costs that are easily quantifiable and ascertainable—that is, quality costs that are captured from recorded, historical transactions. "Optimum quality costs including cost of lost sales" include the same easily quantifiable costs *plus* the cost of lost sales. (Note that from Exhibit 1 the cost of lost sales is one type of external failure cost.)

Exhibit 3 shows the relationships for quality costs when the costs do not include the cost of lost sales (i.e., the only quality costs considered are those from recorded, historical transactions). This graph is similar to the graph in Exhibit 2, except that the horizontal axis represents the number of defective units rather than the level of quality assurance. This modification makes the costs and quality assurance relationships easier to apply in practice. Now, the analysis is in terms of a decrease (increase) in the number of defective units, rather than an increase (decrease) in the level of quality assurance.

As with the graph in Exhibit 2, the vertical axis represents the amount spent on quality costs. Again, all components of prevention and appraisal costs are combined on one curve. Similarly, all components of internal and external failure costs are combined on

Exhibit 3. *Optimum Quality Costs Ignoring Cost of Lost Sales*

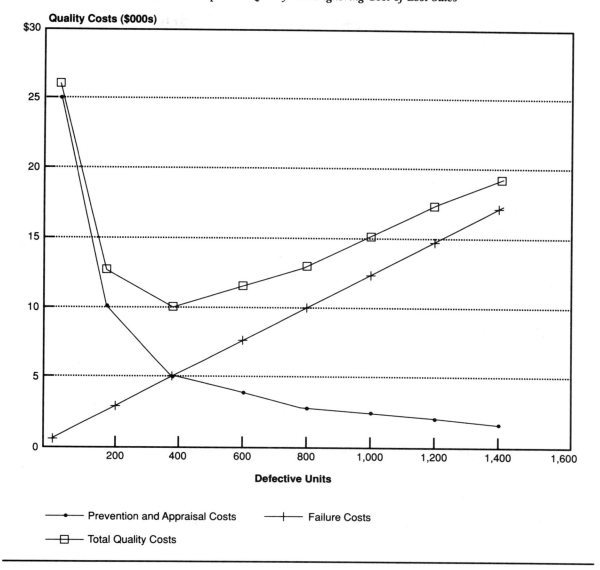

one curve. Since the horizontal axis has zero defective units at the origin, the direction of the slope of the two cost curves differs from the direction of the slope of the corresponding curves in Exhibit 2. That is, the prevention and appraisal cost curve slopes downward, and the failure cost curve slopes upward.

Note several important points about the relationship between prevention and appraisal costs and the number of defective units. The prevention and appraisal cost curve slopes downward because as prevention and appraisal costs decline, the number of defective units increases. Conversely, as prevention and appraisal costs increase, fewer units are defective. Also note that to achieve zero defects, prevention and appraisal costs approach infinity.[6] A final point to note is that prevention and appraisal costs drive the number of defective units, whether the defective units are discovered by the firm or by its customers.

Notice the direct relationship between the number of defective units and failure costs. The failure cost curve slopes upward because as defective units increase, so do failure costs. On the other hand, as defective units approach zero, so do failure costs. Unlike the

Exhibit 4. *Optimum Quality Costs Including Cost of Lost Sales*

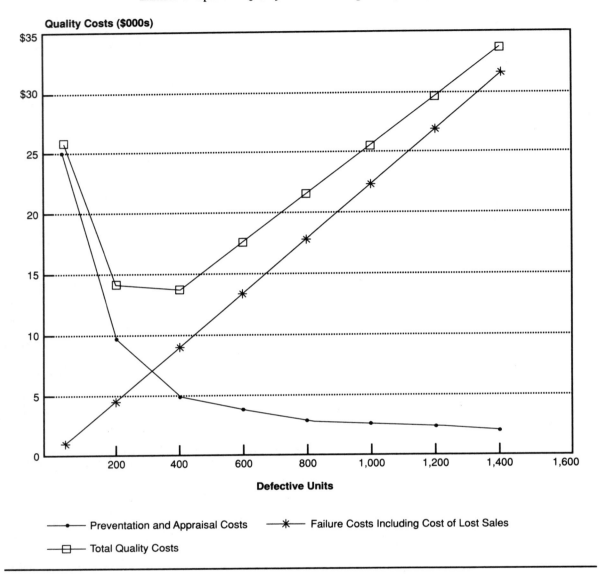

Quality Costs ($000s)

Defective Units

———•——— Prevention and Appraisal Costs   ———*——— Failure Costs Including Cost of Lost Sales

———☐——— Total Quality Costs

---

traditional model in Exhibit 2, the model in Exhibit 3 suggests a linear relationship between failure costs and the number of defective units.

Total costs. The total cost curve in Exhibit 3 represents the total prevention and appraisal costs plus failure costs for each number of defective units. As before, the minimum point on the total quality cost curve shows the optimum to spend on quality costs.

Exhibit 3 shows the indirect, cause-and-effect relationship between the sum of prevention and appraisal costs and failure costs.

To summarize, prevention and appraisal costs affect the number of defective units, and defective units affect failure costs.

In Exhibit 3, the minimum total quality cost is $10,000 when the cost of lost sales is ignored. Therefore, $10,000 would be the optimum quality cost target for the firm.

Effect of cost of lost sales on optimum quality costs

Exhibit 4, by contrast, shows the optimum quality costs that result when the cost of lost sales is included in the model—that is, qual-

Exhibit 5. *Data Points for Failure Costs in Exhibits 3 and 4*

(1) Number of Defective Units	(2) Failure Costs from Recorded Transactions* $12.50 × (1)	(3) Failure Costs from Recorded Transactions Plus Estimated Cost of Lost Sales** (2) + [$10 × (1)]
50	$ 625	$ 1,125
200	2,500	4,500
400	5,000	9,000
600	7,500	13,500
800	10,000	18,000
1,000	12,500	22,500
1,200	15,000	27,000
1,400	17,500	31,500

* Labeled "Failure Costs" in Exhibit 3.
** Labeled "Failure Costs Including Cost of Lost Sales" in Exhibit 4.

ity costs that arise from recorded, historical transactions (as shown in Exhibit 3) plus the cost of lost sales.

The prevention and appraisal cost curve is the same in Exhibit 4 as in Exhibit 3. The line in Exhibit 4 labeled "failure costs including cost of lost sales" includes the same costs in the line labeled "failure costs" in Exhibit 3, but it also includes an estimate of the cost of lost sales.

The data points for failure costs including the cost of lost sales are based on the assumption that the estimated cost of lost sales is $10 times the number of defective units. For example, if the number of defective units is 400 and failure costs based on recorded, historical transactions are $5,000, then failure costs based on transactions plus cost of lost sales are $5,000 + ($10 × 400), or $9,000. If the number of defective units is 1,000 and failure costs based on recorded transactions are $12,500, then failure costs based on transactions plus cost of lost sales are $12,500 + ($10 × 1,000), or $22,500. Exhibit 5 shows the data points for failure costs in Exhibits 3 and 4.

Although failure costs including the cost of lost sales are shown as a linear relationship with the number of defective units, the relationship may be nonlinear. In Exhibit 4, note that the slope of the curve for failure costs including cost of lost sales is steeper than the corresponding curve (i.e., the curve for fail-

ure costs ignoring the cost of lost sales) in Exhibit 3. Therefore, the optimum total quality costs in Exhibit 4 is $14,000, or $4,000 more than the optimum in Exhibit 3.

A comparison of Exhibits 3 and 4 shows that if a company relies on the information based solely on historical (i.e., the easily quantifiable) costs to determine the point at which costs and benefits are equal, the company will spend less to improve quality than it should. This can seriously jeopardize the company's future. Management should spend at least the minimum total quality cost after taking into account the cost of lost sales.

Optimal cost of quality in proper perspective

Modifying the quality cost model to include the cost of lost sales improves decision making. However, management runs the risk of not using the model correctly for today's business environment. Deciding how much to spend on quality costs based solely on the quality cost model may lull management into thinking it has made the best decision for the firm by limiting spending on quality to the minimum amount.

According to the model, the optimum quality cost is always at a point that allows some number of defective units. In Exhibit 4, adoption of $14,000 as the optimal amount of quality costs (i.e., the point at which $1 spent on prevention and appraisal results in $1 saved on failure costs) means accepting about 300 defective units out of total output of 1,600 units, or a quality assurance level of 81.25 percent.

Optimum competitive cost level. Users of the model must be aware that the optimum cost level is not necessarily the optimum *competitive* cost level. Total quality costs determined from this model are only one factor to be considered in deciding how much to spend on quality.

Another important factor that should be considered in deciding how much to spend on quality is the importance of one product to

---

The major categories of quality costs are prevention, appraisal, and failure. Since these costs are interrelated, the trick for management is to determine how much to spend on one category to balance out the amount spent on the others.

---

the success of another product or program. Consider the Hubble Space Telescope. In April 1990, the Discovery astronauts successfully deployed the $1.5-billion Hubble Space Telescope. The hope was that by sending a telescope beyond the distorting atmosphere of the Earth, scientists could make remarkable discoveries about the universe. One camera in the telescope would capture a great breadth of the universe, and another would obtain close-up pictures of the planets.[7]

These high hopes were dashed a few weeks later when a serious defect was discovered in one of the two mirrors that bring light into the telescope. Because of this defect, the pictures from the telescope are blurred. The problem cannot be corrected from the ground. Replacing the mirror is not feasible because astronauts would not be able to put the mirror in place while in orbit. Moreover, returning the telescope to earth risks contamination.[8] A recovery mission is scheduled for 1992 to replace one of the telescope's cameras

with an improved version to regain some of the telescope's capability.[9] The likely source of the defect was a mistake in grinding the glass for the mirror. Thus, a 100 percent level of quality assurance is required in a critical program such as the space program.

Quality as a marketing tool

Allowing minimum costs to determine management's quality objectives may squelch the opportunity to view quality as a marketing tool. Customers now often demand high-quality products. Indeed, W. Edwards Deming warns that management can no longer accept any level of defective workmanship.[10]

Although the fact is not always recognized, quality has become the ultimate marketing tool—indeed, perhaps a survival tool. Quality is not only a means for sustaining and expanding market share, but also the means by which a firm can command premium prices.

According to Armand Feigenbaum, chairman of General Systems, "More than 80 percent of the consumers we surveyed last year [in 1988] said that quality was more important than price. In 1978, only 30 percent said so."[11] Therefore, high quality may increase revenues so much that the increase more than offsets any increased costs to improve quality.

Today, many firms define quality in terms of customer satisfaction or meeting customer needs. This new model places the customer firmly in the equation by including the cost of lost sales in the measurement process. By focusing part of the measurement of quality cost on lost sales, this improved model requires management to bring the marketplace into the quality decision process. ▲

Notes
1. Stephen S. Cohen, director of Berkeley Roundtable on the International Economy, quoted in Otis Port, "How the New Math of Productivity Adds Up," *Business Week* (June 6, 1988): 104.
2. Otis Port, "How to Make It Right the First Time, A Revolutionary New Approach to Quality Control," *Business Week* (June 8, 1987): 142–143.

3. See, e.g., C.U. Chisholm, "Quality Assurance: A Review of Production Practice," *Quality Assurance* (June 1982): 55–60; Thomas P. Edmonds, Bor-Yi Tsay, and Wen-Wei Lin, "Analyzing Quality Costs," *Management Accounting,* (Nov. 1989): 25–29; Richard J. Schonberger and Edward M. Knod, Jr., *Operations Management: Serving the Customer,* 3rd ed. (Plano, Tex.: Business Publications, Inc., 1988); and J.M. Juran, *Quality Control Handbook,* 3rd ed. (New York: McGraw-Hill, 1974).

4. Jack Campanella and Frank J. Corcoran, "Principles of Quality Costs," *Quality Progress* (April 1983): 16–22.

5. Robert Kaplan, *Relevance Lost* (Boston: Harvard Business School Press, 1987).

6. For an excellent argument that it does not require infinite prevention and appraisal costs to reach zero defects, see Arthur M. Schneiderman, "Optimum Quality Costs and Zero Defects: Are They Contradictory Concepts?" *Quality Progress* (Nov. 1986): 28–31.

7. Sharon Begley, Mary Hager, Daniel Glick, Karen Springen, and Andrew Murr, "Heaven Can Wait," *Newsweek* (July 9, 1990): 48–55.

8. Begley, Hager, Glick, et al., "Heaven Can Wait."

9. Craig Covault, "NASA Fights Image, Technical Problems on Hubble Shuttle," *Aviation Week & Space Technology* (July 7, 1990): 16–18.

10. W. Edwards Deming, *Quality, Productivity, and Competitive Position* (Cambridge, Mass.: MIT Center for Advanced Engineering Study, 1982).

11. Janice Castro, "Making It Better," *Time* (November 13, 1989): 79.

Managers' Perceptions About Quality Costs

Lawrence P. Carr and Lawrence A. Ponemon

This column examines how managers view quality costs by comparing the perceptions of controllers and other key managers involved with quality management. The survey used shows that under conditions of worsening quality levels, most managers perceive prevention costs as decreasing and failure costs as increasing. General managers, however, tend to be inconsistent in their views of quality costs, which means that they may incorrectly perceive trade-offs between cost and quality.

Managers today understand that unsatisfactory quality means poor use of resources and, thus, higher costs. They also know that good quality can even reduce overall product costs.

Juran and the ASQC model

The general concept of the cost of quality was first introduced by Joseph Juran in 1951.[1] Juran advanced the view that an optimal quality level can be achieved by balancing the costs associated with product defects against the cost of quality control. Since then, the notion of quality costs has captured the attention of senior managers because of the high costs associated with poor quality. Many industries, for example, report a yearly cost of quality that exceeds 30 percent of sales revenue. As a result, many companies devote considerable resources to carefully tracking and reporting quality costs.[2]

The American Society for Quality Control (ASQC) provides a cost model to guide managers in the design of quality cost accounting systems.[3] Implicit in this model are the behaviors of four different quality cost subcategories as quality deteriorates. This column attempts to validate the ASQC cost model by examining the perceptions that managers have about quality costs in their firms. In particular, the column compares the perceptions of controllers versus the perceptions of other key managers who are involved in quality management.

Background

The ASQC model provides guidelines for defining, categorizing, and monitoring quality cost.[4] Quality cost is divided into two broad subcategories:

- The *cost of control* (which typically includes engineering, inspection, process control, and training costs incurred to prevent poor quality); and
- The *cost of failure to control* (which includes costs that result from poor quality, including rework, scrap, customer service, and warranty expenses).

Cost of control. The cost of control can be further divided into *prevention* cost and *appraisal* cost. Prevention deals with all activities (e.g., training and education) that a company employs to prevent quality problems from occurring. Appraisal refers to the early detection of possible quality control problems, such as inspections of material and process control. For example, companies may spend considerable prevention costs to properly engineer prototypes before they are placed into production. Companies also spend resources on appraisal costs to audit the quality of incoming materials or to inspect the precision levels of equipment before production begins.

Cost of failure to control. The cost of failure to control is caused by intermediate or final

Exhibit 1. *Cost Trade-Off Between Prevention and Correction Controls*

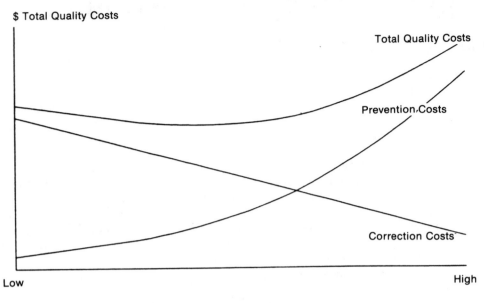

Prevention Cost: Includes both the cost of prevention appraisal activities (e.g., preventive maintenance, material controllers, engineering, lot and sample inspections for incoming materials).

Correction Cost: Includes both the cost of internal and external failure (e.g., rework, scrap, conversions, warranty claims, customer services, customer badwill, opportunity costs).

---

products that do not meet quality specifications. The cost of failure to control also includes two subcategories: *internal* failure cost and *external* failure cost. Internal failure refers to products or services that the company determines to be of unacceptable quality at some stage of the production process, thus requiring rework or resulting in scrap. External failure refers to the consequences of products or services that customers determine to be of poor quality.

Trade-offs

Implicit in the ASQC framework is the idea that balancing the trade-offs in various control activities will greatly improve the overall quality level, yet yield a substantial reduction in total operating costs. That is, a company with poor quality can greatly reduce the costs associated with internal and external failure by adding relatively inexpensive preventive measures.

At a certain point, however, additional prevention costs will only increase total quality costs, as Exhibit 1 illustrates. As Exhibit 1 shows, overall quality control costs at first decline (although at a decreasing rate) as prevention controls are introduced. At the same time, costs of correction decrease. But the rate of improvement in total quality costs continues to diminish until, finally, marginal increases in prevention costs cause increases—rather than decreases—in total quality costs. The minimum of the total quality cost curve (and, thus, the optimal level of control) occurs at the point where the cost of correction and the cost of prevention curves intersect. In other words, more prevention produces comparatively little decrease in correction costs, which means an overall increase in total quality costs.

An understanding of quality cost can help managers identify those areas in the production of goods or services where corrective action will produce major quality improvements and savings. Cost data can be useful in detecting those products that require further engineering and redesign to reduce scrap and reworking cost. Cost data can help identify defective output before materials and labor are committed (and, thus, before costly disassembly and rework become necessary). Finally, quality cost accounting can redirect quality control priorities. For example, cost data can be used in decisions about whether to eliminate inspections at stations where no problems have occurred.

Perception study

Of fundamental importance to the analysis of quality control goals and programs is management's prediction of quality cost behavior in relation to various control levels. This study examines the perceptions of 117 key managers—all involved in various aspects of quality management—about the behavior of the four quality cost subcategories in relation to worsening quality levels. The managers involved in the study were selected from eleven high-technology manufacturing firms in the Northeast. At each company, at least one manager was chosen from each of the following functions:

1. *Accounting.* The divisional controller of the business entity;
2. *Production.* The vice-president of manufacturing;
3. *Marketing and customer service.* The vice-president of marketing or sales; and
4. *General management.* The chief executive officer, chief operating officer, or general manager.

In most of the companies, the controller (or a designated representative from accounting) was not directly involved in the management of quality control programs. In all cases, those chosen from general management were the senior managers in the firms.

Each manager completed a survey under the supervision of the researchers. The managers were asked to express an opinion about the behavior of quality cost subcategories (i.e., prevention, appraisal, internal failure, and external failure) in terms of their own companies. Managers selected one of the seven different cost behaviors shown in Exhibit 2 to

represent the relationship between the behavior of the four subcategories of quality cost and deteriorating quality.

Exhibit 3 illustrates, in percentage bar chart form, the managers' rating of the seven cost behaviors for each of the four subcategories of quality cost. The managers generally agreed about the behavior of prevention costs, internal failure costs, and external failure costs. Their perceptions about appraisal costs, however, follow no discernible pattern.

Managers—especially those in the accounting and marketing functions—generally perceive the cost trade-offs that exist between control and the failure to control quality.

Interpreting the responses. As the graphs in Exhibit 2 show, in the face of worsening quality, about 87 percent of the managers expect prevention costs to decrease (i.e., 87 percent is the sum of the percentages shown for the first three curves shown in Panel A of Exhibit 2); 85 percent perceive internal failure cost as increasing (see Panel C of Exhibit 2), and 80 percent perceive external failure cost as increasing (see Panel D of Exhibit 2).

Further, more than 41 percent of these managers perceive prevention costs as decreasing at a decreasing rate (see Curve 3 in Panel A). More than 48 percent perceive internal failure as increasing at a constant rate, and 36 percent rate external failure as increasing at an increasing rate.

At first glance, the perceptions of the managers in this survey seem consistent with the cost relationships shown in Exhibit 1, in which increased prevention costs at least initially lead to decreases in correction costs.

Varying perceptions of controllers and other managers

Exhibit 4 illustrates in bar chart form, for each subcategory of quality cost, the percent-

Exhibit 2. *Seven Cost Behaviors Associated With Decreasing Quality Levels*

Cost Curves

1. Decreases at an increasing rate

2. Decreases at a constant rate

3. Decreases at a decreasing rate

4. Stays constant

5. Increases at a decreasing rate

6. Increases at a constant rate

7. Increases at an increasing rate

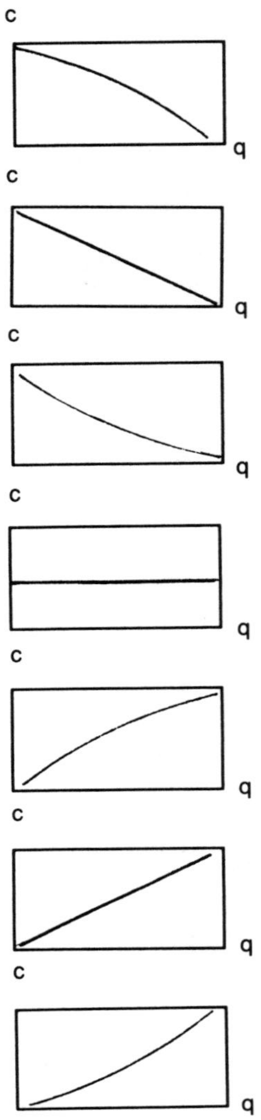

c denotes increasing costs; q denotes worsening quality levels.

---

age cost rating by area of management within the organization. As the exhibit shows, the perceptions of controllers and marketing managers are generally consistent. In terms of the ASQC cost model, controllers and marketing managers are more likely than production or general managers to view quality cost behavior correctly.

For example, more than 68 percent of controllers and 58 percent of marketing managers rate prevention cost as decreasing at a decreasing rate as quality declines (which is

correct), while only 32 percent of production managers and 31 percent of general managers perceive this to be the case. Further, many general managers view the cost behavior of prevention costs quite differently, for 32 percent (wrongly) perceive prevention costs as increasing at an increasing rate.

To better understand why differences in perceptions exist across management areas, interviews were conducted with some of the participants. The salient finding was that controllers and marketing managers seem to un-

Exhibit 3. *Quality Cost Subcategories by Seven Cost Behaviors*

Panel A
Prevention Cost

Panel B
Appraisal Cost

Panel C
Internal Failure Cost

Panel D
External Failure Cost

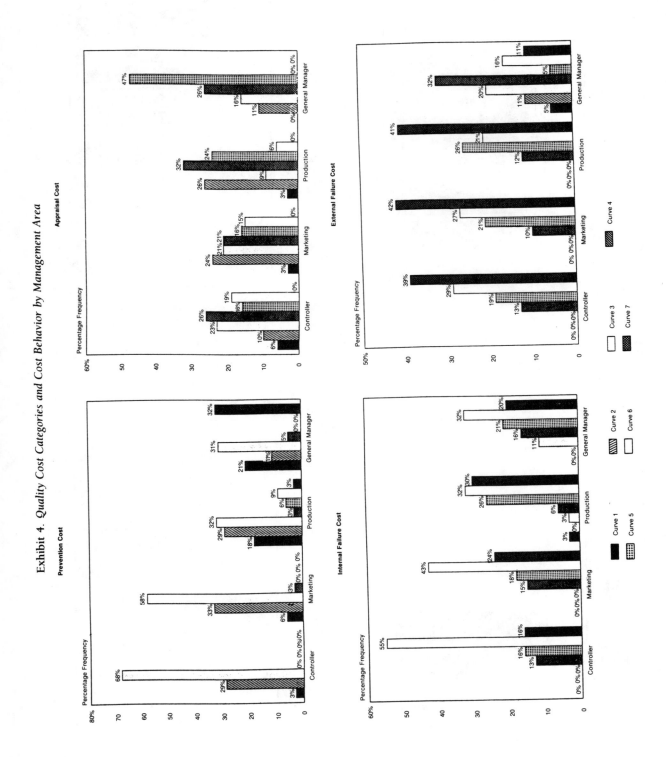

Exhibit 4. Quality Cost Categories and Cost Behavior by Management Area

derstand that prevention controls are incurred to increase quality. Thus, worsening quality generally means that not enough prevention controls are in place. Several of the production and general managers who were interviewed, however, tended to view all quality costs as reactions to poor quality. In other words, as quality improved, all quality costs would decline. Hence, perfect quality meant zero costs (in accordance with the "quality is free" theory).[5]

Conclusion

This article provides evidence that managers—especially those in the accounting and marketing functions—generally perceive the cost trade-offs that exist between control and the failure to control quality. The managers' perceptions suggest that worsening quality occurs (as the ASQC model suggests) as prevention costs decrease and failure costs increase. While most managers seem to have correct perceptions about quality cost, general managers were least able to perceive the trade-offs between cost and quality that exist in terms of the subcategories of prevention costs and failure costs. This finding should be of concern, because differences in how various managers perceive quality costs can lead to conflict and resistance to cost of quality programs.

The responsibility for quality control programs has typically been the domain of production or general management. Controllers or accounting managers support quality programs by providing needed accounting data, but they are often excluded from decisions involving the company's overall strategy for quality. In light of these findings, perhaps controllers and accounting managers should play a greater role in planning quality strategies and in managing quality programs. ▲

Notes
1. J.M. Juran, *Quality Control Handbook* (New York: McGraw-Hill 1951).
2. J. Clark, "Costing for Quality at Celanese," *Management Accounting* 42–46 (Mar. 1985).
3. American Society for Quality Control, *Accounting for Quality Costs* (Milwaukee, Wis.: ASQC 1986).
4. *Id.*
5. P. Crosby, *Quality Is Free* (New York: McGraw-Hill 1979).

PART *L*

Strategic Cost Management

Taking Strategy to the Bottom Line

John Gurrad and Scott Belser

Many companies try to connect strategy with the financial plans that actually guide managers' actions, but few have devised good linkages. Financial plans such as sales quotas, manufacturing plans, and departmental budgets are typically focused on the short term, but financial managers must always follow fundamental corporate strategies. If financial decision making ever becomes isolated from strategy, the company's long-term strategies can be damaged. This case study lays out the steps that one company took to integrate strategic and financial planning.

One of the greatest hazards of strategic planning is the disconnection between a company's strategy and its financial plans. Managers become driven only by making their numbers and not by achieving strategic goals; strategy becomes just a game.

Strategic planning and finance must work together and relate closely to each other. Senior managers well understand the potential dangers of separating strategy from practical financial planning. Without close linkage between the two, both disciplines lose much of their value.

Strategic planners must build their ideas on realistic financial constraints and on an assessment of opportunities. Plans that rely on overoptimistic assumptions about costs, prices, or capital requirements are useless. In fact, impractical plans can be harmful to achieving strategic objectives. They may distract managers from beneficial plans that can be implemented. In addition, they may lessen managers' belief in the value of strategy and discourage them from long-range thinking.

Financial managers' plans must follow fundamental corporate strategy; strategy is the underlying driver of finance. If isolated from strategic drivers, finance-oriented decisions can easily damage a company's long-term objectives. Cost-cutting plans that reduce research investments can hurt the company's long-term technology. Short-term profit thresholds can prevent penetration of valuable new markets that are slow to develop.

Financial plans are typically short-term focused. Some common forms of financial planning—sales quotas, manufacturing plans, departmental budgets—are usually oriented toward only one year. A solid strategic planning process forces companies to consider the long-term effects of their decisions.

Foreign companies, especially those in Asia, seem better able to align financial goals with long-term strategic interests. CEOs, CFOs, and senior planners of US companies must devote increasing attention to overcoming this strategic and financial disconnect.

Concerns about the integration of strategic and financial planning have recently become important for American President Companies (APC), a $2.5-billion container transportation company headquartered in Oakland CA. Its ships carry container cargo between Asia, the Middle East, and North America; an extensive double-stack rail network delivers freight within North America.

A critical upgrade

Traditionally, the company had only limited and sporadic long-range planning (e.g., for major vessel investments). It primarily relied on annual financial plans. However, recent

Exhibit 1. *APC's Integrated Planning Process*

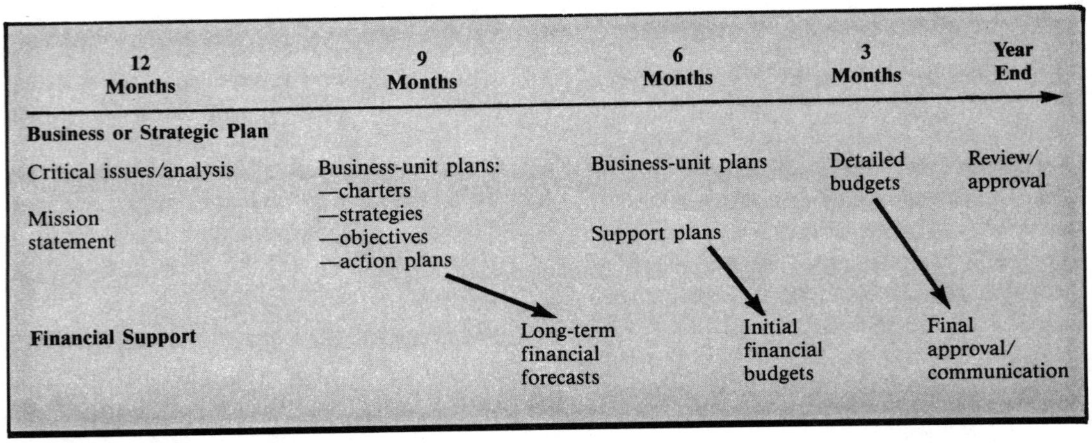

12 Months	9 Months	6 Months	3 Months	Year End

Business or Strategic Plan

Critical issues/analysis

Mission statement

Business-unit plans:
—charters
—strategies
—objectives
—action plans

Business-unit plans

Support plans

Detailed budgets

Review/ approval

Financial Support

Long-term financial forecasts

Initial financial budgets

Final approval/ communication

---

industry trends and a disappointing financial performance forced APC to improve all its planning. Some of these factors include the following:

- Companies supported by foreign governments pose strong low-price competition.
- Pacific Rim trade growth is slowing and new trade patterns are emerging.
- Customer transportation requirements are becoming more demanding.
- Market differentiation is more difficult to achieve.
- Information technology is increasing the cost of providing quality service.

Senior management was determined to upgrade and link business planning across APC. It set forth a process that is now well on its way to being implemented.

The APC process explicitly seeks to ensure close coordination of all planning throughout the company. Among its key tenets:

1. *Focus on both long- and short-range plans.* The business planning process is continuous, designed to link general strategies, annual business plans, and ultimately short-range financial plans. The most important link is to the budget, which reflects the business plan in financial terms.

2. *Align corporate strategies with business-unit plans.* With operations in many countries, APC has a number of different business

units and international operational units. Therefore, a key goal is to ensure good coordination among the company's dispersed organizations.

3. *Develop strategies by involving and communicating broadly with employees.* On one hand, the process works to ensure that all employees know the company's fundamental direction and their personal priorities in achieving those objectives. Good communication from top management is critical. On the other hand, the process also seeks the participation and ownership of employees in strategy development. Good upward communication is also crucial.

4. *Link organizational objectives with individual objectives.* The process calls for individual action plans to align with corporate business plans. In this way, individuals can be held accountable for their contribution to the plan's success.

5. *Monitor business plans against concrete actions and measurable standards.* Successful implementation requires a clear way to determine whether plan goals are achieved. To the maximum extent possible, the business plans should include action plans and objectives (i.e., success measures that are both verifiable and quantitative). Such measures should then be monitored on an ongoing basis for reward or corrective action.

The planning schedule

The company has used these general principles to design a process that coordinates annual business and financial planning with long-range planning. It is a year-long process composed of five principal steps (see Exhibit 1).

☐ **Step one: Initiate planning and set overall goals.** In early February of each year, senior corporate and business-unit executives meet to consider the company's long-range direction and goals. The meeting typically includes the top 25 to 30 corporate and business-unit managers. They gather offsite to review a detailed situation analysis, which contains information on industry and market trends, customers, competitors, and the company itself. They identify and discuss the critical strategic issues facing the company in the next three to five years and reexamine the company's mission statement, strategies, and objectives in light of the situation analysis and critical issues.

The product of these sessions includes an overall assessment of the company's strengths, weaknesses, opportunities, and threats (a SWOT analysis); a modified definition of the core business-mission statement; and, if necessary, revised strategies and objectives.

"In early February of each year, corporate and business-unit managers gather offsite to review information on industry trends, customers, competitors, and the company itself."

APC's executive committee works with the business planning department to refine the work of the 25 to 30 members of the APC senior management group. By the end of March, it approves a final version of the corporate mission statement, general strategies, and long-range objectives.

In later years of the planning cycle, underlying corporate positions such as the mission statement or general strategies require only affirmation and fine-tuning. They are expected to remain valid for three to five years. The company can give proportionately greater attention to annual action plans and financial implications.

☐ **Step two: Business-unit plans.** Beginning in April, the business units (American President Lines, APL Land Transport, and APL Information Services) use the corporate plans to develop their own specific plans. Senior managers within each unit meet to define their business-unit charters, which are similar to the corporate mission statements but specific to business-unit circumstances.

Over the next two months, the business units also develop their own general strategies and long-range objectives; these are then aligned with the corporate plan. In addition, business units form teams to develop year-by-year, step-by-step action plans. The executive committee approves their work by the end of May.

A number of managers throughout the organization participate in the planning process. The business planning department communicates initial results from senior management's meeting to the field organization. Field managers provide their input. In one instance, the top 40 managers within one of the company's business units (American President Lines) held a first-time-ever meeting in Asia to finalize their charter, strategies, and objectives and to organize special teams to help define action plans.

During this period, the business units also begin a crucial step: they start to quantify the financial impact of their objectives and action plans. Wherever possible, they estimate the revenues and costs associated with activities included in the plans.

☐ **Step three: Annual plans.** The long-range plans developed in the winter and spring form the basis for annual planning starting in June. The business units and key corporate support functions (e.g., human resources, systems, finance) define their annual business plans and align them with long-range objectives. The annual business plans include key activities, internal and external assumptions, and broad financial forecasts. They define resource requirements and set priorities. By mid-September, the executive committee approves final plans.

☐ **Step four: Budgets.** After approval of annual business plans, the business units and support functions develop detailed budgets. These budgets "price out" the actions included in the business plans.

☐ **Step five: Final approval.** By early December, the executive committee reviews and approves final budgets for all levels of the company. The board of directors also reviews major elements of plans and budgets. The plans become effective upon final board ratification.

Making planning work

The company's planning process includes several key features. First, senior management has made it very clear to the entire organization that the integrated business planning process has its full support. The CEO sponsored the development of the planning process. Other members of the senior management team attend many of the planning sessions with middle managers. Periodic review by the executive committee demonstrates continuing interest in the results of the planning.

Second, the business planning department took great care in developing a successful planning process. With senior executives' endorsement, a cross-functional team devoted significant effort to defining a workable process with broad support. The team interviewed line managers, studied external sources, and gradually refined their proposals for inputs, outputs, and formats before finalizing their recommendations. This concern for process also included a follow-up survey during the initial planning phases. The survey recorded line managers' feedback and formed the basis for further modifications.

In general, the business planning department plays a significant role in facilitating all aspects of the process. (In the follow-up survey, respondents rated process facilitation as the best aspect of the experience.) APC has small planning departments at the corporate level and in each of the major business units. The directors of business planning lead development of the overall process and help coordinate planning at the business-unit and corporate levels. In addition, the directors communicate interim results and get feedback from the field organization to increase the field's understanding and input to the plans.

Third, the planning process builds on a solid foundation of managers' communication skills. During the late 1980s, APC began a major initiative to implement a quality program throughout the company. A key aspect of the initiative was increased experience in

---

"A follow-up survey indicated line managers felt that developing measurable objectives and realistic action plans was difficult and too time-consuming."

---

group problem-solving and consensus building. Managers across the company had been meeting several times a year to discuss key problems and solutions. The resulting improvement in teamwork and communication skills were critical to the success of the company's overall planning efforts.

The remaining challenges

Planning at APC is still evolving. Senior management expects that ongoing adjustments will be necessary as circumstances change and the organization gains more experience with planning. Additional efforts will continue to resolve the final issues that remain. These include the following:

☐ **Unrealistic expectations.** One potential pitfall is expecting too much too soon. Real organizational change often requires several years. There is always the temptation to demand faster change and quicker success. The organization may become discouraged if problems persist.

An initial follow-up survey indicated a sense of frustration among line managers; they felt that developing measurable objectives and realistic action plans was difficult and too time-consuming. APC's planning staff are working with line managers to refine the estimates of the time required to develop objectives and action plans.

Senior management and planners must be careful to manage expectations. They must avoid organizational burnout and temper enthusiasm to accomplish the plan's objectives.

☐ **The right information.** Another significant pitfall in any action planning is making decisions without the right information. An invaluable result of APC's planning has been to focus its needs for information. Important information was sometimes not readily available. In other instances, the information required additional analysis before being used. As a result, many long-range action plans included a multiyear program of gathering the right data, analyzing this data, and developing more specific action plans based on solid information.

Companies should carefully consider their needs to develop a useful strategic data base. APC is working to strengthen

- Internal data, especially on costs and operating statistics.
- Customer data, such as customer surveys.
- Competitor data, especially on costs.

☐ **Quantification and measurement.** A continuing concern in planning is effective measurement. A key element of APC's measurement program is setting quantitative targets that can be independently observed. However, the company's efforts to be more quantitative have proved to be challenging. (Many US companies have experienced similar difficulties in adopting the quantitative techniques of Japanese organizations.)

In some cases, managers have been reluctant to become too specific in their objectives. As success criteria become more concrete, individuals can be more readily held accountable for their performance. Managers may become uncomfortable or afraid that measures will be used negatively. This reluctance has compounded the difficulties in defining quantitative standards.

The planning staff is working with managers to define the kinds of positive standards they use to judge performance. They anticipate that a set of quantified measures will emerge over the next several years.

☐ **Management involvement.** Another issue is ensuring the right balance of management involvement. APC management is convinced

that broad participation by managers at many levels is vital to success. Without real participation, there is little chance for ownership and commitment to the plan. Involvement in the planning process also increases better communication and understanding of basic corporate strategies.

At the same time, senior management must be visibly involved. By adding a generalist perspective, their participation in meetings is critical for resolving key disputes and showing support for the planning process.

The danger is that senior management leadership that is too strong may discourage participation among down-the-line managers. Middle managers may be reluctant to discuss ideas that contradict the views of senior management, particularly if they are strongly stated.

APC is still exploring the best ways to enlist line involvement. Meetings in which senior managers are not present have sometimes been found to encourage more creative thinking. Planning staff have also solicited individual views—either directly or through the mail.

"A continuing concern in planning is good measurement. Yet, managers may become uncomfortable or afraid that measures will be used negatively."

The final APC process may very well evolve into a mix of forums for participation. Some face-to-face meetings may include senior management; others may not. Electronic communications, such as voice mail, fax, or E-mail, are additional alternatives.

☐ **Individual incentives.** A major pitfall of planning is a failure to provide incentives for implementation. APC is currently launching a program to integrate action plans into its individual performance system. In several business units, individuals' annual reviews include evaluations of their contributions to accomplish the action plans. Thus, monitoring of the business plan will occur concurrently with monitoring of individual activity. APC management expects several years to be needed for full integration.

The experience at APC has shown that strategic and financial planning can be integrated more completely if there is a clear management intention to do so. The competitive environment of the 1990s makes it imperative that strategy drive finance—but in a way that reflects financial realities.

When management recognizes the need for integration, it must establish a solid planning process. The effective process must include a closely coordinated schedule, the willing cooperation of all managers, and rigorous follow-up. ▲

Invest in a High-Yield Strategic Plan

Arnold S. Judson

Successful implementation of strategy depends on how effectively certain changes can be made to operating systems. For one thing, performance measurement systems institutionalize the status quo at the functional or departmental level. For strategy to be successful, senior executives must first acknowledge the barriers that block lasting change from occurring in their organizations, then help transform the way that people, processes, and systems work.

Most senior executives admit that they continue to be frustrated with the low yield from their investment in strategic planning. I estimate that U.S. firms are currently spending well over $10 billion annually in analyzing their industries, markets, and competitors, and then formulating plans for their strategic business units (SBUs) and their corporations. Yet studies suggest that fewer than 10 percent of these plans ever get implemented as intended.

Why is this track record so poor? There are at least three fundamental reasons. One is that the senior executives who actually formulate strategic plans underestimate what it takes to execute them. They often fail to appreciate the nature and magnitude of the many changes that must be made in how their organization, people, processes, and systems work in order to achieve the improvements in performance associated with a particular strategy.

Consider a large engineering/construction firm that decided to change its strategy because its traditional business of designing and building nuclear generating plants for electric utilities had dried up. Top management, in addition to its traditional business, decided to target smaller-scale projects and provide ongoing maintenance services. The company failed in its efforts to implement this strategy. The organization, systems, and procedures designed to handle projects of enormous scale proved unable to develop the nimbleness and responsiveness required for small projects. Further, the customer service mindset and associated behavior needed to provide effective maintenance was alien to the firm's culture.

A second reason for failures in implementation is that managements fail to specify in sufficient detail the work required to execute strategies: who must do what, when, and with what resources and accountabilities. In order for such work to get done, every person involved needs to understand what must be done differently, how, why, and when, along with the resources available. Almost every strategic plan I have ever seen either fails to describe this information or treats it in vague terms.

Strategies also fail to be implemented for a third reason: Managements do not realign measures, controls, information, rewards, and communications to support new strategies. All these processes, systems, and procedures are the products of past history and tend to be already in place and often well established in the way the organization works. They may or may not be appropriate to support new strategies, especially when these call for changes in direction. When existing systems and processes are misaligned with the new strategies, their power can easily undermine or defeat efforts at implementation.

A common example is the budget. The budget process is often decoupled from the strategy formulation process. If there are insufficient funds in the budget to meet the needs of strategy execution, it is the budget that typically prevails at the expense of the strategy.

Revise the operating system

Although each of these three deficiencies constitutes a barrier to successful strategy implementation, it can be transformed into a gateway. The key to this gateway is that successful strategy implementation depends on how effectively certain changes can be made to operating systems.

Every SBU depends on one or more operating systems within the organization to carry on its business and to execute its strategies. Almost every strategy is aimed at improving business performance in one or more dimensions: faster growth, more share of market, better returns, higher profits, etc. Typically, such strategies call for the organization as a whole, with each of its component departments and the people in each department, to operate differently.

For example, one strategy may require new products and services that better meet customers' needs to be brought to market in half the time. Another strategy requires substantial improvements in the quality of market offerings. A third strategy may press for more aggressive pricing, as a result of greatly reduced costs.

Successful implementation of such strategies often requires fundamental changes in the behavior of the existing operating system(s). Each includes all the functions, people, technology, work flows, policies, procedures, and institutional systems (e.g., planning, information [including performance measures], control, rewards, communications) and the way these interact to carry on the business. Each operating system has its own culture and performance capabilities (strong and weak), including an inherent ability to resist change. Any operating system tends to have a high level of inertia.

One element in any operating system is exceptionally powerful in perpetuating established behavioral norms. This is the set of performance measures institutionalized at the function or departmental level. These measures provide the day-to-day indices by which each department's managers and employees both determine the objectives and priorities for allocating personal time and effort, and assess the adequacy of both individual and departmental performance.

It is difficult to anticipate accurately how any changes required by a business strategy will affect the operating system (e.g., changed functional roles, changes in how functions must interact, changed priorities, new technology, etc.). It takes extraordinary managerial effort—including a keen understanding of what drives successful implementation—to achieve the desired changes.

Successful strategy execution requires changes in the relevant operating system(s) at two levels. One level is systemic. For example, a plan might call for the installation of work cells in a manufacturing process, the development of a greater sensitivity to and emphasis on customers and service, or the redesign of a new product introduction process. Once these systemic changes have been achieved, a monitoring procedure based only on the plan itself would signal that implementation was complete.

Yet the gains intended by such changes would not be realized until a consistent change in the way the operating system works had been achieved over time. Thus, full implementation of a strategy requires the completion of two phases: (1) initial *installation* of changes to the operating system specified by the plan; and (2) making these installations *operational* over time.

In my experience, the key to successful strategy implementation by an operating system lies in its ability to focus on a relatively few key issues and to maintain this focus for a substantial period of time—long enough to achieve the required resolutions after the completion of the installation phase.

At the other operating system level of individual manager, supervisor, and employee, successful strategy implementation often requires durable changes in personal behavior. These changes typically require each individual to replace familiar, well-established activities with modified or new ones. Often, new skills must be learned. The impetus for such changes in behavior is altered priorities and the need to develop and sustain focus on a few key issues and tasks.[1]

Even when there is a strong, widely shared commitment to carry out a strategy, initial good intentions quickly fade. Implementation breaks down as normal day-to-day pressures and crises cause people to shift their priorities and diffuse their efforts. What begins as an attempt to carry out a particular set of actions to implement a strategy soon degenerates into business as usual. Only some actions get installed, and those that are apparently complete never see full realization in the operational phase.

There are three powerful antidotes to these implementation barriers. Measures and controls carefully aligned to focus everyone's attention on the areas of gain intended to be achieved by the strategy must be established—not only at the systemic level but also within each department. These measures must then be coupled with a systematic feedback and implementation progress monitoring process, and to the reward and compensation system.

Implementation failures

When formulating strategy, why have so many executives failed (1) to understand what changes must be put in place to improve the way their organizations work; (2) to specify the work required to make these changes; and (3) to realign established processes, systems, and procedures? Essentially, these failures can be attributed to the following points.

Few senior executives I have worked with perceive that the essence of successful strategy implementation depends on their ability to change profoundly how their organizations, people, systems, and processes work. They tend to ignore that their organizations are made up of a collection of overlapping operating systems, combinations of which support each SBU. They seldom perceive that achieving strategic objectives almost always requires fundamental and lasting changes in the way these operating systems work. And they fail to understand the subtlety, complexity, and power of the many forces at work within each operating system, all of which combine to sustain the status quo.

Often, the most powerful forces are deeply rooted in the company's culture. A leading paint manufacturer, dismayed by an eroding market share, embarked on a strategy aimed at recapturing customers. Several market studies revealed that customers no longer could distinguish this company's superior paint quality from the adequate quality offered by its many competitors. Attracted by the lower prices set by the competition, customers were no longer willing to pay the premium price for the leading manufacturer's superior-quality paint.

> *"A leading paint manufacturer's effort to launch a strategy based on aggressive price reductions failed. Its entire operating system was attuned to producing premium-quality paint for premium prices."*

An effort to launch a strategy based on aggressive price reductions failed. Many years of proud conviction that the superiority of its paint commanded a premium price led to the company's stubborn refusal to accept the findings of several market studies. Its entire operating system was attuned to producing premium-quality paint for premium prices.

Senior executives frequently lack detailed knowledge of how their operating systems actually work to support strategy execution. Such knowledge is essential to specify the work required to make the necessary changes in these operating systems, which will ensure that strategies are actually implemented. These are typically changes to work flows, systems, procedures, practices, processes, and structure.

Usually, executives who formulate business strategy are far removed from operations. They seldom know what and how many changes made to elements of the operating system will have sufficient leverage to change the way the entire system works. This lack of detailed knowledge is exacerbated when the executive comes from another company or from another industry. However, managers and supervisors at lower levels in the hierarchy who do have this knowledge are seldom involved in formulating either strategic or operating plans.

Senior executives often assume that when their company's intended strategy is based on a sound understanding and careful analysis of the environment, industry, markets, competition, and the company's strengths and weaknesses, everyone required to execute this strategy will readily accept and enthusiastically do what is necessary to ensure that the strategy is successfully implemented. Unfortunately, such assumptions are seldom justified.

"A cultural characteristic in U.S. industry seems to be a craving for quick, painless fixes to difficult problems."

Because middle- and lower-level managers and supervisors are more aware than senior executives of the difficulties entailed in changing operating systems in order to execute a new strategy, the credibility of the strategy often suffers. When such managers and supervisors fear that they may have more to lose than to gain from the required changes to the operating system, their behavior may become more resistant than supportive.

U.S. executives tend to have a distaste for complexity. A cultural characteristic in U.S. industry seems to be a craving for quick, painless fixes to difficult problems.

Unfortunately, each operating system in a company is made up of many different elements (e.g., structural functions, work flows, people, systems, processes, etc.) that interact in complicated, subtle ways. Achieving desired changes in how such operating systems function to support strategy execution requires an understanding of the many forces at work, a recognition of their complexities and ambiguities, and a willingness to engage them.

Transform barriers into gateways

There are five steps senior managers can take to transform the major barriers to successful strategy execution into gateways to achieve their strategic objectives.

First, executives must define each operating system within their organization that is relevant to carrying out a particular business strategy. In a relatively small organization engaged in a single business and housed in a single facility, the operating system *is* the entire organization. But often the organization is large, engaged in several different businesses, each with its own strategy, and housed in many dispersed facilities. Identifying and matching operating systems to businesses and strategies is more difficult.

In such instances, the starting point is often an SBU. Then one must identify all the functions, work flows, processes, systems, and facilities required to support that SBU's business and execute its strategy. The boundaries of each operating system will seldom coincide with what appears in organization charts.

The second step involves identifying the special demands or strategic imperatives made by the strategy on its supporting operating system(s). For example, a strategy aimed at achieving greater market penetration may require greater flexibility in pricing and greater emphasis on satisfying customers with after-sales services. Such a strategy will demand from the supporting operating system(s) both more emphasis on reducing total costs and improved flexibility in the system's ability to respond to customers' service requirements.

Priorities can be determined by assessing the gap between the urgency of the strategic imperative and the system's current level of performance relevant to each imperative. The greater the gap, the higher the priority.

The third step is to identify both drivers and obstacles to making changes in the operating system, so as to close the gaps identified by the strategic imperatives.

Some initial objective research is usually necessary to develop a comprehensive picture or how the operating system is currently working. This information can then be examined systematically by a group of senior-, middle-, and lower-level managers and supervisors, who represent the key players in the operating system. Such a group can readily identify dysfunctional areas and their underlying causes. These areas can then be prioritized by their potential to change total system behavior in the desired directions.

The fourth step is to substitute a new kind of operating plan, which will describe what needs to change. An operating plan is the appropriate vehicle for describing what needs to change, why, how, when, with what resources, and with what accountabilities. Such a plan must be driven by the business strategy and closely aligned with it. This is achieved by using the SBU to define the operating system(s) and by using its business strategy to define the demands being made on the operating system.

The objectives for the operating plan can then be developed by relating the major causes for dysfunctions in the operating system to the strategic imperatives. These imperatives are also the basis for selecting the

---

"No operating plan should be regarded as valid for more than six to nine months."

---

strategies that will provide the foundation for the operating plan, along with the action plans for executing these strategies. Collectively, these action plans describe what must be done to implement the business strategy.

By enlisting and mobilizing the collective intelligence of the key players in the operating system to formulate this kind of operating plan, two distinct benefits are achieved. One is that the plan itself is founded on a solid understanding of the detailed workings of the operating system. Thus, the plan is realistically based, highly credible, and on target.

The other benefit is a buy-in by key managers and supervisors who must carry out the plan and make the required changes to the operating system. Because the operating plan is "owned" by those who formulated it, its successful execution is assured by the high level

of understanding and commitment developed by those responsible and accountable.

A fifth step senior executives can take is to put in place mechanisms that will ensure effective execution of the operating plan. These mechanisms are systematic processes for measuring, tracking, and monitoring the progress of plan implementation, along with updating and revising the operating plan (when appropriate).

Measures must be devised and established for the operating system as a whole and for each organizational function or department within that system. These should measure accomplishment against plan goals, both for the plan as a whole and for each individual strategy or program in the plan. Such measures, coupled with a systematic process for reviewing and discussing the experience of actually executing each step in the operating plan's action programs, are the most powerful mechanisms I know to sustain implementation momentum and focus.

A monitoring procedure should be instituted whereby all the managers accountable for operating plan implementation (including those accountable for each action step or task) meet at least quarterly to share and discuss experiences and accomplishments as they execute the plan. Each formal review session should also include a review of performance as a function of the measures employed, along with a reconsideration of the relevance of the measures themselves.

Each such review should include a reconsideration of the plan itself and any desirable additions or modifications indicated by the experience gained in implementation. No plan should be regarded as valid for more than six to nine months. Such a monitoring procedure will ensure that the plan remains vital and relevant over time.

Conclusion

By changing the way senior executives view and practice strategy implementation, they can effectively transform barriers to business strategy into gateways for successful execution.

By recognizing that strategy execution depends on management's ability to change how the relevant operating systems function, and by appreciating what is involved in achieving durable change, senior executives can avoid the trap of underestimating the complexities and effort required to implement strategy. By involving middle- and lower-level managers and supervisors in formulating operating plans and providing detailed action programs, senior executives can ensure that everyone

---

"Senior executives must value the need to achieve buy-in for the strategy from those who must make it happen."

---

responsible for carrying out the strategy will have individual road maps.

By addressing the problem of transforming operating system behavior to achieve large system change, senior executives can ensure that budgets, controls, rewards, and information are on the agenda as the operating plan is formulated. In this context, these systems and processes are considered and realigned if

appropriate to support business strategy implementation.

Senior executives will be successful in improving the probabilities that their strategies will be executed only if they abandon the notion that middle- and lower-level managers and supervisors will have the same perceptions of business strategy, its underlying rationale, and its urgency as their own. Instead, they must assume the opposite. They must value the need to achieve buy-in for the strategy from those who must make it happen. ▲

Note
1. Such efforts to change individual and small-group behavior are often met with resistance. How such resistance can be minimized is discussed in my book, *Changing Behavior in Organizations: Minimizing Resistance to Changes* (Cambridge, Mass.: Basil Blackwell, 1991).

Strategic Cost Management: Tailoring Controls to Strategies

Vijay Govindarajan and John K. Shank

Strategic cost management can be defined as the use of cost information to do the following: help formulate and communicate strategies; carry out tactics that implement those strategies; and then develop and implement controls that monitor success at achieving strategic objectives. Management control systems are, ultimately, tools to implement strategies. Since strategies differ in different types of organizations, management controls should be tailored to the requirements of specific strategies. This article explains how.

One important role of internal accounting information in a business is to facilitate the *development and implementation* of business strategies. Under this view, business management is a continuously cycling process consisting of the following four stages:

1. Formulating strategies;
2. Communicating those strategies throughout the organization;
3. Developing and carrying out tactics to implement the strategies; and
4. Developing and implementing controls to monitor the success of the implementation steps, and hence the success in meeting the strategic objectives.

Cost information plays a role at each of these stages. From this perspective, strategic cost management (SCM) can be thought of as the managerial use of cost information *explicitly* directed at one or more of the four stages of the strategic management cycle. Giving explicit attention to the strategic management *context* distinguishes SCM from managerial accounting.

Previous articles have explained value chain analysis and cost driver analysis—tools that are designed to help in the *formulation* of strategies.[1] This article discusses the role of control systems in the *implementation* of strategies.

Management control systems

Management control systems are tools to implement strategies. Since strategies differ in different types of organizations, controls should be tailored to the requirements of specific strategies. The logic for linking controls to strategy is based on the following line of thinking:

- For effective execution, different strategies require different task priorities, different key success factors, and different skills, perspectives, and behaviors.
- Control systems are measurement systems that influence the behavior of those people whose activities are being measured.
- Thus, a continuing concern in the design of control systems should be whether behavior induced by the system is consistent with the strategy.

The first part of this article defines the concept of strategy and describes "generic" strategies that business units can adopt. The second part of the article discusses how to vary the form and structure of control systems in accordance with variations in generic business-level strategies. The final part of the article contrasts the view of controls given with conventional management accounting practices.

Concept of strategy

Strategy has been conceptualized as the process by which managers, using a time horizon of three to five years, evaluate external environmental opportunities and also internal strengths and resources to decide on *goals* as well as *a set of action plans* to accomplish these goals.[2] Thus, a business unit's strategy depends on two interrelated aspects:

1. Its mission or goals; and
2. The way the business unit chooses to compete in its industry to accomplish its goals—i.e., the business unit's competitive advantage.

Mission. Turning first to the mission, consulting firms (e.g., Boston Consulting Group,[3] Arthur D. Little,[4] and A.T. Kearney[5]) and also academic researchers[6] have proposed the following three missions that a business unit can adopt:

- *Build.* This mission implies a goal of increased market share, even at the expense of short-term earnings and cash flow. A business unit that follows this mission is expected to be a net user of cash: that is, the cash flow from its current operations would usually be insufficient to meet its capital investment needs. Business units with "low market share" in "high growth industries" typically pursue a "build" mission (e.g., Apple Computer's Macintosh business and Monsanto's biotechnology business).
- *Hold.* This strategic mission is geared to the protection of the business unit's market share and competitive position. The cash outflows for a business unit that follows this mission generally equal the cash inflows. Businesses with "high market share" in "high growth industries" typically pursue a "hold" mission (e.g., IBM in mainframe computers).
- *Harvest.* The harvest mission implies a goal of maximizing short-term earnings and cash flow, even at the expense of market share. A business unit that follows the harvest mission is a net supplier of cash. Businesses with "high market share" in "low growth industries" typically pursue a "harvest" mission (e.g., American Brands in tobacco products).

Competitive advantage. In terms of competitive advantage, Porter[7] has proposed the following two generic ways in which businesses can develop sustainable competitive advantage:

- *Low cost.* The primary focus of this strategy is to achieve low cost relative to competitors. Cost leadership can be achieved through approaches such as economies of scale in production, learning curve effects, tight cost control, and cost minimization in areas such as R&D, service, sales force, or advertising. Firms that follow this strategy include Texas Instruments (in consumer electronics), Emerson Electric (in electric motors), Chevrolet (in automobiles), Briggs and Stratton (in gasoline engines), Black and Decker (in machine tools), and Commodore (in business machines).
- *Differentiation.* The primary focus of this strategy is to differentiate the product offering to create something that customers perceive as unique. Approaches to product differentiation include: brand loyalty (Coca Cola in soft drinks), superior customer service (IBM in computers), dealer network (Caterpillar Tractors in construction equipment), product design and product features (Hewlett-Packard in electronics), or product technology (Coleman in camping equipment).

Business unit mission

The planning and control requirements of business units differ according to the strategies they pursue. This section discusses how control systems should be designed to achieve the various missions of business units.

As noted earlier, the mission for ongoing business units could be to build, hold, or harvest. These missions constitute a continuum, with "pure build" at one end and "pure harvest" at the other end. For effective implementation, there should be congruence between the mission chosen and the types of controls used. The control-mission "fit" is developed using the following line of reasoning:[8]

- The mission of a business unit influences the uncertainties that its general manager faces and the short-term versus long-term trade-offs that the manager makes.
- Management control systems can be systematically varied to help motivate managers to cope effectively with uncertainty

and make appropriate short-term versus long-term trade-offs.

- Thus, different missions often require systematically different management control systems.

Mission and uncertainty

Build units tend to face greater environmental uncertainty than harvest units for several reasons:

- Build strategies are typically undertaken in the growth stage of a product life cycle, whereas harvest strategies are typically undertaken in the mature/decline stage of the product life cycle. Factors such as the following change more rapidly and are more unpredictable in the growth stage than the mature/decline stage of the product life cycle: manufacturing process; product technology; market demand; relations with suppliers, buyers, and distribution channels; number of competitors; and competitive structure.
- An objective of a build business unit is to increase market share. Since the total market share of all firms in any industry is 100 percent, the battle for market share is a zero-sum game; thus, a build strategy pits a business unit into greater conflict with its competitors than does a harvest strategy. Since competitors' actions are likely to be unpredictable, this contributes to the uncertainty faced by build business units.
- Both on the input side and on the output side, build managers tend to experience greater dependencies with external individuals and organizations than do harvest managers. For example, a build mission signifies additional capital investment (greater dependence on capital markets), expansion of capacity (greater dependence on the technological environment), increase in market share (greater dependence on customers and competitors), increase in production volume (greater dependence on raw material suppliers and labor market), and so on. The greater the external dependencies that a business unit faces, the greater the uncertainty it confronts.
- Since build business units are often in new and evolving industries, the experience of build managers in their industries is likely to be less. This also contributes to the

greater uncertainty faced by managers of build units in dealing with external constituencies.

Mission and time span

The choice of build versus harvest strategies has implications for short-term versus long-term profit trade-offs. The share-building strategy includes:

- Price cutting;
- Major R&D expenditures (to introduce new products); and
- Major market development expenditures.

These actions are aimed at establishing market leadership, but they depress short-term profits. Thus, many decisions that a manager of a build unit makes today may not result in profits until some future period. A harvest strategy, on the other hand, entails maximizing short-term profits.

The following sections discuss how the form and structure of control systems might differ across business units with different missions.

Strategic planning

Several design issues need to be addressed for a strategic planning process. There are no hard and fast answers about these design choices; instead, the answers tend to depend on the mission that the business unit is pursuing (see Exhibit 1).

When the environment is uncertain, the strategic planning process is especially important. Management must think about how to cope with uncertainties, which usually requires a longer-range view of planning than is possible in an annual budget. If the environment is stable, there may be no strategic planning process at all, or only a broad-brush strategic plan. Thus, strategic planning is more critical for build business units than it is for harvest business units. Nevertheless, strategic plans may still be necessary for harvest business units, because a company's overall strategic plan must encompass all its businesses to effectively balance cash flows.

Capital deployment. In screening capital investments and allocating resources, the systems may be more quantitative and financial for harvest units. A harvest business unit operates in a mature industry and does not offer

Exhibit 1. *Different Strategic Missions: Implications for Strategic Planning*

	Build	Hold	Harvest
Importance of strategic planning	Relatively high	→	Relatively low
Formalization of capital expenditure decisions	Less formal DCF analysis; longer payback	→	More formalized DCF analysis; shorter payback
Capital expenditure evaluation criteria	More emphasis on nonfinancial data (market share, efficient use of R&D dollars, etc.)	→	More emphasis on financial data (cost efficiency; straight cash on cash incremental return)
Hurdle rates	Relatively low	→	Relatively high
Capital investment analysis	More subjective and qualitative	→	More quantitative and financial
Project approval limits at business unit level	Relatively high	→	Relatively low

tremendous new investment possibilities. Hence, the required earnings rate for such a business unit may be set relatively high to motivate managers to search for projects with truly exceptional returns.

Since harvest units tend to experience stable environments (with predictable products, technologies, competitors, and customers), discounted cash flow (DCF) analysis often can be used with confidence. The required information used to evaluate investments from harvest units is primarily financial.

A build unit, on the other hand, is positioned on the growth stage of the product life cycle. The corporate office wants to take advantage of the opportunities in a growing market, so the corporate officers may set a relatively low discount rate to motivate managers to forward more investment ideas to the corporate office. Given the product and market uncertainties, the financial analysis of some projects from build units may be unreliable. For such projects, nonfinancial data are more important.

Budgeting

Implications for designing budgeting systems to support varied missions are contained in Exhibit 2.

A key issue is how much importance should be attached to meeting the budget in evaluations of a business unit manager's performance. The greater the uncertainty, the more difficult it is for superiors to regard subordinates' budget targets as firm commitments and to consider unfavorable budget variances as clear indicators of poor performance.[9] There are several reasons for this, as the following sections explain.

Predictability of profit targets. First, performance evaluation presupposes establishment of accurate profit targets. Targets that can serve as valid standards for subsequent performance appraisal require the ability to predict the conditions that will exist during the coming year. If these predictions are incorrect, the profit objective will also be incorrect. Obviously, these conditions can be predicted more accurately under stable conditions than under changing conditions. The basic effect of uncertainty is to limit the ability of managers to plan or make decisions about activities in advance of their occurrence. Thus, the greater the uncertainty, the more difficult it is to prepare targets that can become the basis for performance evaluation.

Exhibit 2. *Different Strategic Missions: Implications for Budgeting*

	Build	Hold	Harvest
Role of the budget	More a short-term planning tool	———————▶	More a control tool ("document of restraint")
Business unit manager's influence in preparing the annual budget	Relatively high	———————▶	Relatively low
Revisions to the budget during the year	Relatively easy	———————▶	Relatively difficult
Roles of standard costs in assessing performance	Relatively low	———————▶	Relatively high
Importance of such concepts as flexible budgeting for manufacturing cost control	Relatively low	———————▶	Relatively high
Frequency of informal reporting and contacts with superiors	More frequent on policy issues; less frequent on operating issues	———————▶	Less frequent on policy issues; more frequent on operating issues
Frequency of feedback from superiors on actual performance versus the budget	Less often	———————▶	More often
"Control limit" used in periodic evaluation against the budget	Relatively high (i.e., more flexible)	———————▶	Relatively low (i.e., more flexible)
Importance attached to meeting the budget	Relatively low	———————▶	Relatively high
Output versus behavior control	Behavior control	———————▶	Output control

Knowledge about cause-effect relationships.
Second, since efficiency refers to the amount of output per unit of input, evaluations of a manager's efficiency depend on a detailed knowledge of the outcomes associated with given management actions—that is, knowledge about cause-effect relationships. Better knowledge about cause-effect relationships exists under stable conditions than under uncertain conditions. Therefore, judgments about efficiency are more difficult under uncertain conditions.

Use of financial performance indicators.
Third, the emphasis of financial performance indicators is on outcomes rather than on process. Managers control their own actions, but they cannot control the states of nature that combine with their actions to produce outcomes. In a situation with high uncertainty, therefore, financial information does not adequately reflect managerial performance.

Less reliance on budgets in build units

Since build units tend to face higher uncertainty than harvest units, less reliance is usually placed on budgets in build units than in harvest units.

Example. In the late 1970s, the SCM Corporation adopted a two-dimensional yardstick to evaluate business units: bottom-line performance against budget was one dimension, and performance against specific objectives

Exhibit 3. *Different Strategic Missions: Implications for Incentive Compensation*

	Build	Hold	Harvest
Percent compensation as bonus	Relatively high	⟶	Relatively low
Bonus criteria	More emphasis on nonfinancial criteria	⟶	More emphasis on financial criteria
Bonus determination approach	More subjective	⟶	More formula based
Frequency of bonus payment	Less frequent	⟶	More frequent

was another. The ratios of the two were made to vary according to the mission of the business unit. For instance, evaluations of pure harvest units were based 100 percent on budget performance. Evaluations of "pure hold" units were based 50 percent on budget performance and 50 percent on completion of objectives. Finally, evaluations of pure build units were based 100 percent on completion of objectives.[10]

Other differences in the budget process. The following additional differences in the budget process are likely to exist between build and harvest units:

- In contrast to harvest units, budget revisions are likely to be more frequent for build units because of the more frequent changes in the product or market environment.
- Managers of build units may have relatively more input and influence in the formulation of budgets than managers of harvest units. This occurs because build managers operate in rapidly changing environments and have better knowledge of these changes than senior management. The stable environments of harvest units make the knowledge of the manager less important.

Incentive compensation system

In designing an incentive compensation package for business unit managers, questions such as these need to be resolved:

1. What should the size of incentive bonus payments be relative to the base salary of

general managers? Should the incentive bonus payments have upper limits?
2. What measures of performance (e.g., profit, return on investment, sales volume, market share, or product development) should be employed as the basis for determining a general manager's incentive bonus awards? If multiple performance measures are employed, how should they be weighted?
3. How much reliance should be placed on subjective judgments in deciding on the bonus amount?
4. How often (e.g., semiannually, annually, biennially) should incentive awards be made?

Decisions about these design variables are influenced by the mission of the business unit (see Exhibit 3).

Bonus-to-base salary ratio. As for the first question, many firms follow the principle that the riskier the strategy, the greater the proportion of the general manager's compensation in bonus compared to salary (the "risk/return" principle). They maintain that since managers in charge of more uncertain situations should be willing to take greater risks, those managers should receive a higher percentage of their remuneration in the form of incentive bonuses. Thus, reliance on bonuses is likely to be higher for build managers than for harvest managers.

Which performance measures to use. As for the second question, when an individual's rewards are tied to performance according to certain criteria, his behavior is influenced by the desire to optimize performance with respect to those criteria.

Some performance criteria (e.g., cost control, operating profits, cash flow from operations, and return on investment) focus on short-term performance, whereas other performance criteria (e.g., market share, new product development, market development, and people development) focus on long-term profitability. Thus, linking incentive bonus to the former set of criteria tends to promote a short-term focus on the part of general managers, whereas linking incentive bonus to the latter set of performance criteria is likely to promote a long-term focus.

Given the differences in the time horizons of build and harvest managers, it may be inappropriate to use a single, uniform financial criterion (such as return on investment) to evaluate the performance of every business unit. Rather, it may be preferable to use multiple performance criteria, with differential weights applied for each criterion depending on the mission of the business unit.

Example. "General Electric Company and Westinghouse Electric Corporation, for example, are tailoring compensation packages to the different 'missions' of their individual businesses.

Both GE and Westinghouse have mature as well as young businesses. In the mature businesses, short-term incentives might dominate the compensation packages of managers, who are charged with maximizing cash flow, achieving high profit margins, and retaining market share. In the younger businesses, where developing products and establishing marketing strategies are most important, non-financial measures geared to the execution of long-term performance might dictate the major portion of managers' remuneration."[11]

Use of subjective judgments. As for the third question, in addition to varying the importance of different criteria, superiors must also decide on the approach to take in determining a specific bonus amount.

At one extreme, a manager's bonus might be a strict formula-based plan with the bonus tied to performance on quantifiable criteria (e.g., X percent bonus on actual profits in excess of budgeted profits). At the other extreme, a manager's incentive bonus might be based solely on the superior's subjective judgment or discretion. Alternatively, incentive bonuses might be based on a combination of formula-based and subjective approaches.

Performance on most long-run criteria (e.g., market development, new product development, and people development) is clearly less amenable to objective measurement than performance on most short-run criteria (e.g., operating profits, cash flow from operations, and return on investment). Since, as already noted, build managers—in contrast to harvest managers—should focus more on the long run than on the short run, build managers are typically evaluated more subjectively than harvest managers.

Frequency of bonuses. Finally, the frequency with which bonuses are paid influences the time horizon of managers. More frequent bonus awards encourage concentration on short-term performance, since they have the effect of motivating managers to focus on those facets of the business that they can affect in the short run. Less frequent calculation and payment of bonuses encourage managers to take a long-term perspective. Thus, build managers tend to receive bonuses less frequently than harvest managers.

Example. Premark International (which was formed in 1986 in a spin-off from Dart & Kraft, Inc.) adopted the design of an incentive bonus plan for the general manager of its Tupperware division, whose mission was to build market share: "[If you award the bonus annually], Tupperware could reduce advertising and promotional activities and you can look good in profits that year. Then the franchise starts to go to hell. If you're shooting for an award after three years, there's less tendency to do things short term."[12]

Business unit competitive advantage

A business unit can choose to compete either as a differentiated player or as a low-cost player. The choice of a differentiation approach rather than a low-cost approach increases uncertainty in a business unit's task environment for three reasons.

First, product innovation is likely to be more critical for differentiation business units than for low-cost business units. This is partly because of the fact that a low-cost business unit, with its primary emphasis on cost reduction, typically prefers to keep its product offerings stable over time, whereas a differentiation business unit, with its primary focus on uniqueness and exclusivity, is likely to engage in greater product innovation. A business unit with greater emphasis on new product activities tends to face greater uncertainty since the business unit is betting on unproven products.

Second, low-cost business units tend to have narrow product lines to minimize inventory carrying costs and to benefit from economies of scale. Differentiation business units, on the other hand, tend to have a broader set of products to create uniqueness. Product breadth creates high environmental complexity and consequently, higher uncertainty.

Third, low-cost business units typically produce no-frill, commodity products—these products succeed primarily because they have lower prices than competing products. By contrast, products of differentiation business units succeed if customers perceive that the products have advantages over competing products. Since customer perception is difficult to learn about and since customer loyalty is subject to change because of actions by competitors or for other reasons, the demand for differentiated products is typically more difficult to predict than the demand for commodities.

The specifics of the control systems for low-cost and differentiation business units are similar to the ones described earlier for harvest and build business units. This is so because the uncertainty facing low-cost and differentiation business units is similar to the uncertainty facing harvest and build business units.

Examples. Digital Equipment Corporation (DEC) followed a differentiation strategy, whereas Data General followed a low-cost strategy. The control systems in these companies differed accordingly. DEC's product managers were evaluated primarily on the basis of the quality of their interaction with their customers (a subjective measure), whereas Data General's product managers were evaluated on the basis of results, or profits. Further,

DEC's sales representatives were on straight salary, while Data General's salesmen received 50 percent of their pay on a commission basis. Salaried compensation indicates behavior control, and commission compensation, outcome control.[13]

A broad-based chemicals manufacturer used differentiated management controls focusing on the differing key success factors for its yellow dye unit (which followed a cost leadership strategy) and its red dye unit (which followed a differentiation strategy). The performance of the manager in charge of yellow dye was evaluated closely according to *theoretical* standard costs rather than currently achievable standard costs. The results of this tight financial control were remarkable: Within two years, actual cost for yellow dye decreased from $5.72 per pound to $3.84 per pound, thus giving the yellow dye unit a major cost advantage. By contrast, since the key strategic issue for red dye was product differentiation rather than cost leadership, the management control reports for the red dye unit focused on product leadership variables (e.g., milestone reporting on the development project for hot spray dyeing) rather than on cost control variables.[14]

Additional considerations

Although tailoring controls to strategies has a sound logic, designers of control systems need to be cognizant of several potential problems.

The changing environment. First, a business unit's external environment inevitably changes over time, and a change in the operating environment might imply the need for a shift in strategy. This raises an interesting issue. Success at any task requires commitment. The strategy-control "fit" is expected to foster such a commitment to the current strategy. However, if the control system is too closely related to the current strategy, it could result in overcommitment, thereby inhibiting managers from shifting to a new strategy when they should.

Examples of declining industries that have been transformed into growth industries include the major growth of Arm & Hammer baking soda, which was once in the decline stage of the product life cycle, and the surge in demand during the 1980s for fountain pens, which were once considered an obsolete product.

The following examples in the radio, musical instrument, and motorcycle industries illustrate the problems of overcommitment when there is a close fit between strategy and controls:

Examples. "Financially oriented U.S. manufacturers once treated the radio as essentially a dot on the product portfolio matrix. Convinced that every product has a life cycle, they viewed the radio as having passed its peak and being a prime candidate for 'milking.' Starved for investment funds and resources and being subject to tight financial controls, the radio died in a self-fulfilling prophecy. On the other hand, Japanese radio manufacturers such as Matsushita (Panasonic) and Sony—ignoring or unaware of product life cycle and portfolio theories—obstinately believed in their product's value. The division heads of these firms had no option but to extend the life of the product since to do otherwise would mean dissolving their divisions, which was an untenable option. So they pressed their engineers, component manufacturers, and marketing people for new ideas . . . Today the portable radio-cassette and Sony Walkman stores are part of business folklore."[15]

Yamaha in the musical instrument market in the United States and Honda, Kawasaki, Suzuki, and Yamaha in the motorcycle market in the United States and in Europe have successfully destroyed the dominance of incumbent manufacturers that concentrated on milking their products for profit in a stagnant market.[16]

Thus, there is an ongoing dilemma: How to design control systems that can simultaneously maintain a high degree of commitment to—as well as a healthy skepticism regarding—current strategies.

Mission and competitive advantage. Second, we have discussed mission and competitive advantage as separate characteristics. However, business units have both a mission and a competitive advantage that, in some combinations, may result in a conflict regarding the type of controls to be used. As Exhibit 4

Exhibit 4. *Fits and Misfits in Control System Design*

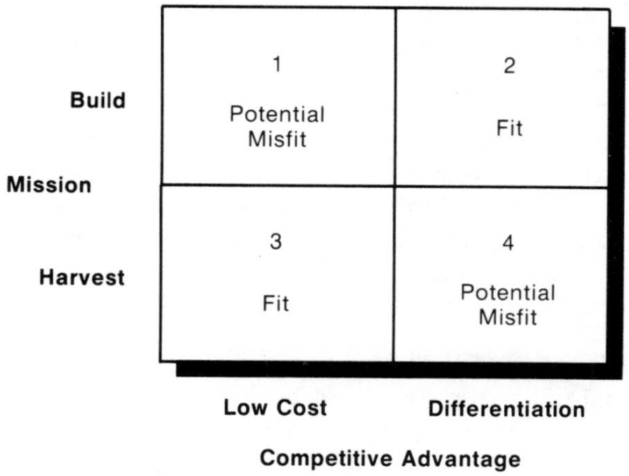

demonstrates, the ordinal classification of mission and competitive advantage yields four distinct combinations. There is an unconflicting design in cells 2 and 3.

Both of these cells have a similar level of uncertainty, which suggests a similar control system design. Cells 1 and 4, however, have conflicting demands; designing a control system that fits both is difficult. Several possibilities exist. It might be possible to change the mission or competitive advantage so that they do not conflict from the standpoint of systems design (i.e., move the business unit to cell 2 or cell 3). If this is not feasible, perhaps either mission or competitive advantage is more critical for implementation and would, therefore, dominate the choice of the appropriate type of control. If mission and competitive advantage are equally important, control system design becomes especially difficult. Here, control systems cannot be designed for the mission or competitive advantage in isolation without incurring costs.

Administrative problems and dysfunctional effects. Third, explicitly differentiated controls across business units might create administrative awkwardness and dysfunctional effects, especially for managers in charge of harvest units.

Many harvest managers believe that their career prospects within their companies are somewhat limited. While corporate managers in most diversified firms may find it rational to harvest one or more of their businesses, every company wants to grow at the overall firm level. Thus, as one goes higher in the corporate hierarchy, skills at successfully executing a build strategy become more important than those of successfully executing a harvest strategy. From a career perspective, this likelihood tends to favor managers currently in charge of build businesses.

Example. The following speculation regarding who might succeed Walter Wriston as the next CEO of Citicorp appeared in *The Wall Street Journal* nearly three years *before* the actual announcement of his successor: "Ironically, Mr. Theobald may not get to the top precisely because he runs a division that has always been a big money maker for Citicorp, its institutional division. Unlike his two competitors, who are charting new courses for Citicorp, Mr. Theobald is simply carrying forward a tradition of profiting handsomely from making loans to corporations and governments, domestically and abroad."[17] Subsequent events confirmed these speculations.

Given these possibilities, harvest managers may perceive their roles as being less important. Explicitly designing tight controls over harvest strategies compounds this problem.

System designers might consider two possibilities to mitigate this problem. First, as part of the planning process, they might avoid using such harshly graphic and negative terms as "cash cow," "dog," "question mark," and "star" and instead use terms such as "build," "hold," and "harvest." The former are "static" terms that do not convey missions as well as do "dynamic," action-oriented terms such as "build," "hold," and "harvest."

Second, to the extent possible, a harvest manager should be given one or more products with high growth potential. Doing this should prevent managers from becoming typecast solely as "harvesters." Corning Glass Works follows this policy of assigning a growth-oriented product to a manager who is in charge of a harvest business.[18]

Summary

This article argues that the role of management control depends on the strategy being followed and that effective control systems are differentiated depending on strategy. For example, carefully engineered product standard costs are likely to be a very important ongoing management control tool for a firm that follows a cost leadership strategy in a mature, commodity business. But for a firm that follows a product differentiation strategy in a market-driven, rapidly growing, fast-changing business, carefully engineered standard manufacturing costs may well be much less important.

It is not surprising that monitoring R&D productivity is much more important to a company like Merck than manufacturing cost control. On the other hand, a better system for monitoring R&D costs would not gain much attention in a company like International Paper, which employs many accountants to track manufacturing cost variances on a regular monthly basis. Although cost information is important in all companies in one form or another, different strategies demand different control perspectives.

It is interesting to compare the SCM perspective about the role of cost information with the perspective that is more prevalent in management accounting today. The theme in management accounting texts today has been the same for thirty years. That theme was first articulated by Simon and others,[19] who coined three phrases to capture the essence of management accounting:

- Scorekeeping;
- Problem solving; and
- Attention directing.

Although these specific words are not always preserved, these three objectives still come through frequently in today's textbooks—as they also clearly did when the Controllers Institute (which now is the Financial Executives Institute) commissioned a team of faculty from Carnegie Tech (which now is Carnegie Mellon) to study the elements of effective controllership.

The point is not to deprecate per se this long-standing common starting point, but rather to emphasize how much our conception of *what* we do starts with our consensus about *why* we do it. Each of the three well-known roles involves a set of concepts and techniques that are implicitly assumed to apply to all firms, if perhaps in varying degrees. For example, standard cost variances are a key tool for "attention directing," and contribution margin analysis is a key tool for "problem solving."

Because the three roles are not seen as varying across firms depending on strategic context, the relevance of the related tool concepts also is not seen to vary across firms. If agreement could be reached that *why* we do management accounting differs in important ways depending on the basic strategic thrust of the firm, it would be a much easier transition to see that *how* we do management accounting should also reflect the basic strategic thrust.

Even if management accounting in most companies today is still heavily involved with conventional tasks, this need not be true in the future. Management accounting as it is reflected in management control systems can and should be redirected to explicitly consider the strategic issues that a firm faces. ▲

Notes

1. John Shank & Vijay Govindarajan, *Strategic Cost Analysis* (Chicago: Richard D. Irwin 1989); and John Shank & Vijay Govindarajan, "Strategic Cost Management and the Value Chain," *Journal of Cost Management* (Winter 1992): 5–21.
2. See, e.g., K.R. Andrews, *The Concept of Corporate Strategy* (Homewood, Ill.: Dow-Jones Irwin 1971); H.I. Ansoff, *Corporate Strategy* (New York: McGraw-Hill 1965); Alfred A. Chandler, *Strategy and Structure: Chapters in the History of American Industrial Enterprise* (Cambridge, Mass.: The MIT Press 1962); C.W. Hofer & D.E. Schendel, *Strategy Formulation: Analytical Concepts* (St. Paul, Minn.: West Publishing Co. 1978); and R.E. Miles & C.C. Snow, *Organizational Strategy, Structure and Process* (New York: McGraw-Hill 1978).
3. B.D. Henderson, *Henderson on Corporate Strategy* (Cambridge, Mass.: ABT Books 1979).
4. R.V.L. Wright, *A System for Managing Diversity* (Cambridge, Mass.: Arthur D. Little, Inc. 1975).
5. C.W. Hofer & M.J. Davoust, *Successful Strategic Management* (Chicago, Ill.: A.T. Kearney, Inc. 1977).
6. R.D. Buzzell & F.D. Wiersema, "Modelling Changes in Market Share: A Cross-Sectional Analysis," *Strategic Management Journal* (Jan.-Feb. 1981): 27–42; and Hofer & Schendel, *Strategy Formulation*.
7. Michael E. Porter, *Competitive Strategy* (New York: The Free Press 1980).
8. This section draws from an extensive body of research that has focused on strategy implementation issues at the business-unit level. Some of the key references are: V. Govindarajan, "A Contingency Approach to Strategy Implementation at the Business Unit Level: Integrating Management Systems With Strategy," *Academy of Management Journal* (Sept. 1988): 4, 31, 828–853; V. Govindarajan, "Implementing Competitive Strategies at the Business Unit Level: Implications of Matching Managers to Strategies," *Strategic Management Journal* 10 (1989): 251–269; V. Govindarajan & Joseph Fisher, "The Interaction Between Strategy and Controls: Implications for Managerial Job Satisfaction" (working paper, The Amos Tuck School of Business Administration, Dartmouth College 1989); V. Govindarajan & J. Fisher, "Impact of Output Versus Behavior Controls and Resource Sharing on Performance: Strategy as a Mediating Variable," *Academy of Management Journal* (June 1990): 259–285; V. Govindarajan & J. Fisher, "Incentive Compensation, Strategic Business Unit Mission, and Competitive Strategy" (working paper, The Amos Tuck School of Business Administration, Dartmouth College 1991); V. Govindarajan & A.K. Gupta, "Linking Control Systems to Business Unit Strategy: Impact on Performance," *Accounting Organizations and Society* 9, No. 4 (1985): 51–66; A.K. Gupta & V. Govindarajan, "Business Unit Strategy, Managerial Characteristics, and Business Unit Effectiveness at Strategy Implementation," *Academy of Management Journal* 27 (1984): 25–41; A.K. Gupta & V. Govindarajan, "Build, Hold, Harvest: Converting Strategic Intentions into Reality," *Journal of Business Strategy* 4, no. 3 (1984): 34–47; G.E. Hall, "Reflections on Running a Diversified Company," *Harv. Bus. Rev.* (Jan.-Feb. 1987); R. Sata & M.A. Maidique, "Bonus System for a Balanced Strategy," *Harv. Bus. Rev.* (Nov.-Dec. 1980); John K. Shank & V. Govindarajan, *Strategic Cost Analysis* (Homewood, Ill.: Irwin 1989): chs. 6, 7; J.K. Shank & V. Govindarajan, "Profit Variance Analysis: A Strategic Focus," *Issues in Accounting Education* 4, No. 2 (Fall 1989); Robert Simons, "The Relationship Between Business Strategy and Accounting Control Systems: An Empirical Analysis," *Accounting Organizations and Society* (July 1987): 357–374.
9. See V. Govindarajan, "Appropriateness of Accounting Data in Performance Evaluation: An Empirical Evaluation of Environmental Uncertainty as an Intervening Variable," *Accounting Organizations and Society* 9, no. 2 (1984): 125–135.
10. Hall, "Reflections on Running a Diversified Company," at 88–89.
11. "Executive Compensation: Looking to the Long Term Again," *Business Week* (May 9, 1983): 81.
12. L. Reibstein, "Firms Trim Annual Pay Increase and Focus on Long Term: More Employers Link Incentives to Unit Results," *The Wall Street Journal* (Apr. 10, 1987): 25.
13. B. Uttal, "The Gentlemen and the Upstarts Meet in a Great Mini-battle," *Fortune* (Apr. 23, 1979): 98–108.
14. Shank & Govindarajan, *Strategic Cost Analysis*, at 114–130.
15. K. Ohmae, "The Long and Short of Japanese Planning," *The Wall Street Journal* (Jan. 18, 1982): 28.
16. B.G. James, "Strategic Planning Under Fire," *Sloan Management Review* (Summer 1984): 57–61.
17. J. Salamon, "Challenges Lie Ahead for Dynamic Citicorp After the Wriston Era," *The Wall Street Journal* (Dec. 18, 1981): 1.
18. Richard F. Vancil, "Corning Glass Works: Tom MacAvoy," in F.F. Vancil, *Implementing Strategy* (Boston: Division of Research, Harvard Business School 1982): 21–36.
19. Herbert Simon, et al., *Centralization Versus Decentralization in Organizing the Controller's Department* (New York: The Controllership Foundation, Inc. 1954).
20. A modified version of this article will appear in the forthcoming book by the authors, *Strategic Cost Management* (New York: The Free Press 1993).

Strategic Cost Management and the Value Chain

John K. Shank and Vijay Govindarajan

The value chain for any firm in any business is the linked set of value-creating activities—from basic raw material sources to the ultimate product or service that is delivered to consumers. This article explains how to construct and use value chains. It uses a real-world study from the airline industry to highlight the fact that the strategic cost management (SCM) insights that emerge from value chain analysis are different from—and better than—the insights available from traditional management accounting approaches.

This article begins by defining the value chain concept, contrasting it with the value-added notion, and demonstrating its power. Then, the methodology for constructing and using a value chain is introduced. The case study is presented to illustrate the power of value chain analysis. The final part of the article explains how the value chain concept is the overarching framework for strategic cost management and how activity-based costing and similar cost management tools can be usefully accommodated within the value chain concept.

One of the major themes in strategic cost management (SCM) concerns the focus of cost management efforts: How does a firm organize its thinking about cost management? In the SCM framework, managing costs effectively requires a broad focus that Michael Porter calls the "value chain"—i.e., the linked set of value-creating activities.[1] This focus is external to the firm, with each firm viewed in the context of the overall chain of value-creating activities of which it is only a part, from basic raw material to end-use consumers.

In contrast, traditional management accounting adopts a focus that is largely internal to the firm, with each firm viewed in the context of its purchases, its processes, its functions, its products, and its customers. In other words, management accounting takes a value-added perspective that starts with payments to suppliers (purchases) and stops with charges to customers (sales). The key theme is to maximize the difference (i.e., *the value added*) between purchases and sales. The strategic insights yielded by value chain analysis, however, differ significantly from—and are superior to—those suggested by value-added analysis.

The concept

Porter notes that a business can develop a sustainable competitive advantage by following one of two strategies:[2]

- A low-cost strategy; or
- A differentiation strategy.

Low-cost strategy. The primary focus of a low-cost strategy is to achieve low cost relative to competitors (i.e., cost leadership). Cost leadership can be achieved through such approaches as:

- Economies of scale in production;
- Experience curve effects;
- Tight cost control; and
- Cost minimization in such areas as research and development (R&D), service, sales force, or advertising.

Firms that have followed this strategy include Texas Instruments in consumer electronics, Emerson Electric in electric motors, Hyundai in automobiles, Briggs and Stratton in gasoline engines, Black and Decker in machine tools, Commodore in business machines, K-Mart in retailing, BIC in pens, and Timex in wrist watches.

Differentiation strategy. The primary focus of a differentiation strategy is to create something that customers perceive as being unique. Product uniqueness can be achieved through such approaches as brand loyalty (Coca Cola in soft drinks), superior customer service (IBM in computers), dealer network (Caterpillar Tractors in construction equipment), product design and product features (Hewlett-Packard in electronics), or technology (Coleman in camping equipment). Some firms that have followed a differentiation strategy include Mercedes Benz in automobiles, Stouffer's in frozen foods, Neiman-Marcus in retailing, Cross in pens, and Rolex in wrist watches.

Whether or not a firm can develop and sustain cost leadership or differentiation depends fundamentally on how the firm manages its own value chain relative to those of its competitors. Both intuitively and theoretically, competitive advantage in the marketplace ultimately derives from providing better customer value for equivalent cost or equivalent customer value for a lower cost. Thus, value chain analysis is essential to determine exactly where in the firm's segment of the chain—from design to distribution—costs can be lowered or customer value enhanced.

The value chain framework

The value chain framework is a method for breaking down the chain—from basic raw materials to end-use customers—into strategically relevant activities in order to understand the behavior of costs and the sources of differentiation. As noted earlier, a firm is typically only one part of the larger set of activities in the value delivery system. Suppliers not only produce and deliver inputs used in a firm's value activities, but they importantly influence the firm's cost or differentiation position as well. Similarly, distribution channels have a significant impact on a firm's value activities.

As is discussed more fully below, gaining and sustaining a competitive advantage require that a firm understands the *entire* value delivery system, not just the portion of the value chain in which it participates. Suppliers and distribution channels have profit margins that are important to identify in understanding a firm's cost or differentiation positioning, because end-use customers ultimately pay for all the profit margins throughout the value chain.

Strategic implications

Exhibit 1 provides a conceptual value chain for the paper industry. The distinct value activities (such as timber, logging, pulp mills, paper mills, and conversion plants) are the building blocks by which this industry creates a product of value to buyers. It is possible to quantify the economic value created at each stage by identifying the costs, revenues, and assets for each activity. Every firm in Exhibit 1—A, B, C, D, E, F, and G—must construct a value chain for the total paper industry, breaking the total value in the chain into its fundamental sources of economic value. Such an analysis has potential strategic implications for every competitor in this industry:

- If competitor A (a fully integrated company) calculates the return on assets (ROA) at each stage of the chain by adjusting all transfer prices to competitive market levels, it could highlight potential areas where the firm could more economically buy from the outside (which is the strategic choice of make versus buy). For example, most "fully integrated" forest product companies still use independent loggers to cut their trees on the way to their mills.
- With a complete value chain, competitors B, C, D, E, F, and G might be able to identify possibilities to integrate forward or backward into areas that can enhance their performance. Westvaco, for example, has stopped manufacturing envelope paper, although it still owns a large envelope converter. Champion International has sold its envelope converting business but still produces envelope paper.
- Each value activity has a set of unique cost drivers that explain variations in costs in that activity.[3] Thus, each value activity has its unique sources of competitive advantage. Companies are likely to face a different set of competitors at each stage: Some of these competitors would be fully inte-

Exhibit 1. *Value Chain in the Paper Products Industry*

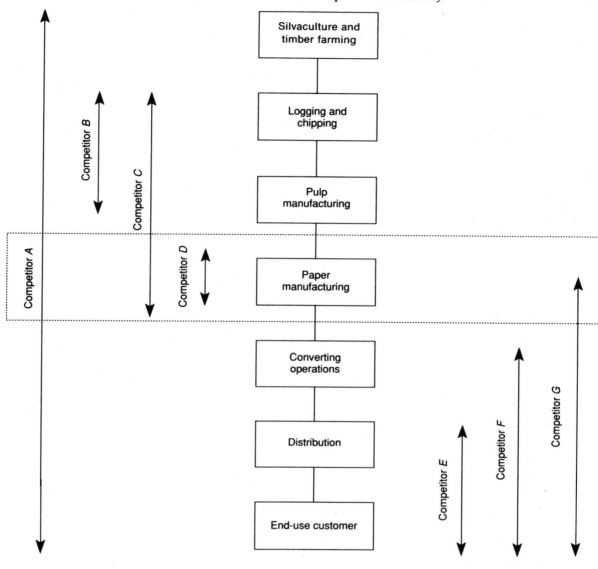

grated companies, and some of them would be more narrowly focused specialists. For example, company D faces competition from A, C, and G in the paper manufacturing stage. Yet A, C, and G bring very different competitive advantage to this stage of the value chain vis-à-vis D. It is possible for D to compete effectively with A, C, and G only by understanding the total value chain and the cost drivers that regulate each activity. For example, if "scope" (vertical integration) is a key structural driver of paper

mill cost, A has a significant advantage, and D a significant disadvantage in this marketplace.

• The value chain analysis helps to quantify buyer power (for B, C, and D) and supplier power (for E, F, and G) by calculating the percentage of total profits that can be attributed to each stage in that chain. This calculation can help firms identify ways to exploit linkages with both their suppliers and their customers to reduce costs, enhance differentiation, or both.

Value chain vs. value-added analysis

The value chain concept can be contrasted with the internal focus that typically is adopted in management accounting. Management accounting usually takes a value-added perspective, as noted earlier. From a strategic perspective, the value-added concept has two big disadvantages:

1. It starts too late; and
2. It stops too soon.

Starting cost analysis with purchases misses all the opportunities for exploiting linkages with the firm's suppliers. Such opportunities can be dramatically important to a firm.

Supplier linkages

The differences between a value chain perspective and a value-added perspective can be seen clearly in the context of scheduling problems that can arise if a firm ignores the complete value chain. The automobile industry provides a good example.

A few years ago, a major U.S. automobile manufacturer began to implement just-in-time (JIT) management concepts in its assembly plants. Assembly costs represented 30 percent of sales. The company reasoned that use of JIT would eliminate 20 percent of these costs, because assembly costs in Japanese automobile plants were known to be more than 20 percent below those in U.S. plants. As the firm began to manage its factories differently in order to eliminate inventory buffers and waste, its assembly costs began to drop noticeably. But the firm experienced dramatic problems with its major suppliers, who began to demand price increases that more than offset the savings in the assembly plants. The automobile firm's first response was to chide its suppliers and tell them that they, too, needed to embrace JIT concepts for their own operations.

A value chain perspective revealed a much different picture of the overall situation. Of the automobile company's sales, 50 percent were purchases from parts suppliers. Of this amount, 37 percent were purchases by the parts suppliers, and the remaining 63 percent was value added by the suppliers. Thus, suppliers actually were *adding* more manufacturing value to the automobiles than the

assembly plants (63 percent × 50 percent = 31.5 percent, versus 30 percent). By reducing buffer inventory and requiring JIT deliveries by suppliers, the company had placed major strains on its suppliers. As a result, the suppliers' aggregate manufacturing costs went up more than the company's assembly costs went down.

The reason, once identified, was very simple. The assembly plants experienced huge and uncertain variability in their production schedules. One week ahead of actual production, the master schedule was more than 25 percent wrong 95 percent of the time. When inventory buffers are stripped away from a highly unpredictable production process, the manufacturing activities of the suppliers become a nightmare. For every dollar of manufacturing cost that the assembly plants saved by moving toward JIT management concepts, the suppliers' plants spent much more than one dollar extra because of the schedule instability.

Because of its narrow, value-added perspective, the automobile company had overlooked the ramifications that its scheduling changes had on its suppliers' costs. Management had ignored the fact that JIT requires a partnership with suppliers. A major factor in the success of JIT at a Japanese automobile assembly plant is stable scheduling for suppliers. Whereas the U.S. plant regularly missed schedules only one week in the future by 25 percent or more, Japanese plants vary by 1 percent—or less—from schedules that are planned four weeks in advance.

A failure to adopt a value chain perspective doomed this major effort to failure; ignorance of supply chain cost analysis concepts on the part of the automobile company's management accountants proved very costly. These scheduling ramifications might have been handled better if management accountants in the automobile industry had been taught value chain concepts somewhere in their accounting education.

Beneficial linkages (i.e., linkages with suppliers and customers that are managed in such a way that all parties benefit) can also be tracked more accurately with value chain analysis rather than with value-added analysis. For example, when bulk chocolate began to be delivered as a liquid in tank cars instead of as ten-pound, molded bars of chocolate, industrial chocolate companies (i.e., the suppliers) eliminated the cost of molding bars and packing them, but they also saved candy makers the cost and trouble of unpacking and melting the solid bars of chocolate.[4]

Customer linkages

In addition to starting too late, value-added analysis has another major flaw: It stops too soon. Customer linkages can be just as important as supplier linkages; stopping cost analysis at the point of sale eliminates all opportunities for exploiting linkages with customers.

Exploiting customer linkages is the key idea behind the concept of life-cycle costing.

Exploiting customer linkages is the key idea behind the concept of life-cycle costing. *Life-cycle costing* is a costing concept that argues for including all the costs incurred for a product—from the time when a product is conceived until it is abandoned—as part of the product cost Life-cycle costing thus deals explicitly with the relationship between what a customer pays for a product and the total cost that the customer incurs over the life of the product. A life-cycle costing perspective on the customer linkage in the value chain can lead to enhanced profitability. Explicit attention to post-purchase costs by the customer can lead to more effective market segmentation and product positioning. Designing a product to reduce post-purchase costs of the customer can be a major weapon in capturing competitive advantage. In many ways, the lower life cycle cost of imported Japanese automobiles helps to explain their success in the U.S. market.

There are other examples in which the linkage between a firm and its customer is designed to be mutually beneficial and the relationship with the customer is viewed not as a zero-sum game but as a mutually beneficial one. A case in point is the container in-

dustry. Some container producers have constructed manufacturing facilities near beer breweries and deliver the containers through overhead conveyers directly onto the customers' assembly line. This practice results in significant cost reductions for both the container producers and their customers by expediting the transport of empty containers, which are bulky and heavy.[5]

Missed opportunities

Just as many cost management problems are misunderstood because of failure to see the impact on the overall value chain, many management opportunities are missed in the same way. The paper industry again provides an example of these missed opportunities when a value-added, rather than a value chain, analysis is applied.

In the late 1980s, U.S. suppliers of paper to envelope converters lost profits because they were caught unawares by a significant change in the value chain of the envelope converter. The shift from sheet-fed to roll-fed envelope finishing machines had dramatically changed the raw material specifications for envelope paper.

Although roll-fed machines were not introduced in the United States until around 1980, today they produce more than 60 percent of all domestic envelopes. Roll-fed machines—which are far more expensive to buy, but much less expensive to operate, than sheet-fed machines—can bring substantial overall savings for envelope converters, especially when large volumes of envelopes are produced.

With sheet-fed machines, an envelope company buys large rolls of paper 40–60 inches wide, which are cut into sheets, cut into blanks in die-cutting machines, and finally fed by hand into folding-and-glueing machines. With roll-fed machines, however, the envelope company buys narrow rolls of paper 5–11 inches wide, which are converted directly into envelopes in one combined operation.

Paper manufacturers do not want to complicate their primary manufacturing process by producing the narrow rolls directly on the paper machines. Instead, they use secondary machines called "rewinder slitters" to convert the large rolls of paper from the paper machines into the narrower rolls that the converters who use roll-fed machines now want. Thus, the transition from selling wide rolls to selling narrow rolls has added an additional processing step for the paper manufacturers. The business issue, therefore, is how the change in the customers' (i.e., the envelope company's) value chain should be reflected in paper prices now that manufacturing costs along the value chain have increased because of the envelope company's changed requirements.

Management accounting in the paper industry takes neither value chain analysis nor life-cycle costing into account. Consequently, the additional costs for the rewinder slitter machines are considered just a small part of mill overhead, which is assigned to all paper production on a per-ton basis. For a large, modern paper mill, rewinder slitter cost ranges from 1–7 percent of total cost. The impact on total average cost per ton is less than $10. Little of this cost is variable with incremental production, because the mill always keeps excess capacity in such a small department. (It is only common sense to make sure that $300 million paper machines are never slowed down by a bottleneck at a $2 million rewinder slitter machine.)

The industry norm is to charge $11 per ton extra if the customer wants the rolls slit to the narrow widths (i.e., 11 inches or less). The savings to the envelope converter from roll-fed machines far exceed this extra charge. Unfortunately, the full cost to the paper mill of providing the incremental rewinder slitting service also far exceeds this extra charge. It can cost more than $100 per ton to have an outside subcontractor slit rolls to narrow widths. An external value chain perspective would look at the savings from narrow rolls for the customer and the extra costs to the paper mill and set a price differential somewhere in between. An internal mill costing perspective, however, sees no cost issue at all.

The lack of a value chain perspective contributes to the lack of concern about product costing issues. The $11 surcharge looks like pure extra contribution to profit. The result is an uneconomic price, the impact of which is buried in a mill management accounting system that ignores value chain issues. The op-portunity to more accurately price might not have been missed if the management accountants in the paper companies (like their colleagues in the automobile and candy industries) had been exposed to value chain concepts somewhere in their management accounting education.

A framework of interdependence

The value chain framework highlights how a firm's products fit into the buyer's value chain. Under this framework, for example, it is readily apparent what percentage the firm's product costs are in relation to the ultimate buyer's total costs. The fact that paper constitutes over 40 percent of the total costs of a magazine is very useful in encouraging the paper mill and the publisher to cooperate on cost-reduction activities.

Unlike the value-added concept, value chain analysis explicitly recognizes the fact that the various activities within a firm are not independent but, rather, interdependent. At McDonald's, for example, the timing of promotional campaigns (one value activity) significantly influences capacity utilization in "production" (another value activity). These linked activities must be coordinated if the full effect of a promotion is to be realized. As another example, Japanese producers of videocassette recorders (VCRs) were able to reduce prices from $1,300 in 1977 to $298 by 1984 by emphasizing the impact of an early step in the chain (product design) on a later step (production) by drastically reducing the number of parts in VCRs.[6]

Conventional management accounting approaches tend to emphasize across-the-board cost reductions. By recognizing interdependencies, however, value chain analysis admits to the possibility that deliberately increasing costs in one value activity can bring about a reduction in total costs. The expense that Procter & Gamble incurred to place order-entry computers directly in Wal-Mart stores, for example, significantly reduced overall order-entry and processing costs for both firms.

The methodology

The value chain concept just described has a unique methodology. Its methodology involves the following steps:

1. Identify the industry's value chain, then assign costs, revenues, and assets to value activities;
2. Diagnose the cost drivers regulating each value activity; and
3. Develop sustainable competitive advantage, either through controlling cost drivers better than competitors or by reconfiguring the value chain.

These steps are considered in greater detail in the following sections.

Identifying the value chain

The first step in constructing and using a value chain is to identify the industry's value chain. This step must be executed with the idea of gaining competitive advantage, for competitive advantage cannot be meaningfully examined at the level of the industry as a whole.

A value chain disaggregates an industry into its distinct strategic activities. Therefore, the starting point for cost analysis is to define an industry's value chain, then to assign costs, revenues, and assets to the various value activities. These activities are the building blocks with which firms in the industry create a product that buyers find valuable.

A value chain disaggregates an industry into its distinct strategic activities. Therefore, the starting point for cost analysis is to define an industry's value chain, then to assign costs, revenues, and assets to the various value activities. These activities are the building blocks with which firms in the industry create a product that buyers find valuable.

Activities should be isolated and separated if they satisfy any or all of the following conditions:

- They represent a significant percentage of operating costs;

- The cost behavior of the activities (or the cost drivers) is different;
- They are performed by competitors in different ways; and
- They are likely to create differentiation.

Each value activity incurs costs, generates revenues, and ties up assets in the process.

After identifying the value chain, operating costs, revenues, and assets must be assigned to individual value activities. For intermediate value activities, revenues should be assigned by adjusting internal transfer prices to competitive market prices. With this information, it should be possible to calculate ROA for each value activity.

Diagnosing cost drivers

The second step in constructing and using a value chain is to diagnose the cost drivers that explain variations in costs in each value activity.

In conventional management accounting, cost is primarily a function of only one cost driver: output volume. Cost concepts related to output volume—fixed versus variable cost, average cost versus marginal cost, cost-volume-profit analysis, break-even analysis, flexible budgets, and contribution margin, to name a few—permeate the thinking and the writing about cost.

In the value chain framework, by contrast, output volume per se is seen to capture little of the richness of cost behavior. Rather, multiple cost drivers are usually at work. Further, cost drivers differ across value activities. For example, number of orders received is the cost driver for the receiving activity, number of setups is the cost driver for the production control activity, and number of orders shipped is the cost driver for the shipping activity.

Attempts have been made to create a comprehensive list of cost drivers.[7] In the strategic management literature, in particular, good lists of cost drivers exist.[8] Following these lists, the following list of cost drivers is divided into two categories:

- Structural cost drivers; and
- Executional cost drivers.

These two categories are discussed in the sections below. An attempt is also made below to define which drivers in these two categories can be considered "fundamental" cost drivers.

Structural cost drivers

The first category of cost drivers, structural cost drivers, draws on industrial organization literature.[9] *Structural cost drivers* derive from a company's choices about its underlying economic structure. These choices drive cost positions for any given product group. There are at least five strategic choices that a firm must make about its underlying economic structure:

1. *Scale*: What is the size of the investment to be made in manufacturing, R&D, and marketing resources?
2. *Scope*: What is the degree of vertical integration? (Horizontal integration is more related to scale.)
3. *Experience*: How many times in the past has the firm already done what it is doing again?
4. *Technology*: What process technologies are used in each step of the firm's value chain?
5. *Complexity*: How wide a line of products or services is being offered to customers?

Each structural driver involves choices that drive product cost. Given certain assumptions, the cost calculus of each structural driver can be specified.[10]

Recently, much interest has arisen over activity-based costing (ABC).[11] The ABC analysis is largely a framework to operationalize complexity, which is a fundamental cost driver.

Executional cost drivers

The second category of cost drivers, *executional cost drivers,* are those determinants of a firm's cost position that hinge on its ability to "execute" successfully.

Whereas structural cost drivers are not monotonically scaled with performance, executional drivers are. That is, for each of the structural drivers, more is not always better. Thus, for example, there are diseconomies of scale or of scope: A more complex product line is not necessarily better or necessarily worse than a less complex line. Too much experience can be as bad as too little in a dynamic environment. Texas Instruments, for example, emphasized the learning curve and became the world's lowest-cost producer of obsolete microchips. Technological leadership versus "followership" is a legitimate choice for most firms.

In contrast, for each one of the executional cost drivers, more is *always* better. The list of

> *In the value chain framework, output volume per se is seen to capture little of the richness of cost behavior. Rather, multiple cost drivers are usually at work. Further, cost drivers differ across value activities. For example, number of orders received is the cost driver for the receiving activity, number of setups is the cost driver for the production control activity, and number of orders shipped is the cost driver for the shipping activity.*

basic executional cost drivers includes at least the following:

- *Work force involvement* ("*participation*"): Is the work force committed to continuous improvement (*kaizen* in Japanese)?
- *Total quality management (TQM)*: Is the work force committed to total product quality?
- *Capacity utilization*: What are the scale choices on maximum plant construction?
- *Plant layout efficiency*: How efficient, against current norms, is the plant's layout?
- *Product configuration*: Is the design or formulation of the product effective?
- *Linkages with suppliers or customers*: Is the linkage with suppliers or customers exploited, according to the firm's value chain?

Quantifying the effects of each of these drivers also involves specific cost-analysis issues. Many strategic planners maintain that SCM is moving quickly away from structural drivers and toward executional drivers because the insights from analyses based on structural drivers are too often obsolete and, hence, ineffective.

Fundamental cost drivers

No consensus currently exists on what constitutes "fundamental" cost drivers. One publication, for example, offers two different lists of fundamental cost drivers.[12] Those who see cost behavior in strategic terms, however, agree that output volume alone cannot catch all aspects of cost behavior. Ultimately, how unit costs change because of changes in output volume in the short run is seen as a less interesting question than how a company's cost position is influenced by the firm's comparative position on the various drivers that are relevant in its competitive situation.

Whatever items are on the list of "fundamental" cost drivers, the key ideas are as follows:

1. *Value chain as the broader framework.* The concept of cost drivers is a way to understand cost behavior in each activity in the value chain. Thus, ideas such as ABC are only a subset of the value chain framework.
2. *Volume is not enough.* For strategic analysis, volume is usually not the most useful way to explain cost behavior.
3. *Structural choices and executional skills.* What is more useful in a strategic sense is to explain cost position in terms of the structural choices and executional skills that shape the firm's competitive position. For example, Michael Porter[13] analyzes the classic confrontation in 1962 between General Electric and Westinghouse regarding steam turbines in terms of the structural and executional cost drivers for each firm.
4. *Relevant strategic drivers.* Not all strategic drivers are equally important all the time, though several are probably important in every case. For example, Porter develops a strategic assessment of du Pont's position in titanium dioxide, based primarily on scale and capacity utilization issues.[14]
5. *Cost analysis framework.* For each cost driver, a particular cost analysis framework is critical to understanding the positioning of a firm.
6. *Cost drivers specific to activities.* Different activities in the value chain are usually influenced by different cost drivers. For example, the relevant cost driver for advertising is market share, whereas promotional costs are usually variable. For example, Coca Cola can realize economies of scale in advertising because of its large market share. A price-off by contrast (an example of a sales promotion activity), is strictly a variable cost per unit.

Developing sustainable competitive advantage

The third step in constructing and using a value chain is to develop sustainable competitive advantage. Once a firm has identified the industry's value chain and diagnosed the cost drivers of each value activity, sustainable competitive advantage can be gained either by controlling those drivers better than competitors or by reconfiguring the value chain.

For each value activity, the key questions to ask about developing sustainable competitive advantage are:

1. Can costs in this activity be reduced, holding value (revenues) constant?
2. Can value (revenue) be increased in this activity, holding costs constant?

Cost reduction

By systematically analyzing costs, revenues, and assets in each activity, the firm can achieve both differentiation and low cost. An effective way to accomplish this goal is to compare the value chain of the firm with the value chains of one or two of its major competitors, then identify the actions needed to manage the firm's value chain better than competitors manage their value chains.

Value increase

While continuing the focus on managing the existing value chain better than competitors, a company should devote more effort toward identifying where in the value chain payoffs could be significant. For example, in the mature and highly competitive meat packing industry, Iowa Beef Processors has performed exceptionally well by controlling its processing, distribution, and labor costs. It accomplished these cost reductions by redefining the traditional value chain in this industry:

"Earnings per share [of Iowa Beef Processors] have soared at a compound annual rate of over 23 percent since 1973. The company has achieved this remarkable record by never wavering from its strategy and obsession—to be the low-cost producer of beef.

To that end, it rewrote the rules for killing, chilling, and shipping beef. It built plants on a grand scale, automated them to a fare-thee-well, and now spends up to $20 million a year on renovation to keep them operating efficiently. The old-line packers shipped live animals to the abattoirs at such rail centers as Chicago, but Iowa Beef brought the plant to the cattle in the sprawling feedlots of the High Plains and Southwest. This saved on transportation and avoided the weight loss that commonly occurs when live animals are shipped. Iowa Beef also led the industry in cleaving and trimming carcasses into loins, ribs, and other cuts, and boxing the pieces at the plant, which further reduced transport charges by removing excess weight.

The company has fought tenaciously to hold down labor costs. Though some of its plants are unionized, it refused to pay the wages called for in the United Food & Commercial Workers' expensive master agreement, which the elders of the industry have been tied to for forty years. Iowa Beef's wages and benefits average half those of less hard-nosed competitors."[15]

It is not suggested here that constructing a value chain for a firm is easy, as the above details demonstrate. There are several thorny problems to confront: calculating value for intermediate products, isolating cost drivers, identifying linkages across activities, and computing supplier and channel margins, for example. Despite these problems, it is in every firm's self-interest to construct its value chain. The very process of performing the value chain analysis can be quite instructive. Such an exercise forces managers to ask: "How does my activity add value to the chain of customers who use my product or service?"

Power of value chain analysis: a case study

This section presents a case to illustrate the value chain concept and methodology. This study also demonstrates how value chain analysis differs from conventional management accounting analysis.

In the study, the cost and differentiation positioning of two firms from the airline industry are contrasted by comparing the cost per seat mile of these two airlines in the different

Exhibit 2. *Ajax Airlines Financial Data*

Statements of Income	1988	1987
Sales	$8,800	$7,200
Expenses		
Salaries and benefits	$2,900	$2,400
Aircraft fuel	1,100	1,000
Fleet operations cost (lease and depreciation)	3,900	3,200
Total operating expenses	$7,900	$6,600
Operating income	$900	$600
Interest expense	230	200
Tax	335	200
Net income	$335	$200
Balance Sheets		
Current assets	$2,600	$2,100
Property and equipment	7,000	6,300
Total assets	$9,600	$8,400
Current liabilities	$2,700	$2,000
Long-term debt	3,000	3,000
Equity	3,900	3,400
Total liabilities	$9,600	$8,400

components of their value chains. The analysis offered is based on the published financial statements of the firms discussed.

The value chains of airline competitors are described in both qualitative and quantitative terms. Generally, it can be said that all commercial airlines provide value to customers at the following three stages:

1. By providing reservation information and ticketing services;
2. By operating the aircraft from point A to point B; and
3. By providing other services to passengers before a flight, during a flight, and after a flight arrives.

Each element in the value chain utilizes specific assets and has a specific cost function. Overall return on investment is a result of value added at all three linked stages.

Conventional financial reports reveal nothing about the separate value-creating activities in which the airline is engaged. Exhibit 2 shows a disguised and condensed version of the published income statements and balance sheets of one of the major trunk airlines (which here is fictitiously called Ajax Air-

Exhibit 3. *Ajax Airlines*
du Pont Analysis

	$\dfrac{\text{Net income}}{\text{Sales}}$	$\times$	$\dfrac{\text{Sales}}{\text{Assets}}$	$\times$	$\dfrac{\text{Assets}}{\text{Equity}}$	$=$	$\dfrac{\text{Net income}}{\text{Equity}}$
1988	$\dfrac{\$\ 335}{\$8{,}800}$	$\times$	$\dfrac{\$8{,}800}{\$9{,}600}$	$\times$	$\dfrac{\$9{,}600}{\$3{,}900}$	$=$	$\dfrac{\$\ 335}{\$3{,}900}$
	0.038	$\times$	0.917	$\times$	2.46	$=$	0.086
1987	$\dfrac{\$\ 200}{\$7{,}200}$	$\times$	$\dfrac{\$7{,}200}{\$8{,}400}$	$\times$	$\dfrac{\$8{,}400}{\$3{,}400}$	$=$	$\dfrac{\$\ 200}{\$3{,}400}$
	0.028	$\times$	0.857	$\times$	2.47	$=$	0.059

lines). The statements clearly reveal much that is interesting about the company—but nothing about the value chain. Combining the financial statements with a du Pont analysis (as shown in Exhibit 3) can yield conventional insights, but not much about business strategy.

Profit margins

The du Pont analysis reveals (for one thing) that profit margins at Ajax improved along with sales. That is, the airline was able to sell more tickets, while operating expense declined per dollar of sales. Asset utilization—a critical factor in the airline industry—also improved, as the improved asset turnover (from 0.857 to 0.917 in Exhibit 3) shows. All the while, financial leverage remained constant. So it appears that Ajax Airlines was able to improve both margins and asset utilization, while holding financial risk constant. It would appear that management has done a good job and should continue with its apparently successful growth strategy.

But *how* has Ajax grown? And *how* has the company been able to earn greater margins at a higher level of sales? Where has Ajax added capacity to improve asset utilization? And, finally, what strategy is Ajax pursuing? Financial statement analysis provides no answers to these questions.

Traditional management accounting analysis

Traditional management accounting provides additional information about Ajax Airlines, though it also ignores a value chain perspective. Traditional cost accounting would suggest that, in an industry such as the airline industry with high fixed costs, contribution

analysis is the key. The argument would be that, because fleet cost and compensation for pilots, flight attendants, and ground personnel do not depend on volume in the short run, the airline strategy should be to fill up capacity by aggressive pricing. Once the break-even point is met, most of every incremental dollar of revenue goes straight to the bottom line, because incremental variable cost is probably confined mainly to fuel and food.

Given additional information that is usually supplied in the annual report of most major airline companies, the traditional contribution analysis for a firm can be constructed. Exhibit 4 shows that analysis for Ajax Airlines using seat miles flown as the per-unit metric.

Since incremental cost in the short run is very low, traditional managerial accountants would recommend filling up the unused capacity (as shown in Exhibit 4) at almost any price. But the supplementary financial data show that Ajax Airlines did not pursue this objective. Ajax Airlines was able to charge significantly more for each seat mile flown without improving utilization of the available seat miles, because seat miles flown at capacity utilization stayed constant at 64 percent. This conflicts, moreover, with conclusions drawn from Exhibit 3. That analysis shows that asset utilization improved, while traditional management accounting concludes that it remained constant. This conflict resurfaces when other factors are analyzed, as is discussed next.

Further management accounting analysis

The management accounting analysis in Exhibit 4 reveals that, for the same capacity utilization, Ajax Airlines was able to charge a higher price per seat mile flown while paying more for compensation and equipment (compensation per seat mile rose from $0.042 to $0.045, while fleet operations cost per seat mile rose from 5.6 cents to 6.0 cents). This suggests that, by improving the quality of service and the quality of equipment used, Ajax was able to charge higher prices. Although this conclusion may correspond to what happened, there is no way to be sure that this was the strategy that Ajax actually pursued. (In fact, it probably is not what happened.) Moreover, how can the contradictory conclusions about asset utilization from the

Exhibit 4. *Ajax Airlines*
Contribution Analysis

	1988	1987
Additional Information		
Seat miles flown	65,000	57,000
Available seat miles	102,000	89,000
Asset utilization (load factor realized)	64%	64%
Revenue per seat mile flown	$0.135	$0.126
Compensation per seat mile flown	$0.045	$0.042
Fuel per seat mile flown	0.017	0.018
Fleet operations cost per seat mile flown	0.060	0.056
Total	$0.122	$0.116
Operating profit per seat mile	$0.013	$0.010
Contribution margin per seat mile flown	$0.118	$0.108
Break-even level	$\frac{\$6,800}{\$0.118} = \$57,600$	$\frac{\$5,600}{\$0.108} = \$51,900$
Break-even percent of available capacity	56.5%	58.3%

two different analyses be explained? Also, should the extra revenue from the unused seats flow straight to the bottom line (as both analyses would seem to suggest)?

In an attempt to understand these problems, quite different insights can be gleaned from a value chain analysis, as shown in Exhibit 5. Clearly, Ajax Airlines invested heavily in ticketing and reservations (T&R), probably to improve its computerized reservations system. And—despite a 14 percent increase in seat miles flown (i.e., from 57,000 in 1987 to 65,000 in 1988, as Exhibit 4 shows)—T&R cost per seat mile flown held constant at $0.005 (see the "Costs" section near the bottom of Exhibit 5), though T&R cost is hardly a fixed cost. Presumably, Ajax Airlines is willing to increase T&R costs and assets as a strategic investment in better service.

A value chain analysis also shows that operating an aircraft is not purely a fixed cost, as traditional management accounting suggests. While the number of seat miles flown increased by 14 percent, operating expenses increased by 28 percent (i.e., from $3,900 to $4,980, as the line item labeled "Aircraft operations" in Exhibit 5 shows), so this figure is obviously not a fixed cost. Clearly, therefore, cost drivers other than capacity utilization are at work here, and management evidently does not control them.

The reduction in the asset base (see the line item "Aircraft operations" in Exhibit 5 under the category "Identifiable Property, Plant, and Equipment") is presumed to reflect one more year's depreciation on the aging fleet rather than a strategic change in fleet configuration. Also, it is interesting that cost per seat mile flown has risen about 13 percent (i.e., from $0.068 to $0.077—see the line item "Aircraft operations" in Exhibit 5 under the category "Costs" near the bottom of the exhibit). This is an element in the value chain that seems not to translate easily into value to the customer—the part, that is, that simply involves getting from point A to point B. Apparently, Ajax Airlines has raised the price per seat mile flown mostly to compensate for an increase in fleet operating expenses that has no clear strategic justification.

Customer service expense per seat mile flown has dropped from $0.043 to $0.040. As a straight fixed cost, this expense should have dropped to $0.038 ($0.043 ÷ 1.14, where 1.14 adjusts for the 14 percent increase in seat miles flown), so Ajax Airlines is spending a little more on this activity, as adjusted for volume.

Strategically, Ajax Airlines seems to be hoping that a small increase in aggregate (but not per-unit) customer service expenditures and a better T&R system will justify higher prices in an aging fleet. But increased aircraft operations costs offset most of the profit impact of the increase in revenue per seat mile flown from $0.126 in 1987 to $0.135 in 1988 (see

Exhibit 5. *Ajax Airlines*
Value Chain Analysis

	1988	1987
Sales	$8,800	$7,200
Tickets and reservations	320	300
Aircraft operations	4,980	3,900
Customer service	2,600	2,400
Total expenses	$7,900	$6,600
Identifiable Property, Plant, and Equipment (PPE) Assets		
Tickets and reservations	$2,000	$1,000
Aircraft operations	5,000	5,300
Customer service	0	0
Total	$7,000	$6,300

	Per Seat Mile Flown		Per Available Mile	
	1988	1987	1988	1987
Costs				
Tickets and reservations	$0.005	$0.005	$0.003	$0.003
Aircraft operations	0.077	0.068	0.049	0.044
Customer service	0.040	0.043	0.025	0.027
Total	$0.122	$0.116	$0.077	$0.074
Assets				
Tickets and reservations	$0.030	$0.020	$0.020	$0.010
Aircraft	0.080	0.090	0.050	0.060
Customer service	0	0	0	0
Total	$0.110	$0.110	$0.070	$0.070

"Revenue/seat mile" in Exhibit 4). This result hardly seems to fit the "success story" told by the traditional management accounting analysis. Value chain analysis, however, can yield different insights. The linking of traditional financial analysis with strategic positioning in this way is a critical element in effective financial analysis.

Comparative analysis

It should be noted that the ability to present value chain analyses that are comparative across competing firms increases the value of the technique. Exhibit 6 shows a simple example of the comparative value chain perspective. The exhibit shows a chart that was prepared from publicly available information for two very different major airlines: United Airlines and People Express (in its heyday).

Structured in this way, the difference in strategies between the two airlines becomes obvious. The "no frills" concept of People Express is readily apparent. Specifically, strategic decisions in the five areas listed in the "Value chain elements" column of Exhibit 7 account

for the $13,500 difference in the cost per 10,000 seat miles flown between these two airlines.

A strategy for competitive advantage

Traditional cost analysis focuses on the notion of value added (i.e., selling price less the cost of purchased raw materials) under the mistaken impression that this is the only area where a firm can influence costs. This article argues that value chain analysis provides a more meaningful way to explore competitive advantage.

Value added could be quite misleading for at least three reasons:

1. It arbitrarily distinguishes between raw materials and many other purchased inputs. Purchased services, such as maintenance or professional consulting services, are treated differently than raw materials purchased;

2. It does not point out the potential to exploit linkages (whether between a firm and its suppliers or between a firm and

Exhibit 6. *Value Chain Configurations: A Comparison Between People Express and United Airlines*

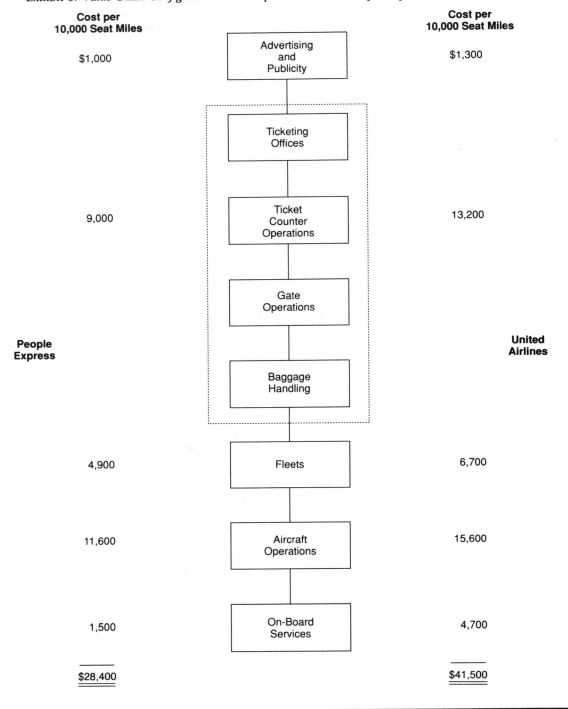

Cost per 10,000 Seat Miles		**Cost per 10,000 Seat Miles**
$1,000	Advertising and Publicity	$1,300
	Ticketing Offices	
9,000	Ticket Counter Operations	13,200
	Gate Operations	
People Express	Baggage Handling	**United Airlines**
4,900	Fleets	6,700
11,600	Aircraft Operations	15,600
1,500	On-Board Services	4,700
$28,400		$41,500

its customers) with a view to reducing costs or enhancing product differentiation; and

3. Competitive advantage cannot be fully explored without considering the interaction between purchased raw materials and other cost elements (e.g., purchasing higher-quality and higher-priced raw material can reduce scrap costs, and thus could lower total costs).

Exhibit 7. *Strategic Inferences From the Value Chains of People Express and United Airlines*

Value Chain Elements	People Express Less Than United Airlines (Cost per 10,000 Seat Mile)	Strategic Differences	
		People Express	United Airlines
Advertising and publicity	$ 300	Heavy promotion to tout low price/no-frills airline	Heavy promotion of full-service airline
Reservations and Ticketing	$4,200	No ticket offices No separate computer reservation system	Ticket offices in downtown locations Extensive computer reservation system
		Secondary airports and terminals No ticket counters (check-in only) Tickets purchased on board the aircraft or from machines No interline tickets Few fare options	Full-service
		First-come, first-serve seating No ticketing at gates	Full-service
		Carry-on space provided Charge for checked baggage No interline baggage	Free baggage checking
Fleet costs	$1,800	Used aircraft ("budget" airplanes)	New aircraft
Flight operations	$4,000	High-density seating Nonunion pilots Smaller crews and more flying hours per day Flight crews paid on dramatically lower scale Flight crews double on ground duties	Union pilots Bigger crews Crews paid on higher scale
Cabin operations	$3,200	Nonunion flight attendants Lower pay scale No first class No meals Charge for snacks and drinks served	Full-service

The focus of the value chain analysis is external to the firm. Each firm is seen in the context of the overall chain of value-creating activities, of which the firm is likely to be only a small part. (There apparently are no firms that span the entire value chain in which they operate.)

In summary, the methodology for constructing and using a value chain involves the following steps:

1. Identify the industry's value chain, then assign costs, revenues, and assets to each activity;

2. Identify the cost drivers that regulate each value activity; and

3. Build sustainable competitive advantage, either by controlling cost drivers better than competitors or by reconfiguring the value chain.

Efforts to simultaneously reduce costs and enhance differentiation are possible by carefully considering costs, revenues, and assets at each value activity vis-à-vis competitors. Cost driver analysis (of which ABC is a subset) is a part of value chain analysis. In SCM, therefore, the value chain provides the overall

Exhibit 8. *Value Chain vs. Conventional Management Accounting—A Summary*

	Traditional Management Accounting	Value Chain Analysis in the SCM Framework
Focus	Internal	External
Perspective	Value-added	Entire set of linked activities from suppliers to end-use customers
Cost driver concept	Single driver ("volume")	Multiple cost drivers • Structural drivers (e.g., scale, scope, experience, technology, and complexity) • Executional drivers (e.g., participative management, total quality management, and plant layout)
	Application at the overall firm level (cost-volume-profit analysis)	A set of unique cost drivers for each value activity
Cost containment philosophy	"Across the board" cost reductions	View cost containment as a function of the cost driver(s) regulating each value activity
		Exploit linkages with suppliers
		Exploit linkages with customers
		"Spend to save"
Insights for strategic decisions	None readily apparent (this is a large reason why the strategic consulting firms always discard the conventional reports as they begin their cost analyses)	Identify cost drivers at the individual activity level, and develop cost/differentiation advantage either by controlling those drivers better than competitors or by reconfiguring the value chain (e.g., Federal Express in mail delivery and MCI in long-distance telephone)
		For each value activity, ask strategic questions pertaining to: • Make versus buy • Forward/backward integration
		Quantify and assess "supplier power" and "buyer power," and exploit linkages with suppliers and buyers

framework; topics such as ABC are components of constructing and using value chains.

The case study provided in this article illustrates that the insights derived from value chain analysis are much different from those suggested by more conventional management accounting tools. Exhibit 8 summarizes the key differences between value chain and conventional management accounting.

The value chain perspective can be used to derive the following insights:

- Since virtually no two companies compete in exactly the same set of value activities, value chain analysis is a critical first step in understanding how a firm is positioned in its industry. Building sustainable competitive advantage requires a knowledge of the full, linked set of value activities of which the firm and its competitors are a part.
- Once a value chain is fully articulated, crit-

ical strategic decisions (e.g., make-or-buy decisions or forward versus backward integration) become clearer. Investment decisions can be viewed from the perspective of their impact on the overall chain and the firm's position within it.
- The value chain analysis helps to quantify supplier power by calculating the percentage of total profits that can be attributed to suppliers. This activity could help the firm identify ways to exploit linkages with suppliers.
- The value chain framework highlights how a firm's product fits into the buyer's value chain. Given this framework, it is readily apparent what percentage the firm's product costs comprise of the buyer's total costs. This information could be useful in encouraging the firm and buyers to work together in cost reduction activities.
- In the final analysis, the simultaneous pur-

suit of low cost and differentiation depends on a sophisticated understanding of the drivers of costs, revenues, and assets at each value activity and the interdependencies between value activities. ▲

Notes

1. Michael E. Porter, *Competitive Advantage: Creating and Sustaining Superior Performance* (New York: The Free Press, 1985): 62–67.
2. Michael E. Porter, *Competitive Strategy* (New York: The Free Press, 1980): 34–44.
3. John K. Shank, "Strategic Cost Management: New Wine, or Just New Bottles?" *Journal of Management Accounting Research* (Fall 1989): 47–65.
4. Porter, *Competitive Advantage,* 88.
5. M. Hergert and D. Morris, "Accounting Data for Value Chain Analysis," *Strategic Management Journal* (June 1989): 175–188.
6. *Ibid.*
7. Porter, *Competitive Strategy,* 70–87.
8. Daniel Riley, "Competitive Cost Based Investment Strategies for Industrial Companies," in *Manufacturing Issues* (New York: Booz, Allen & Hamilton Inc., 1987): 27–34.
9. F.M. Scherer, *Industrial Market Structure and Economic Performance,* 2nd ed. (New York: Rand McNally, 1980).
10. Pankaj Ghemawat, *The Arithmetic of Strategic Cost Analysis* (Boston: Harvard Business School Press, 1986).
11. Robin Cooper, "You Need a New Cost System When . . . ," *Harvard Business Review* (January–February 1989): 38–49; Robin Cooper and Robert S. Kaplan, "Measure Costs Right: Make the Right Decisions," *Harvard Business Review* (September–October 1988): 72–91; Robert S. Kaplan and H. Thomas Johnson, *Relevance Lost: The Rise and Fall of Management Accounting* (Boston: Harvard Business School Press, 1987).
12. [no author], *Manufacturing Issues* (New York: Booz, Allen & Hamilton Inc., 1987): 16–31.
13. Michael E. Porter, *du Pont in Titanium Dioxide* (Boston: Harvard Business School Press, 1986).
14. Michael E. Porter, "GE vs. Westinghouse in Large Turbine Generators," *Harvard Business School Case Series 380-128.*
15. A. Stuart, "Meatpackers in Stampede," *Fortune* (July 29, 1981): 67–73.

Effective Long-Term Cost Reduction: A Strategic Perspective

Michael D. Shields and S. Mark Young

Effective long-term cost reduction is a continuous activity that must be a strategic and cultural priority. In contrast to traditional cost reduction, with its emphasis on expedient and quick reductions in short-term costs because of immediate crises, strategic cost reduction must be part of a competitive strategy that integrates technological and human resource management strategies to provide a coordinated, broad-based, and long-term approach to reducing costs. Long-term competitive cost advantage depends on establishing a culture of continuous improvement of quality, time, and cost through innovation. Long-term cost reduction is most effectively accomplished by continuously learning about target core competencies faster than competitors can and by establishing long-term employment relationships with innovative, multiskilled employees who are paid above-average compensation.

Between the recessions of the late 1970s and early 1990s, several million U.S. managers and workers received significant pay cuts or were laid off because of cost reduction programs.[1] These programs were intended primarily to increase cost competitiveness. The business press described these cost reduction programs in phrases such as "slash and burn," "retrenching," "meat axing," "cutting and slicing," "repositioning," "restructing," "demassing," and "downsizing." In an attempt to justify the overall approach to cost reduction, the term "rightsizing" was coined. It is still unclear whether firms that engaged in these cost reduction programs will experience long-term success, since little systematic empirical evidence exists. Nonetheless, as articles in the business press show, cost reduction programs aimed at reducing the work force are still being implemented.[2]

This article first describes and evaluates the cost reduction programs employed in the late 1970s and throughout the 1980s, then sets forth a more viable basis for effective long-term cost reduction. The ultimate conclusion is that long-term controllable costs are caused (i.e., both increased and decreased) by employees, individually and in groupings, that range from small teams to entire organizations. As a consequence, the key to successful long-term cost reduction is to make cost reduction part of organizational culture—i.e., part of a competitive strategy based on the integration of human resources and technological strategies.

Traditional cost reduction programs

Starting in the late 1970s and throughout the 1980s, most firms relied on traditional cost reduction, which means a collection of crash programs that focus on cutting costs by reducing payrolls and eliminating jobs.[3] The key features of traditional cost reduction are identified in Exhibit 1.

A traditional cost reduction program is typically a distress tactic targeted at all employees. It is triggered in reaction to an immediate threat, such as poor performance, loss of contracts, or price reductions. Some of these programs (especially offshore retreat and diversification, both of which are explained below) are employed in the hope of escaping to places where labor and facilities costs are cheaper. While these traditional approaches often reduce costs immediately, the associated reduction in the value of human assets sets the stage for potential long-term failure. Five frequently used traditional cost reduction programs are described in the sections below; their effectiveness is also analyzed.[4]

Exhibit 1. *Differences Between Traditional and Strategic Cost Reduction*

Attribute	Traditional	Strategic
Goals	Specific	Competitive advantage
Scope	Narrow	Broad
Time frame	Short-term	Long-term
Frequency	Periodic	Continuous
Trigger	Reaction	Proaction
Target	Labor	Entire value chain

The technology approach

The technology approach focuses on replacing direct labor with technology to increase operating efficiency and to reduce the influence of unions. This approach is usually adopted or intensified after performance measures indicate poor performance. But the successful implementation of this approach requires money, time, an effective innovation process, and highly skilled employees—all of which, in firms that are performing poorly, are in short supply.

It is doubtful whether this labor-focused cost reduction—with its emphasis on immediate improvements in direct labor efficiency—can provide sustainable competitive advantage.[5] Its effectiveness is questionable because, in many manufacturing settings, a product's cost of direct labor is typically no more than 10 percent of its sales price. This means, for example, that a 100 percent increase in direct labor efficiency can only reduce a product's total cost as a percentage of its sales by 5 percent. Alternatively, the complete elimination of direct labor can only reduce the product's total cost as a percent of its sales by 10 percent (*assuming* that the substitute for this labor is costless).

Thus, attempts to gain or sustain competitive advantage by reducing labor cost would appear to be weak foundations for a successful cost reduction program. As Hamel and Prahalad[6] point out, the *cost* of labor is rarely a source of sustainable competitive advantage. First, labor is a small percentage of total cost. Second, when the labor force is the key to a firm's competitive advantage, that advantage stems from labor's ability to be innovative through work methods (e.g., through total quality management) and flexibility. More-over, many firms adopt technology-intensive strategies (e.g., computer-integrated manufacturing, or CIM) when they reduce their work force. Importantly, the success of these strategies requires having highly skilled employees who can design, implement, operate, and service these advanced technologies. Unfortunately, these critical human resource issues are ignored or receive only lip service because of short-term cost considerations. Ironically, however, long-term success with technology is determined by how employees work with the technology.

Another important consideration in achieving good performance from a technology-intensive strategy is knowing when and how much should be spent on technological innovation. Evidence indicates that the relationship follows an elongated S shape, with spending related to technology on the x-axis and technological performance on the y-axis.[7] This elongated S relationship indicates that initial spending on technology results in little, if any, increase in performance. At some point, as spending continues to increase, there are dramatic increases in the performance of the technology. Finally, a point is reached at which further increases in spending result in only small (or no) increases in performance as the limits of the technology are hit (e.g., conventional washing machines can get clothes only so clean).

The implication for cost management is that a firm will achieve a better payoff from its spending on technology if it knows where it is on the S curve. For example, when a new technology is first introduced, a firm may decide to stop spending for the new technology when only a negligible increase in performance is obtained. At the other extreme, a firm at the far end of its S curve may fail to realize that it has moved beyond the point at which increased spending will lead to worthwhile increases in performance. The result could be wasted spending as the technology hits its performance limit.

"Lean and mean"

The "lean and mean" approach has been a popular cost reduction program since the 1980s. Firms that follow this approach apply tough policies and controls to reduce the number of employees. A common approach is

Exhibit 2. *Cost Reduction Roller Coaster*

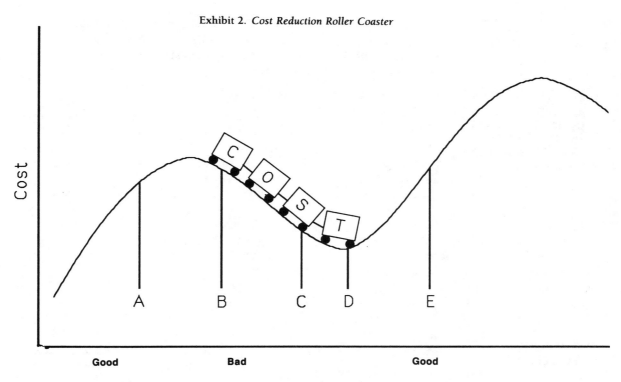

A: As costs rise, the economy goes soft.
B: To reduce costs, cut discretionary programs, reduce work force, etc.
C: Problems develop: moral, motivation, conflict, shortages, delays.
D: To reduce problems and to react to the expanding economy, hire new employees.
E: Incur extra costs to train new employees and to cover learning curve effects.

to employ across-the-board cost cuts through layoffs and reductions in pay and benefits.[8]

An appropriate depiction of the effects of a lean and mean program is a roller coaster traveling through time. The end of the ride can be— and frequently is—a long-term failure, despite short-term thrills and success. Exhibit 2 illustrates the interaction of lean and mean cost reduction efforts and the state of the economy. As shown in Exhibit 2, a firm's costs—total and unit—rise when the economy is "good" and fall when the economy is "bad." We define a good (or bad) economy as one in which there is low (high) unemployment and a growing (shrinking) gross national product.

When the economy is good, the lean and mean approach is not employed; as a result, costs creep up as inefficiency increases and new programs are initiated or expanded. As costs rise across firms, the economy begins to soften as prices become inflated. In response,

firms begin to implement lean and mean programs to cut costs by reducing and eliminating discretionary programs and employees. While there is an immediate cost decrease, adverse effects become noticeable shortly thereafter.[9] The morale, motivation, and commitment of remaining employees begins to decrease. Their stress increases because they worry about being the next ones who will be laid off, and also because they are overworked because of the layoffs.[10] Having fewer employees also leads to coordination problems (e.g., production delays and missed schedules), which can cause decreases in quality and increases in delivery time. Another bad consequence is that the creative and motivated employees leave for better employment opportunities.

In time, the economy begins to expand again as firms' products regain their competitiveness as a result of their cost reduction program. In response, firms abandon their lean

How Effective Are Traditional Cost Reduction Programs?

Recent surveys suggest that traditional cost reduction programs do not meet their objectives.* One survey found that—out of 350 senior managers in 275 companies that, together, make up 26 percent of the U.S. gross national product—half responded that the cost-cutting or restructuring programs at their companies had failed to achieve what had been hoped.

Results of the other survey (this one of managers from 1,005 corporations) found as follows:

- Less than one half of the companies had met their cost reduction targets;
- Only 32 percent had raised profits to an acceptable level;
- Only 21 percent had improved return on investment appreciably;
- 58 percent reported that employee morale was battered;
- 37 percent were having trouble persuading the survivors to remain; and
- 87 percent reported that early retirement programs led to decision by star employees to leave.

* Surveys by the Cresap division of the consulting firm Towers Perrin and by consultant Wyatt Co. cited in Anne Fisher, "Morale Crisis," *Fortune*, Nov. 18, 1991, at 71–72.

increase because the work still needs to be done.[12] The long-term effects of lean and mean programs are like the roller coaster ride shown in Exhibit 2.

Offshore retreat

Many firms have tried to reduce costs by escaping to places (e.g., Asia) that offer the promise of lower labor costs. Many of these firms have found, however, that start-up costs of offshore retreats are higher than expected, while quality and delivery performance are lower.[13] The success of this cost reduction approach often depends on how employees at home are treated and on the vagaries of exchange rates and currency fluctuations. Employee morale at home can be hurt if domestic or local employees are laid off when the firm moves jobs offshore.

Mergers

Mergers purport to create economies of scale by eliminating overlapping employees, products, plants, and overhead. The idea is to build on the strengths of each merging entity, but the result is often that the worst aspects of each firm survive.[14] Problems often occur in assimilating diverse or incompatible management styles, corporate cultures, product lines, and technologies. Frequently, these mergers result in layoffs and compensation reductions, with the result that morale and motivation decrease. Ultimately, the hoped-for economies of scale from the merger are not realized as hidden or unexpected costs arise.

Diversification

Diversification into new industries is an approach that firms often use when they are searching for cheaper operating environments. If a firm expands beyond its core competency, however, it is likely to experience difficulties in developing and implementing new products, technologies, or distribution systems, with the result that costs are higher than expected.[15] The increasing diversity also increases the cost of complexity, which in many cases exceeds the incremental revenue.

When can traditional cost reduction approaches succeed?

Given these five approaches to traditional cost reduction, the question arises: "Are there

and mean programs; they begin to hire employees again and to reestablish or expand programs to reduce the adverse effects of the previous cost reduction programs. As the economy expands, firms continue to hire new employees and to incur associated training and learning-curve costs.[11] The net result is that costs begin to increase again. This cycle keeps repeating, but as time goes on, each new cost peak becomes higher than the previous cost peaks.

Lean and mean is not effective in the long term, because it attempts to reduce costs by reducing workers, but it does *not* reduce the work that needs to be done to make and sell products. While cutting workers, but not work, is a popular approach to traditional cost reduction, it causes an immediate decrease in costs that is usually followed by an

Exhibit 3. *The Sand Cone Model of Cost Reduction*

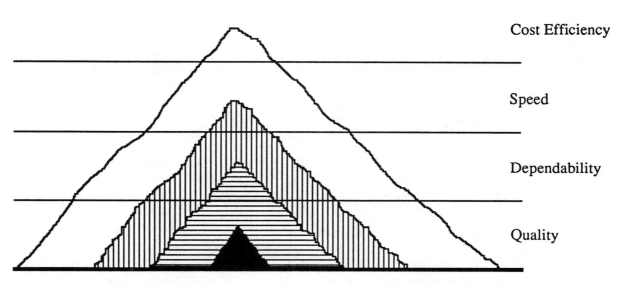

Cost Efficiency

Speed

Dependability

Quality

Source: K. Ferdows and A. DeMeyer, "Lasting Improvements in Manufacturing Performance: In Search of a New Theory," 9 *The Journal of Operations Management* 168–184 (No. 2, 1991).

situations when traditional cost reduction can be effective?" (See accompanying box," How Effective Are Traditional Cost Reduction Programs?") Some managers have found that traditional cost reduction is effective in only the following three situations:

1. When "dressing up" a business for divestiture;
2. When implementing a harvest strategy; and
3. When reducing operating costs—but only when a firm's overall strategic position is good.[16]

While traditional approaches to cost reduction may be effective in these special situations, in general, traditional approaches do not appear to provide a basis for long-term competitive success.

Strategic cost reduction

In contrast to the traditional approach, this article advocates strategic cost reduction as an approach that can provide companies with

better opportunities for creating and sustaining long-term competitive advantage. Strategic cost reduction is a long-term approach that integrates competitive strategy, technological strategies, human resource management strategies, and organizational design considerations to provide a focused and coordinated basis for sustaining competitive advantage. Exhibit 1 compares traditional and strategic cost reduction strategies.

The importance of viewing cost reduction as part of a long-term competitive strategy is reinforced by evidence that Ferdows and De-Meyer provide.[17] Their analysis of 187 European manufacturers indicates that cost reduction is the result of having achieved success with other manufacturing strategies. Specifically, they argue and empirically show that long-term cost improvement is the result of having first achieved improvement in quality, then dependability, and finally speed. There is a cumulative effect by which prior gains influence current gains, a process that can be illustrated as a pile of sand with four layers: quality at the bottom and cost at the top (see Exhibit 3). Increases in quality help increase dependability; then gains in both quality and dependability spur gains in speed. Finally, the cumulative effects of these prior gains result in cost efficiency gains.

Ferdows and DeMeyer also point out that, due to the shape of the pile of sand, achieving a small gain in cost requires successively larger gains for these other aspects of performance (e.g., a 10 percent cost gain may require a 15 percent gain in speed, a 25 percent gain in dependability, and a 40 percent gain in quality). The implication is that long-term successful cost reduction is achieved indirectly—through gains made in other strategically important areas. Thus, the cost reduction strategy should be deeply embedded in the firm's competitive strategy.

Strategic cost reduction occurs continuously and is intertwined with competitive strategy.[18] Ideally, competitive strategies and also cost reduction strategies are derived from analyses of a firm's own value chains and of the value chains of its competitors to identify key activities that offer the best competitive alternatives. Strategic cost reduction is part of a competitive strategy that is focused on improving the performance of key activities and their cost drivers in a firm's value chain.

Focus

Two critical aspects of developing a strategic cost reduction program involve deciding where to focus the program and the mix of methods to use to reduce strategically important costs. Many manufacturing firms achieve competitive advantage from activities that occur before (e.g., R&D) or after (e.g., distribution) manufacturing, rather than in manufacturing itself. For many manufacturers, the most effective strategy to reduce a product's total life cycle cost is to focus cost reduction efforts on those activities that occur before manufacturing begins.[19] For instance, many Japanese manufacturing firms focus their cost reduction efforts on activities that occur before manufacturing begins, because they have found that this gives them the most and the quickest reductions in costs.[20] Quickly reducing costs significantly is crucial to maximizing market share and achieving target cost strategies.[21] Thus, for most firms, initial ef-

forts at cost reduction should be focused on those activities that occur before manufacturing ever begins—i.e., conception, development, and design.

Set of methods

While manufacturing firms use many methods to reduce costs, there is only limited evidence that they are used in coordinated ways to achieve synergistic gains.[22] Thus, an important aspect of developing an effective cost reduction strategy is to identify a set of cost reduction methods that can be used in concert to continuously reduce strategically important costs. The methods selected should be compatible with—and should reinforce—a firm's competitive strategy, culture, and human resource management strategy.[23]

For instance, the implementation of a cost reduction strategy may coincide with the adoption of a competitive strategy and a corporate culture of continuous improvement. A set of methods can be employed to achieve continuous improvement, including activity-based management (ABM), value analysis and engineering, just-in-time (JIT) manufacturing methods, total quality management (TQM), cross-functional teamwork, employee involvement, and employee skill enhancement.[24] Rappaport[25] provides a list of coordinated ways by which a firm can reduce its long-term costs if it is pursuing a cost leadership strategy or a differentiation competitive strategy. Hayes, Wheelwright, and Clark[26] provide examples of how manufacturing firms can use a set of cost reduction methods to achieve synergistic gains in performance.

Trade-offs

In some cases, the strategically important issue is to *increase* cost to achieve other competitive gains. For example, a study by McKinsey and Company found that being six months late to market but meeting the developmental cost budget resulted in actual profits that were one-third lower than budgeted profits.[27] In contrast, bringing a product to market on time but 50 percent over the developmental budget resulted in a profit loss of only 4 percent. The important point of this example is that sometimes it is strategically advantageous to increase costs if doing so can help achieve other competitive gains.

Employees are the ultimate long-term cost driver

Effective cost reduction (especially in the long term) requires changing employees' behavior. In the long-term, the decisions and actions of employees cause costs; only employees can make decisions and take actions to reduce costs. Thus, the key to effective long-term cost reduction is employees—their beliefs, values, and goals. This means that

---

The key to successful long-term cost reduction is to make cost reduction part of organizational culture—i.e., part of a competitive strategy based on the integration of human resources and technological strategies.

---

successful cost reduction depends on establishing and nurturing an appropriate organizational culture, such as one based on continuous improvement and cost consciousness.[28] In the long term, successful cost reduction depends on how well a cost reduction strategy fits with a firm's competitive strategy, culture, and human resource management strategy.

The major reason that traditional cost reduction fails to have a positive long-term strategic impact is that it excludes the value of having employees who are broadly and deeply skilled—employees who work together and are committed to the long-term success of a firm. This human resource management approach is one of the most important reasons for the comparative success of Japanese firms. For example, one key to the success of Japanese firms has been their treatment of human resource management as long-term and strategic; human resource management is an important, if not *the* most important, part of their competitive strategy.[29]

The importance of employees as long-term cost drivers can be illustrated based on a discussion of quality improvement. Many firms have adopted the approach of trying to improve quality and reduce the cost of quality by substituting technology for people. But,

behind all this technology are employees who design, operate, and service it. Technology can produce products that are only as good as the employees who develop and operate the technology—software programmers, machine technologists, design engineers, and others.

In the long term, the way to improve product quality and reduce the cost of quality through technology is to use technology to supplement high-quality employees. Technology will work better if it is complemented by employers who are highly educated, highly skilled, highly motivated, and committed to continuous improvement. All the innovation that is necessary for technology to be effective comes from humans. Having creative employees is important because, when trying to sustain competitive advantage through technology, technology does not stand still. Technology-intensive firms must continuously innovate to improve existing technology or to introduce new technology; otherwise, they will fall behind their technology-intensive competitors.

Three prerequisites to realizing the maximum benefits to be derived from long-term cost reduction efforts of employees are: having good top management, having a cost culture, and offering long-term employment. Each provides an important and necessary contribution to the establishment of an organizational setting in which employees are willing and able to make strategic cost reductions. The next sections discuss how top management, cost culture, and long-term employment affect long-term costs. Later sections explain how organizational cost drivers affect strategic cost reduction.

Top management

Top management must take the initiative in decision making and action to demonstrate to other employees and stakeholders that they are serious about improving the competitive position of the firm.[30] Top management should be prepared to set examples by taking tough action (e.g., taking a bigger reduction in pay than do the workers, laying off senior executives before laying off line workers, and eliminating executive perks) and getting involved with all employees. Top managers should take these actions to show that they are aware of the problems other employees face and that top management cares about employees and their fate during tough times.

One important determinant of success is the ability of top management to establish *strategic intent*, which means that they must provide *leadership* to achieve a *vision* by exploiting *core competencies*.[31] Top management must provide the leadership that makes all employees committed to achieving this strategic intent.[32] Top management must discuss strategic problems, challenges, and opportunities with employees. Finally, top management must set a steady course of action, set clear targets, and establish review mechanisms.

Top management must establish strategic goals for cost reduction. These goals should be based on supporting or reinforcing the firm's core competencies and competitive strategy. For example, top management may decide that the best way to reduce cost and to increase both quality and flexibility in the long-term is by exploiting the firm's competence in mechanical, manufacturing, and software engineering by implementing CIM. Accompanying this introduction would be a change in the human resource management strategy to increase employees' knowledge of how to use the new technology. For example, direct labor employees could be retrained to become machine technologists and monitors.

Cost culture

Top management must also develop a cost-conscious culture. The goal of a cost-conscious culture is continuous improvement of quality, time, and cost through innovation. Achieving this goal can be aided by redesigning the organization to focus attention on key factors that have to do with sustaining continuous improvement strategies. The acid test of a cost-conscious culture is whether employees are motivated to take actions that reduce long-term costs but expose them to short-term risk. An example is a culture in which workers are willing to be innovative enough to eliminate their own jobs because they believe that they will then be assigned to more challenging and rewarding jobs.

Eight ways to develop a cost culture. Eight key ways to develop a cost culture are as follows:[33]

1. Have top management demonstrate daily to employees the importance of reducing costs to the firm's success.
2. Hire the best-qualified employees. These employees can then develop high-quality activities and products, because long-term total cost with high quality is less than long-term total cost with low quality.
3. Empower employees through participation, involvement, and autonomous, cross-functional work teams.
4. Increase the levels of education, training, retraining, and cross-training provided to employees to increase and broaden their skills, commitment, and innovation.
5. Motivate employees to break existing paradigms (e.g., eliminating existing constraints rather than optimizing within them).
6. Communicate horizontally more than vertically; eliminate conflicting bureaucratic messages; focus all employees' communication on two or three keys to success; reduce the number of rules, policies, and standard operating procedures; and provide scoreboards for continuous feedback.
7. Link compensation to cost reduction (such as gains in productivity and efficiency, achievement of target costs, and improvement over the previous period's costs).
8. Provide all employees with continuous feedback about competitors' costs, their own performance, and the performance of other teams.

Traditional cost reduction means a collection of crash programs that focus on cutting costs by reducing payrolls and eliminating jobs.

Train[34] provides an interesting description of a firm with cost problems that is struggling—philosophically and politically—with whether to implement a traditional cost reduction program (i.e., deep across-the-board cuts). Analysis of this case by senior executives and consultants illustrates why and how such

Exhibit 4. *Organizational Cost Drivers*

Structure

- Number of work units
- Number of functional departments/horizontal layer
- Number of profit centers
- Number of distribution channels
- Number of product lines
- Number of vertical levels in organization
- Number of operating facilities
- Number of products produced at more than one facility
- Number of employees

Process

- Planning and control processes
- Employee involvement and participation
- Total quality management
- Capacity utilization
- Plant layout and its efficiency
- Product configuration
- Linkages between suppliers and/or customers
- Education and training programs
- Activity-process sequence (linear, concurrent)
- Management style
- Number of internal transactions
- Number of external transactions
- Number of meetings
- Number of trips
- Number of memos sent or received
- New product sales/total sales
- [Number of new employees + number of exited employees]/total employees

---

situations should be a strategic cultural priority that is dealt with by methods like the eight outlined above.

Long-term employment

Many firms have found that the best way to realize the maximum potential from all employees to reduce long-term costs is to establish a long-term employment relationship in which both employees and the employer can adjust to changing circumstances.

For example, a human resource strategy that is based on long-term employment, cross-training of employees, continuous education, job rotation, and work teams creates an organizational skill set that provides a firm with the flexibility to adapt quickly to changes, opportunities, and threats. Having broadly skilled employees also increases flexibility when product and activity volume decrease and it becomes necessary to rearrange employee work assignments. The bottom line is that if firms want employees to be committed to long-term cost reduction, they must make long-term commitments to their employees. An employee's commitment will extend only as far into the future as his expected employment benefit horizon (e.g., including pension benefits).

Avoiding layoffs. Many firms have found that it is in their best interest not to lay off workers as a means of cutting costs.[35] Over a period of time, it is cheaper to keep excess employees. For example, the employees can be put to work on projects that will improve efficiency or eliminate non-value-added activities; alternatively, they can be provided with additional training. Some firms have used excess workers to lay the groundwork for an expected expansion in business by having them prepare the firm to use new technologies. This proactive approach can help a firm adapt faster when the business environment improves.

Laying off employees causes motivational problems for the remaining employees and, when business improves, the firm must incur the cost of hiring and training new employees who will probably not be as effective and efficient as were the employees who were laid off. Thus, while laying off employees may bring about an immediate reduction in cost, over a period of several years, it could become the more costly alternative because of the roller coaster effect.

When a company must lay off employees, a program should be implemented to maintain (if not increase) the morale of the remaining employees. Imberman[36] suggests a three-step program:

1. *Define the sources of the firm's competitive problems.* In many cases, this requires changing the corporate culture to accept the problems for what they really are. Changing the culture will help the survivors establish a shared vision of what is required for success, which usually requires communication and innovation.
2. *Initiate action to solve the problem.* This requires realistic challenges and experiments. It is critical that employees believe that to solve these problems they must work smarter, not harder or longer.
3. *Increase employees' skills.* This is accomplished through education, training, retraining, and cross-training.

Organizational cost drivers

An organization is a collection of people. Based on the view that employees are the ultimate long-term cost driver, it is a natural extension to see an organization as an important long-term cost driver. If an employee causes and reduces costs, then groups of employees will also cause and reduce costs.

Organizations group employees into teams, departments, divisions, and similar groupings to efficiently and effectively accomplish activities. The way in which employees are organized affects the long-term cost structure. The diversity of operating units and their boundaries (e.g., functional or geographical boundaries) affect a firm's complexity (e.g., its number of parts and their interrelationships), which, in turn, affects long-term costs. Some have offered ABM as a solution to reducing the cost of complexity, because ABM focuses on eliminating non-value-added activities and reducing the number and frequency of cost drivers.[37] Gingrich and Metz[38] provide examples of how to reduce the cost of organizationally induced complexity by making changes in organizational structures and processes.

Organizational cost drivers include organizational structure, organizational process, and organizational learning. Examples of organizational cost drivers include vertical structure, horizontal structure, work units (e.g., individuals versus teams), educational programs, process sequence (e.g., linear versus concurrent), and culture and management style (e.g., decentralization, a vertical chain of command, or entrepreneurial); see Exhibit 4.

Firms adapt their organizational structure and processes over time in response to various challenges and opportunities. Many of the contemporary changes to these organizational cost drivers are intended to increase a firm's speed, flexibility, quality, and innovation. Organizational structure and process significantly affect what and how fast an organization learns.

Organizational cost drivers determine a significant percentage of a firm's long-term cost structure and its competitive position. It is difficult to identify any one of these cost drivers as being the most significant. Nonetheless, they act in concert to determine long-run costs. Thus, organizational cost drivers should be the focus of a cost reduction strategy.

A specific example of how these cost drivers affect long-term costs can be seen in the case of a large aerospace firm whose cost structure was analyzed by a well-known strategic consulting firm. This consulting study predicted that unit operating costs could be reduced by 47 percent if the aerospace firm changed its cost drivers as follows:

- A 17 percent reduction could be achieved if the firm adopted a focused manufacturing strategy and flattened the organizational structure;
- A 6 percent reduction could be achieved if the firm implemented efficient cross-functional communication; and
- A 24 percent reduction could be achieved if the firm switched product design structures (e.g., by implementing concurrent engineering) and emphasized throughput time (e.g., by adopting JIT and cycle time management).

A more general example is based on Skinner's argument[39] that a manufacturing firm's cost reduction efforts are most effective when they focus on structure and process. Skinner advances the view that cost reduction and improvements in productivity are based on a "40-40-20" rule concerning the sources of competitive advantage: That is, about 40 percent of the possible advantage stems from long-term manufacturing structure (e.g., number, size, location, and capacity of facilities) and basic approaches to materials and work force management. Another 40 percent comes from equipment and process technology (e.g., JIT, TQM, and flexible manufacturing systems). Only about 20 percent is derived from traditional approaches to productivity improvement (e.g., those that focus on labor). The implication of this argument is that the key to successful long-term manufacturing cost reduction is to focus on improving organizational cost drivers.

Organizational structure

Organizational structure is how responsibility for activities is differentiated horizontally and vertically. These structures evolve over time in response to changing opportunities and challenges.

Exhibit 5. *Temporal Changes in Vertical Organizational Structures*

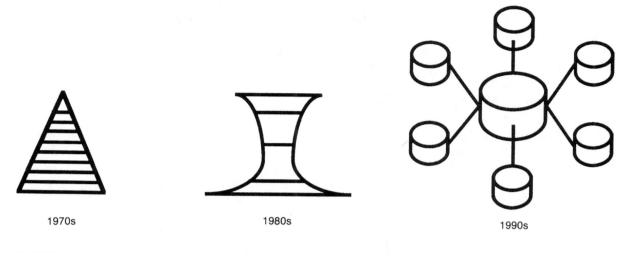

1970s   1980s   1990s

For example, throughout the 1970s, most firms were structured like a pyramid with many vertical layers (see the left-hand side of Exhibit 5). This structure was used to transmit information vertically between the top and the bottom layers of the firm. Humans were the key communicators, and an extensive vertical hierarchy was needed to increase the probability that effective and efficient communication occurred. The limiting factor was the horizontal span of control within a vertical layer. For example, assuming a horizontal span of control of ten, if there are 1,000 workers at the bottom level of a pyramid, the firm's vertical structure would consist of at least three additional vertical levels with 100 first-level supervisors, ten second-level supervisors, and one third-level supervisor (e.g., the CEO). Extrapolating this analysis to firms with 100,000 workers indicates that they will have at least six vertical layers with at least 11,110 employees between the top and bottom vertical layers. An important detrimental consequence of these pyramidal structures was slow and distorted vertical communication, which reduced the quality of outputs and increased their time-to-market and cost.

A significant change began in the 1980s. The introduction of new information processing and communication technologies (e.g., personal computers, facsimile machines, and local area networks) allowed the tops and bottoms of pyramids to communicate more directly. This greatly reduced the need for middle managers. Firms therefore began to transition their vertical structures from the pyramid form to the hourglass form (see the middle figure in Exhibit 5). This change is continuing in the 1990s. Now it is predicted that in the future companies will be organized like flat networks, as the figure on the right-hand side of Exhibit 5 illustrates.[40] While these flatter vertical structures reduce costs because fewer managers are needed, that is not their primary strategic benefit. These flatter structures speed up and increase the quality of information exchange, which (in turn) results in getting products of higher quality and lower cost more quickly to customers.

Horizontal structure. A significant portion of the cost of complexity arises from how firms are horizontally structured. Many firms are organized horizontally by product, geography, or function. This creates a firm that is fragmented and has a series of narrow goals or visions (e.g., one for each horizontal unit). One result is myopic, short-term management. This fragmentation also reduces a firm's speed and flexibility.

The most common organizational structures consist of many horizontal layers. These can create functional barriers, especially if information is intended to flow vertically rather than horizontally. One way to reduce the cost of this horizontally induced complexity and rigidity is to design the firm so that the primary organizational structure is horizontal. The intention of this organizational approach is to break down the functional barriers that impede the horizontal flow of information.

It is important that information flow horizontally at the lowest level possible (i.e., rather than up to a high level in the organization, where senior managers make decisions that are then channeled back down to the function areas). The importance of keeping the information down at the local level is highlighted by the fact that it is employees in the field or on the shop floor who are most aware of problems and how to resolve them. Thus, firms should consider organizing so that the various functional employees can regularly meet to exchange information, quickly solve problems, and coordinate action.

A traditional cost reduction program is typically a distress tactic targeted at all employees. It is triggered in reaction to an immediate threat, such as poor performance, loss of contracts, or price reductions.

Another way to reduce the cost of horizontal complexity is to tear down the functional lines and horizontally reorganize the firm into cross-functional teams that have broad responsibility for all aspects of a product.[41] These local employees are better able to deal with product diversity and process complexity. A firm is better off not transmitting this complexity upward to senior managers, who are often not as intimately familiar with the details as local employees. Besides, transmitting information vertically increases time, and hence cost. The goal is to reduce the cost of horizontal communication, which could also increase quality, speed, learning, and flexibility by breaking down functional barriers (e.g., through concurrent engineering). The result of this change in horizontal structure is an expected decrease in long-term costs.

Firms can also reduce their long-term costs by organizing horizontally based on groups of activities.[42] For example, Prahalad and Hamel[43] argue that to achieve global competitive advantage, an effective basis for horizontal structuring is to organize based on core competencies. Core competencies are activities or knowledge that a firm has that make it a world-class performer.

Appropriate groupings of activities into horizontal units can reduce the costs of coordinating across diverse functions; they can also focus each grouping of activities on a customer (whether the customer is internal or external). An example of this is a Navy supply center that, after introducing ABC, found that its previous functional structure resulted in processes that were cost inefficient.[44] In response, the supply center changed its organizational structure so that it was based on groupings of activities that were required to deliver completed services to customers. The supply center also increased employees' training in team building and statistical quality control. Within two years, the supply center found that its operating costs had decreased, that delivery performance had increased, and that no layoffs were necessary. Using an ABM approach to organizational design also allows a firm to analyze how expected long-term costs vary depending on how the various activities are aggregated and linked together to form linear and parallel processes. A further advantage of an ABM approach to organizational design is that the activity representation of a firm fits nicely with value chain analysis.[45]

Some Japanese firms are now designing their organizational structures and management accounting systems based on horizontal relationships. Accounting systems are being designed primarily by product line rather than by functional areas.[46] The basic unit of design is a product line, with functional areas nested within each product line. These firms have decentralized responsibility for costs and defined cost centers based on product lines. The advantage of this horizontal organization is that it clearly divides responsibility for products, activities, and costs. Since the organization and its accounting system are designed based on products rather than functional areas, most costs are direct to products,

Exhibit 6. *An Example of How Organizational Cost Drivers Can Reduce Long-Term Costs*

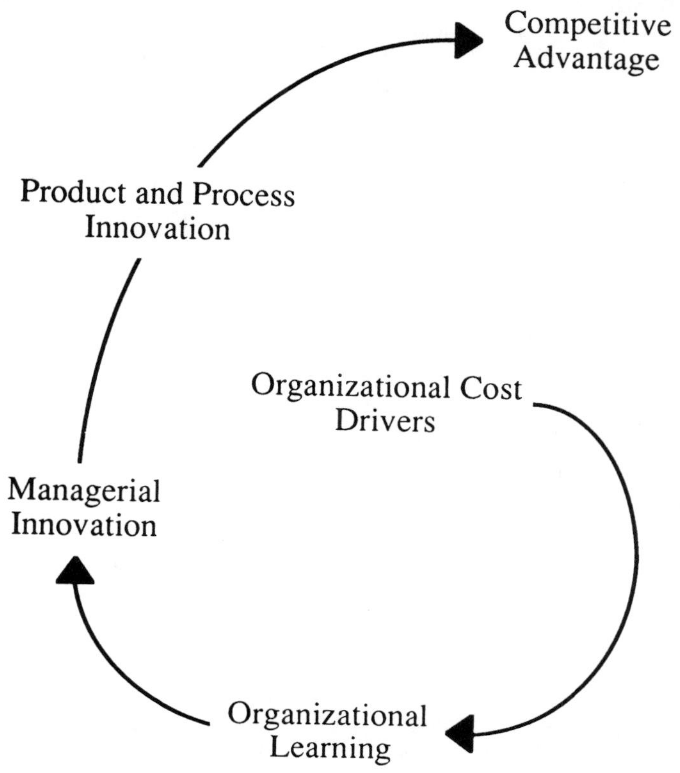

which significantly reduces the amount of costs that are allocated to products. To reduce costs, these Japanese firms have a continuous improvement strategy for each product line.

Organizational processes

Organizational design also includes developing processes to accomplish and coordinate activities. In the strategic consulting literature, *executional cost drivers* are thought to affect the ability of a firm to implement action successfully.[47] These cost drivers include work force involvement (which means participation, culture, and commitment to continuous improvement), total quality management, capacity utilization, plant layout efficiency, product configuration, and exploiting linkages with suppliers and customers (e.g., through JIT and electronic data interchange). As discussed above, how activities and employees are linked determines the basic processes within an organization and,

hence, how—and how much—they drive organizational costs.

Organizational learning

Exhibit 6 provides a general example of how organizational cost drivers affect long-term costs. The idea behind this example is that the rate of organizational learning determines whether a firm can sustain a competitive cost advantage. To do so requires that the firm learn about a core competency (e.g., new product technology or manufacturing process technology) faster than its competitors.[48] Important sources of organizational learning are educational programs, R&D, information systems, budgeting and performance evaluation systems, and cross-functional teams.

Organizational learning occurs when a firm learns about its environment and how to make it better. Organizational learning also deals with how this learning is stored in organizational memory for future use.[49] Much of management accounting can be interpreted as strategies for organizational learning. For example, budgeting is a processs that organizations use to solve problems (i.e., to learn better ways to manufacture and market products to achieve desirable financial outcomes), to share this information across vertical and horizontal levels, and to serve as an organizational memory for storing this information.

Organizational cost drivers (e.g., vertical and horizontal structures and processes, culture, and education programs) determine the type and rate of organizational learning because they affect the type and extent of communications and problem solving by various parts of a firm (Exhibit 6). For instance, a firm learns faster about product and process interactions when it is structured according to concurrent engineering guidelines rather than function (e.g., according to design, engineering, and manufacturing). Organizational learning affects the rate of managerial innovation (e.g., learning about total quality management), which then serves to promote process and product innovation (e.g., product designs with no quality defects and manufacturing processes that minimize the occurrence of errors).[50] The result is a sustainable source of competitive advantage that derives from learning faster and better than competitors can about core competencies and about process and product innovation. Thus, an important source of long-term cost reduction is organizational learning, which (in turn) is determined by how an organization is structured and the processes that occur within the structure.

Conclusion

The central idea that this article develops is that effective long-term cost reduction is a continuous activity that is a strategic and cultural priority. In contrast to traditional cost reduction, with its emphasis on expedient and quick reductions in short-term costs in response to immediate crises, strategic cost reduction is part of a competitive strategy that integrates technology and human resource management strategies to provide a coordinated, broad-based, and long-term approach to reducing costs.

Firms will be better long-term performers if they can get off the short-term cost reduction roller coaster. Long-term competitive cost

advantage depends on establishing a culture of continuous improvement of quality, time, and cost through innovation. Long-term cost reduction is most effectively accomplished by continuously learning about target core competencies faster than competitors can and by establishing long-term employment relationships with innovative, multiskilled employees who are paid above-average compensation. ▲

Notes
1. R.M. Tomasko, *Downsizing—Reshaping the Corporation for the Future* (New York: AMACOM 1987).
2. "The New Executive Unemployed," *Fortune*, Apr. 8, 1991, at 36–48.
3. P. Richardson, *Cost Containment: The Ultimate Advantage* (New York: The Free Press 1988).
4. *Id.*
5. W. Skinner, *Manufacturing: The Formidable Competitive Weapon* (New York: John Wiley & Sons 1985); also G. Hamel & C. Prahalad, "Strategic Intent," *Harv. Bus. Rev.* 63–76 (May–June 1989).
6. Hamel & Prahalad, "Strategic Intent," *supra* note 5.
7. R. Foster, *Innovation—The Attacker's Advantage* (New York: Summit Books 1986).
8. R. Henkoff, "Cost Cutting: How To Do It Right," *Fortune*, Apr. 9, 1990, at 40–49.
9. Business International Research Report, *Strategic Cost Reduction: How International Companies Achieve Cost Leadership* (Geneva: Business International S.A. 1987); Henkoff, "Cost Cutting," *supra* note 8.
10. T. Jick, "The Stressful Effects of Budget Cuts in Organizations," in L. Rosen, *Topics in Managerial Accounting* 267–280 (New York: 3d ed., McGraw-Hill Ryerson Limited 1984).
11. B.C. Ames & J.D. Hlavacek, "Vital Truths About Managing Your Costs," *Harv. Bus. Rev.* 140–147 (Jan.-Feb. 1990).
12. Henkoff, "Cost Cutting," *supra* note 8.
13. Richardson, *Cost Containment: The Ultimate Advantage, supra* note 3.
14. *Id.*
15. C. Prahalad & G. Hamel, "The Core Competence of the Corporation," *Harv. Bus. Rev.* 79–91 (May–June 1990).
16. Business International Research Report, *Strategic Cost Reduction, supra* note 9.
17. K. Ferdows & A. DeMeyer, "Lasting Improvements in Manufacturing Performance: In Search of a New Theory," 9 *The Journal of Operations Management* 168–184 (No. 2 1991).
18. Business International Research Report, *Strategic Cost Reduction, supra* note 9.
19. M.D. Shields & S.M. Young, "Managing Product Life Cycle Costs: An Organizational Model," *Journal of Cost Management* 39–52 (Fall 1991).
20. T. Makido, "Recent Trends in Japan's Cost Management Practices," in *Japanese Management Accounting*, Y. Monden & M. Sakurai, eds. (Cambridge, Mass.: Productivity Press 1989); M. Tanaka, "Cost Planning and Control Systems in

the Design Phase of a New Product," in *Japanese Management Accounting*.

21. C. Berliner & J. Brimson, *Cost Management for Today's Advanced Manufacturing: The CAM-I Conceptual Design* (Boston: Harvard Business School Press 1988); Makido, "Recent Trends," *supra* note 20; R. Cooper & M. Sakurai, "How the Japanese Manage Overhead" (unpublished paper, Harvard Business School, 1990); Toshiro Hiromoto, "Another Hidden Edge—Japanese Management Accounting," *Harv. Bus. Rev.* 22–27 (July–Aug. 1988); M. Sakurai, "Target Costing and How to Use It," *Journal of Cost Management* 39–50 (Summer 1989); Tanaka, "Cost Planning," *supra* note 20; F. Worthy, "Japan's Smart Secret Weapon," *Fortune,* Aug. 12, 1991, at 72–75.

22. Shields & Young, "Managing Product Life Cycle Costs," *supra* note 19.

23. A. Majchrzak & M. Rahimi, "Transitioning to CIM Systems: Effects of Human Factors and Resources Management," in *Success Factors for Implementing Change: A Manufacturing Viewpoint*, K. Blanche, ed. (Dearborn, Mich.: Society of Manufacturing Engineers 1988); D. Opalka & J. Williams, "Employee Obsolescence and Retraining: An Approach to Human Resource Restructuring," *The Journal of Business Strategy* 90–96 (Spring 1987); H. Thompson & R. Scalpone, "Managing the Human Resource in the Factory of the Future," 5 *Human Systems Management* 221–230 (1985); R. Hayes, S. Wheelwright, & K. Clark, *Dynamic Manufacturing* (New York: The Free Press 1988); R. Schuler & I. MacMillan, "Gaining Competitive Advantage Through Human Resource Management Practices," *Human Resource Management* 244–255 (Fall 1984).

24. Shields & Young, "Managing Product Life Cycle Costs," *supra* note 19.

25. A. Rappaport, *Creating Shareholder Value* Chap. 4 (New York: The Free Press 1986).

26. Hayes, Wheelwright, & Clark, *Dynamic Manufacturing, supra* note 23.

27. "A Smarter Way to Manufacture," *Business Week,* Apr. 30, 1990, at 110–117.

28. M.D. Shields & S.M. Young, "A Behavioral Model for Implementing Cost Management Systems," *Journal of Cost Management* 17–27 (Winter 1989); Shields & Young, "Managing Product Life Cycle Costs, *supra* note 19.

29. V. Pucik & N. Hatvany, "Management Practices in Japan and Their Impact on Business Strategy," in *Advances in Strategic Management* Vol. 1, 103–131 (Greenwich, Conn.: Jai Press 1983).

30. Business International Research Report, *Strategic Cost Reduction,*" *supra* note 9; Richardson, *Cost Containment, supra* note 3.

31. Hamel & Prahalad, "Strategic Intent," *supra* note 5; Prahalad & Hamel, "The Core Competence," *supra* note 15.

32. R. Walton & G. Susman, "People Policies for the New Machines," *Harv. Bus. Rev.* 98–106 (Mar.-Apr. 1987); Shields & Young, "Managing Product Life Cycle Costs," *supra* note 19.

33. Richardson, *Cost Containment,*" *supra* note 3; Shields & Young, "A Behavioral Model," *supra* note 28; Henkoff, "Cost Cutting," *supra* note 8; E. Lawler, G. Ledford, & S.

Mohrman, *Employee Involvement in America: A Study of Contemporary Practice* (Houston: American Productivity & Quality Center 1989); E. Lawler, *High-Involvement Management: Participative Strategies for Improving Organizational Performance* (San Francisco: Jossey-Bass Publishers 1986).

34. A. Train, "The Case of the Downsizing Decision," *Harv. Bus. Rev.* 14–30 (Mar.-Apr. 1991).

35. B. Saporito, "Cutting Costs Without Cutting People," *Fortune*, May 25, 1987, at 26–32; Schuler & MacMillan, "Gaining Competitive Advantage," *supra* note 23.

36. W. Imberman, "Managers and Downsizing," *Business Horizons* 28–33 (Sept.-Oct. 1989).

37. Berliner & Brimson, *Cost Management for Today's Advanced Manufacturing, supra* note 21; P. Turney, "How Activity-Based Costing Helps Reduce Cost," *Journal of Cost Management* 29–35 (Winter 1991).

38. J. Gingrich & H. Metz, "Conquering the Costs of Complexity," *Business Horizons* 64–71 (May-June 1990).

39. W. Skinner, "The Productivity Paradox," *Harv. Bus. Rev.* 55–59 (July-Aug. 1986).

40. P. Drucker, "The Coming of the New Organization," *Harv. Bus. Rev.* 45–53 (Jan.-Feb. 1988); R. Miles & C. Snow, "Organizations: Concepts for New Forms," *California Management Review* 62–73 (Spring 1986); J.B. Quinn, T. Doorley, & P. Paquette, "Beyond Products: Services-Based Strategy," *Harv. Bus. Rev.* 58–67 (Mar.-Apr. 1990); H. Thorelli, "Networks: Between Markets and Hierarchies," 7 *Strategic Management Journal* 37–51 (1986).

41. Shields & Young, "Managing Product Life Cycle Costs," *supra* note 19.

42. C.J. McNair, "Interdependence and Control: Traditional vs. Activity-Based Responsibility Accounting," *Journal of Cost Management* 15–24 (Summer 1990); M. Hammer, "Reengineering Work: Don't Automate, Obliterate," *Harv. Bus. Rev.* 104–112 (July-Aug. 1990).

43. Prahalad & Hamel, "The Core Competence," *supra* note 15.

44. D. Harr, "How Activity Accounting Works in Government," *Management Accounting* 36–40 (Sept. 1990).

45. J. Shank & V. Govindarajan, *Strategic Cost Analysis* (Homewood, Ill.: Richard D. Irwin 1989); M. Hergert & D. Morris, "Accounting Data for Value Chain Analysis," 10 *Strategic Management Journal* 175–188 (1989).

46. Cooper & Sakurai, "How the Japanese Manage Overhead," *supra* note 21.

47. D. Riley, "Competitive Cost-Based Investment Strategies for Industrial Companies," *Manufacturing Issues* (New York: Booz, Allen & Hamilton Inc. 1987).

48. R. Stata, "Organizational Learning—The Key to Management Innovation," *Sloan Management Review* 63–74 (Spring 1989); P. Senge, "The Leader's New Work: Building Learning Organizations," *Sloan Management Review* 7–23 (Fall 1990).

49. C. Fiol & M. Lyles, "Organizational Learning," *Academy of Management Review* 803–813 (1985); B. Levitt & J. March, "Organizational Learning," 10 *Annual Review of Sociology* 319–340 (No. 4 1988).

50. C. Fine, "Quality Improvement and Learning in Productive Systems," *Management Science* 1301–1315 (Oct. 1986).

Glossary

ABC See *activity-based costing.*

Absorption costing A method of costing that assigns all or a portion of the manufacturing costs to products or other cost objects. The costs assigned include those that vary with the level of activity performed and also those that do not vary with the level of activity performed.

Activity 1. Work performed within an organization. 2. An aggregation of actions performed within an organization that is useful for purposes of activity-based costing.

Activity analysis The identification and description of activities in an organization. Activity analysis involves determining what activities are done within a department, how many people perform the activities, how much time they spend performing the activities, what resources are required to perform the activities, what operational data best reflect the performance of the activities, and what value the activity has for the organization. Activity analysis is accomplished by means of interviews, questionnaires, observation, and review of physical records of work.

Activity attributes Characteristics of individual activities. Attributes include cost drivers, cycle time, capacity, and performance measures. For example, a measure of the elapsed time required to complete an activity is an attribute. (See *cost driver* and *performance measures.*)

Activity capacity The demonstrated or expected capacity of an activity under normal operating conditions, assuming a specified set of resources and a long time period. An example of this would be a rate of output for an activity expressed as 500 cycles per hour.

Activity cost assignment The process in which the cost of activities are attached to cost objects using activity drivers. (See *cost object* and *activity driver.*)

Activity cost pool A grouping of all cost elements associated with an activity. (See *cost element.*)

Activity driver A measure of the frequency and intensity of the demands placed on activities by cost objects. An activity driver is used to assign costs to cost objects. It represents a line item on the bill of activities for a product or customer. An example is the number of part numbers, which is used to measure the consumption of material-related activities by each product, material type, or component. The number of customer orders measures the consumption of order-entry activities by each customer. Sometimes an activity driver is used as an indicator of the output of an activity, such as the number of purchase orders prepared by the purchasing activity. (See *intensity, cost object,* and *bill of activities.*)

Activity driver analysis The identification and evaluation of the activity drivers used to trace the cost of activities to cost objects. Activity driver analysis may also involve selecting activity drivers with a potential for cost reduction. (See *Pareto analysis.*)

Activity level A description of how an activity is used by a cost object or other activity. Some activity levels describe the cost object that uses the activity and the nature of this use. These levels include activities that are traceable to the product (i.e., unit-level, batch-level, and product-level costs), to the customer (customer-level costs), to a market

This glossary is based on the Computer Aided Manufacturing-International, Inc. (CAM-I) "Glossary of Activity-Based Management," edited by Norm Raffish and Peter B.B. Turney, CAM-I is a not-for-profit membership organization with offices in Arlington, Texas, and Poole, England. Norm Raffish is a manager with Ernst & Young in Woodland Hills, California. Peter B.B. Turney is chief executive officer of Cost Technology in Portland, Oregon.

(market-level costs), to a distribution channel (channel-level costs), and to a project, such as a research and development project (project-level costs).

Activity-based cost system   A system that maintains and processes financial and operating data on a firm's resources, activities, cost objects, cost drivers, and activity performance measures. It also assigns cost to activities and cost objects.

Activity-based costing   A methodology that measures the cost and performance of activities, resources, and cost objects. Resources are assigned to activities, then activities are assigned to cost objects based on their use. Activity-based costing recognizes the causal relationships of cost drivers to activities.

Activity-based management   A discipline that focuses on the management of activities as the route to improving the value received by the customer and the profit achieved by providing this value. This discipline includes cost driver analysis, activity analysis, and performance measurement. Activity-based management draws on activity-based costing as its major source of information. (See *customer value.*)

Allocation   1. An apportionment or distribution. 2. A process of assigning cost to an activity or cost object when a direct measure does not exist. For example, assigning the cost of power to a machine activity by means of machine hours is an allocation because machine hours are an indirect measure of power consumption. In some cases, allocations can be converted to tracings by incurring additional measurement costs. Instead of using machine hours to allocate power consumption, for example, a company can place a power meter on machines to measure actual power consumption. (See *tracing.*)

Assignment   See *cost assignment.*

Attributes   Characteristics of activities, such as cost drivers and performance measures. (See *cost driver* and *performance measure.*)

Attribution   See *tracing.*

Avoidable cost   A cost associated with an activity that would not be incurred if the activity was not required. The telephone cost associated with vendor support, for example, could be avoided if the activity were not performed.

Backflush costing   1. A costing method that applies costs based on the output of a process. The process uses a bill of material or a bill of activities explosion to draw quantities from inventory through work-in-process to finished goods. (Backflushing can occur at intermediate stages as well as for finished goods.) These quantities are generally costed using standard costs. The process assumes that the bill of material (or bill of activities) and the standard costs at the time of backflushing represent the actual quantities and resources used in the manufacture of the product. This is important, since no shop orders are usually maintained to collect costs. 2. A costing method generally associated with repetitive manufacturing. (See *repetitive manufacturing* and *standard costing.*)

Benchmarking   See *best practices.*

Best practices   A methodology that identifies an activity as the benchmark by which a similar activity will be judged. This methodology is used to assist in identifying a process or technique that can increase the effectiveness or efficiency of an activity. The source may be internal (e.g., taken from another part of the company) or external (e.g., taken from a competitor). Another term used is *competitive benchmarking.*

Bill of activities   A listing of the activities required (and optionally, the associated costs of the resources consumed) by a product or other cost object.

Budget   1. A projected amount of cost or revenue for an activity or organizational unit covering a specific period of time. 2. Any plan for the coordination and control of resources and expenditures.

Capital decay   1. A quantification of the lost revenues or reduction in net cash flows sustained by an entity due to obsolete technology. 2. A measure of uncompetitiveness.

Carrying cost   See *holding cost.*

Competitive benchmarking   See *best practices.*

Continuous improvement program   A program to eliminate waste, reduce response time, simplify the design of both products and processes, and improve quality.

Cost Accounting Standards 1. Rules promulgated by the Cost Accounting Standards Board of the federal government to ensure contractor compliance in accounting for government contracts. 2. A set of rules issued by any of several authorized organizations or agencies, such as the American Institute of Certified Public Accountants (AICPA) or the Association of Chartered Accountants (ACA), dealing with the determination of costs to be allocated, inventoried, or expensed.

Cost assignment The tracing or allocation of resources to activities or cost objects. (See *allocation* and *tracing*.)

Cost center The basic unit of responsibility in an organization for which costs are accumulated.

Cost driver Any factor that causes a change in the cost of an activity. For example, the quality of parts received by an activity (e.g., the percent that are defective) is a determining factor in the work required by that activity because the quality of parts received affects the resources required to perform the activity. An activity may have multiple cost drivers associated with it.

Cost driver analysis The examination, quantification, and explanation of the effects of cost drivers. Management often uses the results of cost driver analyses in continuous improvement programs to help reduce throughput time, improve quality, and reduce cost. (See *cost driver* and *continuous improvement program*.)

Cost element An amount paid for a resource consumed by an activity and included in an activity cost pool. For example, power cost, engineering cost, and depreciation may be cost elements in the activity cost pool for a machine activity. (See *activity cost pool, bill of activities*, and *resource*.)

Cost object Any customer, product, service, contract, project, or other work unit for which a separate cost measurement is desired.

Cost of quality All the resources expended for appraisal costs, prevention costs, and both internal and external failure costs of activities and cost objects.

Cost pool See *activity cost pool*.

Cross-subsidy The improper assignment of costs among cost objects such that certain cost objects are overcosted while other cost objects are undercosted relative to the activity costs assigned. For example, traditional cost accounting systems tend to overcost high-volume products and undercost low-volume products.

Customer value The difference between customer realization and sacrifice. *Realization* is what the customer receives, which includes product features, quality, and service. This takes into account the customer's cost to use, maintain, and dispose of the product or service. *Sacrifice* is what the customer gives up, which includes the amount the customer pays for the product plus time and effort spent acquiring the product and learning how to use it. Maximizing customer value means maximizing the difference between realization and sacrifice.

Differential cost See *incremental cost*.

Direct cost A cost that is traced directly to an activity or a cost object. For example, the material issued to a particular work order and the engineering time devoted to a specific product are direct costs to the work orders or products. (See *tracing*.)

Direct tracing See *tracing*.

Discounted cash flow A technique used to evaluate the future cash flows generated by a capital investment. Discounted cash flow is computed by discounting cash flows to determine their present value.

Diversity Conditions in which cost objects place different demands on activities or activities place different demands on resources. This situation arises, for example, when there is a difference in mix or volume of products that causes an uneven assignment of costs. Different types of diversity include: *batch size, customer, market, product mix, distribution channel*, and *volume*.

Financial accounting 1. The accounting for assets, liabilities, equities, revenues, and expenses as a basis for reports to external users of the information. 2. A methodology that focuses on reporting financial information primarily for use by owners, external organizations, and financial institutions. This methodology is constrained by rule-making bodies such as the Financial Accounting Standards Board (FASB), the Securities Exchange Commission (SEC), and the American Institute of Certified Public Accountants (AICPA).

First-stage allocation　See *resource cost assignment.*

Fixed cost　A cost element of an activity that does not vary with changes in the volume of cost drivers or activity drivers. The depreciation of a machine, for example, may be direct to a particular activity, but it is fixed with respect to changes in the number of units of the activity driver. The designation of a cost element as fixed or variable may vary depending on the time frame of the decision in question and the extent to which the volume of production, activity drivers, or cost drivers changes.

Flexible factory　The objective of a flexible factory is to provide a wide range of services across many product lines in a timely manner. An example is a fabrication plant with several integrated manufacturing cells that can perform many functions for unrelated product lines with relatively short lead times.

Focused factory　The objective of a focused factory is to organize around a specific set of resources to provide low cost and high throughput over a narrow range of products.

Forcing　Allocating the costs of a sustaining activity to a cost object even though that cost object may not clearly consume or causally relate to that activity. Allocating a plant-level activity (such as heating) to product units using an activity driver such as direct labor hours, for example, forces the cost of this activity to the product. (See *sustaining activity.*)

Full absorption costing　See *absorption costing.*

Functional decomposition　Identifies the activities performed in the organization. It yields a hierarchical representation of the organization and shows the relationship between the different levels of the organization and its activities. For example, a hierarchy may start with the division and move down through the plant, function, process, activity, and task levels.

Holding cost　A financial technique that calculates the cost of retaining an asset (e.g., finished goods inventory or a building). Generally, the calculation includes a cost of capital in addition to other costs such as insurance, taxes, and space.

Homogeneity　A situation in which all the cost elements in an activity's cost pool are consumed by all cost objects in proportion to an activity driver. (See *cost element, activity cost pool,* and *activity driver.*)

Incremental cost　1. The cost associated with increasing the output of an activity or project above some base level. 2. The additional cost associated with selecting one economic or business alternative over another, such as the difference between working overtime or subcontracting the work. 3. The cost associated with increasing the quantity of a cost driver. (Also known as *differential cost.*)

Indirect cost　The cost that is allocated—as opposed to being traced—to an activity or a cost object. For example, the costs of supervision or heat may be allocated to an activity on the basis of direct labor hours. (See *allocation.*)

Intensity　The cost consumed by each unit of the activity driver. It is assumed that the intensity of each unit of the activity driver for a single activity is equal. Unequal intensity means that the activity should be broken into smaller activities or that a different activity driver should be chosen. (See *diversity.*)

Life cycle　See *product life cycle.*

Net present value　A method that evaluates the difference between the present value of all cash inflows and outflows of an investment using a given discount rate. If the discounted cash inflow exceeds the discounted outflow, the investment is considered economically feasible.

Non-value-added activity　An activity that is considered not to contribute to customer value or to the organization's needs. The designation "non-value-added" reflects a belief that the activity can be redesigned, reduced, or eliminated without reducing the quantity, responsiveness, or quality of the output required by the customer or the organization. (See *customer value* and *value analysis*.)

Obsolescence   A product or service that has lost its value to the customer due to changes in need or technology.

Opportunity cost   The economic value of a benefit that is sacrificed when an alternative course of action is selected.

Pareto analysis   The identification and interpretation of significant factors using Pareto's rule that 20 percent of a set of independent variables is responsible for 80 percent of the result. Pareto analysis can be used to identify cost drivers or activity drivers that are responsible for the majority of cost incurred by ranking the cost drivers in order of value. (See *cost driver analysis* and *activity driver analysis*.)

Performance measures   Indicators of the work performed and the results achieved in an activity, process, or organizational unit. Performance measures may be financial or nonfinancial. An example of a performance measure of an activity is the number of defective parts per million. An example of a performance measure of an organizational unit is return on sales.

Present value   The discounted value of a future sum or stream of cash flows.

Process   A series of activities that are linked to perform a specific objective. For example, the assembly of a television set or the paying of a bill or claim entails several linked activities.

Product family   A group of products or services that have a defined relationship because of physical and production similarities. (The term *product line* is used interchangeably.)

Product life cycle   The period that starts with the initial product specification and ends with the withdrawal of the product from the marketplace. A product life cycle is characterized by certain defined stages, including research, development, introduction, maturity, decline, and abandonment.

Product line   See *product family*.

Profit center   A segment of the business (e.g., a project, program, or business unit) that is accountable for both revenues and expenses.

Project   A planned undertaking, usually related to a specific activity, such as the research and development of a new product or the redesign of the layout of a plant.

Project costing   A cost system that collects information on activities and costs associated with a specific activity, project, or program.

Repetitive manufacturing   The manufacture of identical products (or a family of products) in a continuous flow.

Resource   An economic element that is applied or used in the performance of activities. Salaries and materials, for example, are resources used in the performance of activities. (See *cost element*.)

Resource cost assignment   The process by which cost is attached to activities. The process requires the assignment of cost from general ledger accounts to activities using resource drivers. For example, the chart of accounts may list information services at a plant level. It then becomes necessary to trace (assuming that tracing is practical) or to allocate (when tracing is not practical) the cost of information services to the activities that benefit from the information services by means of appropriate resource drivers. It may be necessary to set up intermediate activity cost pools to accumulate related costs from various resources before the assignment can be made. (See *activity cost pool* and *resource driver*.)

Resource driver   A measure of the quantity of resources consumed by an activity. An example of a resource driver is the percentage of total square feet occupied by an activity. This factor is used to allocate a portion of the cost of operating the facilities to the activity.

Responsibility accounting   An accounting method that focuses on identifying persons or organizational units that are accountable for the performance of revenue or expense plans.

Risk   The subjective assessment of the possible positive or negative consequences of a current or future action. In a business sense, risk is the premium asked or paid for engaging in an investment or venture. Often, risk is incorporated into business decisions through such factors as cost of capital, hurdle rates, or the interest premium paid over a prevailing base interest rate.

Second-stage allocation   See *activity cost assignment.*

Standard costing   A costing method that attaches costs to cost objects based on reasonable estimates or cost studies and by means of budgeted rates rather than according to actual costs incurred.

Sunk costs   Costs that have been invested in assets for which there is little (if any) alternative or continued value except salvage. Using sunk costs as a basis for evaluating alternatives may lead to incorrect decisions. Examples are the invested cost in a scrapped part or the cost of an obsolete machine.

Support costs   Costs of activities not directly associated with production. Examples are the costs of process engineering and purchasing.

Surrogate activity driver   An activity driver that is not descriptive of an activity, but that is closely correlated to the performance of the activity. The use of a surrogate activity driver should reduce measurement costs without significantly increasing the costing bias. The number of production runs, for example, is not descriptive of the material-disbursing activity, but the number of production runs may be used as an activity driver if material disbursements coincide with production runs.

Sustaining activity   An activity that benefits an organization at some level (e.g., the company as a whole or a division, plant, or department), but not any specific cost object. Examples of such activities are preparation of financial statements, plant management, and support of community programs.

Target cost   A cost calculated by subtracting a desired profit margin from an estimated (or a market-based) price to arrive at a desired production, engineering, or marketing cost. The target cost need not be the expected initial production cost. Instead, it may be the cost that is expected to be achieved during the mature production stage. (See *target costing.*)

Target costing   A method used in analyzing product and process design that involves estimating a target cost and designing the product to meet that cost. (See *target cost.*)

Technology costs   A category of cost associated with the development, acquisition, implementation, and maintenance of technology assets. It can include costs such as the depreciation of research equipment, tooling amortization, maintenance, and software development.

Technology valuation   A nontraditional approach to valuing technology acquisitions that may incorporate such elements as purchase price, startup costs, current market value adjustments, and the risk premium of an acquisition.

Throughput   The rate of production of a defined process over a stated period of time. Rates may be expressed in terms of units of products, batches produced, dollar turnover, or other meaningful measurements.

Traceability   The ability to assign a cost directly to an activity or a cost object in an economically feasible way by means of a causal relationship. (See *tracing.*)

Tracing   The assignment of cost to an activity or a cost object using an observable measure of the consumption of resources by an activity. Tracing is generally preferred to allocation if the data exist or can be obtained at a reasonable cost. For example, if a company's cost accounting system captures the cost of supplies according to which activities use the supplies, the costs may be traced—as opposed to allocated—to the appropriate activities. Tracing is also called *direct tracing.*

Unit cost   The cost associated with a single unit of a product, including direct costs, indirect costs, traced costs, and allocated costs.

Value-added activity   An activity that is judged to contribute to customer value or satisfy an organizational need. The attribute "value-added" reflects a belief that the activity cannot be eliminated without reducing the quantity, responsiveness, or quality of output required by a customer or organization. (See *customer value.*)

Value analysis   A cost-reduction and process-improvement tool that utilizes information collected about business processes and examines various attributes of the processes (e.g., diversity, capacity, and complexity) to identify candidates for improvement efforts. (See *activity attributes* and *cost driver.*)

Value chain The set of activities required to design, procure, produce, market, distribute, and service a product or service.

Value-chain costing An activity-based cost model that contains all activities in the value chain.

Variance The difference between an expected and actual result.

Variable cost A cost element of an activity that varies with changes in volume of cost drivers and activity drivers. The cost of material handling to an activity, for example, varies according to the number of material deliveries and pickups to and from that activity. (See *cost element, fixed cost,* and *activity driver.*)

Waste Resources consumed by unessential or inefficient activities.

Willie Sutton rule A reminder to focus on the high-cost activities. The rule is named after bank robber Willie Sutton, who—when asked "why do you rob banks?"—is reputed to have replied "because that's where the money is."

Work cell A physical or logical grouping of resources that performs a defined job or task. The work cell may contain more than one activity. For example, all the tasks associated with the final assembly of a product may be grouped in a work cell.

Work center A physical area of the plant or factory. It consists of one or more resources where a particular product or process is accomplished. ▲

Index

Q

Q factor, E1-9

Quality. *See also* Total quality management (TQM)
cost of, B2-6, 8–9
customer's definition of, K1-1–4
measuring, G1-3
as nonfinancial measures, H3-5

Quality control, JIT and, C3-6–7

Quality costs, K4-1–8
ASCQ model, K5-1–7
cost of control and, K5-1
description of, K4-1–2, K5-1–2
failure to costs, K5-1
manager's perceptions about, K5-1–7
optimum, K4-3–8
traditional model of, K4-2–4

Quality of work life, improving, J6-1–5

R

Raw materials, JIT and, C3-8

Reasonably predictable (RP) costs, G2-1

Reconfiguration, C4-7

Recurring expenses, C4-4

Regulatory compliance, aerospace and defense (A&D) contractors and, B6-8

Reichheld, Frederick F., E2-5

Relevant costs, A4-1

Reliability, as nonfinancial measures, H3-4–5

Replacement decisions, G4-3

Research and development (R&D). *See also* Product design
ABM and, B3-1–6
activities in, B3-5
budgeting for discretionary costs and, G2-1, 4
marketing and, B3-3–4
project structures and, B3-6
value-added and non-value-added activities in, B3-1, 5

Residual linking, G3-5

Resource categories, B5-3–5
consumption basis for, B5-3–4
engineering relationships and, B5-11–12
organizational units and, B5-3
reconciling activities at, B5-11
spending profiles of, B5-10–11

Resource category costs, B5-4–5

Resource drivers, definition of, J1-9

Resources
cellular manufacturing systems and, C4-4, 7–9
definition of, B6-2

Responsiveness to customers, of nonfinancial measures, H3-5

Restructuring
comprehensive approach to, J5-1–5
cost driver analysis and, B2-9
downsizing, B2-9–10
empowerment vs. enforcement and, B2-9
managerial, J5-4–5
through FACT analysis, B2-6–9

Return-on-investment (ROI)
performance measures and, H2-2–3
transfer pricing and, I3-4

Rewards, performance measures and, H2-6

Rework, JIT and, C3-7

Roach, Stephen, B2-2, B2-9, B2-11

Robinson, James D., III, B2-1

Robinson-Patman Act, I1-3, I2-1, 5

Robotics, B1-1
FMS and, C6-3

Robust quality, K4-3

Rockwell International, E1-9

Rodgers, Buck, E4-1

Rolex, L4-2

Routing, unidirectional, C4-3–4

Rsd, A1-5, A6-2–3
in cost assignment view of ABC, A1-3

S

Salespeople, tactical pricing and, I1-7

Sasser, W. Earl, E2-5

Scientific Information Center (SIC), F4-4

SCM Corporation, L3-5–6, 10

Scorecard approach to performance measures, H1-1–6, H3-1

Scrap and rework, JIT and, C3-7

Sears, D4-4

Second-wave companies, D4-1

Seiko Epson, D1-3

Self concept, U.S. and Japanese attitudes compared, F2-2

Self-managed work teams, J6-1–3

Service. *See also* Customer service
manufacturing as a, D1-4

Service defectors, E4-3